OXFORD READINGS IN CLASSICAL STUDIES

The series provides students and scholars with a representative selection of the best and most influential articles on a particular author, work, or subject. No single school or style of approach is privileged: the aim is to offer a broad overview of scholarship, to cover a wide variety of topics, and to illustrate a diversity of critical methods. The collections are particularly valuable for their inclusion of many important essays which are normally difficult to obtain and for the first-ever translations of some of the pieces. Many articles are thoroughly revised and updated by their authors or are provided with addenda taking account of recent work. Each volume includes an authoritative and wide-ranging introduction by the editor surveying the scholarly tradition and considering alternative approaches. This pulls the individual articles together, setting all the pieces included in their historical and cultural contexts and exploring significant connections between them from the perspective of contemporary scholarship. All foreign languages (including Greek and Latin) are translated to make the texts easily accessible to those without detailed linguistic knowledge.

OXFORD READINGS IN CLASSICAL STUDIES

Persius and Juvenal
Edited by Maria Plaza

Horace: *Odes* and *Epodes*
Edited by Michèle Lowrie

Horace: *Satires* and *Epistles*
Edited by Kirk Freudenburg

Thucydides
Edited by Jeffrey S. Rusten

Lucan
Edited by Charles Tesoriero, with Frances Muecke and Tamara Neal

Xenophon
Edited by Vivienne J. Gray

The Religious History of the Roman Empire
Pagans, Jews, and Christians
Edited by J. A. North and S. R. F. Price

Greek and Roman Historiography
Edited by John Marincola

Tacitus
Edited by Rhiannon Ash

Latin Panegyric
Edited by Roger Rees

Propertius
Edited by Ellen Greene and Tara S. Welch

Herodotus: Volume 1
Herodotus and the Narrative of the Past
Edited by Rosaria Vignolo Munson

Herodotus: Volume 2
Herodotus and the World
Edited by Rosaria Vignolo Munson

Sport in the Greek and Roman Worlds: Volume 1
Early Greece, the Olympics, and Contests
Edited by Thomas F. Scanlon

Sport in the Greek and Roman Worlds: Volume 2
Greek Athletic Identities and Roman Sports and Spectacle
Edited by Thomas F. Scanlon

The Roman Historical Tradition
Regal and Republican Rome
Edited by James H. Richardson and Federico Santangelo

Flavian Epic
Edited by Antony Augoustakis

The *Epistles* of Pliny
Edited by Roy Gibson and Christopher Whitton

Greek Lyric
Edited by Ian Rutherford

Sallust

Edited by
WILLIAM W. BATSTONE
and
ANDREW FELDHERR

OXFORD
UNIVERSITY PRESS

OXFORD
UNIVERSITY PRESS

Great Clarendon Street, Oxford, OX2 6DP,
United Kingdom

Oxford University Press is a department of the University of Oxford.
It furthers the University's objective of excellence in research, scholarship,
and education by publishing worldwide. Oxford is a registered trade mark of
Oxford University Press in the UK and in certain other countries

© Oxford University Press 2020

The moral rights of the authors have been asserted

First Edition published in 2020

All rights reserved. No part of this publication may be reproduced, stored in
a retrieval system, or transmitted, in any form or by any means, without the
prior permission in writing of Oxford University Press, or as expressly permitted
by law, by licence or under terms agreed with the appropriate reprographics
rights organization. Enquiries concerning reproduction outside the scope of the
above should be sent to the Rights Department, Oxford University Press, at the
address above

You must not circulate this work in any other form
and you must impose this same condition on any acquirer

Published in the United States of America by Oxford University Press
198 Madison Avenue, New York, NY 10016, United States of America

British Library Cataloguing in Publication Data

Data available

Library of Congress Control Number: 2019953282

ISBN 978-0-19-879098-3

Links to third party websites are provided by Oxford in good faith and
for information only. Oxford disclaims any responsibility for the materials
contained in any third party website referenced in this work.

Preface

It became clear to the editors early on that there were many, many possible versions of this collection that would have been of great use to students of Sallust. If the one we ultimately produced is among them, much credit for that goes to friends and colleagues who offered their own suggestions about what it should include, especially Christina Kraus and David Levene, as well as the anonymous referees for Oxford University Press. We wish that we could have included more of those suggestions, and by far the hardest task we faced was choosing what to leave out.

We thank too the authors who allowed us to republish their works and variously took the trouble of updating, correcting, and reformatting their contributions: Ulrike Egelhaaf-Gaiser, Erik Gunderson, Christina Kraus, Antonio La Penna, David Levene, and Patricia Osmond. Financial support from the Magie Fund of the Princeton Classics Department, and from the Department of Classics at the Ohio State University made it possible to employ assistants to help with translation and editing. Stephen Blair prepared the translations from German, and Gemma Storti from Italian. William Little contributed to editing several articles. Caitlin Mongrain prepared the index of passages cited, and the production of the final manuscript was overseen with exemplary care and dedication by Emma Curran. Kathleen Coleman graciously offered many suggestions for improving the translation of Chapter 2. At Oxford University Press Charlotte Loveridge and Georgina Leighton have provided valuable assistance, advice, and encouragement.

Translations of Greek and Latin have been added to the body of the text wherever they were absent from the original publications, except in cases where the meaning is obvious from the context or the text is cited to illustrate a purely stylistic point. All infelicities in those translations, as in the chapters originally published in German or Italian, are the responsibility of the editors. L. D. Reynolds's now standard *Oxford Classical Text* of Sallust was published in 1991, and it was not practicable to standardize all citations to conform to it. So too fragments of the *Histories* are identified with Maurenbrecher's numeration and users of Ramsey's excellent new Loeb volume are referred to the concordance it contains.

Contents

List of Illustrations	ix
List of Abbreviations	xi

1. Introduction   1
   William W. Batstone and Andrew Feldherr

2. Sallust: Diction and Sentence Structure, Narrative Style and Composition, Personality and Times   24
   Kurt Latte

3. The Moral Crisis in Sallust's View   85
   D. C. Earl

4. A Traditional Pattern of Imitation in Sallust and his Sources   104
   R. Renehan

5. The Accounts of the Catilinarian Conspiracy   116
   Eduard Schwartz

6. Intellectual Conflict and Mimesis in Sallust's *Bellum Catilinae*   141
   William W. Batstone

7. The History of Mind and the Philosophy of History in Sallust's *Bellum Catilinae*   166
   Erik Gunderson

8. Sallust's *Catiline* and Cato the Censor   214
   D. S. Levene

9. Jugurthine Disorder   244
   Christina S. Kraus

10. Sallust's *Jugurtha*: An 'Historical Fragment'   272
    D. S. Levene

11. Sallust's *Jugurtha*: Concord, Discord, and the Digressions   306
    Thomas Wiedemann

12. *Non sunt conposita verba mea*: Reflected Narratology in Sallust's Speech of Marius
    Ulrike Egelhaaf-Gaiser — 316

13. On the Introduction to Sallust's *Histories* — 340
    Friedrich Klingner

14. The *Histories*: The Crisis of the *Res Publica* — 350
    Antonio La Penna

15. The Faces of Discord in Sallust's *Histories* — 371
    Andrew Feldherr

16. Princeps Historiae Romanae: Sallust in Renaissance Political Thought — 400
    Patricia J. Osmond

Bibliography — 445
Acknowledgements — 477
Index of Passages — 479

List of Illustrations

16.1. Miniature from an early fourteenth-century Bolognese copy of *I fatti di Cesare* illustrated by the Maestro di Gherarduccio. Florence, Biblioteca Riccardiana, MS 1538, fol. 3r (by permission of the Ministero dei Beni e delle Attività Culturali e del Turismo) — 404

16.2. Map illustrating Sallust's *excursus* in B.J. 17–19 on the regions, cities, and peoples of North Africa, in a 1433 copy of San Concordio's translation of the *Bellum Iugurthinum*. Rome, Biblioteca Corsiniana, MS 1860, fol. 27v (by permission of the Biblioteca dell'Accademia Nazionale dei Lincei e Corsiniana) — 406

16.3. Alexander Barclay presenting his translation of Sallust's *Bellum Iugurthinum* to Thomas, duke of Norfolk. Woodcut, from the first edition (London, [1522]), sig. a 4v. Williamstown, MA, Chapin Library, Williams College (by permission of the Williams College Special Collections) — 427

16.4. Portrait of Sallust on a Roman contorniate in the collection of Fulvio Orsini, with other drawings and notes. *Imagines et elogia virorum illustrium* (Rome, 1570), p. 90 (by permission of the Ministero dei Beni e delle Attività Culturali e del Turismo) — 432

List of Abbreviations

ANRW	Temporini, H., et al. (eds.) (1972–). *Aufstieg und Niedergang der römischen Welt.* Berlin and New York: De Gruyter
BnF	Bibliothèque nationale de France
C	Clark, A. C. (1907). *Q. Asconii Pediani Orationum Ciceronis quinque enarratio.* Oxford: Oxford University Press
CAH	(1970–2005). *Cambridge Ancient History*, 14 vols., 2nd edn. Cambridge: Cambridge University Press
CERL	Consortium of European Research Libraries
CIL	(1893–). *Corpus Inscriptionum Latinarum.* Berlin: Reimer
FGrH	Jacoby, F., Fornara, C. W., et al. (eds.) (1923–). *Die Fragmente der griechischen Historiker.* Leiden: Brill
FRHist	Cornell, T. J., Bispham, E. H., Rich, J. W., and Smith, C. J. (eds.). (2013). *The Fragments of the Roman Historians*, 3 vols. Oxford: Oxford University Press
H	Haines, C. R. (transl.) (1919). *The Correspondence of Marcus Cornelius Fronto with Marcus Aurelius Antoninus, Lucius Verus, Antoninus Pius, and Various Friends*, 2 vols. Loeb Classical Library. Cambridge, MA: Harvard University Press
ILS	Dessau, H. (ed.) (1892–1916). *Inscriptiones Latinae Selectae*, 3 vols. Berlin: Weidmann
ISTC	Incunabula Short Title Catalogue, British Library
J	Jocelyn, H. D. (1967). *The Tragedies of Ennius. The Fragments Edited with an Introduction and Commentary.* Cambridge Classical Texts and Commentaries 10. Cambridge: Cambridge University Press
L	Lindsay, W. M. (ed.) (1913). *Sexti Pompei Festi De verborum significatu quae supersunt cum Pauli epitome.* Leipzig: Teubner
LHS	Leumann, M., Hofmann, J. B., and Szantyr, A. J. B. (1965) *Lateinische Grammatik*, vol. 2, *Lateinische Syntax und Stilistik.* Rev. by A. Szantyr. Munich: Beck
M	Maurenbrecher, B. (ed.) (1891–3). *C. Sallusti Crispi Historiarum reliquiae*, 2 vols. Leipzig: Teubner
OLD	Glare, P. G. W. (ed.) (1982). *Oxford Latin Dictionary.* Oxford: Clarendon Press
OPAC-SBN	Online Public Access Catalogue, Servizio Bibliotecario Nazionale
ORF	Malcovati, H. (1953). *Oratorum Romanorum Fragmenta Liberae Rei Publicae.* 3rd edn. Turin: Paravia. (4th edn. 1976)

List of Abbreviations

P	Peter, H. (1914). *Historicorum Romanorum Reliquiae*, 2 vols., 2nd edn. Stuttgart: Teubner
RE	Wissowa, G., et al. (eds.) (1893–1978). *Paulys Real-Encyclopädie der classischen Altertumswissenschaft*. Stuttgart: Metzler
RIS	Muratori, L. A. (ed.) (1723–51). *Rerum Italicarum scriptores ab anno aere christianae 500–1500*. Milan: Typographia Societatis Palatinae. (New series: Carducci, G. and Fiorini, V. (eds.) (1990–). Città di Castello: Lapi.)
TLL	(1900–). *Thesaurus Linguae Latinae*. Leipzig: De Gruyter
VDH	Van den Hout, M. P. J. (1999). *A Commentary on the Letters of M. Cornelius Fronto*. Leiden: Brill

Journal abbreviations are those used in *L'Année Philologique*.

1

Introduction

William W. Batstone and Andrew Feldherr

Sallust wrote at a transformational moment both in the history of the Roman state and in the story of how that history was represented. His two surviving monographs and the now fragmentary *Histories* were produced in the late forties and early thirties BCE. Nearly a decade of wars and the violent deaths of leading political figures marked a sharp break from the years when the historian himself had been an active participant in public life. Any future order, or even the end of civic violence, could not be confidently foreseen. The subjects he chose for his works—Catiline's conspiracy in 63 BCE, the botched war fifty years earlier against Jugurtha, and the struggle to redefine the Roman political order after the dictatorship of Sulla—focus on critical moments that themselves raise questions about the continuities between present and past in Roman history. They are also, especially when viewed from the time when Sallust wrote, stories of failure and futility, where even temporary successes like the eventual capture of Jugurtha and the defeat of Catiline all take their place within a larger process leading to 'the devastation of Italy'(*vastitas Italiae*, *B.J.* 5. 2). The attention he gives to describing and diagnosing the decline and fall of the Roman political order has been among the most important aspects of his legacy.

His work also constitutes an anxious refoundation of the writing of history in Rome, in a way that simultaneously reveals the pressures of these events on any attempts to represent them and questions historiography's ability to escape from those pressures. Sallust's writings reflect the violence of the times in which they were written most obviously through their own polemical energy. In the first word of the *Jugurtha* the historian proclaims the falsity of other voices. The narrative of the *Catiline* competes with exaggerated accounts and rumours of the crimes of its protagonist while it founders on the unknowability of the role played by some dark and powerful actors. Establishing the truth of a new account of the past by refuting versions that were in some way more appealing or better known had been an authorizing strategy of history writing from its beginning.[1] But Sallust's own evocation of the context in which he writes adds a new level of complexity to such gestures. While his readers may well recognize Sallust's efforts as an urgent proclamation of the distinctness of his own representation of events, an alternative response would be to consider whether Sallust's story can escape being assimilated to its tendentious and self-serving rivals. For as the preface to the *Catiline* makes clear, it is not only the author who is a product of his times but his audience as well: their anxieties about their own status and reputation affect their willingness to accept claims about others' virtues and vices (*B.C.* 3. 2). And beyond the difficulties of knowing the truth among all these false tales, and of conveying that truth to readers disinclined to believe it, Sallust highlights how the very language through which he presents his account has been transformed by the history he relates. Competing rhetorical appropriation of the same common terms—virtue, friendship, 'the public good'—by rival factions had evacuated those words of stable meanings. 'We have lost the true words for things,' laments Cato in the speech he gives arguing for the execution of Catiline's co-conspirators (*B.C.* 52. 11), but should we take this statement itself as a true representation of the historical conditions in which Sallust wrote, or recognize it as yet another rhetorical strategy deployed by Cato? Thus, while the battle in Sallust's works seems initially to be waged with dishonest rivals, we may well conclude that the writer is ultimately at war with himself,[2] as every attempt to set his voice apart from the historical contingencies that limit its authority—to record history rather than make it—seems further to implicate him in the very struggles he condemns.

A brief survey of what can be known about Sallust's biography[3] conveys how the political violence of the late Republic might have seemed an inescapable aspect of Roman public life.[4] Jerome's *Chronicle*

---

[1] Marincola 1997: 218–36.   [2] See Batstone 2010b.

[3] For the ancient evidence, see Kurfess 1981. Succinct surveys of his life can be found in Ramsey 2007 and Schmidt, 2008. Syme 1964 relates his political views to his class and background.

[4] The seminal work on violence in the Republic is Lintott 1999, now in a second edition, 1999; see also Nippel 1995. The standard survey of the period from Sulla to the outbreak of civil war in 49 is Gruen 1974. For the transformation of the Republic from 60 BCE to 14 CE, see Syme 1939, 1952. Much work has been done since these magisterial studies, but they remain crucial. Recent important work on violence in the late Republic includes Mouritsen 2017, Steel 2013, Wiseman 2009, Morstein-Marx 2004, Millar 1998, and Brunt 1988. Flower 2010 reconceives the history of the Republic and has much to say about violence both lethal and non-lethal.

Introduction 3

(1930) reports that he was born at Amiternum in the Sabine territory in 86 BCE,[5] just after the Social War (which might have brought his family to Rome[6]) and the year of the seventh consulship of Marius. This was the year that Marius, the dominant figure of Sallust's *Jugurtha*, died. Sallust was to end his *Jugurtha* in 104 BCE, at the beginning of Marius' second consulship, 'when all the hopes and power of the state were entrusted to him'. Marius' own ending, in the year of Sallust's birth, reveals the bitter irony of this conclusion: after returning again from Africa, this time as an exile, Marius, with his co-consul Cinna, slaughtered and beheaded the supporters of Sulla, and died fourteen days into his term. Sallust was born into a world of violence. He would have been in his third year when Sulla marched on Rome for the second time, in his fifth at the time of Sulla's proscriptions, and about 8 at the time of the dictator's death in 78 BCE. The conclusion of the Slave War against Spartacus, punctuated by the crucifixion of six thousand of his followers along the Appian Way from Rome to Capua, came when Sallust was 15. When he was turning 20, Pompey was sent east to fight Mithridates, and the turbulence of the middle sixties began: tribunes' bills, political trials, fierce competition at the polls, and violence. In 63 BCE, Cicero was consul: the Catilinarian conspiracy became a war, and Cicero ordered the conspirators killed in Rome. Sallust would have been about 23. He offers no sign that he was at Rome at the time.

Sallust's earliest traceable involvement in political life comes eleven years later, and one year after the so-called 'first triumvirate'[7] had been destabilized by the death of Crassus. At the beginning of 52 BCE, the demagogue Clodius was killed in a brawl orchestrated by his rival, Milo; his body was placed in the Senate house and burned. The 34-year-old Sallust seems to have been involved. Cicero said that he and Q. Pompeius Rufus called him a thief and a murder; he in turn called them 'abject and desperate men'.[8] We hear also that he settled his quarrel with Cicero and

---

[5] This has been questioned, as regards both place and date (Syme 1964: 13–15), but most accept 86 as the likely year of his birth.

[6] Schwartz 1897 proposed that the family left Amiternum and hid in Rome to avoid the violence of the Social Wars. If so, Sallust may have been born and raised in Rome.

[7] This modern designation no longer finds favour with historians; see Sanders 1932.

[8] See Cic. *Mil.* 47. Asc. 37. 16–21 C lists three tribunes, Q. Pompeius, C. Sallustius, and T. Munatius Plancus, involved in disruptive public gatherings (*inimicissimas contiones*). With reference to Cicero's remark, Asc. 49. 24–50. 1 C names two tribunes, Q. Pompeius Rufus and C. Sallustius, *abiecti homines ac perditi*, who accused Cicero of being a thief and a murderer; with reference to Clodius' pyre in the Senate house, he names Plancus and Pompeius.

Milo (Asc. 33 C). In 50 BCE he was removed from the Senate by Appius Claudius (Dio 40. 63. 4). We do not know why.

In 49 BCE, when Sallust was 37, Caesar's civil war broke out. He joined Caesar and with Minucius Basilus commanded two legions in Illyricum, where he was defeated (Oros. 6. 15. 8). We next hear of Sallust in 47 BCE, when he was sent to Campania to appease troops who were demanding pay and dismissal. This time he narrowly escaped with his life, although the two senatorial envoys who were with him were killed. He seems to have been praetor designate in 47 and assumed the office of praetor the next year (Broughton 1948: 76–8, Dio 42. 52), and so, at 40, he regained his senatorial seat. During the African campaign he secured supplies for Caesar from the island of Cercina. But this sole military success does not seem to justify Caesar's next move: he appointed Sallust as the first governor for the new province of Africa and as proconsul with three legions under his command. Dio Cassius gives the following tendentious account of the outcome:

> [Caesar] delivered the Numidians to Sallust, nominally to rule, but really to harry and plunder. At all events this officer took many bribes and confiscated much property, so that he was not only accused but incurred the deepest disgrace, inasmuch as after writing such treatises as he had, and making many bitter remarks about those who fleeced others, he did not practise what he preached.
>
> (43. 9. 2–3)

Upon his return to Rome, he was charged with extortion and bribery. The charges were not pressed; a later rhetorical exercise attacking Sallust claims it was because he had bribed Caesar (*Inv. in Sall.* 3. 19). In any event, he was not expelled from the Senate for a second time, but retired to his house and gardens to write history. Caesar was assassinated when Sallust was 42. Nothing is known of his final years, and it is only a reasonable compromise of the contradictions in Jerome that places his death in 35 BCE (*Chron.* 1981), at the age of 51. Since Sallust describes himself as turning to history 'after I had decided to keep the remainder of my life far from public affairs' (*B.C.* 4. 1), we date all of his works from the period between 44 and 35 BCE, with the general assumption that the *Catiline* came first, because of its more explicit presentation of the author's aims, and the *Histories* last, because of their larger scale. The little that survives of the final book of that work allows for debate about whether they were completed, and if not, what conclusion Sallust had in mind. These years were anything but free from partisan conflict, as Caesar's successors, Octavian and Antony, struggled first against his assassins and then against one another. Other than some very doubtful

Introduction 5

evidence connecting Sallust with Ventidius Bassus, one of Antony's lieutenants, there is no trace of any political activity on the part of the historian during this period.[9] Yet for all the historian's claims of impartiality, it may be that the authoritarian turn in Roman politics under the triumvirate provides as fruitful a context for understanding the political tenor of his work as the times when he held office himself.[10]

How any of these events shaped the way Sallust presented Rome's history would become a framing question for his modern readers, as many of the works collected here will reveal. This uncertainty is only increased by the way he introduces both of the monographs. His prologues, which Quintilian criticized for their irrelevance ('he began with prologues that do not pertain to history at all', *nihil ad historiam pertinentibus principiis orsus est, Inst.* 3. 8. 9), have a problematic relationship both to history in general and to the histories that follow in these works. The prologue to the *Catiline* seems to project a world in which *virtus* is effective in accomplishing great deeds and the memory of these deeds is both long-lasting and a compensation for death. Later, however, in the same work Sallust will question these very assertions: the talent of Greek historians has made the actions of Athens somewhat greater than they actually were, and the Roman suffered a lack of historians because they preferred action over writing. Furthermore, the *Catiline* itself seems to be an example of viciousness and twisted *ingenium* producing actions for which Sallust will provide a long-lasting memory. Similarly, the *Jugurtha* offers a totalizing ethical claim: that it is a mistake to think life is ruled by chance and *fortuna* rather than *virtus*, that the *ingenium* produces immortal deeds, that the soul is the ruler of the human race and has power over all things. But not only is this explicitly contradicted by Sallust himself in the *Catiline* ('in all matters fortune is the master', *fortuna in omni re dominatur, B.C.* 8. 1): it is also contradicted by Sulla (known as *Felix*, something like 'blessed with the favour of the gods' or 'the Fortunate') when he speaks to Bocchus about turning over Jugurtha ('fortune generally rules over human affairs', *humanarum rerum fortuna pleraque regit, B.J.* 102.9) and by the narrative

---

[9] Fronto 122 VDH (= II 136 H) describes Ventidius as either having imitated Sallust in a speech proclaiming the victory over the Parthians for which he celebrated a triumph in 38 BCE or having employed him as a ghost writer. On the passage and the history of its interpretation, see Leisner-Jensen 1997 and Vassiliadès 2015.

[10] Syme 1964: esp. 121–37 and 214–39, also the discussion of Perl 1969. For summaries of the state of the question, see McGushin 1992: 20 and Vassiliadès 2015 with bibliography. Many scholars claim to find references to the triumviral period in all of Sallust's writings. For a recent attempt to read the *Histories* as providing analogies to the period of the triumvirate, see Gerrish 2019.

itself, which twice turns upon fortune and chance: Marius begins his political career because 'by chance at Utica a fortune teller said that he should go to Rome to test his fortune; all would be well' (*haruspex dixerat:...fortunam quam saepissume experiretur; cuncta prospere eventura, B.J.* 63. 1. 1),[11] and after Sulla's own emphasis on the role of fortune in events, Bocchus' crucial decision to betray Jugurtha to the Romans comes only after a long series of reversals and changes of intention, as the conflicting emotions of desire (*lubido*) and fear (*metus*) gain control over the king (*B.J.* 108. 3). While Sallust does not mention chance in the closing scene, it certainly seems that Sulla was, once again, lucky and his claim that fortune rules human affairs was more accurate than he knew. In this and other ways Sallust problematizes the relationship between what history should be and what it is, between what we say about it and what happens in writing it.

Similarly, he raises questions about the search for the truth and even the knowability of the facts. Was Crassus involved in the Catilinarian conspiracy? When Tarquinius says that he was (*B.C.* 48. 3), fear, money, and self-interest compel the Senate not only to claim that it was not true, but then to investigate why Tarquinius lied. From this point until the *equites* at the Temple of Concord draw their swords on Caesar (*B.C.* 49. 4) it is impossible to disaggregate wholly fact from rumour: did Tarquinius lie? Was Cicero behind it? Was Caesar behind it? Would naming Crassus help or hurt the conspirators? Would Cicero lie about Crassus when he would not lie about Caesar? Was Crassus telling the truth about Cicero? Why did the *equites* draw their swords? Did they believe the rumours or were they trying display their patriotism as a refutation of their perceived fickleness?[12]

Rumours and beliefs and self-deception become consistent features in the *Catiline* and lie at the juncture between the story the work has to tell and its own claims to historical veracity. If history presents itself as a true version of what actually happened, why does Sallust repeat rumours, especially ones that he claims are not true or not likely to be true? Surely what Catiline actually did, what the public record records, was bad enough? The speech he gives to his fellow conspirators with all witnesses removed (*B.C.* 20. 1) is relatively standard fare in ancient historiography, but why do we need drinking of human blood, especially when Sallust will tell us that there is not much evidence for it (*B.C.* 22. 5)? The answer seems to be: because some said that Cicero's supporters had made it up to help mitigate the hatred men felt for him. Not only does the rumour

---

[11] See further Avery 1967 and Gilbert 1973.

[12] This is elaborated in Batstone 1990 (revised as Chapter 6 of this volume). See also Batstone 1986.

Introduction 7

potentially characterize Catiline through innuendo, but such innuendo itself draws attention to how (dis)information spread in the period. The *Catiline*, again and again, becomes a patchwork of speculation, letters, speeches, rumours, and deceptions.

The problem expands to include the speeches by Caesar and Cato: the former sees in history a record of how even good beginnings can become the precedent for vicious actions, while the latter finds in the ferocious morality of a father killing his son the proper precedent for killing the Catilinarians. These speeches are followed by a comparison of these two men, both men of 'prodigious *virtus*, dissimilar character' (*ingens virtus, divorsis moribus*, 53. 6). But even the comparisons cannot avoid the rhetoric of invective and hostility. To take one example: 'Caesar achieved glory by giving, helping, forgiving; Cato by not offering bribes' (*Caesar dando sublevando ignoscundo, Cato nihil largiundo gloriam adeptus est*, B.C. 54. 3). How is 'not offering bribes' a complementary virtue to 'giving, helping, forgiving'? It seems to be virtuous only to the extent that it accuses Caesar's generosity of being a form of bribery. And, perhaps more disturbing, we have one report that he was flexible on the matter: Cato did not reject bribery in an effort to defeat Caesar in 60 BCE when he ran for the consulship.[13] What presents itself as 'dissimilar character' (*divorsis moribus*) under the rubric of 'prodigious virtue' (*ingens virtus*) turns out to be the competitive rhetoric of the forum and its accusations. Similarly, the deliberative speeches of Caesar and Cato not only offer different solutions to the problem presented by the captured conspirators, but they look at history and moral action from different perspectives. What good is history, if it can yield only a deadlock between the unyielding moral certainty of Manlius Torquatus and the mutability of time that changes good beginnings into bad precedents? And outside the speeches themselves, as they look to the forties, who was right? Or were both wrong?

The problem of knowing what happened and how to understand events becomes in Sallust the readers' problem and the problem that readers themselves will create. One of the things that makes the writing of history such a challenge is the readers. They are located in time and context, and they will suspect the motives of the writer. In the *Catiline*, as the writer seeks an equivalence between words and deeds, these imagined readers accuse the historian of malevolence and 'envy' (*invidia*) when he criticizes, of lying (*ficta pro falsis*) when he praises *virtus* (B.C. 3. 1–2).

---

[13] See Suet. *Div. Iul.* 19: on the election of Bibulus to the consulship, 'not even Cato denied that bribery, under such circumstances, was for the public good' (*ne Catone quidem abnuente eam largitionem e re publica fieri*).

In the *Jugurtha* the memorializing function of history, its record of exemplary actions by exemplary men (*B.J.* 4. 5–6), faces a greater danger: who today competes with his ancestors in virtue? Even the 'new men' depend upon intrigue and theft (*B.J.* 4. 7).

But Sallust's attack on his own times and criticism of his readers does not leave him unscathed. To a large extent, the history of readers of Sallust is a history of accusations relating to his own life and the tendentious purposes of his history. At least since the 'Letter to Caesar' and the 'Invective against Cicero' (since Syme, generally thought not to be by Sallust: see below pp. 14–5), hidden political motives have been inferred from his writing. The pseudo-Ciceronian counter-invective against Sallust turns to his character and his entire life. Dio comments on the historian's rapaciousness; Gellius (*NA* 17. 18), citing Varro (Sallust's older contemporary) remarks: 'Sallust the writer of that stern and unbending style, in whose history we see the marks of the censor created and brandished, was caught by Annius Milo committing adultery, beaten thoroughly with whips, and sent away only after he had paid a fine'. Such invective has been largely discounted as evidence by Sallust's biographers precisely because both acts and charges of extortion and adultery were omnipresent in Roman politics at the time, but it points to a paradox of ancient historiography, which becomes particularly acute in the case of Sallust: first-hand knowledge of political life and high public status contributed to the historian's authority. However, that authority could be undermined if he seemed to use his historical work to settle personal scores.[14] The relationship between the historian's biography and his work was thus highly contestable. The author of a history could be blamed for too great a separation from politics, and for too close a connection with it.

---

[14] The history of Sallust's reception bears out Sallust's fears: Beni 1622, Mommsen 1856: vol. 3, 177n., (Permalink: http://www.deutschestextarchiv.de/book/view/mommsen_roemische03_1856?p=187) and Schwartz 1897 all thought Sallust falsified history to exculpate Caesar; they have been followed by Last 1948 and MacKay 1962. Scaliger 1561, Voss 1627: 74–6, Brosses 1777: 144 praised his writings as those of an objective and sincere historian. It is not often observed that Mommsen's enormously influential verdict appears only in a footnote. For the history of Sallust's scholarly reception up until the 1930s, see Schindler 1939; Leeman 1965 remains an important resource, supplemented by Ramsey 2007. Broughton 1936 thought his representation of Cicero displayed his own fears of reprisal, while Stone 1999 saw a wise, courageous consul; Katz 1983 detected a guilty conscience; Syme 1964: 104–11 finds honesty in Sallust's defence of Caesar and antipathy that was far from denigration in his treatment of Cicero. Such ways of reading Sallust can be traced back to the *Invective* and the letters (assuming, as is usual today, that they are spurious).

In Sallust's works, the relationship between authorship and activity not only becomes an explicit subject but is presented in a way that reveals this contentiousness. The opening of the *Jugurtha* shows how the pressures of the time make Sallust's activity as a historian uniquely valuable (or perhaps worthless) and difficult. He refuses to make the expected generic claims about the *virtus* of history—although he alludes to them—on the grounds that contemporaries would accuse him of arrogance for extolling his own *studium* (4. 2). Instead, he defends himself against charges of *otium* by coupling his task with that *studium*, claiming that the memory of past deeds (*memoria rerum gestarum, B.J.* 4. 6), like the wax images of ancestors, kindles the flame that aspires to *virtus*. It is a page taken from the *pro Archia*,[15] but even as such it draws him into the world where writing subjects one to personal attack of the same sort that would be triggered by public actions. The boundary between the politics of writing and the politics of action is blurred. *Otium*, the context for literary composition, has become more beneficial to the Republic than its alternative (*negotia*, 4. 4). And yet even the author's defence of his *otium* in this upside-down Republic might be reversed by the nature of public life. For those who strive to win office now, to earn *honores* in the old-fashioned way, are so deaf to the lessons of the past that one wonders who the recipients of history's benefits will be.[16]

The way Sallust had introduced his biography in his historiographic debut, the *Catiline* (*B.C.* 3. 3–4. 2), sets the stage for this provocative view of what it meant to write history, and presented it in terms that were, if anything, more radical. There arguments about the historian's life seem no longer simply to perpetuate political conflicts, nor to politicize the act of writing history by measuring the value of literature against deeds in the public sphere, but to instigate a tension between interpreting the historian's text on the basis of his actual political biography and allowing his words to recompose that biography. Sallust reduces his own story to abstract battles against political forces. *Fama* and *invidia* here not only refer to the duplicitous power of language but come to embody it. Such a presentation might be understood again as an authorizing strategy, distancing Sallust's treatment of contemporary figures from charges of favouritism and bias, or as a programmatic introduction to the problems of language that replay these struggles on a higher plane and make it harder to separate the virtuous from the vicious. But Sallust's life is more than abstracted: it is also borrowed. The phases of his disillusionment

---

[15] *propter otium ac studium*, Arch. 3. 14.
[16] For other recent treatments of this much-studied passage, see esp. Grethlein 2006a and Egelhaaf-Gaiser 2010 (= Chapter 12 of this volume).

with politics reproduce the experiences of Plato described in his autobiographical *Seventh Letter*.[17] Readers who recognize this allusion have many strategies available for interpreting it. Does this reference actually justify Sallust and align his project with Plato's? Or does it mark his self-defence as borrowed, removed from particulars? Does it reveal a good conscience or a guilty conscience? Does it whitewash his past or show that Sallust's life matters as it illuminates the conceptual patterns of history his work will trace? Such patterns may indeed reveal a new understanding of the world they describe, or the language in which virtue might be expressed enters the text only after its meanings have been stripped through its competing uses in political rhetoric.[18]

The same competing use of political rhetoric sneaks into the text in a form of intratextuality. In excusing himself for the mistakes of his youth, he remarks that he was just a young man (*adulescentulus*) whose youth had been seized by a corrupt ambition (*ambitione conrupta tenebatur*,[19] *B.C.* 3. 4). The passage is filled with those moral abstractions that made war upon the Republic and upon his 'unwarlike' (*inbecilla*) youth when

---

[17] See Vretska 1976: vol. 1, 96 and Egermann 1932: 27, and Renehan 1976 (= Chapter 4 of this volume) and 2000.

[18] How the preface to the *Histories* had depicted the work of the historian is very difficult to say given the fundamental uncertainties involved in its reconstruction (see the discussion in La Penna and Funari 2015: 119–128, whose own ordering of the fragments is quite radical). In comparison to the monographs' evocations of *omnes homines* (*B.C.* 1. 1) and the *genus humanum* (*B.J.* 1. 1), the opening of the *Histories* strikingly narrows the focus to the story of a particular people, the Romans, in a particular time period. In generic terms too this may seem to avoid the disorienting effect of those earlier introductory gestures, which Quintilian would describe as irrelevant to history. The *Histories*, however, possessed a completely different form and scale. Where the monographs challenge their audience to contextualize their tightly bounded subjects, annalistic history initially seems to stress continuities of both subject (following on from previous consulships) and author (especially if Sallust's period continued the work of Sisenna), the *Histories*' beginning may well have challenged that sense of being part of an integrated whole (see Chapter 15). Certainly the preliminary narrative emphasized the forces that rent rather than united the Republic. There are a couple of hints as well that larger questions about the place of history writing in relation to politics may also have featured in its opening. The catalogue of historiographic virtues assigning brevity to Cato and truthfulness to Fannius (*H.* 1. 4M) strikingly departs from generic precedent by mentioning previous historians by name. And as Scanlon 1998: 201–3 suggested, this gesture may have a further polemical edge as a rebuttal to Cicero's various catalogues of historians, which had graded them entirely on their approximation to oratory (see also McGushin 1992-4: 67–70 and Petrone 1976: 62–3). The tension between historiography and oratory would be even more notable if La Penna is correct in assigning fragments critical of rhetoric (*H.* 4. 54 and Fronto 148. 8 VDH) to the preface (see La Penna and Funari 2015: 121–5, citing La Penna 1973 and 1985).

[19] The phrase can also be read as 'his youth was corrupted and controlled by ambition'. In the slippage from 'corrupt ambition' to 'corrupted youth' there is some uncertainty about where the moral blame lies.

he was carried away with *studium* for the Republic. Toward the end of the *Catiline* this collocation of terms reappears. Cato is recommending the death penalty, and as part of his rhetoric of shame he imagines that some in his audience would want leniency. His sarcastic and mocking reason for having pity on the captured conspirators is 'the little young men made errors through ambition' (*deliquere homines adulescentuli per ambitionem*, *B.C.* 52. 26). It is as if Sallust has Cato attack him and his self-exoneration. Why? Perhaps this just shows how unrestrained Cato's rhetoric is, how little he understands about the Republic and *imbecilla aetas*. Perhaps it suggests that Sallust shared more with the captured conspirators than he can actually admit,[20] that he just barely rescued himself from disastrous decisions: 'and so when my spirit took a rest from many troubles and dangers and I decided that for me the rest of my life should be held far from the Republic' (*igitur ubi animus ex multis miseriis atque periculis requievit et mihi relicuam aetatem a re publica procul habendam decrevi*, *B.C.* 4. 1). It cannot be uninteresting that the only other *adulescentulus* in the *B.C.* is Caesar himself. It is to such resonances and the choices they raise that the text of Sallust's life story alerts his readers.

Questions about the continuities between a public career, a literary career, and the text that grapples with both provide a good introduction to Sallust's scholarly reception over the last century because they echo precisely one of the most important debates within it: whether he was primarily a politician or primarily an author. Is his particular version of events best explained as arising from partisan political motives, so that history writing becomes politics by other means? Or is he inspired by an understanding of Roman historical development, or indeed by a philosophical conception of human aims, to present the events of the past in a particular way? The beginnings of this debate may be traced within this volume; on one side stands Schwartz's (1897) magisterial demonstration of the inconsistencies between what Sallust says about Catiline and other information that has come down to us; on the other, the concluding pages of Klingner's (1928) interpretation of the prologue to the *Histories*, with their assertion that Sallust's pessimistic account of recent history reflects a serious intellectual purpose shaped in response to other literary representations of that past.[21]

---

[20] See Katz 1983 on Sallust's guilty conscience, a reading that may derive from similar comment about Thucydides in Collingwood 1961: 29, 'In reading Thucydides I ask myself, What is the matter with the man, that he writes like that? I answer: he has a bad conscience.'

[21] See Becker 1973 for a fuller account of the stages in this debate.

In Klingner's case, then, the prioritization of Sallust as someone reflecting on politics rather than directly engaged in a political struggle still, understandably, points beyond the complexities of the textual representation to the real intentions of the author. The same tendency also marks one of the most original attempts to connect the literary aspects of Sallust's works with his historical context, by Kurt Latte (1935). Unlike Klingner's emphasis on the work's ideological content, however, Latte, in a manner that seems reminiscent of the new formalist tendencies in contemporary art history, constructs his Sallust from the very texture of the writing, and then embeds the resulting psychic portrait in a powerful, if also impressionistic account of the mental world of the late Roman Republic. His work stands in contrast not only to historicizing approaches to Sallust built on facts rather than words, but also explicitly to literary analyses that treated the description of stylistic features as an end in itself. His organic account of Sallust contains at once one of the most comprehensive and interesting analyses of the way Sallust writes and a thrillingly ambitious, if controversial attempt to imagine the sources of that style in the social realities of the age.

During the period when critical debate about Sallust focused on his ultimate motives for writing, the nature and function of Sallust's prefaces became a key piece of evidence. If Sallust's historical monographs themselves stand out for their tight focus, his prefaces deal in the broadest terms with fundamental ethical issues. We have already encountered Quintilian's surprise in finding historical works begin in this way, and he compares them instead to the practice of epideictic orators. For readers arguing that Sallust's presentation of events was governed by ideas, the distinctive breadth of these beginnings provides powerful support, and much work has been done to establish an intellectual background that gives coherence to their ethical content, arguing variously for the pre-eminence of Plato and/or the Stoics as Sallust's sources, and to demonstrate their thematic importance for the historical narratives that follow.[22] Hard-line advocates for the politically engaged Sallust, and also those who find an emphasis on demonstrating philosophical principles incompatible with the representation of historical truth, have

---

[22] Tiffou 1973 offers a comprehensive reading of the monographs as a playing out of the moral ideas presented in the prefaces. La Penna 1968: 15–67 (originally 1959) gives a thorough summary of the earlier scholarship on the proems. Egermann 1932 argued for the philosophical bona fides, and direct Platonic inspiration, of the prefaces; Pantzerhielm 1936 for a Stoic intermediary. Leeman 1954–5 uses the prefaces to understand the historiographical principles the works manifest. See also Rambaud 1946 and Syme 1964: 240–3.

had little patience with such work.[23] They have argued that the ideas are a pastiche of commonplaces, and point to evidence from Cicero's writings that such prefaces were simply detachable rhetorical pieces and were not expected to relate closely to the specific work they introduce. Recent approaches tend to treat the significance of the prefaces as more of a literary than a historical problem that would be capable of final proof or disproof. Batstone, for example, in Chapter 6, sees the very challenges of finding coherence in the moral arguments of the *Catiline* as a model and signal for the uncertainties that will confront the reader in the work to come.[24] Others might connect the incongruity between the recovery of narrowly historical truth and the transhistorical claims of the prefaces with the debate about the nature of historiography itself and the tensions between reflection and engagement in Sallust's self-presentation. Indeed Earl's (1972) argument that the form of the prefaces specifically recalls the esoteric works of Aristotle, which were very much a recent discovery in late republican Rome, proves particularly thought-provoking in this context. For it not only underlines the newness of these beginnings but also potentially connects this unfamiliarity with the thematic problem of relating Roman history to universalizing discourses, as well as suggesting the role of imported Greek models in this project. As in the case of Thucydides, whose work seems to have enjoyed a recent vogue when Sallust was writing, engagement with Greek sources seems less to complement his assimilation of archaizing features from the Latin tradition than to point a contrast between old and modern intellectual models.[25]

Also closely connected to the interpretation of the prefaces is the study of the ethical content of Sallust's works more broadly. Both his emphasis on moral causes for historical events and the inclusion of passages that evoke the presentational methods of diatribe and satire would become distinctive parts of the historian's legacy and make his work particularly influential for both revolutionary and, thanks to his idealization of the past and anxieties about civil discord, counter-revolutionary polemic.[26]

---

[23] 'In all the watery wastes of Sallustian scholarship there is no more stagnant pool than the literature on the *prooemia*' Badian 1971: 103.

[24] Less deconstructive readings that also take the presentation of ideas in the prefaces seriously include Woodman 1988b: 121–2 and Feeney 1994. For an analysis of how the imagery of the preface to the *Catiline* anchors it thematically to the rest of the work, see Krebs 2008.

[25] For an approach that harmonizes Greek and Roman ideas in the prefaces, see Syme 1964: 242, with further bibliography.

[26] A comprehensive history of Sallust's influence on later political thought remains to be written, as far as we know. On the early modern period, see Fontana 2003 and Osmond 1995 (= Chapter 16 of this volume); for British and American political ideas of the eighteenth century, see Hardy 2007. For two recent attempts to rehabilitate Sallust as a political thinker, see Connolly 2014: 65–114 and Hammer 2014: 145–89.

His portrait of contemporary decline was particularly congenial to Christian critics of Roman worldliness, and Augustine engages closely with his works in the *City of God*.[27] Because Sallust claims to give a historical picture of the moral and political climate of early Rome, and his archaizing style seems to offer access to an ethical language uninfluenced by Greek philosophical considerations, Sallust's works have been mined for information about the development of political and ethical ideas during the Republic. However, no easy line can be drawn between the political mobilization of Sallust's depiction of Rome's moral history—its reception, so to speak—and its academic study. For example, a groundbreaking re-evaluation of Sallust's intellectual seriousness as a historian, published in the first years of the Nazi regime, begins chillingly with author's expressed hope that his study will contribute to 'keeping the exemplary patriotism of the Romans before the eyes of the German people'.[28] In a different historical context, Joy Connolly (2014) makes Sallust's work central to a presentation of Roman republicanism that engages with theories of political action in the wake of the Occupy movement. In this volume, investigation of this dimension of Sallust's writings is represented by a work characterized by its 'objectivity'[29]; D. C. Earl's analysis of the traditional elements in Sallust's ethical ideas and the historian's understanding of contemporary politics has been one of the most influential in English. His is, of course, a fundamentally historical project in locating the complexities and contradictions it describes in the thought of the author rather than the strategies of its textual presentation. And subsequent arguments that Sallust's writings, consciously or unconsciously, challenge the possibility for restoring or even representing ancient *virtus* provide a productive perspective for re-examining his approach. Conversely, his way of understanding the formulation of the text will offer a persuasive alternative for many readers.

In addition to the debate about the significance of the prefaces, another controversy fundamental to arguments about Sallust's motives for writing involves the status of the non-historiographic material that also survives under his name. This consists of a rhetorical attack on Cicero (paired with a 'Ciceronian' attack on Sallust) and two letters

---

[27] For the reception history of the *Histories* in antiquity and beyond, including their use by Christian writers, see La Penna's prolegomena to La Penna and Funari 2015: 1–42. On Augustine see conveniently O'Daly 1999: 240–6, also Marin 1997, Taisne 1997, and Harding 2011.

[28] 'die vorbildliche Staatsgesinnung des Römertums dem deutschen Volke gegenwärtig zu halten' Schur 1934: Foreword.

[29] Cf. Rutledge 1964: 137: 'austere in its objectivity'.

offering advice to Caesar. The first has long been recognized as a school piece (paired with a pseudo-Ciceronian response), but consensus on the letters has proven harder to achieve. For those who want to argue that a political agenda subtends the monographs and histories, they seem to provide external corroboration for both Sallust's views and his aims to put them into effect. The contrary position considers these pieces as consequences rather than explanations of what Sallust says in his authentic works, as rhetorical exercises drawing on the language and themes of the monographs. And for those convinced the *Letters* are forgeries, arguments about Sallust's views that took them as evidence were a fortiori inadmissible (the stakes in the debate about the *Invective* are considerably lower). And so different understandings on the status of the *Letters* tended not only to divide advocates of Sallust the pamphleteer from those of Sallust the historian/thinker but also to isolate national communities of Sallust scholarship from one another. In Italy and Germany, the letters were generally treated as authentic, while in the UK they were considered forgeries and left out of account. It was one of the lasting contributions of Syme's 1964 monograph on Sallust, the last general book on this author in English, to eliminate such divisions with a magisterial demolition of arguments for the letters' authenticity which has been widely, if not universally accepted.[30]

The various attempts to revive Sallust's reputation from the charges of being, on the one hand, a propagandist for Caesar and, on the other, a *littérateur* rather than a serious historian came to fruition in the 1960s with three synoptic monographs which completely changed the terms of the debate about Sallust: Büchner's *Sallust* (1960), Syme's *Sallust* (1964), and La Penna's *Sallustio e la rivoluzione romana* (1968). All three aim

---

[30] A few points of reference for exploring this long scholarly controversy: Last 1923, whose argument against the authenticity of the *Letters* was very significant in the UK, gives a survey of the earlier history of the question; Fraenkel 1951 provides stylistic arguments for rejecting Sallustian authorship of the *Letters*; Syme1964: 314–51, as stated above, made a comprehensive case against all three works being genuine, including a substantial review of the then recent arguments, and marked a decisive turning point in scholarship. See also Ernout 1962, another strong opponent of the genuineness of all three works. Key defences of the authenticity of the *Invective* and the *Letters* include Vretska 1961: vol. 1, 12–15 and 38–48, and Büchner 1967 and 1982: 20–88 and 468–72. Since Syme, agreement can be found in Németh 1992, Thraede 1977 and 1978, Becker 1973, and Lebek 1970. Seel 1966 found the *Letters* genuine but the *Invective* not; Pasoli 1970 agrees that the *Letters* are Sallustian, as do Paananen 1975, Voit 1982, Compagno 1991, and Schmid 1993. There is also a very useful overview in Schmal 2001: 24–30, whose own position that the controversy is insoluble is itself challenged as defeatist by Woytek 2004, himself convinced that the *Letters* cannot be Sallustian. Samotta 2009 is a recent example of an interpretation of Sallust's political beliefs that does employ evidence from the *Letters*; see esp. p. 18, n. 22, with further bibliography. See also Santangelo 2012.

not so much to heal the breach beween the politician and writer as, in extensive treatments of the work's historical content and style, to point out the inadequacy of the competing formulations: as Syme puts it, 'Sallust is at the same time an artist, a politician, and a moralist.'[31] And the task of all three books may be fairly described as giving a rich literary and historical contextualization for this newly integrated author. Both Syme and La Penna rebut portrayals of a narrowly tendentious Sallust through a combination of detailed analyses of his narratives and a more complex and frankly realistic picture of Roman political thought and action during the period. For Syme, this largely involves prosopographical investigation, broadening the dramatis personae of the works to reveal the more complex and flexible political positions that were available, and, especially valuably disproving the idea that Sallust had deliberately diminished Cicero's role in the Catilinarian conspiracy out of political enmity. Syme was the only one of the three who was primarily a historian, and yet his description of Sallust's style, one of the fullest and most accessible in English, becomes the capstone of the book in its demonstration of the tools that Sallust used to give unified expression to his own personality and his view of the times. By contrast both La Penna and Büchner had worked mostly in the field of philology, and thus in a sense travelled a reverse path in relation to Syme's. A particularly striking contrast in La Penna's case comes from the very different conception of history he brings to his analysis of Sallust's views. A Marxist emphasis on social and political forces overshadows the alignment of individual political actors in his understanding of Roman politics. His Sallust is shaped by his background as a member of the Italian upper classes, at once shut out by the Roman aristocracy but also out of sympathy with truly destabilizing revolutionary movements. Perhaps as a result of this ideological inspiration, he presents a more optimistic Sallust, who can construct heroes (like the Sertorius of the *Histories*) as well as shades of villainy. And because his own explanatory model relies on terms and concepts that had no place in Roman historical discourse, a tension arises between his account of Sallust's motives and the historian's own. As opposed to a Sallust who knew very much what he wanted to say, even if he could not always get the facts right, such analysis suggests a necessarily imperfect understanding on the part

---

[31] Given the difficulty of excerpting a work so uniform in tone and quality, whose methodology is so inseparable from its practice, and whose arguments have been so influential, we have decided instead to trust that Syme's *Sallust*, now widely available in paperback and furnished with an excellent introduction by Mellor, will remain an essential and accessible point of reference and comparison for all readers of this volume.

of the historian, and, in a pleasingly Sallustian way, implies how his representations of the past are constrained by the historical conditions under which he wrote. Büchner differs from the others in his acceptance as genuine of the texts Syme bluntly labels 'the false Sallust'. But instead of using the *Letters* as a glimpse into the author's actual political agenda, by taking into account their (alleged) dating some half a decade before the historical works, Büchner makes them the starting point in the author's evolution from a partisan pamphleteer to a more reflective political thinker. Büchner's approach is also the most literary of the three in that he devotes much of his book to the representational means Sallust uses to express these higher political truths, and his discussions of the speeches within the works have been particularly valuable.

Despite the many differences between these scholars' understanding of Sallust and his times, from the role of abstract ideas in his writings to whether personal agency or economic forces best account for Sallust's historical views, their shared synthesis of the writer and the politician found general acceptance. This new phase in Sallust studies saw a shift of focus to the production of scholarly commentaries that have remained standard resources ever since: Vretska's (1976) on the *Catiline*, and Koestermann's (1971) on the *Jugurtha* in German, and McGushin's on the *Catiline* (1977) and the *Histories* (1992–4) with Paul's (1984) on the *Jugurtha* in English. But at the same time new theoretical explorations of historiography as a genre combined with specific arguments in the field of Classics to challenge again fundamental assumptions about the relationship between literary form and both historical content and, ultimately, the relation of the historical author to his text. The tensions between historical and literary approaches to Sallust would re-emerge, but the battleground would shift from Syme's question of 'who was Sallust?' (1964: 3) to the works themselves and the validity of conflicting interpretative models for understanding them. Hayden White in the 1970s argued that, far from being the means of conveying information, the literary form in which history was written possessed its own 'content', implicitly challenging the dichotomy observable in the structure of Syme and La Penna's books between the histories and their style.[32] If the narrative form of history inevitably imposes a plot on the events it depicts, then even though we grant that an author can choose that form, as Sallust highlights the brevity of his monographs, he may no longer be easily said to control its significance.

---

[32] In addition to his magnum opus *Metahistory* (1973), White's ideas on historiographic form may be most readily approached in the essays collected in his 2010 volume. For other recent discussions of history and literature, see Jenkins 1991 and Batstone 2009.

This theoretical reprioritization of the formal aspects of any historical work in relation to its informational content was complemented in the field of Classics by historicizing approaches to writing history as a literary practice. In 1979, T. P. Wiseman tackled the problem of how the detailed information about Rome's early development presented by historians like Livy could have been preserved, given that these events were centuries earlier than any written narrative that might have been available to Livy or his antecedents. His solution was that such accounts had been bulked out not through access to any now lost sources, but by the same techniques developed by rhetoricians for creating verisimilar narration. A. J. Woodman (1988b) did not confine his discussion to historians like the Roman annalists, often suspected of excessive credulity, but argued that even writers like Thucydides, who seemed to predict the intellectual rigour of the modern academic historian, understood their work primarily in rhetorical terms. Their ultimate aim was not the representation of the past as it really was but building narratives that accomplished the effects prescribed for public speakers: teaching, delighting, and inspiring their audiences (though much room was left for polemic among different practitioners of the genre for which of these aims ought to take precedence).

This redefinition of historiography as fundamentally a rhetorical practice gave a new status to formal analyses, now freed from the assumption that historical narratives mattered only because of, or were in large measure predetermined by, their informational content. Sallust's manipulation of narrative form had often been studied as evidence for his efforts to distort the truth. Now, though, these narratives could be seen as literary structures worthy of analysis without such a priori assumptions about their function. And attention to the effect of a text on its audience, together with its distancing from an external truth that might seem to guarantee its coherence or rationality, expanded the range of narrative models scholars were willing to entertain: for example, Levene's argument that the *Jugurtha* is structured as a fragment, or Kraus' analysis of the same work as focused on a protagonist who ultimately defies representation. For the *Catiline*, such an approach is exemplified by Batstone's account of the work as a 'rhetorical artifice' which challenges the audience's sense that the past is knowable or that the moral certainty Sallust seems to offer can be securely obtained.[33] Those portions of Sallust's narratives that had no close connection to what was taken to be Sallust's main interest in Roman politics, especially

---

[33] See Chapter 6 of this volume.

the geographical excursus in the *Jugurtha*, also assumed a new importance within the semantic economy of his works. While Latte too had focused on the interpretative difficulties that result from the perpetual oscillation Sallust creates between antitheses, these new analyses, rather than leading to psychohistory, imagine authorial strategies to engage his readers or to reproduce the experience of the paradoxical and disruptive nature of the events described.

Yet in one respect these same tendencies of Latte's work point to another influential recent development in Sallustian scholarship. For while Levene and Kraus grant a greater role to the audience as interpreters of events, they also operate with a strong model of authorial intention. But if Sallust's narrative is shaped by his times, whether through their effect on his mental and emotional structures or because his perspective derives from social processes that he cannot stand apart from to describe, as Marxist analysis would suggest, or even because the language or formal structures he uses have changed their meanings, as Cato complains, then limits emerge to the control the designing author implied by the rhetorical model of ancient historiography can exert over his work. History again comes to shape Sallust's narrative, not as its content, the truth he is bound to tell, but as the context for its production and reception. Thus, in place of a Sallust structuring his text to emphasize the irreconcilability of the antitheses it creates, for Gunderson the 'interaction between mind and history brings into question the sovereignty of Sallust's own *ingenium*'.[34]

L'Année philologique lists over three hundred publications on Sallust so far in the twenty-first century. And while their number and diversity challenge generalization, some of the trends in current scholarship may be usefully understood in relation to the trajectories of investigation we have been sketching. The increasing scope won in the last decades of the previous century for scholarship that privileged questions about historical writings' textual aspects over their value as information has continued to open historiography to approaches more common in the study of other literary genres. The question of how intertextuality, the hermeneutic relationship between literary texts, operates in historiography has received considerable attention. In place of an instrumental approach that conceived of a historian as 'using' either sources of information or stylistic models for presenting that information, the works that scholars had identified as contributing to the composition of a history came to be studied rather as presences determining how that

---

[34] See Chapter 7, p. 211 et passim.

history was read.[35] Yet for all that historiographers' interest in intertextuality derives in large part from its importance in the study of Latin poetry, it can in practice equally highlight the distinctiveness of history's generic claim to authority based on the truth of its representations. Someone struck by the similarity between two epic accounts of a duel would, for example, be less likely to think it arose because both were describing the same 'real' event. And, while battles and political rebellions may seem more believable if they conform to a reader's experience of how such episodes are typically handled, the recollection that two historians differ in specific details or that Sallust's description of a Roman siege recalls what Thucydides said of a completely different event can provide a sharp reminder of the inevitable subjectivity of even the most scrupulous historian and of the inevitable distance between any event and its textual representation. Reading history against this polyphonic textual background can thus emphasize an author's capacity to clarify his audience's understanding of his own work or to confront them with its contradictions; but it can also introduce new challenges to the 'sovereignty of [the historian's] *ingenium*' as other authorial voices emerge through his own.[36]

Sallust provides a particularly rich subject for such an approach. The explicitness of many of his evocations of earlier writers had created a long tradition of identifying Sallust's 'models', and comparisons with Thucydides in particular feature regularly in accounts of his style and attitudes.[37] And questions about how his Thucydidean affinities differentiate Sallust from earlier Roman historians, or how his Roman priorities refract allusions to the Athenian historian, reveal how the Thucydidean presence in his text folds into larger concerns about Roman identity and cultural transformation in his work.[38] Indeed, the relationship between Sallust and Thucydides has been a particular focus of recent scholarship. That this scholarship includes both Meyer's argument that in Pompey's letter (*H.* 2.98M) Sallust conveys a highly nuanced message about civil-war

---

[35] Some important methodological discussions of intertextuality within ancient historiography include Damon 2010, Levene 2010: 82–163, O'Gorman 2009, and Pelling 2013.

[36] Gunderson 2000: 119 (= Chapter 7, p. 211 of this volume).

[37] On Sallust's imitation of Greek authors, see, e.g., Avenarius 1957, Perrochat 1949, and the path-breaking works of Renehan 1976 (= Chapter 4 of this volume) and 2000; on Sallust's Roman antecedents, see Skard 1956. On Thucydides, see to the works cited below in nn. 39–40, esp. Scanlon 1980.

[38] Although it never uses the word and predates the rise of explicitly intertextual readings in Latin studies, Levene 2000's analysis of the complexity of Sallust's allusions to the elder Cato (Chapter 8) is an exemplary demonstration of how this approach bears on the coherence of the historian's own voice and attitudes.

Rome through the 'allusive imitation' of Nicias' letter in Thucydides (7. 11–15),[39] and Grethlein's observation of a fundamental difference between Sallust's narrative voice and Thucydides' itself demonstrates the openness of the method and its ability to convey very different conceptions of authorship.[40]

Attention to other literary aspects of Sallust's work has also highlighted its polyphony and complexity. Sallust's reliance on the direct representation of speeches and documents in all of his works to convey reflection on events had long been noted. But the more immanent voices conjured up by these embedded rhetorical performances stand in an uncertain relationship to the narrative voice of the historian. And as that voice has itself been understood as a literary phenomenon or as the manifestation of the actual author's political views, 'intratextual' comparisons can address questions about the nature of historiographic representation itself, especially its capacity to stand apart from politics, and about the historian's understanding of the past in relation to those articulated at the time.[41] Readings explicitly informed by narratological theory provide a language for extending the exploration of the presence of the author in the text and the relationship between history and its telling. Grethlein, again, has set out a productive framework for addressing these questions by highlighting how ancient historians manipulate the intrinsic potential opposition between a hindsight that understands events as causes and effects and a reconstruction of how events were perceived by participants at the time who had no access to any teleological perception of what they were undergoing. His treatment of Sallust himself highlights the variety and perhaps the openness of the historian's representation of the past, as it shuttles between the mimetic priorities of the *Jugurtha*, which reproduces the confusions of that baffling war, to what he sees as the emphasis of the *Catiline* on fitting the specific event into a larger understanding of Roman history as a whole.[42]

Yet the Sallustian text with most to gain from these new trends may prove to be his fragmentary masterpiece the *Histories*. Until very recently

---

[39] Meyer 2010; the quoted phrase is taken from Scanlon 1980: 97.

[40] 'While the Thucydidean style evokes the impression of the events telling themselves, the voice of the Sallustian narrator reinforces the gap between narrative and events' Grethlein 2006b: 322–3. Also Döpp 2011, Gärtner 2011a, 2011b, and 2011c, and Spielberg 2017.

[41] See esp. Egelhaaf-Gaiser 2010 (= Chapter 12 of this volume) and the other essays in Pausch 2010; also Batstone 2010a and 2010b, Dué 2000, Feldherr 2012 and 2013, and Sklenář 1998, as well as the work on the *Histories* cited below.

[42] Grethlein 2013: 268–308; for other explicitly narratological approaches to Sallust, see esp. Batstone 2009 and Miller 2015.

this was a difficult text both to study and to teach. No new edition of the fragments had appeared since Maurenbrecher's in 1893. Yet beginning in the 1990s a series of important works offered updated and expanded presentations of and commentaries on this material: McGushin (1992–4) provided a translation and historically oriented commentary (although unfortunately without the Latin text), Funari (1996) re-edited all the fragments preserved indirectly, through citation, with a full philological commentary,[43] and has since begun a complete multivolume edition of all the fragments with La Penna and Funari (2015), and finally Ramsey (2015) produced an invaluable edition for the Loeb Classical Library with English translation. This renewed attention to the text and ordering of the fragments has coincided with increasingly nuanced understandings of the relationship between the historian's viewpoint and the perspectives embedded in the rhetorical set pieces that constitute the fullest excerpts from the work to prompt new evaluations both of the historical value of his text for the crucial decade of the seventies and of Sallust's own political aims.[44]

The authors of this introduction are very conscious of their own participation in a specific moment in the history of Sallust's reception. How much is the image of a Sallust disjoining the representational and rhetorical dimensions of his writing conditioned by the penultimate directions the literary turn in historiographical studies has taken? It would certainly be a challenge to explain to many of the scholars whose works we have included. Or can we claim that the terms of such inquiry are but new manifestations of the 'difficult task' that Sallust himself makes of historiography? The very debates about how context determines reading extend from the first century BCE to the present problem of balancing a Sallust through whom we perceive events and ideas against a Sallust who ultimately highlights the struggle to obtain any such certainties from language and narrative. In this perspective, everyone reading Sallust, however much they search for impartiality, risks repeating the struggle of the historian to free himself from the conflicts about which he writes, which by his own account of his life would make writing history a repetition of living it. The spoils for such a perpetual battle to disembed the text from its histories include the perception that Sallust matters not simply as a test case for chronicling

---

[43] Funari 2008 complements this work with an edition of the fragments preserved in codices and papyri.

[44] On the speeches, see especially Adler 2006, Gärtner 2011a, Meyer 2010, Rosenblitt 2011, 2013, and 2016, Speilberg 2017, and Steed 2017. For Sallust and contemporary politics, see Gerrish 2019 and, on the 70s BCE, Rosenblitt 2019.

different ways in which scholars of the last hundred years have approached their task, but as an author whose work provokes us to ask questions that will always matter in thinking about history and its representations: how do we know the truth of what happened? Can narrative explanations ever tell us about more than the point of view from which they were formulated? How can history be an action as it represents actions? How do we, as readers and writers, match words and deeds?

2

Sallust

Diction and Sentence Structure, Narrative Style and Composition, Personality and Times

Kurt Latte

I. DICTION AND SENTENCE STRUCTURE

The idiosyncratic language of Sallust, so clearly distinct from the prose of its day, has provoked countless studies.[1] Of those not confined to particular phenomena such as asyndeton or chiasmus, the overwhelming majority are purely descriptive and are motivated more by grammatical than by stylistic investigations. Of its more general aspects, only the relationship of Sallust's language to archaizing or colloquial Latin and consequently to the contemporary emergence of Atticism has received thorough discussion. No attempt has yet been made to isolate from this abundance of data those elements which determine the effect of Sallust's style and to connect them with the way he shapes his narrative. The following account is limited to a few examples which are representative of Sallust's style and consciously omits less prominent features. It starts from the impression made on the reader and seeks its explanation in the writer's intellectual make-up.[2]

---

[1] Latte's monograph has been very lightly abridged by the editors: some supporting examples which Latte quoted in full are here merely given as references, and an occasional note treating textual controversies has been omitted where recent editions render it irrelevant.

[2] The *Letters to Julius Caesar*, the authenticity of which has been so fervently discussed in recent years that they threaten to distract attention from the principal works, are deliberately left out of account. I preferred to set out the writer's particular stylistic character based on works of undoubted authenticity; to apply these findings to the *Letters* would require a study of its own, which hopefully can soon be conducted elsewhere. The change in Sallust's use of

Every stylistic study of an ancient author does well to attend first to the testimonies of the ancient tradition, even though it cannot stop there. These are abundantly available for Sallust and reveal that he had a well-established place within Roman literary history as a paradigm for certain stylistic qualities; the judgements hardly differ from one another. His archaism is emphasized already by his immediate contemporaries, at first as a criticism. Asinius Pollio, in a work dedicated to the subject,[3] accused Sallust of 'excessive imitation of archaic diction' (*nimia priscorum verborum imitatio*, Suet. *Gramm.* 10); the grammarian Pompeius Lenaeus called him 'a most unlearned thief of archaic and Catonian words' (*priscorum Catonisque verborum ineruditissimum furem*, ibid. 15. 1). Imitation of Thucydides was also recognized early; Velleius calls him the 'rival of Thucydides' (*aemulus Thucydidis*, 2. 36. 2; cf. Quint. *Inst.* 10. 1. 101, Sen. *Contr.* 9. 1. 13). The archaizing period of the second century CE, conversely, cannot praise him enough. Fronto recommends him to Marcus Aurelius as a model (I 14 H, 44 VDH); Gellius, of course, reaches a similar judgement (*NA* 4. 15. 1). Even the closely related boldness of his neologisms was observed; Valerius Probus makes use of it to justify an obviously false conjecture (Gell. *NA* 1. 15. 18; fr. I Aistermann). Fronto, moreover, admired the architecture of his work (*structe...historiam scripsit*, 'he wrote history in a structured way', II 48 H, 132 VDH), a judgement which will find confirmation in what follows. Even Sallust's predilection for antithesis did not escape Fronto: 'Sallust used decorously arranged antitheses: "of others' property greedy, of his own prodigal, with sufficient eloquence but too little wisdom" (*B.C.* 5. 4); and with wordplay that was not strained or trivial but restrained and elegant: "masker and unmasker"' (*Sallustium antithetis honeste compositis usum: 'alieni appetens, sui profusus, satis eloquentiae, sapientiae parum'; paronomasia etiam non absurda neque frivola, sed proba et eleganti: 'simulator atque dissimulator'*, II 158 H, 100 VDH). We may assume that the disdain expressed for idle word-spinning was directed at Seneca, given the well-known antipathy towards him during this archaizing period; indeed, Fronto elsewhere finds fault with Lucan's *iusque datum sceleri* ('legality bestowed to crime', 1. 2) by contrast to Sallust's formulation *omne ius in validioribus esse* ('all legality belongs to the stronger', *H.* 1.18 M): without

---

language, which Löfstedt 1933: 290 treated with customary sensitivity, is left aside for a different reason. Proofs of this kind are much easier to establish in the study of word choice and syntax than in that of style proper, in which great differences are hardly to be expected over the short span of less than ten years lying between the *Catiline* and the *Histories*, above all for a writer who composes as self-consciously as Sallust.

[3] Perhaps the *Epistula ad Plancum*, Gell. *NA* 10. 26. 1.

regard for the heavy rhythm of the Sallustian phrase, it is evidently the overblown artifice of expression that he finds offensive in Lucan; *iura dare* is otherwise used to express jurisdiction over subject peoples, whereas here it must mean 'authority is entrusted to criminals'; in addition there is the use of the abstract *scelus* in place of Sallust's concrete *validiores*. We find a similar appraisal of the relationship between Seneca and Sallust in a detailed discussion of *brevitas*, which has always been considered the most distinctive feature of Sallust's style. Quintilian, who admits its appropriateness to historiography but cautions against its use in oratory, speaks of the 'Sallustian brevity and his "broken off" style' (*Sallustiana **brevitas** et abruptum sermonis genus, Inst.* 4. 2. 25) and of those imitators of Sallust who make themselves 'hard to understand because of their abbreviated endings' (***praecisis** conclusionibus obscuri*, ibid. 10. 2. 7); his opponent Seneca speaks of 'thoughts cut short and words ending earlier than expected' (*Ep.* 114. 17, ***amputatae** sententiae et verba **ante exspectatum** cadentia*). One noticed in him, then, a premature breaking off of sentence conclusions which hampered the flow of the rhythm.[4] A Ciceronian like Quintilian and a representative of the 'new' style of the Neronian period are agreed in their criticism of this tendency. This fact is important since Seneca's language at first glance appears to have much in common with Sallust's, and no less a figure than Eduard Norden (1898: 1. 310) has voiced the judgement that Seneca's assessment of Sallust's faults could as well be applied to the philosopher's own style. Again, it is necessary to distinguish the historian's style from similar phenomena in order to make the emphasized in ancient criticism once once more clear to us.

At *B.C.* 15. 5 Sallust represents Catiline's outward appearance: *igitur colos **ei exanguis**, **foedi oculi**, **citus** modo, modo **tardus** incessus: prorsus in facie voltuque vecordia inerat* ('his complexion was bloodless; hideous his eyes; now swift, now slow his gait, and overall in his face and expression madness was present'). The description is given in two clipped segments focused on substantives and chiastically arranged; the brevity of the cola, which consist almost entirely of emphatic words (only *ei* in the first colon and *modo~modo* in the second stand in the middle, without emphasis), gives the expression a forceful, penetrating quality.

---

[4] *verba bene cadunt* and the like are the principal technical expressions for clausula rhythm; cf. Cic. *Orat.* 170, *infracta et amputata loquuntur*, and in contrast to that 168, *contiones saepe exclamare vidi, cum **apte verba cecidissent***. But the passages about Sallust must not be taken to refer only to his avoidance of rhythmic clausulae, but rather also to the absence of similarly constructed parallel cola. 'Roughness of harmony' is a sign of Thucydidean style (Dion. Hal. *Ep. ad Amm.* 2. 2, τὸ τραχὺ τῆς ἁρμονίας; cf. Cic. *Or.* 32).

Prorsus introduces the concluding sentence, which once again has a bipartite structure, although *facies* and *voltus*, the more general and the more specific terms, appear practically as synonyms in juxtaposition to one another and show again the importance the writer attached to such duality. A somewhat analogous passage appears in Seneca's description of Caligula: *tanta illi palloris insaniam testantis **foeditas** erat, tanta oculorum sub fronte anili latentium **torvitas**, tanta capitis destituti et emendaticiis capillis aspersi **deformitas**; adice obsessam saetis cervicem et **exilitatem** crurum et **enormitatem** pedum* ('so great was the hideousness of the pallor bearing witness to his insanity, so great the cruelty of the eyes lurking beneath his old woman's brow, so great the ugliness of his head, bald and scattered with prosthetic hair; add to that a neck covered in bristles and the thinness of his legs and the hugeness of his feet', Constant. 18. 1). The structure is quite similar: after three sentences linked to each other through anaphora and the assonance of abstract nouns ending in -*itas*, there follows a similarly tripartite conclusion, in which again both of the last cola are linked by sound patterns. However, the difference from Sallust is apparent: Sallust avoids assonance of final syllables, which lends a playful quality to the whole expression, whereas Seneca famously loves it so much that he does not shrink from using neologisms to produce this effect.[5] The depiction of Catiline is oriented entirely towards physical, outwardly visible characteristics; only in the final sentence does *vecordia* ('madness') connect these characteristics to the conspirator's mental state. For Caligula we get far more sharply observed details, but the expression consistently highlights their effect on the viewer: not *pallor* ('paleness') but *palloris foeditas* ('the hideousness of his paleness') and likewise not *torvi oculi* ('cruel eyes') but *torvitas oculorum* ('the cruelty of his eyes'). Thus, the sensory impression, the physical reality, retreats behind the projected mental state and the interpretation. Finally—and here we reach perhaps the essential difference—Seneca's sentences have their emphasis at the end; the cola are ordered in parallel (genitive—participle—subject) and conclude in every case with a word of similar meaning; the variety of the expression serves only to hammer home the same impression of ugliness with ever-changing turns

---

[5] *torvitas* and *enormitas* are neologisms. Sallust has only one construction of the kind, B.J. 66. 2, *volgus... seditiosum atque **discordiosum** erat* (for the more usual *discors*). There is nothing in Sallust comparable to the distribution of echoing clause-endings. The alliterative correspondences that are frequent in him are of a different kind, such as *fluxa atque fragilis* (B.C. 1. 3), *metus atque maeror* (B.J. 39. 1), *pollens potensque* (B.J. 1. 3; see Kroll 1927: 300). These are partly formulaic and were already popular in the oldest Latin prose as linguistic ornamentation (Fraenkel 1922: 360) and are thus an archaizing element in Sallust.

of phrase. In Sallust, by contrast, we find a kind of pendulum motion: the emphatic beginning passes through an unemphatic middle to an emphatic conclusion, and this impression of swinging to and fro is emphasized through the chiastic arrangement of parts. Compared with this, it is perhaps of less importance that Seneca is far more verbose and employs empty verbs like *erat* or *adice* for the sake of syntactic completeness.[6]

Sallust's fondness for chiasmus has long been recognized.[7] A few examples will suffice here: *eos... laetos modo, modo*[8] *pavidos animadvorteres; ac sicuti* **audiri** *a suis aut* **cerni** *possent,* **monere** *alii alii* **hortari**, *aut* **manu** *significare aut* **niti** *corporibus* ('you would have seen them **happy** now, now **sad**; and as they were able to be **heard** by their own troops or **seen**, **warned** some, others **exhorted**, or with **hands made signs** or **strove with bodies**', *B.J.* 60. 4); *consulibus* **insidias tendere**, **parare incendia** | *opportuna* **loca** *armatis hominibus* **obsidere** || *ipse cum telo esse, item* **alios iubere** | **hortari** *uti semper intenti paratique essent* || *dies noctisque* **festinare, vigilare** | *neque insomniis neque labore* **fatigari**. ('for the consuls **traps he sets** | **he readies arson** | suitable **places** with armed troops **he occupies** || **he himself** with weapon stands, and so **others he orders** | **he encourages** them to be always tensed and ready || day and night **he hastens and is wakeful** | neither by wakefulness nor labour is **he wearied**', *B.C.* 27. 2; cf. also *B.J.* 36. 2 and *B.C.* 11. 4). The last example is already more artfully constructed: the two segments marked at the end with a double bar fall into three units, of which in each case the first two are more tightly bound to each other through chiasmus, while the last colon, separated by a single bar, reverses the word order of the one immediately preceding it; moreover, in one of these concluding cola the verb occurs last (*obsidere*), and in the other first (*hortari*), so that their chiastic relation to each other is made apparent. The conclusion to the passage, like the two preceding clauses, is composed of two parallel phrases; in both cases the thought is expressed once positively and once negatively; mercilessness and pillaging, restless activity and indefatigability stand side by side. This handful of examples already shows that the purely formal rhetorical figure of antithesis in Sallust

---

[6] By way of illustration, the attempt may cautiously be made to translate the Seneca passage into the style of Sallust. It would perhaps run something like this: *foedus illi pallor insaniam testans, oculi sub fronte anili torvi, caput calvom raro et infecto capillo, postremo cervix saetosa, exilia crura, pedes enormes.*

[7] The material is in Steele 1891: 13ff. See also Kroll 1927: 300.

[8] *modo...modo* is almost always chiastic, as Kroll recognized (ibid.); to the only exception mentioned by him (*B.C.* 56. 4) one must add *B.J.* 57. 4 as well.

corresponds to a peculiarity in his arrangement of ideas, which restlessly tosses the listener between antithetical terms.

This principle can explain a form of simple sentence which is closely related to the chiastic expressions just analysed: *fiducia augeri nostris coepit et promi lingua* ('**confidence** began **to be increased for our troops** and **expressed in their speech**', *H.* 3. 36 M), *ubi se **dolis fatigari** videt neque ab hoste **copiam pugnandi fieri*** ('when he saw that **he was being worn out with tricks** and from the enemy **no opportunity for battle was forthcoming**', *B.J.* 56. 1); *ex summa laetitia atque lascivia, quae diuturna quies peperat, repente omnis **tristitia** invasit* ('after **the greatest joy and abandonment**, which the long period of inactivity had produced, suddenly **sadness** invaded all', *B.C.* 31. 1); *neque plane ocultati humilitate arborum et tamen incerti, quidnam esset* ('**neither completely hidden** on account of the lowness of the trees and **nevertheless unclear as to what** was there', *B.J.* 49. 5; see also, for example, *B.C.* 7. 7 and 33. 3). The difference from the previously discussed sentence type is that here there is a single pair of contraries; the result is the simpler form *a–b–a*, in place of the *a–b–b–a* of chiasmus. But the movement of the sentence and the distribution of emphasis are similar. Beginning and end are forcefully stressed; between them lies a weakly stressed element containing explanatory qualifiers and syntactic fillers. The arc can be further stretched, so that the contraries are distributed between two adjacent clauses: *quoi (Metello) quamquam **virtus, gloria** atque alia optanda bonis superabant, tamen inerat **contemptor animus et superbia*** ('although Metellus possessed **virtue, glory**, and all other things good men choose in abundance, nevertheless there dwelled in him a **contemptuous spirit and pride**', *B.J.* 64. 1); *pro victoria satis iam pugnatum, reliquos labores **pro praeda** fore* ('the fighting has already been enough **for victory**, the remaining efforts would be **for plunder**', *B.J.* 54. 1; see also *B.J.* 13. 1). Two sentences are even joined in this way: *non peculatus aerari factus est neque per vim sociis **ereptae pecuniae**, quae quamquam gravia sunt, tamen consuetudine iam pro nihilo habentur; hosti acerrumo **prodita senatus auctoritas, proditum imperium vostrum** est* ('**no theft from the treasury** occurred **nor** through violence from the allies was **money plundered**, which crimes, though serious, are now considered trivial because of our habituation: to our bitterest enemy **betrayed was the Senate's authority, betrayed your command**', *B.J.* 31. 25). The repeated negation in the first part and the anaphora in the second ensure that the corresponding double clauses stand out to the ear.

Nor is it only antitheses that can bracket sentences in this way; often the thought returns to its starting point. *B.C.* 20. 9 shows an intermediate stage: *nonne* **emori per virtutem** *praestat quam vitam miseram et inhonestam, ubi alienae superbiae per ludibrium fueris,* **per dedecus amittere?** ('is not **to die through courage** better than a life that is wretched and dishonourable **to lose through shame?**'). The opposed terms *virtus* and *dedecus* are both paired with a verb of dying. Synonyms balance each other at B.C. 5. 8: *incitabant praeterea corrupti civitatis mores quos pessuma et divorsa inter se mala* **luxuria atque avaritia vexabant** ('**provoking** him too were the corrupted morals of the state, which the two worst and contradictory evils, **luxury and avarice, were undermining**'). The clauses do not correspond in their syntactic function: Catiline is the object of *incitabant*, while *mores* is the object of *vexabant*. But for the ear, the likeness of form and meaning at its beginning and end binds the sentence together. Elsewhere Sallust achieves a similar effect by repeating a word: *quoniam* **armis** *bellum parum procedebat, insidias regi per amicos tendere et eorum perfidia* **pro armis** *uti parat* ('since the campaign was making no progress **by arms**, he prepared to set a trap for the king through his friends and use treachery **in place of arms**', B.J. 61. 3). At times the echo is purely formal: *ab* **imperatore** *consulto trahi* (*bellum*) *quod homo inanis et regiae superbiae* **imperio** *nimis gauderet* ('**by the commander** the war was dragged on deliberately because a vain man with the pride of a king enjoyed **command** too much', B.J. 64. 5). Even here the intention, in light of this pattern, is unmistakable.

While in these cases the emphasis is placed at the beginning and end of the sentence, elsewhere in Sallust we find sentence structures in which two strongly emphasized groups come together directly in the middle: *quod ei per* **maximam amicitiam maxima copia** *fallundi erat* ('because through **the greatest friendship the greatest power** of deceiving was his', B.J. 61. 4), *finis meos advorsum* **armatos armis** *tutatus sum* ('my lands against **the armed by arms** I defended', B.J. 110. 6; cf. also B.J. 63. 4, B.J. 67. 1, and B.J. 110. 2). This constitutes a kind of inversion: the emphasized words are pushed inwards from both ends; in place of the overall pendulum motion seen in the sentence structures treated above, we have here two halves whose climaxes meet in the middle, while the low points lie at beginning and end.

What all the forms discussed share is that two ideas which either oppose each other or belong together are strongly emphasized by their placement at both ends of the sentence or in the middle. This is frequently, but by no means always, achieved through syntactically equivalent components (i.e. nouns with nouns). This preference for duality of expression explains a number of other features familiar to every reader of Sallust.

He is fond of structuring tripartite sentences in such a way that the first two parts link themselves together, or that the third splits itself again into two parts: *interea plebs coniuratione patefacta* . . . *Catilinae consilia execrari, Ciceronem ad caelum tollere;* | *veluti ex servitute erepta* **gaudium atque laetitiam** *agitabat* ('meanwhile the people, when the conspiracy was revealed cursed the plans of Catiline, praised Cicero to the stars; | as if rescued from slavery experience **happiness and exaltation**', *B.C.* 48. 1; cf. also *B.C.* 21. 2). The 'Law of Increasing Components',[9] according to which the longest units in a multipartite expression are pushed to the final position, is not a sufficient explanation. This is shown by cases in which the first segment itself is extended, e.g., ***consulares omnes itemque senatus magna pars*** *sententiam eius laudant,* | *virtutem animi ad caelum ferunt, alii alios increpantes timidos vocant* ('**all the consulars** and **a great part of the Senate** too praise his opinion, exalt to the skies the virtue of his soul, while they charge one another with timidity', *B.C.* 53. 1; cf. also *B.J.* 70. 5). Moreover, the last segment can be extended in other ways than through a bipartite expression. How much importance Sallust placed on this principle is shown in *B.C.* 48. 1 (above) by the fact that, contrary to his usual pursuit of brevity, he places the synonyms *laetitia* and *gaudium* beside each other. Groupings of this sort are indeed quite common for him.[10] 'Face and expression' (*facie voltuque, B.C.* 15. 5) has already been singled out; for other pairs of synonyms, cf. *B.C.* 38. 4, *B.C.* 39. 4, *B.J.* 30. 4, and *B.J.* 31. 2.[11] Nor can such expressions be accounted for sufficiently as imitations of old Latin formulaic turns of phrase;[12] rather, they are rooted in Sallust's most distinctive stylistic tendencies.

The same aim for duality also effectively governs his characteristic variation of particles. He transforms tripartite expressions into bipartite ones by joining two of the members more closely together though the selection of particles: *alii volgum effusum oppido caedere,* **alii** *ad portas festinare,* **pars** *turris capere* ('**some** slaughter the crowd poured out from the town, **some** rush to the gates; **part** seize the towers', *B.J.* 69. 2), *oleastro* **ac** *murtetis* **aliisque** *generibus arborum* ('with wild olive **and**

---

[9] Cf. *LHS*: 722–6, and in addition the careful analysis of Lindholm 1931.

[10] The fact is already emphasized in ancient stylistic criticism: *Valerium Probum audivi haec dicere, usum esse Sallustium* **circumlocutione quadam poetica** *et cum dicere vellet, hominem avaritia corrumpi, corpus et animam dixisse* ('I have heard Valerius Probus say that Sallust employed an almost poetic form of circumlocution, and when he meant that a man was corrupted by avarice used to say "body and soul" were corrupted', Gell. *NA* 3. 1. 5). It is amusing to read Favorinus' resistance against this incontestable observation in the Gellius passage: he clings to the rigid formula of Sallust's *brevitas*.

[11] More at Kroll 1927: 301.

[12] So Kroll (ibid.), citing Hache 1907: 21, and Fraenkel 1922: 359ff. On these 'exhaustive doublings' in old Latin, see the fine work of Haffter 1934: 53ff. He too (81 n. 1) understands the phenomenon in Sallust as the 'continuation of old-Latin historiographical diction'. On the intensive force of pleonasms, see Löfstedt 1933: 175ff.

myrtles, **also** with other sorts of trees', *B.J.* 48. 3; cf. also *B.J.* 31. 10, *B.J.* 43. 4, and *B.J.* 74. 1). A further consequence of these efforts is the occasional splitting up of simple sentences, a process in which Sallust's preference for paratactic expressions is, of course, also at work: *emissae eo cohortes Ligurum quattuor et C. Annius praefectus* ('four cohorts of Ligurians were dispatched there, and C. Annius the prefect', *B.J.* 77. 4), to which one may compare the usual formula in Caesar: *Caesar postero die T. Labienum legatum cum iis legionibus, quas ex Britannia reduxerat in Morinos... misit* ('the next day Caesar sent the legate T. Labienus with the legions which he had brought back from Britain against the Morini', *Gall.* 4. 38). *B.C.* 50. 1 is similar: *dum haec in senatu aguntur et dum legatis Allobrogum... praemia decernuntur* ('while these things were being decided in the Senate and while rewards were decreed for the ambassadors of the Allobroges'), whereas something like *quibus rebus cognitis a senatu... praemia decernuntur* would correspond to the typical style of historiographical narrative. Everywhere we encounter the same basic tendency in the shaping of his thoughts.

The desire to introduce pairs of opposites is so strong in Sallust that it occasionally emerges with no regard for context. The magnificently dark conclusion to the *Catiline* portrays the horrors of the Civil Wars The victors roam the battlefield: 'Turning over the enemy corpses, some discover a friend, part find a host and relative; there were also those who recognized their personal enemies' (*volventes hostilia cadavera amicum alii, pars hospitem et cognatum reperiebant; fuere item, qui inimicos suos cognoscerent, B.C.* 61. 8). The term 'friends' is subdivided into *amici, hospites,* and *cognati*; this triad is once again converted by the word order into a dyad, set in opposition through the conjunction of *alii–pars*. Then comes the sentence about *inimici*, in contrast to this whole group. It can no longer serve to increase revulsion at these horrors; after the slaughtered friends and relatives, its effect is rather flat, and there can be no doubt that it is inserted purely for the sake of the antithesis. Sallust similarly begins the description of Africa at *B.J.* 17. 1: *res postulare videtur, Africae situm paucis exponere et eas gentis, quibuscum nobis bellum aut amicitia fuit, attingere. Sed quae loca et nationes ob calorem aut asperitatem, item solitudines minus frequentata sunt, de iis haud facile compertum narraverim.* ('the occasion seems to require that I describe the location of Africa and touch on those peoples with whom we are hostile or allies. But of the places and tribes that are less visited because of heat or the harshness of the land or likewise uninhabited regions, I would not easily give an account'). The statement that he will only discuss the tribes that have come into contact with the Romans makes it self-evident that he will omit unexplored regions; if he, nevertheless, repeats this thought in a whole new sentence, the expansiveness is only explicable on the grounds of his striving after antithesis. This observation also resolves a difficulty in the famous opening chapter of the *Catiline*. It begins with the proposition that human beings should strive for glory in order not to resemble animals. In 1. 3 he elaborates that one should seek this glory 'by means of genius rather than strength' (*ingenii quam virium opibus*). This could have followed immediately after the first sentence. In any case, one expects as a transition: 'What distinguishes human beings from animals is the mind.' Instead, Sallust offers: *sed*[13] *nostra omnis vis in animo et corpore sita est, animi imperio, corporis servitio magis utimur; alterum nobis cum dis, alterum cum beluis commune est* ('but all our power is divided between mind and body; we more employ the mind for control and the body for service; the one we have in common with gods, the other with beasts'). Here the pairing of *corpus* and *corporis servitium* is immediately very striking; the progress of the thought suffers from the fact that the body, only just clearly indicated and repudiated in *ventri oboedientia* ('obedient to the belly'), now appears again on an equal footing, only to be again denounced once and for all in the concluding sentence, which with *beluae* ('beasts') recalls *pecora* ('herds') in 1. 1. The slight unevenness of this sentence becomes understandable only in light of the parallels cited above. Even more subtle is *B.C.* 20. 7: *ceteri omnes, strenui, boni, nobiles* **atque ignobiles** *volgus fuimus* ('all the rest of us, serious, good men, both noble **and commoners**, were simply a rabble'), where E. Schwartz (1897: 571 n. 2 (= Chapter 5, p. 130 n. 42 in this volume)) wanted to delete *atque ignobiles*. This kind of complementary figure of speech also occurs in authors with quite different stylistic aims.

The picture that has emerged so far of Sallust as stylist is quite consistent. The sentence structures that characterize his language all show the same inclination towards bipartite division of expression, which usually corresponds to an opposition of ideas. The thought process does not stride steadily forward, as in Cicero or Caesar; nor, as in Seneca, does it unfold in parallel sentences, which, with striking variation, force the same thought upon the listener. Rather, it constantly swings back and forth between contraries, which sometimes roughly collide with each other, sometimes appear as the extreme boundaries of the movement of the sentence. The result is a great restlessness of expression; the simple line of the classical sentence is replaced with a

---

[13] *sed* here, as at *B.C.* 25. 1 and often in Sallust, simply serves the continuation of the thought. Kunze 1897: 3. 1. 55ff.

frenetic hither and thither, which the voice of the reciter must follow, and which is only rarely relieved by simpler forms.

It is fitting at this point to ask how far Sallust's other stylistic traits fit in with the conclusions just reached. Here the treatment may be briefer since the features we are dealing with have long been recognized. The frequency of the tricolon asyndeton in Sallust seems at first glance to contradict these results. Such asyndeton occurs mostly with substantives or infinitives, less frequently with adjectives and prepositional phrases, e.g. *impudicus adulter ganeo, manu ventre pene* ('the wastrel, adulterer, glutton, with hand, stomach, penis', *B.C.* 14. 2; cf. also *B.J.* 14. 20, *B.J.* 14. 23, and *B.C.* 58. 11). The pattern is widespread in old Latin, already in the well-known prayer at Cato, *Agr.* 141: *agrum terram fundumque; prohibessis defendas averruncesque* ('field, earth, and farm may you guard, protect, and sweep clean').[14] In Sallust it has a particular stylistic function: it occurs wherever especially vivid depiction is desired. Thus, it involves either synonyms—as at *B.C.* 59. 5, *appellat hortatur rogat* ('he names, encourages, asks') or *B.C.* 19. 4, *imperia iniusta superba crudelia* ('commands unjust, arrogant, cruel'; cf. also *B.J.* 49. 4)—or rapidly fired-off keywords meant to encompass suggestively the entire scope of a concept: *in sanguine ferro fuga* ('in blood, steel, flight', *B.J.* 14. 9); *animus aetas virtus* ('mind, age, virtue', *B.C.* 58. 19). The individual components are often quite fixed for Sallust and return again and again: *gloriam honorem imperium* (*B.C.* 11. 2), *gloria imperium potentia* (*B.C.* 12. 1), *avidus potentiae honoris divitiarum* (*B.J.* 15. 4; cf. also *B.C.* 20. 14, 58. 8). Thus, in such lists, the effect comes more from the fullness of expression than the individual elements; through the asyndeton the three words melt together into a unity, which is most clearly expressed by the fact that the group is often treated as *one* colon: *tum Catilina polliceri tabulas novas | proscriptionem locupletium || magistratus sacerdotia rapinas | alia omnia, quae bellum atque lubido victorum fert ||* ('then Catiline promised absolution of debts, | the proscription of the wealthy || magistracies, priesthoods, booty | and all other things which war and the whim of victors bring ||', *B.C.* 21. 2). Here it is clear that the two shorter cola that begin the sentence correspond to the two longer ones, of which one is the tricolon (just as, e.g., at *B.C.* 54. 3). Thus, it in no way disrupts a sentence structure built around double cola but rather reinforces the impression of restlessness we receive from Sallust's style.

The lack of concinnity and avoidance of familiar expressions aims at the same effect. It has been observed that in combinations of adjective

---

[14] Cf. Leo 1906: 6ff.

and substantive Sallust prefers to reverse the usual order: *designati consules* (*B.C.* 18. 2); *quidam L. Tarquinius* (*B.C.* 48. 3); *Africum mare* (*H.* 2. 2 M; cf. Reckzey 1888; Kroll 1927: 299). The tendency goes further: the *triumviri rerum capitalium* (judicial officials) are for him *vindices rerum capitalium* (*B.C.* 55. 5); for 'proclaim consul' instead of *consulem creare, renuntiare,* or *designare* he prefers the rarer *declarare* (*B.C.* 24. 1, *B.J.* 27. 4, and *B.J.* 63. 4).[15] Where the consul usually goes to Rome *ad comitia habenda* ('to hold elections'), he says *Calpurnius Romam ad magistratus rogandos proficiscitur* (*B.J.* 29. 7); the old adage *malum consilium consultori pessumum* ('a bad plan is worst for its planner')[16] in his work goes *prava incepta consultoribus noxae esse* (*H.* 1. 77. 1 M). While familiar expressions act on the reader like minted coins that one accepts without much thought, their reshaped versions in Sallust demand a heightened attention and do not allow his audience to relax. Similar is the effort to construct sentence units of similar stylistic function in syntactically different ways—Sallust's so-called 'inconcinnity' (*inconcinnitas*). This is observable in Sallust from the smallest sentence components to the construction of entire periods: *neque per vim, neque insidiis* ('neither through violence nor with treachery', *B.J.* 7. 1); *recte atque ordine* ('correctly and in order', *B.C.* 51. 4). Several recurring types can be distinguished. There is variation in number (singular replaced by plural): *fidem, fortunas* (*B.C.* 16. 2), *fama atque fortunis* (*B.C.* 33. 1), *glande aut lapidibus* (*B.J.* 57. 4); also in the verb: *iuventus... discebat, magisque... habebant* (*B.C.* 7. 6); variation in case: *plerosque militiae, paucos fama cognitos* ('most known for military service, few by reputation', *B.J.* 84. 2), *armorum aliquanto numero, hostium paucorum potiti* ('in possession of a fair number of arms, but few enemy troops', *B.J.* 74. 3); in verb tense (*B.C.* 20. 1, *B.J.* 20. 1) and voice: *priusquam exercitus aut* **instrui** *aut sarcinas* **conligere**... *quivit* ('before the army could be drawn up or strap on their packs', *B.J.* 97. 4; cf. *B.C.* 53. 3); and finally, an especial favorite of his, in the particles introducing correlative clauses: *pars–alii, pars–reliqui, modo–interdum* (*B.J.* 55. 8, *B.J.* 62. 9, as above). But the same principle also dominates in more extensive units: *praemissus orator et subdole speculatum Bocchi consilia* ('sent ahead as a pleader and secretly to spy out Bocchus' plans', *B.J.* 108. 1); *existumans publice privatimque aere alieno oppressos* (*Allobroges*) *praeterea* **quod** *natura gens Gallica bellicosa esset, facile eos ad tale consilium adduci posse*

---

[15] The rigidity of constitutional terminology in Latin makes the phenomenon especially striking in this field. Kroll (1927: 299 n. 2) also notes *sociorum et Lati* for *nominis Latini* (*H.* 1.55. 12 M; cf. *B.J.* 84. 2) and *ex consili decreto* for *de consilii sententia* (*B.J.* 62. 5).
[16] Otto 1890: 90.

('reckoning that being overwhelmed with debt publicly and privately, and since the Gallic race was naturally warlike, the Allobroges could be easily persuaded to accept such a plan', *B.C.* 40. 1). He is particularly fond of this juxtaposition of a substantive object with an entire sentence: *neque maius aliud neque praestabilius invenias magisque naturae industriam hominum quam vim aut tempus deesse* ('nor would you find anything greater or more outstanding, and that effort rather than force or time is lacking to human nature', *B.J.* 1. 2; see also Kroll 1927: 287).[17]

The avoidance of familiar, customary expressions is perhaps clearest in Sallust's archaisms. We have already repeatedly encountered elements of his writing style that have their models in older Latin prose. Usually this is simply connected with the Atticizing tendencies of the period, which is all the more justified since Sallust, alongside his imitation of old Latin prose, Cato's above all, notoriously models his work on Thucydides'. Doubtless, without the classicizing fashion of the time his idiosyncrasy would have revealed itself in other forms of expression; but, in the context of the present work, this realization does not absolve us from asking what effect the writer was trying to achieve with his preference for older forms of expression. For Sallust did not by any means take over all the characteristics of his models indiscriminately. For example, rhyming clauses, which he avoids (see above, p. 27, n. 5), occur quite frequently in archaic Latin;[18] apparently they seemed ill suited to the desired dignity of his narrative. Beyond his orthography, which is more a visual than an aural effect,[19] what he adopted was mostly the use of a number of words in obsolete senses, such as *tempestas* for *tempus* ('time'), *facinus* for *factum* ('deed'), *ingenium* meaning 'quality' (*H.* 3. 26 M), *memorare* meaning 'say'—as well as words which were already absent from the living language, such as the negative particle *haud*,[20] *cognomentum*,[21] *fluxus, transenna* (*H.* 2. 70 M). The frequent use of iteratives (*imperitare, ostentare, rogitare*), which he shares with Cato, belongs here as well.[22] Even a passage from the Twelve Tables is quoted as if part of the everyday stock of language: *quia illi in tanto malo vita integra fama*

---

[17] There is no shortage of Catonian examples: *pleraque Gallia duas res industriosissime persequitur, rem militarem et argute loqui* ('warfare and talking cleverly', *Orig.* fr. 34 P).
[18] Leo 1898: ii. 29–30. For Cato: Norden 1898: 1. 167 and *Or.* 57. 1 Jordan = 212 *ORF.*
[19] Even those who wrote *adversus* probably pronounced a sound comparable to the 'o' in English 'worth'; the sound in between 'u' and 'i' in *maxumus* was still pronounced differently from the normal 'i' in the time of Claudius, as shown by his attempt to introduce a special character for it (Buecheler 1915: 1. 12ff., Quint. *Inst.* 1. 4. 8).
[20] Wackernagel 1924: ii. 256.   [21] Cf. *TLL* III 1494, 16.
[22] Cato comes first to mind; Skard 1933: 68 reckons this among the poetic elements in Sallust that derive from Ennius, which can hardly be right.

potior fuit, **inprobus intestabilisque** *videtur* ('because in such great misfortune he considered life preferable to an unsullied reputation, he seems **wicked and despicable**', *B.J.* 67. 3; cf. *XII tab.* 8, 22). Sallust may have felt himself justified in such a usage since his model Cato had used a passage from an ancient legal text in quite a similar way, apparently in a description of the Carthaginian legal system (*Orig.* fr. 81 P = 85 *FRHist*). Even his sentence formation is influenced by Cato. Hence Sallust's frequent use of *tum vero* to introduce a sequential clause: *confecto proelio, tum vero cerneres...* ('when the battle was finished, then indeed you might see...', *B.J.* 61. 1; cf. *B.J.* 94. 3, *B.J.* 106. 6); compare a sentence from Cato's speech *de aedilibus vitio creatis* (67.5 Jordan = 217 *ORF*; see also Kroll 1927: 297 n. 2): *inter offam et herbam,* **ibi vero** *longum intervallum est* ('between the mouthful and the sprout, there indeed is a long distance'). In Sallust, the effect is merely a little old-fashioned and laboured, while in Cato it sprang with delicious freshness from the attempt to visualize the length of the process by which the plant in the field is fashioned into the prepared dish. This sharp demarcation of the sequential clause, which hampers the even flow of the period, has a close relative in the preference for parataxis. This is particularly significant for Sallust since it reveals a desire for segmentation which distinguishes his sentence construction from that of the true archaic style: *animus... neque vigiliis neque quietibus sedari poterat;* **ita** *conscientia mentem excitam vastabat* ('his soul could not be stilled awake or asleep; **so** did conscience destroy an irritated mind', *B.C.* 15. 4; cf. *B.J.* 54. 4, and *B.J.* 99. 2-3.). The temporal particles *post, postremo,* and *deinde* are used in the same way (first observed by Kroll 1927: 284). These breaks are not indiscriminately inserted 'to hang an addendum on at the end' (so Kroll, ibid.), but rather are quite deliberately placed in the service of ordering the elements of the sentence. At both *B.C.* 44. 1 and 46. 3, an asyndetic group of proper names is followed by a final one tacked on with *item*; the writer's intention is revealed by the fact that both times something is reported in the subsequent material which distinguishes that person's fate from those of the others. But while here there are substantial reasons for the emphasis, in other cases the motives are purely stylistic: *Volturcius interrogatus de itinere de litteris, | postremo quid aut qua de causa consili habuisset, || primo fingere alia, dissimulare de coniuratione* ('Volturcius asked about his journey, and the letters, | **finally** what his plan was and why, || at first made up some things and lied about the conspiracy', *B.C.* 47. 1). Here *postremo* serves to set apart the final, longer element from the two shorter ones placed asyndetically side by side, and thus to achieve the design that we have come to recognize as typical for Sallust. *B.C.* 51. 33 is similar: *uti quisquam domum aut villam, postremo* *vas aut vestimentum aliquoius concupiverat* ('as each had come to desire the house or villa, finally the dishes or clothing of another'; cf. *B.J.* 31. 23). He thus adopts the old Latin locution *postremo* to mark the conclusion to a list, with no implication of a temporal relationship (*B.C.* 61. 5, *B.J.* 10. 2, *B.J.* 14. 18, *B.J.* 35. 5; cf., for example, Plaut. *Trin.* 613, 622; Caecil. 204 R). Nevertheless, a comparison may reveal how different a paratactic series looks in Sallust from one in Cato. Fronto (II 150 H, 123 VDH) quotes Cato as follows: *interea unamquamque turmam, manipulum, cohortem temptabam, quid facere possent, proeliis levibus spectabam cuiusmodi quisque esset; si quis strenue fecerat, donabam honeste, ut alii idem vellent facere, atque in contione multis verbis laudabam. Interim aliquot pauca castra feci* ('meanwhile I used to make trial of each squadron, maniple, cohort, what they were able to accomplish, in light skirmishes I was looking to see of what sort each was; if anyone had given his all, I would reward him honourably so that others would be willing to do the same, and I would praise him extensively in assemblies. During that time I pitched some few camps,' 35 *ORF.*). Here is Sallust: *Metellus in isdem castris quadriduom moratus saucios cum cura reficit, meritos in proeliis more militiae donat, univorsos in contione laudat atque agit gratias, hortatur ad cetera, quae levia sunt, parem animum gerant: pro victoria satis iam pugnatum, reliquos labores pro praeda fore* ('Metellus remained in the same camp for four days while he tended the wounded, rewarded the deserving in battles according to military custom, praised and thanked all in the assembly, and encouraged them to bear the same spirit regarding the tasks that remained, which would be easy: they had already fought enough to secure victory: their remaining efforts would be for spoils,' *B.J.* 54. 1). In Cato we are first given two sentences constructed in parallel, of which the second, with *proeliis levibus spectabam*, explains the *temptabam* of the first in greater detail; since, in the supplementary indirect question, a single soldier replaces the collective regiments being tested, the bestowing of honours and the praise in front of the ranks is appropriately placed next and justified, with truly Catonian iciness, by the fact that it serves as a spur to the others; then, with *interim*, a further and frequently cited means of solidifying military discipline is loosely attached. The sentence construction naturally follows the progress of thought, and, although the deliberate correspondence between *donabam honeste* and *multis verbis laudabam* is unmistakable, nevertheless the overall impression is that the thoughts are arranged within the series in the order in which they occurred to Cato. A deliberate architectural scheme lending form to the entire passage is not to be found. With Sallust it is quite different. The description rises from individuals (*saucios-meritos*) to the collective (*univorsos*); at the same time, the structure of the sentences changes from parallelism to increasingly marked chiasmus, reaching its climax in the final sentence. Thus, two pairs of sentences are bound together, the second pair with reversed placement of the verb (... *agit gratias, hortatur*...), and the final sentence, the main point of the *cohortatio*, functions as a conclusion towards which the entire construction builds. By means of parataxis a unity of composition is achieved which is in no way inferior to the hypotactic Ciceronian period. This result is made possible only through the writer's deliberate planning of the whole in advance. The desire and the ability to create expansive unified structures reveals that the work of the Ciceronian age had not vanished without a trace in this new generation, and clearly distinguishes Sallust's archaizing sentence construction from the truly archaic.

It is customary to count his extended use of the historical infinitive among Sallust's archaisms.[23] In this he became a model for subsequent historians, and statistically he makes more frequent use of the construction than anyone after him, even Tacitus;[24] the first examples of the passive historical infinitive and the infinitive in subordinate clauses appear in his work. The phenomenon must not merely be recorded as a fact of historical syntax. It is now certain that the historical infinitive is to be understood as an old substantive clause.[25] Its use in Sallust reveals a consistent stylistic intention throughout. He piles on these forms wherever it is necessary to sketch the agitated motion of the masses in moments of struggle and unrest or the disquiet of an individual with curt, abbreviated strokes (B.C. 31. 3, 60. 4, B.J. 12. 5, 101. 11.; B.C. 17. 1, B.J. 72. 2. More at Perrochat 1932: 51ff.). Often a brief sentence with a finite verb serves as a conclusion (*B.C.* 60. 4, *B.J.* 12. 5, 96. 2-4). Elsewhere, too, he prefers substantival expressions. *B.J.* 100, a passage of twenty-four Teubner lines, has only the following finite verbs in a main clause: *decreverat* (1), to explain a motive; *curabat, locaverat, explorabant* (2/3), and *cogebat* (4) in the description, and *coercebat* and *aiebant* (5) in a similarly parenthetical treatment of Marius' behaviour during the entire campaign. In the course of the narrative proper there are only the four imperfects in 2-4; everything else is related in substantival clauses.[26] Stretches of such

---

[23] Most recently Schuster 1926: 240-1.
[24] Perrochat 1932: 66. This sensitive study begins from the sketchy nature of the historical infinitive ('forme d'expression esquissée') and accurately assesses its stylistic value in all essential points.
[25] Kretschmer 1910: 270ff.; Wackernagel 1920: 1. 268ff.
[26] The chapter begins *dein Marius uti coeperat in hiberna*. Ahlberg, along with manuscripts *CBm*, inserts an *it* to complete the sentence. But this is very weakly attested, and it is likelier that a finite verb was meant to be supplied than that one was left out. Alongside

overwhelmingly uniform character are rare even for Sallust; more frequent are passages in which the finite verb is added rather for the sake of syntactic completion than its meaning. In *B.C.* 23. 1–3, for example, only four finite verbs occur, three of which are auxiliary verbs (*fuit*, *erat*, *coepit*); and even the fourth bears no special emphasis, *huic homini non minor vanitas inerat quam audacia* ('the man possessed no less vanity than ambition'). This device cannot be explained merely by pointing to literary fashions. The run of substantive clauses, usually joined by asyndeton, interrupts the calm progression of the historical report; their accumulation hastily drives an abundance of unelaborated ideas past the reader. The narration seems abrupt and hurried. Such passages signify a change in the pace of the presentation. The resulting unevenness serves the same artistic purposes as the phenomena discussed above.

It has become clear that Sallust's archaism, too, is not merely the mask of a stylistic virtuoso interchangeable with any other, in the way that, say, the writers of the second century CE were able to switch models at will. Rather, it is for him a means of expressing his authorial identity, and is substantially transformed in his hands. The effect of this style on a generation accustomed to the measured flow of the classical period must have been different from what it was in the middle of the second century BCE; what had then corresponded to everyday speech was now perceived as exotic and surprising and increased the impression of restlessness that Sallust's style produced; the short sentences, once the natural mode of speech, the subdivision through particles rather than hypotaxis, and the preference for substantival sentence forms all lent a rapidity of movement to the expression and disrupted the steadily measured course of the words. Throughout, the archaic formal elements have been forged into a unified style.

The same conclusions apply to Sallust's Graecisms and imitations of Thucydides.[27] In this domain, Sallust goes as far as the Latin language permits. Already in antiquity expressions like *quae res secundae amant* ('which prosperity favours', *B.J.* 41. 3) and *quae ira fieri amat* ('which anger is prone to accomplish', *B.J.* 34. 1) had been labelled Graecisms (Quint. *Inst.* 9. 3. 17; cf., for example, Thuc. 2. 65. 4, ὅπερ φιλεῖ ὅμιλος ποιεῖν; Thuc. 3. 81. 5, οἷον φιλεῖ ἐν τῷ τοιούτῳ γίγνεσθαι). The usage is doubtless influenced by Greek, but Sallust has not gone so far as to

---

substantival clauses like *B.J.* 100. 2, *Sulla cum equitatu apud dextumos*, and 4, *ipse armatus intentusque*, one is reluctant to eliminate a third example in the same passage through conjecture. At any rate, a verb here would be an unemphatic syntactic supplement, which even on account of its scope would hardly carry weight.

[27] See Löfstedt 1933: 412ff.

attempt the impersonal construction. He is more daring at *B.J.* 84. 3, *neque plebi militia volenti putabatur* ('military service was not thought appealing to the people') and *B.J.* 100. 4, *uti militibus... labor volentibus esset* ('that work be agreeable to the soldiers'), based on the Greek phrase βουλομένῳ μοι ἦν, etc., a construction which Sallust introduced into Latin literature and was subsequently imitated by Livy, Tacitus, and later writers.[28] Very bold calques occur as well: *B.J.* 8. 1 *complures novi atque nobiles* ('many youths and nobles') only becomes intelligible when one translates back to νέοι, since Latin does not use *novus* to mean *iuvenis*.[29] Though in these cases it is clearly the unusual expression that attracts him and it would be unjustified to name a particular model, nevertheless the influence of Thucydides on his sentence structure is unmistakable,[30] above all in the incongruence with which, after a collective subject, he sometimes employs the plural verb and other times switches between the two numbers (*B.C.* 7. 4, *B.C.* 23. 6, and *B.C.* 56. 5). An even harsher *constructio ad sensum* occurs at B.C. 18. 2: *coniuravere pauci... de qua quam verissume potero dicam* ('many conspired..., about which I will speak as truly as I can') where the noun *coniuratio*, antecedent of the feminine *qua*, must be extracted from the verb (as Sallust perhaps understood a φυλακήν to be supplied out of the previous φυλάσσοντες at Thuc. 7. 28. 2; cf. Thuc. 1. 22. 1). Likewise at *B.C.* 56. 5 (*servitia, quoius copiae*) and *B.J.* 102. 6 (*populo Romano... melius visum... tutiusque rati*), the shift from singular to plural recalls examples in Thucydides (5. 73. 1, 6. 37. 1, and, for the *B.J.* passage, cf. 1. 110. 4). The Greek historian may also be the model for the roughness with which Sallust expects a verb of related meaning to be supplied from previous material: *quam rem alii in superbiam vortebant, alii bonum ingenium contumelia accensum esse* ('which some judged arrogance, while others [judged] that his good character was set ablaze by the insult', *B.J.* 82. 3), where a generic verb of judgement must be extracted from *vortebant*; similarly *plerique in parte tertia Africam posuere, alii tantummodo Asiam et Europam* [sc. *partes orbis putavere*] ('most have placed Africa in the third part, others [consider] Asia and Europe the only

---

[28] Cf. *LHS*: 100, as well as Priscian 18. 169 p. 285, 1 Hertz.

[29] The commonly accepted explanation (*homines*) *novi* [i.e., 'new men' as opposed to 'nobles'] is contradicted by the sense: only a connection with influential members of the Roman nobility is of importance to Jugurtha. The placing of *novi* first also precludes taking it, on the analogy of the expressions handled above, as a complementary expression; it would then need to come after the word that evokes it. [Most now accept the older understanding of the phrase Latte rejects (eds.).]

[30] The characterization of Thucydides' diction given by Dionysius of Halicarnassus (*Ep. ad Amm.* 2) can be transferred almost entirely to Sallust; evidently the theory had been standard a generation earlier as well.

[parts of the world]', *B.J.* 17. 3). So at Thuc. 1.17, οὕτω...ἡ Ἑλλὰς... κατείχετο μήτε κοινῇ φανερὸν μηδὲν κατεργάζεσθαι κατὰ πόλεις τε ἀτολμοτέρα εἶναι ('thus Greece as a whole was prevented from accomplishing anything conspicuous and its component cities became less adventurous'), the sense of exerting an effect is all that is preserved from the verb of prevention. This all springs from the previously observed inclination towards expressions that avoid parallelism. Sallust's preference for unusual constructions even leads him to take over pure Graecisms from his model. Thus, he seems to have been the first to venture the brachylogic use of *in* with the neuter form of an adjective (*in maius celebrare*, *B.J.* 73. 5; cf. Thuc. 1. 21. 1, ἐπὶ τὸ μεῖζον κοσμοῦντες; and consequently *H.* 2. 69, 3. 14, 1. 5 M). In that usage the imperial period followed him;[31] he stands alone in using the expression *proelium in manibus facere* ('to fight hand to hand', *B.J.* 57. 4, modelled on Thuc. 4. 43. 2 ἦν ἡ μάχη...ἐν χερσὶ πᾶσα).

While everything cited so far fits easily with the character of Sallust's style, the last form of imitation reaches beyond it to an expression that seems at first very disconcerting. He borrows entire sentences from his model or imitates their rhythm in a completely different context.[32] One may compare *B.C.* 6. 5, *magis dandis quam accipiundis beneficiis amicitias parabant* ('more by giving than receiving favours did they obtain friendships') with Thuc. 2. 40. 4, οὐ γὰρ πάσχοντες εὖ, ἀλλὰ δρῶντες κτώμεθα τοὺς φίλους ('not by receiving but by performing benefits let us gain friends'). Here a thematic connection is still perceptible: Thucydides' praise of Athens is transferred to Rome, but elsewhere the imitation is purely formal: *ut merito dicatur genitos esse, qui neque ipsi habere possent res familiaris neque alios pati* ('so that deservedly a generation is said to have been born which is able neither to retain its inherited wealth nor to allow others to do so', *H.* 1. 16 M); cf. Thuc. 1. 70. 9, ξυνελὼν φαίη (τις) πεφυκέναι ἐπὶ τῷ μήτε αὐτοὺς ἔχειν ἡσυχίαν μήτε τοὺς ἄλλους ἀνθρώπους ἐᾶν ('one might say in sum that they were born neither to have peace themselves nor to allow other men to have it').[33] The fruits of other authors are occasionally harvested in a similar way. Often the political speeches of Demosthenes are used: *B.C.* 52. 21-2, *sed alia fuere, quae illos (maiores) magnos fecere, quae nobis nulla sunt...pro his nos habemus...* ('but there were other things which made our ancestors great,

---

[31] Hand 1836: iii. 350-1.

[32] The passages are collected in Mollmann 1878, overall a diligent and insightful work. He was preceded in this by G. Kortte in his commentary (1724), with his customary learning but lacking acute judgement; even in Mollmann there is still too much.

[33] Cf. also *B.J.* 31. 17~Thuc. 2. 61. 6; *B.J.* 7. 5~Thuc. 2. 40. 3; *B.J.* 44. 5~Thuc. 3. 81. 5; *B.C.* 38. 3 (also *H.* 1. 12 M)~Thuc. 3. 82. 8.

which we do not possess... in their place we have...'; cf. Dem. *Phil.* 3. 36, ἦν τι τότ', ἦν, ὦ ἄνδρες Ἀθηναῖοι, ἐν ταῖς τῶν πολλῶν διανοίαις, ὃ νῦν οὐκ ἔστιν,... νῦν δ'..., 'there was, there was, Athenians, something then in the thoughts of the multitude which exists no longer,... now, instead...'). This example is especially striking because only the outward surface of the opposition is taken over; the content differs entirely. In another passage as well he borrows the form of a polished sentence from the Athenian orator, while the content is changed to suit the context: *B.J.* 85. 12, *gerere quam fieri tempore posterius re atque usu prius est* ('to accomplish is later than to become [sc. consul] in respect to time, but in fact and utility comes first'; cf. Dem. *Olynth.* 3. 15, τὸ γὰρ πράττειν τοῦ λέγειν καὶ χειροτονεῖν ὕστερον ὂν τῇ τάξει, πρότερον τῇ δυνάμει καὶ κρεῖττόν ἐστιν, 'action, though later than speaking and elections in the order of time, is first in importance and greater').[34]

This dependency reveals something more than the mere wish to be seen as a Roman Thucydides. One may compare the identical procedure in neoteric poetry, where the aim is to lend the verse the same flow that was so striking in the Greek original. Just so, Sallust's concern with Greek literature was very strongly limited to formal considerations: the close relationship between form and content that made up the essence of the great Greek author begins to loosen for him. Pre-minted forms stand at the ready for any purpose at all and can take on content of various types. Sallust yielded to the temptation of employing them more frequently than any prose author before him; not until Tacitus, in the correspondence demonstrated by Mommsen of single, pointed phrases between his *Histories* and Plutarch, does one again encounter the like.[35] As powerful a master of language as he was, this dependency betrays a certain weakness of original creativity in comparison to the surging abundance of Cicero. Though he possessed the capacity to select the style that was suited to him, he would have been unable to create it on his own.

One word more is needed by way of addendum on the question of vulgarisms in Sallust. Since Wölfflin (1876: 146) coined the often repeated phrase 'vulgar, democratic Latin', the attempt has continually been made to point out colloquial elements in Sallust, with no regard to the assertion of Quintilian, who explicitly testifies to the laborious polish

---

[34] Cf. *H.* 1. 55. 15 M~Dem. *De cor.* 97.
[35] Mommsen 1905-13: 7. 240. It has been overlooked, in the spirited discussion of the question, that the same relationship obtains between certain 'truly Tacitean' expressions and the orators preserved in the elder Seneca. Evidently generations had worked towards the perfection of individual sayings that achieved their final form in Tacitus.

of his style.[36] W. Kroll (1927: 280) gets credit for having objected to this 'misunderstanding of the nature' of ancient literary prose: 'Whoever consciously archaizes and Hellenizes, indeed, whoever composes a historical work at all worthy of the claim to be literature, does not write vulgarly, not even in isolated phrases.' The well-known overlap between archaic and vulgar Latin admittedly makes the error understandable, but Kroll has shown that an old Latin provenance can be established for the majority of cases adduced for this purpose.[37] Colloquial expressions intended by the author to be perceived as such are nowhere to be found. At one point, this negative conclusion can even be directly supplemented by a piece of evidence to the contrary. At *B.C.* 44. 5, Sallust incorporates a document into his narrative which is also preserved in Cicero, *Cat.* 3. 12: a letter of Lentulus. The two versions differ in some details, and on the basis of our knowledge of epistolary style in the Ciceronian age there can be no doubt that the one that appears in the speech is, if anything, closer to the original wording than Sallust's. If any inclination towards 'vulgar', or rather 'colloquial', expression were detectable in him, one would expect that his alterations to this passage would betray it. The text in Cicero runs: *qui sim scies ex eo quem ad te misi. cura ut vir sis et cogita quem in locum sis progressus; vide ecquid tibi iam sit necesse et cura ut omnium tibi auxilia adiungas, etiam infimorum* ('You will know who I am from the one I have sent to you. Be brave and consider how far you have gone; look out if you need anything now, and take care to acquire all assistance, even from men of the lowest class'). Out of this Sallust makes the following: *qui sim ex eo quem ad te misi cognosces. fac cogites, in quanta calamitate sis et memineris te virum esse. consideres quid tuae rationes postulent. auxilium petas ab omnibus, etiam ab infumis*. First of all, he replaces the colloquial *scire ex* or *de aliquo*, 'to learn from somebody', which is quite common in Cicero's letters[38] but absent from his philosophical works as well as from Caesar, where the more correct *cognoscere* is used; at the same time, the informal placement

---

[36] Quint. *Inst.* 10. 3. 8: *sic scripsisse Sallustium accepimus; et sane manifestus est etiam ex ipso opere labor* ('that [sc. by revising] is how we hear that Sallust wrote, and the effort is clear from his work'). Quintilian presents the opinion as a traditional one, to which he appends his own observation with *etiam*. There must have existed biographies of Sallust at that point, of which that of Asconius is mentioned on one occasion (Ps.-Acr. *ad Hor. Serm.* 1. 2. 41, presumably from a more complete edition of Porphyrio). Assertions about the working methods of an author belong to the commonplaces of ancient biography: so Donat. *Vit. Verg.* 22 (p. 14, 13 Diehl), *Vit. Pers.* 8. It is thus overwhelmingly probable that Quintilian owes his information to a *Vita* (see also Norden 1898: 1. 202).

[37] See also Skard 1933: 4.

[38] *Fam.* 9. 17. 1, *Att.* 12. 22. 2, more in Marx 1905: 2. 270 ad 757; cf. also Plaut. *Capt.* 297, *Curc.* 257.

of the verb near the beginning is substituted by its normal position, also conspicuously preferred by Sallust elsewhere.[39] The next sentence offered two parallel imperatives; both are altered to yield dissimilar forms, and in addition the typically epistolary *cura ut*[40] is replaced with *memineris te...esse*, from a more elevated literary register. The reason for his reordering of the two sentences is not discernible. The words *quem in locum sis progressus* and *ecquid tibi iam sit necesse* display that vagueness which is at home in all spoken language, which does not trouble to search out the most fitting expression and can content itself with hints, which the listener easily fleshes out through familiar facts.[41] Sallust replaces both of these with more informative phrases. Finally, in the concluding sentence, the carelessly repeated *cura ut* is omitted for the sake of brevity and *adiungas* ('acquire') replaced with *petas* ('seek')—without any clear explanation, since Sallust often uses *adiungere* similarly (*B.C.* 24. 4, *B.J.* 70. 2). If, indeed, not all Sallust's changes can be explained as corrections of colloquial usages, a substantial portion can. This is a confirmation that he consciously avoids vulgar turns of phrase.

II. NARRATIVE STYLE AND COMPOSITION

Every representation of events takes a selection from the abundance of actual occurrences and orders the pieces arbitrarily within certain boundaries. Scholarship on Sallust thus far has been concerned with the selection itself, essentially as a means to understand Sallust's political affiliation. His artistic aims have only received attention in so far as they concern his relationship to Hellenistic historiography. How far the patterning that distinguishes his construction of individual sentences also determines his method of narration remains to be examined.

Battle scenes in Caesar are as a rule quite consistently presented in a linear progression; we hear of the enemy only at the moment in which their actions have an effect on the Romans; whatever earlier actions are essential for the audience to understand what is happening are reported in a subordinate clause. The battle in Britain at *B Gall.* 4. 32 is a good example: Caesar sends a legion to forage; the apparently peaceful situation, indicated by the details of barbarians working in the fields or doing business with the Romans in the camp, is emphasized in a subordinate

---

[39] Kroll 1927: 298.   [40] *TLL* s.v. 1499, 11; cf. 1498, 81.
[41] Cf. Hofmann 1926: 165ff.

clause before the announcement of a dust cloud by the troops on watch gives the first sign of an attack. The account of Caesar's subsequent preparations requires only this one piece of information; not until he has advanced so far that he sees his troops in combat with the enemy do we learn in a brief sentence what has happened in the meantime. In 34 the narration is carried to a conclusion with the same directness. Chapter 33 is interposed in between because the general, constantly attentive to the weaponry of his opponent, desires to give an extensive account of the tactical use of chariots among the Celts of Britain. This section has nothing to do with the account of the battle. The remainder hangs together as a seamless depiction of events in the order in which they were perceived by the commanding officer; the vantage point and direction of the gaze are fully uniform throughout the entire passage.[42] Let us compare a few battles scenes from Sallust. *B.C.* 60 reports the decisive battle between Catiline and the troops of the state. One is immediately struck by the frequent change in subject: *Petreius–hostium exercitus* ('the army of the enemy'), *veterani* ('the veterans')–*illi* ('the Catilinarians'), *Catilina–Petreius, Manlius et Faesulanus–Catilina*. This should not be put down merely to grammatical variation, for the list makes clear how the names of the opponents alternate. On closer inspection, even the lead-up to the battle is presented entirely differently from how it is in Caesar. Instead of a single, unified plot, two actions from two sides come together. Petreius gives the signal for the attack and orders the troops forward; 'the army of the enemy does the same' (*idem facit* **hostium exercitus**). Next a sentence without an explicit subject describes their impact (*concurrunt*). As the battle begins, it is again presented as an alternation of attacks and counter-attacks: 'the veterans... press forward, the Catilinarians... resist' (*veterani... instare, illi... resistunt*). A description of Catiline follows, in historical infinitives that highlight the essential circumstances, rounded off with a brief and almost epigrammatic judgement (60. 4). A passage of almost equal length (60. 5) corresponds to this, presenting the counter-measures of Petreius that decide the battle. He breaks through the centre, where Catiline is fighting, and then turns against both of the wings. The deaths of the commanders are then reported in reverse order, first those of the commanders of the Roman wings, Manlius and Faesulanus, then Catiline's. In this way, the fate of the protagonist forms the conclusion. With each change of subject, the perspective of the narrator changes as well; what we hear of Catiline's activity could not possibly have been perceived by his opponent during the fight. The battle is not conceived as the

---

[42] Cf. Oppermann 1933: 41; Fränkel 1933: 36.

deliberately guided struggle of one party towards victory, but rather as a restless surging back and forth between two hostile masses, until the decision finally brings the action to a halt. This narrative order is by no means exceptional for Sallust. *B.J.* 101 depicts an attack on the Roman army by the united forces of Jugurtha and Bocchus. Corresponding to the two enemies are two commanders on the Roman side, Marius and Sulla. With this doubling, the construction of the whole becomes more complicated than in the Catiline passage just mentioned. The account begins when the scouts, who have guarded the Romans during their march, appear from all sides and rush towards the army. **Marius**, unsure from which direction the attack will come, brings the troops to a halt without changing formation (101. 1–2). An initial movement thus threatens the army from without and comes to a standstill with the general. The next sentence describes **Jugurtha**, his expectations, and the arrangement of his forces. Then the narration returns to the Romans, this time to **Sulla** (commanding the right wing, 100.2). Under attack, he launches a counteroffensive against the troops of the Mauri—the reader's gaze is now pointed in the opposite direction to that of the first sentence—while a portion of his cavalry confines itself to defence (4). Then **Bocchus** attacks the Roman rear (5). Only now do we hear that **Marius** is in the forefront doing battle with Jugurtha (6). This information comes in an independent clause and for a moment distracts our attention from the rearguard, to which the narration then returns. **Jugurtha** makes his way there in order to spread fear among the Romans through the false report of Marius' death. In two antithetical sentences the effect on the Romans (*milites*) and the enemy (*barbari*) is depicted (7). Now the Romans are about to yield, when **Sulla**, who meanwhile has routed his opponents, returns from his pursuit and falls on the flank of the Mauri (8). Once again an action, the Roman resistance this time, progresses from the periphery towards the heart of the melee. The flight of the enemy commanders is then contrasted: **Bocchus** escapes immediately; **Jugurtha** only after desperate resistance. Finally, **Marius** too appears in the rear, having driven back the enemies facing him. With this the struggle is decided along the entire line of battle. A concluding sentence portrays, in antithetical substantive clauses, pursuers and fugitives on the broad battlefield; the motion finally comes to rest with the striking sentence 'Everything, as far as the eye could see, was covered with spears, arms, and corpses, and the ground around them stained with blood.' The unceasing variation is notable; twice the sequence Marius–Jugurtha–Sulla–Bocchus sweeps past us, to be finally rounded off with the two generals Marius and Jugurtha; in between, the anonymous masses of Roman and barbarian soldiers are named a single time. The disorderly chaos of an attack devolving into a series of individual skirmishes finds masterful expression in this depiction.

But it is also clear how differently Caesar would have shaped the same narrative: either the whole would have been viewed from the vantage point of the rearguard, with all the other skirmishes presented as marginal, or he would have presented the actions of the commanding officer as the dominant line to which everything else was subordinated. In Sallust, the unity of the event is dissolved into a multiplicity of individual actions running together with one another, which become the more visible through the partial change of orientation within the landscape. It is almost as if the space itself participates in this sense of motion, as the reader's gaze is alternately drawn from the distant horizon of the African plain towards the tight-knit mass of Romans in the middle, and from here back again into the openness where the pursuit takes place and into which the routed fugitives vanish without a trace. The events, struggling to break free from one another, are unified only by their simultaneity; and as if Sallust had perceived the same, he emphasizes this relationship through numerous particles (*interim–dum–tum–dein–simul–ubi–simulque–iamque . . . cum–statim–atque interim–denique–tum*), which almost pedantically highlight the temporal relationship.

How the presentation of space conforms to the principle of constant variation that dominates Sallust's narrative becomes particularly clear in his descriptions of the terrain. Once again, a comparison with Caesar brings Sallust's distinctiveness to the fore. *B Gall.* 2. 18 describes the setting of the battle with the Nervii. The hill on which the Roman camp stands slopes down to the river Sambre; on the other side the ground rises again, treeless for 300 metres and thereafter covered with a thick forest that hinders visibility. Here the gaze of the observer travels from a particular vantage point on the Romans' side straight out over the landscape, taking in first the nearer and then the farther parts.[43] In Sallust this unity is broken up: *erat . . . flumen oriens a meridie nomine Muthul a quo aberat mons ferme milia viginti tractu pari . . . **media** autem planities deserta* ('there was a river called the Muthul rising from the south from which the mountain, running parallel, was separated by nearly twenty miles . . . but the plain in the middle was desert', *B.J.* 48. 3). First the outermost boundaries are indicated and only then the plain lying between. The elements at *B.C.* 59. 2 are arranged in the opposite order: *planities erat inter sinistros montis et ab dextra rupe aspera* ('the plain lay between mountains on the left and the sharp rock on the right'). The depiction of a military procession is also fitted to this pattern: *Manilium in dextra, Faesulanum quendam in sinistra parte curare iubet.*

---

[43] See Oppermann 1933: 37ff.

ipse...adsistit ('Catiline ordered Manilius to be in charge on the right and a certain man from Faesulae on the left...he himself stood...', *B.C.* 59. 3; cf. also *B.J.* 45. 2, *in agmine in primis modo, modo in postremis saepe in medio adesse*, 'in the line of march he was present now in front, now in the rear, and often in the middle', where, moreover, the order is meant to illustrate Metellus' sudden appearance, here one moment, there the next). Admittedly, most of Sallust's descriptions of place are too short to allow for any division at all.

To confirm the insight just reached, and to meet the objection that such an antithetical arrangement occurs in battle scenes only because the subject matter demands it, a few other narrative passages may be briefly examined. At *B.C.* 26 the account of Catiline's defeat in the consular elections begins with the plans of the conspirator, culminating in the attacks on Cicero (26. 1). Next come Cicero's defensive measures, divided between his efforts to win over first Fulvia and then his colleague C. Antonius. The last sentence returns to Cicero's own person with the description of the guards with whom he surrounds himself. Clearly *circum se praesidia amicorum...habebat* ('he was keeping a garrison of friends around him', *B.C.* 26. 4) comes as a response to *insidias parabat Ciceroni* ('he was plotting traps for Cicero', *B.C.* 26. 2). Catiline's schemes return to form the conclusion (*B.C.* 26. 5). Here, alongside the complicated forms we have just seen, we have a simple *a–b–a* arrangement, which likewise has its equivalent in his sentence structures (see p. 29 above). The antithesis Cicero–Catiline, in constant alternation, also governs the next chapter. First the conspirator's measures to foment revolution in Italy and the dispatching of Manlius are reported (*B.C.* 27. 1), then his actions in Rome, which lead up to the meeting at Laeca's house and the attempt to assassinate Cicero (*B.C.* 27. 2–28. 2); this is followed by the defensive reaction, in which Curius at first plays an active role (*B.C.* 28. 2–3). Again the scene changes: Manlius' activities in Etruria are now depicted (*B.C.* 28. 4). Only then, introduced by a sentence summarizing the events in both Rome and Etruria, comes the consul's counterblow, which secures the conferral of dictatorial authority (*B.C.* 29). Similarly, a description of the quarrel between Jugurtha and his adoptive brothers takes the form of a verbal exchange between Hiempsal and Jugurtha (*B.J.* 11. 3–4, 5, 6, 7–9); the narration of the Φίλαινοι (*B.J.* 79. 5–10) moves repeatedly back and forth between the Carthaginians and Cyreneans. Here a comparison with the way Valerius Maximus shapes the episode (5. 6 ext. 4) is instructive: in his account, the Cyreneans' suggestion that the Carthaginians be buried alive at the boundary follows immediately after they accuse them of cheating, whereas Sallust puts the Carthaginians' request for other terms in between. At the beginning, too, Valerius speaks only of the departure of the Carthaginians; Sallust mentions both parties in independent clauses.

Similar also is the digression on the political struggles in Rome since the overthrow of Carthage. The excursus at *B.J.* 41-2 develops out of an opposition between the nobility and the populace. After an introductory passage, which contrasts the periods before and after the war in the middle (*B.J.* 41. 2-3) and is rounded off by an antithesis (*optaverant-adepti sunt*), there follows a series of short sentences that set the behaviour of the *nobilitas* and of the *populus* against one another. Only once are the two groups brought together, to be opposed to the *res publica* as a single entity (*B.J.* 41. 5, end). This first section (*B.J.* 41. 5-8) is concluded with an account of the situation arising from these oppositions, given in Sallustian fashion in historical infinitives (*B.J.* 41. 9). In terms simply of diction, to this point the two sides are designated with synonyms (*nobilitas-populus, nobilitas-plebis vis, paucorum arbitrium-populus, imperatores cum paucis-parentes **militum***); but now the Gracchi, whose entrance is prepared by the generalizing sentence at *B.J.* 41. 10, emerge from the nobility itself as champions of the plebs; the terms used up so far occur once more in a transitional subordinate clause (*B.J.* 42.1, vindicare **plebem** in libertatem et **paucorum** scelera patefacere,* 'to liberate the plebs and expose the crimes of the oligarchy'), in the manner in which Sallust often uses the alternation of pairs to establish their connection (see pp. 51-53 and 58-59 below). What follows is dominated by the new antithesis, which is basically identical to the first (*Ti. et C. Gracchus-nobilitas, B.J.* 42. 1, *Gracchis...animus-nobilitas, B.J.* 42. 2-4), until the author, concluding with a generalizing sentence, returns to his theme. Through the articulation of its individual components, the digression as a whole is split into two large sections with clearly demarcated conclusions, in which respectively the *plebs* and the Gracchi appear as opponents of the nobility. They are of about the same length, and stylistically as well quite noticeably differentiated: while the first section portrays the unease of the general uprising in very short sentences, the second begins with an expansively sweeping period that joins the fates of the two brothers together as a unit before pursuing that of each individually; in what follows as well more capacious sentences prevail, and the antitheses are accordingly now placed farther from each other. Thus, the compositional structure that governs the course of thought in the component passages is repeated on a larger scale.

In light of what has been said above, it will seem self-evident that Sallust constructs his comparative character sketches of Caesar and Cato in such a way that the traits of the one are compared with those of the other sentence by sentence (*B.C.* 54. 2-6), particularly since Plutarch in his syncrises generally proceeds no differently; but whereas Plutarch compares similarities, here contrary traits are juxtaposed with one another. Elsewhere too his character sketches show an idiosyncratic construction. Sempronia is described at *B.C.* 25 in such a way that her vices form the centre of the passage (3–4), surrounding which her noble pedigree and beauty (2) and her intellectual gifts (5) form an introduction and conclusion. While the portrait here is divided into larger segments, Sallust constructs the famous characterization of Sulla (*B.J.* 95. 3ff.) out of the smallest antithetical components. High nobility, but ruined family; education and lofty spirit, but love of pleasure and even greater love of glory; profligate when idle, active where action is needed; clever and eloquent, but accessible to friends; an opaque dissembler, but generous. The conclusion to the whole is formed by a sentence that contrasts the judgement of him before and after the Civil War. Again, the opposition becomes clear when one compares a characterization by Livy in which he does not, as so often, paint only in bright colours: that of Hannibal at 21. 4. Here, in an almost schoolmasterly way, the brilliant gifts of the young hero are given first (21. 5–8) and thereafter his faults. The only antithesis, and a purely formal one at that, comes in the last sentence of the first section—*princeps in proelium ibat, ultimus conserto proelio excedebat* ('he was the first to go into battle and the last to withdraw after battle was joined'). Nor is this an invention of Livy; he merely applies to Hannibal a long-traditional expression from Greek rhetoric's repertoire of conceits.[44]

The construction of the speeches also conforms to the basic principles of Sallustian composition we have observed. It is, however, often more involved, as several pairs of antitheses are artificially intertwined. The speech of Philippus in the *Histories* is a good example (*H.* 1. 77 M).[45] The opening immediately introduces a doubled set of opposites: war–peace, Lepidus–the senatorial party; an internal connection between them is established through Lepidus' appearance as representative of the rebellion, while the senators are confronted with their shameful passivity. The

---

[44] Lys. 16. 18 μετὰ τῶν πρώτων μὲν τὰς ἐξόδους ποιούμενος, μετὰ τῶν τελευταίων δὲ ἀναχωρῶν ('making sorties among the first, retreating with the last'); Aristid. Or. 46. 191. ἔσχατος μὲν ἀνεχώρει μετὰ ἐσχάτων Ἀθηναίων, οὐ τὴν αὐτὴν τάξιν φυλάττων, ἥνπερ ὅτε ἐκπλεῖν ἔδει· τότε μὲν γὰρ πρῶτος ἦν ἐν πρώτοις ('last he retreated with the last Athenians, but he did not keep this position when it was necessary to sail forth; then he was first among the first'). Neither Aristid nor Livy is necessarily dependent on Lysias; the phrase was certainly repeated more frequently than we can detect and surely not invented for the excellent Mantitheus of Lysias.

[45] The analysis of Ullmann 1927: 42 contents itself with identifying the rubrics of *suasoriae* in this and in the other speeches.

first antithesis is set up in the opening clauses: *vellem rem publicam quietam esse...sed contra seditionibus omnia turbata sunt* ('I would prefer the Republic be tranquil...but on the contrary all has been thrown into confusion by rebellions'); the beginning of section 2, *bellum atque arma, quamquam* **vobis** *invisa, tamen quia* **Lepido** *placent sumenda sunt* ('war and arms, although detestable to you, must nevertheless be taken up because they are pleasing to Lepidus'), establishes the connection with the second antithetical pair. Once again the speaker recalls the first sentence with *pacem praestare-bellum pati* ('peace is foremost...to endure war'); then the following passage elaborates on this connection: *M. Lepidus...exercitum habet-vos...pacem optatis* ('M. Lepidus possesses an army...you are hoping for peace'). Now the speaker picks up the second opposition (*vobis-illi, adeptus est (Lepidus)-tribuistis (senatores)*), which leads to a description of the behaviour of the senatorial majority in which the word *pax* ('peace') is repeated twice (5). This prolonged attention to the Senate has a purpose, for the speaker himself now steps forward as its antithesis: *equidem-ceterum illi* ('I for my part...yet they'). The slack policy of the majority is responsible for Lepidus' dominance; the thought likewise takes the form of an antithesis (*at tum erat Lepidus-nunc est*, 'yet then Lepidus was...now he is') and opens into a powerful depiction of the dangers threatening Rome's power (7-8). The connection to the war and peace motif now occurs again, only fleetingly and in a subordinate clause (*quibus quies in seditionibus, in pace turbae sunt*, 'who have calm during rebellion, and disturbances in peace'). Then the speech turns again to the senators with a call to action (9). This is still more urgently repeated at 12-13, but in between comes a description of Lepidus (10-11), in which the catchwords *ex pace et concordia ad arma civilia* ('from peace and concord to civil war') appear anew in an emphatic position (10). Towards the end of 13 they are taken up again, and again attached to the opposition insurgent-Senate: **pax et concordia** *disturbantur palam, defenduntur occulte,* **quibus illa placent,** *in armis sunt,* **vos** *in metu* ('**peace and concord** are disturbed openly but defended in secret; those who prefer this are in arms, you in fear'). The speaker then switches to Lepidus; an abundance of antitheses lending emphatic expression to impassioned indignation culminates in a direct address (14-16). With renewed effort he then appeals again to the Senate; here one of the two pairs of opposites occurs in a slightly altered form: peace is replaced with *verba*, 'mere words', which here signifies much the same since, as he has shown, any action must be a counteroffensive. This expression, too, has been prepared already by the introduction, with **legatos** *pacem concordiam* at 5 recalled by **legatos** *et decreta* here (17). In continually new turns of phrase Philippus now drives this antithesis home to his audience (*verbis arma temptabitis*, 'you will challenge weapons with words'; *dilectus habiti-legatos et decreta paratis*, 'an army has been enrolled... you are readying embassies and decrees'; *pacem-bellum*, 'peace—war'; *armato Lepido vos inermos*, 'with Lepidus armed you unarmed'; *illi a vobis pacem, vobis ab illo bellum suadet*, 'he urges you to make peace with that man, but he urges that man to make war on you', 17-18). He then forces a choice upon his listeners with two groups of sentences introduced with almost the same words (*haec si **placent***, 'if these are pleasing', 19; *sin libertas et vera magis **placent***, 'but if liberty and truth please more', 20). The recommendation (22), given in the stiff formulae of the official style, forms the conclusion, which contrasts with the agitation of the actual speech by its calmness and cool objectivity.

This overview shows that the development of the thought is essentially based on a single opposition, which takes on a deceptive appearance of multiplicity only through the variation in terminology. Within this opposition, the argumentation progresses towards its goal, and the crowding together or thinning out of the antitheses indicates a hastier or slower pace to the discourse, increases or relaxes its urgency. As in passages of historical narrative, the restlessness of the movement is often stilled with a concluding sentence: so the actual proposal, with its calmer formality, comes here at the end of the entire speech.

The construction in the letter of Pompey is different. The opening contrasts the behaviour of Pompey with that of the Senate, and at the same time a purely hypothetical situation with the actual one (*H.* 2. 98. 1 M). At the end of this longer period comes the key word 'hunger', which dominates the letter in multiple variations. For the two passages that follow list the general services of Pompey and the army to Rome (2) and his particular achievements in this war (4-6), concluding both times with the thought: *you* have done nothing of the sort, but rather exposed us to hunger (*quom interim a vobis per triennium vix annuos sumptus datus est*, 'when meanwhile for three years you have scarcely granted us our annual expenses', 4; *pro quis o gratissimi patres, egestatem et famem redditis*, 'in return for which, most obliging senators, you have rewarded us with deprivation and hunger', 6). The last section, recalling the opening, again describes the situation of the army and the general; this time the enemy army serves as a comparison, not without a scarcely concealed threat (7-8); their exhausted means are highlighted through contrasts both spatial (Spain-Gaul) and temporal (*superiore anno*, 'last year', 9). Yet another reprise of the main antithesis (*ego-reliqui vos*) forms the transition to a repetition of the threat that introduced the passage. Thanks to the preservation of a palimpsest from Orleans, we know that Sallust presented the oppositions in the letter even more incisively, in that he carries them over immediately into the historical narrative:

> This letter was read aloud to the Senate at the beginning of the next year. But the consuls made a deal concerning the provinces assigned to them by the Senate: to Cotta went Nearer Gaul, Sicily to Octavius. Then the next consuls L. Lucullus and M. Cotta, deeply disturbed by the letter and message of Pompey,... saw to securing wages and reinforcements by every means. (*H.* 2. 98D M)

The structure of this letter is distinct from the passages treated so far in the unequal length of its two opposing parts. Not including the opening, three passages of increasing length are devoted to Pompey's achievements, and at the conclusion of each the contrast with the Senate is drawn in a few brief words; it is all the more effective when the persistent inactivity of the government is opposed in almost the same words to the ever more expansively described accomplishments of the general and the ever more desperate emergency of the army. The last section, beyond its relation to the whole speech, takes on its own formal unity thanks to the recurrence of the same ideas at its beginning and end. It seems an illustration of Pompey's rebukes when the outgoing consuls' busying themselves about their provinces is made to intervene between the receipt of the letter and dealing with its demands. We have already often encountered such apparent discontinuities in the course of a narrative, and we see in this case how Sallust is capable of exploiting it to reveal his unspoken judgement of events.

How far can the distinctive compositional principles we have observed help in understanding the overall construction of Sallust's work? Reitzenstein 1906: 87–8. made a well-known attempt to demonstrate that Sallust's monographs were structured as dramas in five acts. He supports this argument with a passage from Cicero's letter to Lucceius where he says that what he went through in the period between his consulship and return from exile, which he proposes to the historian as the subject for a monograph, was 'like a drama, possessing various **acts** and many changes of plans and circumstances' (*quasi fabula: habet enim varios **actus** multasque <mut>ationes et consiliorum et temporum, Fam.* 5. 12. 6). From these words Reitzenstein adduces a Hellenistic theory equating the structure of such monographs with that of tragedy and therefore transfers Horace's famous doctrine of five acts to historiography. The word *varius* alone shows that Cicero has in mind the colourful vicissitudes of eventful destinies, and Lauckner 1911: 59ff. has convincingly shown that the letter to Lucceius employs precisely the

Sallust: Narrative Style and Composition 55

peripatetic-Hellenistic theory of historiography that Sallust rejects (see pp. 66–67 below). It is, therefore, not to be expected that it would be an important factor in the overall construction of the monographs. But above all, this division of Sallust's works into five parts is itself rather forced. It is true that the later portion of the *Jugurtha* easily falls into three segments grouped around the principal active figures, Metellus, Marius, and Sulla; but since Reitzenstein himself must concede that his first act (5–26) is 'artistically' divided in two by the massive excursus on Africa, his argument about the work's structure does not quite persuade. Likewise, in the *Catiline* this structure can only be achieved by disregarding the divisions indicated by the author himself. Thus, the concluding portrait of the atmosphere at Rome in light of the danger at *B.C.* 31. 1–3 is robbed of its compositional function by extending the second 'act' as far as 39. 5; chapters 39. 6–43, moreover, do not belong under the heading 'collapse of the conspiracy' but rather describe the ominous extension of the calamity into the unforeseeable future; furthermore, Reitzenstein himself quite rightly emphasizes that the long passage at *B.C.* 36. 4–39. 5 is there to create a structural break. It does not help to simply move the break to a different spot to forestall the objection; this segment can be united neither with the foregoing nor with the subsequent act. On the whole, in light of everything we have already seen of Sallust's methods of representation, a structure composed of such large, isolated segments appears foreign to his design.

By contrast, the alternation between actions that affect one another is unmistakable. After the introduction to the *Catiline* (*B.C.* 1–4) comes an exposition that in essence dwells on the conspirators (*B.C.* 5–22). It begins with a characterization of Catiline (*B.C.* 5. 1–8) and gains context from a sweeping treatment of cultural history (*B.C.* 5. 9–13). After this, the story of Catiline does not immediately resume; rather, a description of the circle around him is developed out of the portrait of general moral decay (*in tanta tamque corrupta civitate*, 'in so large and so corrupt a citizenry', *B.C.* 14). Not until then does the narrative return to the protagonist (*B.C.* 15), only to dwell once again, with an explicit glance backwards (*ut supra diximus*, 'as we said before'), on the activities of the co-conspirators (*B.C.* 16). The actual plot begins with the naming of the participants at the first meeting, and thus at the moment of conspiracy (*B.C.* 17), but it resumes only with the meeting at *B.C.* 20-2 containing the great speech of Catiline, a scene which begins with one of those backward-pointing phrases characteristic of Sallust (*quos paulo ante memoravi*, 'those whom I mentioned a little before'). An account of the first conspiracy is placed in between (*B.C.* 18–19). This arrangement makes it hard to believe that Sallust was principally concerned with the progression of the narrative. It need hardly be comprehensively demonstrated that the fluid transitions and references here produce an artistic unity that scarcely conceals the constant departures from the straight storyline. The only explanation of this phenomenon is that in the construction of the whole work as well Sallust yielded to that same inclination towards constant alternation between leading characters we have already established for individual episodes; the way in which we are told one minute of Catiline and the next of his partners in crime corresponds precisely to the jumping from one military commander to another on the same side traceable in his battle narratives. In comparison with the examples from the *Jugurtha* given above (see pp. 47–48), however, it must be acknowledged that Sallust's artistry had here not yet reached its peak: the position of the individual pieces within the whole seems decidedly arbitrary, and other arrangements could have been at least as well justified as this one.

After the great assembly, which also gives an impressive portrait of Catiline's personality through his speech, the reaction sets in, again divided into two: the garrulous indiscretion of Curius and Fulvia (*B.C.* 23. 1–4) and the resulting election of Cicero to the consulship (*B.C.* 23. 5–24. 1) follow in sequence. Next comes a return to Catiline, whose plans are described at *B.C.* 24. 2–4 and 26. 1. In between the portrait of Sempronia intervenes (*B.C.* 25). This has been prepared for by the mention of women among Catiline's associates but has no connection at all to what follows. Indeed, it is so unorganically integrated that some external reason for its insertion has long been sought. It is particularly awkward that *his rebus comparatis* ('after these preparations'), at *B.C.* 26. 1, refers back to 24 as if chapter 25 were simply not there. Since there is only one brief reference to Sempronia elsewhere in the narrative (*B.C.* 40. 5), Schwartz 1897: 564 and 570 (= Chapter 5, pp. 124 and 130 in this volume) rightly explains her prominence here as an attack on her son D. Brutus, one of Caesar's assassins.[46] This accounts for the mention of Sempronia but not its placement in the work. Evidently the constant alternation between Catiline and the other conspirators which dominated the previous section is still at work here, before the new opposition that displaces it has been fully developed. Now, however, at *B.C.* 26. 2–4, the countermeasures of Cicero link up with the plot of Catiline. This marks the beginning of open conflict (*B.C.* 26. 5). Catiline's attempts end in failure at Rome (27–28. 3), while in Etruria the movement is initially successful (28. 4). On the defensive, Cicero pushes through the *senatus consultum*

---

[46] See also Münzer 1920: 272–3.

ultimum (*B.C.* 29), and an alarming new report leads to the deployment of troops throughout Italy (*B.C.* 30). Finally, the agitated mood at Rome is described (*B.C.* 31. 1–3). The opponents, Cicero and Catiline, clash directly in a meeting of the Senate, but no decision is reached (*B.C.* 31. 4–32. 1). Once again a counteraction follows, as the Senate proclaims the conspirators 'public enemies' (*B.C.* 36. 2–3). A broad overview (*B.C.* 36. 4–39. 5) highlights this outcome and shows the danger at its highest point. After this, the negotiations with the Allobroges (*B.C.* 39.6–41) demonstrate the threatening spread of the conspiracy; it begins to infect the provinces as well (*B.C.* 42); the conclusion of the episode returns to Rome, where the original negotiations took place (*B.C.* 43). The betrayal and arrest of the Allobroges (*B.C.* 44–5) stand at the beginning of the next counteraction, followed by the capture of the Catilinarians (*B.C.* 46.1–5) and the proceedings in the Senate (*B.C.* 46. 6–9), interrupted only by a description of the change of attitude among the people (*B.C.* 48. 1–2). After another feeble attempt at resistance (*B.C.* 50. 1–2), the decisive Senate meeting, distinguished by the two great speeches of Caesar and Cato, leads to the death sentence and execution of the conspirators (*B.C.* 50. 3–53). From the interplay of action and reaction in this section, greater clarity gradually emerges about the goals of the conspiracy, but also confusion (as Sallust represents it) thanks to the suspicions against certain eminent men. A final section (*B.C.* 56–61) brings the story of Catiline to a close in an essentially unified movement; for he again stands at the centre of events and gets the second great speech which structurally corresponds to the first (*B.C.* 20). Only brief passages are devoted to depicting the troops of the state (*B.C.* 57. 2–4, *B.C.* 59. 4–6).

This overview of the content of the monograph reveals the narrative's rapid alternations back and forth between the conspirators and the senatorial party. Three large units can be discerned: preparations (*B.C.* 5–22), the struggle to expose the conspiracy (*B.C.* 23–55), and the demise of Catiline (*B.C.* 56–61); the end of each section is marked by speeches (both I and III by a speech of Catiline, II by the debate between Caesar and Cato). In the first section, the narrative constantly moves between Catiline and his co-conspirators, in the second between the Catilinarians and the senatorial party. Only in the third does Catiline take the leading part for a relatively long stretch, but even here accounts of the senatorial army temporarily distract attention from the actual hero, to say nothing of the construction of battle narratives (see p. 46 above). This compositional form was important enough to Sallust that he was willing for its sake to add some strokes of free invention to his overall picture, such as the account of the first meeting of the conspirators; he needed this scene, as is now clear, as an effective conclusion to his first section, and the redating of the meeting at Laeca's house also becomes explicable from this perspective.[47]

The construction of the *Bellum Iugurthinum* shows itself to be similar, except that the composition here is more coherent and the progression calmer; a more mature artistry is discernible. An uninterrupted movement carries the background story as far as the demise of Hiempsal and the division of the kingdom between Adherbal and Jugurtha (*B.J.* 5–16). The excursus on the geography of Africa follows on naturally from this (*B.J.* 17–19). Jugurtha's opponents here are first Micipsa, then his cousins; the speech in this portion is therefore given to Adherbal. The next section stretches from *B.J.* 20 to 42 and is clearly bounded by the concluding observations on the party system of the Roman state (*B.J.* 41–2). Here Jugurtha is opposed to the Roman Senate and people; in quite short units the misdeeds of Jugurtha and the inadequate resistance to them in Rome follow upon one another: *B.J.* 20–1 Expulsion of Adherbal—*B.J.* 21. 4–22 Discussions in the Senate, embassy to Africa—*B.J.* 23 Countermeasures of Jugurtha—*B.J.* 24–5 Discussions in the Senate, repeated embassy to Africa—*B.J.* 26 Fall of Cirta, death of Adherbal—*B.J.* 27–8. 3 Renewed discussions in Rome, entrance of Memmius, bribery—*B.J.* 28. 4–29 Peace agreement in Africa—*B.J.* 30–32. 1 strengthened opposition in Rome, speech of Memmius—*B.J.* 32. 2–35 Jugurtha in Rome—*B.J.* 36–8 Defeat of A. Albinus in Africa—*B.J.* 39–40 Energetic resolutions in Rome. The growing opposition to the weak policy of the Senate and the ever-increasing insolence of Jugurtha define the movement in this section, which accordingly has its climax in the speech of Memmius, the leader of that opposition. The constant alternation is made clear formally as well through the change of setting, now Rome, now Africa. At this point Metellus emerges as the Numidians' opponent (*B.J.* 43–79); this long section is divided in two: at *B.J.* 62 it reaches an apparent conclusion with the nearly complete defeat of Jugurtha, while the actual conclusion, in Sallustian fashion, is indicated through an excursus (*B.J.* 78–9, on the Syrtes and the Philaeni). In between, the narrative switches in the familiar way between the Roman attack and the Numidian king's resistance: *B.J.* 43–5 Metellus' preparations—*B.J.* 46–7 First acts of aggression in an apparent state of peace—*B.J.* 48–53 Counterattack of Jugurtha, first battle—*B.J.* 54–62 Fighting around Zama and apparent conclusion. The new operation now provides an opportunity to introduce Marius with an account of his youth and

---

[47] On the other often discussed chronological inaccuracies in Sallust, see Seel 1930: 46ff. who quite correctly sees them as simple errors.

machinations (*B.J.* 63-5); only after this is the actual plot resumed with Jugurtha's victory at Vaga (*B.J.* 66-7).—*B.J.* 68-9 Revenge of Metellus—*B.J.* 70-2 Bomilcar's attempted treachery. In between, the election of Marius is inserted, which points back to his entrance and forward to the coming section, *B.J.* 74-7. With another defeat of Jugurtha, the victories at Thala and Leptis, the activities of Metellus come to an end. The beginning of the next section, which extends to the conclusion of the work, is marked by the entrance of a new opponent: at *B.J.* 80-1 Jugurtha succeeds in drawing Bocchus into the war. As Marius' plots in the preceding section had prepared the way for this one, so here a brief passage (*B.J.* 82-3) brings Metellus' story to its conclusion. The new general, still in Rome, is only now introduced and characterized through a speech (*B.J.* 84-86. 3). What follows is divided into two sections, of which the first (*B.J.* 86. 4-94) reports the victorious advances of Marius, while the second (*B.J.* 96-101) contains the desperate but unsuccessful resistance of the local kings. These are separated by the characterization of Sulla (*B.J.* 95), who now steps into the foreground for the final negotiations with Bocchus (*B.J.* 102-13), though without completely displacing Marius in the author's design. This is shown in the last chapter, where the consul's name is emphatically placed at the end. At the same time, the synopsis given there of the empire's overall situation is meant retroactively to situate the events in Africa within the course of Roman history. Sallust wants to narrate the destiny of the Roman people, not of Jugurtha.

The breaks that were detectable in the *Catiline* have vanished in the *Jugurtha*; though the constant change of viewpoint remains here as well, the transitions are carefully justified. An explicit backward reference like *sicut supra memoravi* ('as I reported before') occurs only at *B.J.* 84. 1 and serves to connect Marius' appearance as consul with his election at *B.J.* 73. 6-7.[48] In general, the divisions match the changes in Jugurtha's main opponent; excursus serve to demarcate the sections, and speeches distinguish the most important opposing figures.

In Sallust, a coherent ordering pattern determines the relationship of the individual elements of the narrative to one another as much as it does the components of the sentence. Nowhere else does this pattern return in such an unambiguous form, and this justifies recognizing in it the

---

[48] This formula, which Sallust loves, modelled on the Polybian προειρημένος ('the aforementioned', under the influence of the Polybius imitator Sempronius Asellio?), is used nowhere else in the *Jugurtha* to bridge a leap in the narrative; at *B.J.* 96. 1, the backward reference to Sulla's arrival (*B.J.* 95. 1) is minimal, since only the characterization of Sulla comes between.

individual style of the author. The picture that emerges from the distribution of material, however, requires some elaboration. An attempt must be made to identify the principles according to which he made selections from the mass of available facts or reshaped the tradition; for this aspect of his work, too, can within certain limits be considered as subject to Sallust's choice. Previous treatments have primarily examined this question in terms of his political bias, without thereby reaching a generally accepted or satisfactory result.[49] The following remarks place the emphasis on stylistic considerations.

The monographic form, first of all, necessarily requires an accentuation of the principal characters. Jugurtha can serve as an example. The personality of the Numidian prince is thrown into relief by every means; the wickedness of his behaviour stands out all the more since the indigenous Numidians who oppose him are reduced to mere shadows. The war in which, according to Livy (*Per.* 62), Hiempsal fell becomes an assassination (*B.J.* 12). Massiva, whom Posidonius called a 'second Jugurtha' (Diod. 34 fr. 34a), appears in Sallust as a harmless exile (*B.J.* 35). If, after the murder, Sallust has Jugurtha leave Rome *iussus a senatu* ('at the command of the Senate', *B.J.* 35. 9), while according to every other account he fled in secret (Diod. 34 fr. 34a, Liv. *Per.* 64, App. *Num.* 1), it is to illustrate his criminal brazenness.[50] It should perhaps also be borne in mind here that Sallust consistently depicts Jugurtha as an unlawful usurper; it does not seem to have been noticed that according to the line of succession given by Livy (29. 29. 6), the legal situation in the Numidian royal house was at the very least doubtful: there Gala is followed not by his son Masinissa, but 'according to the native custom' (*more gentis*) by his brother Oezalces, apparently the eldest member of the royal family; he would be succeeded by his son Capussa, and only then would the claim of the young Masinissa come into effect. Accordingly, as the eldest living grandson of Masinissa, Jugurtha would have a stronger right to the throne than his cousins, or at the very least an equally strong one. The only counterargument would be his illegitimate birth (*B.J.* 5. 7), which in a royal harem might not carry all that much weight (cf. *B.J.* 80. 6). However, such considerations ascribe to the historian a comprehensive reading of the sources which we perhaps should not assume. Even if he was aware of all the facts at our disposal, our methods still do not allow an unintentional adjustment of events

---

[49] The charges against Sallust are collected in Lauckner 1911 and Bosselaar 1915. Both are under the spell of their conception of Sallust as a tendentious falsifier.

[50] That the passage contains a 'humiliation of the senate' (Lauckner 1911: 42) can hardly be accepted.

according to the demands of his narrative to be clearly distinguished from a deliberate departure from the tradition available to him. One might more easily attribute the incorrect account of Marius' *cursus honorum* (*B.J.* 63. 4–5, by contrast with Plut. *Mar.* 5. 1–2) to the desire to heighten the impact of his first appearance. The displacement of the oracle Marius received at Utica on the way to the elections (Plut. *Mar.* 8. 8) to the beginning of the episode (*B.J.* 63. 1) perhaps springs from the same intention. Considering that this passage begins the section in which Marius emerges as the chief opponent to the protagonist, Sallust's motive for the alteration is just as likely to be of an artistic nature as to result from political bias.

More productive for our purposes is an examination of what Sallust leaves out. We may hope to detect this process of selection most clearly in the earlier monograph, thanks to the rich source material on the Catilinarian conspiracy available to us from the Ciceronian period. Moreover, since it may be assumed that Sallust was familiar at least with the speeches of Cicero, omissions in comparison to material available to him there must be regarded as intentional. If we compare Sallust's account of the Senate meeting on 8 November 63 (*B.C.* 31. 5–32) with the rest of the tradition, it becomes clear that Sallust passes over all factual details relating to the Senate's procedure. He mentions neither the time of the session and its setting, the temple of Jupiter Stator (Cic. *Cat.* 1. 11, 1. 33; 2. 12), nor the actual course of the debate, with the conspirator's call for a vote in the Senate (Cic. *Cat.* 1. 20). The Senate's attitude is likewise only very briefly depicted: 'all cried out and called him a public enemy and a parricide' (*obstrepere omnes, hostem atque parricidam vocare*, *B.C.* 31. 8). The consulars' moving away from Catiline at his entrance is missing (Cic. *Cat.* 1. 16, 2. 12). How uncertain the position of the majority in response to Cicero's revelations really was can be seen in the initial silence at the consul's question whether Catiline ought to leave the city; only through the trick of posing the same question about Q. Lutatius Catulus was it possible to move the Senate to express an opinion (Dio 40. 5a; see also Münzer, *RE* XIII 2091; cf. Cic. *Cat.* 1. 21, *Mur.* 51). Of this, too, Sallust says nothing. As a result, the entire episode becomes a confrontation between the consul and Catiline. Cicero's speech is passed over with an allusion to its publication, in keeping with the common practice of ancient historians.[51] But not even the conspirator's initial silence, over which the great orator so exulted

---

[51] Baehrens 1926: 40 has rightly corroborated this by pointing to Livy 45. 25. 3 and *Per.* 49. One may add Tac. *Ann.* 15. 63, *quae in vulgus edita eius* (*Senecae*) *verbis invertere supersedeo* ('I forego transforming what Seneca has issued in his own words').

(*Cat.* 2. 13, *Orat.* 129), is reported. Instead Catiline appears much more composed and duplicitous than in reality. Absent is the threat attested in Cicero (*Mur.* 51): 'the Republic had two bodies, one weak with a weak head, the other strong but without a head; to this, while he was alive, if it would be deserving of him, a head would not be lacking' (*duo esse corpora rei publicae, unum debile infirmo capite, alterum firmum sine capite; huic, si ita de se meritum esset, caput se vivo non defuturum*). In place of this ambiguous statement comes the adroit comparison between the patrician and the 'lodger-citizen' (*inquilinus civis*) of Rome, which reveals the man's utter dangerousness. Not until he realizes that his cause is hopeless does he leave the session, with an outcry whose graphic power reveals the force of his hatred ('I shall put out my conflagration by pulling down the building', *incendium meum ruina extinguam, B.C.* 31. 9). It is well known that Catiline used these words on an earlier occasion in response to Cato (Cic. *Mur.* 51); Sallust did not scruple to transfer them here because they seemed to provide a more fitting conclusion than the allusive remark about the headless state. It is also not quite certain whether the accusation of being a 'lodger-citizen' was made on this occasion; Appian, whose source Sallust used,[52] mentions it only as a slogan of the general agitation against the consul (*B Civ.* 2. 2).[53]

A great economy in the portrayal of individual details is immediately visible. The merely factual, whatever was inessential to the picture or easily supplied by Roman readers through their knowledge of the procedure at Senate meetings, is left out. Likewise, all irrelevances which might distract from the two principal actors are omitted; the attitude of the audience spontaneously breaks through only once, in a short sentence. Further, the majority of the accusations hurled at Cicero by Catiline are indicated only with a brief *maledicta alia*; it cannot be doubted that, in keeping with the usual practice of the time, this conceals invective whose repetition Sallust considered inconsistent with the dignity of his history. We thus receive a simplified, stylized picture of the proceedings which makes no claim to photographic fidelity. Only the depiction of Catiline engages the author's interest, the change in his attitude from the moment when he comes into the Senate 'with the aim of dissimulating or of exculpating himself' (*dissimulandi causa aut sui expurgandi, B.C.* 31. 5), through his failed attempt to win over his peers with a hypocritical appeal to his nobility, up to the unrestrained outbreak of rage, forms the true subject of the scene. Everything else is brought in only as far as is necessary for comprehension. For that

---

[52] Schwartz, *RE* II 223.   [53] On this, see Schwartz 1897: 606.

Sallust: Narrative Style and Composition 63

reason, the depiction of Catiline's deliberations is deferred to the following sentence.

The great Senate meeting of 5 December (*B.C.* 50. 3–53. 1) is treated in a very similar manner. Once again location and date are missing; only the armed guards are mentioned.[54] Apart from the presiding magistrate's putting the question, we hear only the opinion of the *consul designatus*, Silanus, that the conspirators should be put to death. The further course of the hearing, in which a number of consulars aligned themselves with Silanus (Cic. *Att.* 12. 21. 2), is not reported, nor is Cicero's renewed intervention with the *Fourth Catilinarian*. The mitigation of the proposal, to which Silanus himself assented, is presented immediately after his first vote, although it in fact took place after Caesar's speech (Suet. *Caes.* 14. 1).[55] After the resolution to execute the conspirators, the subsequent attempt to bring Caesar's proposal for the seizure of their property to a vote as well is omitted (Plut. *Cic.* 21. 5). By this means the reader's entire attention is concentrated on the great debate between Caesar and Cato; only the ultimate outcome of the proceedings is reported in another brief passage (*B.C.* 53. 1). After this, the Caesar-Cato antithesis is continued in the character portraits of both. Instructive too is a comparison between the depiction of the Catilinarians at *B.C.* 14. 1–4 and its model, the famous description Theopompus[56] gives of Philip II's circle. Sallust had this in mind and simply lifted his second sentence from it: *quod si quis etiam a culpa vacuos in amicitiam eius inciderat, cottidiano usu atque illecebris facile par similisque ceteris efficiebatur* ('but if anyone even free from fault fell into his friendship, by daily habit and by enticements he was easily made like and equal to the rest', *B.C.* 14. 4; cf. εἰ δὲ καὶ μὴ τοιοῦτός τις <ὢν> ἐληλύθει, ὑπὸ τοῦ βίου καὶ τῆς διαίτης τῆς Μακεδονικῆς ταχέως ἐκείνοις ὅμοιος ἐγίνετο, 'even if someone who was not of this sort came to Philip, he quickly became like those on account of the Macedonian lifestyle and habits', F 224). Sallust begins with a longer period listing the five types of Catiline's comrades. The first four are subdivided into two groups, and the initial pair is held together verbally through introductory particles (*quicumque–quique*), as well as by content: bankrupts are the subject of both clauses, first those who have impoverished themselves through their vices and profligacy, next those whom bribes have landed in debt. The second group contains criminals of all kinds; the connection is loose, and both its components are tacked

---

[54] See Stein 1930: 15–16.
[55] [In fact Sallust's statement at *B.C.* 50. 4 looks forward to a later stage in the debate (eds.).]
[56] *FGrH* 115 F 224–5.

on with a mere 'moreover' (*praeterea-ad hoc*): these are (1) condemned parricides and the sacrilegious, and those who fear conviction for these crimes, and (2) those who survive through murder and perjury. The latter are scarcely distinguishable from the first group. By way of conclusion comes a category which actually encompasses all the others (*omnes quos flagitium egestas conscius animus agitabat*, 'all whom disgrace, want, or a guilty mind impelled'). The distinction is thus unclear and is accomplished more by grammatical form than by content in order to achieve a tight structure and by means of an apparent abundance of groups to conceal the fact that they summon up only very generalized notions. Theopompus is hardly more specific: robbery, murder, perjury, and deception, along with the pederasty only vaguely hinted at in Sallust, form the principal accusations. The description, however, is nearly four times as long. The role of the compositional structure is filled by a progressive heightening of the tone, whose build-up ultimately culminates in the mythological comparison to Centaurs and Laestrygonians. To every vice he adds its negative complement (e.g. τὸ μὲν ἀληθεύειν καὶ ταῖς ὁμολογίαις ἐμμένειν οὐκ οἰκεῖον αὐτῶν ἐνόμιζον, τὸ δ' ἐπιορκεῖν καὶ φενακίζειν ἐν τοῖς σεμνοτάτοις ὑπελάμβανον, 'to tell the truth and to abide by what they swore they did not consider their business, but they took it upon themselves to break oaths and to swindle in the most holy places'). Thus, he creates an impression of unchecked abundance, next to which Sallust's concision seems oppressive; the graceful puns and Gorgianic antitheses,[57] which are constantly elaborated into perfect formal symmetry, give the account a swaying rhythm which renders Theopompus' anger against Philip's companions less persuasive.

The narratives of the Jugurthine War show a similar stylization. In the surprise attack by the inhabitants of Vaga against the Roman occupying forces (*B.J.* 66. 2–67) only the commanding officer T. Turpilius Silanus, whose fate Sallust will treat at a later point (*B.J.* 69. 4), is mentioned by name. Nothing about the preparations for the betrayal is related beyond the choice of date and the prevailing attitude of the population. Neither the occupation of the citadel nor the closing of the gate receives more than an incidental mention to make clear the total success of the attack. The essential content of the passage is exclusively the interaction between unarmed Romans and the crowds that close in on them. Here, too, he relates only few concrete details, such as the participation of

---

[57] A comparison with Sallust's manner of writing shows how little is expressed by the basic designation of an 'antithetical style'.

women and children on the rooftops; the remainder deals in generalizing expressions which could just as well apply to any conflict of this type, and in shaping which Sallust presumably took creative licence.

Truly vivid, realistic details are rare in his descriptions and mostly derive from his source, such as the depiction of the sleeping Nabdalsa at the discovery of Bomilcar's conspiracy (*B.J.* 71. 1ff.), or the mountaineering skills of an unnamed Ligurian (*B.J.* 94. 2ff.). In the *Catiline* they are completely absent. Here despite the archaizing language we find a profound contrast to the delight in factual abundance and variety which appears in Cato's *Origines* and characterizes the truly archaic period.

This effort to simplify events has had two consequences, which have long been recognized: inaccuracies, beyond those already described, find their way into his account either unintentionally or deliberately. This includes the collapsing of Marius' three campaigns into two (already criticized by Mommsen 1855: 2.140n), and probably also the replacement of P. Sulla as candidate for the consulship with Catiline himself in the account of his first conspiracy (*B.C.* 18; see Baehrens 1926: 55). Second, it leads to an economy in the introduction of supporting characters. E. Schwartz 1897: 563 (= Chapter 5, p. 124) has observed that each figure is mentioned at least twice, and the rare exceptions to this rule, such as C. Flaminius (*B.C.* 36. 1), are cited as names only, without the reader being expected to seek further information. The aim is not abundance of material but highlighting what is significant. Another phenomenon is equally important for the overall effect, namely, restraint in the representation of pathetic scenes. A comparison of the scene where Fulvia learns of the conspiracy (*B.C.* 23. 3–4) with the highly embellished version of Diodorus (40. 5) illustrates the difference particularly well. Sallust says only *Fulvia insolentiae Curi causa cognita* ('Fulvia, having learned the reason for Curius' high and mighty manner'); the Hellenistic historian, however, paints an elaborate scene:

> She was amazed at his words and could not discern the reason for his threat; nevertheless the young woman retained her proud bearing. But during their conversation, while she drank with him, she addressed him with artful flattery and begged to hear what his words betokened. And he told her out of love, to win her favour, the whole truth.

Here Sallust's dry statement has grown into a seduction tale of refined expansiveness, which is perhaps the invention of Diodorus' unknown model. Sallust not only avoids the erotic and the obscene entirely[58] (recall

---

[58] The only exception is, of course, *B.C.* 14. 2, *quicumque... manu ventre **pene** bona patria laceraverat* ('and those who had laid waste to their inheritance with hand, gut, and

his dismissal of the gossip concerning the Catilinarians' pederasty, *B.C.* 14. 7), but also restricts as much as possible the portrayal of horrific scenes. It is true that he reproduces, with the scepticism customary among ancient historians in such cases, the rumour that the Catilinarians drank human blood to seal their conspiratorial brotherhood (*B.C.* 22). But the execution of the conspirators (*B.C.* 55. 5) is dispatched in one brief and matter-of-fact sentence, and that of Jugurtha is not reported at all, even though the image of the Numidian falling into insanity and roughly abused by his Roman executioners yet clinging to life with all the dogged energy of his nature would have offered quite an effective conclusion (Plut. *Mar.* 12. 4–5). The words *civitas magna et opulens cuncta poenae aut praedae fuit* ('the whole great and wealthy city was given over to punishment or plunder', *B.J.* 69. 3) conceal within themselves the execution of the entire council of Vaga (App. *Num.* 3). At the end of the *Catiline*, it is not mentioned that the head of the fallen rebel commander was cut off and sent to Rome (Dio Cass. 37. 40. 2). The narration of the death of Hiempsal breaks off at the point where he is discovered hiding in a cottage (*B.J.* 12. 5). Next comes the single sentence: 'the Numidians brought his head...to Jugurtha' (*Numidae caput eius...ad Iugurtham referent*), from which the young king's fate must be inferred. It is instructive to compare with this spare representation the picture Tacitus gives of the death of Vitellius, whom the soldiers discovered in a very similar situation (*H.* 3. 84–5): here we are spared no detail of the disgrace with which the dethroned emperor goes to meet his death. The report is meant to shock through its depiction of the vicissitudes of human existence, although any sympathy for Vitellius is far from the author's intention.

In this respect Sallust consciously differs from the Hellenistic historians and their ealier Roman imitators, such as Cornelius Sisenna.[59] These

---

penis'), where the word *penis* is offensive not only to modern sensibilities (Cic. *Fam.* 9. 22. 2). Naturally the coarse word is meant to illustrate the debasement of the Catilinarians, but it seems additionally that Sallust was following an older model in using it. Piso Frugi in his *annales* (fr. 42 *FRHist* = fr. 40 P) had spoken of young men 'devoted to their penises' (*peni dediti*), perhaps in a description of the moral decline around the year 154 (cf. fr. 40 *FRHist* = fr. 38 P). It is possible in any case that this description, along with that of Theopompus (see p. 63 above), supplied colouring for Sallust's own picture.

[59] Sisenna's 'detailed portraiture of the hideous' was already brought out by Mommsen 1856: 1856: 3.611) with respect to fr. 14 *FRHist* (= fr. 103 P): *innoxios trementibus artubus repente extrahis atque in labro summo fluminis, caelo albente* ('suddenly you drag out the innocent with trembling limbs and on the highest bank of the river, as dawn is brightening'). See also fr. 33 *FRHist* (= fr. 45 P) and, for the erotic element, fr. 32 *FRHist* (= fr. 13 P): *mulierem missa fide ac pietate propter amoris nefarii lubidinem obstitisse* ('that a woman who had cast away loyalty and piety stood in his way on account of her lust for a criminal love affair').

Sallust: Narrative Style and Composition

wanted primarily to stir the reader's emotions, even at the cost of truth (Plut. *Per.* 28. 3), and to compete with the genres of high poetry in their portrayal of the cruel games that Fortune plays with humanity. The devastation of captured cities (Polyb. 2. 56. 6, by way of Phylarchus), scenes of torture (Polyb. 2. 59. 1), and executions are indispensable to this style, as are lovingly detailed accounts of emotional processes.[60] All this is deliberately left aside in Sallust. He avoids the suspense produced by novelistic narration; instead, he wants to bring out the essentials in a condensed outline, refraining from a confusing abundance of detail. Colourful scenes play no role, at least in the two monographs; it stands out as remarkable when he at one point contrasts the victory celebration of drunken barbarians in the flickering light of their campfires with the silence of the Romans waiting in the darkness for the signal to attack (*B.J.* 98. 5ff.). Individual details almost always serve a special purpose: thus, the description of the honours Metellus had bestowed upon himself in Spain (*H.* 2. 70 M) are meant to illustrate the decline of Roman traditions. A personal stake in events and leading figures like the one that animates Cato's famous account of the heroic action of M. Caedicius (fr. 76 *FRHist* (= fr. 83 P)) is nowhere apparent. Instead, his writings are permeated by a reflectiveness which is the distinctive feature of his representation. All these traits derive especially from his imitation of Thucydides. E. Schwartz 1897: 560ff. (= Chapter 5, pp. 121–5 in this volume) who first accurately assessed Sallust's relationship to Hellenistic historiography, draws the conclusion 'that in Sallust's time there existed a classicizing Greek theory of historiography, which, in specific contrast to the showiness of Hellenistic novels, demanded a return to the lofty, purely political manner of Thucydides, contemptuous of the artistic expectations of the masses, and took its laws from him' (p. 565, = Chapter 5, p. 125 in this volume). He points out that the same model had a very similar effect on Dio Cassius.[61] It is still unclear to what extent the critical observations of the time extended beyond purely stylistic matters such as diction and figures of speech and sense; the books of Dionysius of Halicarnassus on the Attic historians offer nothing more than this, and the evidence for any theoretical treatment of composition and narrative technique in historiography is generally scanty. There is much that we can only ascribe to a fine literary sensibility developed through meticulous reading of a model, just as the perfection of Hellenistic versification was not transmitted in any theoretical textbook. In any case, Sallust's close affinity to his Greek predecessor is as clear in his representational technique as it is in his language.

---

[60] Schwartz 1896b: 114.   [61] *RE* III 1690.

This aim is particularly perceptible in the more abstract portions of the works. As Thucydides embeds the archaeology within his account of the beginnings of the Peloponnesian War, so Sallust, after the opening chapters of the *Catiline*, inserts a review of Roman history from the foundation of the city (*B.C.* 6–13). His dependence is made all the more conspicuous through the echo at 6. 5 of Thuc. 2. 40. 4 (see p. 42 above). Even the extensive moral descriptions which provide the accompaniment to his narrative have their counterpart in the famous chapters at Thuc. 3. 87ff., relating the descent into savagery brought on by the Peloponnesian War. Here the very hues in which Sallust paints the situation at Rome are sometimes adopted wholesale. The keywords of *B.C.* 10. 3–5, 'greed' and 'ambition' (*avaritia* and *ambitio*; *pecuniae-imperi cupido*), recur at Thuc. 3. 82. 8 (πλεονεξία–φιλοτιμία). At *B.C.* 38. 3 an entire sentence is simply taken over from the corresponding place (see p. 42 n33 above). Its immediate continuation is deployed at *B.J.* 42. 4 and 41. 5 (cf. Mollmann 1878: 3–4.). It is thus not surprising to meet with an echo even in the speech of Cato at *B.C.* 52. 11: *iam pridem nos vera vocabula rerum amisimus...malarum rerum audacia fortitudo vocatur* ('we have long since lost the true words for things,...audacity in evildoing is called "bravery"'; cf. Thuc. 3. 82. 4, τὴν εἰωθυῖαν ἀξίωσιν τῶν ὀνομάτων ἐς τὰ ἔργα ἀντήλλαξαν τῇ δικαιώσει. τόλμα μὲν γὰρ ἀλόγιστος ἀνδρεία φιλέταιρος ἐνομίσθη, 'they changed the customary estimation of words in relation to things at their discretion. Thus heedless zeal was considered loyal courage'). It is more disconcerting when a battle scene from the Greek historian recurs with clear verbatim echoes; not only does the 'teichoscopia' before Zama (*B.J.* 60. 4) borrow the description of the spectators' changing attitude (*B.J.* 60. 2) from Thuc. 7. 71. 3, but even such a tiny detail as the spectators' involuntary bodily movements (*B.J.* 60. 4) is faithfully copied. Most remarkable, however, is the fact that the praise of Roman virtue which resounds so insistently through Sallust's writings largely employs expressions that derive from Greek authors and were originally coined for Athens.[62] The most important model here was not Thucydides but the *Panegyricus* of Isocrates. With *B.C.* 7. 6 *gloriae maximum* **certamen** *inter ipsos erat* ('the greatest contest for glory was among themselves') compare Isoc. *Paneg.* 79 τὰς στάσεις ἐποιοῦντο πρὸς ἀλλήλους,...ὁπότεροι φθήσονται τὴν πόλιν ἀγαθόν τι ποιήσαντες ('they used to direct their strife against one another,... which should be the first to do some good for the city'; cf. also *B.C.* 9. 2 and Isoc. *Paneg.* 85); with

---

[62] In what follows there is some room for doubt about whether the passage quoted is Sallust's direct model for a particular phrase although borrowings from the same texts mutually corroborate each other. As far as the intertextual relationship is concerned, there is the possibility that long-fossilized commonplaces are here being put to use.

Sallust: Narrative Style and Composition 69

B.C. 9. 5, *beneficiis magis quam metu imperium agitabant* ('they exercised power through benefits rather than fear'), compare Isoc. *Paneg.* 80, τῷ ποιεῖν εὖ προσαγόμενοι τὰς πόλεις, ἀλλ' οὐ βίᾳ καταστρεφόμενοι ('winning over cities by good deeds, but not overturning them with violence').[63] Moreover, at the opening of the chapter, the sentence about good customs that mean more than good laws (*B.C.* 9. 1) is a formula employed on countless occasions to represent the purity of a primitive people (Tac. *Germ.* 19. 5 and Gudeman 1916: ad loc., as well as Stat. *Silv.* 3. 5. 88). The idea expressed in between, on the contrast between the expenditure for temples to the gods and that for private dwellings, occurs at Dem. 3. 25–6. It returns at greater length at *B.C.* 12. 3.[64] Thus, almost the entire intellectual content of the chapter can be recognized as the product of Sallust's reading. Something similar can be said of individual sentences, which he rearranged as he saw fit: a very famous passage of Plato's *Menexenus* (247d) appears at *B.J.* 85. 49; the *Cyropaedia* at *B.J.* 10. 4 (= 8. 7. 13) and 107. 1 (= 3. 3. 45), and a very famous passage of Plato's *Menexenus* (247d) appears at *B.J.* 85. 49, the *Cyropaedia* at *B.J.* 10. 4 (= 8. 7. 13) and 107. 1 (= 3. 3. 45), and the *Memorabilia* at *B.C.* 13. 3 (= Mem. 2. 1. 30). the *Memorabilia* at *B.C.* 13. 3 (= *Mem.* 2. 1. 30). More important is the fact that the introductory chapters of the *Catiline* rely almost entirely on borrowed ideas and formulae. The comparison with animals whose gaze is fixed on the ground notoriously comes from Plato (*Rep.* 9. 586a). The thoughts on the priority of the mind are found in the proem of Isocrates' *Panegyricus* and, more specifically in relation to animals, again later in the same work (48); the notion of glory as the only worthwhile goal of human life has the same source (76). The intervening sentences (*B.C.* 1. 2), as Egermann 1932: 44 has shown, offer a paraphrase of a famous passage of Plato's *Phaedo* (80a), but with the important difference that one well-known sentence (*alterum nobis cum dis, alterum cum beluis commune est*, 'the one we share with gods, the other we have in common with beasts') appears here as a simple assertion, whereas in Plato it serves as one link in an argumentative chain with a different aim. Even where Sallust speaks of his personal experiences, a similar dependency on Platonic expressions may be observed.[65] The

---

[63] Similarly, from Rome, Cic. *Off.* 2. 27 (i.e. Panaetius); cf. Dahlmann 1934: 19.

[64] Here, too, the transfer to Rome had already taken place before Sallust; not only Horace (*C.* 2.15. 13) expresses the same thought, but also Cicero in his speeches (*Flacc.* 28; cf. *Mur.* 76). It is quite possible that it was already present in the famous speech of P. Rutilius Rufus *De modo aedificiorum*, to which Augustus insistently drew attention (Suet. *Aug.* 89. 2); the quotation from Demosthenes would suit his Greek education well, and its appearance in three later authors who apparently were independent of each other would be easily explained.

[65] Noticed by Mollmann 1878: 18. See also Egermann 1932: 27ff.

opening sentence is, once again, taken over almost verbatim: 'but as a young man initially, like many others, I was borne by my zeal towards politics, and there many things opposed me' (*sed ego adulescentulus initio sicuti plerique studio ad rem publicam latus sum, ibique mihi multa advorsa fuere*, B.C. 3. 3; cf. Pl. *Ep.* 7. 324b, νέος ἐγώ ποτε ὢν πολλοῖς δὴ ταὐτὸν ἔπαθον· ᾠήθην, εἰ θᾶττον ἐμαυτοῦ γενοίμην κύριος, ἐπὶ τὰ κοινὰ τῆς πόλεως εὐθὺς ἰέναι. καί μοι τύχαι τινὲς τῶν τῆς πόλεως πραγμάτων τοιαίδε παρέπεσον, 'when I was young I had the same experience as many others. I thought that as soon as I became my own master I would go into politics right away. But changes in the affairs of the city intervened'). Youth as an excuse for early errors comes from here as well (*imbecilla aetas* = κἀγὼ θαυμαστὸν οὐδὲν ἔπαθον ὑπὸ νεότητος, 'and I experienced nothing surprising, considering my youth', 324d). The retreat from political life together with the justification of the decision on account of the corruption of the state (*B.C.* 3. 3, 4. 1) has its parallels later in the letter (325c ff.). There can be no doubt of a direct relationship; thus, Sallust is here styling himself as a second Plato, but he proves himself a master of literary artistry through the dexterity with which he gives the clear reference to Athens' political situation an ambiguous turn to make it conform to his own compromised personal history (*multa mihi advorsa fuere*).

It is clear that Sallust subscribes to the need for a historian to infuse his material with political reflection, but that he largely meets this need with borrowed ideas. His own reflections on events are thus neither unmediated nor vigorous enough to cast aside this support. In this area he could be accused of lack of invention. His procedure, moreover, shows a significant difference from Thucydides. While the Greek historian seeks to unearth the power dynamics lurking behind processes and determining all political life or dialectically elucidates the pros and cons of a decision, Sallust's thinking is oriented towards moralizing observations which are basically unsuited to politics. A comparison between two very similar sentences is telling: *nobis dissensiones* **vitio** *humani ingenii evenere* ('our dissensions arose through a flaw of human nature', H. 1. 7) vs ἐπέπεσε πολλὰ καὶ χαλεπὰ κατὰ στάσιν...γιγνόμενα μὲν καὶ ἀεὶ ἐσόμενα, ἕως ἂν ἡ αὐτὴ **φύσις** ἀνθρώπων ᾖ ('many harsh circumstances occurred during the conflict... things that happen and always will as long as the nature of human beings is the same', Thuc. 3. 82. 2). Where Thucydides, as a student of the Sophists, coolly recognizes a tendency of human nature, Sallust introduces the judgemental term 'flaw' (*vitium*). The tone of the censor sounds throughout his writings, but is quite different from the bracing impartiality of judgement found in Cato, his most obvious model. Approval, which the former censor bestows just as readily as reproach, is utterly absent from Sallust, with the single exception of the great syncrisis of Caesar and Cato in the *Catiline*. Rather, the historian prefers to observe that individual deeds and events occurred in accordance with habits, or in keeping with the way men generally behave in such cases (*B.C.* 30. 2, 37. 2; *B.J.* 15. 5, 25. 3, 66. 2, 93. 3, 96. 3); almost without exception this is said with contemptuous disapproval.

This tendency intensifies the impression of darkness and hopelessness which Sallust's writing generally creates and thus contributes to the overall picture. In his conception of history, time is the only constant element. Its progress accompanies the change in events while the setting and course of the action continually shift and while blow and counter-blow succeed one another. Within this to and fro the momentary victory of one party may occur, but no peace, no goal striven after and reached, which might offer real closure. The *Catiline* ends with the deep dejection of the victors, and even the final sentence warns of the strife that is tearing the state apart. At the end of the *Jugurtha*, the threat of the Cimbri suddenly emerges and summons Marius to new battles. The last sentence achieves a similar effect, with the assurance that *at that time* all the power and all the hope of Rome rested with Marius. The reader knows how little Marius' subsequent career matched these expectations. History is here viewed as the unceasing struggle between men at war with one another. It may result in a shift in power relations, but no change in the situation. That the main forces in the narrative are always individuals contributes to this effect; for Sallust 'only the individual has any significance, the circumstances not at all'.[66] The masses of the displaced who make his rise possible disappear behind the figure of Catiline, just as the parties of the post-Gracchan period vanish behind Memmius and the leaders of the Senate. Thus, the enduring cause of political conflict is obscured in favour of its alternating, successive representatives; history disintegrates into a series of individual struggles and becomes accidental and meaningless. This is true not only of the episodes he takes as the subjects of his narratives, but also of the overall image he constructs of Rome's development. In each of the three works he gives a brief overview of general decline down to the present. Fundamental, as Klingner 1928: 181ff. (= Chapter 13, pp. 343ff. in this volume) has shown, is the conception of Posidonius that the removal of the external threat of Carthage allowed all the forces of self-interest and discord to run wild. In the Rhodian philosopher, however, the glowing picture of a happy prehistory stands at the beginning, and the whole tends towards the renewal of the state by

---

[66] Schwartz 1897: 574 (= Chapter 5, p. 133 in this volume).

Sulla. Sallust 'has broken off the resolution to the decline in Posidonius' schema without replacing it with a new one' (ibid.: 187, = Chapter 13, p. 348 in this volume). The decline thus becomes incalculable and aimless; all the efforts and struggles he chronicles cannot check the decay; individuals merely gratify their personal ambition or lust for profit within it. The picture of decline is presented so pitilessly that it appears almost malevolent. Sallust can transpose it essentially unchanged into the mouths of Rome's enemies expressing their hatred, such as Jugurtha (*B.J.* 81. 1) or Mithridates in his letter to Arsaces (*H.* 4. 69 M). The pessimistic tone of this conception of history outweighs the differences in how Sallust formulates it between his three works. While in the *Catiline* (*B.C.* 6–7) the disappearance of external tasks diverts a restless need for action towards personal ends, in the *Jugurtha* (*B.J.* 41–2) and even more clearly in the *Histories* (*H.* 1. 11–12 M) it is only the fear of threats from abroad that holds Rome in line.[67] Behind Sallust's representation, then, stands a conviction of human worthlessness and the meaninglessness of history. This is corroborated by our observations about the judgement of events in his writings. But this investigation already leads us from the effect of the works to the man who composed them.

III. PERSONALITY AND TIMES

Our treatment of Sallust's characteristics as a writer has yielded a consistent picture: language and representation are harsh, mannered, and disharmonious; composition through antitheses prevails from the smallest sentence elements to the structuring of scenes and of entire works. Deep unrest and hopeless bitterness emanate from his narrative. But this tone is not a sign of weak resignation; rather, a deliberate artistic intention forces the course of events almost violently into a compositional structure which appears with such rigidity in no other Roman historian. One seems to sense how the author's extreme exertion conceals inner tensions he cannot reconcile.

We know enough of Sallust's outward life and of contemporary trends to be able to make sense of this attitude. The young man from

---

[67] The psychological interpretation of these facts can vary; while Klingner sees in them a progressive darkening in the author's thinking, Seel 1930: 77ff. claims to recognize a growing resignation and indifference. One should perhaps also consider that the first treatment of this theme, with the expansive description of the 'good' period, stands closest to his model, as we might expect. Later, this way of thinking became more familiar, and was therefore more pointedly expressed.

Amiternum moved to Rome, like so many other Italians, with the ambition of climbing the political ladder. His aims were thoroughly personal: glory and wealth; to what extent he believed in the partisan ideologies, which by then had become empty, remains unclear. Philosophical studies during his youth can be taken for granted at that time; he himself testifies to having turned away from them at an early age (*B.C.* 4. 2), and the fact is confirmed by the allusions to Plato.[68] But it would be a slander to associate him with the neo-Pythagorean mysticism of the circle of Nigidius Figulus,[69] not because the spiritualism practised there would be inconceivable for a pupil of Greek philosophy, but rather because throughout his life strong political differences separated him from the adherents of that superstition.[70] The quaestorship followed and the tribunate in 52, during which he was conspicuous for wildly inflammatory speeches on the occasion of the murder of Clodius (Asc. 49. 6–8, 49. 24–50. 1, and 51. 10–11 C). As a result, he was expelled from the Senate by the censor Appius Claudius Pulcher in the year 50. With that, his career was, for the time being, at an end. During the Civil Wars, Caesar employed him as he did others whose careers had been wrecked; the dictator was not choosy about whom he exploited so that one must be cautious in drawing conclusions from this about his opinion of Sallust. With no especially brilliant achievements to show for himself, Sallust nevertheless received the reward of proconsular *imperium* in the recently created province of Numidia. We may consider it certain that he trafficked in extortion there (Dio Cass. 43. 9. 2), but he was allowed to keep

---

[68] See pp. 69–70 above. The evidence given there shows that his reading did not penetrate very deep: the *Menexenus*, the *Phaedo*, and the Seventh Letter are among the texts most frequently read in antiquity. Even the echoes of Thucydides are not evenly distributed over the entire work: the introduction, funeral oration, and III 81ff. are obviously preferred. The case is similar with other authors: Isocrates' *Panegyricus*, the third *Philippic* and the third *Olynthiac* of Demosthenes, and the *Cyropaedia* and *Memorabilia* of Xenophon can be demonstrated with certainty. There is also a very famous passage from Theopompus (see p. 63 above). It is naturally unjustifiable to assume that the scope of his reading ended there, but one sees at any rate which monuments of Greek prose were in his mind while he was writing.

[69] See Regenbogen 1932: 8.

[70] The connection is recorded only in the invective falsely attributed to Cicero (5. 14), a late rhetorical composition; its basis was a biography of Sallust which in Suetonian fashion uncritically mixed hearsay and truth; the speech naturally incorporated only what was discreditable to Sallust. Nigidius was a strict aristocrat; Appius Claudius Pulcher, who was likewise involved in necromancy (Cic. *Tusc.* 1. 37, *Div.* 1. 132) and presumably belonged to this circle as well, had expelled Sallust from the Senate. Similar accusations were indeed levelled against the democrat Vatinius (Cic. *Vat.* 14—one immediately thinks of the *sacrilegium Nigidianum*, whose name Cicero declines to mention out of decency), but the connection is too weak to support the questionable tradition.

what he had stolen; Caesar's indifference in such matters provided no check to his hangers-on. But with that the road to political influence was once more closed to him, this time for ever. From then on he lived as a private citizen in his villa amid the *horti Sallustiani*, which even into the imperial period enjoyed great celebrity. His historical works date only from this time.[71]

Even without further evidence, anyone familiar with Roman life will infer from these facts that giving up political power was a painful rupture for Sallust. And the explicit confession that he inserts into the personal section of the proems of both monographs confirms this. The desire for fame is quite openly admitted as the driving motive for all his activity. Out of the antithesis between mind and body in the introduction to the *Catiline*, he develops the injunction to seek fame through the power of the soul, not the body; a commonplace sentence on the transience of earthly beauty and riches justifies the preference for an enduring reputation based on *virtus* (*B.C.* 1. 4; cf. p. 33 above). Then, rather circuitously, he establishes that in the course of history the superiority of the mind to mere bodily strength was first discovered in war; the same applies in peace as well, as one should now expect. But *B.C.* 1. 4 had already equated mental power particularly with *virtus*, and the formulation *virtus animi* (*B.C.* 1. 5) continues that association. Thus, Sallust, with an unconscious switch between the two meanings of *virtus*, can here substitute moral uprightness for mental strength and subsume 'effort' (*labor*), 'self-control' (*continentia*), and 'fairness' (*aequitas*) within the notion of *virtus animi*. The overview of great world empires at the beginning leads to the conclusion that rule (*imperium*) always passes to the best. Only then does he resume: *virtus* prevails not only in the state but in every activity; to whomever is *indoctus et incultus* ('unlearned and uncultured', *B.C.* 2. 8), the mind is a burden, the body a source of enjoyment. Here at last the antithesis of the opening is resumed with a clear echo (*dediti ventri* = *ventri oboedientia*, *B.C.* 1. 1), and the motif of fame resurfaces as well: only the one who 'seeks renown for some outstanding deed or worthy skill' (*praeclari facinoris aut artis bonae famam quaerit*, *B.C.* 2. 9) is truly alive. We have thus returned by a roundabout detour to the starting

---

[71] The individual pieces of evidence for his life are carefully assembled in Funaioli *RE* I A 1918ff. He overlooks Porphyr. *Hor. serm.* 1. 1. 102: (*Nomentani*) *libertum Damam nomine cocum Sallustius Crispus historiarum scriptor fertur centenis milibus annuis conductum habuisse* ('Sallustius Crispus, the historian, is said to have hired a freedman of Nomentanus, Damus by name, as a cook for one hundred thousand sesterces a year'). This remark must stem from the biography that Porphyrio used (see p. 44, n., 36 above). But that does not make it reliable, and it can at best reveal the image that the subsequent generation had of the proprietor of the *horti Sallustiani*.

point, without the depth of the ideas introduced in between justifying the extent of their treatment. For Sallust has said no more than that war depends more on mental than on physical faculties and that every productive activity in life requires mental capacity. The middle piece 1. 5–2. 6 can only be explained if the concepts *virtus* and *animus* were primarily associated in his mind with the political sphere. The next section confirms this, for the assessment of mental activity we receive here is oriented towards the state: *pulchrum est bene facere rei publicae, etiam bene dicere haud absurdum est....et qui fecere, et qui facta aliorum scripsere multi laudantur* ('it is a noble thing to do good for the Republic, and even to speak well is not trivial...many are praised, both of those who have acted and who have recorded the actions of others'). The rest of the chapter sets the difficulty of the historian's task in its proper light. The claim here, seemingly introduced only by the familiar antitheses, is basically outrageous: the historian is elevated right alongside the maker of history. The introduction to the *Jugurtha* shows that for him this claim was entirely serious. In the two opening chapters, the keywords of the *Catiline* return somewhat rearranged, sometimes with direct verbal echoes. The decision to avoid political activity follows, this time much more decisively taken (it is noticeable how the passing years have confirmed this sequence of thought). But at one point the connection to the historian's personal experience becomes even more insistent, namely, when he defends himself from the charge of 'inactivity' (*B.J.* 4. 3, *inertia*). Not only does the realm of political action appear reduced to cultivating personal networks (*salutare plebem et conviviis gratiam quaerere*, 'to greet the people and seek favour at banquets'), but Sallust also bitterly recalls what type of person came into the Senate after him (*B.J.* 4. 4); the old defeat obviously still rankles. The conclusion is this time even more resolute: 'greater advantage will come to the state from my leisure than from the work of others' (*maius commodum ex otio meo quam ex aliorum negotiis rei publicae venturum*).

Thucydides, who came to historiography by way of similar experiences, had never made a similar claim for all his proud self-assurance as a political thinker. Its appearance in his much humbler successor therefore requires explanation. Sallust speaks of *his* task and of *his* life; it is therefore justifiable to look for the answer in his personal position. For the old-fashioned Roman, politics was the sole path to distinction. Only this counted as a worthy activity for a man of high standing: everything else is play, *ludus*, good enough to fill an idle hour. Indeed, the language itself possessed no term for this; in order to speak of such times in one's life it was necessary to resort to negative periphrases, like the bon mot of the elder Africanus attested in Cato: *numquam se plus agere, quam nihil cum ageret* ('he was never more active than when he was performing no action', Cic. *Rep.* 1. 27 (fr. 130 *FRHist.* = fr. 127 P)). The senator writes history as well—but in old age, at the end of his political career, and even then he still has concrete, practical ends. He wants to educate the rest of the world about Rome, like Fabius Pictor, or he carries on his struggles with domestic opponents in this medium, as the work of the elder Cato developed into a covert justification of his career. With this exception, no native Romans appear as authors in what we know of early Latin literature, let alone members of the nobility.[72] Of course an upper-class man like Q. Lutatius Catulus, victor over the Cimbri, might compose verses on the side; but this occupation does not stand at the centre of his life, and he would reject the notion that the renown of his name should be somehow bound up with it. The study of philosophy and literature had been part of education since the second century, but the adult is supposed to hold these things at a distance. Anyone who cannot tear himself away from them at the appropriate time and turn to the tasks of the forum becomes suspect (Polyb. 31. 23. 11). When Ennius' Neoptolemus declares, 'I must be a philosopher, in a few respects, for philosophy in general is not pleasing' (*philosophari est mihi necesse, sed paucis, nam omnino haud placet, Scaen.* 22 J²), he could count on the total assent of his audience. Those with such education try, if anything, to conceal it from the multitude. Even more than two generations later Cicero does not consider it advisable to be able to recall the name of Polyclitus instantly in front of the jury (Cic. *Verr.* 5.5). Only in the middle decades of the first century is there any loosening of this stricture.[73] This is a sign that the old ways of life were declining. Its point of departure was the zeal for life of a young generation to whom contact with the Greeks offered relief from burdensome pressures and who were no longer willing to let their personal longing for pleasure and joy be stifled by the constraints of their ancestry. It is not so much from a new engagement with the intellectual as from the discovery of new spheres of interaction between people that the new poetry sprang. The same boundless energy that appears in the brutal tyranny of the provincial governor and the heedless avarice of the Roman merchant now also extended itself into the realm of the erotic: hence the poetry of Catullus. In their devotion to the moment,

---

[72] Eloquence, which serves essentially political ends, can here be left out of consideration; the composition of technical works always possessed validity.

[73] Knoche 1934: 102ff., esp. 117–18, has demonstrated how the old Roman concept of fame as connected with statecraft expands during this period and comes to encompass nonpolitical fields; one reason for this, as he rightly emphasizes (117), must be sought in the partisan conflicts that made a straightforward assessment of political action impossible.

the members of this generation display a vitality which no longer wishes to, and perhaps no longer can, be tamed and subordinated to the collective. Emotion liberated itself from the shackles in which Roman *gravitas* had bound it, but the segment of society that it affected remained small. For this circle, poetry becomes the means to express the new sensibilities, but when these are exhausted, it collapses into lifeless imitation. Dead, irrelevant knowledge and refinement of form then compensate for the lack of substance. And, after all, it was only a small and deliberately isolated group that cultivated this poetry. Thus, the reach of the movement was limited in scope and in content from the very outset, and for this reason it could not win the struggle to justify a new way of life. But it seems doubtful whether the neoterics intended any such thing. For all the self-assurance with which they tend to speak of the eternal importance of their own creations, poetry is after all by their own intentions only a game, *nugae*, a sideline to the political activity which, for Calvus, Cornelius Gallus, and perhaps Cinna too, was still the true duty of the Roman. Only those who came to this circle unburdened by the demands of family tradition could surrender themselves to poetry as unconditionally as Catullus did, and even then only while young. Cicero gives us the verdict of even educated Romans when he claimed 'that he would have no time to read lyric poets even if his lifespan were doubled' (*negat Cicero, si duplicetur sibi aetas, habiturum se tempus quo legat lyricos*, Sen. *Ep.* 49. 5).[74] Lucretius considered it self-evident that his patron Memmius would have no time for his poem when politics called (Lucr. 1. 42). Even such a confirmed bookworm as M. Terentius Varro still undertook a military command at 60. Only a small handful of individuals built themselves a life apart, in deliberate opposition to the demands of ancestry and custom that confronted a high-born Roman.

We first encounter this type of new man in Cicero's friend Atticus, especially in the picture that his lesser comrade in learning, Cornelius Nepos, sketched of his life. To be sure, it was not so much intellectual considerations as the powerful influence of the Marian turmoil which made the young Pomponius aware of the dangers and meaninglessness of political participation in a state that was tearing itself to pieces. He travelled to Athens and did not return until time had dissolved all the ties that bound him to the political life, when his age had ruled out a conventional *cursus honorum*. From this point, his relationships with men of the most diverse political parties remained purely personal, and he turned down every attempt to drag him into politics with genial

---

[74] Tragedy, too, for him, is a 'more trivial skill' than eloquence (*levior ars*, *Brut.* 3).

determination. Atticus' constant readiness to help, his universally acknowledged selflessness, served as substitutes for the connections that others had acquired in public service, and protected him from the dangers to which such a deliberate isolation is vulnerable in times of civil strife. The necessary condition for such a life is the absence of all passions, the serenity of the spectator who sympathetically offers whatever assistance is in his power, but whose personal safety even the emergency of the closest friend cannot endanger. Moreover, this path was only opened at the cost of renouncing glory, and only when one knew how to extricate oneself early on from the vexatious hunt for office. Thus, in Atticus' existence there was certainly greater scope for intellectual occupation than was the case with other Romans of the time, but it never prevailed because he lacked the total devotion that could take him from enjoyment to creativity. Many aspects of his portrait anticipate the centuries to come, but in his own time he remained a curiosity to be tolerated; everything necessary to light the way to a new humanity was lacking in him.

In Cicero, however, the conflict is visible in all its tragic grandeur. Filled with burning ambition, he strove for political influence. All his thoughts were focused on this possibility; all his studies in Greece were preparation for it. A position such as the Scipios once occupied in Rome might have appeared to the young man of Arpinum as the fulfilment of all his desires. But he lacked that toughness with which the younger Scipio could endorse and execute whatever political necessity demanded, even when he personally shuddered at it. More and more the world view of Greek philosophy took control of him and hindered that unreflecting action which was all too necessary for his success. This is clearest, perhaps, in the provincial governorship he unwillingly accepted in 51 BCE. Upright dealings and personal selflessness are the guiding principles of his time in office, and we may believe him when he writes to his trusted friend that the work itself pleased him, not only the reputation it brought (*Att.* 5. 20. 6). Such refinement of moral feeling, which finds satisfaction in living up to absolute principles without regard for practical consequences, is essentially un-Roman; it would bring Cicero into constant conflict with an environment that allowed such an attitude no scope for effectiveness. Nevertheless, he failed to draw the conclusions to which a related viewpoint had led Atticus. That would have required a break with his past, a rejection of the reputation as statesman to which he felt himself entitled, a determined reorientation towards an utterly new form of existence. And that he could not achieve. Even in his later works he speaks of his activity as a writer in much the same terms in which Romans had always spoken of such things, as 'restrained and honourable leisure' (*otium moderatum et honestum, Brut.* 8) or describes a conversation during a visit to Caesar as containing 'nothing serious, a lot of literary discussion' (σπουδαῖον οὐδὲν...φιλόλογα multa, *Att.* 13. 52. 2). Only during periods when political activity has been rendered impossible does he turn to contemplation. In the year of Caesar's consulship, when he seems to have considered his separation from politics as temporary, his statements sound quite definitive: 'O, my dear Atticus, let us fall upon those splendid pursuits and for a while return to that place we never should have left' (*incumbamus, o noster Tite, ad illa praeclara studia et eo, unde discedere non oportuit, aliquando revertamur, Att.* 2. 16. 3). His flexible nature holds out the comfort of this new situation, even if a note of indignation is audible:

> For a long time now I was weary of steering, even while it was still possible; but now that I am forced to leave the ship—now that I have not set the helm aside, but had it snatched from me—I wish to watch the shipwreck from the land; I wish, as your friend Sophocles says, 'to hear the downpour beneath a roof with sleeping mind' (κἂν ὑπὸ στέγῃ πυκνῆς ἀκούειν ψακάδος εὑδούσῃ φρενί). *Att.* 2. 7. 4.

He is even inclined to joke: 'Cicero the philosopher greets Atticus, the statesman' (Κικέρων ὁ φιλόσοφος τὸν πολιτικὸν Τίτον ἀσπάζεται, *Att.* 2. 12. 4). Clearly he recognized the decision before him. He could have found the antithesis between these two paths set out by Greek philosophers from as early as Plato in the *Theaetetus*;[75] he himself alludes to Theophrastus and Dicaearchus in the first passage and shortly thereafter presented both ways of life in *De re publica* (1. 26ff.). But how little it occurred to him then to draw for himself the ultimate conclusions from such words is shown by the altered tone in which, fourteen years later, and now broken by the death of his daughter, he speaks of his philosophical work. Here it is plain that it offers only a poor substitute for what he has lost. Now he avoids the resolute profession he voiced so easily in 59 BCE. Engagement with philosophy is forced by necessity into the foreground; a letter to Varro from the year 46 BCE declare that where it had once been his recreation (*delectatio*), it is now his salvation (*salus*). 'If nobody will employ our efforts in the state', he continues, 'then we will write and read *republics*, and, if not in the Senate house and the forum, then in books, as the most learned men of old used to do, we will dedicate our work to the state and research customs and laws' (*Fam.* 9. 2. 5; cf. 9. 3.2). Speaking to Varro, he attempts to justify his enforced literary activity from a political perspective; but one can glimpse what he really

---

[75] See Boll's (1920) fine address. Jaeger 1928: 390.

thought of it in occasional phrases which involuntary slip out in the letters to his confidant: 'I'm busy with philosophy here; what else do I have left?' (*quid enim aliud? Att.* 15. 13. 6); 'I've composed two lengthy tracts here; it's the only way I can abstract myself from this wretchedness' (*a miseria quasi aberrare, Att.* 12. 44. 4). The frequently misunderstood comment on his literary production during this period must also be interpreted in light of these sentiments: 'They are only transcriptions; they require less trouble; I only have to add the words I have in excess' (*Att.* 12. 52. 3). The deep bitterness with which the statesman and orator speaks of the excess of words that he has at his command now that the forum and Senate are closed to him is unmistakable. As soon as the death of the dictator made political activity possible again, everything else falls away. It is forgotten that he had once followed up a remark of Caesar's by praising his own services to the development of the Latin language as a national achievement far exceeding the storming of a Ligurian fort, even if the latter earned the honour of a triumph (*Brut.* 255). Even for the Roman in whom Hellenic thinking was more alive than in anyone else of the period, the *vita contemplativa* remains a stopgap and a form of resignation.

When we return to Sallust from this overview of the period and the possibilities it offered, the meaning of those remarkable prologues is more clearly discernible. In his conception, too, statecraft and politics are presented as the single appropriate sphere of activity for the Roman.[76] The loss of this possibility struck him a blow all the heavier since he had set all his hopes on it. The switch to an intellectual existence thus remained for him only a bitter necessity. It was not granted to him, as it was to Cicero, to lose himself at least for fleeting moments in the joys of artistic creation; he never forgot that this occupation was only a substitute. The ardour of his intention might affirm its value; that is why he exaggerates its significance beyond all measure. At no time in his life had philosophy become a truly vital force; the ideas with which he supports his claim are, as has been shown, not original, but borrowed; they possessed no influence on the conduct of his life. Nevertheless, he felt the need to compose the events of his life in retrospect, to shape the picture of himself that would live on in later ages. Thus, he puts on, half playfully, the mask of Plato, and perhaps he himself even forgets for a while the gulf separating his past as a demagogue on the streets of Rome from the man who turned away from the state of his time because his moral principles could endure no compromise. The more he thus forgot

---

[76] Seel 1930: 21 briefly points to this way of interpreting the prologues.

his own responsibility for his fate and saw himself as an innocent victim, the more he burned with hatred for the age and the society in which he had suffered calamity. His choice of material is not coincidental. We know that, with the help of an outline prepared for him by Ateius Philologus, he selected from all of Roman history the subjects that seemed to suit his purpose (Suet. *Gramm.* 10). If continuing from where Sisenna left off perhaps determined the subject for his great *Histories*, still in both of the monographs he was completely free. Nevertheless, the world depicted in both is the same: the horrific last century of the Republic, with its reckless partisan struggles, its fragmentation and selfishness. He obviously took a bitter satisfaction from dwelling on this period and passing on its image to the future in the darkest hues. The depravity of the state in which he was forced to live becomes his justification.

The complement to this attitude toward the recent past is his admiration for archaic Rome. This above all supplies the background against which the period depicted stands out. Its real motive is not a love for the vanished virtues but the desire to attack a depraved present, denouncing which was essential for Sallust's self-affirmation. Thus, he takes upon himself the style and attitude of a second Cato the Censor. The literary trend toward classicism made this possible, but provided only the external form within which the mood that masters him takes shape; under other circumstances it would have expressed itself in quite a different way, but nonetheless equally. For, despite all his archaizing, Sallust remains a man of the last century BCE, and a tension is visible between the form he adopts and his nature which had already been noticed in antiquity. Varro (Gell. *NA* 17. 18) pointed out the discrepancy between the censorious strictness of his writings and the moral lassitude of his life. This is apparent also in individual phrases that speak of the worthlessness of riches (*divitiarum...gloria fluxa atque fragilis*, 'the glory of wealth is transient and uncertain', *B.C.* 1. 4). Elsewhere he depicts the decay of the old customs with the words *paupertas probro haberi, innocentia pro malevolentia duci* ('poverty is considered an offence, and harmlessness is believed a kind of malevolence', *B.C.* 12. 1), which apply exactly to his own conduct. But the opposition goes much deeper; it permeates the entire work. His paratactic sentence construction strives for a division and order which is foreign to the archaic period (see pp. 38–9 above); his narration lacks that abundance of detail which exposed the early period's curiosity and youthful rejoicing at the world (see p. 65 above). The same is true of his attitude to ancestral virtue, the *virtus maiorum*. If to portray it he borrowed the ornaments from speeches in praise of Athens (see pp. 68–9 above) without being aware of the difference, this does not exactly suggest sincere ties to the ideal he praises. The changes in traditional Roman concepts that were then taking place under the influence of Greek thought[77] drew him too along in their thrall; his image of the old Roman character remains conventional and tied to the present. Not only does he ascribe virtues to the ancestors which can scarcely be reconciled with their sober rigidity, but his understanding of their lifestyle is likewise limited. Nowhere does one so clearly sense the distance that separates his thinking from that of the archaic Roman as when he lets slip the confession that he considers agriculture to be a slavish occupation (*agrum colundo aut venando, servilibus officiis*, B.C. 4. 1). Whoever speaks this way was never touched by the spirit of the introductory chapters of Cato's *De agricultura*. The conceptual world of a noble Roman of Sallust's day stands here in the sharpest contrast to Cato's statement that 'our elders, when they praised a good man, praised him thus, "a good farmer, a good cultivator"' (*maiores nostri... virum bonum quom laudabant, ita laudabant, bonum agricolam, bonum colonum*, Agr. 1. 2).[78]

The glowing picture of ancient Roman ways that Sallust had painted for himself offered him no inner stability; to measure himself by those standards was far from his intention. It appears much more as an element of his style which serves predetermined narrative ends. But even in this capacity its effectiveness is limited. Apart from the characterization of Cato in the *Catiline*, he never offers the reader an extensive example of those virtues; the impressions with which his works leave us are of quite another kind. At the centre of both monographs stand criminal natures exaggerated into enormity with calculated artistry. Faithlessness and betrayal influence the progress of the plot at decisive moments. The author dwells with particular relish on all ambivalence and hesitation: Cicero's conflicting feelings at the discovery of the conspiracy (*B.C.* 46. 2) and Micipsa's worries over the threat to his children posed by Jugurtha's growing popularity (*B.J.* 6. 2) are described with obvious empathy. But few passages are of such unsettling penetration as those in which he depicts a human being haunted without respite. Catiline, whom a crime against his own son drives on to further atrocity (*B.C.* 15. 4), Jugurtha, who, terrified at having been betrayed by his most intimate circle, does not dare to linger in any one place (*B.J.* 72. 2)—these are images that never release their hold on the reader.

---

[77] For an individual case, see Dahlmann 1934: 19–20.
[78] The contrast was, as far as I know, first emphasized by Egermann 1932: 77 n. 2.

The reason is to be sought in Sallust's own nature. It was always denied him to resolve the conflict into which his fate had led him. His thoughts go back and forth between the memory of the hopes of his youth and the only task still left available to him, between the ideal of true Romanness which he was powerless to make his own and the comfortless present. The restless disposition that fills him shapes the rhythm of his sentences and the form of his narrative. The consistent effect that his works project testifies to the force with which this tension pervaded his entire being. It testifies as well to the force of will with which he was able to tame the constant oscillation of his style within a carefully composed structure. Perhaps this quality, which he never mentions among the merits of the Romans, is what is most Roman about him. Sallust the man was destroyed by the contradiction between the only form of action possible in his world and his own special situation; Sallust the author found his particular style precisely in this contradiction. Neither abundance of ideas nor richness of artistic techniques distinguishes him; both are reused more often than is common elsewhere among ancient authors. But it is precisely in this monotony that the dark character of his narration achieves its effect; it shows no small artistry that he was able to produce works of such cohesive unity.

The harsh fate of the entire generation that stands at the end of the Roman Republic is nowhere made clearer than in Sallust. The old Roman ways of life and values are still so strong that the individual cannot escape them. But the men on whom the weight of these demands falls have become more complicated and can no longer force their more refined and sensitive souls into submission to this rigid norm. The state which once could rightly demand this sacrifice is no more; in its place, a grim partisan machine swallows all who come in contact with it and drags them down into its maelstrom. There is no longer any space apart from it in which people can fashion their lives, much less the possibility of recognition for such behaviour. Even those with the sense to remain aloof from political activity kept in their hearts the gnawing accusation of neglected duty. It is precisely in the finest minds that a conflict arises which deprives their lives of rest. They must admit to themselves that the conventional forms of activity have become meaningless, and yet they find no new ones that they can enthusiastically approve. Those at the boundary between two epochs cannot enjoy that inner security which is natural to people of other ages. Compared with this distress of the soul, the external existential threat posed by the Civil Wars almost seems to retreat, although it alone is great enough to account for the bitterly painful strain one finds in all contemporary portraits. Not until the imperial period, with its new ordering of things, was this burden, too, lifted from people's shoulders, when all real political action was reserved for the ruler. It was not the power of an individual or a group that succeeded in winning recognition for a new form of existence; rather, the transformation of social relations created a space for the development of new schools of thought which would previously have languished. For this reason a new generation, much weaker in its vitality, succeeds where the previous one had failed. Vergil, Horace, and Livy discover for themselves an attitude to intellectual activity which is no longer resignation but the proud consciousness of actively upholding the Roman way and the Roman name in a different field from the political. Thoughts that we only rarely find in Cicero now become quite common; the poet's claim to lasting renown sounds more convincing in Horace than in the neoterics or even Lucretius. There even emerges now a purer relationship to Roman history than Sallust could have had. The bitterness of partisan struggles, with its flood of hatred and defamation, now belonged to the past; for the new generation, the old oppositions had become lifeless. Livy had never held office; he was an utterly apolitical being, lacking all understanding of the harsh realities of historical events. This is precisely why he shaped his account of Rome's prehistory into a myth of the greatness of the ancestors, where the mind could find respite from the confusion of recent times. The deep hopelessness with which Sallust had watched the now meaningless progress of history gave way to heroic transfiguration.

3

The Moral Crisis in Sallust's View

D. C. Earl

In both the *Bellum Catilinae* and the *Bellum Jugurthinum* Sallust consistently represents the whole history of the Roman Republic down to 146 BCE as one of unbroken *concordia*, *boni mores*, and *virtus* both at home and abroad.[1] That this picture is highly idealized needs little demonstration. For the earlier part of the second century BCE alone our sources contain numerous references to trouble with the armies,[2] misconduct by provincial governors and commanders in the field,[3] the growth of wealth and luxury,[4] demoralization and unrest at home.[5] It is consequently of considerable interest that Sallust in the *Historiae* modifies this unhistorical view. The turning point is still the removal of the *metus hostilis* with the destruction of Carthage.[6] But before this date Sallust here distinguishes a period of *discordia* with the expulsion of the kings, the *metus Etruscus*, a further period of *discordia* representing

---

[1] e.g. *B.C.* 9. 1–3; *B.J.* 41. 2.
[2] In 198 BCE, Livy 32. 3. 2–7; 195 BCE, Cato frr. 17–18 *ORF*; 190 BCE, Livy 34. 56. 9; 187 BCE, Livy 39. 6. 5–6; 182 BCE, Livy 39. 38. 6–12, 40. 1. 4, 40. 16. 9; 180 BCE, Livy 40. 35. 7, 40. 39. 4, 40. 40. 14, 40. 41. 8–11; 177 BCE, Livy 41. 10. 6–10; war with Perseus, Livy 42. 32. 7–35. 2, 43. 11. 10, 43. 14. 7.
[3] 190 BCE, Cato frr. 58–65 *ORF*; Livy 35. 3, 35. 20. 6, 35. 21. 7ff., 36. 38, 37. 46. 1–2; Cato fr. 66 *ORF*, Livy 37. 57. 9ff.; 173 BCE, Livy 42. 3. 1–11, 42. 10. 5, 42. 28. 12; 42. 7. 3–9. 6, 42. 10. 9–15, 42. 21. 1–22. 8; 171 BCE, Livy 43. 2. 1–12; 42. 3. 1–4, Cato frr. 154–5 *ORF*; war with Perseus, Livy 43. 1. 4–12, 43. 4. 5–13, 43. 5. 1–10, 43. 6. 2–3, 43. 7. 5–8, 43. 10, *Per.* 43; 154 BCE, Livy *Per.* 47; Val. Max. 6. 9. 10, Festus 360 L; 151 BCE, App. *Hisp.* 51–5, 59–61.
[4] Livy 39. 5. 14–17, 39. 7, 45. 40. 1, Polyb. 38. 35. 4, Vell. Pat. 1. 9. 6, Diod. Sic. 31. 8. 11, Plut. *Aem.* 32. 3, 38, Cato frr. 173–5 *ORF*, Gell. *NA* 2. 24. 1–6, Plin. *HN* 10. 139, Ath. 6. 108, 6. 274C, Macrob. *Sat.* 3. 13. 13, 3. 16. 4, 3. 17. 3–5.
[5] Livy 39. 8–19; cf. McDonald 1944: 11ff.; Livy 39. 44. 9; cf. 39. 42. 5–43. 5; De Sanctis 1923: 600ff.; Plut. *Cat. Mai.* 16–19; Livy *Per.* 48; Val. Max. 2. 4. 2; Vell. Pat. 1. 15. 3; Livy 34. 56. 9, 43. 16. 1–16; Polyb. 35. 4; App. *Hisp.* 49.
[6] *H.* 1. 11, 12, 16 M.

the struggle of the orders, and, finally, between the second and third Punic Wars, a period of *optimi mores* and *maxima concordia* under the influence of the *metus Punicus*. This is in strong contrast to the picture of the early Republic presented in *Bellum Catilinae* 7–9, and it has been taken as showing an increased pessimism on Sallust's part. In view of the highly fragmentary state of our text of the *Historiae* certainty is impossible, for the speeches and epistles cannot be taken as evidence of Sallust's own opinions. Clearly his earlier neglect of the struggle of the orders, in particular, did not arise from ignorance, for Memmius in the *Bellum Jugurthinum* (31. 17) refers to the secession of the *plebs*, while the works of the elder Cato, to whom Sallust was notoriously indebted, would have given him ample reason to correct his idealized view. Further, in *Bellum Catilinae* 9. 1, we read, of the early Republic, *concordia maxuma, minuma avaritia erat* ('harmony was very great, greed was very small'). The interpretation of the phrase *minuma avaritia* is of importance here. Did Sallust mean it to be taken at its face value as meaning that even in this state of *virtus* a certain amount of *avaritia* was already present, although unimportant beside the prevailing *concordia*? That is, did Sallust already recognize that his view was unhistorical? Or does *minuma* here stand for nothing more than *nulla*, being used solely to provide a neat phrase with *concordia maxuma*? With regard to Sallust's supposed increased pessimism, it is relevant to observe that already in the *Bellum Jugurthinum* he had been prepared to admit that the *novi homines* had turned out to be no better than the *nobiles*. Moreover, if such is the reason for his modifications, why should he retain his artificial and unhistorical view of the period between the second and third Punic Wars? It seems more likely that the modifications of the historical scheme in the *Historiae* represent nothing more than a response to criticism of his earlier idealized view as published in the *Bella*. Even so, the central point remains. The period of idealization is limited, but the idealization continues.

Even more significant is that Sallust, in choosing 146 BCE as his turning point, rejected a strong and, by his time, well-established tradition that by the middle of the second century Rome had undergone a crisis from which she never recovered and that the processes which eventually destroyed the Republic had already begun to work.

Thus, the annalistic tradition represented in Livy and drawing on contemporary material ascribes the crisis to the return of Manlius Vulso's army from Asia in 187 BCE.[7] The booty and luxurious habits

---

[7] Livy, 39. 6. 7. With *et quae tum magnificae supellectilis habebantur, monopodia et abacos Romam advexerunt* ('and they brought to Rome items of furniture then considered splendid, one-footed tables and sideboards') cf. *triclinia aerata abacosque et monopodia Cn.*

they brought back formed *luxuriae peregrinae origo* ('the origin of foreign luxury') and *semina futurae luxuriae* ('seeds of future luxury'). Polybius, however, while of the opinion that from 200 BCE onwards there was some change in moral standards, places the crisis in the years after Rome had achieved universal dominion, that is, after 168 BCE.[8] Writing of the desire of the young Scipio Aemilianus to lead a virtuous life, he contrasts it with the general deterioration of morals at the time. As examples he gives homosexuality, whoring, and elaborate and costly banquets. Such debauchery arose from contact with Greek dissoluteness during the war with Perseus, and now burst into flame. The reasons given are, firstly, that the destruction of the Macedonian monarchy gave rise to the belief that undisputed and universal dominion was now assured to Rome and, secondly, the immense difference made both to public and to private life by the importation into Rome of the wealth of Macedonia.[9] Thirdly, the annalist L. Piso, although he seems to have given an account of the return of Manlius Vulso similar to that of Livy, dated the moral collapse to 154 BCE. This, at least, seems to be the inference from Pliny's cryptic remark *M. Messalae C. Cassi censorum lustro, a quo tempore pudicitiam subversam Piso gravis auctor prodidit* ('During the censorship of M. Messala and C. Cassius, from which time the great writer Piso related that all moral shame was overthrown').[10] This bare statement does not make clear the reasons for Piso's choice of this particular date, although the censors were themselves not such as to inspire confidence, but Polybius says that the Senate's chief motive in declaring war on Dalmatia was that it did not wish the citizens to become enervated by a long peace, it being now the twelfth year since the war with Perseus. The intention was by declaring war to renew the spirit and enterprise of the Romans.[11]

Manlium Asia devicta primum invexisse triumpho suo... L. Piso auctor est ('Lucius Piso reports that Gnaeus Manlius first carried bronzed couches and sideboards and one-footed tables in his triumph after the conquest of Asia'), Plin. *HN* 34. 14 = Piso fr. 36 *FRHist* (= 34 P). With *tum coquus... in pretio esse et, quod ministerium fuerat, ars haberi coepta* ('then cooks began to be valued and what had been a chore became an art') cf. Cato's speech against a certain Lepidus in 184 BCE *cum ait statuas positas Ochae atque Dionysodoro effeminatis qui magiras facerent* ('when, he reports, statues were set up to the effeminate Ocha and Dionysodorus, who practised cookery'), Fronto II 2 H, 227 VDH = Cato fr. 96 *ORF*. On increased attention to cuisine after 187, see Cato fr. 146 *ORF*, Plut. *Cat. Mai.* 8. 1, 18. 1; Polyb. 31. 25. 5; Ath. 6. 274–5.

[8] Cf. Brink and Walbank 1954: 103ff.
[9] Polyb. 31. 25. 3ff.; cf. Diod. Sic. 31. 26, Polyb. 6. 57. 5 (in a theoretical context).
[10] Plin. *HN* XVII, 244 = Piso fr. 40 *FRHist* = 38 P; cf. Fest. 285 L.
[11] Polyb. 32. 13. 6. For the censors, see Val. Max. 2. 4. 2, Livy 43. 1. 4–12. Their proposal to build a stone theatre was opposed by P. Scipio Nasica as *inutile et nociturum publicis*

None of these accounts precludes the possibility of the truth of the others. Livy's *semina futurae luxuriae* ('seeds of future luxury'), Polybius' moral corruption, and Piso's *pudicitia subversa* ('moral shame overthrown') can be formed into a coherent series of increasing moral decline, as Pliny saw.[12] The passage from Livy on the effects of Manlius Vulso's army clearly derives, in part at least, from the same source as Piso's account and is supported, where Piso is lacking, by the evidence of Cato. Polybius' account of the moral results of the war with Perseus occurs in his description of the early life of Scipio Aemilianus, in which he is at pains to emphasize that, although Scipio was averse from the traditional method of training for public life and winning public notice, he was nevertheless aiming at the same goal as his contemporaries and submitting himself to the dictates of *mos maiorum*, to the aristocratic ideal of *gloria* won by *egregia facinora* in public service.

It may be suggested, therefore, that these passages represent what may be conveniently termed a senatorial tradition of the second century. This suggestion is, perhaps, supported by the circumstance that, although the writers appear to be concerned mainly with the morality of the individual, each has chosen a point which is also marked by a decline in public conduct: the indiscipline of Vulso's army and the complaisance of its general; the insubordination of the army in Macedonia, the oppression of its generals, who even defied the authority of the Senate, the desecration of Q. Fulvius Flaccus, the oppression of the Statielli by M. Popillius Laenas, and the discontent at Rome; the events of the Spanish wars, particularly the panic and cowardice of the young nobles and the outrages of L. Licinius Lucullus and Ser. Sulpicius Galba—although it was a peculiarity of Roman thought generally to represent political crises as moral ones.

Although Sallust rejects this tradition, he could not have been unaware of it, or at least of part of the evidence on which it was based. The extent of Sallust's debt to the elder Cato was much remarked in antiquity.[13] This debt is usually represented as one of language,[14] but an acquaintance with the language of Cato implies a knowledge of the subject matter expressed in this language. The remarks in the *Bella* and *Historiae* on the demoralization which tends to follow prosperity can be paralleled in the

---

moribus ('useless and harmful to public morality'), Livy *Per.* 48; cf. Val. Max. 2. 4. 2, Vell. Pat. 1. 15. 3. For other similar occurrences this year, see Livy, *Per.* 47, Val. Max. 6. 9. 10; Fest. 360 L; Livy, *Per.* 48.

[12] *NH* 33. 148; cf. Flor. 3. 13.
[13] e.g. Suet. *Aug.* 86, Fronto I 4 H, 56 VDH.
[14] e.g. Quint. *Inst.* 8. 3. 29; Suet. *Gram.* 10.

fragments of Cato.[15] This may be nothing more than the independent use of a historical commonplace, but Cato also seems to have been the chief source for the account of the foundation and early history of Rome which appears in the *Bellum Catilinae*.[16] Much of the tradition of the moral crisis of the second century goes back ultimately to Cato, especially to his censorship in 184 BCE, which, directed particularly against luxury and moral decline, had been commemorated by a statue set up in his honour with an inscription recording how he had restored the tottering Republic.[17]

But while Sallust should not have been unaware of this tradition of the second century, he seems to have been concerned with a different aspect of the period from that which appears prominently in Cato, Livy, Polybius, and Calpurnius Piso. The time between the second and third Punic Wars is described as that when the Roman people *optimis moribus et maxima concordia egit* ('acted with the best morals and greatest harmony') and *concordia* is common to all three Sallustian accounts of this period. Further, it was *concordia* which united the motley collection of foreigners and aboriginal tribes into a *civitas*.[18] It was *concordia*, especially between Senate and *populus*, which was the particular characteristic of the Republic when *virtus omnia domuerat* ('*virtus* had overcome everything', B.C. 7.5).[19] It was *concordia* which was destroyed by the rise of *partes* and *factiones* after the destruction of Carthage, when men, basing their actions, not on *virtus*, but on *lubido* expressed as *ambitio* and *avaritia*, tore the *res publica* asunder in pursuit of their selfish ends. It is a principle of government that *concordia parvae res crescunt, discordia maxumae dilabuntur* ('with harmony small affairs grow, with discord the greatest collapse', *B.J.* 10. 6).

It is clear from the analysis of the Roman constitution which Polybius gives in Book 6 of his *History* that Sallust was justified in thus stressing the lack of serious friction between the Senate and the *populus* in the first half of the second century BCE. But this *concordia* was only one factor in a complex political situation which also included the disputing factions of the nobility, the increase in public and private wealth, and a certain moral decline. By ignoring these other aspects and concentrating on *concordia*, Sallust has produced an overgeneralized and idealistic account.

---

[15] e.g. *B.C.* 10. 1, *B.J.* 41. 1, *H.* 1. 11, 12 M, Cato *Orig.* fr. 87 *FRHist* (= 95*a* P); fr. 122 *ORF*.
[16] Cf. Serv. *Aen.* 1. 6 = Cato *Orig.* fr. 63 *FRHist* (= 5 P). On Sallust's debt to Cato, see Brunnert 1873, Ernout 1949.
[17] Plut. *Cat. Mai.* 19. 4, Scullard 1951: 152ff.   [18] *B.C.* 6. 2.   [19] *B.J.* 41.

The result is that Sallust postdates the various stages of moral decline as compared with the 'senatorial' tradition. The latter is concerned with the introduction of *luxuria* from Greece, its growth, and the moral degeneration consequent on it. For Sallust, *luxuria* is a comparatively late development in the process of decline. But both Sallust and the tradition agree that the agent of the first importation of *luxuria* was an army from Asia, in the annalistic account represented by Livy that of Manlius Vulso, for Sallust that of Sulla.[20] The two accounts are closely similar both in their descriptions of the lax discipline of the armies and in listing articles of luxury. Both, too, insist that the occasions mentioned were the first on which a Roman army came into contact with such luxury. Whatever may be the truth about the Livian version, in Sallust's case this can hardly be true. The general picture of the indiscipline of Sulla's army may well be correct, but there is ample evidence in Polybius, Livy, and the annalists that this was not the first time that an army of the Roman people had so conducted itself. *Primum* here may be only rhetorical colour and the whole sentence with its reference to *sacra profanaque omnia polluere* ('to pollute everything, sacred and profane') nothing more than a commonplace. On the other hand, it may represent an effort on Sallust's part to be consistent, since his overconcentration on *concordia* had led him to reject the tradition of the growth of *luxuria* in the earlier second century.

A further example of the results of Sallust's overgeneralized view of the second century may be seen in his comments on the nobility after the destruction of Carthage and the murder of the Gracchi: *paucorum arbitrio belli domique agitabatur; penes eosdem aerarium provinciae magistratus gloriae triumphique erant* ('action was taken at home and in war by the decision of the few; the treasury, the provinces, magistracies, honours, and triumphs were in the hands of the same men,' *B.J.* 41. 7). The same idea is expressed both by Catiline and by C. Memmius.[21] While it was certainly true for Sallust's own time, it was no new thing. His comment that the nobility in the time of Marius passed the consulship from hand to hand within itself and that no *novus* was so famous or had such *egregia facta* that he was not considered unworthy of that honour and, as it were, unclean, although the emotional colour of *indignus* and *pollutus* may belong more nearly to his own day, is equally applicable to the second century.[22]

---

[20] Livy 39. 6. 5ff., Sall. *B.C.* 11. 5–6.   [21] *B.C.* 20. 8, *B.J.* 31. 20.
[22] *B.J.* 63. 6; cf. Catiline's jibe: *M. Tullius, inquilinus civis urbis Romae* ('Marcus Tullius an immigrant citizen of the city of Rome,' *B.C.* 31. 7).

The explanation of Sallust's idealistic account of the earlier second century lies, then, in his isolation of *concordia* as the aspect of the political situation which seemed to him the most important, overconcentration on which led him to neglect other factors which seem relevant to his treatment of his theme. If the second century before 146 BCE was a time of *optimi mores* arising necessarily from political *concordia* and, ultimately, from *virtus*, then the tradition of the growing moral degeneration of this period must be rejected. In other words, Sallust is here a victim of his own generalization.

Sallust's choice of the destruction of Carthage as the turning point in Roman history set a fashion.[23] It appears in all three works, allied with the theory of the *metus hostilis*, the removal of which led to a breakdown of *virtus* and thus of *concordia*.[24] The use of this theory forms a test case for Sallust's general attitude to philosophic ideas. It is not surprising to find that it has been derived from Posidonius.[25] But the idea was a commonplace in ancient thought and appears as such in Xenophon, Plato, Aristotle, and frequently in Polybius.[26] Most important is the tradition which connects it closely with the famous debate between the elder Cato and Scipio Nasica on the destruction of Carthage, in which Nasica is said to have urged the preservation of Rome's great enemy precisely on the grounds that the maintenance of Roman discipline depended on the existence of an external threat.[27] It has been suggested that this tradition derives from some philosophical interpretation of Roman history and is, therefore, to be dismissed as unhistorical.[28] But the same idea is ascribed to Q. Caecilius Metellus by Valerius Maximus and by Appian to Scipio Africanus.[29] The latter is said to have urged the third treaty with Carthage because he considered it sufficient to deprive her of her supremacy. There were also some, Appian continues, who thought that he wished to keep a neighbour and rival as a perpetual

---

[23] Cf. Plin. *HN* 33. 150, Vell. Pat. 2. 1. 1, Flor. 1. 33. 1, 1. 34. 18, 1. 47. 2, August. *De civ. D.* 1. 30, Oros. 5. 8. 2. For 146 BCE as an epoch in popular thought in the provinces, see Sherwin-White 1939: 234–5, especially the Sibylline verses which refer not only to the Romans' love of money but also to the destruction of Corinth, not even mentioned by Sallust.
[24] *B.C.* 10. 1, *B.J.* 41. 1, *H.* 1. 11, 12 M; cf. Gelzer 1931: 271ff.
[25] Klingner 1928: 165ff.
[26] Xen. *Cyr.* 3. 1. 26, Pl. *Leg.* 3. 698Bff., Arist. *Pol.* 7. 1334a-b, Polyb. 6. 18, 6. 57. 5, 31. 25. 3ff., 32. 13. 6.
[27] Flor. 1. 31. 5, App. *Pun.* 69, and, much extended, Plut. *Cat. Mai.* 27, Diod. Sic. 34. 33. 3–6; cf. Bikerman 1946: 150, Gelzer 1931: 273ff., Aymard 1948: 109 n. 12, Scullard 1951: 241–3.
[28] e.g. from Posidonius; cf. *FGrH* 87 F 112.
[29] Val. Max. 7. 2. 3; App. *Pun.* 65.

menace to Rome to preserve Roman discipline and to ensure that she never became overbearing and careless because of the greatness of her prosperity. He adds that Cato, when not long afterwards he was condemning Roman severity towards the Rhodians, declared that this was, in fact, Scipio's view. Now, while Cato's actual quotation from Africanus is not preserved, there exist fragments of his speech *Pro Rhodiensibus* which allude both to the enervating effects of prosperity and also to a theory of the *metus hostilis*.[30] The same notion again lies behind Polybius' story that the Senate undertook the Dalmatian war to check the increasing enervation due to twelve years' peace.[31]

That the theory of the *metus hostilis* was common in ancient political thought and, indeed, something of a rhetorical commonplace does not prove that Nasica did not share it. Rather, it makes it at least possible for him to have advanced it, although not in the elaborate version found in Plutarch and Diodorus.[32] Indeed, point would have been added to his words by his turning against Cato an argument which the latter had already used in the case of Rhodes to defeat a proposal not very dissimilar from that which he was now urging. In any case, there was nothing new in the idea in the second century BCE nor was it ever a very profound theory.

It seems probable that this is the source of Sallust's account of the effects of the destruction of Carthage. The debate between Cato and Nasica was famous and the theory of *metus hostilis* a commonplace. In any case, he would have been familiar with Cato's published speeches. The Posidonian version seems to have laid great stress on external consequences. According to Diodorus, Nasica held that fear of Carthage would not only promote discipline and peace at home, but would also make Rome govern her subjects more moderately and clemently, while the removal of the threat would stimulate their hatred against the provincial governors.[33] In the theoretical passages in which Sallust treats of the *metus hostilis* this aspect is barely mentioned and appears elsewhere only where appropriate to the immediate subject, as in the *Letter of Mithridates*. Sallust is concerned almost entirely with internal consequences, in particular with the destruction of *concordia*.

There is, however, an important difference. It seems that Nasica advocated the preservation of Carthage to check a degeneration of

---

[30] Cato, frr. 163, 164 *ORF* = *Orig.* fr. 87–8 *FRHist* (= 95a–b P); cf. fr. 121 *ORF*, from the speech *Ad Litis Censorias* of 184 BCE.
[31] Polyb. 32. 13. 6.   [32] Cf. Gelzer 1931: 284–5; contra, Gsell 1913–28: 3. 331.
[33] Diod. Sic. 34. 33. 4–6; cf. Scullard 1951: 242.

which signs were already apparent.[34] The tradition of the moral crisis of the earlier second century and the many extant fragments of Cato's speeches attacking the growing luxury and corruption at Rome support on general grounds the view that this was Nasica's purpose.[35] For Sallust, on the other hand, 146 BCE marks not an intensification of an already existing corruption, but the very beginning of it, the moment when, for the first time, *saevire fortuna ac miscere omnia coepit* ('fortune began to rage and mix everything up', *B.C.* 10. 1).

There is some evidence for believing that a decline in public morality did take place. Polybius, for instance, in his earlier books, especially 6, probably written about 155 BCE, speaks with respect of the high standard of honesty and the incorruptibility current among the ruling nobility. In the later books, however, composed perhaps not earlier than the 140s and probably after the destruction of Carthage, passages occur which show a falling away from this standard.[36]

Again, the censorship which Polybius' friend and patron Scipio Aemilianus conducted in 142 BCE was, despite the inertia of his colleague, of unusual severity.[37] The fragments of his speeches at this time attest his concern at the general abandonment of the standard of *mos maiorum*, the growth of vice and luxury, and the *avaritia* and misgovernment of magistrates in the provinces.[38]

In the same year as Carthage, Corinth was destroyed, and in the years afterwards the Spanish wars dragged on. The earlier years of these wars had been marked by unrest at home, indiscipline in the armies, and incompetence and bad faith on the part of the generals. The later years show the same features. In 144 BCE serious riots occurred because of heavy recruiting. A tribune even attempted to prevent the consul from marching to Spain and in 138 the consuls were actually imprisoned by the tribunes C. Curiatus and S. Licinius for refusing to make certain exemptions from the levy.[39] In Spain itself, Q. Servilius Caepio, consul in 140, risked mutiny by his strict discipline when campaigning against the Vettones and Callaici.[40] When Scipio Aemilianus succeeded to the

---

[34] App. *Pun.* 69, Plut. *Cat. Mai.* 32. So, apparently, also the Posidonian version; cf. Diod. Sic. 34. 33. 4–6.
[35] e.g. Cato frr. 69–71, 96, 110, 131, 145–6, 174–5, 224, 247, 254 *ORF*.
[36] 38. 5. 1ff., 31. 25. 3ff.; cf. Brink and Walbank 1954: 97ff.
[37] Dio Cass. fr. 76, Val. Max. 6. 4. 2; cf. *De vir. ill.* 58. 9.
[38] Gell. *NA* 6. 20. 1 = Scipio fr. 13 *ORF*; Cic. *De or.* 2. 260; Gell. *NA* 5. 19. 15, 6. 12. 1 = Scipio fr. 17 *ORF*, fr. 19 *ORF*; cf. Livy *Oxy. Per.* 55; Val. Max. 6. 4. 2, 8. 1. 1; cf. Cic. *Mur.* 58; *Div. Caec.* 67; Livy *Oxy. Per.* 55.
[39] Cic. *Leg.* 3. 20, Livy *Per.* 55, *Oxy. Per.* 55; *CAH*[1] 8. 377.
[40] Livy *Per.* 54, *Oxy. Per.* 54, 55, Val. Max. 9. 6. 4, App. *Hisp.* 70.

command in 134, he found the army corrupted by licence and luxury and so demoralized by defeat that the usual camp following was augmented by soothsayers and diviners whom the soldiers were continually consulting.[41] After forbidding various objects and practices at variance with military life, he was forced to devote much of the year to restoring discipline and training the army.[42] Nor did many of the generals offer a good example. For instance, Q. Pompeius, consul in 141, concluded a treaty in 139 with Numantia in return for thirty talents of silver. The treaty was declared invalid by the Senate, but the money was not returned.[43] There is evidence, too, of peculation elsewhere than in Spain. In 140 D. Iunius Silanus was accused by the Macedonians and when the case was remitted to his natural father, T. Manlius Torquatus, Silanus committed suicide.[44] At Rome itself, L. Hostilius Tubulus became notorious for accepting bribes while presiding over the *quaestio de sicariis* ('standing tribunal for murder trials') as praetor in 142. When prosecuted by P. Mucius Scaevola, he went into exile and took poison on his recall.[45] As evidence of the continued growth of luxury we may instance the *Lex Didia sumptuaria* of 143.[46]

All this shows a situation which is disquieting enough, but certainly not new. The imprisonment of the consuls and the trouble about the levies in 138 BCE repeated the pattern of events in 151.[47] The indiscipline of Aemilianus' troops recalls that of his father's army in Macedonia.[48] Examples of peculation and bad faith on the part of generals and governors can be cited from the beginning of the century onwards, while the whole period after the second Punic War saw a continuous influx of wealth into Rome and an ever-increasing standard of living.[49]

The evidence clearly does not support Sallust's contention that the fall of Carthage marked a sudden descent to corruption at Rome. Rather, it suggests a slow decline of standards throughout the second century which aroused the concern both of the reactionary Cato and the more liberal Scipio Aemilianus. Individual cases of corruption occur throughout the century, and it seems unlikely that immediately after 146 the majority of the nobles were given over to *ambitio* and *avaritia*. Certainly, the protracted length of the Spanish wars and the incompetence of the

---

[41] Livy *Per.* 57, App. *Hisp.* 84–5.   [42] Livy *Per.* 57, App. *Hisp.* 85–6.
[43] Cic. *Font.* 23, *Off.* 3. 109, *Fin.* 2. 54, Livy *Per.* 54, Vell. Pat. 2. 1. 5, Val. Max. 8. 5. 1, App. *Hisp.* 79, 83.
[44] Cic. *Fin.* 1. 24, Livy *Per.* 54 and *Oxy. Per.* 54, Val. Max. 5. 8.
[45] Cic. *Att.* 12. 5b, *Nat. D.* 1. 63, *Fin.* 2. 54, 4. 77, 5. 62, Asc. 23 C.
[46] Macrob. *Sat.* 3. 17. 6.   [47] Polyb. 35. 4, App. *Hisp.* 49, Livy *Per.* 48.
[48] Livy 42. 32–5, 43. 11. 10, 43. 14. 7.
[49] Cf. the authorities cited in Earl 1961: 41 n. 2–5.

generals struck a severe blow to the prestige of the Senate which had emerged from the Punic Wars with its power and authority greatly enhanced, but this is not to say that the Senate as a body was corrupt or willfully self-seeking.

It is noticeable that Sallust, although he is quite clear as to when corruption began at Rome, makes it less clear how or why this occurred as soon as the *metus Punicus* was removed. Vague references to *fortuna* and to *otium atque abundantia earum rerum quae prima mortales ducunt* ('leisure and the abundance of all things which mortals consider the most important')[50] do not constitute reasons. Further, Sallust seems to have been completely unaware of a serious objection to his scheme of *virtus*. If Rome was kept in a state of *virtus* merely by the existence of an external threat and if this state of *virtus* automatically came to an end with the removal of this threat, this can hardly be regarded as true *virtus*. True *virtus*, in Sallust's sense or in any other, should surely be independent of external compulsions. Sallust's adoption of the theory of the *metus hostilis* involves him in a fundamental difficulty, and it is hard to see him here, at least, as a serious philosophic historian. Rather, the theory, together with the complementary, but distinct idea of the enervating effects of unchecked prosperity, would seem to have been taken over from his sources.

The question then arises, how far is Sallust's choice of the destruction of Carthage as the turning point conditioned by his view of the years which precede this event. Having through overconcentration on *concordia* produced an idealized account of the earlier second century as a time of predominant *virtus* both in the individual and in the state, which leads him to ignore the evidence in Cato and elsewhere for a certain degeneration of public and private morality, he has then to explain how within a few years Rome had reached the position in which the Gracchan revolution, in its political aspects, was possible. To take the Gracchi themselves as marking the turning point would not explain, for instance, why the *nobiles* came suddenly to abandon their *virtus* and both to call forth the actions of the Gracchi and to react to them in the way they did. In a state of *concordia maxuma* ('the greatest harmony') in which *virtus omnia domuerat* ('*virtus* had overcome everything', *B.C.* 7.5), the action of the Gracchi and the reaction of their opponents would be alike incomprehensible.

It seems that Sallust, committed to finding between an ideal period of *concordia* and *virtus* and the undoubted reality of the Gracchan intervention a point at which the former declined into a state where the other

---

[50] *B.C.* 10. 1–2, *B.J.* 41. 1.

was possible, chose the destruction of Carthage partly as the outstanding event of the time and more especially since arguments closely suited to his purpose had been advanced on that occasion by Scipio Nasica.

The theoretical analysis of decline expressed in general terms in the *Bellum Catilinae* is worked out in terms of Roman history in the digression which occupies chapters 41 and 42 of the *Bellum Jugurthinum*.[51] This begins with a statement of Sallust's idealized view of the second century BCE. The removal of the fear of Carthage gave rise to peace and the abundance of the things which men prize most highly.[52] This in turn brought *lascivia atque superbia* ('licentiousness and arrogance') manifested in *mos partium et factionum* ('practice of parties and factions'), that is, *ambitio, cupido imperi*.

Two features in particular call for comment, the phraseology used and the continuing oversimplification. To describe the immediate effects of the destruction of *concordia* Sallust employs a suggestive formulation: *coepere nobilitas dignitatem populus libertatem in lubidinem vortere, sibi quisque ducere trahere rapere* ('the nobles began to twist their dignity into unbridled desire, the people did the same to their liberty; each man appropriated, stole, plundered for himself', *B.J.* 41. 5). For the meaning of *dignitas* adequate literary evidence exists only from the late Republic, when, in a political sense, it signifies either a particular office or the prestige acquired through holding an office.[53] It includes the idea both of the worthiness of its possessor and of the respect inspired by this worthiness.[54] *Dignitas* differs from *gloria* in that it attaches to a man permanently and is inheritable by his descendants. A man may inherit the *dignitas* of his ancestors but, strictly speaking, he can only emulate their *gloria*, which arises from the individual's *egregia facinora* ('eminent deeds').[55]

Since it was inheritable, *dignitas* was closely allied with *nobilitas* and both rested ultimately on the tenure of public offices. The idea of *nobilitas* first began to be formulated in the second century BCE. At the same time the nobility tended to become more and more exclusive and to control strictly those offices on which *nobilitas* rested. As a result, *dignitas*, like *nobilitas*, became identified with the distinctions and preserves of the nobility and became the prerogative of the *nobiles* alone.

---

[51] For the theoretical analysis, see Earl 1961: 13ff.
[52] Sallust consistently ignores the Spanish wars in his references to *otium* after 146 BCE, another example of his oversimplification arising from too close adherence to an artificial historical scheme.
[53] Wegehaupt 1932: 22ff. For *dignitas* in Sallust, see Earl 1961: 69–75.
[54] Ibid. 9ff., 17–18, 19.   [55] Ibid. 12ff.; cf. Heinze 1925: 30.

This is the background to Sallust's remark. The *dignitas* of the nobility rested on their control of public life.[56] This power they abused,[57] so that their *dignitas* came to mean reckless and unjust domination.[58]

Inherent in the position of the nobility had always been the danger of a conflict between *dignitas* and *libertas*. As early as Plautus this danger had been recognized, at least so far that *leges* which assured the *libertas* of the individual might be overborne by *mos maiorum* drawing its power from *auctoritas* and *dignitas*.[59] The danger lay dormant so long as the aristocratic concept of *virtus* was observed in its entirety; so long, that is, as the pursuit of pre-eminent *gloria* was tempered by concern for the *respublica*, including *leges* and *libertas*, and the man who claimed *dignitas* was, in Livy's phrase, *haud minus libertatis alienae quam suae dignitatis memor* ('not less mindful of another's freedom than of his own dignity,' 7. 33. 3). As soon, however, as this tradition began to break down, as soon, to use Sallust's terms, as *virtus* declined into *ambitio*, a direct *contentio libertatis dignitatisque* ('struggle for liberty and dignity')[60] was certain to arise and became, in fact, a salient feature of Roman politics at the end of the Republic.

The assertion of the claims of *dignitas* is seen in its most extreme form in the history of the first Triumvirate. All ancient authorities agree that the motive behind this compact was *potentia* and *dignitas*.[61] After the death of Crassus, Pompey and Caesar faced each other, each suspicious of the other and jealous of his own *dignitas*.[62] The Civil War was a struggle for *dignitas*, for Pompey could not bear an equal nor Caesar a superior.[63] It was in defence of his *dignitas*, which he claimed to regard as more important than his life, that Caesar marched on Rome.[64]

---

[56] *B.J.* 41. 7: *paucorum arbitrio belli domique agitabatur; penes eosdem aerarium provinciae magistratus gloriae triumphique errant* ('action was taken at home and in war by the decision of the few; the treasury, the provinces, magistracies, honours, and triumphs were in the hands of the same men').

[57] *B.J.* 41. 8: *praedas bellicas imperatores cum paucis diripiebant; interea parentes aut parvi liberi militum, uti quisque potentiori confinis erat, sedibus pellebantur* ('the generals snatched away the spoils with a few other men; meanwhile the parents or small children of the soldiers, if someone happened to have a more powerful neighbour, were pushed from their homes').

[58] Cf. *B.C.* 11ff., *B.J.* 31, 85, C. Gracchus frr. 48–9 *ORF*, Cic. *Verr.* 2. 5. 175, Plut. *Ti. Gracch.* 8.

[59] Earl 1961: 25–6.   [60] Livy 4. 6. 11.

[61] Flor. 2. 13. 11, Dio Cass. 37. 55. 3–56. 4.   [62] Flor. 2. 13. 14.

[63] Flor. 2. 13. 14, Lucan 1. 125; Caes. *BCiv.* 1. 4. 4; Vell. Pat. 2. 33. 3.

[64] Caes. *B Civ.* 1. 9. 2, 1. 7. 7, 3. 91. 2, Cic. *Att.* 7. 11. 1, *Lig.* 18, *Marcell.* 25, Hirtius *B Gall.* 8. 52. 4, 8. 53. 1.

Against such extreme claims, whether made by the nobility or their opponents, appeal could be made to *libertas*, which, being a vague term standing for a mere minimum of political rights, admitted of many interpretations.[65] It could be invoked in defence of the existing order by individuals or classes in the enjoyment of power and wealth.[66] It could equally be invoked by their opponents. It was on this plea that the young Pompey raised a private army and put down the tyranny of the Marian party.[67] Caesar's other excuse for precipitating the Civil War was precisely *ut se et populum Romanum factione paucorum oppressum in libertatem vindicaret* ('to win freedom for themselves and the Roman people who were oppressed by the faction of the few,' *BCiv.* 1. 22. 5). In Caesar the *contentio libertatis dignitatisque* reached its culmination. He crossed the Rubicon to defend his own *dignitas* and to protect *libertas* from the *dignitas* of his opponents. It is significant that he expected these excuses to meet, if not approbation, at least understanding.

Libertas, in fact, became a political catchword, employed especially by the *populares* in assailing the *dignitas* of the *optimates*.[68] In this passage of the *Bellum Jugurthinum*, *libertas* appears as much the peculiar distinction of the *populus* as *dignitas* of the *nobilitas*. At first, after the destruction of Carthage there was no conflict. Both sides were engaged in perverting their respective distinctions for selfish ends and both were equally guilty of *ambitio*.[69] The assertion of *dignitas* by the nobility was, however, incompatible with the assertion of *libertas* on the part of the *populus*. The nobility, because of its superior power and its control of the machinery of state, was able to oppress the *populus*.

It was from this situation that the great conflict between *libertas* and *dignitas* arose when there were found among the nobility men who preferred *vera gloria* to unjust domination, that is, when the Gracchi *vindicare plebem in libertatem et paucorum scelera patefacere coepere* ('they began to win the freedom of the plebs and expose the crimes of the few,' *B.J.* 41. 10–42. 1). Cicero put matters somewhat differently when he referred to *P. Scipione, qui ex dominatu Ti. Gracchi privatus in libertatem rem publicam vindicavit* ('P. Scipio, who as a private citizen won from the

---

[65] Wirszubski 1950: 14. [66] Syme 1952: 155.

[67] *BAfr.* 22. 2: *paene oppressam funditus et deletam Italiam urbemque Romanam in libertatem vindicavit* ('he won freedom for Italy and Rome when they had been almost completely overwhelmed and destroyed').

[68] Wirszubski 1950: chs. 2 and 3.

[69] *Lubido* in this passage denotes the same thing as *cupido* elsewhere. Sallust appears to use them interchangeably. Since both *ambitio* and *avaritia* are essentially *cupido* and differentiate only in their ends, they naturally go hand in hand; cf. *B.J.* 41. 9.

tyranny of Ti. Gracchus the freedom of the Republic,' *Brut.* 212).[70] No clearer illustration could be found of the extent to which *libertas* had become a mere political slogan. Sallust was not unaware of this, for the phrase *vindicamus in libertatem* ('we win freedom') occurs also in Catiline's speech to his fellow conspirators. A comparison between it and the digression of the *Bellum Jugurthinum* under discussion is interesting. In both a minority, *pauci*, is represented as using its superior resources to achieve a dominant position in the *res publica* and to oppress the rest of the citizens.[71] Indeed, the *res publica* is all but destroyed.[72] Against this oppression both passages invoke *libertas*. But there remains a difference. The Gracchi invoked *libertas* on behalf of the oppressed *plebs*: *vindicare plebem in libertatem* ('to win the freedom of the plebs'). Catiline invokes it for himself and his fellows: *nosmet ipsi vindicamus in libertatem* ('we ourselves win our liberty'). Catiline's *libertas* means *auctoritas* ('authority'), *gratia potentia honos divitiae* ('influence, power, honour, wealth') for himself.[73] His speech is a clear example of the way in which the opponents of whatever party happened to be in power could and did claim that a minority in control, for the moment, of the government was oppressing the *res publica* and exploiting the constitution in its own interests. On the same excuse Pompey raised a private army and Caesar marched on Rome.

Exactly to what extent *libertas* figured in the advocacy of the Gracchan proposals is in the present state of the ancient evidence obscure, but it has been suggested that *aequum ius* ('equal right') and *aequitas* were invoked rather than *libertas* in its full sense.[74] If this were so, then the question arises how far Sallust is describing the Gracchan intervention in the political terminology of a later period. The phrase *vindicare in libertatem* and its cognate *vindex libertatis* seem to belong to the

---

[70] Cf. *Off.* 1. 109: *qui Ti. Gracchi conatus perditos vindicavit* ('who avenged the desperate attempts of Tiberius Gracchus').

[71] *B.J.* 41. 7–8, quoted Earl 1961: 53 n. 56 and 57, *B.C.* 20. 7: *nam postquam res publica in paucorum potentium ius atque dicionem concessit, semper illis reges tetrarchae vectigales esse, populi nationes stipendia pendere,* etc. ('for after the commonwealth passed into the power and jurisdiction of a few powerful men, those men always obtained the tribute of kings and tetrarchs; peoples and nations payed taxes to them').

[72] *B.J.* 41. 5: *res publica... dilacerata* ('the commonwealth torn apart'), *B.C.* 20. 7: *si res publica valeret* ('if the commonwealth were sound').

[73] *B.C.* 20. 7–8: *volgus fuimus sine gratia sine auctoritate, iis obnoxii quibus, si res publica valeret, formidini essemus. itaque omnis gratia potentia honos divitiae apud illos sunt aut ubi illi volunt* ('we were a rabble with no influence or authority, obedient to those who would have feared us if the commonwealth were sound. And so all influence, power, honour, and wealth are in their hands or where they will them to be').

[74] Wirszubski 1950: 44ff.

post-Sullan period.[75] While a few pre-Sullan coins invoke the principle of *libertas*, mainly in connection with the secret ballot, the majority of examples occur after Sulla, culminating in the glorification of *libertas* by M. Brutus, in the persons of his ancestors Lucius Brutus and Servilius Ahala, on the eve of the Civil War, the announcement of the restoration of *libertas* by Caesar, and the continual reference to the restitution of *libertas* on the coins of Brutus and Cassius after the death of the dictator.[76] *Libertas*, it would appear, did not assume its highest importance as a political slogan until the time of Sulla, that is, at about the same time as the terms *populares* and *optimates* became current,[77] and Sallust's phraseology belongs to a later period than that of the Gracchi, when the *contentio libertatis dignitatisque* had reached its height.[78]

Thus far Sallust's formulation shows close similarity to popularist propaganda. But he is prepared to admit that the Gracchi were *ex nobilitate* ('of the nobility'). That the Gracchi were progressive *nobiles* before they became *populares*, that they came of an ancient and famous family,[79] and that Tiberius, at least, at the beginning of his tribunate, was backed by a powerful group of the nobility were all features which tended to be obscured in later writers. The Gracchi, particularly Gaius, were in antiquity regarded as model *populares*,[80] and as the term *nobilitas* ceased to be a technical term denoting status and came rather to be equated with *factio paucorum* and the like, so the *populares* tended to ignore the origins of the Gracchi, while the *optimates* preferred to forget that the first challenge to the power of the ruling oligarchy, which set in motion the disruptive forces of the following century, came from within the ranks of that oligarchy itself.

Sallust's insistence on this point is the more surprising in view of the oversimplification which follows. What the crimes were of which the nobility was guilty, and which were laid open by the Gracchi, he does not detail. Nor, more serious, does he as much as mention the complex social and economic situation which gave rise to the actions of the Gracchi. The depopulation of Italy, the growth of the urban proletariat, and the rise of the commercial classes are all ignored, and the emphasis throughout is on the political aspect alone, as Sallust conceived it, in terms of the

---

[75] e.g. Cic. *Leg. agr.* 2. 2. 4, *Flacc.* 25, *Sest.* 144, *Fam.* 2. 5. 2, 10. 31. 5, *Phil.* 2. 30.
[76] Alföldi 1956: 92.
[77] On these terms, see Strasburger, s.v. *Optimates*, RE XVIII, cols. 773ff.
[78] Wirszubski 1950: 74ff.
[79] As Sallust puts it, *quorum maiores Punico atque aliis bellis multum reipublicae addiderant* ('those whose ancestors had added much to the commonwealth in the Punic and other wars', *B.J.* 42. 1).
[80] e.g. Cic. *Sest.* 105, *Dom.* 24.

decline of *virtus* into *ambitio*, from which sprang the breakdown of *concordia* and the oppression of the *populus* by the superior resources of the nobility. The *socii ac nomen Latinum* ('allies and those of Latin name') and the *equites* are mentioned only in this political context as instruments of the nobility. Even at this level Sallust's version is oversimple. To talk simply of the Gracchi is to ignore the real and important differences between the two brothers. The opponents of Tiberius are described by Plutarch and Appian merely as 'the wealthy' or 'the men of property'.[81] The Latin sources are more explicit and speak of *senatus et equester ordo* ('the Senate and the equestrian order').[82] While the latter term is here something of an anachronism, there is no doubt that in resisting the agrarian law the Senate had the support of many wealthy businessmen who had invested in land in Sicily, Italy, and elsewhere.[83] C. Gracchus, however, contrived to win the emergent *equites* from the Senate by his *Lex de Provincia Asia* and by transferring the *Quaestiones* to their control.[84] Indeed, he is said to have boasted that by organizing the *equites* as a political force by giving them control of the courts he had broken the power of the Senate.[85]

Of equal interest to his recognition that the Gracchi were *ex nobilitate* is Sallust's final judgement on them: *et sane Gracchis cupidine victoriae haud satis moderatus animus fuit* ('the Gracchi clearly did not have a spirit sufficiently moderate because of their lust for victory', *B.J.* 42. 2). They had begun by seeking *vera gloria* ('true glory'), that is, in Sallustian terms, they had aimed at *gloria virtutis via* ('glory by the path of *virtus*'), by achieving *egregia facinora* through *bonae artes* ('honourable skills'). But they too had fallen prey to the all-pervading *cupido* of the years after the destruction of Carthage, years when *haud sane quisquam Romae virtute magnus fuit* ('there was clearly no one at Rome great in *virtus*', *B.C.* 53. 6). Compared with their opponents, however, the Gracchi were *boni*: *sed bono vinci satius est quam malo more iniuriam vincere* ('but for the good man it is better to be overcome than to overcome injury in a wicked way', *B.J.* 42. 3). *Boni*, men of *virtus*, proceed *bonis artibus*, and the difference between the *bonus* and the *ignavus* ('worthless') lies precisely in that the former *vera via nititur* ('struggles on the true path'), while the latter *quia bonae artes desunt, dolis atque fallaciis contendit* ('because

---

[81] Plut. *Ti. Gracch.* 20, App. *B Civ.* 1. 12–13.
[82] Livy *Per.* 58, Vell. Pat. 2. 3. 2.
[83] Cf. Diod. Sic. 34.2–3; Caspari 1913: 184–5, Hatzfeld 1919: 225–6.
[84] Cic. *Verr.* 2. 3. 12, *Att.* 1. 17. 9, 5. 13. 1, *Flacc.* 19, *Leg. Man.* 14–15, App. *B Civ.* 5. 5, Cic. *Verr.* 1. 38, 2. 3. 168, App. *B Civ.* 1. 22.
[85] App. *B Civ.* 1. 22, Diod. Sic. 37. 3. 9.

honourable skills are absent, struggles with fraud and lies', *B.C.* 11. 2).[86] True *boni* would not have acted as the nobility had done.

The result of the suppression of the Gracchi was that *ea victoria nobilitas ex lubidine sua usa multos mortalis ferro aut fuga extinxit plusque in relicuom sibi timoris quam potentiae addidit* ('the nobles used that victory as they desired and got rid of many men with the sword or with exile and on the rest imposed more fear for themselves than power', *B.J.* 42. 4). As after the destruction of Carthage, so after the murders of the Gracchi *lubido* was the guiding principle of the nobility. But what had brought *potentia* by the oppression of the *populus* after 146 BCE after 122 gained the *nobiles* not more power, but the fear of the rest of the community, and gave a new impetus to party strife: *quae res plerumque magnas civitatis pessum dedit, dum alteri alteros vincere quovis modo et victos acerbius ulcisci volunt* ('matters which generally destroy great states while one group wishes to conquer the other in whatever way possible and to take a more bitter vengeance on the conquered', *B.J.* 42. 4).[87]

Thus, Sallust's description of the events immediately following the destruction of Carthage presents two chief aspects. In the first place, these two chapters of the *Bellum Jugurthinum* provide a working out in terms of Roman politics of the conception of the decline of *virtus* and the destruction of *concordia* after the removal of the *metus Punicus*. This account is simplified and compressed to the exclusion of all aspects of the situation other than the political. Social and economic factors, even those which made agrarian reform necessary, are ignored, and attention is directed solely to the theme of *ambitio, avaritia*, and the oppression of the *populus* by the *nobilitas*, in which neither side showed *virtus*. Sallust's procedure here is the same as that employed to describe the years before 146, overconcentration on a generalized and theoretical motivation causing the neglect even of immediate historical factors. In the second place, in his expression of this theme Sallust uses the phraseology of the political vocabulary of the last years of the Republic, especially that related to a conception of a *contentio libertatis dignitatisque*. The opposition of *dignitas* and *libertas* and the phrase *vindicare in libertatem* have been discussed and illustrated at some length. In addition may be instanced the use of *factio* and *pauci*.[88] Politically, Sallust's view of the second century BCE seems to be popularist, as against the rest of

---

[86] Cf. Earl 1961: 10–11, 14.

[87] Cf. *B.J.* 10. 6: *concordia parvae res crescunt, discordia maxumae dilabuntur* ('by concord small states grow; by discord the very greatest dissolve').

[88] *B.J.* 41. 1, 41. 6, 41. 7, 42. 1.

the tradition, which was optimate. Clearly, the rise of the *populares* was synonymous with the end of *concordia*;[89] but the *populares* claimed that it was not they who actually brought *concordia* to an end. It had already ended in 146, and the theoretical reason was the lack of *metus hostilis*. If *concordia* was already ended with the degeneration of the *virtus* of the *nobiles*, then the Gracchi were not destroyers but men who took a natural line in bringing true *virtus* back into its place in the state. But Sallust has gone further. In his view the *populus* was equally guilty with the *nobilitas* of the disruption of *concordia*. The nobility succeeded in its oppression only because it was stronger, and even the Gracchi were not free from *ambitio*.

[89] Oros. 5. 8. 1, unless it is no more than a piece of rhetorical embroidery, shows that in 133 some people, including perhaps Aemilianus, already recognized that *concordia* was in danger: Brink and Walbank 1954: 103 n. 3.

4

A Traditional Pattern of Imitation in Sallust and his Sources

R. Renehan

'We now recognize that in the view of the ancients a poet's originality was not diminished by his use of old material, but rather displayed in his ingenious adaptation of that material to his own purposes; what is true of poetic technique is also true of thought.'[1] What Lloyd-Jones here states of ancient poetry is equally applicable to ancient prose. In the case of Sallust, it was already known in antiquity that his writings contained many imitations of earlier authors, both Greek and Roman; and, while the old sneer of Pompeius Lenaeus, *priscorum Catonis verborum ineruditissimus fur* ('the most unsophisticated thief of Cato's archaic expressions'), is familiar, the judgement of a modern critic, Eiliv Skard, is both fairer and more accurate: 'für Sallust war das Wichtigste nicht, durch Neues zu glänzen, sondern im Bekannten gross zu sein.'[2] In his imitations Sallust does not confine himself merely to borrowing lapidary *phrases* introduced arbitrarily into his work. Rather, his borrowings are sometimes taken from passages which show a *context* similar to that of the corresponding Sallustian passage. To take an obvious example, in discussing the decline of morals at Rome, Sallust makes much use of Thucydides' famous Corcyrean Digression. Perrochat correctly remarks 'Salluste se sert de ces textes [sc. Thuc. 3. 81–5], sur les révolutions et la décadence morale et civique des cités grecques, pour parler de faits analogues à Rome.'[3] Clearly, by taking over expressions which Thucydides uses in his account of Greek *stasis* and applying them to *res Romanae*, Sallust is making an implicit judgement on Rome: as Greece was then, so Rome is now. This technique

---

[1] Lloyd-Jones 1971: 44–5.   [2] Skard 1956: 108.
[3] Perrochat 1949: 15. For Sallust's Greek models, see, in addition to Perrochat's work, the paper of Avenarius 1957: 48–86.

of criticizing indirectly, by means of an artistic use of traditional material, is far more effective than a bald statement of opinion would have been. It seems to have gone all but unnoticed that Sallust is a master of this delicate device. The purpose of the present paper is to attempt to demonstrate his mastery from examples. In each instance an examination of the original context of the borrowed material will reveal a value judgement of Sallust himself, a judgement which has determined the choice of the particular passage to be imitated.

SALLUST AND AESCHYLUS

Sallust's famous σύγκρισις of Caesar and Cato contains the words *esse quam videri bonus malebat* [sc. *Cato*] ('[]Cato's] preference was to be good rather than to seem good', B.C. 54. 6). In view of the often rabid partisanship of the Romans, it has seemed surprising to some that Sallust, who had been one of Caesar's officers in the Civil War, should be so generous in praising the great republican, Cato Uticensis.[4] The words cited above are of course an imitation of a famous verse of Aeschylus, οὐ γὰρ δοκεῖν ἄριστος ἀλλ' εἶναι θέλει ('for he desires not to seem but to be the best', *Sept.* 592). The verse was a very familiar one, as other imitations and citations show. For this reason commentators have been content to assume that Sallust is here rendering a well-known Greek bon mot, whose ultimate source may have been a matter of indifference, or even quite unknown, to him. The assumption is not justified. Consider Shakespeare. Hundreds of his verses and phrases are now common coin in the English language. While it is true that ὁ ἐπιτυχών ('any chance person') may be familiar with only the saying and not the source, a cultured person still knows the play in which, say, 'Sweets to the sweet' first occurred. Sallust was such a cultured, well-read person; the numerous imitations of earlier writers in his works are themselves sufficient proof of that. It is legitimate to assume a priori that he knew the source of the verse which he is imitating here. An inspection of the context in Aeschylus will confirm the assumption.

The words οὐ γὰρ δοκεῖν ἄριστος ἀλλ' εἶναι θέλει are said of Amphiaraus, whose story will be recalled: Amphiaraus had sworn that, whenever he and Adrastus disagreed, he would abide by the decision of his wife Eriphyle.

---

[4] Sallust prepares us at the beginning of the passage for the praise to come: *sed memoria mea ingenti virtute, divorsis moribus fuere viri duo, M. Cato et C. Caesar* (B.C. 53. 6). I do not know whether it is significant that Cato is here mentioned before Caesar.

When Adrastus wished to lead an expedition against Thebes, Amphiaraus opposed it, since, being a seer, he knew that the campaign would cost him his life. Eriphyle, bribed by Polynices, came out in support of the expedition. Whereupon Amphiaraus, faithful to his oath, joined the expedition, preferring to lose his life rather than his honour. The verse which we are considering occurs in a messenger's speech in which it is reported that Amphiaraus is one of the Seven. Here are the beginning verses of Eteocles' reply to the messenger (597–614):

> Alas, the luck which among human beings
> conjoins an honest man with impious wretches!
> In every enterprise is no greater evil
> than bad companionship: there is no fruit
> that can be gathered. The field of doom
> bears death as its harvest.
> Indeed, a pious man, going on board
> as shipmate of a crew of rascal sailors
> and of some mischief they have perpetrated,
> has often died with the God-detested breed;
> or a just man, with fellow citizens
> themselves inhospitable, forgetful of the Gods,
> has fallen into the same snare as the unrighteous,
> and smitten by the common scourge of God
> has yielded up his life. Even so this seer,
> this son of Oecles, wise, just, good, and holy,
> a prophet mighty, mingling with the impious—
> against his better reason—with loud-mouthed
> men who pursue a road long to retrace,
> with God's will shall be dragged to their general doom.[5]

It seems obvious that Sallust must have had this very passage in mind and judged that it applied perfectly to Cato—the just man who came to ruin because of his association with unjust fellow citizens. And like Amphiaraus, Cato, after Thapsus, chose an honourable end of life: βίου πονηροῦ θάνατος εὐκλεέστερος ('Death is less disgraceful than a wretched life'). These agreements are too good to be coincidence. I do not regard it as extravagant to state that Sallust, by his choice of a tragic verse (592) from this tragic context, subtly reveals his belief that his opponent Cato had demonstrated, in life and in death, some of the qualities of a Greek tragic hero.[6]

---

[5] Grene 1959: 283–84.

[6] I point out an excellent example of the practice of reworking and 'capping' older material here. Just as Sallust has taken over a line from Aeschylus, so Tacitus in turn in the *Agricola*—a work inspired in good part by Sallust's monographs—has imitated directly *esse quam videri bonus malebat*. Tacitus says of Agricola that he *maluit videri invenisse bonos*

SALLUST AND CICERO

The resemblance of *B.C.* 20. 9, *quae quo usque tandem patiemini, o fortissumi viri* ('and to what point finally will we endure these things, oh bravest men'), to the famous opening of Cicero's First Catilinarian (*quo usque tandem abutere, Catilina, patientia nostra,* 'to what point finally will you abuse our patience, Catiline') has long been remarked. Whether this is a coincidence or not is disputed. Skard,[7] pointing out that Sallust uses *quo usque* elsewhere (*H.* 1. 77. 17M) and that Livy has *quo usque tandem ignorabitis vires vestras* ('to what point finally will you disregard your own strength', 6. 18. 5), concludes that both historians took the expression from an older *Geschichtswerk* ('historical work'). This is unnecessary and undemonstrable, since *quo usque* is normal— and common—Latin. The present case is different. Observe, first, that the parallelism between the First Catilinarian of Cicero and Sallust's *B.C.* 20. 9 is very close: *quo usque tandem = quo usque tandem; abutere patientia nostra ~ patiemini; Catilina ~ o fortissimo viri*. Neither of Skard's parallels is so close. In Livy 6. 18. 5 there is neither a vocative nor a verb corresponding in sense to *patiemini*; in Sallust *H.* 1. 77. 17 there is no *tandem*. Here again a comparison of the two contexts is decisive. Cicero's words occur (1) in a speech (2) directed against Catiline (3) in condemnation of his conspiracy. In Sallust the words appear (1) in a speech (2) spoken by Catiline (3) in exhortation of his fellow conspirators. It is certain that Sallust was familiar with the First Catilinarian.[8] If he remembered any of it, he would surely have remembered the impressive opening. When he puts into the mouth of Catiline the word *quae quo usque tandem patiemini*, the echo of Cicero must be intentional. Otherwise, we have to maintain that Sallust himself failed to perceive the close parallelism of language and of pointedly opposed contexts. Such a coincidence would be too remarkable to be probable. Rather, the reader is expected to make the association. This is parody. To be sure, as Syme has written, 'If that is malice, it is not very noxious.'[9] Nevertheless, the ironical allusion implies an attitude on Sallust's part toward Cicero—a disrespectful one, and thus the passage becomes a

---

quam fecisse (7. 3). *Bonos* and *maluit* clearly go back to Sallust's *bonus* and *malebat*, not to Aeschylus' ἄριστος and θέλει. (Cf. also *B.C.* 51. 38.) It would perhaps be far-fetched to suggest that Tacitus here intends to compliment Agricola by comparison with Cato.

[7] Skard 1956: 24.

[8] *Tum M. Tullius consul, sive praesentiam eius timens sive ira conmotus, orationem habuit luculentam atque utilem rei publicae, quam postea scriptam edidit* (*B.C.* 31. 6).

[9] Syme 1964: 106.

valuable piece of evidence. Could one imagine Sallust parodying Caesar or Cato? In fact, to the best of my knowledge, this is the only specimen of parody in Sallust: here the Roman Thucydides laughed.[10]

This passage is, incidentally, evidence for something else, if the interpretation presented here is correct. Parody is not practiced *in vacuo*; Sallust wished his readers to savour it. Clearly this would be possible only if Cicero's words were well known not only to Sallust, but to his audience. We may therefore conclude that *quo usque tandem abutere, Catilina, patientia nostra* had already become a familiar quotation at the time of the composition of Sallust's *Catilina*. It has remained such ever since.

SALLUST AND HERODOTUS

Qui [sc. *Iugurtha*] *ubi primum adolevit, pollens viribus, decora facie, sed multo maxume ingenio validus, non se luxu neque inertiae conrumpendum dedit, sed, uti mos gentis illius est, equitare, iaculari* ('And as soon as Jugurtha grew up, physically powerful, graceful features, but by far especially strong in his mind, he did not allow himself to be corrupted by luxury or sloth, but, as is the custom of his nation, practised horsemanship and throwing the javelin,' *B.J.* 6. 1). The final words, describing the customs of the Numidians, seem modelled on Herodotus' description of the customs of the Persians: παιδεύουσι δὲ τοὺς παῖδας ἀπὸ πενταέτεος ἀρξάμενοι μέχρι εἰκοσαέτεος τρία μοῦνα, ἱππεύειν καὶ τοξεύειν καὶ ἀληθίζεσθαι ('They educate their boys beginning from 5 years old to 20 in three things only: horse riding, archery, and truth telling').[11] In Sallust the infinitive *equitare* corresponds to ἱππεύειν and *iaculari* to τοξεύειν; nothing answers to ἀληθίζεσθαι. Recall that for Sallust the Numidians in general and Jugurtha in particular were notoriously treacherous,[12] and the omission will appear no accident. The historian is implying a contrast between the truthful Persians and the deceitful Numidians. The ethnographical and geographical excursus was an essential part of historiography for Sallust; an allusion to Herodotus, the first great model for such excursuses, is not surprising.

---

[10] As, so we are told, Thucydides did once: τινες θαυμάσαντες εἶπον ὅτι λέων ἐγέλασεν ἐνταῦθα (Σ Thuc. 1. 126. 3).

[11] Hdt. 1. 136. I first compared the two passages in Renehan 1962: 257. For a comparable passage, see Hippoc. *Aer.* 17.

[12] *B.J.* 46. 3, *genus Numidarum infidum*; *B.J.* 26. 2, *omnia potiora fide Jugurthae*. See also *B.J.* 46. 8, 48. 1, 53. 6, 56. 5, 61. 5, 91. 7.

A Traditional Pattern of Imitation

SALLUST AND PLATO'S SEVENTH LETTER

Sallust incorporates into the *B.C.* and the *B.J.* a number of imitations of Plato's Seventh Letter; the passages are listed by Perrochat.[13] Here I wish to consider the implications of *B.C.* 3. 3-4. 2, a passage which is under heavy debt to Plato, as the following parallels will show:

B.C. 3. 3: *sed ego adulescentulus initio, sicuti plerique, studio ad rem publicam latus sum, ibique mihi multa advorsa fuere* ('but I, in the beginning as a young man, just like many others, was eagerly drawn to political activity, and there many things were opposed to me').

Ep. 7. 324B: When I was young I expected, as the young often do, that as soon as I was grown up, I should at once take part in the public life of the city. And I was confronted with certain developments in the political situation.

B.C. 3. 4-5: *quae tametsi animus aspernabatur insolens malarum artium...quom ab relicuorum malis moribus dissentirem* ('and although my soul, unaccustomed to wicked ways, spurned these things...since I disagreed with the wicked customs of the others').

Ep. 7. 325A: Seeing, then, all these events, and many other crimes by no means negligible, I was disgusted and withdrew myself from the wickedness of the times.

B.C. 4. 1-2 *igitur ubi...mihi relicuam aetatem a re publica procul habendam decrevi...a quo incepto studioque me ambitio mala detinuerat, eodem regressus statui res gestas populi Romani carptim, ut quaeque memoria digna videbantur, perscribere* ('and so after...I determined that the rest of my life was to be passed far away from politics...I returned to the same study which I had begun and from which wicked ambition had held me back, and I decided to write out the deeds of the Roman people in separate studies').

Ep. 7. 325E-326A and the result was that I, who at first had been full of enthusiasm for a political career, now that I observed all this...became finally dazed by the spectacle...and I was forced to say, in praise of true philosophy, that only by its help can political justice and the rights of the individual ever be discerned.

There are clear indications that Plato's Seventh Letter was known in first-century Rome (as one would have assumed in any event). Cicero quotes a passage from this *praeclara epistola Platonis* ('brilliant letter of Plato') in *Tusc.* 5. 35. 100; he alludes to the same passage in *Fin.* 2. 28. 92. Furthermore J. Souilhé has suggested that Nepos used the Seventh Letter for his life of Dion.[14] Sallust must have realized (and therefore intended) that some at least of his readers would recognize the imitations. How are the two contexts similar? Each is autobiographical and each tells us essentially the same thing. Plato and Sallust have experienced a

---

[13] Perrochat 1949: 48-53.   [14] Souilhé 1931: vii.

comparable misfortune: both with the innocence of youth naively approached τὰ πολιτικά ('politics'), only to become disillusioned with the corruption attendant upon a public career. As a consequence they abandoned politics for more honourable pursuits—the theoretical Greek turning to philosophy and the practical Roman to the composition of history. The similarities are obvious and apt, and it should not be doubted that Sallust intended the comparison to be made. Now Plato, the *deus philosophorum* ('philosophers' god'), was by Sallust's time one of the most revered figures of the ancient world; his motives in renouncing what seemed certain to be a distinguished public career were rightly regarded as noble and above reproach. The reader is meant to draw a similar conclusion about Sallust's motives for renouncing public life. What are the facts? Put baldly, they are as follows. Plato took his leave of politics when he was in his twenties, of his own volition; Sallust, when he was over 40—and then only when charges of corruption obliged him to withdraw from public life. Whatever one thinks of Sallust's morals,[15] it must be said that his use of traditional material here for apologetic purposes is an artistic tour de force. The choice of Plato's Seventh Letter was a brilliant one; it has fooled many readers over the centuries.

SALLUST AND THUCYDIDES

The suggestion that Sallust subtly contrives to have the reader associate him with Plato in the quality of his personal life gains support from the undeniable fact that in historiography he intends a comparable association with Thucydides. Time and again he imitates Thucydides in style and historical attitude; sometimes he translates literally.[16] The Romans were conscious of this; to Velleius Paterculus, for instance, Sallust was *aemulus Thucydidis* ('Thucydides' rival').[17] Read in this light, chapter 8 of the *B.C.*—a chapter which, one must note, could have been entirely omitted without any loss of continuity between chapters 7 and 9—is instructive:

> *Sed profecto fortuna in omni re dominatur; ea res cunctas ex lubidine magis quam ex vero celebrat obscuratque. Atheniensium res gestae, sicuti ego*

---

[15] *B.C.* 3. 4 is revealing: *tamen inter tanta vitia inbecilla aetas ambitione conrupta tenebatur.* Sallust admits therefore to *ambitio*. But compare *B.C.* 11. 1: *ambitio...quod tamen vitium propius virtutem erat*. The only *vitium* which Sallust acknowledges in his own past he goes on to describe as *propius virtutem*! The apologist has unconsciously shown his hand.
[16] See Perrochat 1949: 1–39; Avenarius 1957: 49–56.   [17] 2. 36. 2.

A Traditional Pattern of Imitation

> *aestumo, satis amplae magnificaeque fuere, verum aliquanto minores tamen quam fama feruntur. sed quia provenere ibi scriptorum magna ingenia, per terrarum orbem Atheniensium facta pro maxumis celebrantur. ita eorum qui fecere virtus tanta habetur, quantum eam verbis potuere extollere praeclara ingenia. at populo Romano numquam ea copia fuit, quia prudentissumus quisque maxume negotiosus erat, ingenium nemo sine corpore exercebat, optumus quisque facere quam dicere, sua ab aliis bene facta laudari quam ipse aliorum narrare malebat.*

> But clearly fortune is the master in every thing; she celebrates and obscures all things more in accordance with her fancy than the truth. Athenian history, as I judge it, was quite rich and magnificent, but still somewhat less than its reputation. But because men of great talent were born there, Athenian deeds are celebrated throughout the world as the greatest. So it is that the *virtus* of those who act is considered to be as great as men of brilliant talent are able to exalt it in their words. The Roman people, on the other hand, never had such resources because the most judicious men were the most active, none used his talent without his body, all the best men preferred to act rather than speak, preferred that their good deeds be praised by others rather than themselves tell the stories of others.

The words *Atheniensium res gestae … celebrantur* are obviously modelled on Thucydides 1. 10. 2 and this parallelism provides the clue to Sallust's intention. Sallust is surely implying that in him Rome has at last found her Thucydides. Syme's remarks are to the point:

> Because of the historical and personal situation, [Sallust] might discern a congeniality with Thucydides, which he was impelled to enhance, deliberately. Thucydides knew war and government, he failed as a general, and he wrote in exile. The subject of his history was the empire of the Athenians and how it was brought to ruin.[18]

IMITATION IN SALLUST'S SOURCES

Such are the examples which I have to offer in support of my thesis that consideration of the original contexts of borrowed matter can sometimes disclose a belief or attitude of Sallust himself. If the same technique can be shown to be present in those authors who were Sallust's own sources, it is not unreasonable to maintain that the thesis thereby receives further

---

[18] Syme 1964: 56.

confirmation. Such is the case: I give several specimens from Isocrates, Xenophon, Polybius,[19] and (possibly) Plato.

Of Isocrates Werner Jaeger has written:

> Plato, with the *Apology*, was the first to convert the speech of defence into a literary form in which a great man could defend his 'activity' ($\pi\rho\hat{\alpha}\gamma\mu\alpha$) and thereby utter a confession of faith. The egotistical Isocrates must have been deeply impressed by this new autobiographical pattern, and in the Antidosis speech he adapted it after his own manner. Of course, his life had none of that background of heroic struggle which sets off the noble and steadfast figure of Socrates in the *Apology*; and yet he clearly felt that his position was closely similar to Socrates', for *he took every opportunity to remind the reader of it by verbal imitations of Plato's words and of the accusation aimed at Socrates*.[20]

The parallelism (Isocrates: 'Socrates' :: Sallust: Plato) is striking and needs no comment.

In Book 1. 73–8 Thucydides records an Athenian speech purportedly given at Sparta shortly before the start of the Peloponnesian War; in this speech an attempt is made to explain and justify Athenian foreign policy. The orator points out, inter alia, that, if the Spartans should conquer the Athenians, the hatred which now is directed against Athens would soon be directed against Sparta (1. 77. 6). Many have seen in this a *vaticinium ex eventu* (a theological term for 'a prophecy written after the event'). However that may be, Xenophon in his *Hellenica* (3. 5. 8–15) puts into the mouth of a Theban envoy, pleading at Athens in the year 395 for Athenian assistance against Sparta, a speech which sets forth the fulfilment of this prophecy. This speech must be an intentional parallel to the speech in Thucydides, as Jaeger pointed out in his *Demosthenes*:

> I do not know whether anyone has as yet noticed the fact of the complete parallelism between this speech with its leitmotiv and the speech of the Athenian in Thuc. 1. 77. 6. This parallelism cannot be other than deliberate. To mention but one example, we may point out how Xenophon connects his history with the episode of the Melians in Thuc. 5. 84–115, when dealing with the imminent fall of Athens in *Hell.* 2. 2. 10. Even if one does not see this in Xenophon's general formulation in § 10, the immediately preceding section prevents any misunderstanding; for there Lysander's recolonization of the Melians is referred to expressly. When, in the very same breath,

---

[19] For imitations of Isocrates in Sallust, see Perrochat 1949: 67–72; Avenarius 1957: 79–80. For imitations of Xenophon, see Perrochat 1949: 61–66; Avenarius 1957: 59–64. For an imitation of Polybius, compare *B.C.* 2. 4–6 with Polyb. 10. 36. 5–7; see further Avenarius 1957: 64–6.

[20] Jaeger 1945: 133; the italics are mine.

A Traditional Pattern of Imitation 113

Xenophon makes the Athenians dread the fate of the Melians for themselves, his insistence on this change of rôles is unmistakeably a reference to the argument of the Melians in Thuc. 5. 90 that it is to the interest of the Athenians to let equity reign, as they might easily find themselves in the same situation (καὶ πρὸς ὑμῶν οὐχ ἧσσον τοῦτο ὅσῳ καὶ ἐπὶ μεγίστῃ τιμωρίᾳ σφαλέντες ἂν τοῖς ἄλλοις παράδειγμα γένοισθε ['And for you this is no less important inasmuch as in addition to being the greatest punishment your fall would be a warning for others.']). This prophecy is now fulfilled. We may conclude from these observations that Xenophon regards his work as continuing that of Thucydides in more than the mere fact that it joins on to the earlier work at a definite point of time. *It is obvious that in such passages as these he has striven for unity with Thucydides not only in his description of events, but in his inner attitude as well.*[21]

Paul Friedländer has published an analysis of the famous passage in Polybius (31. 23–30) in which the character and education of Scipio Africanus Minor are described.[22] It was Friedländer's merit to have observed and demonstrated that in this passage the well-known conversation between Polybius himself and young Scipio contains a number of similarities with the conversation of Socrates and the young Alcibiades in the *First Alcibiades*.[23] For details the reader may be referred to Friedländer's paper; I give here only some of his conclusions:

> The event [sc. the conversation between Polybius and Scipio]... evoked the scene from Plato's dialogue in Polybius' mind. He saw Scipio and himself as the more fortunate counterparts of Alcibiades and Socrates. The educational work which he accomplished with the son of Aemilius and consequently with the young Roman nobility he felt to be initiated, directed, and sanctioned by the great example. And he was not mistaken of course.[24]

Once again we may set up a proportion—Alcibiades: 'Socrates' :: Scipio: Polybius. As in Sallust, the proportion is founded on the use of traditional material with reference to the original context. The relevance of Polybius to our study does not end here; in another place Friedländer writes:

> But Polybius not only quotes, uses, and criticizes Plato freely, he enters into a competition with him. Referring to what one may call the central

---

[21] Jaeger 1938: 208 n. 12 (= Jaeger 1940: 204 n. 12); the italics are mine.
[22] Friedländer 1945: 337–51 (= Friedländer 1968: 323–32).
[23] Whether or not the *First Alcibiades* is a genuine work of Plato is a matter of indifference here. It was believed to be genuine and indeed was often used as an introduction to the 'Socratic' philosophy in later antiquity. It is in fact a good introduction for such purposes. My own opinion is that it is spurious.
[24] Friedländer 1945: 347 (= Friedländer 1968: 332).

postulate of the *Republic* (473C–D, 479B–C), the identity of ruler and philosopher, he demands in almost the same words [12. 28. 2–5] that the active statesman write history or that the historian have an active rule in the state: 'Until this happens there will be no end to the ignorance of the historians.' He himself is convinced that in his person are merged the philosopher and the statesman, the statesman and the historian, and his very wording shows how strongly he felt himself to be on a par with Plato.[25]

I do not know whether it has been observed how very similar, *mutatis mutandis*, are the attitudes which appear in Sallust: the contrast between the theoretic life of the philosopher and the practical life of the historian implicit in the use of the Seventh Letter, the combination of 'the philosopher and the statesman, the statesman and the historian' in Sallust himself (so, at least, he would have us believe), the placing of himself, as shown 'by his very wording', on a par with Thucydides as his Roman counterpart. On all this, compare above; here I call attention to the fact that the analogies with Polybius show Sallust to have used, once more, traditional material in a traditional way.

Platonic examples of this technique are more difficult to establish, in part because of the complexity of the man. I confine myself to one possible illustration. Several scholars have called attention to apparent verbal echoes, in the *Apology*, of Gorgias' *Palamedes* and have drawn conclusions therefrom. Coulter summarizes the situation thus:

> In a succinct and important study, Joseph Morr pointed to the verbal echoes in Plato and concluded that they are conscious allusions to the Gorgianic work; by reminding the reader, Morr argued, of an earlier account of a wise man unjustly condemned, Plato endeavored to set Socrates against the larger backdrop of myth, and to enlarge thereby the meaning of his death. Essentially the same view was held by A. H. Chroust in a later study; this scholar made a special contribution by suggesting that the conception of Palamedes as the archetype of the dishonored philosopher was already current and accessible to Plato.[26]

Unfortunately, the question of the relationship of the *Apology* to the *Palamedes* is not an easy one and there are chronological uncertainties. But if these scholars are correct, then Plato also has used older material whose full significance in its Platonic surroundings can only be understood by taking into account the original context.

---

[25] Friedländer 1945: 344–5 (= Friedländer 1968: 330).
[26] Coulter 1964: 269. See Coulter's paper for references and further details. For Plato's attitude to the mythical Palamedes, see Friedländer 1968: 234.

A Traditional Pattern of Imitation

Plato, as Hermann Diels observed,[27] is a Proteus and with this complex genius we begin to wander too far from Sallust, whose literary artifices are simple in comparison. Let us, therefore, conclude here with a respectful wish that our demonstration of the presence of a traditional 'imitation technique' in Sallust may be pleasing, and perhaps even convincing, to the distinguished Latinist in whose honour this paper has been written.

---

[27] I once heard Werner Jaeger attribute this observation to Diels.

5

The Accounts of the Catilinarian Conspiracy

Eduard Schwartz

By the time Sallust published his representation of the Catilinarian conspiracy, more than twenty years had passed since the events he narrated. It was a long time for those who had lived through them. A rift such as that between 1792 and 1815, between 1848 and 1870, lay between the dictatorship of Caesar and the final victory of the Senate. That scuffle with a band of aristocratic troublemakers must have seemed like a storm in a teacup compared with the calamity that reduced the proud edifice of the world-ruling oligarchy to a hopeless pile of rubble.

The man who believed himself to have saved the state in those days maintained a proud confidence in his deeds even into the time when there was 'no longer any commonwealth', and he did not allow the years to destroy the monument to his past which he had erected in his heart. But this was not enough: Cicero missed no opportunity to transmit his deeds to posterity in such a way that he would not come off so badly in the annals as he had in his political life, where the Roman oligarchy, through lesser and greater insults, constantly reminded the honest and vain man of Arpinum that it always had at least as much to offer the greatest rascal born in its centre as it did to the municipal parvenu.[1] The letter to Pompey, the publication of his consular speeches, the incessant mentions of the fifth of December in the Senate and the courts were not enough: he wanted even to read of his glory within his lifetime. The Greek poetry of the day was debased enough that a Κικερωνιάς (the title of a Greek poem about Cicero) need not appear an artistic monstrosity, but his own client Archias left him in the lurch and preferred to sing to Lucullus.[2] The great

---

[1] *Fam.* 1.9.10ff., 7. 7ff.   [2] *Att.* 1. 16. 15.

Posidonius, then old and infirm, declined with a tactful compliment to develop the sketch sent over by his 'friend' into a richly coloured portrait, as would have been expected of his artistry.[3] The critical orator was reluctant to entrust his laurels to the typical scribblers,[4] since even Atticus' pamphlet seemed to him too plain in its classicism;[5] thus, he himself undertook, in the most pompous Greek he was capable of, to compose a memoir about his consulship. In doing so he could invoke the examples of Rutilius Rufus and Sulla; moreover, nothing prevented a Roman from making it clear to the *Graeculi* ('little Greeks', a derogatory diminutive) that not only was he a great man, but he had also mastered their language. Even a Latin memoir[6] was a possibility. What was dubious, however, was his decision to become his own Ennius and to glorify himself in epic; this ran contrary to all tradition, and he himself was uneasy about the project.[7]

Then came the disaster of 58 and the glorious return a year later. But the new alliance of rulers early in the year 56 brought an abrupt end to his rekindled hope of occupying a leading position in the Senate. The consular, who had now discovered that the nobility had no thought of identifying with such a parvenu, preferred to serve the function of a satellite for those in power; but the more bitterly he perceived that the dream of his youth, to enter on an equal footing into the storied, honourable tradition of the Scipios, Metelli, and others, was forever out of his reach—that the same *optimates* who had abandoned him in 58 now once again looked blithely on as he drifted away from Pompey, and to his chagrin flattered Clodius—the more hotly burned his longing to see the great phase of his life, the years in which, as he believed, his destiny was that of Rome, immortalized by the pen of an acknowledged historian in spite of his aristocratic enviers.[8] He wrote a long and showy letter, of which he was quite proud,[9] to a friend of Pompey he was long

---

[3] *Att.* 2. 1. 2.   [4] *Att.* 2. 2. 2.   [5] *Att.* 2. 1. 1.
[6] *Att.* 1. 19. 10.   [7] *Att.* 1. 19. 10.
[8] Originally he wanted to revenge himself on Hortensius with a pamphlet, who must have had a scene with him around then (*Att.* 4. 6. 3), and to throw in his face the 'betrayal' of 58: Hortensius in particular seems to be that 'envier' who advised him in 58 to back down of his own accord, and who warned him about Pompey (*Q. fr.* 1. 3. 8; cf. *Att.* 3. 8. 4, 9. 2, 15. 2, *Fam.* 14. 1, *Dom.* 29, and moreover *Att.* 3. 7. 2, 13. 2, 19. 3, 20. 1, 4. 3. 5, *Fam.* 1. 7. 2, *Red. pop.* 13. 21, *Sest.* 46), holding out the prospect of an immediate return (*Q. fr.* 1. 4. 4). Apparently Cicero had answered Hortensius sharply on that occasion, with the ulterior motive of thereby winning Caesar and Pompey to himself (cf. *Att.* 4. 6. 3 and 4. 5); Atticus was pleased with the insightful strategy and encouraged a pamphlet to make the breach with the *optimates* irreconcilable. Cicero shied away from this: he said he could not betray his hidden intentions, and besides he had no desire to make Hortensius immortal. He preferred a historical narrative of his own fate: his fame was dearer to him than his hatred.
[9] *Att.* 4. 6. 4, *Fam.* 5. 12.

acquainted with, L. Lucceius, with the request to interrupt his historical research and immediately, as soon as possible, to write a history of his deeds, his misfortune, and the atonement he was forced to undergo.

Lucceius was polite enough not to refuse his old acquaintance's request directly,[10] but he never kept his promise, although a year later Cicero reminded him of it and sent a manuscript as the basis for the desired work.[11] In the meantime he had been unable to contain himself and had composed a second poem 'On His Fate', which at first he had reservations about publishing,[12] until finally the author in him, as usual, triumphed over the politician.

Cicero had presented his fame to his contemporaries in outmoded forms: and what else should he have done, struggling as he was for a dying epoch? Atticus knew what he was doing when he urged his friend to reinvent not only the oratorical style, but also the historical; but this was not accomplished by him who saw in history only the means to glorify his own person.[13] Cicero was not spared the distress that, along with the collapse of his political position, his well-deserved literary authority also began to falter. The heightened classicism which Caesar had helped to its position of dominance forgot that not he, but Cicero, had conquered the formlessness of the recent Asianism. The poets of the newer school threw Cicero's verses onto the rubbish heap without a thought; in that period of *Sturm und Drang*, the orator's rattling hexameters were out of fashion before they even saw the light of day. In addition, there was the content: self-praise, panegyric hyperbole to the advantage of his own ego. Thus, these Ciceronian representations of the Catilinarian conspiracy could certainly not be seen as decisive—far from it. However, one must not forget the law of continuity, which applies just as well for historiography as for any other ancient production. Whoever treated the same material after Cicero, however displeased he might been with him, no longer found the material raw, but rather, in a predetermined form: the selection of facts, the groupings were already given. In such a case, an ancient historian will perhaps hollow out the earlier representation, redistribute light and shadow, or rearrange the important factors and motives; but he will never make a *tabula rasa*, never return to the sources anew and erect an entirely new structure from the ground up.

An event such as the Catilinarian conspiracy naturally has its secrets. The question of the men behind the scenes never fell silent and, typically, was never impartially answered. The opponents of Caesar and partisans

---

[10] *Att.* 4. 6. 4.   [11] *Att.* 4. 9. 2, 11. 2.   [12] *Fam.* 1. 9. 23; *Att.* 4.8a.3.
[13] *Leg.* 1. 5ff. The passage must have been composed shortly after the completion of the *De re publica*.

Accounts of the Catilinarian Conspiracy   119

of Pompey circulated quite nasty revelations;[14] Crassus as well had to pay for his enmity towards Pompey. Cicero, who certainly knew a good deal, was cautious in his publications: neither in 60 nor in 56 did he have a reason to make himself enemies. This self-restraint was difficult enough for him, and on more than one occasion—first during Caesar's consulship,[15] then, after Caesar's death, while Antony was in power[16]—he applied his pen to Ἀνέκδοτα (a collection of anecdotes, mentioned in a letter of 3 May 44, and perhaps the same as the 'secret history' mentioned already in early April 59), which, carefully preserved, were meant to attack his enemies at least after his death. This book he quite definitely distinguishes[17] from a plan to treat Caesar's death in the form of a dialogue in the style of Heraclides Ponticus—that is, in such a way that the historical personages themselves appear.[18] Varro was supposed to play a leading role, for which reason he asks to borrow a Varronian dialogue (perhaps the Τρικάρανος ('The Three-Headed', a pamphlet by Varro on the coalition of Pompey, Crassus, and Caesar in 60 BCE)?[19]). In Rome the work was awaited with anticipation;[20] the war with Antony prevented the plan from coming to fruition.

Now, the ancient sources mention a book by Cicero *De consiliis suis*,[21] which is supposed to have contained vicious attacks on his enemies, namely Caesar and Crassus, and to have been published posthumously by his son;[22] the only fragment of it, preserved in two places, blames Caesar and Crassus for having supported Catiline against Cicero in the elections of 64.[23] Because Dio places the composition of the pamphlet immediately after Cicero's return, it cannot have dealt with the events

---

[14] Cf. Suet. *Iul.* 9.   [15] *Att.* 2. 6. 2, 7. 1, 8. 1, 12. 3, 14. 2.
[16] *Att.* 14. 17. 6, *librum meum illum* ἀνέκδοτον *nondum, ut volui, perpolivi.* 16. 11. 3, *librum quem rogas perpoliam et mittam.*
[17] *Att.* 14. 17. 6, *ista vero quae tu contexi vis, aliud quoddam separatum volumen exspectant*; cf. 15. 4. 3 (after he had rejected Atticus' suggestion, in Brutus' name, that he write a speech in celebration of Caesar's murder; cf. 15. 3. 3), '*at*', *inquis*, '*Ἡρακλείδιον aliquid.*' *non recuso id quidem, sed et componendum argumentum est et scribendi exspectandum tempus maturius. licet enim de me ut libet existimes..., me Idus Martiae non delectant.*
[18] *Q. fr.* 3. 5. 1.   [19] *Att.* 15. 13. 3, 16. 11. 3, 12.
[20] *Fam.* 12. 16. 4, *tu, sicut mihi pollicitus es, adiunges me quam primum ad tuos sermones; namque illud non dubito, quin, si quid de interitu Caesaris scribas, non patiaris me minimam partem et rei et amoris tui ferre.* Cf. *Att.* 16. 5. 5.
[21] Asc. 83. 20–2 C *in expositione consiliorum suorum.* Dio 39. 10, βιβλίον... τι ἀπόρρητον συνέθηκε καὶ ἐπέγραψεν αὐτῷ ὡς καὶ περὶ τῶν ἑαυτοῦ βουλευμάτων ἀπολογισμόν τινα ἔχοντι. Charis. p. 146. 31, *in ratione consiliorum suorum.* Otherwise abbreviated *de consiliis suis* or *de consiliis.* Cf. Cic. *Fam.* 5. 12. 9, *nostrorum temporum consilia atque eventus.*
[22] Dio 39. 10, Plut. *Crass.* 13.
[23] Asc. 83. 20–2 C, Plut. *Crass.* 13; see p. 129 below.

of 57; nor can it be identical with the memoir sent to Lucceius, since after the renewal of the triumvirate Cicero would have hesitated to send a libel against Caesar and Crassus to a henchman of Pompey: but it is not impossible that these were the Ἀνέκδοτα written in 44 after Caesar's death, in which the calamity of Caesar, as shown above, cannot have been treated. Dio (or, better, his source) would then have placed the book in the year 57 because it did not extend any further. This assumption causes as little difficulty as the one that Cicero, when he wrote against the 'tyrant', was silent about his political behaviour after the conference at Luca.

This is what was available to Sallust: Cicero's self-praise and the gossip of aristocratic society. As I have said above, the world had become a different one by the time he was writing. And yet one must not forget that great disasters do not tend to rupture with one fell swoop all the intellectual links that connect a new era to a rapidly vanishing one. The personal experience of the older generation is not so quickly uprooted, and a single event, such as the death of a famous man, suddenly makes near-forgotten things current again. It is, for example, quite probable that after Caesar's and Cicero's death the old histories of the sixties were very interesting to the public, and that in particular Cicero's disclosures were avidly read and hotly debated; the alteration in the general world view, however, also asserted itself twice as rapidly. Sallust would doubtless have been in a position to procure himself a great deal of new and reliable material through consultation of the *acta senatus* (records of the actions, discussions, and decisions of the Senate), pamphlet literature, and oral tradition. But one does the ancient writer of history an injustice if one expects from him what belonged to the province of the historical *researcher*, or, according to the ancient terminology, the *grammaticus*. The task of the historian is essentially to produce a work of art, for which he seeks ready-made material. Sallust—who, as an independent *littérateur* in the field of *historia*, a field long accessible to a high-born Roman, sought to recapture the honour he had lost in his political career—was supplied with historical material by a prominent philologist of Greek origin, L. Ateius Philologus,[24] just as Parthenius and C. Iulius Hyginus collected mythological matter for the poets Gallus and Ovid; however, one should not assume that this synopsis of Roman history gave special

---

[24] Suet. *Gram.* 10: *L. Ateius Philologus libertinus Athenis est natus.... coluit postea familiarissime C. Sallustium et eo defuncto Asinium Pollionem, quos historiam componere aggressos alterum breviario rerum omnium Romanarum, ex quibus quas vellet eligeret, instruxit, alterum praeceptis de ratione scribendi.*

attention to the Catilinarian conspiracy. This material was available to Sallust in the form that Cicero had given it.

Sallust's representation of the Catilinarian conspiracy is meant to be a work of art. One may assume offhand that a Roman of Caesar's age, in which the principle of $\mu i\mu\eta\sigma\iota\varsigma$ (the idea that the purpose of a work of art was to imitate action) and learned connoisseurship dominated the artistic discourse, does not produce a work of art following some immanent instinct, under the more or less immediate inspiration of the Muse, but rather consciously follows certain firmly minted principles and rules which some Hellenic doctrine of style abstracted from the models of Hellenic antiquity. This must be accepted all the more readily in light of Cicero's testimony, which deserves absolute credence, that in his day an artistic historiography in the Latin language did not exist—or, more precisely, such a historiography as would do justice to the stylistic sensibility of the time: for it is nonetheless true, though frequently forgotten, that Roman historiography from its very beginning was dominated by a Hellenic historiography which had never been naive.

When one attempts to trace back Sallust's representation to the artistic principles operating within and determining it, it emerges that he stands in sharp contrast to the tendency in historiography that dominates Hellenistic literature from Callisthenes to Posidonius. This is Peripatetic historiography as it was developed, practically, by Callisthenes and Duris, and, theoretically, one may at least suppose, in the writings of Theophrastus and Praxiphanes $\Pi\epsilon\rho i$ $i\sigma\tau o\rho i\alpha\varsigma$ ('Concerning Historical Inquiry'). It emerged from a struggle against, on the one hand, the monotonous formalism of the Isocrateans and, on the other hand, the pseudo-poetic style of Ionic historiography as revived in the time of Alexander; but it is in no way attached to Thucydides, and should probably also be distinguished from that historiography of officers and politicians which emphasized the factual over the artistic—that of king Ptolemy, Hieronymus of Cardia, and above all Polybius. Aristotle himself did not invent this type of historiography; he saw in historical representation only a means, never an end in itself. But the hard judgement he pronounced over historiography as an artistic genre did not eradicate the demand of an educated public to read artistically composed and written works of history, and it would have been astonishing if the Aristotelian doctrine of aesthetic effects and the stylistic principles discovered by him should not have been adapted to this demand. The result of this very rapid adaptation, which indeed was in large part already accomplished during Aristotle's lifetime, is exactly that Peripatetic historiography which rivals tragedy as Aristotle understood it, and which simultaneously took account of the collective spirit of that school which encompassed all knowledge, in that it absorbed what the Ionians had formerly called ἱστορίη ('History'), just as the Master had absorbed Democritus.

The last great exponent of this specifically Hellenistic genre is Posidonius, who, in his treatment of material and in the brilliant colouring of his language, is much more the successor to the great geographical-historical works of Agatharchides than to the pragmatism of Polybius. But this is augmented by something quite idiosyncratic, which was foreign to the Peripatetics with their cool calculation of effects: the dithyrambic swing of the Syrian prophet, who, if not quite deep in sense, was nevertheless sweepingly broad, and who believed that he, though a mixture of Stoic pantheism, Platonic transcendentalism, and Peripatetic knowledge, could bestow a new faith upon the godless world. Already during his lifetime Posidonius had a powerful effect on the Graeco-Roman society then rebuilding itself, and to a still greater degree after the establishment of the world empire at which his world-encompassing doctrine aimed; but those very circles from which Sallust came, the classicists and the Caesarians, faced the last significant writer of the Hellenistic period, the ardent supporter of the Roman oligarchy, with a cool alienation. It alters nothing that the connoisseur easily detects one Posidonian thought after another in the introduction Sallust prefixed to his history of the Catilinarian conspiracy (and thus to his historical output as a whole), such that one could almost be so bold as to use it to furnish an image of a prologue by the Stoic portraitist of world history: since Isocrates' time the prologue had the right to be treated separately. The decisive factor is the method of narration itself, and this is thoroughly different from that of Duris and Phylarchus, Agatharcides and Posidonius. To express myself peripatetically, it lacks ἐνάργεια ('clarity', 'vividness') and πάθος ('emotion', 'passion'). The Peripatetic doctrine of style possesses the art of composing sensational images through the vivid presentation of an abundance of individual moments and the skilful deployment of all aesthetic techniques, and it bequeathed this art, systematically developed, to Alexandrian poetry as well as historiography. The Catilinarian conspiracy offered a fertile opportunity for affecting pieces of this type: one may think of the Senate session of 8 November, 3 December, and 5 December; of the triumphant homecoming of Cicero on the night of 5 December; of the love of Curius and Fulvia. The tragic art of the Peripatetic historian celebrates a glowing triumph whenever such colourful depictions work powerfully on the affect, when sudden changes in fortune, suspenseful περιπέτειαι ('reversals in circumstances), mysterious or horrific scenes titillate the reader's nerves to pangs of delight. Nothing of that in Sallust: and yet how easy it would have been to exploit for these ends Catiline's youth, the secret meetings of the conspirators, the events of the elections in 64 and 63, the failed attack of 7 November, the scenes in Cicero's house on 5 December, or the final desperate struggle, to name just a few. Only a single time does the narrative take a small step towards the gruesome: as the execution of the Catilinarians is about to be told, the dreadful Tullianum is described, but briefly and cursorily as if the author did not consider it of primary importance to send a shiver down the reader's spine; thus, the exception confirms the rule. From the tragedy of the decadent period Peripatetic historians borrowed the figure of Tyche, who, depending on the author's whim, could play the role of blind destiny or poetic justice; and this whole theatrical apparatus became such a firm fixture of the historical style that not even the sober rationalist Polybius could bring himself to cast it off, however strange this last, ghostly remnant of poetry or quasi-poetry appears amid his doctrinaire, unsparing omniscience. Sallust knows no Tyche and no Nemesis. Only once does he seem to forget himself: when he describes how Catiline's grisly bloodguilt drives him on to his last and greatest crime (15). Here the analogue in mind is the tragic $ἄτη$ ('the blindness/recklessness that leads to ruin'); a resonance with, for example, the C. Gracchus of Posidonius,[25] driven to ruin by the Erinyes, cannot be ruled out. It will become clear that this stylistic slip has its own particular cause. For the moment this slip suffices to prove that it was not stylistic inability or ignorance of Hellenistic technique that led Sallust onto such divergent paths. On the contrary, the Hellenistic technique of the historical novel, in large part introduced by Coelius Antipater and further developed by Sisenna, was certainly still at that time the historiographical form that one was likeliest to encounter; whoever, like Sallust, disdained it, did not do so out of inability or by mere coincidence, but rather out of opposition, in order to replace it with something better.

Instead of a series of brilliant, gruesome, theatrically daring images, he presents his plot with a compact rationality, abstaining from every directly aesthetic effect; only indirectly, imperceptibly to the reader, does he heighten interest through concentration on the essential. The narrative is meant to compel the judgement that this historian wants to write history for those with understanding, and will not try his luck on the aesthetic delectation of a large audience. Just as detail is only very sparingly presented, so the reader is given but few dates: only there where they serve to underline the two most outstanding moments, the beginning of the conspiracy and the first taking up of arms by the

---

[25] Diod. 34.28a. Cf. Schwartz 1896a: 799.

insurgent army,[26] or where the impression of especial reliability must be conjured.[27] The author proceeds just as meticulously with the number of personal appearances: he made it a strict law for himself to mention no character only once; each person named by him must appear at least twice.[28] Speeches are put in the mouths only of main figures who are characterized through them: one at the beginning and one at the end by Catiline himself, and one each for Caesar and Cato; in addition to these there is Catiline's letter to Catulus and Manlius' message to Q. Marcius Rex. The characterizations correspond to the speeches, as indeed those of Caesar and Cato are directly attached to their speeches. But while among Catiline's accomplices only the leader of the insurrection army speaks, and that a single time, Catiline's characterization is complemented by that of a woman, Sempronia,[29] and even more strikingly a woman who, although she appears a second time in keeping with the law just mentioned, never decisively intervenes in the course of events. The characterizations of Q. Curius and of Cethegus[30] are not on the same level as the others; these are meant only to explain an element of the plot, and not to awaken the reader's interest in the personality as such. The depictions of morality and mood belong among the characterizations as well. These, too, are carefully balanced against one another and located at significant places. The introduction to the characterizations of Caesar and Cato corresponds to the depiction of the oligarchy at the beginning; in the middle, the popular party is brought to the fore with a longer treatment and two sharply opposed descriptions of the behaviour of the urban mob.[31]

Only a writer in possession of a thoroughly developed historiographical theory could compose like this. That the theory Sallust followed took Thucydides as its point of departure is beyond doubt. The attempt to create an impression of objectivity, the peculiar use of speeches, the contempt for any detail inessential to the statesman prove this, even without the hallmarks of an imitation which strives with all the means at the Latin language's disposal to produce the $\xi\acute{\epsilon}\nu o\nu$ ('strangeness') and the $\sigma\epsilon\mu\nu\acute{o}\nu$ ('solemnity') of the Thucydidean style. But in calling Sallust an imitator of Thucydides, one must not believe one has said everything. For one thing, this alone is not sufficient to explain everything. Neither

---

[26] 17. 1, 30. 1.   [27] 18. 5, 6.
[28] This explains Wirz's observation on the list of conspirators (Wirz 1864: 47). The M. Fulvius Nobilior mentioned here must, according to this rule, be identical with the Fulvius whose death is narrated at 39. 5. As the son of senator who has himself not yet made it into the Senate, he is relegated to equestrian status.
[29] 25.   [30] 23. 1–2, 43. 4.   [31] 31 and 48.

the depictions of morality with their historical retrospectives nor the elaborate characterizations correspond to the method of Thucydides, who, as Bruns [Bruns 1896 (eds.)] has shown, never foregrounds his characters in rounded-off portraits set off from the narration. But even leaving aside this deviation, which, however it may be explained, shows no more than that imitation was oriented towards particular considerations, it is inconceivable that Sallust discovered what was imitable in Thucydides through nothing else than his reading of him, that Sallust himself abstracted from Thucydides the artistic laws he followed. That could only have been accomplished by a Greek, philosophically educated literary critic. I do not know who it was, and I doubt whether we shall ever learn his name; much more important than that is to recognize that in Sallust's time there existed a classicizing Greek theory of historiography, which, in contrast to the pomp of Hellenistic novels, demanded a return to the proud, purely political manner of Thucydides, contemptuous of the general public's need for dramatization, and which derived its laws from him. Tellingly, however, this did not mean that the facts themselves needed to be carefully corroborated according to primary sources; the theory of $\mu\iota\mu\eta\sigma\iota\varsigma$ applied only to the artistic form, not to the scientific research.

As important as the artistic factor is for the evaluation of Sallust, it would be wrong to believe that he intended his historical works to be mere paradigms of a new historiographical theory, as, for example, Caecilius and Dionysius had theirs. What is characteristic of this epoch of Roman literature—that Hellenism provides only the formal theory, while the Romans pour their own life into this mould—reveals itself in historiography as well as in oratory and poetry. Sallust is a political historian not only because a historiography which aims to be Thucydidean must primarily bring out the interplay of politically effective forces, but also much more by virtue of being a Roman, a contemporary of the revolution. In this point even pre-Sallustian Roman historiography distinguished itself from its teacher, Hellenistic historiography, which, rivalling poetry, had grown up in the tranquillity of domestic politics under the Hellenistic monarchs and did not know the passions of partisan struggle, or knew them only in hazy images. By contrast, the frantic struggle of parties and politicians in Rome began at exactly the point when Hellenistic historiography was more and more deeply infiltrating annalistic writing, and it was inevitable that its artistic devices be used not only for aesthetic, but also for political ends. By no means did Sallust abandon the old, traditional ends for the sake of the new techniques; on the contrary, he accomplished those ends all the more securely since his techniques gave the narrative a character so factual and so averse to all gossiping and sensational detail. The finely ramifying veins, the beating pulse of the Sallustian work, will become clearly visible only when it has been shown how his artistic techniques, the economy of his work as a whole, and the structure of his narrative relate to his political intentions.

Sallust belonged to that *perdita iuventus* ('ruined/desperate/hopeless youth')[32] which hoped for salvation from Caesar, and found it in him in only too generous supply. Good Roman society regarded these pirates of the revolution as bitterly as French society did the comrades of Napoleon III, and rejected them after their leader's death unless they possessed some or other instrument of power. Sallust, who had no other claims to reputation than a thrashing in Milo's boudoir, a turbulent tribunate, the flight from Caesar's mutinous veterans, and the plundered province of Africa, was clever enough to recognize that there was nothing more that could be salvaged for him politically, and took up the pen to revenge himself against the arrogant oligarchy whose misdeeds so abundantly counterbalanced and outweighed his own. He had rightly identified the sphere for his abilities: already his first attempt became a political artwork of the highest rank.

L. Catilina nobili genere natus ('L. Catiline, born to a noble family'): these words simultaneously introduce the narrative and his literary battle against the nobility. No opportunity is missed to emphasize the aristocratic pedigree of the conspirators; in the list of participants only the high-born are mentioned (17). Cn. Piso is characterized (18. 4) with the words *adulescens nobilis, summae audaciae, egens factiosus* ('a noble young man, full of recklessness, no money, a partisan'); Curius, *natus haud obscuro loco* ('born in no mean circumstances'), forms a fine pair together with Fulvia, *muliere nobili* ('a noble woman', 23. 1, 3), Cato cries out to his peers in the Senate that *coniuravere nobilissumi cives patriam incendere* ('they conspired, the most noble citizens, to burn down the fatherland', 52. 24), and Lentulus, strangled in the Tullianum, is sounded out with a cutting sneer (55. 6): *ita ille patricius ex gente clarissuma Corneliorum, qui consulare imperium Romae habuerat, dignum moribus factisque suis exitium vitae invenit* ('and so that patrician, from the very famous family of the Cornelii, a man who had held consular power, found an end of life worthy of his character and actions').

---

[32] Cic. *Ad Att.* 7. 7. 6. Asinius Pollio, the parvenu from the land of the Marrucini and by no means a Roman of old heritage, belonged to it as well; his diplomatically oblique confession (*Fam.* 10. 31. 2) is nevertheless clear enough. Caesar's own judgement is representative (Suet. *Iul.* 72).

These are only the superficial sparks of a hatred that burns much deeper. The Catilinarian conspiracy deserves to be narrated 'because the criminal attitude that came to light in it and the danger into which it brought the state were unique in their kind'; thus he momentously concludes the proem. The question immediately arises: how was a character like Catiline able to develop so dangerously? Because his development took place within a fully corrupt and debased oligarchy: this discussion, beginning with the words *incitabant praetera corrupti civitatis mores* ('in addition, the corrupt moral character of the state urged him on') and ending with the epanalepsis *in tanta tamque corrupta civitate* ('in a state so great and so corrupt'), is significantly inserted into the characterization of the protagonist placed at the beginning, in order to leave room for no other idea than that the single cause of the dreadful crime against the state was the degeneracy of the ruling caste. This was fatefully stimulated by the Sullan restoration, which reinstated the government of the nobility. Sulla made greed into the dominant vice, which even destroyed the discipline of the Roman army (11); his *dominatio* ('the domination of Sulla', i.e. the period of his dictatorship, 82–80 BCE) revealed to Catiline the goals for which he strove; his proscriptions did likewise for the Catilinarians (5. 6, 21. 4); his veterans were the future tyrant's hope (16. 4).

Thus, the conspiracy that formed in 64 appears as the natural and inevitable outgrowth of the oligarchy, whose nature is revealed in it. Nobody can fail to be affected by the tightly structured crescendo of this beginning; and yet a small gap in this construction reveals that the entirety is an artificial creation—namely, the very inconsistency, mentioned above, that the Thucydidean historian inserts a motif of the very Peripatetic historiography he otherwise condemns, with his picture of Catiline hounded onto the path of crime by the pangs of his conscience. He was lacking a specific catalyst to set events in motion at precisely *this* time, and he knew no other way to fill this gap than with an exclusively poetic conceit. This betrays that the author himself was uncomfortable with the causal connection he had established, since its combinations destroyed the natural logical coherence of the main tradition.

Since the studies of Wirz[33] and John[34] it is agreed that Catiline did not form his conspiracy until his defeat in the consular elections of July 63 confronted him with the prospect of financial and political ruin. Only with the recognition of this fact does it become possible both to

---

[33] Wirz 1864.
[34] John 1876a and 1876b. I assume familiarity with these treatments in the following.

appreciate the artistry with which Sallust has reshaped his narrative of the beginnings of the conspiracy into a devastating condemnation of the oligarchy and to explain the reason for that stylistic lapse just mentioned. As he had carefully excluded all coincidences in order to develop as strongly as possible the causal relationship between the corruption of the oligarchy and the crime of Catiline, he could not use the negative consequences of an electoral defeat as the cause for the outbreak of the conspiracy, but rather had to resort to an internal psychological process—even leaving aside the ease with which such a process recommends itself to invention. At the same time, he accomplished yet another goal related to his struggle against the oligarchy.

For years Catiline had been a mere tool of Crassus and Caesar in the agitations by which they sought to create a counterweight to Pompey's military power; it was their abandonment of him, as the death of Mithridates in 63 gave hope that the victorious *imperator* ('commander', 'general') might soon return, which drove him to his mad attempt at revolution. These two had engaged him to recruit gangs for the intended coup; they supported his candidacy in 64. Sallust's position in relation to these events was predetermined: Caesar had to be exculpated under any circumstances; Crassus could take the blame. This had the result, first, of elevating Catiline's importance higher than corresponded to the reality, since one of the men who engaged him had to disappear. At the same time this achieved the artistic advantage that the focal point of the whole acquired that captivating quality which always accompanies a villain of the grand style. He made this villain emerge with the finest wickedness from the lap of the oligarchy that bitterly accused Caesar for having used such a man as his tool. Now, it would not have recommended itself to push the date for the invented, spontaneous emergence of the conspiracy up to the year 66, for in this case the period in which it did nothing would be too long; but if it were placed in 64, then the affairs leading up to the elections of this year, which were seriously compromising for Caesar, would disappear; and the single year between this and the consular *comitia* of 63 could then easily be filled with that old standby of rhetorical historiography, the doublet. Of course, it was then unavoidable that in the first conspiracy—that of 66/5—Catiline did not appear alone. But Sallust mitigated the difficulty in that, alongside Cicero the advocate but in contrast to Cicero the rapporteur,[35] he represented the matter as if Catiline had wanted to secure the consulship for Autronius and himself, not for the former and P. Sulla. He then inserted the entire narrative as

---

[35] Cf. Cic. *Sull.* 67ff.

an ancillary episode with one quite significant connection—namely, the mention of the suspicions that Crassus knew about the conspiracy of 64. His share in the events of 66/5 is never considered in the narrative proper: only by way of his reporting the rumour that Cn. Piso was murdered at Pompey's instigation does the clever author allow a gentle shadow—perhaps no more than a shadow of slander—to fall upon the man. Caesar is not mentioned at all. With the auspicious, not to say brazen words *quam verissume potero dicam* ('I will tell as accurately as I can'), all sensationalist divulgences[36] are rejected as idle gossip.

His procedure is quite different when he speaks of the involvement of Crassus and Caesar in the conspiracy of 63. If, like a good advocate, he had simply said nothing when Caesar's case was quite bad, so here, faced with a probably false and at any rate unprovable charge, he moves into an open attack (49): the villainous machinations of the oligarchic leaders, brought on by personal enmity, wanted to plunge the innocent man into ruin. And the Catulus who dared to slander Caesar was the same man whom Catiline honoured with a confidential letter, and to whom he entrusted his children (35). Both are meant to complement each other to yield a far from flattering picture of the celebrated leader of the *optimates* (literally, 'the best', 'the noblest', the name by which the aristocrats referred to themselves)[37] and arch-enemy of Caesar. To understand why Catiline turns to him, one must remember that it was through Catulus' influence that Catiline is supposed to have been acquitted in the trial regarding the Vestals in 73.[38]

It could only heighten the credibility of Caesar's apology if Crassus once again were not entirely whitewashed. Here, too, the historian leaves the matter undecided with refined narrative technique. He speaks of the subsequent denunciation of L. Tarquinius, but says nothing of the most dangerous piece of evidence: the anonymous letter from the conspirators to Crassus, which the latter gave to Cicero;[39] instead he prefers to bring in that ever-ready spy Fulvia. It would have diminished Catiline too much if more than a mere hint of suspicion were to fall on Crassus.

---

[36] Cf. Suet. *Iul.* 9.

[37] Dio 37. 46. 3, i.e., Livy, characterizes him with the words ὁ διαφανέστατα τῶν πώποτε τὸ δημόσιον ἀεὶ πρὸ παντὸς προτιμήσας: the judgement is borrowed, in deliberate contrast to Sallust, from Cicero: cf. *Sest.* 101, *qualis nuper Catulus fuit quem neque periculi tempestas neque honoris aura potuit umquam de suo cursu aut spe aut metu demovere*. Cf. also Cic. *Ad Att.* 2. 24. 4 (from the year 59), *nihil me <iudice> fortunatius est Catulo cum splendore vitae tum hoc tempore*, that is: lucky Catulus, that he died in full bloom before living through these times; the ellipsis is understandable as it is.

[38] Oros. 6. 3. 1.   [39] Plut. *Crass.* 13, *Cic.* 15; Dio 37. 31. 1.

The remarkably unmotivated characterization of Sempronia has already been noticed above, and it leads one to suppose, in light of the rigid economy of the Sallustian work, that it has an interest lying outside the narrative. I think others[40] have been right to suspect that, by way of his mother, D. Brutus, the assassin of Caesar, is the real target here.

As has been shown, Sallust elevated Catiline above the level consistent with the historical reality, but he remains true to his intention of representing him as a villain inevitably sprung from the oligarchy in that he consistently suppresses his anarchistic agitations. In place of the speech by which he aligned himself with the oppressed at the *comitia* of 63,[41] Sallust reports the exhortation to Catiline's ruined aristocratic comrades[42] that they no longer allow a small minority of their peers to usurp all the power of the government and to wallow in aimless luxury. He awards only a marginal importance to the social element and shifts the role of its representative from Catiline onto the leader of the army of the insurrection, C. Manlius: in his message to Q. Marcius Rex, the wretchedness of the truly oppressed receives expression. But this interests him only in so far as it affords him the opportunity for a new attack against the Sullan order, which he carries out in such a way that, with a remarkable reworking of Cicero's account,[43] he casts the Sullan veterans into the background, says nothing at all of their involvement in the electoral campaigning of 63, suppresses the suggestion that Manlius himself belonged to the army settled by Sulla,[44] and instead makes the farmers driven off their homesteads by Sulla's land allocations the heart of the army collected by Manlius.[45] All in all he leaves no doubt that he preferred to see in these elements the same subordinate position as that of Manlius in comparison to Catiline.

The masses of the metropolis appear even worse. A debased, ragtag mob, they watch the collapse of the state with unabashed pleasure. Weighty inculpations are again levelled against Sulla: the noxious effect of his proscriptions had operated through the embitterment of the financially and politically ruined descendants of those ostracized and through the evil example of the wretched parvenus who enriched themselves by the tyrant's victories. The pressure of the oligarchy became intolerable when, in Pompey's absence, no worthy opponent challenged it. But even the leaders of the popular party basically did no more than follow their own interests. The Caesarian publicist betrays himself in the mention of the restitution of the tribunate by Pompey: Caesar's

---

[40] Cf. Stern 1883: 124.   [41] Cic. *Mur.* 50.

[42] At 20. 7 one should read *ceteri omnes boni strenui nobiles, volgus fuimus sine gratia*, etc.; *ignobiles* is evidently an interpolation.

[43] Sal. *Cat.* 2. 20; Cic. *Mur.* 49.   [44] Cic. *Cat.* 2. 20.   [45] 28. 4.

democratic opposition is omitted, and Pompey, the future hero of the senatorial party, is stamped as a democrat.

Thus, the portrait of Catiline's personality and the depiction of the situation in Italy and Rome unite to form a continuous indictment of the oligarchy. The whole culminates in the debate between Caesar and Cato and in the syncrisis of the two. The much-maligned Caesar is the only bastion of lawful freedom, the true refuge of the oppressed: his aim is a wide berth to exercise his superior ability, not the languid pleasure into whose arms the oligarchy hurls itself. With great artistry, the self-sufficient virtue of Cato, which spurns every superficiality and dishonest means, is drawn in contrast to this; one is meant to admire it but consider it impractical, and on the other hand to love Caesar for all his faults; for these benefit not himself but others.

It is quite remarkable, and a proof of the persuasive power of death, that so soon after the death of Caesar and many years before the refounding of the monarchy, the figure of Cato had already become such an ideal of Stoic, unworldly virtue that even an ardent Caesarian, heedless of the sharp attacks with which his master had attempted to destroy this dangerous idol, considered it advisable to set this ideal in all its splendour beside the image of the mighty dictator, and indeed even to model this image after it: for everyone will perceive that in Sallust's syncrisis the portrait of Cato contains the acute, primary strokes, and that the portrait of Caesar merely inverts these. With incomparable skill the brilliance of this ideal is now used to cast the darkest shadow upon the oligarchy, deeper and darker than any that the historian elsewhere casts upon it. If this strict, incorruptible man of the most upright justice cannot rouse the cowardice and greed of the rulers by any other means than by the threat that their property and standard of living are at risk, if he must cry out 'Look on and stand idly by, if you must, while your allies are plundered and the treasury is embezzled, only do not be so honourable as to protect *everyone* in your social class'—then the impartial reader must admit that such a government is irredeemably lost.

Catiline, the nefarious criminal from a noble house; Cato, the lone paragon of virtue; Caesar, the appointed benefactor to the world: the Sallustian artwork culminates in these three figures. This is no coincidence. In the introduction to the syncrisis of Cato and Caesar he enlightens his readers, in dry, unmistakable words, that history is made by only a handful of significant characters. A few brought Rome to greatness; then followed the ages in which there were only mediocrities. This is a cuttingly sharp contradiction of the judgement Cato and Polybius had pronounced, with their deep understanding of the nature of an oligarchic republic: that Rome had not become great through the conscious actions of one man, but rather through a gradual, organic development.[46] Out of this contradiction, this bitter judgement of the time that counted as the most glorious for republicans,[47] there wafts the acerbic hatred of a man who was too talented and too ambitious to accept quietly the role of outcast which republican society had foisted upon him; but there wafts also, out of the word of the servant, the spirit of the master, of the Καῖσαρ βασιλεύς ('Caesar the King') who looked down on his peers with the sovereign contempt of genius, to whom the pride of the Roman Senate was an absurd prejudice and the centuries-old tradition of the nobility a lifeless spectre, who audaciously planned to wrest the nimbus of the *caput orbis terrarum* ('the capital of the world') away from the Capitol.

Caesar's plans were not compatible with *imperium Romanum* ('Roman imperial power'), but with a Graeco-Roman βασιλεία ('monarchy'); a new world was supposed to arise. In the classicism and strict imitation of Greek models with which the Roman youth opposed itself to older Roman literature, he recognized with the sharp vision of a great revolutionary the germ of a new style which was capable of exploding, or at least radically changing, the forms that grew up in the Republic; his intervention helped this opposition to its victory. Sallustian historiography is a part of this struggle of new and old. Not only is the curt, nobly self-restrained, objective Thucydidean in conflict with the sensational, tragic pomp of the Hellenistic historical novel; this is also the struggle of a man of a new age against traditional annalistic writing. The latter, in a nearly endless copiousness which stifled the individual character, had presented the nobility in the style of the tables of magistrates; deeds of war and triumphs followed one upon another in a series; the stable element in this flurry of events and impressions was the Senate, to which the most brilliant and popular annalist, Valerius Antias, consistently gave precedence. There was an oppositional, democratic kind of annalistic history, but it created no new forms; it retained the entire apparatus of oligarchic *annales* (the yearly records kept by the chief priest in Rome) and simply inserted the tribunes in place of the consuls and *patres* ('fathers', a term for senators), so that its falseness stood out more garishly in the contradiction of form and content than its rival, which had stayed true to the old traditions. Sallust is quite different. With smug contempt he pushes aside the robbery of the oligarchic mediocrity;

---

[46] Polyb. 6. 10. 2; Cic. *Rep.* 2. 1. 2.

[47] Cic. *Dom.* 130, *tempus illud erat tranquillum et in libertate populi et gubernatione positum senatus* ('that time was peaceful; it found rest both in the people's freedom and in the Senate's control').

no senatorial debates are reported at length; no list of magistrates is given; everything is concentrated on three pre-eminent personalities. For the revolutionary only the individual has any significance, the circumstances not at all; he rouses especial interest for Catiline when he compels contempt for the oligarchy. In this political, aggressive individualism lurks the reason that drove Sallust to characterize his heroes extensively, in contrast to the truly Thucydidean manner. For him, individual traits are not important in so far as they determine political events: rather, the state, apart from a small, opaque remnant, becomes visible in the personality. The oligarchs' social standing suppressed the individual; the Caesarian accordingly protests against it by pushing this standing, together with the masses, into the background and allowing the most glaring light that his art can produce to fall on individuals.

By now one question above all will have occurred to the reader of this study, to which one may rightly demand an answer: if Sallust had his narrative unfold through individual personalities, then where is that personality who claimed centre stage for himself throughout his lifetime and, more importantly, in the only historical treatments available in Sallust's time—the consul of 63, the hero of the fifth of December, M. Tullius Cicero? He was a personality, he was an individual if anyone was, though admittedly not one in whom the nature of the state could become visible. It was the tragedy of his life that his personality was too good for the sphere which he wanted to conquer for it and which he would not give up trying to conquer. Having grown up in the fresh and unsullied mountain air of his *municipium* (a town in Italy which possessed the rights of Roman citizenship), his chest swelling with the traditional ideal of republican magistracy and the *patres conscripti* ('Conscript Fathers', the chosen or elected fathers, a term for Senators), he set himself the goal of winning acceptance into the thoroughly corrupt nobility; the brilliance of the great tradition blinded the novice with redoubled force when he had climbed to its highest rung, and the mature man remained naive enough to cultivate and cherish the ideal of his youth, although he could neither breathe new life into the nobility nor make that sacrifice which every oligarchy demands: that of one's own individuality. His was too sensitive for that, too sonorous, I should say: Cicero's daemon had so arranged it that he wanted only to act, but perceived sensations with the utmost fineness, and could nurture his sensibility in the stream of eloquence, the wit of conversation, and the confessionality of the letter. He was a modern man, and he was fighting for a dying past. This conflict ruined him politically and robbed him of the statesman's reputation for which he so thirsted; if it did not inwardly destroy him, if Cicero in all his political misery nevertheless, to speak

Pindarically, kept swimming back upwards like the cork on the fishing net, this he owed to the God who had granted him to express what he suffered, to the forthright and rich humanity of his soul, which continually inflames the sensibilities of sympathetic hearts.

The time of unbridled civil war during which Sallust wrote was not suited to the understanding of such a person, and if the Lord saw fit that at least the uniqueness of the great master of language should be spared, so the partisan and mortal enemy of the oligarchy was not in a position to do justice to the speaker whose bloody shadow had become a symbol of the Republic's struggle for life and death. Sallust's history of the Catilinarian conspiracy is not only an attack on the oligarchy, not only a defence of Caesar: in addition, it is carefully premeditated, from the first line to the last, to annihilate the person and the narrative of Cicero.

One fact above all betrays where Sallust stood in relation to Cicero: he does not think him worthy of a characterization of his own, so that for those who have grasped the Sallustian laws of composition he comes to rank even below Catiline. Accordingly, the orator is given no oration. At only one point (31. 6) is a speech, the *First Catilinarian*, alluded to, which he himself had published: that is, strictly speaking the speech ought to be inserted at this point, but this is not necessary, since everybody knows it. The speech is considered with apparently flattering predicates: *orationem habuit luculentam atque utilem rei publicae* ('he produced a speech that was brilliant and useful for the republic'). But the narrative interprets these compliments in an extremely peculiar way. After the relevant events have been recounted, the historian interposes a rather long treatment of the situation of the Roman state at the time. What this means for Sallust's position in relation to the people and the popular party has already been explained above; what is relevant here is his evaluation of the state of affairs created by Catiline's departure. It is represented as among the most dangerous situations that had ever prevailed in Rome; the attitude of the metropolitan masses is such that a success on Catiline's part, indeed even an indecisive battle, is sufficient to bring about the dreaded revolution. And whose fault was this? The reader can only answer: Cicero's, who through his speech forced Catiline to flee the city for his military camp. Certainly the 'brilliant' speech had been 'of service to the state'; and yet, as the reflective reader capable of following the author's gestures must complete the compliment, it was not to the orator's credit. The Sallustian law of composition which inserts speeches at decisive points in the plot proves itself even here, where he only gives the locus of the speech. But he refrains from presenting Cicero giving a speech not only for the reason given above: the force of his attack is only strengthened by his invocation of the real speech published by Cicero himself, as if he were unwilling to be in any way suspected of having invented something to the disadvantage of the exalted saviour of the fatherland.

This flaunting of objectivity is, however, purely show: Sallust has summoned up all his artistry to cast the activity of the consul in the most unfavourable light possible. He does not characterize him directly, but obliquely, through statement of the motives that guide him. Cicero pushes through the *senatus consultum ultimum* ('the final decree of the senate', the name modern historians use for an emergency decree passed by the Senate advising the magistrates to protect the Republic; the term comes from Caesar's mocking reference to this decree as 'the most extreme and final decree of the Senate') out of fear, because he no longer feels safe after the attack of the Catilinarians and because the insurrection of Manlius, about which he is too little informed, seriously worries him.[48] This is well known to be false: the *senatus consultum ultimum* had been passed for a long time already when the assembly of the Catilinarians at Laeca's house took place in the night between 6 and 7 November which preceded the attack. Moreover, Cicero knew full well how things stood with Manlius when he motivated the *senatus consultum ultimum* on October 21: he predicted the beginning of the insurrection to the day,[49] and his prophecy had likewise long been fulfilled when he presented the *First Catilinarian* on 8 November.

With the famous and much-discussed redating of the Catilinarian assembly and the attack, Sallust first of all made Cicero appear to have suspended the rights of the people because of a personal danger to himself. But the sophisticated forgery goes further. It is completely left out that Cicero's precautionary measures thwarted Catiline's attempts at a *coup d'état* on 28 October and 1 November;[50] from what Sallust reports of the decrees of the Senate, together with his depiction of the discontent in the city and his judgement of the situation, one would have to conclude that all the noise had been useless and that driving Catiline out had done a great deal of damage.

The greatest advantage that the redating of the meeting at Laeca's offered Sallust was that the basis of the *First Catilinarian Oration* then vanished into thin air. The truth of the matter was that Cicero first received authentic and extensive information about the plans of the conspirators against the Roman state through the betrayal of this meeting, and then conceived the plan to present this material in the Senate, thus compromising Catiline in such a way that nobody would dare any

---

[48] 29. 1. [49] Cic. *Cat.* 1. 7. [50] Cic. *Cat.* 1. 7. 8.

longer to speak in his favour (as had continually happened up to that point); Catiline would then have no choice but to flee the state together with his supporters and openly raise the flag of revolt. The consul could then calmly wait until the insurgents had been crushed by force of arms and was no longer forced to prosecute a court case against citizens, which, if contained within the legal boundaries, did not promise enough success; if, on the other hand, the case was connected with the disputed state of emergency, it offered the popular opposition a frightening weapon against the consul. The plan miscarried: Catilina indeed fled to Manlius, but he left his supporters behind in Rome and thereby a constant source of worry for the consul. Despite all its triumphalism the second *Catilinarian* clearly radiates annoyance that so few had accompanied Catiline, together with wariness against the accusation that Catiline's departure set a dangerous war in motion. But Sallust tremendously exaggerates this error of Ciceronian politics, in that he not only, with a perfidious interpretation of Cicero's own words, ascribes to it the most disastrous consequences, but also robs it of its factual basis. We find in Sallust not the consul who on the previous day escaped a nefarious attack, to whom a detailed murderous plot has been revealed, but a nervous man simultaneously irritated and frightened by the brazenness of Catiline, who, though under prosecution, nevertheless blithely and shamelessly appears in the Senate. The threat with which Catiline actually erupted at Cato before the consular elections a few months prior is transferred here, and not without careful consideration: the entire subsequent narrative supports the idea that this threat was a hair's breadth away from coming true, that the spontaneous and yet cowardly outburst of the consul had brought the state to the brink of ruin. And to ensure that no one should be consoled by the eventual victory, the account concludes with a gripping depiction of the desperate courage of the Catilinarians, the losses of the victors, the doleful scenes that such a war among citizens always brings with it. The consul's salvation of the state is sounded out not with the joyful fanfare of victory, but with a jarring dissonance.

Once again the historian allows the reader a glimpse into Cicero's soul, after the betrayal of the Allobroges, where he is concerned with striking the decisive blow against the conspirators who remained behind in the city. Powerful anxiety and powerful joy move him; that is, in other words, he does not immediately know what he wants. And this impression remains. Nothing could be more devastating of Cicero's actions on 5 December than the brief words: 'He asked the Senate what should be done with the prisoners; shortly before this, the Senate, at a well-attended meeting, had declared their actions treasonous.' The consul lacks the courage to act on his own after the senatorial decree; thus, he hides behind the Senate. While this criticism is not unjustified,[51] still it is maliciously sharpened by the circumstance that Sallust completely conceals what Cicero said in the Senate: he is nothing other than the oligarchy's hangman, and here, only here, does the intimation of the coming detailed description create a particular sense of horror—not a general horror, but horror at the actions of Cicero the consul. In contrast to this, the stories of the Catilinarians' pederasty and the human sacrifice at the forging of their alliance[52] are repudiated carefully, but with all the more deliberate effect, as bogeyman stories circulated by the Ciceronian party. Not a word on Cicero's triumphant homecoming after the execution, at which the people legitimated his actions. On the contrary, this is immediately preceded[53] by the appearance of the irresolute crowd, which, initially full of fear, then favourable to Catiline, ultimately praises Cicero senselessly to the skies, because he preserved them from the danger of losing the wretched roofs above their heads. The noxious mockery of this depiction of their attitude can only be fully understood when compared with the pompous conclusion to the *Third Catilinarian*.

Throughout his whole life Cicero prided himself on having united the Senate and the equestrian class to protect the state from being overthrown; well into his old age he did not tire of praising the *equites* ('the equestrian class', those Romans who were wealthy but not members of the senatorial class) arrayed on the *clivus Capitolinus* ('Capitoline Hill') before the *curia* (the Senate House) on 5 December as one of the most glorious images of his political career. Sallust not only passes over this achievement of Ciceronian politics with eloquent silence, but also turns that band of armed knights into a horde of unreasoning belligerents, who, robbed of their senses through oligarchic demagoguery, threaten to attack the innocent Caesar. With this representation he directly sides with Cicero's mortal enemies Clodius, Gabinius, and Antony.[54]

There is also no shortage of subtler jabs recognizable only to the attentive reader. The sonorous beginning of the *First Catilinarian* is parodied by Catiline himself with the words *quae quousque tandem patiemini fortissumi viri* ('and, my very brave men, how long finally will we endure these things', 20. 9). According to Lentulus' plan, the tribune L. Calpurnius Bestia should *belli gravissumi invidiam optumo consuli imponere* ('impose on the best consul hatred for the oppressive

---

[51] It should be borne in mind that Cicero himself appeals to the Senate against the attacks of Antony, *Phil.* 2. 11. The controversy, then, was still alive when Sallust wrote.
[52] 14. 7, 22. Cf. Cic. *Cat.* 2. 8; Q. Cic. *Comment. pet.* 10; *Cat.* 1. 16.   [53] 48. 1–2.
[54] *Cat.* 4. 15. 22; *Att.* 1. 14. 4, 17. 10, 18. 3, 2. 1. 7; *Pis.* 7; *Red. sen.* 32; *Sest.* 28; *Phil.* 2. 16.

war', 43. 1). This is derisive irony, not only because the accusation, according to Sallust's version of events, really is fitting, but also formally; for Cicero declared himself very unsatisfied when M. Brutus in his *Cato* awarded him no better predicate than that of an *optumus consul* ('the best consul').[55] On another occasion (29. 1) he writes *neque exercitus Manli quantus aut quo consilio foret satis compertum habebat* ('and he had not really discovered either the size of Manlius' army or its strategy'): one is meant to think of the derisiveness with which Clodius and other urban wits had poked fun at the consul's phrase *omnia comperi* ('discovered everything').[56] But these are only little pinpricks compared to the masterful tactics of the main attack, which holds at a distance every slander that might appear partisan: all the more surely, with cold-blooded, cruel calculation, the laurels of the eloquent consul's glory are plucked apart leaf by leaf.

At no point did the literary destruction of Cicero the politician have such an evident purpose to serve as immediately after his death, when the memory of his accomplishments was once again revived. According to the tradition, his pamphlet *De consiliis*, featuring sharp attacks on Caesar and Crassus, was published then, and I admit to being very impressed with the conjecture already put forth by others[57] that Sallust's historical monograph is a response to this pamphlet, because this so aptly explains the combination of apology for Caesar and attacks on Cicero.

All polemic is determined by the opponent, and the indirect method that Sallust chose—and was compelled to choose, if he did not want to insult the historiographical style—is no exception to this; on the contrary, I venture the supposition, without being able to prove it conclusively, that Sallust added only very little to the material of the Ciceronian memoir and posthumous pamphlet, and essentially limited his activity to correcting the given κεφάλαια ('headings', 'main points') according to his own artistic and political concerns, and—what was exceptionally important to him—pouring them into the linguistic mould that it was up to him to create. His false conception of Catiline is above all only the counterpart to Cicero's. Cicero had elevated Catiline in order to exaggerate the value of his own achievement; he first stamped Catiline as a dangerous revolutionary[58] who for a long time now had fought against

---

[55] *Att.* 12. 21. 1, *hic autem se etiam tribuere multum mihi putat quod scripserit* **optimum consulem**. *quis enim ieiunius dixit inimicus?* ('But at this point he thought he was giving me a great compliment because he had written "the best consul". But what enemy has been less forthcoming?'). Naturally Sallust did not know Cicero's letter to Atticus.

[56] Cic. *Cat.* 1. 10, *Acad. Pr.* 2. 62, *Att.* 1. 14. 5, *Fam.* 5. 5. 2.   [57] Besser 1880: 2.

[58] Cf. *Cat.* 1. 18, 1. 31, 2. 7; *Sull.* 67.

the state, although he knew full well that more powerful persons had originally stood behind him, and suspected as much of the conspiracy of 63;[59] Sallust likewise elevates Catiline, but in order to sting the oligarchy, and he backdates the conspiracy to exonerate Caesar. Cicero boasted of having driven away Catiline through his speech; Sallust acknowledges this, but inverts the assessment of it. Cicero does not conceal that the people were afraid on 8 November,[60] and accepts the gratitude of the same people on the evening of 3 December for his uncovering of the conspiracy. Neither the one nor the other is missing from Sallust, but both are cast in a different light. Much more could be listed here, ...[61]

Livy wrote more than a human lifetime after Sallust. The breadth of the gap between the two can hardly be overestimated. Here the utterly corrupted son of the metropolis, full of spirit, empty of character, a true revolutionary; there the simple provincial, daydreaming of the greatness of a free Rome, the romantic who flees from a straitened present to take refuge in the past. The imperial government of Emperor Augustus has done its work. In the sixties, as Pompey was fighting Mithridates and Tigranes and the Parthian War lurked on the doorstep, envy of one man's military power was stronger in metropolitan political circles than the thought that Rome would have to take on the East, so that a plan to cripple Pompey with a Spanish insurrection was within the realm of possibility; Caesar thought nothing of denationalizing the Senate through the incorporation of provincials, and even toyed with the idea of accepting from the East the royal diadem that Roman prejudice denied him: in the age of Augustus the *Roma* that dominated the world was restored to her old privileges, and the national feeling nurtured by the glory of the new monarchy once again indulged in reminiscences of the conquest of the *orbis terrarum* ('the entire world') by the Republic—of that conquest which appeared to the Caesarian Sallust as the playground of oligarchic mediocrity. As nobody suffered any longer from the oligarchic regime, so vanished that hatred which had flared up so brightly in the Caesarian media, and it was only the logical consequence of the Augustan diarchy that a Roman historian should once again tread in the footprints of annalistic writing and celebrate the nobility and Senate, even turning Pompey into a hero; only a weak and harmless reflection now remained of the old fervency of partisan struggle. This was the atmosphere in which Livy lived and moved. To him the passionate, bitter

---

[59] This I deduce from the outburst against Caesar at *Off.* 2. 84.   [60] *Cat.* 1. 1.
[61] One clause referring to last half of this article, which is not translated for this collection, has been removed from this sentence.

Sallust with his merciless criticism of the oligarchy must have been highly unpleasant, and he did not miss the opportunity, when it presented itself, to offer him a piece of his mind.[62] One should thus expect in advance that his narrative represents a stark contrast to Sallust's; he achieved this most easily by avoiding Sallust and returning directly to Cicero.[63]

---

[62] Dio 43. 9. 2–3: τῷ Σαλουστίῳ λόγῳ μὲν ἄρχειν ἔργῳ δὲ ἄγειν τε καὶ φέρειν ἐπέτρεψεν. ἀμέλει καὶ ἐδωροδόκησε πολλὰ καὶ ἥρπασεν, ὥστε καὶ κατηγορηθῆναι <καὶ> αἰσχύνην ἐσχάτην ὀφλεῖν, ὅτι τοιαῦτα συγγράμματα συγγράψας καὶ πολλὰ καὶ πικρὰ περὶ τῶν ἐκκαρπουμένων τινὰς εἰπὼν οὐκ ἐμιμήσατο τῷ ἔργῳ τοὺς λόγους. ὅθεν εἰ καὶ τὰ μάλιστα ἀφείθη ὑπὸ τοῦ Καίσαρος, ἀλλ' αὐτός γε ἑαυτὸν καὶ πάνυ τῇ συγγραφῇ ἐστηλοκόπησε ('[Caesar] handed [the Numidians over] to Sallust, nominally to rule, in fact to pillage and plunder. Of course, he both received bribes and stole many things. The result was he was both accused and suffered the ultimate disgrace, since having written the kind of treatises he had and having said many harsh things about those who fleece others, he did not in fact practice what he preached. And so, even if he was completely exonerated by Caesar, still in his writings he has carved out as on a tablet an image of himself').

[63] For reasons of space, only the first half of this article has been translated here (as far as the end of page 581 of the original publication). From that point on, Schwartz concentrates on post-Sallustian narratives of the conspiracy, although his comparisons continue to shed much light on what was distinctive in the tone and substance of Sallust's version.

6

Intellectual Conflict and Mimesis in Sallust's *Bellum Catilinae*

William W. Batstone

From historians we expect narratives of what really happened and explanations of why; from moralists we expect some clear notion of right and wrong, of what we should do. Sallust's extreme position as a moral historian and his apparent tendentiousness have led some critics and scholars to read between the lines of his text a narrative of veiled accusations against putative villains and have provoked others, like D. C. Earl, to translate his notoriously 'untidy'[1] exposition into secure moral propositions. What both of these responses to Sallust's text share is the desire to clear up difficulties of exposition, to explain for Sallust what he wanted to say, to make the referent of the text an external, knowable thing in the world (of ethics or events). While these responses may seem to add to our store of knowledge about events and ethics in the late Republic and about Sallust's real opinion, they inevitably distort the rhetorical artifice which Sallust himself emphasized.[2] In addition, these

---

[1] The adjective comes from McGushin 1977: 30. 'The untidiness of expression in this prologue is due partly to the fact that Sallust found it difficult to define *virtus*, a concept which is paramount in his thinking and which governs the content of the introductory section as a whole.' As will become apparent, I offer a modified version of this theory: the untidiness is the rhetorical means by which Sallust forces his reader to face the difficulty (1) of defining *virtus*; (2) of locating its proper function in the world; (3) of assuring it its proper reward. This paper is an extension of the arguments, both interpretive and theoretical, that I have offered in Batstone 1986 and 1988b. Readers are referred to those articles for general theoretical justifications and bibliography.

[2] *tamen in primis arduom videtur res gestas scribere: primum quod facta dictis exequenda sunt*, B.C. 3. 2. See also Batstone 1988b. In fact, the problem of readers who read criticism as spite and praise of great virtue as fiction is addressed directly by Sallust at B.C. 3. 2, as is the other rhetorical problem of 'equalling deeds with words'. This paper will be about both Sallust's relationship to his readers (what his text does to and for the reader) and the

rewritings tend to ignore two important aspects of the events themselves: first, the facts are not easy to find because any conspiracy necessarily involves secrecy and obscurity;[3] second, a secure moral or political position in fact remained elusive: no republican solution was found to the problems troubling the Roman Republic, certainly not a permanent one, but, for Sallust, not even a temporary one.[4]

I would like to look at two aspects of Sallust's rhetorical artifice in terms of these difficulties. I shall try to show that, in addition to the record of events which he does give, Sallust is especially sensitive to the difficulties of knowing about some aspects of the conspiracy. Conflicting possibilities of interpretation and their lack of resolution are used by Sallust to create a mimetic sense of the events and even to convey that obscurity of actors which was in fact part of the conspiracy.[5] In other

relationship of words to deeds (how it does what it does). This is an attempt to return Sallust's readers to the text and away from both his putative partisanship and the search for the objective event. On objectivity, see further Batstone 2009.

[3] Consequently, its interpretation involves the vested interests of observers: *sed ex aliis rebus magis, quam quod quoiquam id conpertum foret, haec fama valebat* ('this report was prevalent more for other reasons than because anyone had discovered it', 14. 7). In the case of Catiline, this fact is complicated by evidence that suggests Sallust himself was not in Rome during 65–63 BCE. and so would have met with report and rumour at almost every step of his own investigations. On Sallust's activity in the 60s, see Earl 1966: esp. 306–11. His conclusions, however, are only speculative; see the important caution of Syme 1964: 28, repeated by McGushin 1977: 1.

[4] Earl 1961 describes Sallust's ethical position as a redefinition of *virtus*, although he notes that this redefinition occurs in the terms of the elder Cato (111, 120). For the problems entailed in this solution, see now Levene 2000. That political action for Sallust became impossible, see *B.J.* 3. 1: *Verum ex iis magistratus et imperia, postremo omnis cura rerum publicarum minume mihi hac tempestate cupiunda videntur, quoniam neque virtuti honos datur neque illi, quibus per fraudem iis fuit uti, tuti aut eo magis honesti sunt* ('But of these [paths to glory] political office and military command, in short all public service seems to me at this time not at all desirable, because neither is political honour given to virtue nor are those men who through fraud enjoyed political office either safe or any more honourable because of it'). It is in keeping with this discussion to note that those who here enjoy *honores* are not *honesti*; those who succeed *per fraudem* are not *tuti*. This view is bleak; for there is neither ethical nor practical reason to become a politician. In the *B.C.*, these problems are further complicated by the heroic actions of Catiline as a military commander in 61. 1–6. Granted that the reference above is to the period when Sallust withdrew from politics some twenty years after the conspiracy, still, as the prologue to the *B.C.* makes clear, the problems of the 40s were already alive in the 60s and at the end of the second century.

[5] This mimesis, however, is not relegated to or focused upon analytic questions, e.g., whether Crassus was involved. It is in large part the atmosphere of secrecy, rumour, and suspicion that was part of the events (see, for example, n. 7 below), although often not of much interest to modern historical analysis. This does not mean that Sallust ignored the analytic questions. The two examples I offer below attempt to cover both areas: the rumours and suspicions of slave revolts and the guilt of Crassus.

words, the words that equal events are not statements of objective truth but a textual labyrinth that reveals shadowy powers at work in the words and actions of men. This only threatens 'history' as such if we think that history is the objective, analytic narrative of what really happened. But history is not that for Sallust, and it cannot be that for us. It is also the experience of uncertainty, deception, reinterpretation and misinterpretation.[6] In a similar way, the 'ethical framework'[7] promised by Sallust's preface finally dissolves in uncertainty. As the context changes and develops, the problem of virtuous action keeps appearing, not as the solved problem we expected to find, but as the continuing and elusive problem it is. This loss of secure ethical bearings, like the disappearance of fact, is another dimension of the historical problem Sallust imagines.[8]

Conspiracy, as Cicero knew well, creates a difficult situation. It retains its potential for success by remaining hidden; and, to whatever extent it is successful, its history can only be written either by those privy to the conspiracy or by the ignorant, working on the basis of probability and belief, or prejudice and spite. A conspiracy as important as Catiline's has long raised questions, not just about Catiline and his hidden supporters but, predictably, about Cicero and his hidden motives in either inventing or exaggerating the conspiracy. This has been treated as a historical problem that involves the credibility of Sallust; I propose here that, while Sallust certainly accepted the conspiracy as fact, he was also fully aware of the fact that gaudy details about the conspirators, as well as the hidden motives of hidden supporters, were a locus for rumour and distortion. In fact, Sallust saw rumour and distortion as part of the historical event.

My first example of rumour and the mimetic use of uncertainty is simple and direct. At 30. 1, Sallust reports that L. Saenius had read in the Senate a letter stating that C. Manlius had taken the field with a large force on 27 October.[9] 'At the same time,' Sallust goes on to say, 'as is usual in such circumstances, some reported portents and prodigies, others claimed that meetings were held, arms were transported, slave insurrections were under way at Capua and in Apulia'.[10] The passage offers an interpretive problem. It mixes plausible with implausible, specific with vague, and by not judging the truth or falsehood of its

---

[6] See Batstone 2009.   [7] McGushin 1977: 291.

[8] For a different analysis of the same repetition and irresolution of the problem of *virtus*, see now Gunderson 2000.

[9] Sallust is careful to say that L. Saenius claimed (*dicebat*) that the letter had come from Faesulae, not because Sallust disbelieves the report, but because such claims are integral to the evidence.

[10] *simul, id quod in tali re solet, alii portenta atque prodigia nuntiabant, alii coriventus fieri, arma portari, Capuae atque in Apulia servile bellum moveri.*

content it creates a problem for the reader which is similar to the problem the Senate faced. The prodigies and portents are dubious; of course, there were meetings—the questions are 'Who was there?' and 'What were the meetings about?'—and, as for the slave insurrections and movements of arms, those are important possibilities. The interpretive problem is further complicated by the aside: *id quod in tali re solet* ('that which customarily happens in such circumstances'). The external perspective which it creates assures the reader that human nature is enough to account for what was said, but what *was* happening? With *id quod in tali re solet*, the text becomes opaque. And Sallust adds further complications: the Senate sends Q. Marcius Rex to Faesulae, Q. Metellus Creticus to Apulia, and two praetors to Capua and Picenum. Human nature may be enough to explain the rumours, but it does not fully explain the Senate: the usual rumours, prodigies, portents, meetings, arms, war. Therefore,....A gap is marked by *igitur*. It all depends on what *in tali re* refers to: the letter that was read, the report of events and prodigies, the actual armed multitude. The Senate is, of course, unsure of what they will find; but we hear later, at 42. 2 of *nocturnis consiliis* (late-night meetings), movements of arms, and disturbances at Picenum, and at 46. 3 that Caeparius was getting ready for his mission of stirring up slaves in Apulia. The specific rumours of 30. 2 are never confirmed or denied; and the report itself is located nicely between Catiline's plans to use slaves (24. 4) and the later confirmed disturbances and Caeparius' mission. It is part of this atmosphere that in 56. 5 we hear that Catiline repudiated the use of slaves. The next time we hear of Q. Marcius Rex, he has received a letter from Manlius and the content of the rumours has been dropped (32. 3–34. 1). What has been happening? The usual events in times of crisis. The Senate offers a reward for evidence about the plot, including freedom for slaves (30. 6). No one comes forward; but the Senate sends gladiators to Capua and other Italian towns in order to remove them from Rome. They post guards in Rome. The whole is dramatic; but it is little concerned with facts about portents, meetings, and slave insurrections. It is, instead, a story of fear, human nature, and uncertainty, even as its elements remain uncertain.

Other examples of Sallust's mimetic and dramatic use of uncertainty could be similarly analysed. For instance, within the space of three sentences (14. 7–15. 2) he reports rumours of Catiline's sexual perversity, which were prevalent 'more for other reasons, than because anyone had evidence of their truth',[11] and rumours that Catiline had murdered his

---

[11] *sed ex aliis rebus magis quam quod quoiquam id conpertum foret haec fama valebat.*

Intellectual Conflict and Mimesis 145

own son, which seem to Sallust to explain the hurried plot. In the first instance, the rumours are questionable because they are an easy extension of other details, and *fama* ('rumour', 'opinion', 'report')[12] has gone too far, not because it is wildly improbable, but precisely because it is believable;[13] in the second, the report seems plausible because it explains subsequent events. Together, the accounts have a mimetic, not an analytic, purpose; that is, their rhetorical juxtaposition uses two instances of uncertainty to suggest that uncertain boundary that lies between what probably happened and what might have happened.

Given this kind of attention to the problems of belief and what cannot be known, it is not surprising to find that even something as crude as a statistical survey confirms the impression that, at a very basic level, the *Bellum Catilinae* (*B.C.*) is about suspicions and rumours. Counting all instances of speaking or reporting, *dico, aio, narro, audio, rumor, fama, comperio*, and, when it refers to speech, *fertur*, we find sixty-four instances in the *B.C.* and ninety-three in the *Bellum Jugurthinum* (*B.J.*). Factoring in the difference in length of the two works, the *B.C.* is half again more concerned with 'what can be said and believed' than the *B.J.* Belief and rumour are part of history, as the *B.J.* shows, but, in dealing with Catiline, Sallust's text places at the heart of the events something which required the continual mention of belief, uncertainty, talk, and secrecy.[14]

The most extensive and complex example of Sallust's use of uncertainty, belief, and fear to create a contradictory but mimetic image occurs at *B.C.* 48. 4–49.4, when the Senate considers charges laid by Tarquinius

---

[12] For an extensive and learned discussion of *fama* in Latin, see Hardie 2012: 1–47; for *fama* elsewhere in Sallust, see Batstone 1986, discussed p. 158 below.

[13] In fact, in the context Sallust seems to give the 'other reasons' that made the rumours believable, both in general (*viri muliebria pati*, 13. 3, and *in tanta tamque conrupta civitate Catilina...*, 14. 1) and in specific (*quicumque inpudicus adulter ganeo manu ventre pene bona patria laceraverat*, 14. 2, and *neque sumptui neque modestiae suae parcere*, 14. 6).

[14] It may be counterargued that in investigating the conspiracy Sallust necessarily relied upon the evidence of contemporaries, and that this is reflected in his frequent report of what was heard. To the extent that the causality implied in this counterargument is correct, it tells us why Sallust was especially aware of the difficulties of rumour and talk; it in no way detracts from that interest. Crassus, at 48. 9, is a good example. However, the implication that Sallust only reflects his contemporary sources is not a sufficient explanation for many of the reports, which are themselves reports not of what was said afterwards but of what was being said at the time. Examples include Catiline's sexual activities (14. 7), the drinking of blood (22. 1–4), Fulvia's information, itself a report (23. 4), the rumours Cicero hears (29. 1), the rumours of October 63 (30. 1), Catulus' claims about the letter of Catiline (34. 3), the revolutionary plans that were reported in December (43. 2), Volturcius' evidence before the Senate (*tantum modo audire solitum*, 47. 1), and the eagle of Marius in Catiline's army (59. 3). All these reports are presented as contemporary rumours, not speculation after the events.

against Crassus. As I have dealt in detail with this passage elsewhere,[15] I shall summarize my argument here. Volturcius, after lying and then being promised immunity, gave evidence to the Senate about the Allobroges, and it was confirmed by the Galli. The next day, a certain Tarquinius is brought before the Senate; he says that he will give evidence if offered immunity. His says the same things Volturcius did about arson, murder, and the enemy's movements. He then adds that he was sent by Crassus to tell Catiline not to be concerned about the capture of Lentulus and Cethegus, but that he should hurry to the city. The air of design which Sallust creates, in part through the suspicious parallelism between Volturcius and Tarquinius, is already part of the problem of interpretation. The senatorial response reveals other problems: 'Some thought the charge incredible; others believed it to be true, but thought that in such a crisis so powerful a man ought to be propitiated rather than aggravated. A large number were under obligation to Crassus in private business deals. They all shouted that the accusation was false.'[16] Crassus' guilt or innocence, here, is obscured and finally lost in the opinions and fears concerning him. Consequently, the narrative can only explain the forces that precipitated the vote, not whether or not Crassus was innocent.

In fact, the passage does not even explain what people thought. When Sallust says that a third group, perhaps even the majority (*plerique*), were tied to Crassus by financial obligations, their real opinions disappear into their financial interests. The vote does not determine fact, nor was the vote itself determined by what people thought: in large part, regardless of what people thought, it was determined by money, power, and self-interest. Just as Crassus' guilt or innocence is obscured by conflicting opinions, so even the real opinions of the senators disappear, first in the fears some had of a powerful man, then in the financial interests of the last clause. One might summarize this by saying some voted what they believed, others voted the opposite of what they believed, and many voted their financial interests and no one knows what they believed. If we unpack the implications of the vote, we discover that, if Crassus was guilty, the liars (who voted the opposite of their belief) were right and the simple truth was overwhelmed by fear and money. On the other hand, if Crassus was innocent, he needed the liars, debtors, and cowards, men who were ignorant of truth but were concerned about violence, money, and their lives, to ensure his own safety. These conflicting possibilities

---

[15] See Batstone 1986.

[16] *alii rem incredibilem rati, pars tametsi verum existumabant, tamen quia in tali tempore tanta vis hominis magis leniunda quam exagitanda videbatur, plerique Crasso ex negotiis privatis obnoxii, condamant indicem falsum esse*, 48. 5.

make it impossible for the reader to know the truth, while fostering uncertainty and suspicions in the reader much like the uncertainty and suspicions of the event: *facta dictis exaequanda* ('deeds are to be equalled by words'). In other words, this combination of uncertainty and suspicion is the event.

Tarquinius is put in chains and silenced. It is no small detail that without a word from Sallust or the Senate Tarquinius' guarantee of immunity is revoked—on the basis of fears, lies, and self-interest. There follows an investigation into who put Tarquinius up to the lie. If Tarquinius is telling the truth, or if we imagine that he tells the truth, we now enter into a meaningless exercise: who convinced the witness who told the truth to lie? There is no way this leads to the truth. And, since the possibility that Tarquinius is telling the truth cannot be excluded, the text at this point is not and cannot be answering the question 'Who got Tarquinius to lie?' Nor is the Senate interested in the answer. The senators only want to put to bed an awkward accusation. And, as the text explores the possible avenues of hope, intention, and manipulation that could account for the hypothetical lie, Sallust puts us in possession of the dark potential and uncertainty of the times, the actors, and the evidence. The possible machinators are Autronius and Cicero, the one a conspirator, the other the man whose name is synonymous with opposition to the conspiracy. And yet both could have had their reasons: Autronius, because the name of Crassus would protect the rest of the conspirators; Cicero, because naming Crassus would *prevent* Crassus from protecting the rest of the conspirators. One reason cancels out the other. They cannot both be factually true, but Sallust is telling us that they were, at least in the opinion of the men of the time, both potentially true. Crassus, it seems, really was that unpredictable, that paradoxical, that hard to read: for Sallust, that is a fact, and that fact is part of the problem, just as it constitutes the event.

The powerful men in Rome in the 60s could not be counted on to protect the state; their motives were as shadowy as their actions. When Sallust erases the possibility of knowledge with conflicting explanations of a lie that might not be a lie, he succeeds again in making his words equal to the events as lived by those who observed them. About the real facts all we can know is that, if it was Autronius who put Tarquinius up to the lie (assuming that it was a lie), then Autronius made a mistake. At least this time Crassus chose not to protect the guilty. This, too, is interesting information, but it is information about the kind of misunderstanding that was possible. Sallust leaves us with the talk of the times: *erant eo tempore qui aestumarent...; alii...aiebant...* ('there were at that time men who thought...others...were saying...', 48. 7–8).

But this is not all: Sallust proceeds to probe the problems of interpretation and obscurity: 'At a later date, I personally heard Crassus himself making the claim that that onerous libel had been put upon him by Cicero.'[17] Crassus would, of course, have taken advantage of the Senate's proclamation, despite the fact that it was a product of fear, not of information or even of belief. And there are other difficulties: how would Crassus have known that Cicero was behind it? Even if Cicero was, Crassus may have had his own reasons for naming Cicero. The very narrative we are reading insists that Tarquinius, Autronius, and Cicero each could have had his own reasons for naming Crassus. The problem is that the real truth about Cicero, like the truth about Crassus, is known only by the guilty; the innocent are ignorant and can only say 'not me' and 'I think' or tell some lies themselves. The facts remain hidden in the conflict of explanations and the private animosities of men of public affairs. But this does not make Sallust's text meaningless; rather, it constitutes its meaning. In knowing the silence, self-interest, lies and possible lies, shadowy powers, and financial implications of an event like this, we actually know more about the conspiracy and the events than we would know if it all became a simple matter of objective fact.[18] This is not a threat to history; it is the history.

If we view Sallust's narrative development in section 48 as one that creates interpretive difficulties out of the extensive potential for *inimicitia* ('hatred', 'political enmity', 'hostility'), secrecy, suspicion, self-interest, and misjudgment, we can better see some of the reasons why Sallust follows this narrative with a story about Caesar. The new section (49) begins, 'But at that very time Quintus Catulus and Gaius Piso tried in vain by entreaties, bribes, and reward to induce Cicero to have a false accusation brought against Gaius Caesar, either through the Allobroges or some other witness.'[19] The sentence is usually taken as the beginning of a new story and is interpreted in the context of a contrast between Crassus, who might have been guilty, and Caesar, who Sallust says was

---

[17] *ipsum Crassum ego postea praedicantem audivi, tantam illam contumeliam sibi ab Cicerone inpositam*, 48. 9.

[18] It is significant that a historian as precise and careful as Gruen could not accept Sallust's swirl of irreconcilable perspectives. Speaking of the Senate, he removes the drama, saying, 'None would allow himself to believe it. At least none would profess to believe it.' He records Autronius' alleged effort to get Crassus to protect the conspirators and Cicero's hostility, and concludes, 'In 63 he [Crassus] promptly collected political debts.' Gruen 1974: 285–6.

[19] *Sed isdem temporibus Q. Catulus et C. Piso neque precibus neque gratia neque pretio Ciceronem inpellere potuere, uti per Allobrobroges aut alium indicem C. Caesar falso nominaretur*, 49. 1.

innocent. That contrast is there, but Sallust connects the two stories more closely: 'But (*sed*) at the same time (*isdem temporibus*)' marks a contrast; something else did not happen. The weight of the sentence falls on the emphatic triplet, *neque precibus neque gratia neque pretio*. The contrast is: Crassus said Cicero was behind the false accusation; but at the same time Cicero could not be induced by prayers, favours or money to lie about Caesar. The false accusation against Caesar appears not just because Sallust wishes to exonerate Caesar, but because he needs it to show Cicero's refusal to condone false accusations. In the context, this story stands in contrast to Crassus' accusation. It does not, however, prove Crassus wrong. Sallust's history here is not a history of facts; the narrative of events dissolves into conflicting accusations and ambiguity. In an unexpected way, Sallust's description of one of history's problems, *facta dictis exaequanda* ('deeds must be equalled by words') has another translation: 'deeds must be made equal to words'. What really happened was all the words about the things that we do not know about. Here, the history of events is reduced to words, what people said and thought, what could be said and thought.

But words create as well as reflect deeds and events. The paragraph ends with armed guards at the Temple of Concord drawing their swords on Caesar as he leaves because they believe the false charges. The symbolism is obvious: the danger to the state (and to concord) of rash belief in plausible rumours by the uninformed and the fickle. The equation of words and deeds here lies in the impossible extrication of truth from this complex of self-interest and ignorance. But even this is not the conclusion to a narrative that creates and explores cognitive dissonance. The soldiers act on the rumours spread by Piso and Catulus, but what, really, were *their* motives. They were moved, 'compelled' Sallust says, either by the magnitude of the danger or by the fickleness of their emotions (*animi mobilitate*), to make clear their zeal for the Republic.[20] It was either a true zeal brought on by a sense of danger or a show of zeal produced by fickle emotions.[21] And one must ask whether the guards were just feeling patriotic that day, or were they moved by the need to show that on that day they were not merely fickle. Such is Sallust's conclusion to a section of narrative in which legal charges have uncovered only fear, power, ignorance, self-interest, and duplicity; in which elections and trials have produced angry men dealing in lies and

---

[20] *seu periculi magnitudine seu animi mobilitate inpulsi, quo stadium suum in rem publicam clarius esset, egredienti ex senatu Caesari gladio minitarentur*, 49. 4.

[21] It is quite possible that the *animi mobilitate* is focalized: compelled by (their knowledge of) how they seem fickle, they made a show by drawing their swords.

false rumours; in which violence and hostility appear at the Temple of Concord. Sallust is presenting powerful images of the decline of Roman society. He is not spreading rumours, but is using them to vivify his picture of suspicion, culpability, plausibility, and uncertainty. The image is poetic, in that it creates in the reader an inability to negotiate and reduce what could be said and believed into a version of the truth; it is mimetic because the obscurity it creates is an imitation of the obscurity of the events and the actors themselves in an era when interpretation more often led into darkness than into light.[22]

I would like to turn now from Sallust's imagining of events and motives hidden and distorted in what people say, believe, and fear, to the opening chapters of his preface and his general discussion of history and the goal of human life. I am interested in particular in the notorious 'untidiness' of the preface and I hope to show that it is more than an attempt to create the philosophical and ethical framework for a fresh concept of *nobilitas* ('excellence', 'superiority', 'nobleness'). It is, finally, a failed attempt. And it is this very progress into failure which is its strength. Readers are made simultaneously to share this failure, as the promise of generalizable ethical certainty remains unfulfilled, and to participate in the failure, as they themselves come to revise, retranslate, and supplement Sallust's words. That these revisions and supplements cannot secure action is both the historical problem Sallust imagines and the experience of his reader. This will mean that the loss of ethical certainty, like any loss, creates a desire for precisely what is missing. In my view, this is the centre of Sallust's moral emphasis. If we cannot have moral certainty, we can at least desire it.[23]

The rhetorical and argumentative movement of the first paragraph is exemplary. Sallust begins: 'All men, who are eager to excel the other animals, ought to strive with all resources lest they pass through their life unnoticed.'[24] 'Familiar and even commonplace material',[25] redolent of the past and the values upon which Rome was founded,[26] the sentence

---

[22] If, as C. W. Fornara claims, history begins as a mimetic investigation into what people say, and if that investigation has as its goal the use of direct speech to clarify the central or opposing issues, in Sallust that same investigation is at times halted by what can be said (rumour, belief, idle talk, plausible accusations, and plausible denials), and the mimesis presents the reader with the unsolved interpretive problem. See Fornara 1983: 29–32.

[23] One recalls Horace, *desiderantem quod satis est*, *Carm*. 3. 1. 25: the moral goal for the life of contentment is to desire what is enough; he does not say you will get it.

[24] *omneis homines, qui sese student praestare ceteris animalibus, summa ope niti decet, ne vitam silentio transeant.*

[25] McGushin 1977: 30.

[26] Ibid. 31 on *sese student praestare* and *summa ope niti*.

makes a fine promise of recognized, generalizable, universal truth: 'all men' he says, and he speaks of extreme effort, *summa ope niti* (in Ennian words that have spoken of Roman achievement and effort for over one hundred years, and will speak again in Vergil's *Aeneid*[27]); he speaks of propriety, *decet*, of glorious action, *ne vitam silentio*, of nature and the essential contrast between men and animals. But the beginning is deceptive; it is precisely that world of recognized, generalizable truth that will be problematic. While asserting ethical propriety, the text has omitted the very terms that will orient action toward acceptable goals and an acceptable *gloria* ('glory', 'fame', 'renown'). The central term, *summa ope*,[28] may promise the freedom of full exertion sanctioned by generalizable moral truth, and, indeed, its archaic flavour may seem to recall a world in which the selection of means was not a problem; but in the world Sallust addresses, it is the selection of means which is the very problem that needs addressing. *Summa ope* hides, or should hide, a prohibition,[29] and that prohibition is suggested in the sentence's ending: the animals who pass their lives in silence become herd animals (*pecora*), heads bowed down (*prona*) and obedient to their bellies (*ventri oboedientia*). This contrast and the reining in of *summa ops* become the focus of the next sentence. The contrast between men and animals appears now in the traditional dichotomy of body and mind, *corpus/animus*,[30] and as a contrast between gods and beasts: we have a soul in common with the gods, and a body in common with beasts. The problem of *summa ops* (which we may note appears here in a new form as *nostra omnis vis* ['all our power'], where *omnis* seems to gloss *summa*) is now restrained. 'And so it seems to me more correct to seek glory with the resources of mind than those of physical strength.' The term *rectius*, 'more correct', acts as a gloss and corrective to *decet* ('ought to', 'it is proper') in the first sentence. It also recalls and corrects the 'prone animals', in that it means 'more upright', and it recalls the 'mind's authority', *animi imperio*, in that its root meaning is 'to rule' (*regere*, as in *rex*, 'king'). While this sorting out of

---

[27] Ennius *Ann.* 151 Sk.; Vergil *Aen.* 12. 552: *summa nituntur opum vi.*

[28] *ops*, generally of the 'puissance de l'homme politique' (see Hellegouarc'h 1963: 237); the singular is used in reference to military strength, resources, favour, and, of course, wealth. See *OLD*, s. v.; see also the discussion of Hellegouarc'h, which emphasizes the statistical, but not absolute difference between the usage in the singular and in the plural.

[29] Consider something as ordinary as running for office, canvassing for votes. *Ambitio*, the literal term, is also used for the drive that informs such activity, 'ambition', but for Sallust that drive is hazardous: *quod tamen vitium propius virtutem erat* ('a vice which nevertheless is rather close to a virtue', 11. 1).

[30] *Animus* refers to the mental or spiritual element in man and is regularly paired with the physical body.

resources is happening, other minor redefinitions occur: *animi imperio* becomes *ingeni opibus*; *corporis servitio* morphs into *virium opibus*. What began with *summa ope* ('the greatest power/strength', 'all resources') ends with a rejection of *virium opibus* ('resources of strength', 'physical powers'). The process of redefinition uncovers the inadequacy of Sallust's original universalization at the same time that it restrains the promise of free and full exertion towards a goal. It also requires of the reader a nimble movement among synonyms and recalibrations.

In a parallel movement, the goal of life, *ne vitam silentio transeant* ('not to pass through life in silence/unheralded'), is also redefined. At first the retranslation seems innocent, *gloriam quaerere* ('to seek glory'), the positive version of *ne... silentio*; but *gloria* expands the final goal: 'not passing through life in silence' is inadequate to the goal of living. Because life is short (*vita ipsa qua fruimur brevis est* ('the life itself which we enjoy is short')), it cannot offer the true measure of *gloria*. We should leave a record that lasts as long as possible: *memoria quam maxime longa*. The physical life which we enjoy cannot compare with *gloria* and *memoria quam maxime longa*. And so we should not enjoy that life, with its transient pleasures, wealth and beauty: we should not enjoy the life which we enjoy.[31] The reading process redefines 'enjoyment' (*fruimur*) as well as *summa ope, ne... silentio, vita,* and *gloria*. We should seek *gloria*, but not all *gloria*; it is not this life but eternity that is our real concern. Here, a paragraph that began with an echo of Ennius, ends with a broken and repaired hexameter: *divitiarum et formae gloria* ('the glory of wealth and beauty') sounds like a hexameter up to a diaeresis before the fifth foot, but then the rhythm crumbles with *fluxa atque fragilis est* ('flows away and breaks apart'). Then, Sallust concludes, *virtus clara aeternaque habetur* ('*virtus* is held bright/clear/manifest and eternal'), and we hear the cadence of the hexameter from third foot to end. All seems to be repaired. But it is not. The commentators tell us that in this sentence *habetur* ('is held') means, 'is held as a possession'.[32] But there is no guarantee that it does not or will not mean, 'is believed to be/is held to be'. *Gloria* itself is unaccountably and ominously absent from this new formulation, and the next time Sallust uses *habere*, it will certainly mean 'is thought to be'; and in this instance the judgment is almost certainly

---

[31] See 2. 8: *quibus profecto contra naturam corpus voluptati, anima oneri fuit, eorum ego vitam mortemque iuxta aestumo, quoniam de utraque siletur,* 'The life and death of those for whom contrary to nature the body is a pleasure and the soul a burden I consider to be equal, since there is silence about both.' Here, silence is the silence that comes after death.

[32] Ramsey 2007 ad loc.; 'is a possession', McGushin 1977 ad loc.; 'wird zum herrlichen und ewigen Besitz', Vretska 1976 ad loc., citing Jacobs.

a moral error: *lubidinem dominandi causam belli haberi* ('lust for domination was considered a reason for war'), 2. 2 (see also 5. 6, 8. 4). In the brief compass of four sentences, Sallust has radically shaken the consoling promise of ethical certainty offered by his opening sentence. 'All men ought to strive with all resources' has become 'Men ought to strive with mental vigour' and then 'with the resources of their *ingenium*' (literally, 'one's innate nature, disposition, or talents', often, like 'talent', with a positive connotation).[33] 'Lest they pass through their lives unnoticed' has become 'since life is short, lest they be unnoticed long after death', and then their *virtus*, that resource upon which they build that eternal *gloria*, may only be thought eternal; *virtus* may not have permanence; it may be an illusion. The whole is a process of redefinition and retranslation, and it is also a process of loss.[34]

Let me anticipate here an objection: is it not obvious that Sallust did not mean that one should use every resource or court all forms of *gloria*? Agreed. Not only is it true that Sallust did not mean all resources for any glory, but it seems to me the text counts on the reader's feeling that despite what it says the statement of ethical propriety can be securely written with the understanding that the resources must be qualified, the goal narrowed, and *fortuna* ('chance', 'luck', 'fortune', even 'fate') taken into account. The reader is made to fill ellipses, or, better, to feel that, of course, they were already filled (or could be filled) with the proper ethical orientation and the proper exclusions. And yet, at every step, with every new translation and every renegotiation of the meaning, new problems and new inadequacies appear. *Summa ope* must account for the dangers of *vis corporis* ('physical power') or *venter* ('the stomach'); *gloria* must be able to accommodate the notorious false evaluations of men and the exaggerations of excellent writers (8. 4). At the end of the first paragraph, there may seem to be adequate and apparently secure retranslations. *Summa ope* must mean *ingeni opibus*; *ne vitam silentio* must mean *ut memoria quam maxume longa*, or better *aeterna*. But the apparent

---

[33] Throughout the preface, one must ask how this applies to Catiline: should he use all his political and military resources? Should he use the resources of his *ingenium*? We will hear that it was *ingenio malo pravoque*, 5. 1. We will also hear that *gloria* and *fama* depend on writers and that *virtus* is judged by rhetoric, 8. 2–4.

[34] This process of replacement and loss is thematized by Cato's remark that we have lost the true meaning of words; see 52. 11 and below, p. 157. See also Sallust's complaint at 12. 1: *paupertas probro haberi, innocentia pro malivolentia duci coepit* (note *haberi* again meaning 'is [wrongly] held to be'), and 38. 3, all recalling Thucydides 3. 82. 8. Beyond its thematization, the problem of replacement haunts Sallust's text in the repetitions of the word for one thing in the place of another: *pro* occurs 39 times compared with Cicero's *Catilinarian Orations*, where it appears 14 times. Note as well *probro* above.

adequacy of these retranslations is only part of the rhetorical trap. It engages the reader in an effort to get *summa ope niti decet* right. More modification is on the way: of course, *ingeni opibus* must mean *boni ingeni opibus* ('with the resources of a good *ingenium*'); and, as mentioned, the goal of eternal fame for *virtus* may be just a mistaken belief (one thinks of the *fama atque invidia* ('reputation and envious ill-will') that troubled Sallust himself, 4. 1; and not only that, but by writing it up in his monograph Sallust makes sure that the *invidia* will follow him as long as readers read the *B.C.*). Furthermore, the *B.C.* as history makes it eminently clear that the moral imperative does not apply to everyone: surely not to Catiline, and surely not to the resources of a *malum pravumque ingenium* ('a wicked and twisted mind', 8. 2). And things get darker when we add the problems of writing history: how difficult it is to write, the troublesome readers who misunderstand, the distortions writers of great *ingenium* will create in, say, the comparison of Roman *gloria* with Greek *gloria*. Consequently, when the preface fails, as it will, to secure human exertion and goals, the reader's own resources will also seem to have failed to articulate a clear ethical proposition about action and *virtus*. That, I think, describes the motivation and outcome of Earl's project (Earl 1961) and is one of the reasons why commentators and interpreters have so consistently gone back to the text, rewritten Sallust, and filled his ellipses.[35]

Returning to the text, we find that the second paragraph offers a test case. McGushin comments, '1. 5–2. 6 applies the general principle enunciated in 1. 1–4 to the sphere of government (*imperium*).'[36] The goal of human endeavour was stated in 1. 3 as *gloria* and *memoria quam maxume longa*. And here Sallust's investigation into the relative value of *vis corporis* ('physical power') and *animi virtus* (*virtus* of mind) comes to an unequivocal conclusion: *conpertum est in bello plurumum ingenium posse* ('it was discovered in war that *ingenium* was most powerful', 2. 2). But the investigation which demonstrates the priority of *ingenium* and *animi virtus* puts the display of *animi virtus* in a troublesome context. It

---

[35] See, for instance, the conclusion of Earl 1961: 111, 'Sallust's political thought, then, centres on a concept of *virtus* as the functioning of *ingenium* to achieve *egregia facinora*, and thus to win *gloria*, through *bonae artes*.' This conclusion, we shall see, is satisfactory neither as a prescription nor as a description. Sallust makes it especially clear that *ingenium ipsum* has little to do with *virtus*; that even a *bonum ingenium* may be impeded from *egregia facinora*; that *facinora* at times must be the inactive life of a historian (and that requires a defence); and that there is no necessary connection between *ingenium*, *gloria*, *facinora*, and *bonae artes*. Catiline is a case in point. His *ingenium* is *malum*; his *gloria* endures at least as long as Sallust's and does so because of Sallust.

[36] McGushin 1977 ad loc.

was, Sallust says, at first unclear whether military success depended more on physical strength or *animi virtus: certamen fuit, vine corporis an virtute animi res militaris magis procederet* ('there was a contest as to whether military affairs succeeded more because of bodily strength or mental virtue'). Consequently, rulers availed themselves of their own particular talents: *divorsi pars ingenium, alii corpus exercebant* ('in different ways some exercised intelligence, others the body', 2. 1). It was a time when life was passed without the disruption of *cupiditas* ('desire', 'greed', 'appetite'): *sua quoique satis placebant* ('each was quite pleased with their own possessions', 2. 1). McGushin notes 'the exclusion of a stage of primitive simplicity from the arena of worthwhile activity' since 'the exercise of *ingenium* in the pursuit of *gloria*' is what defines worthwhile activity for men.[37] But the situation is more complex: some did exercise *ingenium* and *virtus animi*. But that was not, in itself, sufficient to settle the dispute. Furthermore, men may have lacked *cupiditas*, but that lack is itself a moral good, as is the stability found in *sua quoique satis placebant* (cf. the instability when corruption sets in: *quod si regum atque imperatorum animi virtus in pace ita ut in bello valeret, aequabilius atque constantius sese res humanae haberent, neque aliud alio ferri neque mutari ac misceri omnia cerneres* ('But if *animi virtus* of kings and military leaders prevailed in peace as in war, human affairs would be more equitable and stable, and you would not be seeing things carried off in different directions and everything changing and confused,' 3. 1)). The failure of this period between 'primitive simplicity' and true *gloria* is marked by the fact that these *reges* ('kings') and *imperatores* ('generals') have in Sallust's text no names. They did not achieve *gloria* or any form of *memoria*. In fact, when we do get names, both of individuals, like Cyrus, and of states, *Lacedaemonii et Athenienses* ('Spartans and Athenians'), when we finally hear of great political and military success, of *maxuma gloria* and *maxumum imperium*, and when the *certamen* ('contest', 'struggle') is finally resolved in favour of *ingenium*, we reach the resolution only at the expense of leaders who consider that 'lust for domination is a legitimate cause for war', *lubidinem dominandi causam belli habere*, and that 'the greatest glory consisted in the greatest military power', *maximam gloriam in maximo imperio*.[38] Here it is not success which is ambiguous or which creates ethical dangers: it is the quest for *gloria* itself; or, put another way, in Sallust the goal of human life and the reward of history entails false equivalences and moral risk. This would

---

[37] McGushin 1977 ad loc.; see also on *genus hominum agreste*, 6. 1.
[38] Note in *habere* (2. 2) the ominous echo of *habetur* (1. 4).

contradict in the most fundamental way the noble belief that men become divine, godlike, and glorious forever through the exercise of mental virtue. In fact, there is surely a bitter irony in the fact that the success of *ingenium* depends both on *lubido* ('desire', 'passion', 'lust') and a false equation of *gloria* with *imperium* (Sallust's own decision to leave politics and write history can be seen as evidence that *imperium* is not the greatest source of *gloria*; perhaps history is). If the success of that mental virtue depends upon a 'lust for domination' and a false belief that 'the greatest glory consists in the greatest army', then *gloria* and history itself are already tainted.[39] Nietzsche was right when he said that Sallust's 'cold sarcasm against "beautiful words" and "beautiful sentiments" is the enemy of all lofty words and sentiments' (*Twilight of the Idols*, 13. 1). Here that sarcasm turns on the lofty words of his own preface. Readers will have to decide whether this sarcasm is satiric, marking 'the lies our fathers told us', or nostalgic.

As soon as Sallust concludes that *ingenium* is the more important asset in war, he turns to peace and civil government. 'But if the *animi virtus* of kings and generals were to prevail in peace just as in war, then human affairs would be more equitable and steady' (quoted above).[40] The strategic success of *ingenium in bello* ('mental capacity in war') depended upon *labor, continentia et aequitas* ('hard work, temperance, and fairness'); but the specification Sallust leaves out is that restraint and equity compose the posture of the *reges* or *imperatores* only with regard to his own men and state. With regard to other states, *cupiditas, lubido dominandi*, and dissatisfaction with one's own possessions has already characterized the actions of this *animi virtus*. This oversight, however, is itself an effective element in the progress of Sallust's exposition. No sooner does the text overlook *lubido dominandi* than it reappears in *lubido atque superbia* (2. 5), just after *aliud alio ferri* (2. 3) reverses *sua quoique satis placebant*. The moral and political risks of *maxumam gloriam in maximo imperio* are overlooked only to be rediscovered, now in civil *imperium*. If the progress here seems untidy, it is because *lubido dominandi* cannot be tidily relegated to foreign affairs once it begins to motivate *animi virtus*. Indeed, even the term *animi virtus* becomes problematic in the context of *lubido*, but that is a typical Sallustian problem: what exactly is *animi virtus*? If this *virtus* has the capacity for *lubido dominandi*, then the seeds of political turmoil and civil chaos may already be part of the moral

---

[39] On *cupido gloriae, certamen gloriae*, and [*certamen*] *dominationis* in the *Histories*, see La Penna 1968: 301–2 (= p. 360 of this book).

[40] *quodsi regum atque imperatorum animi virtus in pace ita ut in bello valeret, aequabilius atque constantius sese res humanae haberent*, 2. 3.

injunction, *summa ope niti decet, ne vitam silentio transeant* which seemed so secure at the beginning. In any event, when the paragraph ends, *lubido et superbia* are on the attack and fortune is now in control. There is little left of the opening assurance: 'All men...ought to strive with all resources less they pass through their life unnoticed.' All of this, of course, takes on even more problematic connotations when we consider that Catiline here in Sallust's monograph will speak, be spoken of, and win a kind of *gloria* that will last as long as Sallust's.

In a sense the underlying problem is one of definition, of drawing the right boundaries. What did or should *summa ops* mean? What kind of *memoria* should be made *quam maxime longa*? This semantic problem is the analogue of a political problem and the problem of writing history; it involves both knowledge of what things are and should be and control over them and their use.[41] What is *animi virtus* and does it really apply to Cyrus? Can we exercise a full *animi virtus* in foreign affairs without *lubido dominandi* and still achieve *maxima gloria*? The experience Sallust offers is simultaneously one of discovering that some resources (like *summa ope*) must be defined and limited, but that other definitions will not contain what they were meant to contain. Sallust, of course, makes the semantic problem explicitly political in Cato's speech: 'We have long since lost the true names for things,'[42] Cato says, shortly before his own garish rhetoric redefines *misericordia* ('pity', 'compassion', 'mercy') as a form of bribery in which the gift given to the wicked is the blood of innocent men.[43]

But the text throughout undermines the categories it proposes. To return to the preface, Sallust's conclusion about the process by which 'a change in character is accompanied by a change in *fortuna*' (2. 5) is: 'And so it is always the case that *imperium* is transferred from the less good to the *optimus quisque*' ('the best individuals').[44] This is a bitter consolation; it contains the disturbing possibility of irony and another problem of definition. *Optimus quisque* is notoriously ambiguous: redolent of Roman

[41] See further Batstone 1988b.
[42] *iam pridem equidem nos vera vocabula rerum amisimus*, 52. 11. See now Batstone 2010b.
[43] 29. *ne illi sanguinem nostrum largiantur* appears under the argument *hic mihi quisquam mansuetudinem et misericordiam nominat* (52. 11) and is a direct consequence of the concession *sint misericordes in furibus aerari* (52. 12). Thus, Cato may be said to argue: words do not mean what they used to; *misericordia* is misused; but let the senators be what they call *misericordes* when dealing with thieves; let them not be *misericordes* when dealing with our lives, because that amounts to making our blood into a form of *largitio* to the criminals. See further Batstone 1988b and 2010b.
[44] *ita imperium semper ad optumum quemque a minus bono transfertur*, 2. 6.

politics, it suggests both the turmoil in Rome and the fact that Rome herself may have already become a participant in the changes of *fortuna* which affect others.[45] But the term also engages other questions of definition and applications. First, does it refer exclusively to individual leaders within states or to states as imperial powers? Put another way, can the reader, in terms of this proposition, draw an exclusive and safe boundary between foreign and domestic decay? And, furthermore, who are the *optimus quisque*? Are they really those whose strategic success shows a certain *animi virtus*? Is the term itself sardonic, shifting as easily from ruler or ruling class to new ruler or new ruling class as power and *fortuna* do? Was Cyrus *optimus quisque* when his lust for power conquered kings who were satisfied with their boundaries? It is not surprising that at this point Sallust's rhetoric must regroup and change direction, and that, when it does, Sallust attempts a new version of *gloria*: not just any *gloria*, or any *memoria longa*, but 'fame for a brilliant act or good character' (*praeclari facinoris aut artis bonae famam*, 2. 9). These adjectives, however, only reassert the ethical orientation that keeps eluding specification,[46] and they create a new problem: *fama*, which is, of course, already involved in a *praeclarum facinus*.

The problem of constructing an adequate ethical imperative and the inevitable difficulties and revisions required by a new context continue throughout the preface. *Fama* or *gloria* continues to be a problem. The historian, who contributes to *fama*, undertakes a task difficult enough to justify it as an alternative to politics (3. 1–2). However, the difficulties themselves, the *malevolentia et invidia* ('ill-will/hatred and hostile envy') of his audience, only reveal another problem with *gloria* as either the measure or the goal of men's lives. 'When you recount the virtue and glory of good men, those things which each man thinks easy for him to do he hears with equanimity; beyond that he considers them just like fictions as good as false.'[47] What is happening to 'fame for a brilliant act or good character'? Sallust's new career holds the same dangers as those that drove him from his old career: *invidia* and *fama*. The glory of good men tends to be eradicated by a world in which *invidia* attacks not only ethical and political successes but those who try to write the record of those successes.[48]

---

[45] See Plato Rep. 544d–e and Polybius, prol. 3, for the theoretical background that universalizes decline and fortune.

[46] *Praeclari*, of course, reopens the questions of *ne...silentio*.

[47] *ubi de virtute atque gloria bonorum memores, quae sibi quisque facilia factu putat, aequo animo accipit, supra ea veluti ficta pro falsis ducit*, 3. 2.

[48] Soon afterwards, in 6. 3, Sallust will comment on the result of early Roman successes: *sed postquam res eorum civibus moribus agris aucta satis prospera satisque pollens videbatur, sicuti pleraque mortalium habentur, invidia ex opulentia orta est*. The issue is the same:

Later, in chapter 8, Sallust will reveal yet another complication in the nature of *fama*. Not only is it the case that true *fama* is always under assault and may be erased, but the hallmark of written *fama*, the great Athenian historians, simply by virtue of the context in which they appear and their own talents, may, Sallust says, misrepresent *fama*:

> The history of Athens, as I judge it, was quite grand and magnificent, but still a little less than its reputation. Rather, because extremely talented writers appeared there, Athenian deeds are renowned throughout the world as the greatest. Consequently, the virtue of actors is believed commensurate with the illustrious talents of those who were able to aggrandize them with words.[49]

Ingenia, even *praeclara ingenia* ('brilliant/distinguished natural talents), are returned to a world where *fama* may be distorted by the talent (*magna ingenia* ('great natural talents')) of writers. History presents problems for the goal of all men: it is hard to write, hard to read, and may itself be a distortion.

At *B.C.* 3. 3, another form of *fama* and another context is addressed. If the official, written form of *gloria* is a problem because of the context in which it appears and the bias and self-image of readers, so is the more common, unofficial form of *fama* that constitutes a man's reputation. Sallust brings himself forward as an example of the inaccuracies of *fama*; but more than that, it is significant that he claims to be a victim, not of *malum ingenium* ('wicked character'), and explicitly not of *malae artes* ('wicked ways'), but of an impossible context. He abandons an active political life because he cannot win *praeclari facinoris aut bonae artis fama* ('a reputation for a brilliant deed or good character'), not because he was incapable of *praeclara facinora* ('brilliant deeds'). The problem of reaching an acceptable version of the goal originally stated, *ne vitam silentio transeant*, includes not just the problem of appropriate means and appropriate definitions, but the context that bestows or refuses to bestow *fama* of the right type. Sallust's radical revision of *summa ope niti decet* can now appear as a retirement from political life; 'striving with the fullest resources of the *animus*' has become *animus...requievit*, 'my *animus* rested', 4. 1; and his own goal now is only a relative contentment

---

virtue and success create an *invidia* which attempts to destroy them; they create the conditions of their own demise.

[49] *Atheniensium res gestae, sicuti ego aestumo, satis amplae magnificaeque fuere, verum aliquanto minores tamen quam fama feruntur. sed quia provenere ibi scriptorum magna ingenia, per terrarum orbem Atheniensium facta pro maxumis celebrantur. ita eorum qui fecere virtus tanta habetur, quantum eam verbis potuere extollere praeclara ingenia*, 8. 2–4.

with the *gloria* that will come from commemorating others. The very fact that Sallust must defend his retirement and his new profession is not an escape from the problematic context he addresses but an echo of it. Not only does his defence repeat the *fama* and *invidia* of the political endeavours which he has abandoned, but it will continue to do so both elsewhere in the monograph and as long as the monograph is read. Sallust claims that he was just a youngster (*adulescentulus*, 3. 3), his youth was held and corrupted by ambition (*inbecilla aetas ambitione conrupta tenebatur*, 3. 4). But this excuse is exactly what the moralist Cato rejects when he sarcastically mocks those who would excuse the conspirators: 'They made a mistake, the youngsters, through ambition' (*deliquere homines adulescentuli per ambitionem*, 52. 26). It is a bold and provocative move to have the epitome of moral posturing in the late Republic attack the terms of Sallust's own self-exoneration. Does it mark Cato as ignorant of the forces at work? A man misusing words while carried away with anger and righteousness? Or accuse Sallust of having come all too close to the mistakes of the conspirators? Is it the sign of a lingering guilty conscience? A recognition that all these ambitious *adulescentuli* were equally at risk? The promise of full exertion for the sake of public and political *gloria* is a troubled enterprise, and no one can escape its moral dangers.

Sallust's final qualification on *fama* or *gloria* comes as a new version of *memoria quam maxime longa*. Earlier, this was posed as better than the fragile and slippery *gloria* arising from wealth and beauty. *Memoria longa*, as a simple version of what men should do, was conflicted when Cyrus won *maxima gloria* with his *lubido dominandi*. Now, however, another failed application of the formula appears: it is the *Bellum Catilinae* and Catiline himself. For, when Sallust seeks *gloria* for himself as a historian, he must project his own *memoria Catilinae* ('the memory/history/account of Catiline') as something which will endure *quam maxime longa*. Consequently, the length of Sallust's *gloria* is now bound to and indivisible from the length of Catiline's *memoria* and vice versa. *Memoria longa* is what Catiline has achieved, and to this extent it cannot orient action. Sallust explicitly calls Catiline's deed *memorabile* ('worthy of memory/*memoria*'), but here the cause is *sceleris atque periculi novitiate*, 'the unprecedented crime and danger', 4. 4.

Catiline's appearance at 5. 1 subverts in yet another way the effort to secure the terms of conventional ethics. I noted above that *summa ops*, when faced with the duality of *vis corporis* and *vis animi*, required the rejection of *virium opibus* in comparison with *ingeni opibus*. Catiline now appears *magna vi et animi et corporis*. Another formula has failed; or, put another way, in the context of 5. 1 the reader sees that 1. 2

diverted attention in the wrong direction. It was not *vis animi* which was needed at all, it was *bonum ingenium*; and with this specification the ethical orientation is again merely named, not secured or explained.[50] And there are other disturbing implications. What if one does not have a *bonum ingenium*? What, then, can the state or the ethicist do?[51] What is the purpose finally of a proposition like *mihi rectius videtur ingeni quam virium opibus gloriam quaerere* ('it seems to me more upright/correct to seek *gloria* with the resources of one's *ingenium* than one's power) when that is exactly the way in which Catiline seeks what he does seek and gains the long memory of Sallust's monograph, *sed ingenio malo pravoque* ('but with a wicked and twisted *ingenium*'), 5. 1. The problem is not just that it all depends upon accidents of birth, *ingenium*, and accidents of context and *fama*, but that the statement of what we should do, *animi imperio, corporis servitio magis utimur* (we use better the mind's control, the body's servitude') (1. 2), is in fact a statement of what we mostly do do, and perhaps of what we always do regardless. It cannot orient an ethical imperative, like *mihi rectius videtur*, because in the case of a *malum ingenium* it already motivates the ethical problem; and this is what Catiline, *magna vi et animi et corporis sed ingenio malo pravoque* ('with great power of both mind and body but with a wicked and twisted *ingenium*'), reveals. Sallust's text, as it retranslates itself and considers in new contexts the elements of its provisional propositions, grows out of its own inadequacy and keeps creating further inadequacy.

This writing has been described by Quintilian as broken and deceptive.[52] I have been discussing the way in which the propositional content is broken and deceptive, the way in which the semantic problem is part of the political problem and imitates that problem. At every level, the text is a set of stylistic devices that require negotiation, supplements, and reinterpretation. Of the many examples of stylistic deception one could choose, none is more typical than the proposed *gloria* of *ne vitam silentio transeant*. In the context of *summa ope niti* and *animi imperio, corporis servitio*, we have assumed that the glory proposed is for political and military success.

---

[50] Earl's discussion rightly emphasizes *ingenium* in Sallust's political thought. Sallust, however, does not so much 'redefine' *virtus* (even Earl admits that the terms are originally those of Cato the Censor) as disclose its embattled, vulnerable, and helpless condition.

[51] Sallust remains equivocal about this possibility, for later he rejects the life of those for whom *contra naturam corpus voluptati anima oneri fuit*, but his carefully contrived and shifting vocabulary (*animus, vis animi, animi virtus, ingenium, anima*) ultimately escapes a rigid hierarchical scheme, just as it keeps raising the question of definition.

[52] *brevitas et abruptum sermonis genus: quod otiosum fortasse lectorem minus fallat, audientem transvolat, nec dum repetatur expectat*, 4. 2. 45.

Thus, McGushin glosses *silentium*: 'in a passive sense.... They go through life unnoticed, they are *sine gloria* both in their lifetime and after death.... The emphasis is on the activity required.'[53] But the gloss and the need for a gloss indicate that the expression may provoke another interpretation: *silentio* in an active sense. In our eagerness to get the right interpretation of the word as it appears at 1. 1, we have failed to notice and to emphasize that it is this rejected interpretation which motivates the text before us. Sallust's personal version of *ne... silentio* is to write (to speak) what we are reading, and by speaking in this way to deny silence to Catiline's crime.

Let me review what this kind of writing does. Its rhetorical form and assertive presentation seem to offer the security of absolutes, of ethical imperatives, supported by traditional and conventional thought and categories. This 'promise' plays upon a desire for ethical certainty and, in so doing, highlights that desire at the same time that it appears to fulfil it. Consequently, when that certainty begins to be undermined by further developments in Sallust's own text, readers have felt the need to rewrite 'the political thought of Sallust' in order to fill a lack which the text has helped to create. Ethical certainty is not something Sallust offers. In fact, Sallust's history does the opposite. But in doing so, it provokes the reader to invent and impose new versions of certainty that eventually dissolve in contextual negotiations and compromises, as, for instance, when *niti* (1. 1) becomes for Sallust *requievit* (4. 1). It is finally the readers of Sallust who, in exercising their *ingenium* and *virtus*, become or try to become old-fashioned moralists, not Sallust.

Sallust provokes this response by employing a style that is abrupt and deceptive, both in its propositions and in its terms. It ostentatiously requires interpretation beyond the conventional norms of grammar and lexicography. It often seems to mean one thing and comes to mean another thing, or two things. This problem of the meaning and application of words and phrases is a form of negotiation and retranslation in accordance with a changing and shifty context. Broken and deceptive, thus, become terms which summarize Sallust's style, his ethical certainty, and the period whose history he attempts to write. In the *Bellum Catilinae*, Sallust is in part concerned with the impact and intellectual conflict of 'knowing that something is needed' but not 'knowing what is needed'. This is the analogue of knowing that someone was involved but not knowing who.

The ethical and political problems had, of course, no answer. In fact, the *Bellum Catilinae* is a tale of failure. Nothing was solved by the war,

---

[53] And so on, with a reference to *de utraque siletur* at 2. 8.

and, despite Caesar's confidence that the mind unclouded by emotion will always prevail (50. 1–3), neither Cato nor Caesar found a solution to the particular or the general problem. By the late 40s Sallust had seen many failures of *ingenium* and *virtus*. He writes about a lack, about obscurity, and about ambiguous men of power. He himself had already given up. *Mores* vexed him; *fortuna* had changed; *imperium* was, he thought, in danger of slipping away; action now had to be writing; historical glory had now become stories of strange new danger and crime.

The final picture of the *Bellum Catilinae* is, I think, indicative of both the continuing conflict and Sallust's rhetoric. It is common knowledge that Sallust portrays a Catiline who speaks like a seasoned Roman general. His army fought bravely, and, Sallust says, you could have seen 'how much *animi vis* there had been in Catiline's army', *quanta animi vis fuisset in exercitu Catilinae*, 61. 1. All were wounded in the front, and 'Catiline was found far in advance of his men amid a heap of slain foes', *Catilina vero longe a suis inter hostium cadavera repertus est*, 61. 4. Catiline shows in some degree the *ingenium* and *vis animi* in war that was not his in peace. But the whole ends with a strangely pathetic scene, both commemorative of civil war and fraught with its own conflicts and lack of resolution or closure.[54] Romans come to the battlefield and gaze with mixed emotions on the dead. The scene should be closural, resolving and ending a narrative of civil strife, with victory and death. The first dissonance, however, is thematic. Romans come from the camp to plunder, 'many', Sallust says. It is particularly ironic that this war should end with dead Roman citizens as sources of booty. Was that not Catiline's plan, except that he had not planned to be among the plundered? One recalls the image of civil strife, *aliud alio ferri*, that Sallust says invades the state when *continentia et aequitas* are gone.

But more important than these actions, the closural movement should imagine and give space to the mixed emotions provoked by such a war. Those emotions are there, and they are mixed, as one would expect; but they are not quite the right emotions and not mixed in the way one expects. There is no sadness that these men, with all their *vis animi et corporis*, are lost to the state. There is not the more general and common mixture of emotions that civil war must evoke: relief that the war is over, joy that the winners won, sorrow that Romans had to die. Rather, as Romans come to plunder Romans, some see *amici*, some *inimici*. (*amici* are your political and personal friends, people who support you in the

---

[54] See now Levene 1992 on lack of closure in the *B.J.*

Senate; *inimici* are those who oppose you. The term *hostes* is reserved for foreign enemies and opponents in war.) That is to say, they observe, not the remains of a military encounter, but the remains of normal Roman political activity, *amici* and *inimici*, the traditional allegiances and associations that negotiated power and influence in the state. And it is this sight which occasions joy and sadness, *laetitia maeror luctus atque gaudia* ('joy, sorrow, grief, and jubilation'). Sadness over the death of *amici* combines with an ominous joy at the death of *inimici*. The work's final conflict comes after the events of the *bellum* itself are over. It is a failure of closure, as the appropriate feelings of joy and sadness are applied inappropriately and inauspiciously to the remains of the body politic.

ADDENDUM

This is a revised version of an article published in 1990. When it has seemed particularly relevant, I have tried to bring the bibliography up to date. In some places the argument has been only lightly revised, or not changed at all; in other places, I thought some significant revisions would clarify or even expand the argument. At this distance from the original paper, it seems that the issue I was wrestling with was a fundamental one: why write the *B.C.*? If ethical and moral clarity fails, if events of history fade into self-interests and rumour, if neither Caesar's *ingenium* nor Cato's can solve either the immediate problem represented by Catiline or the looming problem of *virtus* and *res publica* (which one might not unfairly call the opposition of Caesar and Cato), then what is the use of history? Surely it has some use; we keep writing it, and so did Sallust, and, despite 'the intentional fallacy' fallacy, we do want to know what Sallust thought he was up to, and we should, and every reader does. Similarly, we want to know what the text is doing, and it may do more or less than the writer thought, hoped, planned. Since this essay was published, some work has taken up similar ideas. Levene 1992 focused on the lack of closure in the *B.J.* and Levene 2000 has explored Cato's diagnosis of decline as implicated in the decline at Rome; Kraus 1999 read the disorder and uncertainties of the *B.J.* as represented in part by Jugurtha as a diagnosis of contemporary Rome and a threat to the writing of history; Gunderson 2000 read many of the contradictions and repetitions in the *B.C.* as categorical and philosophical failures, which entails reading repetitions and blockages as psychological events, as symptoms of a system that does not work but has to be continually reworked. While my conclusions are similar to and compatible with Levene and Kraus, Gunderson takes a strikingly different approach: The text betrays the writer; the reader is the analyst. There are merits and difficulties with that view, just as there are difficulties and, I hope, merits with reading the *B.C.* as a poetic/mimetic image of mind (theory of history, philosophy, morals, politics) running up against the real (world). The writer shapes the text; the reader is the audience. Other scholars have searched for clarity and certainty: Krebs 2008 has tried to revive a philosophical continuity around the image of 'the way'. The writer believes there is a way. Others may read the blockages and problems as a form of authorial disillusionment: The writer no longer believes or believes it is all a lie. Some read the text as immature. Reading will go on, and that is a good thing.

7

The History of Mind and the Philosophy of History in Sallust's *Bellum Catilinae*

Erik Gunderson

A. PROBLEMS

With the assassination of Julius Caesar on the Ides of March in 44 BCE, the fortunes of one of Caesar's lesser political partisans began to wane. Gaius Sallustius Crispus, a minor figure, formerly involved in scandal and now left without a backer, retired from politics and began to write history. His first project was an account of a failed *coup d'état* from some decades before. Sallust recorded the efforts of a thwarted candidate for Rome's highest office named Lucius Sergius Catilina to raise an army of disaffected Romans and foreigners and to install himself and his partisans at Rome. In the end nothing much came of the plot: some were arrested and killed; some fought and died; others who had not been caught in too manifest support of Catiline were suddenly expressing their enmity for the monster.

Albeit brief, the above is perhaps an adequate summary of both text and author. However this summary does not do justice to the methodological significance of this particular text. Indeed, the text begins not with historical questions, but with a discussion of historiographic issues. While one has become by now familiar with readings of history that read a particular historian's philosophy of history out of an author and perhaps in spite of that author's best efforts, Sallust opens his own text with an explicit meditation on history and philosophy. Furthermore, Sallust inserts himself into the history and into the philosophy of history. Thus, with Sallust one cannot merely 'expose' his historical methods: language, philosophy, and autobiography are already themes within the text, not strands to be plucked out of it. Sallust's history, then, is also a history that labours to present an account of the very possibility of

History of Mind and Philosophy of History 167

history and of the historian. Sallust offers a text that grapples with some of the most basic problems of historiography: what are the conditions of possibility for history? What is the history's relationship to its object? What is the place of the historian relative to his project?

Sallust's philosophy of history is less a formal philosophy than it is a collection of statements about the movement of certain abstract qualities in historical time. In particular, the evolution of man's mind or *ingenium* plays a key role in Sallust's philosophical prologue. Sallust also provides an indication of the role of the historian within the terms he has set forth; and the philosophy of mind's role in history has as one of its special cases historiography. Despite the broad implications of such a philosophy for Sallust's own work, Sallust's philosophical introduction has been poorly received: it is charged with being at least trite, and perhaps also wholly extraneous to his narrative.[1] This verdict fails to see the profundity of Sallust's philosophy, and so too does it fail to see that this profundity is a function of the philosophy's intimate connection with the narrative itself.

When we get to the narrative proper, Sallust will employ many expressions and notions that echo the terms of historical cognition that he offers in this prologue. I would like, then, to read the whole of the text of the *Bellum Catilinae* aggressively by way of the dialectic of mind that Sallust himself offers.[2] I wish to plumb his philosophy without becoming overly distracted as to either its originality or its soundness. I will seek instead its structure and its implications in the here and now of Sallust's own project. I will then read the rest of the monograph through the lens

---

[1] While Sallust's remarks have often been characterized as commonplaces, Syme 1964: 241 n. 7 justly resists simple genealogical research here: 'A large number of the "borrowings" and "influences" are insignificant, their accumulation tedious.' Earl 1961: 7 likewise rescues Sallust from his antecedents: 'It is worth while to examine the prologues and to try to discover what Sallust meant from what he wrote and not from one's opinion of his sources and their value.' Tiffou 1973: 34 treats exhaustively of Sallust's prefaces, and he notes that they cannot be removed without a loss to the whole of the work. See also Büchner 1982: 104–5. It is precisely in the coordination or lack thereof between these morsels of philosophy that a tension emerges that produces a strain felt throughout the whole work. Vretska's commentary offers extensive documentation of the antecedents of Sallust's thought. See Vretska 1976: *ad loc.* and compare McGushin 1977: 293–5. Note also Leeman 1954–5: 323–39 and 38–48 for the importance of reading the preface for itself and in its relation to the whole of the work.

[2] Here we will have to entertain the conceptual apparatus of the Hegelian dialectic even if Sallust's version routinely fails in its efforts at sublation. Hegel himself sees already in antiquity a variety of powerful early versions of dialectic in the Sophists, the Socratics, and so forth. In fact, Sallust's thought is perhaps closest to Hegel's portrait of Anaxagoras: the emphasis is on mind, but there is a difficulty in making its relationship to its object truly dialectical. See Hegel 1974.

of these abstractions and 'truths' that Sallust forces upon his reader from the outset.

Sallust writes of revolution and social discord. But this writing takes place within an intellectual apparatus that already bears the marks of a crisis of its own. The historian and his philosophy of history founder in a manner that harmonizes with the troubled world that would be described.[3] Sallust thus winds up mistelling and untelling his tale in a manner that is ironically entirely appropriate to his history, even if this appropriateness is not of the variety Sallust may have intended. I wish to trace the means by which this historian loses his ability to secure principles vital to him, yet in so losing these principles also shows how there is a disturbance in the world that necessitates the loss. In the very narrative difficulties he encounters Sallust reveals that there has been a revolution in the state that succeeded in overturning the mind even as it has failed to seize political power.[4]

Let me be up front here. For reasons that are more fully articulated below, I see in Sallust's text not the performance of authorship as the mastery of intended meaning, but instead the demonstration of the conditions within which such a mastery is lost. The author here becomes a character within a text that radically questions the function of the author as being exhaustive of its own discursive contents. Within this text the author cannot be the one who in the final instance knows.[5]

Sallust's philosophical prologue to his history fails to clarify the historical and conceptual antecedents to the conspiracy. Indeed, a variety of key terms and ideas that are reused in the story of the conspiracy at once fall into disarray. Most importantly, spirit, mind, and memory (*animus*,

---

[3] Compare Hegel 1956: 60 on the necessary relationship between the subjective and the objective, the *historia rerum gestarum* and the *res gestae* themselves. See as well the comments of White 1987: 11–14, where White specifically glosses this passage in terms of a conflict between desire and the law.

[4] One could compare Kraus 1999 on the untidiness of the *Jugurtha*, and the origins and consequences of this untidiness. It should be noted, though, that Kraus herself accepts the claim that the *Catiline* has a 'neat dramatic arc' (218). Here she is following Scanlon 1987: 63.

[5] Compare Foucault 1977. The basis for this kind of close literary/philosophical rereading of Sallust has been laid principally, I believe, by the work of Batstone and the related efforts of Sklenář. My essay, though, is more earnestly engaged with the whole post-structuralist discourse of the 'death of the author'. Though not formally a post-structuralist account, see Kraus 1999: 220 and 244–5 for the suggestion that Jugurtha threatens Sallust's own project in that text. Dillery's review of this essay makes the mistake of conflating that which exceeds authorial intention as the zone of meaninglessness. See Dillery 2007: 'If we treat the slippages and discontinuities of Sallust's narrative as signs of his inability to write coherently about his topic, then all of the meaning of his text would seem to be thrown into doubt.'

History of Mind and Philosophy of History 169

ingenium, and *memoria*)[6] are rendered unstable.[7] Thus, there are crises enough before Catiline himself appears on the scene. When the tale of the conspiracy is finally told, the breaches in the backdrop replay themselves in the historical foreground. Historical agents reiterate the conceptual failures left over from the philosophical and historical prelude. With a crooked rule one builds a crooked house.

These opening chapters hence serve to introduce the historical players in an unexpected sense: it is not only the ambiguity of the conspiracy that has been presaged.[8] Much like the concepts that introduce them, the historical actors too are split, doubled, and compromised. This rather chaotic figuration of contemporary historical agents thus both is and is not a problem of contemporary political life. They are troubled souls because their times are troubling; but they are also disturbed because their historical genealogy is confused. In this sense the problem of telling a history of *virtus* has washed out into the farthest reaches of the monograph: the loss of this and other vital terms amidst the proximate civil disarray redounds back onto the position from which a critical authorship of a version of these events would position itself.

This is the loss not just of memory, but also of the concept of memory in a world where words have lost their ordinary meaning. Such a formulation looks forward to Cato's admonition and reproach levelled at his fellow senators: 'We've long since stopped calling things by their true names' (*iam pridem equidem nos vera vocabula rerum*

---

[6] I will translate both *animus* and *ingenium* with terms that stress these as rational and intellectual words. Tiffou 1973: 143 offers a more precise definition of their relationship in Sallust:

[L'*animus*] représente l'esprit et toutes les qualités qui lui sont attachés, intelligence, intuition, compréhension, raison, etc. L'*ingenium* comprend aussi l'ensemble de ces qualités, mais en tant qu'elles se trouvent chez tel ou tel individu et qu'elles obéissent à un équilibre entre elles qui varie avec chaque cas particulier. Il est, aux yeux de Salluste, susceptible d'être amélioré ou dépravé.

Hence, in concentrating on the more plastic *ingenium* over *animus*, Sallust allows for a history of the vicissitudes of intelligence, reason, and the spirit.

[7] Batstone 1988b: 1–29 shows how 'virtue' or *virtus* is a category that is destabilized in Sallust's comparison of Cato and Caesar later on in the text. Skléna ř 1998: 205–20 follows up on a number of key strands from Batstone's various essays on Sallust.

[8] Batstone 1990: 120 also sees the prologue as failed and hence also as a suitable introduction to the narrative. Batstone, though, thinks the failure pointed and intentional, while I am representing it otherwise. Despite the significant overlap in our concerns, it could fairly be said that I am drawing the precisely opposite conclusions from those reached by Batstone. Nevertheless, I take his work as being the clearest exposition to date of the stakes involved in reading Sallust. The promise of Batstone's method is further revealed in Sklenář 1998.

amisimus, 52. 11).[9] Cato uses the first person but one suspects that he, as author of the sentiment, claims for himself a knowledge of the lost truth of words. Sallust occupies a parallel position vis-à-vis his readers. Sallust marks a loss while intimating a privileged insight into the past. But in neither case does the moralist free himself from a tainted world that taints in turn the very terms that would be used to depict and condemn it. Thus, if it is the function of history to recover the origins from which springs the very discourse of the historian, Sallust provides us with a genealogy that subverts the task of history as recovery of true origins and their narrativization as true story.[10]

In the face of these difficulties, Sallust's work nonetheless stands out as a technique aimed at the recovery of these lost and lamented objects. In this sense, then, the text's failures also mark out a labour of therapy, a process whereby the author points out impossible and traumatic contradictions in the world as part of an effort to work through these difficulties.[11] The text offers up a series of repetitions and abortive attempts at working through its own difficulties. Nevertheless, these efforts will not provide an eventual cure for the text's neurotic symptoms. And yet this same set of tics and preoccupations does allow us to diagnose the points of trauma and to point out a path where a coherent understanding of Roman history can be found.

B. HISTORIOGRAPHY

The opening acts of Sallust's drama focus on the conceptual and historical antecedents of the conspiracy.[12] Sallust's account, though, is a bit

---

[9] See Sklenář 1998: 215–16 for a discussion of the phrase and a review of the pertinent bibliography.

[10] Compare Foucault 1977a: 143–5. And notice as well the requirements laid out by Hegel 1974 that a history of philosophy be a manifestation of the evolution of philosophy itself. That is, the account of the past history of mind is fundamentally bound up with the question of the status of mind as it produces that very account. This is a proposition fundamental to a reading of Sallust as well. And just as *The History of Philosophy* is necessarily a genealogy of Hegelianism specifically, so too is Sallust's philosophy of mind itself necessarily bound to Sallust's specific role as producer of a history of mind. The Sallustian version, though, for me has a much less happy ending.

[11] See Sklenář 1998: 206 for the invocation of 'autologomachy' or a text against itself. My approach is thus in sympathy with Sklená ř's reading of the stakes of the Cato and Caesar speeches.

[12] Leeman 1967: 108–15 usefully analyses the relationship between Sallust's monographs and Roman tragedy. The pitfalls of overworking the 'tragic' reading of Sallust can be found

History of Mind and Philosophy of History 171

irregular. The early sections of the monograph are confusing and strangely organized. First there are a series of grand cosmic statements about the nature of mind and of man; next one learns of prehistorical forms of government; shortly we learn about the author himself; then Catiline appears; but Catiline immediately gives way to a series of sweeping ruminations on Roman prehistory and history read through the lens of 'character' or 'morals' (*mores*). Eventually Sallust gets to the conspiracy proper, but even here the account is tangled.[13]

It will be useful to trace Sallust's course rather carefully. And, setting to one side the broader narrative structure, one is frequently puzzled by the flow of Sallust's ideas from moment to moment. New paragraphs are often added almost paratactically, and it is frequently left up to the reader to decide the nature of the relationship with the preceding ideas.[14] But Sallust's leaping movement between seemingly dissimilar and discontinuous themes should not preclude the suspicion that there nevertheless lurks an association in Sallust's mind that leads him to speak of the one notion near the other. The analysis of a text on *psyche* might do well to borrow one of the basic tricks of psychoanalytic reading.

The first four sections of the *Bellum Catilinae* are given over to a preface about the evolution in man of the relationship between mind and body. The fifth section introduces Catiline. But then the sixth to thirteenth sections return to a demonstration of the evolution of the mind–body duality.[15] This time decadence and luxury are detailed within this

---

in Büchner's summary of the history of efforts wherein Sallust's work was forced into five acts. See Büchner 1982: 246–7.

[13] Syme 1964: 67 usefully summarizes the problem of the narrative flow as follows: 'The structure is complicated. The author has refused to write a biography or reproduce a portion of Roman annals, from 66 to 63. Disdaining the easy way, he wrecks the narrative order and he brings digressions.' Sallust chooses to wreck his narrative; Syme offers an interesting non-solution to the problems I am investigating. Tiffou 1973: 355–77 offers his own and others' summaries of the structure of the narrative. Compare Vretska 1937, which summarizes the state of the question a generation earlier. Büchner 1982: 132–43 specifically addresses the question of Sallust's use of the excursus in the *Bellum Catilinae*. Wiedemann 1993: 48–57 stresses the literary and historical usefulness of digressions in Sallust's *Bellum Iugurthinum*.

[14] For example, *sed* or 'but' frequently opens a paragraph. Sometimes it introduces a digression that will be closed by an *igitur*. Yet *sed* also introduces a paragraph contrasted with one that precedes it: here the 'but' is adversative. Then again, sometimes *sed* is used loosely and may merely introduce a new idea.

[15] Leeman 1967: 111 highlights the abstract and impersonal quality of Sallust's opening. Apart from a few concrete events, 'der Reste ist reine Sittengeschichte, Geschichte der politisch-moralischen Kräfte, dieser in ihrer Dynamik konkret gemachten Abstrakta, die für das römische und speziell das sallustianische Menschenbild so charakteristisch sind.' ('The remainder is nothing but a history of manners, a history of political and moral forces.

broader outline, giving a more moral cast to the abstract portrait. Section 5 stands between these two versions of the history of the mind. Catiline is the name that moves us from the abstract to the concrete. He is the place where it becomes necessary to turn to Roman history as a special and depraved instance of the history of mind.

Yet this prehistory is itself suspect: as Köstermann noted, Sallust's abstract categories subsist in a tension with the facts of Rome's past.[16] Catiline thus also serves as a point at which the past is falsified in the name of a more telling version of the present: the non-truth of Sallust's prehistory serves only the thematics of the *Bellum Catilinae*, not the truth of Roman history as a general, universal history. Sallust is pointedly not a Livy. This tale of a fallen Republic where words have lost their meaning entails as well the loss of a 'true' relationship to the past. Prehistory gets retold so as to produce a present towards which the logic of the past was pointing. The origin is here not a mere fact or pure chance: the origin is that which 'makes possible a field of knowledge whose function is to recover it'.[17]

Before we ourselves look at Catiline let us instead read closely the prologue as a whole. The opening paragraph of the *Bellum Catilinae* introduces the central terms that will be played out in the whole of the work: mind, memory, and virtue. Sallust begins with the nature of man (*B.C.* 1. 1):

> omneis homines, qui sese student praestare ceteris animalibus, summa ope niti decet, ne vitam silentio transeant veluti pecora, quae natura prona atque ventri oboedientia finxit. sed nostra omnis vis in animo et corpore sita est: animi imperio, corporis servitio magis utimur; alterum nobis cum dis, alterum cum beluis commune est. quo mihi rectius videtur ingeni quam virium opibus gloriam quaerere et, quoniam vita ipsa qua fruimur brevis est, memoriam nostri quam maxume longam efficere. nam divitiarum et formae gloria fluxa atque fragilis est, virtus clara aeternaque habetur.

> All mortal men who wish to rise above other creatures ought to make every effort to avoid passing their lives in silence like the herds of animals whom nature made with downcast eyes and slaves to their bellies. But we find the sum of our powers in our mind and in our body: we use the lordship of our minds and more the slavery of our body. The one we share with the gods, the other with beasts. And so I think it proper to use our powers of intellect rather than the force of our body to seek glory and, given this fleeting life of

The interplay of these last has converted abstractions into concrete entities. The process is typical of Roman and especially Sallustian characterization.')

[16] Köstermann 1973: 789–90.　　[17] Foucault 1977a: 143.

History of Mind and Philosophy of History

ours, to produce the longest possible memory of ourselves. For wealth and beauty's fame is frail and transient; but virtue is glorious and eternal.[18]

Man's nature straddles the divine and the bestial. Sallust introduces an additional hierarchy within this divide: the mind is the sovereign principle while the body is servile.[19] These universal verities within the first section of Sallust's work bridge two versions of language, memory, and authorship. Sallust opens with a twofold statement about both the mastery of mind and the role of language as the agent of mastery.

First, in order to rise above beasts, we must not be slaves to our bellies, but instead make some noise for ourselves and avoid a silent life. Yet these beasts are not representatives of mere animality. They are *pecora*, members of a herd. Here they are perhaps under the sovereignty of a herdsman. At the very least, they are members of a collectivity, a corporate body. One's struggle against the stomach and on behalf of the expressive mouth is necessarily a matter of being exceptional, *egregius*, in its etymological sense [lit.: chosen from the herd]. Speech and the man of speech stand aside from and over against a herd or flock, but as related to and not disjoint from the contrasted items. There is not a radical separation here of speech from animality: this sort of beast is only thought of within a hierarchical universe that coordinates the relationship between master and flock, mind and body. In Hegelese, the dialectic of mind necessarily embraces its own negative.[20]

Moreover man's dual nature ensures that there will always be both minds and bodies, but it is the labour of propriety (*decet, rectius*) to strive (*niti*) to produce both speech and the sovereignty of the herdsman. Hence one should compare the bestial men of section 2. 8: 'I reckon their life and death at the same value, since a silence hangs over each' (*eorum ego vitam mortemque iuxta aestumo, quoniam de utraque siletur*). Sallust qua author both declares the brutish silence of their lives and enacts it by marking these lives with a noisome scorn. The lives are not perfectly silent, since they engender constant reproach from without. The exceptional author-herdsman decrees the market value of his subjects and of his flock: Sallust declares that he has no time for men who are

---

[18] The difficulties surrounding the translation of this last clause will be discussed below.
[19] Hock 1988: 13–24 discusses the politics of servility in Sallust. On the mind as master, see especially pages 17–19.
[20] For Hegel the specific problem within the ancient philosophy of mind is the inability of antiquity to think of spirit as developing out of itself. Hegel accordingly criticizes the entire tradition of mind–matter dualities. See Hegel 1974: 38. And yet it is precisely the materiality of matter and the materiality of history that most troubles Sallust's portrait of the history of mind.

subjected to their bellies (*dediti ventri*, 2. 8). And, in so doing he lives up to the obligation of his own *ingenium*: he has both spoken and mastered in the same moment.

Next, if there is an implication of authorship and cognition as authority in the evocations of the word *pecora*, this theme is swiftly resumed and expanded after the assertion that *imperium* is what we share with the divine and that this sovereignty is the lordship of the mind. For Sallust, mind is not neutral cognition: it is knowing as a sovereign act. In the next sentence Sallust draws a conclusion (*quo*), and he sets himself (*mihi*) on the side of the *ingenium* as against brute strength (*vires*). In human affairs one ought to be governed by intellect and to always manifest it. This is how one ought to seek to be exceptional and to win renown (*gloria*); this is how one compensates for the brevity of life by propagating memory of oneself (*memoria*).[21] Riches and beauty pass away, but virtue (*virtus*) is eternal.[22] Sallust knows, writes, and memorializes these truths for his readers.

Let us do some stocktaking and sort Sallust's inventory of concepts as introduced at the opening of the *Bellum Catilinae*. *Gloria* and *memoria* here pass for virtually the same thing. Fame and memory should both also be taken with *virtus*. Similarly, being eternal, *virtus* is properly allied with the divine. The mind offers the path to all three of these, and it is with the mind's help (*opibus*) that we pursue our proper ends. On the other hand, the body falls out on the side of mere life, riches, and beauty. Sallust thus sets carnality, bestiality, and pleasure against mind, divinity, and virtue.

Adamant about these themes, Sallust essentially reiterates the formulation of this first section in the next, when we meet men who are their bellies' slaves (*dediti ventri*). Such a love of pleasure and hatred of the spirit is unnatural (*contra naturam*). Against these are the acts of civilized man, ploughing, seafaring, building. These deeds come from *virtus*. Likewise, men who are not dedicated to their stomachs seek good repute or *fama* and hence *gloria/memoria* as before.[23] Furthermore, *memoria* remains fruitfully ambiguous. It can straddle both the production of lasting *virtus* with one's intelligence by means of a clever deed and the

---

[21] See Tiffou 1973: 108–17 and Earl 1961: 7–9.

[22] And one must everywhere keep in mind that *virtus* will not in the end prove to be a stable concept within Sallust, as Batstone 1988b has so deftly argued and as I shall shortly question again. One can compare a traditional reading like Pöschl 1967, where *virtus* is not seen as a problem for the text.

[23] Earl 1961: 11 also unites mind and *virtus*: '*Virtus*, then, for Sallust is the function of *ingenium* according to certain rules.' We can add to this the proposition that a crisis in *ingenium* necessarily results in a crisis of *virtus*.

History of Mind and Philosophy of History 175

production of knowledge itself in the history of such deeds. In other words, within authorship we have a master trope for mind, memory, and virtue. Here one ought to note that Sallust has used the first person in both of these paragraphs. Sallust repeats *mihi* and deploys the grammatically superfluous *ego*. Of course, it is his own position as author that is being best served: Sallust's own *ingenium* is producing *memoria* here. And, indeed, Sallust's text has had fame and an 'eternal' posterity. But is Sallust's monograph also virtuous or can it be virtuous in its own terms?[24]

Beast and god, body and mind, these sweeping categories have pointed us towards virtue and the virtue of authorship. But *virtus* is in trouble as soon as it arrives on the scene when the word occurs as the finale of the text's opening paragraph. The Latin reads *virtus clara aeternaque habetur*. A casual reading of this sentence would translate it as '*virtus* is considered to be glorious and eternal'. Such a translation, though, is impossible if we are to take Sallust as meaning what we know he must mean. After all of the preceding philosophical grandeur, can the vital and divine object virtue really be a mere object of repute? Thus, we are forced to correct the translation to '*virtus* is glorious and eternal'. The effort of such a task is not very great, but we must nevertheless mark that we have so laboured. For example, compare the traces left behind in Ernout's edition and translation. Ernout translates *virtus clara aeternaque habetur* as 'la vertu, elle, assure la gloire et l'immortalité' (virtue, *this* guarantees glory and immortality'). Ernout's verb vigorously corrects the ambiguity: one is assured and reassured here. But we have to be assured all over again by a footnote appended to the translation: 'Le verbe *habetur* ne doit pas être pris dans l'acception de "être regardé comme", mais marque ici la possession. Comme l'explique Kritz...' ('The verb *habetur* ought not to be taken in the sense "to regard as"; rather, here it marks possession. As Kritz explains...').[25] For his part, McGushin merely asserts that *habetur* 'retains its proper force, "is a possession"'.[26] The baldness of the comment and the ironies of 'retaining the proper' as maintaining possession of 'possession' reveal the ways in which the conceptual difficulties of the Sallustian historiographic apparatus spread like an infection to commentaries on that apparatus.[27]

---

[24] Vretska 1976: 29 notes that the trajectory of Sallust's text leads to the author's virtue and labour from the very opening words. Questioning *virtus* thus tends to put into crisis the whole of the work.

[25] Ernout 1946: 55. Vretska 1977: 46 labours similarly.

[26] McGushin 1977: 34. On the other hand, Batstone 1990: 121 squarely confronts the ambiguities provoked by Sallust's Latin.

[27] Again compare Kraus 1999: 245 for Jugurtha as a sort of 'infection' within Sallustian thought that spreads out to the historiographic level.

Clearly Sallust has chosen an ill-starred construction: the more familiar, albeit improper reading of his construction produces a meaning contrary to his own interests and intentions. In fact, we will have to dispossess *habetur* of its 'proper' force later at 8. 4, where we learn that the Athenians' *virtus* has been overrated (*virtus tanta habetur*). Later on, this 'having' loses what it properly had and becomes a mere semblance that exposes what Athens never in fact had: their *virtus* was not a proper possession but instead a false assignation. In this opening paragraph, *virtus* totters, for a moment: is it properly had or is it merely considered to be had? The reader has to cast about for a bit of *ingenium* on his or her own part in order to make a successful reading.

This is a dangerous sort of supplement, since it both adds to and replaces the category of *virtus*. The philosophical truth of Sallust's so-called commonplaces sustains itself only by being a truth held in common or even borrowed from outside the text. Hence the slip and pun in the translation of *habetur* reproduce themselves at a still higher critical level: one considers *habetur* to be even stronger than 'is a possession'; the commentators consider *habetur* here to be 'to be' because it must be being and not considering. Ernout and McGushin would warn us that it 'must not be taken' in a sense that deprives Sallust of an essential quasi-philosophical 'possession'. Only the resources of our intelligence (*ingeni opibus*) secure *virtus* for Sallust. At least Sallust warned us that such would be required.

Choosing not to linger in this ambiguous moment, Sallust continues in the next section of the text with some more generalizations that explain not only history in general, but this historian in particular. After laying out this initial set of abstract relationships between mind and body in his first paragraph, Sallust continues by examining deeds. Much like people themselves, so also do mortal affairs bear the mark both of force and of intellect. Sallust seeks to examine which aspect predominates in any given situation. He imagines for himself a world where the two are sundered: initially there is a vague contest between force and wit in military matters in the first section. Next Sallust points to an originary moment (*initio*) where kings ruled either by intellect or by the force of their body: *pars ingenium, alii corpus exercebant*. *Initio* raises a question: the beginning of what? The beginning of memory and the beginning of political life coincide here.[28] History begins with sovereignty: at first there were kings. But this sovereignty is not a simple matter like the

---

[28] This is to force *memoria* back into the monograph. This time we read it as retrospective (memory as history) rather than as prospective (memory as future glory).

sovereign divinity of the mind or of virtue. Nor in the case of the prehistorical state does the body play the role of mind's bondsman: in some states body is sovereign. Thus, as soon as Sallust remembers and as soon as Sallust starts to write as a historian, he thereupon recalls the philosophical and ontological split between mind and body all over again. Sallust is writing this passage in the mind–body idiom of the opening paragraph. Sallustian politics becomes both a divine and bestial affair, since both mind and body are sovereign principles in this world. Significantly, the author's object of inquiry is never as pure as *ingenium* itself is: his own mind and memory look back upon a version of politics as a split object, and an object that recapitulates the opening truths of the text and the philosophical degradation of the body.

At this point in Sallust's account, though, the existential superiority and divinity of mind have yet to be proven as meaningful in history. And we need to attend specifically to the transition from the abstract to the concrete and from mythical communities into historical ones. In practical, worldly matters, *ingenium* justifies its claim to a philosophically privileged place only with the advent of the Persian and Greek imperialists (2. 2).[29] Their labours prove that intelligence is the key to military success. These empires offer empirical proof of the mastery of the intellect where formerly the world was filled with two sorts of state, that of the mind and that of the body. The movement from this bifurcated world into the sway of intelligence marks the real advent of history for Sallust. Before the Persians, the Athenians, and the Spartans seek their empires, none of what Sallust has discussed corresponds to real, identifiable historical deeds. Before mind enacts imperial mastery, there is no history, only static hypothetical states waiting to enter history and the structure of history. Empire begins lived history as the history of mind's prowess in these master states when Sallust unites history, mind, and empire.

The emergence of the history of mind by way of mind's historical triumph, though, does not take place without provoking a new crisis. The place that *ingenium* wins for itself is predicated on war. Yet Sallust also depicts war as a falling away from a simple economy of desire: formerly one lived without cupidity, satisfied with one's own possessions (*tum vita hominum sine cupiditate agitabatur; sua quoique satis placebant*, 2. 1). With the advent of desire and specifically the desire for mastery, glory, sovereignty, and intellect also emerge onto the historical stage (*B.C.* 2. 2):[30]

---

[29] See Tiffou 1973: 48.
[30] Glücklich 1988: 23–41 offers an interesting reading of Sallust along the axis of desire.

> postea vero quam in Asia Cyrus, in Graecia Lacedaemonii et Athenienses coepere urbis atque nationes subigere, lubidinem dominandi causam belli habere, maxumam gloriam in maxumo imperio putare, tum demum periculo atque negotiis conpertum est in bello plurumum ingenium posse.
>
> But after Cyrus in Asia and the Spartans and the Athenians in Greece began to subjugate cities and peoples, the desire for mastery became a motive for war. They thought the greatest glory lay in the greatest empire. And then it was finally discovered by way of practical experience that the intellect was the dominant factor in warfare.

Sallust yokes the subjection of other nations, the desire for mastery (*lubido dominandi*),[31] and the imputation of glory to the advent of empire (*imperio*). As well as producing empire, this triad simultaneously offers the condition for the discovery of the position of intellect. Note Sallust's use of *demum*: 'finally' the issue is decided—as if the world had been waiting for an answer—and a hitherto only latent truth makes its way to the fore.

This entry into historical time comes with a modification of man's libidinal economy. One now desires an other; one desires to master him, and in mastery one learns the truth of the mind.[32] One also enters into history by entering into the glory, and hence the memory, occasioned by a vast empire. These two vital Sallustian abstractions are opened up when one's desires turn outwards and away from one's own possessions. These possessions, though, were not even themselves properly objects of desire: they occasioned only satisfaction.[33] And this turning outwards to empire—a turning that is simultaneously an invocation of *lubido*—at last establishes the sovereignty of mind over body: the bestial potentialities in one's own self-satisfied sovereignty wither away as the external and concrete historical empire waxes; formerly some used their bodies, others their minds (*divorsi pars ingenium, alii corpus exercebant*, 2. 1). And here one is reminded of the logic of the opening sentences of the *Bellum Catilinae*. Now, however, the clever have subdued the brutish. And, true to his calling, Sallust commemorates the event by letting mind speak of the silence and subjection that befalls body.

The line of thought has a Hegelian cast to it. For Hegel there is no autonomous independence of mind: mind discovers itself in the other. It discovers itself in desire for mastery, as the master's desire for his slave.[34]

---

[31] Compare Sklená ř 1998: 208 and Büchner 1982: 96. Scanlon 1980: 51 and Vretska 1976: 57 see an allusion to Thucydides here at the expense of the striking quality of the Latin phrase.
[32] Compare Scanlon 1987: 25 for a reading of this passage.
[33] Sallust's portrait of desire as insatiable can be found below.
[34] See Hegel 1977: 111–19.

The master needs the slave to establish his own consciousness as self-consciousness: the moment of forging the master–slave bond is also a moment of self-recognition by way of being recognized by the other. Significantly, Hegel requires this hierarchy and domination as a key element of the scene. Within this scheme the lord has a conjoint relationship to the bondsman as both thing and conscious being.[35] And in an irony with profound consequences within the Hegelian framework, the lord's own consciousness is radically dependent upon the recognition accorded him by his slave: the master cannot be himself without the slave.

Up to this point my portrait of Sallust has often presented the body as a subjected thing and not an agent. But Sallust nevertheless has filled his text with a number of subjected bodily characters who are mastered by the sovereignty of *ingenium*. In other words, Sallust produces historical figures who are made to live out the philosophy of the prologue. Note, for example, the states overcome by the prudent imperialists, our first victory of mind over body and the moment where historical time emerged. Later Sallust introduces Sempronia, who represents femininity and bodily charm.[36] Most importantly there is Catiline himself, a prodigal representative of body who is mastered both by historical events and by the history that tells of him. Conversely, these mastered bodies are not docile subjects. Much like the Hegelian slave, so also do these abject and unlivable objects exert a reciprocal action on the mind that would compass them. In short, neither Catiline nor any other figure of the narrative is a mere body for Sallust, no more than a slave is mere property for his master. The ambiguity of the whole of Sallust's narrative oscillates around this paradox of objectifying subjects: as in Hegel, one does not simply master another and thereby produce sovereign consciousness. As will be seen below, the very desire for mastery qua desire will undo the sovereignty of both author and text.

In Sallust's portrait of the desire for empire, the gratification of the desire for acquisition also gratifies the desire of and for self-consciousness.[37] Hence the history of mind is the history of acquisition,

---

[35] See Hegel 1977: 115.

[36] Sempronia is by no means an unambiguous figure, though. She will be discussed in more detail below.

[37] For a version of Hegel that stresses desire's role, see Kojève 1980: 3–30. Lacan also routinely uses desire and the other in explaining the mirror stage within his psychoanalysis. See, for example, Lacan 1988: 146–7, which is explicitly Hegelian. Similarly, the insistence upon the world of man and desire as the desire of the other in all three authors helps to explain the strange slip of *habetur* in section 1: virtue is considered eternal because it is a standard that only exists within the world of man as structured by desire and the production of alterity.

where mind acquires mastery of an external object by means of which it establishes for itself a truth of itself as both mind and master. Likewise, body is produced as bondsman in the same moment, since the body and its representatives are required to recognize mind as masterful. This recognition both demonstrates and verifies the hierarchy that will subsist between the mind and body. But this history of mind is necessarily a history predicated on lack: mind remains dependent upon something external to it. It requires the other that it masters. Moreover, one cannot conceive of mind without also conceiving of the desire that enables its self-fulfilment by way of acquisition. *Lubido*, then, is a concept indispensable to the philosophy of Sallust's history. Nevertheless, in the course of the *Bellum Catilinae* the economy of *lubido* will be fundamentally uncontrollable by the *ingenium* whose sovereignty Sallust would champion.

This process of mind's mastery is then a tragic one in the moral terms of Sallust.[38] *Ingenium* excels over the body in war. War is itself a function of desire for mastery, and it is only by way of this desire that memory and the mind can realize themselves. Yet, once the war has ended, *ingenium* begins to falter. Sallust wishes that rulers showed the same psychic virtue (*virtus animi*) when they governed their realm as they did when they won it (*B.C.* 2. 3):[39]

> quod si regum atque imperatorum animi virtus in pace ita ut in bello valeret, aequabilius atque constantius sese res humanae haberent, neque aliud alio ferri neque mutari ac misceri omnia cerneres.
>
> Now if kings and generals evinced as much mental virtue in peace as they did in war, mortal affairs would be more equitable and stable. You wouldn't see things whisked off here and there and everything in a state of flux and confusion.

The grammar of the sentence employs the present counterfactual: if they did it, things would be better; and the world would see less chaos and instability. What was once the case is now no longer true: the past bred

---

[38] Here I wish to resume the observation from Leeman as to the affiliation between history and tragedy. Leeman 1967: 114 also emphasizes as a source of this tragedy man's split body/soul nature.

[39] The collocation *virtus animi* produces a nice moment of consolidation between the moral and the intellectual registers. Below, the two will be found at odds with one another. Earl 1961: 16ff. notes the association of *virtus* with virility and aristocracy. Hence the phrase also contains allusions to a presumptive gender and dominant social status for mind. These two registers will likewise be disturbed by the trajectory of intellect in Sallust. Earl would probably not go so far, as he sees in Sallust a redefinition of *virtus* to make it personal and not hereditary. See Earl 1961: 111. Yet this formulation still leaves room for the notion of a legitimate domination patterned after aristocratic mastery.

a present that subverts the principle of its own origin. The mind discovered as masterful in wartime suddenly fails the very men who discovered it once they have won peace. Mind emerges as sovereign only to begin at once to lose the lustre on its crown. What has gone wrong?

An answer is shortly forthcoming, and, ironically, the question of mind again is answered by way of the idiom and grammar of desire. The next sentences purport to be general verities, but they complicate any easy reading of Sallust's relationship to *ingenium*. Sallust explains the problem of bad internal leadership by explaining that sovereignty (*imperium*) is easily retained by those very skills that produced it. Conversely, when idleness, desire (*lubido*), and arrogance replace hard work, self-restraint, and equity, a state's fortunes change with its moral character (*verum ubi pro labore desidia, pro continentia et aequitate lubido atque superbia invasere, fortuna simul cum moribus inmutatur,* 2. 5).[40] The *continentia* and restraint of the prior epoch are replaced by a raw, grasping *lubido*. Ideally, we ought to have states like the original ones, states in which each is pleased with what is his own (*sua cuique satis placebant*, 2. 1). Yet these are the very states in which one did not know the true and glorious virtue of the intellect. It was by leaving those pre-imperial realms behind that we discovered historical time. *Ingenium* was a property with an unknown value there until the desire for mastery arrived on the scene. This desire began history, and it began history as the history of mind.

Now, though, Sallust would put the genie back in the bottle: *lubido* needs to be banished so that the state may return to a static internal harmony. *Lubido* drove one state to invade another, and to discover in the moment of conquest the power of mind as it found the experience of mastery. After winning this empire, *lubido* suddenly invades (*invasere*, 2. 5) the master state, and the *ingenium* won is lost again. Mastery produces mind, knowledge, virtue, and memory, but it also produces their opposites, body, vice, and forgetfulness in the aftermath of its own triumph. That is, mastery also produces servitude as a vital principle logically adjoined to itself and a principle in which it fundamentally participates; and, where an external object is wanting, a state reproduces the master–slave dialectic in such a way as to divide itself internally. And if such a reading seems to force Sallust's text to mean what is perhaps only implied at this juncture, section 10 reiterates this scheme explicitly and

---

[40] Compare Scanlon 1987: 64–5. Scanlon also draws attention to the parallel with Polybius 10. 3. 6. See also Due 1983: 113–39 for the connection between Sallust and Polybius. Scanlon 1980 explores in detail the connections between Sallust's thought and that of Thucydides.

in specific reference to Rome itself: the sack of Carthage devastated Roman morals. Mind's victory spells its own defeat.

At the present level of abstraction Sallust insists that a state that falls prey to its own involuted *lubido* splits into bad, bodily subjects and good, mental lords. After complaining of the decay of virtue during peacetime, Sallust next talks of the virtue of the arts that produce the world itself as mastered and obedient to men's wills. He declares that agriculture, seafaring, and building are all a function of virtue (*quae homines arant navigant aedificant, virtuti omnia parent*, 2. 7). Set against the practitioners of these virtuous arts, one finds vice-ridden men who are slaves to their bodies (*dediti ventri*, 2. 8) and so many ignorant clods (*indocti incultique*). One sort of citizen is a master of intellect and uses it to subdue and to render the world livable. The other sort of man obeys not the sage and his mind but instead fails even to recognize another's virtue. He serves instead his body and lives a life bereft of the tokens of *ingenium*. Like the *pecora* before him, his life of the gut is brutish and unmemorable (*siletur* as opposed to *famam*). This whole passage reproduces the logic of the opening lines. Also, it recalls the pre-imperial condition where some states used their minds and others their bodies; only now we have two different kinds of citizen within the same state.

The mind–body rift endlessly reproduces itself in Sallust's world. Fortunately, this internal civic split will be retold in a positive light shortly when the Roman *patres* ('fathers') intelligently master the hardy bodies of a martial youth in section 6. At this point in the text the hegemonic state is now master of others but also master and slave within itself: an empire is won; *lubido* invades the victors; the state's fortune changes. Hereupon Sallust imagines for us peacetime activities that reproduce the mind–body and master–slave split all over again. This state may be the lord of an empire, but it is itself now filled with moralists and wastrels, representative of virtuous mind and of depraved body.[41]

However it is only within decadence that this diagnosis becomes possible and hence historiography is enabled: the inscription of history emerges where the *ingenium* of the master state splits off from itself. That is, though the master state represents *ingenium* by the very fact of its successful *imperium*, its internal mind–body split produces a mind that masters and knows the truth of the state's own *ingenium* and *imperium*. In other words, the masterful state manifests *ingenium* but this is not yet consciousness as self-consciousness. The mind that reflects on mind comes in the wake of this sovereignty.

---

[41] Wiedemann 1993: 54–5 notes the connection between mental and political disorder in Sallust's *Bellum Iugurthinum*.

Sallust himself occupies this cognitive role, as he presently intimates. The realization of *ingenium* inaugurated history as the history of empire. Moreover, writing history itself allows for the enactment of both *ingenium* and *imperium*. There is a sovereignty of moral cognition here. Or, for our purposes, a sovereignty of the reactionary historian: the will to know is simultaneously a will to power. Within the decadent master state the *ingenium* of its *ingenium* resides at the theoretical position from which history as virtuous memory emerges with a desire to master (*lubido dominandi*) this faltering political and moral order. Only in a Rome where there are bodies in need of mastering and minds striving to know and to control in the same moment do we find historians.

These sections also give an account of the author.[42] The author and the place of the author are here inseparable from the ethics of history and historiography. And this ethics participates in the full matrix of virtue, memory, and intelligence spelled out earlier. Here history is necessarily the inscription of a memory that would repress unnatural desire and cleanse the state. Yet we will see that this is a project that can never succeed, for it is only by desire's operation that the conditions for historical reflection emerge. Sallust insists that the historian be read as a part of his own history. And, given that Sallust has required of his reader that he examine the genealogy of mind and memory as precursors to the understanding of Catiline, his gesture towards autobiography enfolds the author within the same process: what makes for a Sallust? What of the one who knows and tells of that prodigious body and its wicked deeds? The ambiguities of *ingenium* and its emergence here explicitly challenge our ability to read Sallust as an authority. Sallust's philosophy of mind and his philosophy of history come to undermine the very sage who formulated both.

Is it better to do a great deed or to record it? Above deeds announced the *ingenium*; and when they do, they are likewise masterful deeds. This is the unreflective act as an expression of mind. This historian reflects on such acts: his is reflective consciousness as self-consciousness. Sallust's own position as author allows him to evince the two highest human goals as he produces virtuous and glorious memory while also manifesting cognition itself. Sallust calls out for a recovery of that economy of desire where the deed announced the *ingenium* and where conquest was the proper deed of *ingenium*.[43]

---

[42] Compare the remarks of Due 1983: 113–24.

[43] See, though, Richter 1973: 755–80 for a reading of Sallust's 'archaic' style that stresses the novel and invented qualities of this prose. Sallust is nowhere simply reactionary: the present always complicates any relationship to a departed past. The past is not a mere

Sallust first grapples with the difficulty in evaluating doing and writing in section 3. In this later passage writing initially seems to be subordinate to doing. Yet writing is potentially more difficult than the deed. Writing must not only equal it, but also produce memory for the deed in the act of telling, making, and assigning *virtus* and *gloria*.[44] And in this process, history brings to completeness the *ingenium* of the deed by announcing this intelligence within the broader moral and intellectual matrix that separates men from beasts across a divine and masterly gulf. The *ingenium* of the doer thus needs the *ingenium* of the writer to guarantee *memoria* and *fama* for it. Hence Sallust's history is a history of the mind in the fullest sense: not only does he wish to record mind's deeds, but the act of recording them is itself one of mind's acts. The writer even has a hidden advantage over the doer, since writing's detachment from doing renders it more purely cognitive and less corporeal than actual virtuous action.

Sallust's account of the philosophy of authorship is immediately succeeded by a presentation of the author himself. Sallust follows his evaluation of historiography with an account of his own life. This life lives out the principles that have come before. Accordingly, Sallust comes to embody as lived truth the principles he has just recounted. Sallust comes of age in a society where shame, abstinence, and virtue have been replaced by boldness, free-spending, and greed (*nam pro pudore, pro abstinentia, pro virtute audacia largitio avaritia vigebant*, 3. 3). The grammar of the sentence and the tenor of the sentiments invite comparison with the tottering master state above. The domestic ambiguity of the relationship between mind and body is transferred from the state into its citizen Sallust.

The struggle within Sallust takes place at the level of the mind (*animus*). Will Sallust corrupt his mind with bodily vice, or will he evince *virtus animi*? Desire again intervenes, and again it produces a mixed result. Sallust longs for honour (*honoris cupido*), but his longing leads him into the same ill-repute that truly wicked men find. The desire for honour ought to be attached to the desire for mastery and the desire for fame, since honour in this context certainly means political advancement and its attendant spectacle of dominion. Sallust's qualified *cupido*, an *honoris cupido*, leads him into the same pitfalls as those whose desire was unqualified: mere *cupido* which produced avarice and a whole host of attendant vices. That is, one needs to compare the workings of *lubido*

---

object, but instead an object engaged in a dialectic with the present and with the mind that contemplates it.

[44] Such would be a rather active translation of the Latin phrase *ubi de magna virtute atque gloria bonorum memores* (3. 2).

from above: *lubido dominandi* yields *imperium*, while mere *lubido* is a sign of a bodily and bestial invasion made into the organizing principals of the state. In each instance, for both the state and for Sallust the man, even properly qualified desire ends up in shame. For though men once lived content with their own possessions, their *lubido dominandi* eventually destroyed the conditions of this satisfaction.

In Sallust's case the discomfiture he suffers engenders a turning away from political activity and towards writing. In section 4 Sallust rejects servile pursuits (*servilibus officiis*), agriculture, and hunting. Ironically, agriculture was one of the activities that manifested virtue in section 2. Now this activity becomes merely corporeal and servile when contrasted with authorship and intellectual activity. Writing thus appears again to have an advantage over doing. Sallust also sees the writing as a sort of doing, for he scorns idleness: 'I had no intention of wasting in folly and idleness a "gentleman's leisure"' (*non fuit consilium socordia atque desidia bonum otium conterere*, 4. 1).[45] Indeed, the personal idleness or *desidia* of this passage should be compared to the *desidia* used of the decay of the state in section 2: when idleness replaces labour, fortune and morals both suffer a reversal. By being busy over his writings, Sallust guards his own *fortuna* and *mores*.

Instead of lolling about, Sallust will return to the point from which he lapsed (*eodem regressus*): he will write of the deeds of Rome; and in so writing, Sallust makes a second bid at evincing political virtue.[46] He will transcribe Roman history by taking events individually, and recording those that seem worthy of memory (*memoria digna*). Here the bestowing of memory stands in opposition to servile activities. History and memory are a master's pursuits. Sallust is particularly well suited to such mastery because he is free (*liber*) from the hopes, fears, and partisanship of Roman civic life. This *liber* then plays with the idea of servility that precedes it. The historian is free where the partisan is a slave. In fact, active engagement in civic life is suspect because it is so entangled with these corrupt and corrupting desires and fears: political life as a whole is thus lived under the mark of irrationality and subjection.[47] The historian is positioned above the fray, and his production of virtuous memory forms the proper activity of sovereign intellect. The very act of writing his

---

[45] I am taking *bonum otium* as quasi-sarcastic given the way that Sallust frames it with terms whose resonances are so clearly negative.
[46] Syme 1964: 2 remarks that for Sallust 'his writing is also a continuation and a kind of revenge' after the end of his political career.
[47] This notion also cuts against the virtue of the primary Roman knower/doer of section 8. Sallust the historian profits, but Roman politics and virtue lose at the same time.

history both produces and manifests his liberty; or so, at least, Sallust would have us believe. But we must bear in mind that the master is never a consciousness that lives in independence of the slave. Indeed, his own self-consciousness is radically dependent upon the servility of the other. In Sallust's case, then, the perilous youthful labour contained within *honoris cupido* has been transmuted into a *cupido intellegendi* ('a desire to understand') which is also a *lubido dominandi*. Sallust knows; Sallust writes; Sallust masters. Sallust returns to politics, to the scene of prior defeat. He uses his liberty to enter political life's slave trade all over again.

C. HISTORY

The play of abstractions from Sallust's opening pages proceeds well into the action proper. The history Sallust offers unfolds within the terms of the philosophy of mind *cum* philosophy of history with which Sallust opens. The many paradoxes and difficulties of that intellectual apparatus likewise fittingly presage the unusual telling of the historical action. The crisis of concepts becomes a crisis of doers and deeds. And much as the philosophy ought to have been rather more clear-cut than it was found to be on closer inspection, so also will the interpretation of historical events suffer from similar ambiguities.

The conceptual tensions that marked the opening sections of the *Bellum Catilinae* play themselves out in the body of the text by way of a confused and confusing narrative structure. Nothing is told directly, and everything proceeds by fits and starts as the text doubles objects and doubles back on itself. The knowledge produced by our moralizing historian requires immoral objects, historical bodies that its mind may master. In fact, Sallust declares that he cannot tell the history of Catiline without first telling of his character (*de quoius hominis moribus pauca prius explananda sunt, quam initium narrandi faciam* ('a few things must be made clear about the character of this man before I being my narration'), 4. 5). Hence the fifth section of the work recounts the great force of Catiline's mind and body. The force of Catiline's mind and body are striking: his physical hardiness is almost supernatural, and his mental wickedness is profound. But this force does not bespeak any virtue, for his *ingenium* is rotten and depraved (*malo pravoque*). Sallust's narrative of the history of *ingenium* thus chooses as its privileged case the tale of a wicked mind. Without the monster, Sallust would not bestir his own wit. Much as the sovereignty of mind itself emerged in the case of mastering other states, so also does the emergence of the historian's intellect arise where there is an occasion for mastery.

Catiline as the start of Sallust's history offers a strange and false start. The introduction of Catiline does not lead at once to the story of his conspiracy; instead, both the portrait of Sallust himself and the first glimpse of Catiline stand as concrete representatives both interrupting and exemplifying the philosophy of mind. Sallust says in section 4, 'Therefore I will briefly and as accurately as I can tell of the conspiracy of Catiline' (*igitur de Catilinae coniuratione quam verissume potero paucis absolvam*, 4. 3). Why the 'therefore' though? It is explained by the next clause, 'for I feel that this act was particularly memorable for the novelty of the crime and of the danger' (*nam id facinus in primis ego memorabile existumo sceleris atque periculi novitate*, 4. 4). Yet Sallust must also be referring back to that which immediately precedes the introduction of Catiline, namely his own choice to write history. Prior to that notion we find the representation of historiography as itself a pursuit complementary to doing great deeds. And prior to this argument Sallust gave his maxims on mind, body, and virtue. Thus, we have made our way to Catiline by way of cosmic truths, truths about historiography, and truths about the author. And, as will be seen below, Sallust both demonstrates and falsifies every one of these concepts that lead up to the introduction of Catiline's name and his deed. The reflections on universal truth that the tale of the conspiracy of Catiline occasions, then, are not themselves established as either universal or true, though the weight of these notions is felt throughout the whole of the text.

Catiline here serves for the first time the role he plays throughout the narrative. He is a non-originary origin: his name stands at the place of emergence for a project and a set of themes that are not properly about him or his. Clearly Catiline inaugurates neither the history of mind nor Sallust's choice of history as a profession. In fact the introduction of Catiline in section 5 does not even serve to introduce Catiline's conspiracy. Instead, Sallust will shortly jump away and write the history of immoral antecedents that leads up to Catiline. And this prehistory of Catiline is effectively a third retelling of the prehistory of *ingenium*.

Catiline's own career as a historical agent does not spring from either his own wicked mind or from his soiled body. Instead, the career of Catiline begins with Sulla, namely a sovereign from a still earlier generation of Roman history. Sallust makes the following claim: after Sulla's mastery in the 80s BCE, a tremendous desire for seizing the state fell upon Catiline (*hunc post dominationem L. Sullae lubido maxuma invaserat rei publicae capiundae*, 5. 6). Sallust uses a familiar idiom. We have domination (*dominatio*), desire (*lubido*), and an invasion of *lubido* (*invaserat*).

Catiline, then, is akin to the idle master state above, for he is smitten by desire in precisely the same manner. But what sort of state does Catiline reside in? It is a state that rules an empire and hence a state that once evinced *ingenium*. It is also a Rome that once was led by prudent fathers.[48] Recently, though, politics had been disrupted. Rome was not just a master, but it was also mastered. And this dominion left in its wake the potential for a Catiline. Catiline follows upon the passing of Sulla, a dictator, a master who mastered his fellow citizens, put his political enemies to death, and redistributed their wealth to greedy and grasping partisans.

It is not too surprising that a Sulla leaves behind him the conditions for further unrest and other villains. But Sallust says that it is Catiline who is supposed to be the new one. We were promised *novitas* ('newness, unprecedented novelty') in Catiline's story, and yet we will keep on not finding it. One might argue that Sallust meant not that Catiline was new but only that the crime and danger were new. Yet surely the Roman state had been threatened with as bad or worse before Catiline cooked up his scheme. Indeed, Sulla's dictatorship would offer a fine example of crime and danger. Nevertheless, Sallust will not evaluate Sulla's *dominatio* as to its novelty. Catiline is clearly not radically new: the kingly rule of Rome (*regnum*) that he seeks for himself is inspired by the prior servitude of Rome under Sulla.[49] Likewise, note that Catiline's promises to his followers are themselves hardly novelties. Instead they are decidedly commonplace: 'Then Catiline promised the cancellation of debts, the proscription of the rich, magistracies, priesthoods, booty, and all the rest that war and a victor's lust (*lubido*) brings with it' (*tum Catilina polliceri tabulas novas, proscriptionem locupletium, magistratus, sacerdotia, rapinas, alia omnia, quae bellum atque lubido victorum fert*, 21. 2).

What comes of starting the history of Catiline's conspiracy with Sulla's successful desire for mastery over Rome? Formerly Cyrus' and the other empires began history with their *lubido dominandi*. They produced both historical time and the truth of mind's mastery as the structuring principle of human history. In other words, Sallust has once again told in section 5 the contents of sections 2 and following, where he recounted the realization of *ingenium* in empire. This time proper names have been added even though Sallust's own has been omitted. And with this specificity we also find a new confusion: the relationship between civil war and *ingenium*.

---

[48] These *patres* can be found in 6. 6. They will also be discussed at greater length below.
[49] Compare Vretska 1976: 134.

Sulla's *dominatio* inaugurates an inverted and involuted historical structure. War was the proving ground for *ingenium* before, but now war has turned into civil war, and civil war can only allow for the victory of *ingenium* at the expense of some of the citizen body. The master state again becomes both master and slave within itself, but this time the sovereignty of the master is unjust. Sulla is not a virtuous mind mastering lazy bodies: Sulla sought mastery over any whom he might master.

Such is Sulla's bequest. Sulla's heir Catiline does a novel deed by pursuing a second mastery of Rome. Note, then, the inversion of historical precedents in his programmatic statement at 4. 4: Sallust gives priority to the son over the father; Sallust makes Catiline novel. Moreover, Sallust will speak of Catiline's desires even though Catiline is himself only the seed planted in the progress of Sulla's own lusts. A rereading of section 5. 6 will help to drive this point home. In 5. 6 the name of Sulla and the word *lubido* stand next to one another, and we can wilfully retranslate the Latin to force the text to speak its own subtext: 'After the dominion, Sulla's incredible lust for seizing the state invaded Catiline' (*hunc post dominationem L. Sullae lubido maxuma invaserat rei publicae capiundae*, 5. 6). Both mastery and desire become part of the grammar of post-Sullan Rome.

Sallust does not proceed along this line of thought opened up by the introduction of Sulla and Catiline. Instead, Sallust halts his history. He has already doubled back somewhat and retold one section in another when he adapted section 2 in section 5. But now Sallust will go back even farther and retell everything from the start, changing his account only by adding a few proper nouns. Accordingly, Sallust backs up to the beginning of Roman history and the founding of Rome. Previously history proper started with foreign states seeking to gain empires. Here history starts as the city is settled. And this time Sallust's history will take into account the necessity of internal strife.

Aeneas and his fellow Trojan survivors founded Rome. This is the story of origins that Sallust repeats (*urbem Romam, sicuti ego accepi, condidere atque habuere initio Troiani*, 6. 1). Sallust loosely appends an addition to this version.[50] With the Trojans in this new state there were also the Aborigines, the indigenous populace, a wild, lawless, stateless people living in anarchy (*cumque his Aborigines, genus hominum agreste, sine legibus, sine imperio, liberum atque solutum*, 6. 1).[51] These two

---

[50] I accept the reading *cumque his* which, along with the variants *iis* or *eis*, is the paradosis.

[51] The term anarchy as a translation for *liberum atque solutum* was inspired by Ernout 1946: 60.

radically diverse populaces come together to form a whole, namely Rome. But note how the Aborigines do not understand *imperium*. In the terms of our other prehistory, they resemble a body to which mind has been applied. The advent of the Trojans and (Greek) culture serves as the beginning of civilization for these people and for the city of which they form half. The state of Rome lives and flourishes in the same terms as does a man: its mixes beast and god, body and mind.

Sallust next describes the appearance in Rome of a hegemonic class of prudent men, the 'fathers' or *patres*. Age has made them weak in body, but their *ingenium* is hardy with wisdom (*quibus corpus annis infirmum, ingenium sapientia validum erat*, 6. 6). The mind–body contrast thus recurs, but this time mind rules over body and does not participate in it. Indeed, the feeble *patres* have little choice in the matter, for their bodies could not live up to the demands that might be placed upon them. These 'fathers' are so named either for their age or for the sort of concern they show for their subjects (*hi vel aetate vel curae similitudine patres appellabantur*, 6. 6). But age is only a cipher for the domination of mind over body, of *ingenium* over *corpus*. These fathers seek to maintain the governance of mind over body where theirs is the mind and youths have the body. Father is to son as Trojan is to Aborigine. Similarly, to translate all of this into the imperial idiom from above, the sovereign *ingenium* of the *patres* requires as its external empire the bodies of the young. Finally, as has already been noted, there is a similar sort of 'paternalism' with Sallust's own position as knower and historian vis-à-vis history as a political project: he knows/writes because his body is impotent in the political arena.

In this period the bodily virtues of the youth advance at a rapid pace. The youth of Rome are hardy in war and they learn soldiering by applying themselves to camp life. The martial tenor of the city is the product of a lust for glory (*cupido gloriae*) that arrived in Rome. This arrival is, of course, a parallel one to the invasion of a desire for domination found above. In this case as well the desire is turned outwards. It is a desire to strengthen Rome by mastering external states. This desire is also explicitly contrasted with a depraved domestic lust: youth of this period took more pleasure (*lubidinem*) in the beauty of arms and in the cavalry than in prostitutes and parties.[52] War, the proving ground for *ingenium*, offers the venue for the proper use of the body. The body the *ingenium* of the *patres* would have for itself is the martial body, the body

---

[52] *magisque in decoris armis et militaribus equis quam in scortis atque conviviis lubidinem habebant*, 7. 4.

as instrument of mastery in both the active and passive senses of the word. And in this mastery there is a beauty and pleasure that surpasses sensuality and carnal indulgence. In those fleshy pleasures Sallust finds not the mind's body, but the body's body. Against this decadence, the desire for glory in Sallust's old Rome produces a desire for a martial youth and a masterful class of fathers. Accordingly, in section 43 Sallust will even accuse the conspirators of contemplating mass parricide: these sensualists in agitating for political revolution seek to destroy the proper relationship between mind and body and father and son.

For Sallust glory appears again and again under the sign of the intellect: a healthy father–son relationship fosters glory, and the name of the father governs mind and knowledge in Rome. The relationship between glory and paternal sovereignty, though, speaks not just to Rome's history, but it also reiterates on a different plane the privileges Rome's historian Sallust would claim for himself and the mastery sought by his own mind. Not surprisingly Sallust casts a most favourable verdict upon this fanciful version of old Rome.[53] He declares that at that time virtue was the universal master (*virtus omnia domuerat*, 7. 6). When father masters son and mind masters body, this *dominatio* is lived as virtue's acme. Sulla has yet to invert and redefine dominion.

Sallust has done a tidy job of consolidating the mixed quality of the Roman state. There are lawless Aborigines to whom culture is applied. There are also raw youths whom paternal intellect and imperial designs keep virtuous. Yet Sallust immediately doubles back on himself and ceases to entertain such hierarchical binarisms. Sallust's structuralism becomes both historically and conceptually post-structuralism when the dominion of *virtus* collapses in his next paragraph. There fortune reigns as the supreme mistress (*sed profecto fortuna in omni re dominatur*, 8. 1). Fortune's wanton whim (*lubido*), not truth, governs the fame that men's affairs meet (*ea res cunctas ex lubidine magis quam ex vero celebrat obscuratque*, 8. 1) This clause brings into crisis key elements of Sallust's abstract conceptual apparatus upon which he has expended so much labour. Glory, memory, the intellect, and historiography again seem on the verge of collapse. This new and wanton *lubido* invades the scene of history as a force hostile to truth and anarchic in its tendencies.

Again desire plays a crucial role in Sallust's thought, and once again Sallust is thinking of Athens: formerly the Athenians were one of the first imperialists, now they are evoked as historians. The Athenians did many

---

[53] I call it a fanciful Rome because once again we are in an almost prehistoric time: there is no specific date attached to these events, nor are there any proper names of Romans representative of the era. All we know is that this is 'early Rome'.

fine things, but their reputation exceeds the acts themselves. The great intellects (*magna ingenia*) of Athenian authors become a problem for Sallust. The case has been different with Rome. Romans have been men of action: the wisest men were the busiest, and nobody exercised his wit without also exercising his body.[54] The Roman unites mind and body. It is Greek to split the two. The wisest Roman is *ipso facto* the least likely to speak of his wisdom. This way of putting things seems agreeable at first sight, but a second glance raises questions. This sentence, which reads like an endorsement of old Roman virtue, violates a proposition from the very opening of the monograph: silence is bestial, while mind produces language, virtue, and fame.

This line of argumentation is not one which Sallust himself pursues in this passage. On the contrary, Sallust is seeking to commend the old Romans for what they really were. Their *ingenium* was virtuous, and it enacted this virtue. On the other hand, the Greeks have an *ingenium* that outstrips the deeds of which they speak. With this attack of *lubido* in the register of *ingenium*, the possibility for a decadent knowledge emerges. One recalls that only a moment ago the father thought and the son did. However, Sallust now would retreat back to a position where knowing and doing coincide and the deed declares the *ingenium*. This is the old Roman *virtus*. Sallust's Athenians give rise to doubts about the veracity of history and historians: those who can't do, write.[55]

Yet this is the very formula that Sallust gave for his own literary production. His exile from active political life inaugurated his inscription of contemporary political history. Sallust was the impotent, yet intelligent father, and the raw facts of history were the unruly sons that he would set in order. But now history may announce a *virtus* that was never there (*ita eorum qui fecere virtus tanta habetur, quantum eam verbis potuere extollere praeclara ingenia* ('Accordingly the virtue of men who acted is valued in proportion to the capacity that remarkable genius had to extol it'), 8. 4). History may reflect only fortune's whim and an author's excessive cleverness.

However Sallust himself is making a return to the fertile ambiguity of the phrase *virtus clara aeternaque habetur*. Sallust gives back to the old, silent Roman the eternal and proper possession that was lost as the historian declares and commemorates the doer's *virtus*. Back in section 2 *virtus* seemed almost to become mere reputation until we corrected the

---

[54] *prudentissumus quisque maxume negotiosus erat, ingenium nemo sine corpore exercebat*, 8. 5.

[55] Above and again below I argue that Sallust is a doer in his own right, but the performative aspect of historiography is not immediately at issue here.

translation; here *virtus* is merely an illusion granted by the power of the historian's language. *Virtus* is a possession of the historian, his *ingenium*, and his language. And yet a 'proper' history would refuse this kind of proprietorship and instead demarcate *virtus* as another's possession. History must not be an onanistic reflection of the historian's mind upon itself at the expense of the object. Instead, history must in a reasoned manner reveal the reason of events themselves and assign praise to the sensible and virtuous masters of historical events.

The objects of history ought to be real. The historian should record with his *ingenium* the deeds produced by the hierarchy and harmony of an agent who expresses his own *ingenium* by way of a deed. The intellect of the historian then offers memory and glory to a deed that was already virtuous and the virtuous effusion of a prudent deed: a course is traced from deed to doer, to writer, and back again. Properly, one finds a circuit of intellect and cognition. But the irruption of fortune and her desire upsets all of this. Mind and body are separated, and the masterful hierarchy that persists between the two no longer seems secure. Who will be the subject of the verb *dominare*? Will it be *virtus* or will it be *fortuna*? And one cannot forget the *dominatio* of Sulla either. Sallust's history of mind turns upon the vicissitudes of these various versions of mastery.

This section of the text exerts a stress upon the woof of Sallust's monograph. It doubles his thinking back to an unhappy point. He retreats to an earlier version of the agent and the agent state that is pre-Roman in his own terms. He also retreats to an earlier and faulty version of *virtus*. How can Sallust extract himself from this mess? Tellingly, he cannot. This section emerges after notice had just been given in section 7 that to go on in detail about Roman military success would take us too far afield from Sallust's project. Section 8 was supposed to get us closer to the goal, but it teaches us nothing about Catiline or about Rome. Instead, as we draw closer, we lose sight of *virtus* and of the virtue of history. We draw closer to a failure. Section 9, though, returns to the same sort of praise of early Rome as had been suspended in section 8.

The observations about fortune are rendered an interruption. They are out of place here. Attentive reading of the Latin leads to this conclusion; but, at the same time, such a reading also leaves room for suspicions to the contrary. Thus, the 'as I was saying' (*igitur*) that opens section 9 is used in the sense of a resumption after a parenthesis introduced by 'but' (*sed*), not as a marker of a logical conclusion (*igitur* as 'therefore'). Again a careless reading of our Latin leads to disaster. If section 9 began with an *igitur* as 'therefore' in its logical sense rather than an *igitur* in its structural sense, the glory of martial Rome would become dependent upon fortune's *lubido* not on Rome's own *ingenium* and *virtus*. Sallust very nearly says outright a fear that haunts the whole of his text: perhaps all that really matters in the world is desire and desire's mastery.

The noble history of Rome comes to an end of sorts with the end of its foreign wars. As soon as the last of her enemies is vanquished, the virtues that Rome once evinced vanished. The *ingenium* that ruled in war was unable to sustain itself in peace. It actually needed war to save it from the peace it won by way of war. With the fall of Carthage and other foes, wealth and greed suffuse the Roman spirit. Sallust is about to tell of the history and philosophy of mind as per section 2, but this time Roman history is adduced to demonstrate the vicissitudes of mind.

Sallust again invokes fortune: fortune began to rage and to set all in confusion (*saevire fortuna ac miscere omnia coepit*, 10. 1). The first fit of fortune brought with it a perverse desire and an unsavoury relationship between *ingenium* and truth as historians turned into liars. This time fortune also brings desire along with her, but this time this desire is figured as greed, the indulgence of pleasures, and the triumph of body over mind.[56] The libidinal economy of Sallust's work has hitherto proved treacherous, and fortune's second and lust-filled assault presages still further confusion.

Amidst this venal Rome, *ingenium* suffers a twofold reverse. With the growth of lust for money, there soon followed a lust for power (*igitur primo pecuniae, deinde imperi cupido crevit*, 10. 3). Sallust's argument here and in the surrounding paragraph makes it clear that he means that men seek power for its own sake or power without regard for others or the consequences. And yet this formula for depraved authority lies a bit too close to the salutary longing for empire that got mind, history, and the sovereignty of the mind in history started in the first place: *lubido dominandi* produced *imperium* and verifies the superiority of mind. Here, base gratification comes first with money and then it spreads into the spirit. The desire for rule ought to start in the latter register, though, and then keep in check the former. Money ought to be incidental as glory instead guides a virtuous Roman's steps. Sovereignty was once a sovereign principle; now it is a corrupt and derivative one, since here bestial and bodily desires seek out *imperium*. Everything is indeed being set in confusion. Mind is no longer master.

---

[56] Scanlon 1980: 41–7 covers the varied roles *fortuna* plays in Sallust's work, though Scanlon's effort to unite Sallust's uses is perhaps somewhat forced. Note that fortune is good when it is either made or mastered, or when it is cognizant of virtue (*meliores sequitur*). It is bad where its *lubido* is in control. Hence fortune itself plays into the master–slave dialectic and is not itself a term with an independent value.

History of Mind and Philosophy of History 195

Intelligence suffers a second and still more profound setback in the face of ambition. Language is sundered from *ingenium*. Ambition makes men have one thing in their hearts and another on their lips (*aliud clausum in pectore, aliud in lingua promptum habere*, 10. 5). It gives them a fair face rather than a fair heart (*ingenium*).[57] Ambition has ties as well to glory, but only in its crassest version where one seeks personal advantage and individual fame. Fortune's tantrum has disrupted the foundations of glory, memory, and history. Fortune can detach the *ingenium* from the deed in Athenian historians or in ambitious Romans. In both cases words fail to correspond to the truth. Yet Sallust himself was once and is now a man of ambition. So too is he a historian. What then of his speech in such a world?

According to Sallust, political ambition wrecks the Roman *imperium*. But *imperi cupido* was itself a consequence of the savagery of fortune. And in these phrases one hears echoes of the author's autobiography: he had a *honoris cupido*. He writes in consequence of its frustration. And Sallust writes to further Roman glory even as he knows fortune can falsify historical texts produced by precocious *ingenia*. Sallust writes as fortune's son, a product of the world fortune created—Sulla and other specific Romans are forgotten here—and as a son destined to celebrate or obscure only in accordance with fortune's *lubido*. The author yields up vital aspects of his authority the more entangled he becomes in the structuring structures of his history.

Naturally, fortune is merely serving as a scapegoat. The dialectic of mind as per Sallust does not in fact require chance in order to make things go awry. Victory over all of one's foes is the logical conclusion of the proper exertion of *ingenium* and the will to mastery. Sublime Roman *ingenium* has to subdue foreign decadence and its bestial, bodily creed by way of the verification of the postulate that war proves precisely this very mastery of mind. The frontier must eventually close in such a process. But as soon as Sallust's Rome runs out of foes, it falls into a snare of *ingenium* that he has laid out for it in his prehistory. The unoccupied state naturally faces a crisis where it must either redeploy the *ingenium* it found in war or it must fall prey to an invasion of *lubido* and chaos.[58]

The masterful destiny of *ingenium* ultimately threatens mind's very sovereignty. Ambition has emerged as a synonym for *lubido* in this state: it takes the same grammatical construction, it invades (*invasit*). Specifically, it invades like a pestilence (*quasi pestilentia*). Accordingly the good

---

[57] *magisque voltum quam ingenium bonum habere*, 10. 5.
[58] Compare the construction of section 2 with the sentiments here in section 10.

lubido dominandi that discovered *ingenium* produces as its ironic logical consequence a bad *lubido imperi* that represents ambition as the ambition to rule one's fellows and to gratify one's greed at the same time. The end of *ingenium* is the subversion of all that *ingenium* would champion. One starts with the divine and ends with the bestial, the false, and the wanton.

Wantonness and sexual depravity are the point towards which Sallust is leading us. Even though his narrative doubles back on itself yet again here, the logic nevertheless advances. In section 11 Sallust retreats from his broad condemnation of Rome and picks up instead at an earlier historical point, where things had only begun to go bad. Sallust redefines ambition in this period as an ambiguous failing and one not quite so bad as avarice.[59] And here ambition is a mixed quality, since it induces men to strive for good ends, but sometimes by bad means. In order to make this point, Sallust has once again to redefine a term. In a text where Cato complains about words losing their meaning, it is the author himself who constantly redefines his own key terms as he elaborates the conceptual/historical backdrop of his central narrative.

Imperium meant a wicked sort of mastery a page before; now it takes its more usual and positive translation of 'political office'. In order to advance farther into Sallust's text, we need to forget for the moment that ruling itself has perhaps become a bad thing. We need to forget, among other things, Sulla. As has been mentioned above, the ellipse of Sulla and the history of that period is an enabling moment of forgetfulness for Sallust's narrative. Sallust may record and memorialize (*memorare*), but he can do so only by forcing his readers to have a selective memory. With Sallust's rewritten version of ambition and rule, we return to a safe zone of binary potentials that can be resolved in either direction: there is a good version of each.

Not surprisingly, the stamp of the *ingenium* is found on good ambition and good sovereignty. On the other hand, the mark of the body disfigures these two terms. And here the body is specifically read as effeminacy. Thus, we have on the one side wisdom and the refusal of lust-filled avarice[60] and so also the refusal of wisdom to move past the desire for glory and honour and into avarice and *cupido/lubido*.[61] One is meant to go only so far and no farther along the path of desire. The man who succumbs to greed and loses his gender illustrates the alternative: greed is a poisonous thing, and it effeminizes mind and body (*ea, quasi*

---

[59] *magis ambitio quam avaritia*, 11. 1.
[60] *avaritia pecuniae studium habet, quam nemo sapiens concupivit*, 11. 3.
[61] One should, though, recall Sallust's own *honoris cupido* in section 3.

venenis malis imbuta, corpus animumque virilem effeminat, 11. 3). The manly mind and body are and always have been the mind where the *ingenium* pursues war and the honour of war. When engaged in these pursuits mind, memory, and history remain true, virile, and authoritative. With greed, manly self-presence of mind and body evanesces.

By stepping back, Sallust was able to advance us towards an understanding of the history of mind: now this history has had sexuality added to it as one of its key elements. Effeminate greed is boundless (*infinita*). If we take the term *infinita* literally, we see that the problem is a loss of self-identity with the loss of the outside–inside polarity and perhaps also the (male) master–slave dialectic. Both of these pairs have enabled the progress of Sallust's thought and his history. Against this, greed destroys the lines of demarcation and proprietorship (*fines*) drawn around Sallust's abstract conceptual apparatus. With greed, *habetur* comes into crisis all over again: it can be neither being nor a proper possession; instead 'having' only points towards more acquisition and even criminal getting. The non-self-identity of effeminacy—or, literally, greed—is signalled by its inaccessibility to accumulation or diminution.[62] In effeminate greed one loses the comparative degree and with it notions like number and hierarchy. This condition also points towards the figures of chaos that have filled the text of late as fortune has raged and set all in confusion.

The inaugural scene for this state of affairs brings us back to a familiar figure. Sallust attaches the name of Sulla to this process wherein greed emasculates Rome. Sulla's career brings to life the themes and the thematic crises that Sallust has been evoking. Sulla begins the end of virtue much as he launched Catiline and the history of his conspiracy started above. Sulla takes his army to Asia. In this proverbially rich and luxurious land he indulges his soldiers; pleasure makes them soft (*molliverant*).[63] There for the first time (*primum*) a Roman army learned to love, drink, admire luxury, plunder, and outrage the gods.[64] Sallust joins softness, sexual pleasure, and loss of control in drink. Added to these is a grasping and wanton relationship to goods, a greed that does not honour public or private, sacred or profane. It is *infinita*, the soft, feminine greed of Sulla's Asian Roman army.[65] The violated boundaries of this image

---

[62] *neque copia neque inopia minuitur*, 11. 3.

[63] See Boyd 1987: 187–90 for an extended discussion of Rome's Asian problems in Sallust.

[64] *ibi primum insuevit exercitus populi Romani amare, potare, signa, tabulas pictas, vasa caelata mirari, ea privatim et publice rapere, delubra spoliare, sacra profanaque omnia polluere*, 11. 4.

[65] All of this is supposed to make the army faithful to Sulla (*quo sibi fidum faceret*, 11. 5). Compare the programme of Catiline in section 14 in which he indulges the pleasures of his men to win their loyalty.

only correspond to the dangerous transgressions in Sulla's own career. He wins the state by way of arms. But arms ought only to conquer another state, not Rome itself. Arms ought to be turned outwards, and they ought to consolidate *ingenium*, not serve the body. Sulla falls as a predator upon the goods of others. But the conquered others are fellow Romans, not foreigners.

The next two sections turn all of Rome into Sullan veterans; an Asian and effeminate decadence has overtaken the city. Luxury, greed, and arrogance invade (*invasere*) the youth of Rome. They plunder, outrage the gods, and fall a prey to pleasure. They lust after others' goods (*aliena cupere*) and they sully their own bodies with desire as they lose sight of modesty (*pudorem*) and chastity (*pudicitiam*). The catalogue of vices corresponds in every detail to those that Rome's young soldiers had had induced in them when Sulla educated them in pleasure in Asia. In this Rome sovereignty is mistaken for oppressing another (*proinde quasi iniuriam facere, id demum esset imperio uti* ('It was just as if in offering abuse one finally made use of one's power to command'), 12. 5). *Imperium* in this instance has to take the simple meaning that it has several times above: exercising authority and the legitimate exercise of office. Just as we ought to divinely exercise the *imperium* of our intellect, so ought we to properly use the authority of our command. This, then, is the moment in Roman history that bridges the neutral use of the term with the illegitimate phrase 'lust for power' (*cupido imperi*). Sexual and monetary chaos and indulgence infect or invade the sanctuary of office. The sovereignty of mind fails in the citizen and with it the good sovereignty of the state. Sulla makes Romans into Asians; boundless greed obliterates Roman *fines*; and both the mental and the political versions of *imperium* are perverted.

Ingenium and *imperium* totter together. And in this movement Sallust claims that he has lost the ability to tell and to commemorate. The statement is meant to have a purely local effect, and, similarly, it is a rhetorical hyperbole, not a 'serious' claim. Nevertheless, let us ask if Sallust does in some sense not mean just what he says. The virtuous memory that he ought to produce in his telling cannot be achieved. Instead in section 13, his powers as an author seem as if they are about to fail him. Only a fellow witness could believe the facts that Sallust would capture in his history (*nam quid ea memorem, quae nisi iis qui videre nemini credibilia sunt* ('for why should I mention those things which no one would believe except those who saw them'), 13. 1). The anarchy of desire is ineffable and unintelligible otherwise. Mountains are levelled; seas are filled. Men are used as women; and women take all comers. The register of the body is transformed from a realm of needs into one of luxurious indulgence: weariness, thirst, and hunger lose their meaning.[66]

Sallust concludes that when a man's spirit is suffused with wickedness, desires (*lubidines*) almost surely follow (*animus inbutus malis artibus haud facile lubidinibus carebat*, 13. 5).[67] This sentiment can be read in several directions and dimensions. Sallust indicates that vice in the mind yields vice in the body. Hence the wicked of spirit are wicked in their flesh. But the movement of this logic is opposite to the flow of the arguments that precede it. Previously bad bodily *lubido* corrupted the *ingenium* and the *animus*. So where do wicked practices (*malae artes*) strike first, the body or the spirit? Do wicked ways appease my body and infect my mind, or do they suffuse my mind and then invite *lubido*? That is, according to Sallust's previous arguments, one might have expected *malae artes* to be ciphers for *lubido* and not probable antecedents. The whole history of mind in Sallust has hitherto always been a history of the erotic economy to which the mind belongs. Thus, the notion here that a corrupt heart precedes a vile body conceals for the moment the fallible nature of the mind and its susceptibility to desire.

Nevertheless, this moment does recall the logic of the scene of vice's inception at Rome when a bad *animus* corrupts the body politic and fills it with desires. Sulla, the commander, the conqueror, and hence the representative of *ingenium*, conquers the Republic with his arms. I would argue that it is actually in this prior scene that Sallust loses his narrative abilities. Hence Sallust's claim that he cannot describe the world of section 13 emerges as a consequence of Sulla's legacy, not because of the actual prodigies of that age. For Sallust does describe well enough the vice he imagines to be incredible in post-Sullan Rome. Yet, on the other hand, Sallust fails to adequately represent the inception of the Sullan period. First, when actually describing that period, Sallust merely says that the state is recovered (*recepta*). But this return of Rome is achieved by way of the introduction of an illegitimate brand of sovereignty and by the death of other generals. Hence, Sulla offers not a recovery but instead a revolution. And the recovering of the 'proper possession' does not mean the recovery of *virtus* but instead its undoing.

---

[66] See 13. 3: *sed lubido stupri ganeae ceterique cultus non minor incesserat: viri muliebria pati, mulieres pudicitiam in propatulo habere; vescendi causa terra marique omnia exquirere; dormire prius quam somni cupido esset; non famem aut sitim, neque frigus neque lassitudinem opperiri, sed ea omnia luxu antecapere.*

[67] This corrupt spiritual situation is thus antithetical to Earl's much-cited characterization of the essence of *virtus* wherein it is 'the functioning of *ingenium* to achieve *egregia facinora* and thus to win *gloria* by the exercise of *bonae artes*'. See Earl 1961: 16.

Secondly, the transition from rule to unjust rule is left strikingly opaque: as Sallust describes it, despite a good start, Sulla produced a bad outcome (*bonis initiis malos eventus habuit*, 11. 4). We then learn what ills succeeded Sulla's victory; they are the desiring and rapacity that spread out into all of Rome. But as we learn the 'what', we lose both the 'why' and Sulla as the agent. Hence everybody (*omnes*) gets greedy, plunders, longs, etc. Sulla has a bad outcome, but he is divorced from the consequences of his own action here. Why does Sallust refuse to spell out either why the beginning was good or how Sulla let things go sour? Sulla the agent loses all contact with his deed: on one side, things go well; on the other side, consequences are bad. Intervening between these moments is the recovery of the state by arms (*armis recepta re publica*, 11. 4).

In the paradoxes and ambiguities of this phrase Sallust obscures the crisis of his history of Rome and of mind. Note how Sulla is only the implied subject of the action, not the expressed one. Arms ought to be the site where either mind or body reigns. And, more importantly, victory in arms ought to betoken a victory of mind. But Sulla's victory is no victory: it is a recovery. Likewise Sulla's victory has no victor: there is no Sulla in this clause. Thirdly, Sulla's victory does not reveal whether mind or body has been at work. Presumably we ought to think first of the *ingenium*: Sulla is a magistrate and hence a representative of the hegemonic and authoritative *ingenium* that established Rome as a master state. Similarly, Sulla is a successful general, and hence also a man who would be expected to have used mind to vanquish body. Yet Sulla's victory brings only an attack of *lubido*, not a promotion of the *ingenium*. Bodily failings run rampant in the wake of the 'recovery' of the state.

The baleful attack of *lubido*, though, is not represented as coming from within. Instead, despite the implications of the subordinate clauses that depend upon the victory of Sulla, the scene suddenly shifts. The Asian army is introduced. They are Romans who have become un-Roman away from Rome. When they return, they spread effeminacy and luxury throughout the city until all have been schooled in the failings of the body. Body rules mind—no, body conquers mind. Body has a *lubido dominandi* that sends it in from Asia to win for itself an *imperium* over Rome. This formula is an inversion of the initial trajectory of the movement of mind out into empire: now body comes back from the provinces and vanquishes the Roman *ingenium* at home.

Sulla's civil war produces a radical inversion of the Sallustian conceptual apparatus. Sallust even has trouble figuring it as a civil war. Is it a civil war or just a return or a recovery? Does vice invade from without or does it arise within Rome and Romans? Furthermore, is Sulla mind or body? And lastly, how does the closing of the frontier play into this?

Above, it is suggested that the outward progress of *ingenium* is checked when the last enemy falls; or if it is rash to speak of total peace, *ingenium* suffers when enough enemies have fallen for a sense of security to emerge. This peace then allows men of arms to lay them down long enough to begin enjoying their acquisitions.[68] Then the relationship between *ingenium* and body is no longer easily decided. An ambiguity in the *lubido dominandi* emerges: the desire for acquisition promotes virtue, where the desire of enjoying or using what one acquires promotes vice. Military life now ceases to be the ready means of the domination of a hegemonic mind as a general over an obedient body.

Is Sulla's civil war the product of desire for domination residing within the *ingenium* that no longer has an external object towards which it may be directed? Yet, in the successful attainment of Sulla's desire for domination, it is desire itself that wins, not the sovereignty of mind. Even Sallust's abuses of the action of fortune can be read as a deflection here: it is fortune's chaotic desire, the impersonal action of an abstraction, that ruins Rome. It is not the personal action of a concrete Roman, Sulla; nor is it the action of *ingenium* fulfilling itself that spells disaster.

In civil war the hierarchical inside–outside distinction that strongly governed the initial political life of man has disappeared. And as this distinction between foe and Roman disappears, other polarities evanesce in its wake and vital distinctions lose value. This Rome loses the boundaries that segregate thine from mine, sacred from profane, man from woman, mind from body, and beast from man. For Sallust this series of failures is marked by figures of desire. Lusts of one sort or another surround the moment of the loss of these distinctions. The most sweeping reversal is perhaps the sickness suffered from money where body and mind both go from virile to feminine in section 11. The mastery of the virile mind over the martial body turns into the feminine body lording it over an insatiable spirit. In Sallust's terms, civil war causes Rome to lose its mind and to live within an anarchic and bestial bodily economy.

And while Sallust himself speaks of the lust for goods in section 13 as ineffable, it is the prior lust of Roman mastery over Roman that causes his narrative to falter more noticeably. He cannot tell the tale of this moment clearly. Sallust obscures Sulla and his deed. Indeed, to speak directly of either would require a radical re-examination of the axiomatic principles of the sovereignty of mind. Sallust's preface points towards Sulla and explains him only by way of the ambiguities and contradictions

---

[68] Scanlon 1980: 33 highlights the function of war in Sallust: 'Sallust appears to have adopted a scheme describing linear decline resulting from the removal of *metus hostilis* and breakdown of *virtus*.'

of that preface. Memory, glory, and virtue hang upon the possibility of Sallust's ability to know and to write of Rome, but Sallust loses the possibility of authoritative history in the wake of civil war, or, more generally, in the wake of desire. In section 13 Sallust confesses too late that his text makes sense only in the terms of the loss of *ingenium* in a Rome ruled by post-Sullan *lubidines*. Furthermore, Sallust the historian has attached his own intellectual biography to this Rome, and he himself reads as a man whose mind is troubled by the spectre of the body. He speaks as an authority in a world where *imperium* and *ingenium* have gone awry. He speaks, that is, as a man who may be no authority at all.

D. THERAPY AND CURE

Insufficient justice will have been done to Sallust's work if we stop after pointing out its inadequacy relative to its own conceptual framework. There is more to reading critically than merely catching the author at his weakest moments. Instead, new questions arise that direct us to seek out the reasons why such difficulties should have been encountered at precisely these points. One also wonders if these problems do not themselves yield a sort of paradoxical virtue or perform a species of unexpected work. And perhaps the work is sufficiently beneficial towards certain ends so as to have converted the difficulties themselves into a productive part of Sallust's project even as they simultaneously seem to be points at which he founders. In other words, why these failures? And does Sallust suffer a total loss?[69]

With the end of the thirteenth section, Sallust is ready to talk of Catiline and the conspiracy at length. But he is ready to talk of Catiline only after he has first rendered the truths of Catiline himself as derivative ones. The history of *ingenium* and desire in the abstract and the narrative of Sulla in the concrete are the points in which Sallust has the most invested. Sulla is a sort of incurable sickness. Sallust cannot speak clearly of him; yet Sallust firmly embeds his history within a matrix inaugurated and enabled by Sulla.[70] Hence giving the truth of the Catilinarian

---

[69] It will be worthwhile to recall that, in contrast to the lines of thought I am pursuing, Batstone 1990 argues that Sallust means for his text to be broken in fundamental ways.

[70] Sulla also is the key to the non-Roman fraction of Catiline's army. For different reasons, both the victims of Sulla and his colonists evince a *cupido* and a *lubido* that make them amenable to Catiline's purposes in section 28. Notice the latent formula whose logic is in keeping with the rest of the narrative: Sullan extra-Roman desires would invade the state.

conspiracy or answering any of its mysteries will never unfold the truth of some novel crime, nor will it offer a cure for the sickness of Roman life. The telling of the tale of Catiline is more the indulgence of a symptom than the route to a cure.[71]

In this regard, one might fruitfully compare Freud on repetition:[72] for Freud, the forgotten and repressed is remembered in action;[73] or, for present purposes, the repressed is remembered in the narrative of Sallust. Sallust tells and retells his broken themes as if they would somehow be made whole merely by their iteration. Yet *lubido* and its ruin seem ever less likely to be banished the more Sallust talks of them. And though I am suggesting that Sallust's narrative seeks to act as a sort of talking therapy in which Sallust seeks to heal the losses suffered by *virtus* and *ingenium*, the concomitant crisis in memory results in a condition where Sallust 'repeats during the treatment all his symptoms'.[74]

No matter how many times Sallust offers another version of *ingenium* and mind's mastery, he nevertheless does not solve the crises of the text; rather, he exacerbates them. In this comparison, one has to take Sallust as both patient and doctor. But this does in some measure correspond to Sallust's own assertion that the writing of history is a way to cure his impotence relative to actually performing historically significant acts. On the other hand, Sallust is a physician apparently unable to heal himself. There are peculiarities in the telling of the Catilinarian conspiracy that on this reading become more intelligible as returns to the site of the original crisis. The logic they fall within and the narrative to which they more properly appertain are not one which lies over in the camp of the conspirators. Instead, the erratic movement of the narrative of Catiline tells a second tale that fits in perfectly with the lines of thought traced out in the opening sections.

We return to Catiline after our brief glimpse of him from section 5. He was sandwiched between Sallust's autobiography and the first complaints about Sulla. The company he kept there was as telling as his associates here. His satellites are schooled in vice and softness in precisely the terms Sulla indulged his veterans.[75] Next, in section 15, Catiline's women friends are listed. In fact, the first proper names to be directly associated with Catiline are those of fallen women.[76] The bodily depravity that will mark the whole of his conspiracy takes shape first in the form of personal

---

[71] Newbold 1990 offers a rather unsatisfying psychological reading of Sallust that relies on predetermined categories and word counts.
[72] Freud 1963a: 157–66.   [73] Ibid. 160.   [74] Ibid. 162.
[75] Forms of *docere* cluster around Catiline. See sections 16 and 17.
[76] See Boyd 1987: 197.

and feminine lapses. Indeed, in section 24 Catiline attaches to himself a number of promiscuous women who will incite the urban mob. Physical bodies are intended to arouse the depraved metaphorical body of the state.

And, later, when we read of Sempronia in section 25, we have both an interruption in the tale of the conspiracy and the insertion of another sort of double for Catiline.[77] Her manly boldness (*virilis audacia*) and clever wit are put to use in the field of luxury. Her clever and manipulative sexual aggressivity correspond nicely to the bodily politics of the morally inverted Catiline, who would employ the mind to first spoil the body and then win for it illegitimate political power.[78] Similarly Sempronia's vices recall the confusion both of post-Sullan Rome and of the boundlessness of lust. The crisis of the comparative degree detailed above repeats itself in Sempronia. She is surrounded by violations of the decorum of the comparative. In her short section one reads the words *elegantius, cariora, minus,* and *saepius*: 'more elegant', 'more dear', 'less', and 'more often'. In each case she transgresses the bounds of propriety set out by these terms: she played the cithara and danced more elegantly than a good woman should; she held everything dearer than honour and chastity; it was not clear whether she spared her purse or her reputation less; she sought men more often than she was sought out.[79] The *lubido* of Sempronia sets all boundaries into confusion: one does not know precisely what she did, only that she was 'out of line', as one might say. Sempronia thus recalls the language of *fortuna* and of fortune's *lubido* as well as the problem of the relationship between desire and boundaries (*fines*) in general.

---

[77] Sempronia's brief appearance has provoked endless commentary of which I can only offer some highlights. For Syme 1964: 69 the quality of interruption predominates: she 'has no part in the action' and the choice to include her 'cannot fail to arouse curiosity or disquiet'. Later Syme wonders, 'What is this lady doing in the pages of Sallust?' See Syme 1964: 133. Perhaps, though, this unpleasant arousal is just what we ought to feel before her *ingenium*. Compare the strained efforts of Tiffou to offer an explanation for Sempronia at Tiffou 1973: 366 n. 43. Cadoux 1980: 93–122 takes more time and trouble but eventually dismisses her on page 120. Earl 1961: 90 and Büchner 1982: 134–5 offer an interpretive advance by integrating Sempronia's biography into the major themes of the narrative. One can compare here Paul 1985: 9–22. Boyd 1987 offers the most sophisticated collection of observations on Sempronia that fit her firmly into Sallust's narrative.

[78] Boyd 1987: 193 summarizes the ties between luxury, effeminacy, and moral decay in Sallust: 'Indulgence in *luxuria* results in physical effeminacy complementing the moral denigration within, and *virtus* loses its true meaning.'

[79] *litteris Graecis Latinis docta, psallere saltare elegantius quam necesse est probae, multa alia, quae instrumenta luxuriae sunt. sed ei cariora semper omnia quam decus atque pudicitia fuit; pecuniae an famae minus parceret, haud facile discerneres; lubido sic adcensa, ut saepius peteret viros quam peteretur,* 25. 2–3.

Moreover, with Sempronia we have another disturbing figure who recalls Sallust himself. First, she too is a literary figure, an author of sorts; she knows her Greek and Latin; she performs. Similarly she shows much promise in her birth and ability; only she goes and stays astray, where Sallust erred only to return to propriety. And, lastly, there is even a verbal echo between Sallust's description of the virtue of history and Sempronia's own intelligence. Sempronia has 'no mean intellect' (*ingenium haud absurdum*, 25. 5), while Sallust had said of history that speaking well of the state is 'no mean project' (*haud absurdum est*, 3. 1). Hence the emblem of this bodily, depraved, and effeminate revolution is not radically other than the 'manly intellect' (*uirile ingenium*) that would both record and refuse her. Sallust's monsters ever recall the legitimate in their very illegitimacy.

If Catiline and his cronies seem only to be a resumption of the themes introduced with Sulla, so also is the whole conspiracy of Catiline only a retelling of itself. Sallust informs us in section 18 that there was actually a prior conspiracy. The conspiracy that he now recounts is just another version of the first plot. Once again we lose the novelty of Catiline's crime, the novelty that makes him worth writing of and that Sallust says incites him to write.[80] First, the conspiracy in the *Bellum Catilinae* resembles the education of the Sullan veterans where Catiline schools his men in vices first taught by Sulla to his troops. Next, the conspiracy resembles its own immediate antecedent, a prior conspiracy of Catiline and Piso. For, as Sallust suddenly explains in section 19, there was an earlier attempt on the state with motivations and principal agents strikingly similar to the events of this later conspiracy. So much for the 'novelty of the crime' (*sceleris novitas*) Sallust had promised us. Moreover, Piso in that first conspiracy reads like a Catiline. Writing a tragedy to succeed a farce is a historical fallacy according to Marx's famous supplement to Hegel;[81] but this is just what we find Sallust doing, and the odd spin put upon history by Sallust serves purposes that are other than those that would dictate genres. Faced with too many monsters and too many crimes, Sallust writes the horror into the last link of the chain so that he may avoid addressing directly those first causes that would

---

[80] A kind interpretation of this passage would say that this conspiracy is really only part of Catiline's conspiracy. But why speak of it thus and here? Why bury it and/or stumble over it? Sallust had no compunction about giving the history of the world as a preface to the main narrative; why could not Piso have rubbed shoulders with Sulla as immediate antecedents sandwiched between the universal and the specific?

[81] See Marx 1978: 9: 'Hegel remarks somewhere that all the events and personalities of great importance in world history occur, as it were, twice. He forgot to add: the first time as tragedy, the second as farce.'

hobble his own ability to write history at all. For the route back to these causes brings into question the status of the *ingenium* of the historian himself.

Catiline is not just a double for Sulla or the murderous Piso; he also resembles Sallust and Cicero. When he speaks to his partisans, his oratory is filled with the very stuff of which legitimate discourse is spun. In section 20 and Catiline's speech *ingenium* and *animus* figure prominently. There is an echo of the famous tirade against Catiline made by Cicero.[82] Catiline even refers to manly intellect (*virile ingenium*) in a collocation that his historian would love to claim for himself. Desire and the desire for wealth are destroying Rome and producing chaos,[83] says Catiline. The *lubido* of the wealthy is infinite and insatiable: it is unable to conquer itself in its vastness (*tamen summa lubidine divitias suas vincere nequeunt*, 20. 12). Catiline preaches from the same hymnal as does Sallust. Naturally one is invited to suspect Catiline of cunning and cynicism here: he distorts language to his own ends. In fact, in the next section *ingenium* grapples with *lubido* in a parody of their original encounter as the *ingenium* of Catiline's speech is supplemented by and triumphs by means of promises of debt relief; Catiline's band now imagines that war will allow it to slake its greed. Of course, by now Sallust's readers know that war is the symptom of money troubles, not the cure for them. Catiline's parody of rhetoric and hegemony is enabled by a world that has lost the relationship between key notions.

On the other hand, in his final scenes, Catiline's last speech before his heroic end suddenly heals the breaches in the conceptual apparatus of the whole narrative: battle gives Catiline a martial *virtus* that spills into a moral and manly *virtus*. In short, Catiline is recovered to manly *ingenium* by the labour of warfare, and the abstract mechanics of the *Bellum* end on a rather happy note. But the narrative proper is here tinged with desperation and futility, as Syme observed.[84] The dissonance between these two registers indicates that the restoration of the structure of *virtus* and *ingenium* is tainted. Civil war may have proven something about Catiline's character, but it cost the state dearly. Again one can think of Sulla: he verified certain truths, but the proof soon turned into a poison

---

[82] *quae quousque tandem patiemini, o fortissumi viri* (20. 9) sounds suspiciously like *quousque tandem abutere, Catilina, patientia nostra?* (Cicero, *Cat.* 1. 1) as commentators have long noticed. See McGushin 1977: *ad loc*. Of course, it is entirely possible that Cicero was himself offering a parody of Catiline's rhetoric when he opened the first Catilinarian.

[83] Catiline employs the same trope of luxury used by Sallust above when he talks of filling seas and levelling mountains.

[84] Syme 1964: 68.

for the state. Catiline's return to civil war reiterates the verities and the sickness of Sulla.

Cato may complain that we have lost the 'true names for things' (*vera vocabula rerum*), but this is less a loss of words than it is an unanchoring of the language of virtue. Mind and mastery have drifted into the camp of vice. And yet this is the world from which we find not just a Catiline speaking, but also a Sallust writing—writing, indeed, of Catiline speaking. Sallust cannot finally control and consolidate the authority of his own message, since its lived antithesis employs the same phrasing. Speech or, more generally, language has become an insufficient token of virtue. Perhaps Catiline's words are mere cynicism in the face of the true version of the same message offered aright by Sallust. But this thesis cannnot itself fully satisfy us: Sallust's own message about virtue was itself incoherent; and it was incoherent because of Sulla/Catiline. That is, it is not sufficient to say that in the later speeches Sallust stages Catiline as specious. It is also important to realize that Catiline produces a Sallust who is himself suspect.[85]

As at the beginning of the monograph, it is the deed that reveals the *ingenium*. We know of Catiline's wickedness more from what he does than what he says. Language is likewise separated from *ingenium* here, as it was in section 8 above. Where the Athenians spoke beyond their deeds, Catiline speaks contrary to his. And Catiline's cleverness—a cleverness on loan from his biographer, of course—turns back against Sallust to the extent that Sallust's own text becomes a vehicle for a message of virtue that nevertheless does not enact that virtue. And yet Sallust's text neither speaks well of the state nor does well by it. Indeed, it ends with a scene of Roman uncertainty about how to react in the face of Catiline's defeat. Sallust's own readers are left similarly uncertain about how to digest both the slaying of Roman by Roman and the consequences of such for *virtus* and *ingenium*. And here we need not see Sallust as writing a text that misperforms, but instead as penning an impotent text.

Does his history act as a noble deed? Does it perform virtuous memory as the act of a virile and authoritative *ingenium*? Certainly it tries, but the *Bellum Catilinae* simultaneously spells out the impossibility of establishing such connections within its own logical and historical dictates. And it is in the false speech of a Catiline that we discover one element of the performative impotence of language per se. Catiline makes a rousing speech about defending one's rights, but his men can only be spurred to

---

[85] This line of thought accordingly parallels Sklenář's version of Sallust against himself, but it reads this theme at a different point, arguing for Catiline instead of the Caesar/Cato pair as producing revision and split within the text.

action by promises of debt cancellation and the like. Similarly, Sallust himself tells a tale of Catiline in a noble idiom, but the historical residues of other wars and of other 'lusts of the victorious' (*lubidines victorum*) have disrupted not only the efficacy of such a narrative but even the meaning of the terms that Sallust employs. What does *ingenium* mean in this world? How can Sallust write of things only a fellow witness could understand? What sort of virtuous response are Sallust's readers supposed to make in the face of this narrative? Is mind's tragedy the fact that it comes to know itself too late and only after its inner will to power has already evolved into a tainted civil war that displaces manly self-mastery?

The whole of Sallust's monograph cannot escape from the legacy of speech that would be a deed. Indeed, the comparison with drama that Leeman stresses brings to mind the Greek etymology of drama by way of 'doing', τὸ δρᾶν. And, keeping with the Greek, one is invited to read this history as the imitation of a deed (μίμησις πράξεως), but an imitation that aspires to itself be a 'doing'.[86] Sallust writes in order to produce something, to do well by speaking well (*bene facere, bene dicere*). And this doing is a sort of cognitive mastery where the historian's mind holds sway. Recalling Hegel, consciousness and self-consciousness emerge in the historian's masterful domination of his subject matter as writing performs self-consciousness. It declares both the ego and the sovereignty of the ego by way of subjecting history to itself. Sallust's history of mind attempts to subdue the thematics of the body and of desire. In order to be true to his own opening philosophical conceits, Sallust must master Catiline. This observation allows us to see why Sallust himself needs to play such a prominent role in his own story. Yet we can no longer give a simple interpretation to any of the key categories in Sallust's narrative. And this ambiguity renders suspect the unique sovereignty of historical knowledge.

For example, it is specifically Sallust's *conscientia scelerum* ('consciousness of wickedness') that drives him to tell where he can no longer do. Here I have ironically borrowed the phrase *conscientia scelerum* from section 5. 7, where consciousness of his own wickedness drives Catiline to further depraved acts. Awareness and criminal self-awareness form a durable dyad in Sallust, and such an association has remained with us throughout his work. The problem of knowing and doing comes to a head in section 15. The stain of kindred blood maddens Catiline and drives him to further criminal deeds (*B.C.* 15. 2–5):

---

[86] See Syme 1964: 2 again.

postremo captus amore Aureliae Orestillae, quoius praeter formam nihil umquam bonus laudavit, quod ea nubere illi dubitabat timens privignum adulta aetate, pro certo creditur necato filio vacuam domum scelestis nuptiis fecisse. quae quidem res mihi in primis videtur causa fuisse facinus maturandi. namque animus inpurus, dis hominibusque infestus, neque vigiliis neque quietibus sedari poterat: ita conscientia mentem excitam vastabat. igitur colos exanguis, foedi oculi, citus modo, modo tardus incessus: prorsus in facie voltuque vecordia inerat.

Finally a love for Aurelia Orestilla seized Catiline. She was someone whom no good man ever praised for anything but her looks. Since she was hesitant to marry Catiline because she feared having an adult stepson, it is taken as a fact that Catiline killed his son and so made way for his criminal nuptuals. Indeed, this seems to me to have been the principle reason for hastening the crime (*facinus*). For Catiline's spirit (*animus*) was tainted, and it despised gods and men alike; neither wakefulness nor sleep brought it peace. Thus a guilty conscience (*conscientia*) laid waste to his agitated mind. Therefore, he was pallid, his eyes were bloodshot, his gait was now swift, now slow. In short, madness was readily visible in his face and countenance.

In this passage the difficulty with *facere* and its derivatives comes to the fore. In many instances one is asked to translate Sallust's use of *facinus* as 'deed' by way of a typical appeal to etymology over more familiar uses. But Catiline's deed is always criminal. Hence *facinus* routinely slips into its rather more common translation throughout Sallust's text.[87] In this passage Catiline's murder drives him to do another 'deed' that will be the same one of which Sallust says he wishes to write. Doing and criminal doing converge in the son's death.[88]

Catiline is multiply motivated: it is Sulla who inspires him; and then it is lust; and then murder. All of these motives, though, are not just joined in Catiline's own biography, but they have been found to be linked themes in Sallust's own thought. Catiline embodies the sick logic of history itself. Specifically, Sulla is both a figure of desire and of kin-slaying. Thus Sulla is already both lust and murder, and Catiline's motives converge around Sulla. So also does Sallust's text as a whole even as it purports to be the story of Catiline and not Sulla. The kin-slaying in Rome's own past drives Sallust himself to write. Sallust proceeds down a narrative trail where his step is now swift, now slow. The

---

[87] Compare the twin use of *periculum* in sections 2. 2 and 4. 4: in the first instance *periculum* is mere 'experience', and it is derived from *experior* by way of an etymological play, a *figura etymologica*. In the second passage, *periculum* means 'danger' as soon as Catiline's name is attached to it.

[88] Think also of the original *patres* who governed Rome and the parricide of revolution: the mutual relations of father and son are a durable metaphor in Sallust.

erratic gait of the text staggers in sync with Catiline himself; but it is Sallust himself who marked out the time in this deranged waltz.

At the start of his narrative Sallust seemed to indicate that the historian's job was to speak well of the state. But Sallust the historian has not spoken well: he has told of crime and criminals, *male dicens de male facientibus*. In so doing Sallust recapitulates the tragedy of *ingenium* as a whole: mind has needed a fallen body. Sallust the knowing historian needed to speak of the prodigious and prodigal body of Catiline. Mind desires mastery of the body and the world. Yet, in this moment of desiring (*cupido*), there is opened up a space for a disruptive 'invasion' that precipitates the undoing of mind's unquestioned mastery. Sallust wants to know and hence to master Catiline and the sickness he represents. But Sallust's desire participates in the logic he has himself spelled out. When the desire for mastery applies itself to another Roman in civil war, both mind and body are ruined. In such circumstances what does *ingenium* really know? What can it really do? Sallust's 'War of Catiline' is also a 'War against Catiline' waged by the pen. And as a species of civil war the text itself succumbs to its disastrous logic.

The *Bellum* is a curiously told tale. It starts with a tangle of abstractions. It proceeds by fits and starts as it digresses and repeats itself before it can come to its ostensible subject matter. In the course of this initial movement and in the telling of the conspiracy proper, though, the moral investment of history has been secured. There runs in strange parallel to this history another, more practical tale. A story of simple Machiavellian interest also runs alongside the tale of intellectual, moral, and sexual crisis. Perhaps Catiline is merely a frustrated candidate for the consulship. Maybe Crassus and other prominent Roman aristocrats look for personal gain in the prospect of destabilizing Roman civic life. It may be that some of these nobles take an active, yet covert part in the conspiracy. Meanwhile, the commoners might not be foolish, feminine, or depraved: they might only seek economic relief from the predations of the upper class.[89]

The practical tale of scattered interests felicitously uniting for a brief power play has received a second place in Sallust's telling. The reason for this narrative structure has already been indicated: Sallust has an investment in the morality of history. He indulges this interest and would assert that it ought to be one shared by all Romans. Thus, where he

---

[89] Sections 38 and 39 offer the longest sustained segment of this kind of historiography in the monograph. Syme, who sees many advances rather than lapses in Sallust's age, concludes of the historian that 'he interpreted a process of economic change and political adjustment in terms of morals; and he fell an easy prey to conventional notions about old Roman virtue'. This is Syme 1964: 17.

knows of the possibility of amoral history, he strives instead for a history that turns on the antipodes of morality and immorality. And yet Sallust's narrative techniques undermine the possibility of any such history. Sallust offers instead a rhetorical history whose narrative ambiguities reproduce the hermeneutic ambiguity of the confused Roman civic life in which the historian finds himself.[90] In other words, at several different levels Sallust's text provokes the question 'Where is truth where there is no virtue?'

Sallust suffuses his narrative with the language of virtue, and the morality of the text would somehow itself enact a lost morality of Rome. The archaic language and nostalgic thought of Sallust strive towards the rehearsal of a virtue whose death the Catilinarians have effected even where they have not seized the state. Sallust rehearses a metaphysics of morals for himself and his Roman readers that would enfold the conspiracy within its compass. Sallust would constitute history as a moral object in declaring the immorality to which Rome has descended, as the virtuous memory of history's mind achieved the reversal of immorality by branding it with its very name. The Sallustian 'speech act', though, resembles more the Derridean critique of Austin than Austin's ideal:[91] Sallust's version of the performative utterance is enabled only within the space of the failure of virtuous thought to secure virtuous action.

The gulf between the text and the world is one that Sallust will never be able to bridge. His history declares the philosophical truths of mind to which it must be true, but this same history instead proves the impossibility of such a philosophy of mind. This impossible philosophy is unattainable not only in the terms of Roman history, though. The very relationship between mind and its object cannot be grounded in Sallust's terms. Sallust's desire for narrative and cognitive mastery unleashes a dialectical engagement with its own object. And the course of this interaction between mind and history brings into question the sovereignty of Sallust's own *ingenium*.

There is a sort of melancholy in this turning. Sallust talks as if there has been a loss of a love object. Moreover, one comes to see that this loss is most likely the loss of an object within himself, not just within Rome.[92] But history cannot recover this object, for a variety of reasons. First, the

---

[90] This line of thought follows Batstone 1986: 105–21. On page 116 Batstone concludes, 'For Sallust, research and interpretation, the acquisition of facts, "Was Crassus guilty?" had become a problem.'
[91] See Austin 1975 and Derrida 1988.
[92] Compare Freud 1963b: 166 and 168.

problem of the active powers of narrative or the lack thereof remains insurmountable for Sallust. Next, the telling of the tale of Catiline may rehearse the crisis and seek to assuage the wound suffered by virtue, but this story lies to the side of the site of the first trauma that is attributed to Sulla.[93] Thirdly, the dialectical movement of *ingenium* in Sallust requires the very crisis that would be overcome. And, lastly, to write history is to use the mastery of *ingenium*. Writing thrives in the very space of practical failure, and Syme can justly speak of a 'delectation in disillusionment' on the historian's part:[94] Sallust retains his own intelligence at the price of losing its possibility in the world.

Or has Sallust retained his *ingenium*? *Ingenium* is of itself melancholic, and it plays the role of an object always lost; *ingenium* thrives on oppositions between inside and outside, master and slave, mind and body, male and female that cannot be sustained. The operation of the other, and specifically of the desire of the other, prevents the consolidation of *ingenium*. The libidinous invasion of desire into the self redivides the self. This doubled self then reproduces the binary logic of opposition that structures the universe; it is a logic operant both within the state and within the individual. The radical self-identity of mind, and of mind as solely masterful, virtuous, and male, cannot be sustained within this scheme. Yet, ironically, it is this very dynamic of the splitting and resplitting of *ingenium* that enables the position occupied by Sallust as knower, father, and mind even as his speech cannot act, nor can his body. Nor does Sallust's knowledge have the efficacy of a divine cognition where knowing is akin to doing since it knows a truth or a reality; Sallust's historical knowledge is always too late and impotent.

For Hegel the master is not truly masterful in his consciousness. It is the mastered one, the slave, who holds the true key to full self-consciousness, since in his absolute subjection and in his relationship to labour through time, he has the path to a higher condition opened up to him.[95] Sallust writes a history that longs for a cure for a movement whereby mind is always about to fall into body. The sovereignty of mind as master in Sallust revolts against the implications of the servile body and all of its associates, the lower classes, women, the non-Roman, et al. Yet, in a way, there is a logic, a labour, and a dialectic in which these

---

[93] This is only to say that Sulla is the first named villain, not that the movement of the history of mind is not already flawed before Sallust gives vice a name.
[94] See Syme 1964: 256.
[95] See Hegel 1977: 117–19. Compare Lacan 1977: 99–100, where the master–slave relation is translated into the bond between therapist and patient in the psychoanalytic venue.

slaves participate. And it is through the reading of the tale of these oppressed and repressed objects that we can arrive at a higher plane of understanding of the history and the historian, a clearer conception of the structure of mind and memory in post-Sullan Rome. The dialectical movement that allows for the simultaneous transcending and annulment (*Aufhebung*) of reason in Sallust opens up for us a new opportunity for the exercise of our own wit even where its mastery of the body of the text is admitted to be incomplete and ripe for another revolution in its turn. The mind that tries to master Sallust can never feel secure in its sovereignty.

Sallust's efforts and their methodological significance have a contemporary relevance even in their failure. Sallust's problems and his attempts at a solution bring into stark relief the perils and the products of a historical narrative that evinces a will to knowledge and to mastery. The historian's desire to write and to comprehend becomes a project that compromises the position from which the author would write. However this 'postmodern' crisis of knowledge is not even a modern crisis: it is classical and rhetorical. One needs to reconsider the extent to which the antiquity of such a difficult relation between subject and object should form a part of our own understanding of the epistemological problems of historiography. If, indeed, the postmodern condition is characterized by an 'incredulity towards meta-narratives',[96] we ought to consider this case of a metanarrative that labours to get itself off the ground. The problem of writing an authoritative metanarrative that justifies historiography is already a problem for Sallust as he entangles himself in questions of sovereignty, repetition, and desire. These are the very sorts of concepts with which contemporary critical discourses engage. But in so doing are we at best being post-classical or at worst merely classical?

[96] Lyotard 1984: xxiv.

8

Sallust's *Catiline* and Cato the Censor

D. S. Levene

That Sallust owed a considerable debt to the writings of Cato the Censor[1] was observed in antiquity,[2] and the observation has often been discussed and expanded on by modern scholars.[3] The ancient references to Sallust's employment of Cato are mainly in the context of his adoption of an archaic style, and specifically Catonian vocabulary. But the choice of Cato as a model had an obvious significance that went beyond the purely stylistic.[4] Sallust's works articulate extreme pessimism at the moral state of late republican Rome, and do so partly by contrasting the modern age with a prelapsarian time of near-untrammelled virtue, brought to an end only by the fall of Carthage and the consequent dominance of Roman power, which in turn led to moral corruption. Similarly, Cato famously stood in his own day for moral rectitude—and

---

[1] References in this paper to the fragments of Cato's *Orationes* are according to the ORF numbering. References to the fragments of the *Origines* are according to the numbering of P. Fragments of Cato's other works are cited from Jordan 1860. Versions of the ideas developed in this paper have been tried out previously on audiences in Durham, Leeds, and Oxford, and I am grateful for the comments that I have received on those occasions. I should also like to thank for their help Christina Kraus, Damien Nelis, Clemence Schultze, and Tony Woodman.

[2] Quint. *Inst.* 8. 3. 29: *nec minus noto Sallustius epigrammate incessitur: et verba antiqui multum furate Catonis, / Crispe, Iugurthinae conditor historiae* ('Sallust is equally the object of attack from the famous epigram: "And you, the great thief of the words of ancient Cato, / Crispus, the creator of the Jugurthine history"'); Suet. *Aug.* 86: *verbis, quae Crispus Sallustius excerpsit ex Originibus Catonis* ('words, which Sallustius Crispus extracted from Cato's *Origines*'); Suet. *Gram.* 15: *Sallustium historicum...priscorum Catonisque verborum ineruditissimum furem* ('the historian Sallust...an utterly uneducated thief of ancient vocabulary (especially Cato)'); Fronto, *Ad M. Caesarem* 4. 3. 2: *M. Porcius eiusque frequens sectator Sallustius* ('M. Porcius and his constant disciple Sallust').

[3] For example Deltour 1859; Bruennert 1873; Ernout 1949; Skard 1956: 75–107; Lebek 1970: 291–335.

[4] See, e.g., Deltour 1859: 43–7; Egermann 1932: 77–8; Ernout 1949: 61; Earl 1961: 44–5.

specifically appealed to past virtue as the standard to which he wished to hold his contemporaries.[5] Sallust, by writing in a Catonian style, aligns himself with that tradition.

However, recent studies of Sallust have tended to stress that his moral position is more complex and nuanced than might appear from a superficial reading: that although his prefaces and explicit statements on the state of Roman morality would point the reader towards a simple picture of ancient virtue overtaken by utter corruption, the detail of his narratives leads one to draw different conclusions, so that even apparent villains such as Catiline will exhibit exceptional heroic qualities.[6] The object of this paper is to show that the Catonian allusions in the *Catiline* fit into this pattern: far from reinforcing a simple moral dichotomy of present vice and past virtue, they combine systematically to precisely the opposite effect, and indeed provide us with some of the central paradoxes through which the work must be interpreted. The loss of the great bulk of Cato's writings means that there are likely to be numerous allusions to him that we fail to recognize; but even from what we have, a clear and systematic pattern emerges. I shall be focusing on three sections of the *Catiline* in particular in which the Catonian references are especially charged: (I) Sallust's initial programmatic statements (1-4); (II) the so-called Archaeology (6-13); and (III) the debate between Caesar and the younger Cato on the punishment of the conspirators (51-4).

I. THE PROGRAMME

Sallust begins the *Catiline* with a passage (1-2) which, highly unusually for a historical work in the ancient world,[7] contains no clear reference either to the topic of the work or even to history as a genre,[8] but rather sets out a series of moral dichotomies pitched at a stratospheric level of generality. Man/beast, mind/body, virtue/vice are all placed before the reader and correlated to one another.[9] To surpass the beast, one must

---

[5] For example, Cato, *Orationes* frs. 18, 58, 144, 200, 221-2, *Carmen de Moribus* frs. 1-2; Cic. *Div*. 1. 28; Plut. *Cat. Mai.* 20. 5. See Astin 1978: 100.

[6] Examples include Scanlon 1987; Batstone 1988b; Wilkins 1994; Kraus and Woodman 1997: 10-50.

[7] Cf. Earl 1972.

[8] Naturally, history is in fact covertly alluded to from the start, with, for example, the stress on the avoidance of 'silence' (1. 1), and the importance allotted to 'memory' (1. 3), but it is only in retrospect that their relevance to the genre of the work becomes apparent. On *silentium* in this passage, see Woodman 1973.

[9] Cf. Leeman 1954: 325-8.

seek not physical rewards, but rather *virtus*, which is eternal (1. 4); both body and mind are necessary for success (1. 2, 1. 7, 2. 1), but it is essential that the mind must be in charge (1. 2, 2. 2, 2. 3). Failure in this regard is equated with the lapse of virtue into vice (2. 5), as well as with the beast-like behaviour of sloth and gluttony (1. 1, 2. 5, 2. 8).

Nothing in this should of itself make one think of Cato. It is true that his own moralistic approach had a good deal in common with Sallust's here: for example, Sallust's specific focus on gluttony and sloth, both of which (but especially the former) had been famous objects of Cato's attacks.[10] Sallust (2. 5) speaks of restraint (*continentia*) and justice (*aequitas*) being taken over by lust (*lubido*) and arrogance (*superbia*)—likewise an area with which Cato had shown himself especially concerned.[11] However, there are no recognizable allusions to surviving portions of Cato's work; and while various earlier writers have been canvassed as the sources of Sallust's general thought in these chapters, it is clear that many of the particular ideas expressed are regular ancient commonplaces: thus, the fact that they overlap with Cato's expressed attitudes proves nothing.

However, when we reach the following chapters, in which Sallust first mentions the writing of history directly, describes his own political career, and gives his reasons for taking up historiography, we instantly find something more pointed (2. 9-3. 2):

> sed in magna copia rerum aliud alii natura iter ostendit. pulchrum est bene facere rei publicae, etiam bene dicere haud absurdum est; vel pace vel bello clarum fieri licet; et qui fecere et qui facta aliorum scripsere multi laudantur. ac mihi quidem, tametsi haudquaquam par gloria sequitur scriptorem et auctorem rerum, tamen in primis arduom videtur res gestas scribere.

> But in the great range of affairs nature shows different people different routes. It is a fine thing to act well for the state; it is not a preposterous thing even to speak well for it.[12] One may become famous in peace or war, and of those who have acted and of those who have written of the acts of others, many are praised. And indeed to me, although far from equal glory attends a writer and a doer of deeds, nevertheless writing about deeds seems to me outstandingly difficult.

The phrase *rei publicae bene facere* is unusual and not otherwise attested in extant Latin[13]—apart from being used by Cato of his own deeds in a

---

[10] Cato, *Orationes* frs. 78, 132, 139, 142, 144, 146, *Carmen de Moribus* frs. 2-3; Plut. *Cat. Mai.* 7. 1, 9. 5, *Apophthegms* 198D; cf. Cato, *Orationes* fr. 111. See Astin 1978: 91-2.

[11] Cato, *Orationes* frs. 58, 173, 177, 224. See Astin 1978: 90, 95-6.

[12] This interpretation of *bene dicere* has been questioned, but see Leeman 1954: 329.

[13] More common are related phrases of the form *beneficium in rem publicam*: see Hellegouarc'h 1963: 168 n. 11.

striking section of his speech *De sumptu suo*: it looks as if Sallust is alluding to that here.[14] The immediate conclusion might be that Sallust is contrasting himself as an historian who 'speaks well' with Cato as one who 'acted well'. However, Cato was manifestly someone who both acted *and* spoke—indeed, the very fact that his writings are the source of the allusion that Sallust is making demonstrates this. The contrast rather appears to be that, as Sallust goes on to explain, his own attempt at a political career was prevented through the corruption of the society around him (3. 3–4. 1), and so he returned to his initial intention of writing historiography (4. 2).[15] The specific words in which he expresses his determination to write history, moreover, link his own writing to Catonian historiography in particular: he says *statui res gestas populi Romani carptim...perscribere* ('I decided to write out the deeds of the Roman people selectively,' 4. 2), which recalls the opening words of Cato's *Origines* (*si ques homines sunt, quos delectat populi Romani gesta discribere*, 'if there are any people whom it delights to describe the deeds of the Roman people', fr. 1). Expressions like *res gestas populi Romani* are, naturally, paralleled elsewhere, but the general phrasing here is close,[16] and Sallust's intention expressed in the following sentence to write about the Catilinarian conspiracy 'briefly' specifically suggests the Catonian manner (*paucis absolvam*).[17] In other words, the implication is that whereas Cato was able to prove himself in both speech and deeds, Sallust is being Catonian in the only sphere that the corruption of contemporary society now allowed.[18]

The implications of this passage extend further still. For a Roman reader, *bene dicere* in its immediate context would most naturally be taken to refer not to historiography, but to oratory. However, having introduced the phrase, Sallust immediately shifts the antithesis from 'doing' vs 'speaking' to 'doing' vs 'writing'.[19] His historiographical enterprise is thus not linked narrowly to the imitation of Cato as an historian:

---

[14] Cato, *Orationes* fr. 173; cf. Skard 1956: 82; Vretska 1976: 86.

[15] This is the usual interpretation of the passage. See, however, Kraus and Woodman 1997: 15 for the alternative suggestion that the 'return' is to be interpreted not as Sallust resuming a prior literary activity, but as a return to politics via the medium of historiography: cf. my discussion, p. 218 below.

[16] Note the examples at Herkommer 1968: 66–7.

[17] Sallust later used similar phrasing to describe Cato as he had himself here in the *Catiline*: *Romani generis disertissimus paucis absolvit* (*Histories* 1. 4); see Herkommer 1968: 155. Nepos describes Cato as recounting wars *capitulatim* (*Cato* 3. 4): the precise significance of this is controversial, but it too probably indicates the brevity with which Cato summarized his narrative: see Astin 1978: 218; Chassignet 1986: xv–xvi. Chassignet 1986: xvi further suggests that *capitulatim* points to Cato's selectivity in deciding what to write; if so, it may be that *carptim* in Sallust likewise suggests a Catonian mode of writing.

[18] Cf. *B.J.* 4. 4, and see Marincola 1997: 139.   [19] Leeman 1954: 329.

historiography and oratory are here effectively equated, for all that Sallust's work proves to be in the former genre alone. But the paradox is then expanded: for the term that he uses for 'doer' as opposed to 'writer'—*auctor rerum*—would itself naturally be taken to signify 'historian'.[20] In setting up a contrast between himself and Cato, Sallust collapses together the different aspects of the Censor's career: language normally applied to historians is used to describe political and military activity, while the language that would normally apply to oratory is linked to the writing of history—in effect, the three are equated. As we shall see, this is significant: the role of Cato for Sallust's work will not be confined to his history or indeed his writings alone.

The moral tone adopted in the opening chapters takes on a particular focus in the light of these Catonian allusions. While there was (as far as we can tell) no reason on an initial reading to link this tone to Cato's ideas, once it has been established that Sallust is not merely writing history, but is setting himself up to write it following Cato in particular, the coincidence of various of the topics of that initial moralizing with those famously adopted by Cato himself throughout his career appears to align Sallust with Cato not only in manner, but in topic: an interpretation of history is at hand along Catonian moral lines. This is especially so given the simple fact that such an apparently abstract moral discussion proves to be the preface to a history: it reminds the reader of the single historian who was famous above all for the moral approach that he took to both his life and his works.

However, there is a further aspect to Sallust's allusions to Cato in this section. At 4. 1 he describes his choice of a writing career in negative terms:

non fuit consilium socordia atque desidia bonum otium conterere, neque vero agrum colundo aut venando, servilibus officiis intentum aetatem agere.

It was not my plan to waste good leisure in idleness and sloth, nor even to spend my life concentrating on agriculture or hunting, the duties of slaves.[21]

---

[20] Leeman 1954: 329. Some MSS do in fact read *actorem rerum*, avoiding the ambiguity, and this reading is accepted by a minority of scholars (most notably Vretska 1976: 88–9). However, most editors have accepted *auctorem*, which has good MS authority and is supported by the quotations in Gell. *NA* 4. 15. 2 (in two of the three major MSS) and Charisius, *Gramm*. 1. 215. 28 (Keil): the corruption of *auctorem* to *actorem* in this context seems more likely than the contrary.

[21] This is the usual interpretation of the sentence. Delz 1985 argues that it should be translated 'nor even by agriculture or hunting to spend my life concentrating on the duties of slaves'. On this interpretation, Sallust is not directly referring to a landowner's engagement in agriculture as 'slave's work', but is simply saying that one who does engage in it spends an excessive amount of time *supervising* slaves. However, even on Delz's

The general sentiment of the importance of occupying one's *otium* in a proper fashion is a Roman commonplace, but in the context of historiography it recalls once again Cato's comments at the opening of the *Origines*.[22] However, the specific application of the sentiment to agriculture looks distinctly odd in the light of this, since agriculture was one of the chief activities with which Cato was associated, and which he saw as an especially proper activity for an upper-class Roman.[23] Moreover, this image of agriculture as especially bound up with traditional virtue was one that had survived into the Roman ideology of Sallust's own day: Livy 3. 26. 7–10 is only the most famous instance. For Sallust to refer to it in such a fashion appears to run against the whole tenor of the Catonian allusions in this section.[24] While aligning himself with Cato, he appears to be denying that he can, like Cato, unite in himself the qualities of the man of action and the man of letters; but he also suggests that one of the spheres in which Cato distinguished himself was not in fact a proper component of virtue at all. In other words, at the same time as presenting a Catonian conception of virtue, he appears to be questioning whether Cato himself met those standards. Something here appears not quite to fit.

interpretation Sallust's rejection of the Catonian lifestyle, while couched in less directly dismissive language, is still sufficiently remarkable to require comment.

[22] Cato *Orig.* fr. 2 (from Cic. *Planc.* 66): *etenim M. Catonis illud, quod in principio scripsit originum suarum, semper magnificum et praeclarum putavi, clarorum hominum atque magnorum non minus otii quam negotii rationem exstare oportere* ('for I always thought that point of Marcus Cato that he wrote at the opening of his *Origines* is a splendid and distinguished one: that famous and great men ought to have available an account of their leisure [*otium*] no less than of their business [*negotium*]').

[23] This is not merely a modern association owing to the chance that Cato's *De Agricultura* is the only one of his works that survives complete: it is also referred to in the fragments of his other writings (esp. *Ad Marcum filium* fr. 6: *vir bonus...colendi peritus*; *Orationes* fr. 128: *ego iam a principio in parsimonia atque in duritia atque industria omnem adulescentiam meam abstinui agro colendo, saxis Sabinis, silicibus repastinandis atque conserendis*), and, most importantly, is singled out as one of his major qualities by the ancient testimonies of his life—e.g. Nep. *Cato* 3. 1, Livy 39. 40. 4, Quint. *Inst.* 12. 11. 23, Plut. *Cat. Mai.* 25. 1; cf. Cic. *Sen.* 51–60.

[24] Various explanations have been canvassed: for example, Egermann 1932: 78 sees it as an example of Sallust drawing on Plato (but that in itself seems to be something that requires explanation in the light of the apparent contradiction with the ethos established elsewhere in the section). Syme 1964: 45–6 suggested that it was only modern agriculture to which Sallust objected, and hypothesized that there might be a response to the praise of agriculture put by Cicero into the mouth of Cato in *De Senectute* 51–60. (But how could a reader tell from the words *agrum colundo* that it was this sort of agriculture, and not the agriculture praised by the real Cato, that was the object of Sallust's attack?) Vretska 1976: 108–9 has several suggestions: one (from Earl 1965: 234) is that it was only farming as an *exclusive* occupation that was being objected to (but that hardly fits the blanket comment *servilibus officiis*); another is that it is *manual* labour that is being referred to in this way (but here too *agrum colundo* hardly has such a narrow connotation).

II. THE ARCHAEOLOGY

Separated from the preface only by the short character sketch of Catiline comes the Archaeology—the account of the earlier history of Rome (6–13). As the name suggests, it is to the Thucydidean model that scholars have often referred this passage; yet its opening (6. 1) recalled Cato above all:

> Cato in Originibus hoc dicit, cuius auctoritatem Sallustius sequitur in bello Catilinae: primo Italiam tenuisse quosdam, qui appellabantur Aborigines. hos postea adventu Aeneae Phrygibus iunctos Latinos uno nomine nuncupatos. (Servius, *ad Aen.* 1. 6 = Cato, *Origines* fr. 5)
>
> Cato says this in his *Origines*, and Sallust in the *Catiline* follows his authority: the first inhabitants of Italy were called Aborigines; afterwards, the arrival of Aeneas united them with the Phrygians, and they took on the single name of Latins.

Servius here is witness to the fact that Roman readers saw Cato underlying the opening sentence of Sallust's Archaeology. When taken in conjunction with the Catonian allusions that appeared when Sallust established his theme in the preceding chapters, it seems clear that Sallust is creating a set of expectations about his treatment of the past: his summary of Roman history will be presented along Catonian lines.

And indeed that is what emerges as the Archaeology proceeds. The account of the growth of the Roman state sets out the early Romans' virtues in language which draws on and expands the moral tone adopted in the preface. The stress on *virtus* (6. 5, 7. 2, 7. 5, 8. 4, 9. 2), on the union of mind and body (8. 5) under the control of the former (6. 6, 7. 1), on justice (9. 3, 10. 1) and *labor* (7. 4, 7. 5) all indicate that the earlier abstractions are being given a concrete expression in the history of Rome; linked to these is a further set of virtues for which antique Rome is praised, including generosity and willingness to pardon (6. 5, 7. 6, 9. 5); there is a great stress on military virtues more generally (7. 4–7, 9. 2–4), as well as private frugality (9. 2). The importance of military virtue was a central theme of Cato's writings (which included a handbook *de re militari*),[25] as was his support of justice and opposition to political corruption and abuse of power;[26] and his extensive recommendations of frugality and attacks on luxury are too well known to require much comment.[27] This last theme

---

[25] See Astin 1978: 96–7, 184–5; also Cato, *Orationes* frs. 148, 186, and Plut. *Cat. Mai.* 20. 4, 20. 7–8. On the high military reputation of Cato among later Roman writers, see Astin 1978: 49.

[26] For example, Cato, *Orationes* frs. 94, 136, 154, 173, 177, 224. See Astin 1978: 63–4.

[27] It is central to Plutarch's *Life*; see also Cato, *Orationes* frs. 110, 128, 141, 174, 185, 213; cf. Polyb. 31. 25. 5; Nep. *Cato* 2. 3; Livy 39. 2–4. See Astin 1978: 91–104.

comes to the fore in the second part of Sallust's Archaeology, where, following the fall of Carthage, he describes the lapse into vice of late republican Rome. These vices can in some respects be seen as the obverse of the virtues of early Rome: in all the respects in which Rome had excelled, Sallust now shows its degeneracy, reinforcing the polarized picture of present virtue and past vice.[28] But it is on luxury that he focuses, and luxury which he suggests lies at the heart of the vices of his contemporaries (11. 3–13. 2)—a clear Catonian theme. It is true (cf. p. 216 above) that many of these topics are not shared exclusively by Cato and Sallust but are regular commonplaces; however, the linking of them all together here in a narrative which has a recognizably Catonian opening and which was written in a recognizably Catonian style strongly suggests that the whole picture of Roman history is being presented by Sallust in distinctly and recognizably Catonian terms.[29]

This impression is further reinforced by one formal feature of the Archaeology. Cato was famous for the fact that in the later books of the *Origines*, he narrated wars without naming the generals in them:[30] for him, it appears, it was the collective achievement of the Roman people that mattered, rather than the glorification of individuals. It is therefore noteworthy that Sallust in the whole Archaeology does not name a single individual between Aeneas at the beginning of his account (6. 1) and Sulla at its chronological end (11. 4).[31] In between, individual Romans are referred to, but only by sidelong allusion rather than direct naming. The allusions are clearly recognizable, but at the same time self-consciously oblique: the reader will therefore see the omission of the names as pointed, and so associate them with Cato's similarly self-conscious omissions.[32]

Thus, of early Rome, following its foundation, Sallust says *res eorum civibus moribus agris aucta* ('their state grew in citizens, customs, and territory', 6. 3), a clear allusion to its first three kings: Romulus (who attracted immigrants and united Rome with the Sabines), Numa (who established Rome's legal and religious system), and Tullus Hostilius (who conquered Rome's 'parent' city of Alba Longa). The sense that Cato's manner is being followed here is reinforced by the fact that Sallust is actually imitating Cato's phrasing directly at this point—see *Origines* fr. 20: *eodem convenae conplures ex agro accessitavere.*

---

[28] Cf. Leeman 1967: 111–13.
[29] Cf. Hinds 1998: 34–47 for a discussion of how even standard topoi may in particular contexts shade into and incorporate very specific allusions to earlier texts that employed them.
[30] Nep. *Cato* 3. 4; Plin. *HN* 8. 11.   [31] Cf. La Penna 1968: 118.
[32] See Cato *Orig.* fr. 83 for an extended example of Cato's practice in this area, along with the discussion by Astin 1978: 232–3.

eo res eorum auxit. The power of the kings is said to have turned *in superbiam dominationemque* ('to pride and domination', 6. 7), leading to the foundation of the Republic—an allusion to the last king of Rome, Tarquinius Superbus. At 9. 4 we are told *in bello saepius vindicatum est in eos qui contra imperium in hostem pugnaverant quique tardius revocati proelio excesserant* ('in war people were more often punished for fighting the enemy against orders and when recalled departing from battle too slowly'). The person who was famously punished in Roman history for fighting contrary to orders was the son of Manlius Torquatus, executed by his father in 340 BCE, and this is manifestly an allusion to him.[33] Here too the passage is introduced by a phrase that appears to imitate Cato directly (*seque remque publicam curabant*, 9. 3;[34] cf. Cato, *Orationes* fr. 21, *arbitror rem publicam curare industrie summum periculum esse*).[35] This suggests once again that Sallust is writing history in a self-consciously Catonian manner.

This last allusion, however, points to something disquieting in Sallust's Catonian narrative. It is true that Sallust here is treating the *imperia Manliana* as a limiting case: the fact that punishments were recorded for such things rather than for cowardice proves that early Romans conducted war with *audacia* (9. 3). Nevertheless, it is a surprising example for him to introduce, given that its traditional connotations at Rome were far from positive: it was regularly used as an exemplum of strictness excessive to the point of cruelty.[36] An allusion to it thus seems

---

[33] Commentators (e.g. McGushin 1977: 85) sometimes refer it also to the son of the dictator Postumius, who (allegedly) was similarly executed by his father: see Diod. Sic. 12. 64. 3; Livy 4. 29. 5; Val. Max. 2. 7. 6; Gell. *NA* 1. 13. 10, 17. 21. 17. However, the association with Manlius was far more common (e.g. Cic. *Sull.* 32, *Fin.* 1. 23, 1. 35; Val. Max. 2. 7. 6, 6. 9. 1, 9. 3. 4; Verg. *Aen.* 6. 824–5; Sen. *Controv.* 9. 2. 19, 10. 3. 8; Gell. *NA* 9. 13. 20) and indeed proverbial, even to the point that Livy uses the fame of that version to deny the historicity of the Postumius story (4. 29. 6). That Sallust's readers would have linked the reference here to Manlius in particular is suggested by the pointed phrase *contra imperium* (on the use of the word *imperium* as a covert reference to Manlius, see Nisbet 1959: 73–4), and above all by Sallust's own later reference to Manlius in almost identical language at 52. 30 (see further pp. 233–4 below).

[34] It is possible that the archaism of the double -*que* is also relevant here, but note Lebek 1970: 307 n. 29.

[35] It is even possible that the general sentiment was inspired by Cato *Orig.* fr. 82 (*imperator noster, si quis extra ordinem depugnatum ivit, ei multam facit*, 'our general, if anyone goes outside the line to fight, fines him'), as suggested by Steidle 1958: 7 n. 6. However, the specific situation envisaged in that fragment appears to be different, and the loss of its context makes any connection no more than a tentative possibility.

[36] See Skutsch 1985: 317; Berry 1996: 201–2. Feldherr 1998: 105–11, in a detailed study of Livy's treatment of the Manlius episode (8. 7), argues that the narrative brings out a positive side as well as a negative one to Manlius' actions. Even Feldherr's analysis, however, emphasizes the inherent ambivalence of the episode, and moreover assumes that a Roman

rather strange in the context of the Archaeology, since it would tend to undermine the rigorous dichotomy between the virtuous past and the vicious present, reminding the reader of actions in the past that were at best morally complex and at worst entirely unacceptable.

Nor is this the only point at which the Catonian manner of writing works against the apparent moral clarity of the narrative. One might feel that the fact of imitating Cato was itself problematic. As was said above (pp. 214-15), Cato addressed moral strictures against his contemporaries, contrasting them with the virtuous men of the past. Yet Cato also lived precisely at the time when, according to Sallust's scheme, Rome was in a state of pristine virtue. Nor is this something that could easily be overlooked, for Cato famously died on the point of Carthage's destruction—the moment that, for Sallust, marks the transition from virtue to vice (see pp. 224-5 below). The very imitation of Cato might appear to endorse the contradictory notion that the earlier Republic was not uncomplicatedly virtuous, but contained the same moral degeneracy that Sallust identifies with the later period.

This paradox is especially apparent when one looks at Sallust's account of the corruption of the troops of Sulla at 11. 4-8. The description here appears to draw on the opening of Cato's speech in defence of the Rhodians (*Orationes*, fr. 163; see further pp. 234-5 below): in particular, note the final sentence (11. 7-8): *quippe secundae res sapientium animos fatigant: ne illi corruptis moribus victoriae temperarent* ('for in fact success troubles the minds of the wise: still less would those men, with their morals corrupted, set bounds to victory'). Cato began his speech with the words: *scio solere plerisque hominibus rebus secundis atque prolixis atque prosperis animum excellere atque superbiam atque ferociam augescere atque crescere* ('I know that in favourable, prosperous, and successful times most men's minds swell and their arrogance and insolence grows and increases'); and shortly afterwards added: *secundae res laetitia transvorsum trudere solent a recte consulendo atque intellegendo* ('prosperity is accustomed through joy to push people aside from proper deliberation and understanding'). In other words, Cato was warning his contemporaries against precisely the flaws that Sallust associates with Rome in decline.

On the face of things, of course, Sallust's position is not self-contradictory. For one thing, he does accept that even 'the wise' (*sapientium*) are capable of being troubled by success, thus allowing the possibility that even the virtuous Romans of the past might at least have been at risk;

---

audience would in the first instance identify with the victim, and would be repelled by the consul's actions even as they learned a lesson from them.

moreover, Cato *did* succeed in persuading his audience not to be carried away by their victory (see p. 238 below). However, the detail of Cato's words undermines that conclusion, since he treats the Rhodian case as atypical, and presents the dangers of success as something that people of his day *did* usually succumb to. So too Sallust's statement in 11. 5 that Sulla *exercitum... contra morem maiorum <u>luxuriose nimis</u>que liberaliter habuerat* ('had treated his army, contrary to ancestral custom, luxuriously and too generously') appears problematic in the context of the Rhodian speech, where acting *luxuriose*, far from being something that the Romans of Cato's day eschewed as a matter of course (as implied by *contra morem maiorum*), is something that Cato needed specifically to warn them against (*Orationes*, fr. 163: *neve haec laetitia <u>nimis luxuriose</u> eveniat*, 'and lest this joy turn out too luxuriously'). The parallel vocabulary combines with the general sentiments to recall Cato in a highly problematic way: the imitation itself undercuts the idea that in the middle Republic the vices of Sulla's day were absent.

This conclusion may perhaps be reinforced by the opening of the account of Sulla, where, speaking of the depredations of the proscriptions, Sallust says *rapere omnes, trahere* (everyone seized, carried off). The collocation *rapere trahere* is surprisingly uncommon in extant Republican Latin, but it is found elsewhere in Sallust in a similar context (*B.J.* 41. 5),[37] and earlier appeared in Plautus (*Trin.* 288; cf. *Persa* 410) as part of an attack on contemporary public morality. All these passages share the feature that the words are not merely placed in conjunction, but in asyndeton, and La Penna argues that this is not coincidence: that *rapere trahere* was a political slogan of the 180s of those combating official corruption, and specifically a slogan associated with Cato.[38] If this is correct (and La Penna's arguments, though based on indirect evidence, are strong), then Sallust begins his account of Sulla's dictatorship—the climactic moment of Roman decline according to his model—with a phrase that directly recalls Cato's moral campaigns against the corrupt of his own day. Here, once again, the idea that the destruction of Carthage was the root cause of Roman moral collapse is undermined: Cato's Rome before the fall of Carthage, contrary to the overt tenor of Sallust's narrative, has uncomfortable similarities to Sulla's Rome after it.

But the identification of the destruction of Carthage with the moral decline of Rome is more problematic still. Sallust, in selecting this

---

[37] Also Sall. [*Ad Caes. sen.*] 2. 3. 4: even though the author is highly unlikely to be Sallust, he regularly employs Sallustian phraseology. See La Penna 1987: 103–4.
[38] La Penna 1987.

particular event as a turning point in Rome's history, goes against the majority opinion up to his day, which had regarded the first onset of decline as rather earlier.[39] The precise connection that he is making between the destruction of Carthage and the moral decline of Rome is admittedly not entirely clear. In his later works he directly states that the mechanism is 'fear of the enemy' (*metus hostilis*): that it is necessary for a state to have an enemy in order to keep it virtuous, since total security leads to moral corruption.[40] According to this theory, Carthage represented the last threat to Rome: once it had gone, there was no further constraint to keep the Romans on a moral path. However, this is not stated in so many words in the *Catiline*; what is said here is slightly different (10. 1–2):

> sed ubi labore et iustitia res publica crevit, reges magni bello domiti, nationes ferae et populi ingentes vi subacti, Carthago aemula imperi Romani ab stirpe interiit, cuncta maria terraeque patebant, saevire fortuna ac miscere omnia coepit. qui labores pericula, dubias atque asperas res facile toleraverant, iis otium divitiae, optanda alias, oneri miseriaeque fuere.

> But when the state had grown through labour and justice, great kings were mastered in war, fierce nations and mighty peoples overcome by force, Carthage, the rival of Roman power, utterly perished, all seas and lands lay open, then fortune began to rage and confound everything. To those who had easily endured labours, dangers, and doubtful and difficult circumstances—to them leisure and wealth, things desirable at other times, were a source of burden and wretchedness.

Some commentators take the reference to 'fortune' here to be a demonstration that Sallust in the *Catiline* saw the central mechanism in the fall of Rome not in the sort of rational psychological terms implicit in *metus hostilis*, but rather as the workings of the irrational power of fortune bringing it down.[41] However, the entire argument of the passage, taken in its context, implies a close causal connection between Rome's attainment

---

[39] Earl 1961: 42–6; McGushin 1977: 87–8.

[40] *B.J.* 41. 2–3, *Hist.* 1. 11–12; the phrase *metus hostilis* appears in *B.J.* 41. 2, and *metus Punicus* in *Hist.* 1. 12.

[41] So, e.g., La Penna 1968: 39, 232–3; Bonamente 1975: 144–9. See, however, Latta 1988, who has a similar, but more nuanced position: he denies the relevance of *metus hostilis* (cf. also n. 43 below), but argues that *fortuna* does not represent an *external* irrational power, but the psychological irrationality which causes the Romans' moral collapse at the moment of their imperial success. Latta's position is thus not far from Heldmann's (notes 42 and 43 below), in that he accepts that Sallust is presenting a close (albeit not inevitable) connection between unchallenged power and moral decline (esp. pp. 274–5), but his analysis of the role of *fortuna*, and hence of the general causal sequence, is somewhat different.

of unchallenged world power and the decline in Roman morals.[42] It is true that this connection is not attributed directly to *metus hostilis*, but *metus hostilis* was a standard explanatory mode in antiquity, and thus some connection along the general lines of the moral dangers of unchallenged success after the fall of Carthage would be assumed, even if the detailed mechanism is not precisely spelled out;[43] and the singling out and naming of Carthage suggests strongly the central importance of its destruction in this historical analysis.

But in the light of this it is somewhat disturbing to recall the historical tradition as to *why* Carthage was destroyed. It was above all, according to later writers, the responsibility of none other than Cato himself, who famously ended every speech, on whatever subject he was being consulted, with the opinion that *delenda est Karthago* ('Carthage must be destroyed'). He was, however, opposed by Scipio Nasica, who likewise ended his speeches by advising that *servanda est Karthago* ('Carthage must be preserved'). And the reason that Nasica gave for this opinion, according to the tradition, was in fact *metus hostilis*—that Rome needed Carthage to survive as an enemy in order to preserve its own virtue.[44] By selecting the fall of Carthage as the turning point for Rome, Sallust alludes to this famous debate.[45] But his doing so is stunningly

---

[42] See especially the careful argument of Heldmann 1993: 93–117, who relates the notion of *fortuna* in this passage to 2. 5, *fortuna simul cum moribus immutatur* (108–9), arguing that it represents only the turn of events resulting from a change in Rome's morals, not an independent irrational force.

[43] Earl 1961: 47–8 and Vretska 1976: 203–6 set out the theme's earlier history: both refer this passage uncomplicatedly to *metus hostilis*. Heldmann 1993: 110–12 has certain reservations about this, arguing that Sallust deliberately avoids stating the concept so as not to attribute the earlier rise of Rome to external factors rather than to the Romans' intrinsic virtue, as the earlier part of the Archaeology had indicated (cf. Latta 1988: 277, though his general analysis is different—see note 41 above). According to Heldmann, the reason that *fortuna* is introduced is in order to cover the lack of a precise description of how the causal connection between imperial success and moral disaster is operating. However, I cannot go along with Heldmann in his further suggestion (pp. 105–6) that Sallust's phrasing leaves it ambiguous whether the destruction of Carthage or some earlier date formed the real turning point. The phrase *aemula imperi Romani* directly before *cuncta maria terraeque patebant* shows that it is Carthage that Sallust is identifying as the single barrier to Rome's unchallenged success, while the emphatic *ab stirpe interiit* points to its final destruction as the single key moment in the creation of that success.

[44] The earliest attestation of the story is in Diod. Sic. 34. 33. 3–6; the original source is usually thought to have been Posidonius (e.g. Hackl 1980), but it may go back to Rutilius Rufus (e.g. Gelzer 1931: 270–2). Its historicity is defended by Gelzer and attacked by Hoffmann 1960; but, in either case, the story must have been firmly established in the historical tradition by Sallust's day.

[45] According to Skard 1956: 81, the phrase *nationes ferae et populi ingentes* (10. 1), with which this passage is introduced, is an imitation of Cato, *Orationes* fr. 164. 4: *multos populos*

paradoxical. His account demonstrates that Nasica was right in his predictions of the appalling effect on Rome of destroying Carthage. And Cato, the very man whom he has consistently been using as his model for his account of the virtues of early Rome, was disastrously wrong—to the point of being the prime, though unwitting mover in destroying the Roman morality that in his writings and his life he had consistently advocated. Sallust's employment of Catonian topics and a Catonian style of writing in the Archaeology thus cannot be taken as a simple endorsement of Cato's approach to Roman history and Roman morals, for at the vital moment Cato's attitudes and policies are shown by Sallust as destructive of all that he—and Sallust—had apparently stood for.

III. CAESAR AND CATO

With these considerations in mind, let us now turn to our third key passage: the debate between Caesar and the younger Cato, along with the famous syncrisis that follows it. It is with the syncrisis that I shall begin (53. 6–54. 6):

> sed postquam luxu atque desidia civitas corrupta est, rursus res publica magnitudine sui imperatorum atque magistratuum vitia sustentabat ac, sicuti †effeta parentum†, multis tempestatibus haud sane quisquam Romae virtute magnus fuit. sed memoria mea ingenti virtute, divorsis moribus fuere viri duo, M. Cato et C. Caesar... iis genus aetas eloquentia prope aequalia fuere magnitudo animi par, item gloria, sed alia alii. Caesar beneficiis ac munificentia magnus habebatur, integritate vitae Cato. ille mansuetudine et misericordia clarus factus, huic severitas dignitatem addiderat. Caesar dando sublevando ignoscundo, Cato nihil largiundo gloriam adeptus est. in altero miseris perfugium erat, in altero malis pernicies. illius facilitas, huius constantia laudabatur. postremo Caesar in animum induxerat laborare vigilare; negotiis amicorum intentus sua neglegere, nihil denegare quod dono dignum esset; sibi magnum imperium, exercitum, bellum novom exoptabat ubi virtus enitescere posset. Catoni studium modestiae, decoris, sed maxume severitatis erat; non divitiis cum divite neque factione cum factioso, sed cum strenuo virtute, cum modesto pudore, cum innocente abstinentia certabat; esse quam videri bonus malebat.

> But after the state had been corrupted by luxury and sloth, the country on the other hand thanks to its greatness supported the vices of generals and

---

et multas nationes. If so, it would reinforce the idea that the reader is to see the passage with Cato in mind; but see *contra* Vretska 1976: 200.

officials and, as if their ancestral qualities had been exhausted [?], in many generations there was barely anyone in Rome outstanding in virtue. But in my recollection there were two men of great virtue, but different characters: Marcus Cato and Gaius Caesar.... They were almost equal in family, age, and eloquence; their grandeur of spirit was the same, as was their glory, but they differed in other respects. Caesar's greatness was seen in his kindnesses and generosity, Cato's in his uprightness of life. Caesar became famous through his gentleness and pity; Cato had severity to give him dignity. Caesar obtained glory by giving, relieving, pardoning, Cato by his lack of bribery. In the one was a refuge for the unfortunate, in the other a danger for the evil. Caesar was praised for flexibility, Cato for constancy. Finally Caesar had inculcated into his mind work and wakefulness, attention to his friends' affairs to the detriment of his own, the refusal of nothing that was worth the giving; he desired for himself a great command, an army, a new war in which his virtue might be manifest. Cato concentrated on moderation, decency, and above all severity. He did not compete in wealth with the wealthy or in partisanship with the partisan, but competed with the active man in courage, with the moderate man in decency, with the blameless man in self-restraint. He preferred to be good than to seem so.

One may observe that Sallust here begins by recalling the Archaeology's model of the collapse of Roman morality, with the loss of virtue from the state. When, against that background, he asserts that within his recollection Caesar and Cato *did* possess great virtue, he invites the reader to link their qualities to those of the Roman past, to the perfect virtue of the earlier Republic that he had described before: the word *virtus* is stressed here, as there (cf. p. 220 above). And this is further reinforced by the fact that many of the different qualities ascribed to Caesar and Cato do indeed recall different aspects of the qualities ascribed to the early Romans. Thus, Caesar's qualities include *beneficiis* (54. 2: cf. 6. 5, 9. 5),[46] *ignoscundo* (54. 3; cf. 9. 5), and *laborare* (54. 4; cf. 7. 5, 10. 1–2); and, of course, it is in war that he seeks to exhibit his *virtus* (54. 4; cf. 7. 4). Cato shows *innocentia* and *pudor* (54. 6; cf. 12. 1) and is described as competing in *virtus* (54. 6; cf. 9. 2), while the final phrase—that he preferred to be good than to seem so—shows him as the reverse of the Romans in decline depicted after the fall of Carthage (54. 6; cf. 10. 5).[47] Both Caesar and Cato thus would appear for Sallust to be the modern exemplars of ancient virtue.

---

[46] This connection is seen by Shimron 1967: 331–2. However, he tries to convert it into a criticism of Caesar by suggesting that Sallust meant this as a virtue only in foreign affairs; but note 6. 5, *domi militiaeque*.

[47] Vretska 1976: 635–6. The phrase is, of course, also a direct imitation of Aesch. *Sept.* 592: on the implications of the imitation see Renehan 1976: 97–9.

Sallust's Catiline *and Cato the Censor* 229

Yet against this one must set other aspects of Sallust's description. The opening phrases encourage us to see both Caesar and Cato as equal possessors of *virtus*, but in different ways (*divorsis moribus*). Nothing in the Archaeology prepares us for such an idea. There *virtus* appears to be a unitary phenomenon: either one possesses it or one does not. There is no suggestion there of the possibility found in the cases of Caesar and Cato: antithetical qualities separated out into different people, yet each equally counting (so it would appear) as *virtus*. If ancient virtue is to be seen in Caesar and Cato, it appears to have been fragmented.[48]

Moreover, it is not only virtue in general that appears to have been fragmented here, but the virtue of Cato the Censor in particular. Cicero addressing the younger Cato in *Pro Murena* 66 had described the Censor as follows:

> quemquamne existimas Catone, proavo tuo, commodiorem, communiorem, moderatiorem fuisse ad omnem rationem humanitatis?...si illius comitatem et facilitatem tuae gravitati severitatique asperseris, non ista quidem erunt meliora, quae nunc sunt optima, sed certe condita iucundius.
>
> Do you consider that anyone was more agreeable, more affable, more moderate than your great-grandfather Cato in every aspect of humaneness?... If you sprinkle his civility and flexibility onto your seriousness and severity, those qualities will not indeed be improved, since they are now excellent, but at least seasoned more pleasantly.

The importance of the interaction of harsher and softer virtues was a standard Roman topos: Cicero here shows that it was associated with the Censor in particular (see also p. 230 below for an indication that Sallust may have had the *Pro Murena* in mind when writing this syncrisis).[49] The younger Cato of the syncrisis is recognizably the same character as Cicero addressed; while the additional virtues ascribed to his great-grandfather are here applied to Caesar alone. There are other allusions also. It is well known that the statement that Cato did not 'compete in wealth with the wealthy' is derived from a saying of the Censor himself about his own behaviour: 'I prefer to strive in virtue with the most virtuous than in wealth with the richest and in avarice with the most avaricious.'[50] The younger Cato is thus described in terms that recall his great-grandfather.

---

[48] Cf. Leeman 1967: 113–14; McGushin 1977: 311. On the internal conflicts and contradictions in Sallust's presentation of *virtus* in the syncrisis, see above all Batstone 1988b. My argument in these paragraphs may be seen as in some respects complementing Batstone's discussion.

[49] On the relevance to the syncrisis of the descriptions of Cato the Censor in *Pro Murena*, see Batstone 1988b: 18–19, 22–3.

[50] Plut. *Cat. Mai.* 10. 4.

But so too is Caesar: in an earlier passage of *Pro Murena* (32) Cicero says of the Censor *quo quidem in bello virtus enituit egregia M. Catonis, proavi tui* ('in that war the noble virtue of your great-grandfather M. Cato was manifest'). Sallust appears to be alluding to that phrase in his description of Caesar here (54. 4). Caesar and the younger Cato are splitting between them the qualities of Cato the Censor.

Moreover, ancient virtue as well as being fragmented appears to have some problematic gaps. In the cross references connecting the qualities of Caesar and Cato with those of the Romans of the Archaeology, there are three striking omissions. The key virtues assigned to Caesar and Cato are *mansuetudo* and *misericordia* for Caesar, and *severitas* for Cato: this is especially significant in the context of the Catilinarian debate, where the point at issue is precisely whether Caesar's lenient approach or Cato's severe one is more appropriate.[51] Yet none of these key virtues appears at all in the Archaeology: nothing there allows us to judge whether Caesar's gentleness and pity or Cato's severity makes the one or the other the true heir to the heroic past. Conversely, the virtue of *aequitas* or *iustitia*, which plays a central role in the Archaeology (9. 3, 10. 1; cf. also p. 220 above),[52] is ascribed to neither man here: we are not allowed to draw the easy conclusion that either Caesar or Cato, in advocating their respective policies towards the conspirators, has justice on his side. If the syncrisis in some sense places the seal on the debate scene, it does so only by leaving the points at issue troublingly open.

What, then, of the debate itself? It is striking that, in one sense, the arguments of Caesar and Cato fail to engage with each other. Caesar concentrates the bulk of his fire on the question of precedent, and largely lets the wider issues of the immediate danger to the state and the viciousness of contemporary Rome go by the board. Cato, on the other hand, deals almost entirely with the moral degeneracy of his contemporaries, and their consequent failure to respond to the threat posed by Catiline; the question of precedent is generally ignored by him. Of this latter speech it has often been observed that its language and themes correspond closely to the moral and political analysis that Sallust had earlier put forward in his own voice, and that accordingly the reader

---

[51] It is true that Caesar at 51. 1–4 (in imitation of Diodotus at Thuc. 3. 48. 1) denies that in arguing for leniency he is swayed by *misericordia*, but the very stress on this quality in the syncrisis suggests that he is being disingenuous, as indeed does the fact that the phrase *mansuetudine et misericordia* in 54. 2 alludes to Cato's use of similar phrases at 52. 11 and 52. 27 to describe the claims of those opposing the conspirators' execution.

[52] On the centrality of *aequitas* and *iustitia* in Sallust's picture of Rome's rise to power, see Heldmann 1993: 55–7, 102–5.

is left with the distinct impression that Sallust is endorsing Cato's opinion on the necessity of executing the conspirators (see further p. 241 below).[53]

Cato's speech is not only Sallustian, however: it also appears to be Catonian. Near the start Sallust writes (52. 4; cf. 52. 35):

> nam cetera maleficia tum persequare, ubi facta sunt; hoc nisi provideris ne adcidat, ubi evenit, frustra iudicia inplores: capta urbe nihil fit relicui victis.
>
> For other crimes you may pursue when they occur; but this one, unless you take care that it does not happen, when it arises, you will beg in vain for justice: once a city has been captured nothing is left for the defeated.

This closely resembles Lycurgus, *Against Leocrates* 126:[54]

> τῶν μὲν γὰρ ἄλλων ἀδικημάτων ὑστέρας δεῖ τετάχθαι τὰς τιμωρίας, προδοσίας δὲ καὶ δήμου καταλύσεως προτέρας.
>
> For in the case of other wrongs vengeance must be arranged afterwards, but in the case of treachery and overthrow of the people it must be beforehand.

However, there is nothing in Lycurgus corresponding to Sallust's final phrase; and it is worth pointing also to a saying of Cato, itself dependent upon Lycurgus, quoted by Veg. *Mil.* 1. 13 (= Cato, *De Re Militari* fr. 3):[55]

> in aliis rebus... siquid erratum est, potest corrigi; proeliorum delicta emendationem non recipiunt, cum poena statim sequatur errorem.
>
> In other matters... if there is any mistake, it can be corrected; but the faults of battles do not allow correction, since the penalty follows them instantly.

The quotation, as Jordan suggests,[56] presumably comes from Cato's *De Re Militari*, which Vegetius cites (probably indirectly) several times elsewhere.[57] It adapts what was originally a political statement to a military context. The context in Sallust is itself, of course, a political one not dissimilar to Lycurgus'; however, the imagery he employs (*persequare, capta urbe, victis*) is military. This suggests a double allusion, a 'two-tier reference' via Cato's work back to Lycurgus', carrying with it some of the connotations of both.[58] The use of such military phrasing is especially important in establishing the conspirators not merely as an internal threat, but as the equivalent of an external enemy such as those

---

[53] See, e.g., Steidle 1958: 24–5; Earl 1961: 97–8; Drummond 1995: 74.
[54] See Vretska 1976: 568 for a close comparison of the Sallustian and the Lycurgan passages.
[55] Skard 1956: 86–7.   [56] Jordan 1860: 81.
[57] On Cato and Vegetius, see Milner 1993: xvii–xviii, 15.
[58] On this allusive technique in Latin literature, see McKeown 1987: 37–45.

about whom the Censor was writing: however, as will shortly be seen (pp. 234-8 below), the implications of such an equivalence are more double-edged than may at first sight appear.

Various other sentiments in the speech have also been suggested to depend on sayings of the Censor;[59] and the phrase used of Cato following his speech, *clarus et magnus habetur* ('he was thought famous and great'), links that speech to his great-grandfather, who used a similar phrase allusively of himself at the opening of the *Origines* (fr. 2, quoted above, p. 219).[60] Moreover, there is a strong overlap between certain themes and phrases of this speech and that put into the mouth of the elder Cato at Livy 34. 2-4—in particular, 52. 7 is very close to Livy 34. 4. 1-2.[61] It is, of course, possible that Livy is here imitating Sallust; but the fact that this speech in Livy appears in some other respects to be employing Catonian phraseology and ideas[62] makes it plausible to suggest that similarities between it and Sallust are the result of both authors depending on Catonian models—or at any rate that Livy saw this speech in Sallust as being significantly Catonian. Cato's attack on contemporary Roman *mores*, like Sallust's in his own voice (see pp. 223-4 above), thus recalls the Censor's similar attacks on his own contemporaries.

But if Cato's speech is generally being written by Sallust to appear 'Catonian', one allusion in it is more problematic. At 52. 8 Cato says, *qui mihi atque animo meo nullius umquam delicti gratiam fecissem, haud facile alterius lubidini male facta condonabam* ('I who would never have given any indulgence to myself and my mind was not going to excuse easily the evils of another's lust'). This recalls a saying of the elder Cato quoted by Plut. *Cat. Mai.* 8. 9 (cf. *Apophthegms* 198E): συγγνώμην ἔφη διδόναι πᾶσι τοῖς ἁμαρτάνουσι πλὴν αὑτοῦ ('he said that he pardoned every sinner except himself'). However, Sallust in alluding to this saying reverses its sentiment. His Cato, very pointedly unlike the Censor, holds others to the same

---

[59] For example, Skard 1956: 87 sees the sentiments of 52. 12 (*sint sane, quoniam ita se mores habent, liberales ex sociorum fortunis, sint misericordes in furibus aerari*) as recalling Cato, *Orationes* fr. 224 (*fures privatorum furtorum in nervo atque in compedibus aetatem agunt, fures publici in auro atque in purpura*), and in an intricate argument (pp. 87-9) suggests that 52. 22 may likewise come from Cato. Both of these, however, are less certain.

[60] So Skard 1956: 81; also Vretska 1976: 609, who points out that the collocation is surprisingly uncommon.

[61] Skard 1956: 90-1.

[62] That Livy wrote Cato's speech in 34. 2-4 in a style to resemble Cato is argued at great length by Paschkowski 1966: 107-25, 248-67; cf. Tränkle 1971: 11-16, who denies Paschowski's claim that the speech is stylistically Catonian, but argues that its arguments and themes are nevertheless derived from Cato's writings. Briscoe 1981: 40-2 is sceptical of the overall argument, but accepts some of the individual references (cf. also his notes on 34. 2. 13-13. 3, 34. 3. 9, 34. 4. 2, 34. 4. 3, 34. 4. 14).

standards as those to which he holds himself. And this is especially important when we recall that 'pardoning' (*ignoscundo*) is a quality that in the syncrisis is ascribed to Caesar, and a respect in which he recalls the virtues of primitive Rome (see p. 228 above). As before, Caesar as well as Cato is shown by Sallust as exhibiting 'Catonian' characteristics; Cato himself, for all his Catonian speech, partially lacks such characteristics.

Cato's speech is problematic in another way. As was said above, his response to Caesar misses Caesar's key argument about precedent (on which, see further pp. 234–41 below). Caesar claimed that executing the conspirators was contrary to ancestral precedent. Although Cato's final *sententia* refers to 'ancestral custom' (52. 36: *more maiorum*), the only point at which he directly challenges this argument of Caesar's is at 52. 30–1:

> apud maiores nostros A. Manlius Torquatus bello Gallico filium suom, quod is contra imperium in hostem pugnaverat, necari iussit, atque ille egregius adulescens inmoderatae fortitudinis morte poenas dedit: vos crudelissumis parricidis quid statuatis cunctamini?
>
> Among our ancestors Aulus Manlius Torquatus in the Gallic war ordered his son to be killed, because he had fought the enemy against orders. That noble young man was executed for excessive courage: are you hesitating what you should decree for the cruellest parricides?

This is the sole exemplum that Cato brings forward to show that executing the conspirators conforms to Roman tradition. Yet it is a very uncomfortable example. It is the very story that Sallust alluded to in the Archaeology, and which, as I suggested above (pp. 223–3), was usually seen by the Romans as an example not to be imitated but avoided: an example of strictness excessive to the point of cruelty.[63] Its introduction in the Archaeology appeared to show something disturbing underlying Sallust's Catonian history. Similarly, the very fact that it recurs here, in identical language (note 9. 4: *eos qui contra imperium in*

---

[63] It is true that Cic. *Sull.* 32, like Cato here, uses Torquatus as an example to justify the execution of the conspirators. However, the logic in Cicero is rather different. In the *Pro Sulla* the focus is less on the use of Torquatus as a precedent, but rather on the inappropriateness of Torquatus' descendant (the prosecutor in the case) blaming Cicero for an action that was more justified than his ancestor's. Moreover, in Cicero the justification is in both cases prospective: Torquatus killed his son 'to strengthen command over others' (*ut in ceteris firmaret imperium*), and similarly the state killed its enemies 'in order not itself to be killed by them' (*ne ab eis ipsa necaretur*). In Sallust, on the other hand, the focus at this point in the speech is on the death penalty as a *punishment* (*quod is contra imperium in hostem pugnaverat, inmoderatae fortitudinis morte poenas dedit*), which thus appears to be trying to address directly—however inadequately—Caesar's claim that such a penalty was unprecedented.

hostem pugnaverant), as the sole example that Cato brings to counter Caesar's arguments about precedent, in effect demonstrates the opposite of what it was meant to prove: far from endorsing the execution of the conspirators as part of Roman tradition, it indicates the degree to which such a policy runs against what was best in that tradition.

The same point further emerges from Caesar's speech, where there are several examples to demonstrate that showing mercy to the conspirators would be correct according to precedent. Three such precedents in particular, however, are worth looking at more closely. He twice (51. 22, 51. 39–40) refers to the *lex Porcia de provocatione*, which provided sanctions to protect citizens from flogging. It is not certain that Cato the Censor was the actual promulgator of this law, but it looks at least plausible from *Orationes*, fr. 117: *si eum percussi, saepe incolumis abii; praeterea pro re publica, pro scapulis atque aerario multum rei publicae profuit* ('If I struck him, I often departed unharmed; besides it was a great profit to the state in defence of the state, the shoulders, and the treasury').[64] Hence the reference to this law here is especially pointed: the policy shortly to be advocated by the younger Cato will be going not only against Roman precedent in general, but the precedent set by his famous ancestor in particular. Once again, it is Caesar as much as the younger Cato who can claim to be the Censor's heir.

A similar conclusion may be drawn from Caesar's citation of Roman treatment of the Rhodians (51. 5):

> Bello Macedonico, quod cum rege Perse gessimus, Rhodiorum civitas magna atque magnifica, quae populi Romani opibus creverat, infida atque advorsa nobis fuit; sed postquam bello confecto de Rhodiis consultum est, maiores nostri, ne quis divitiarum magis quam iniuriae causa bellum inceptum diceret, inpunitos eos dimisere.

> In the Macedonian War, which we waged with King Perses, the great and magnificent state of Rhodes, which had grown with the help of the Roman people, was faithless and against us. But when the war ended and consideration was given to the Rhodians' case, our ancestors sent them away unpunished, so that no one should say that the war was undertaken more for the sake of their wealth than of their wrongdoing.

This alludes to what was probably Cato's most famous speech, famous not least because he actually incorporated it into his historical narrative

---

[64] There were in fact three *leges Porciae* on this subject from the early second century BCE: the precise details are unclear. Not all of the laws were passed by Cato the Censor, and it is possible that none was, but the evidence suggests that he was certainly associated with them in some way. See Astin 1978: 21–3.

in the *Origines*:⁶⁵ his defence of the Rhodians. Here too Caesar shows himself to be acting according to Catonian precedent in particular:⁶⁶ the younger Cato is implicitly doing the contrary. Moreover, Cato's speech, according to Gell. *NA* 6. 3. 52, itself appealed to past precedent in support of its case:⁶⁷ by alluding to it here, Caesar not only models himself upon Cato, but indirectly bolsters his argument that the whole weight of Roman tradition was on the side of mercy—Caesar is following Cato, who in turn was acting in accordance with ancestral values.

But it is worth considering the detail of Cato's speech further (it is the speech of his for which the longest fragments and testimonia survive). He opened with a striking generalization (*Orationes*, fr. 163, cited as the opening of the speech by Gell. *NA* 6. 3. 14):

> scio solere plerisque hominibus rebus secundis atque prolixis atque prosperis animum excellere atque superbiam atque ferociam augescere atque crescere. quo mihi nunc magnae curae est, quod haec res tam secunde processit, ne quid in consulendo advorsi eveniat, quod nostras secundas res confutet, neve haec laetitia nimis luxuriose eveniat. advorsae res edomant et docent, quid opus siet facto, secundae res laetitia transvorsum trudere solent a recte consulendo atque intellegendo. quo maiore opere dico suadeoque, uti haec res aliquot dies proferatur, dum ex tanto gaudio in potestatem nostram redeamus.

> I know that in favourable, prosperous, and successful times most men's minds swell and their arrogance and insolence grows and increases. Hence I am now greatly concerned, since this war has been so successful, lest something adverse turn out in deliberation which might undermine our success, and lest this joy turn out too luxuriously. Adversity overcomes and teaches what needs doing; prosperity is accustomed through joy to push people aside from proper deliberation and understanding. Hence I emphatically say and recommend that this matter should be postponed for a few days, until we return from such great joy to self-mastery.

First of all one should note the resemblance of this to the opening of Caesar's own speech a few lines earlier (51. 1):

> omnis homines, patres conscripti, qui de rebus dubiis consultant, ab odio amicitia, ira atque misericordia vacuos decet.

> All men, senators, who deliberate about doubtful matters, ought to be free from hatred, friendship, anger, and pity.

Caesar's opening words here reproduce both the form and the general sentiment of Cato's famous opening; hence the direct references to the

---

⁶⁵ See Livy 45. 25. 3; also Gell. *NA* 6. 3. 7.   ⁶⁶ Syme 1964: 112–13.
⁶⁷ Gell. *NA* 6. 3. 52: *nunc mansuetudinis maiorum, nunc utilitatis publicae commonefacit.*

Rhodians shortly afterwards emphasize the extent to which Sallust is presenting Caesar as following a Catonian model.[68]

Furthermore, Cato began his speech with a warning of the dangers of success, which leads people into *superbia* and *ferocia*: joy can turn out *luxuriose* (cf. p. 224 above). In its immediate context this is simply advising the Romans to delay for a few days after their victory to allow themselves to make their decision calmly. However, it also has other overtones: of the commonplace of the undesirability of unchallenged power for a state, and of the connection between this and moral collapse. That Cato had this idea in mind is apparent from the fragment that follows (*Orationes*, fr. 164, which Gell. *NA* 6. 3. 15 indicates to be the argument that immediately succeeds the one above), where this point is made directly:[69]

> atque ego quidem arbitror Rodienses noluisse nos ita depugnare, uti depugnatum est, neque regem Persen vinci. sed non Rodienses modo id noluere, sed multos populos atque multas nationes idem noluisse arbitror atque haut scio an partim eorum fuerint qui non nostrae contumeliae causa id noluerint evenire: sed enim id metuere, si nemo esset homo quem vereremur, quidquid luberet faceremus, ne sub solo imperio in servitute nostra essent. libertatis suae causa in ea sententia fuisse arbitror.

> And I indeed consider that the Rhodians did not want us to fight the matter out in the way in which it was fought out, nor did they want King Perses to be defeated. But it was not only the Rhodians who did not want it, but I consider that many peoples and many nations did not want the same thing; and my view is that it was not as an affront to us that some of them did not want it to turn out like this, but they were afraid that if there was no man whom we feared, we would do whatever we pleased, lest they be under our sole rule in slavery to us. I consider that it was for the sake of their liberty that they held this view.

The same point emerges also from a controversial passage of Appian (*Pun.* 65):

> εἰσὶ γὰρ οἱ καὶ τόδε νομίζουσιν, αὐτὸν ἐς ʽΡωμαίων σωφρονισμὸν ἐθελῆσαι γείτονα καὶ ἀντίπαλον αὐτοῖς φόβον ἐς ἀεὶ καταλιπεῖν, ἵνα μή ποτε ἐξυβρίσειαν ἐν μεγέθει τύχης καὶ ἀμεριμνίᾳ. καὶ τόδε οὕτω φρονῆσαι τὸν Σκιπίωνα οὐ πολὺ ὕστερον ἐξεῖπε τοῖς ʽΡωμαίοις Κάτων, ἐπιπλήττων παρωξυμένοις κατὰ ʽΡόδου.

> There are also those who think that Scipio wanted for Roman self-control to leave a neighbour and counterbalance as a fear to them for ever, so that they would never act insolently in the magnitude of fortune and freedom from

---

[68] Lebek 1970: 305. [69] Cf. Bellen 1985: 31.

care. That Scipio had this intention was declared to the Romans not long after by Cato, upbraiding them for having been provoked over Rhodes.

On this reading, Appian records that Cato in the course of this speech referred to the treaty that Scipio Africanus had made with Carthage in 201 BCE, and actually attributed Scipio's motives to a desire for—in effect—*metus hostilis*. However, the text here is uncertain. Hoffmann persuasively argues that we should follow the oldest MS (V) in reading the second sentence, καὶ τόδε οὕτω φρονῆσαι τὸν Σκιπίωνα ὃ οὐ πολὺ ὕστερον ἐξεῖπε τοῖς 'Ρωμαίοις Κάτων, ἐπιπλήττων παρωξυμένοις κατὰ 'Ρόδου ('And [they think that] Scipio was thinking the same thing as Cato not long after declared to the Romans, upbraiding them for having been provoked over Rhodes').[70] On this interpretation, Cato made no reference to Scipio or Carthage: Appian is simply comparing his own (anachronistic) explanation of Scipio's policy with comments that Cato made in a different context—namely at the opening of his speech quoted above.

However, even on Hoffmann's reading, Appian's evidence is significant for our understanding of Sallust. Even if Cato did not discuss Carthage in terms of *metus hostilis*, it is clear from Appian that Cato's opening statements in the speech were read (at least by later generations) as an important and famous generalization about the dangers of prosperity that one might appropriately *cite* in the context of *metus hostilis*. Caesar's allusion to Cato's speech here is thus doubly significant: it is not only that he identifies his own policy with that of his opponent's ancestor, but more specifically that the Censor's arguments on behalf of the Rhodians were famously prefaced by a warning that closely recalls the analysis that Sallust in the Archaeology had established as the key to Roman history. Sparing the Rhodians was Cato's way of resisting the decline into immorality that prosperity brings, and which Sallust has told us finally took hold with the destruction of Carthage: Sallust implicitly aligns Caesar with this policy.

That the reader is to make this connection is reinforced by the fact that immediately after his account of Rhodes, Caesar discusses Carthage directly (51. 6):

> item bellis Punicis omnibus, quom saepe Carthaginienses et in pace et per indutias multa nefaria facinora fecissent, numquam ipsi per occasionem talia fecere: magis quid se dignum foret quam quid in illos iure fieri posset quaerebant.
>
> Likewise in all the Punic Wars, although the Carthaginians often committed many horrendous crimes in peace and during truces, they [the Romans]

---

[70] Hoffman 1960: 318–23; *contra* Bellen 1985: 28–9.

never took the opportunity to do such things themselves: they looked more for what would be worthy of themselves than what could justifiably be done to others.

In the context of the *Catiline* this is extremely disquieting. It recalls Sallust's statement in the Archaeology that *accepta iniuria ignoscere quam persequi malebant* ('having received an injury they preferred to pardon it than pursue it', 9. 5); yet ultimately, as Sallust has already told us, Rome did not leave Carthage unpunished but destroyed it. It might thus seem a strange example for him to have Caesar cite as an exemplum of Roman mercy, since it could appear to be no less an exemplum of the contrary. But in fact it is dreadfully appropriate, because, in Sallust's account, the destruction of Carthage was disastrous for Rome—and that destruction was the work of Cato the Censor.[71] Sallust alludes in rapid succession to the Censor's two most famous interventions in foreign affairs: the Rhodians, where he successfully argued for mercy; and Carthage, where he successfully argued for destruction—and Roman morality fell in its wake. The younger Cato, in arguing for the execution of the conspirators, *will* be acting in the manner of the Censor—but it was through that aspect of the Censor that the morality he espoused was destroyed.

But Caesar's concentration on precedent has further implications. He argues not only that the execution of the conspirators would be contrary to past precedent, but also that it would itself provide a dangerous precedent for the future (51. 26–36):

> illis merito adcidet quicquid evenerit; ceterum vos, patres conscripti, quid in alios statuatis considerate. omnia mala exempla ex rebus bonis orta sunt. sed ubi imperium ad ignaros eius aut minus bonos pervenit, novom illud exemplum ab dignis et idoneis ad indignos et non idoneos transfertur. Lacedaemonii devictis Atheniensibus triginta viros inposuere qui rem publicam eorum tractarent.... nostra memoria victor Sulla quom Damasippum et alios eius modi, qui malo rei publicae creverant, iugulari iussit, quis non factum eius laudabat? homines scelestos et factiosos, qui seditionibus rem publicam exagitaverant, merito necatos aiebant. sed ea res magnae initium cladis fuit. nam uti quisque domum aut villam, postremo vas aut vestimentum aliquoius concupiverat, dabat operam ut is in proscriptorum numero esset. ita illi quibus Damasippi mors laetitiae fuerat paulo post ipsi trahebantur, neque prius finis iugulandi fuit quam Sulla omnis suos divitiis explevit. ego haec non in M. Tullio neque his temporibus vereor, sed in

---

[71] It is worth observing in this context that the phrase *nefaria facinora* that Caesar uses to describe the crimes of Carthage appears to be a Catonian one: see *Orationes*, fr. 59; cf. frs. 62, 177.

magna civitate multa et varia ingenia sunt. potest alio tempore, alio consule, quoi item exercitus in manu sit, falsum aliquid pro vero credi. ubi hoc exemplo per senatus decretum consul gladium eduxerit, quis illi finem statuet aut quis moderabitur?

Whatever happens to the conspirators, they will deserve it. But you, senators, think about the precedent you are setting. All evil precedents have arisen from good measures. But when power passes to those ignorant of the case, or the less good, that new precedent is transferred from those cases which are merited and appropriate to those that are unmerited and inappropriate. The Spartans after the defeat of the Athenians placed over them thirty men to control their state.... In our memory when the victorious Sulla ordered the slaughter of Damasippus and others like him, who had grown as an evil to the state, who did not praise his deed? They said that wicked and divisive men who had harassed the state with their uprisings had rightly been killed. But that was the start of great disaster. For as each person desired someone else's house or estate, and in the end vessel or garment, he took care that the person was placed on the list of the proscribed. Thus, those who had rejoiced in the death of Damasippus were shortly afterwards dragged off themselves, and there was no end to the slaughter before Sulla had glutted all his followers with wealth. My fears are not about Marcus Tullius or about now, but in a great state characters are many and varied. It can be that on another day, under another consul who likewise has control of an army, something false is believed to be true. When, following this precedent, the consul draws his sword by senatorial decree, who will set a limit to him or who will control him?

The phrase *vas aut vestimentum* recalls Cato, *Orationes* fr. 174: *neque mihi aedificatio neque vasum neque vestimentum ullum est manupretiosum neque pretiosus servus neque ancilla. si quid est quod utar, utor; si non est, egeo* ('I have neither any building nor vessel nor garment of value nor expensive slave or maid. If there is anything I may use, I use it; if there is not, I go without it').[72] The Romans of Sulla's day have indeed abandoned Cato's prescription of simplicity and lack of covetousness; when he presents Caesar as warning against it, once again Sallust is aligning his position with the best of Catonian morality.

---

[72] Skard 1956: 80. Vretska 1976: 551 denies the Catonian allusion on the grounds that the phrase *nec vas nec vestimentum* appears also in Ter. *Haut.* 141, suggesting that it is a general archaic formula. However Terence might well himself have been imitating Cato's phrase (as, indeed, is suggested by *ancillas servos* in his next line): the speech in question (the *De sumptu suo*) was probably delivered in 164 (Astin 1978: 107–8), while the *Heautontimorumenos* was first performed in 163. It should also be pointed out that word *aedificatio* immediately preceding in Cato makes the parallel with Sallust that much closer (note 51. 33: *domum aut villam*).

But what is the significance of Caesar's final comment? A common view is that Sallust is here covertly hinting at the behaviour of the triumvirs—and especially Octavian—in 43.[73] This interpretation is, however, challenged by Drummond on several grounds: that Octavian's army was privately raised, that the proscriptions were not the result of a consul drawing his sword under a senatorial decree, and that *falsum aliquid pro vero credi* is hard to parallel in 43; he further argues that the 'senatorial decree' in question is not the *senatus consultum ultimum*, as usually thought, but a decree such as that proposed by Silanus at 50. 4.[74] Drummond's own view (35) is that 'the strong military colour of the passage reflects, at a more general level, the violent atmosphere of 44–3'.

Drummond's objections to the thesis that this is a specific allusion to Octavian are strong; but is he right to deny that there is a specific allusion here at all? The reason that scholars have generally sought a precise allusion is that Sallust's language appears to lead in that direction. The pointed contrast between *his temporibus* and *alio tempore*; the emphatically placed *potest*, the apparent precision of *item*, and the implied foreknowledge in *ubi... eduxerit*, all add up to a strong impression that Sallust, writing of course with hindsight, is directing the reader to some very precise future event. Yet it is also undeniable that there is *no* event between 63 and 42 that fits Caesar's description in every detail. This combination of apparent precision and absence of correspondence to any single event does more than simply reflect a general atmosphere of violence: it has the effect of inviting the reader to relate Caesar's description simultaneously to various particular events that correspond to it in some degree. There is no reason why the proscriptions of the Second Triumvirate should be the only, or even the primary, referent of the passage (the allusion to Sulla's proscriptions is simply one example of good precedents leading to bad actions in general): there are several other events that correspond even more closely. Examples include several with the *senatus consultum ultimum*—for, even if we accept Drummond's argument that the decree at issue here is not the *SCU*, Caesar's words simply refer to a consul acting *per senatus decretum*, and this can clearly cover the *SCU* exactly as it can any other senatorial decree. Thus, in 48 the *SCU* was passed by the Senate and used by Caesar's consular colleague Servilius to kill Caelius and Milo, who had raised street riots in support of a programme of debt relief; in the

---

[73] For example Syme 1964: 121–3; Pöschl 1970: 385; Vretska 1976: 552.

[74] Drummond 1995: 33–6; also 79–81 for the argument that Sallust is not presenting the *senatus consultum ultimum* as relevant to the Caesar-Cato debate.

following year the same decree was passed against the tribune Dolabella, and many of his supporters were massacred by Antony, acting as *magister equitum* under Caesar's dictatorship. Both of these cases involved magistrates in command of an army killing Roman citizens without trial, just as Caesar describes in Sallust; and while the correspondence is not exact (cf. p. 240 above), it is at least as close as any of the other possibilities. In other words, the evil future actions which Caesar fears will follow this precedent will be as much as anything the work of Caesar himself.

Does all of this mean that Sallust is endorsing Caesar's analysis, and implying that Cato was wrong to argue for the conspirators' execution? The close correspondence between Cato's moralistic analysis of Rome in his speech and Sallust's own (see pp. 230-1 above) makes that unlikely. Rather the conclusion is far more paradoxical—and far more pessimistic. Catiline *does* represent a threat to Rome that has to be met in the most extreme manner; hence his treatment as in effect a foreign enemy (see pp. 231-2 above), with the implicit parallels between him and the earlier enemies of Rome that Rome—led by Cato the Censor—had the opportunity to spare or destroy. But, precisely *because* Catiline is a threat to Rome, he is something that can enable the Romans to act morally: he is an enemy, and so a challenge to the security of Roman power of the sort that can galvanize the Romans to virtue. But, as an enemy, he needs to be destroyed—and so Rome will once again be secure from threat, and morality will once again perish. Roman history is being replayed, and a Cato is, in effect, playing the same role. Just as the Censor used his full moral weight to argue for the destruction of Carthage—and so led to the downfall of morality—so the younger Cato is arguing for the destruction of the conspirators—and this will lead, among other things, to the excesses of Caesar, Cato's ultimate foe. As Sallust had indicated in his preface (2. 5-6), virtue leads to its own destruction.[75] Caesar meanwhile is himself the heir to the Censor in a different way: he unsuccessfully deploys Catonian precedents of mercy and forbearance—but that very lack of success will provide him with precisely the precedents that will enable the least Catonian sides of his career to come to the fore.

---

[75] Cf. Vretska 1976: 606-7: 'Catos Antrag zwar einen Brutherd moralischen Verfalls für den Augenblick vernichtete, aber ein böses exemplum für die Zukunft wurde, Caesars Antrag zwar dieses exemplum vermieden, vielleicht—so dürfen wir weiter denken—die späteren Ereignisse verhindert oder ihnen doch ein naheliegendes exemplum genommen hätte, für den Augenblick aber der Verschwörung hätte starken Auftrieb geben können.'

IV. CONCLUSION

Cato the Censor is thus not imitated casually by Sallust, but his life and works provide some of the central paradoxes through which the *Catiline* is to be understood. It is from the allusions to the Censor that we can understand that the apparently simple—not to say simplistic—morality of the preface and the Archaeology merely provides a starting point for the genuine complexity of Sallust's moral analysis. The preface sets up the *Catiline* as a Catonian moral history, but contains indications that in the world in which Sallust works Cato's combination of moral activity and moral writing is no longer possible; moreover, Sallust even hints that Catonian morals are not themselves uncomplicatedly desirable. He follows this up in the Archaeology with an abridged history of Rome that is overtly presented along Catonian lines. However, his selection of the fall of Carthage as the crucial turning point for Rome undermines this, both because Catonian allusions to moral problems demonstrate that, contrary to the overt tenor of the narrative, some of the problematic elements of Rome after the destruction of Carthage were already paralleled prior to its destruction and because of Cato's own central role in that destruction. Even in the apparent perfection of the Republic, virtue was not as pure as Sallust suggested, and ultimately it was that very virtue that led to its own downfall. Likewise, Caesar and the younger Cato reflect in their debate the different aspects of the Censor: Caesar argues for Catonian mercy at the expense of Catonian rigour, Cato for the reverse. In the censor these elements were combined; here they are fragmented and separated into contradictory opposites. But here, as before, the policy of moral rigour is the one that wins out at the end, for a genuine threat to the life of Rome has to meet a firm response. Catiline is that threat, as Carthage was before him; removing that threat removes the moral order that made such a victory possible in the first place, and instead allows Rome to accelerate into further disaster.

ADDENDUM

This paper was originally published in 2000. Since then, there has been a great deal of scholarship on the *Catiline*, but nothing which would lead me to change anything I wrote. My identification of Catonian passages in Sallust, my argument that these are highly significant for interpreting the meaning of the work, and above all my analysis of the central paradox that results from those Catonian allusions—namely the extreme tension between the historical Cato's advocacy of the destruction of Carthage and Sallust's identification of the destruction of Carthage as the watershed that led to the collapse of Roman morality—appear to have been generally accepted in more recent scholarly literature. In this addendum, I shall simply refer to some of the most important pieces that have developed in interesting new directions the themes I discussed.

Batstone 2010b extends my account of the fragmentation of virtue in the work (an account which I partly developed from his earlier work: see Batstone 1988b) with a powerful discussion of the instability of the evaluations of virtues made in and by Caesar and Cato in particular, and the consequent paradoxes and failures of their arguments. Feldherr 2012 moves from my account of the fragmentation of virtue to consider the fragmentation of historical perspectives in the Caesar-Cato debate; on a related note, Grethlein 2013: 268–308 examines the *Catiline* as a teleological narrative, specifically drawing on my account of Caesar's speech to argue that it sets up an alternative view of Roman history. Other explorations of the issues I addressed in the article include Melchior 2010, who discusses how *metus hostilis* is rendered problematic when foreign states like Carthage are deemed equivalent to Roman 'enemies' like Catiline. Feldherr 2010 considers Livy's use of Sallust at the defeat of Carthage in Book 30, which (he argues) sets up a series of resonances with Cato himself and with Sallust's use of him. Bruggisser 2002 examines the single concept of *audacia* in Sallust, noting how its positive evaluation in the context of the Archaeology becomes problematic and contested when it is adduced in the speeches of Catiline, Caesar, and Cato.

9

Jugurthine Disorder

Christina S. Kraus

I. DISCORDIA

Sallust's second monograph, written probably in the late 40s BCE, tells the story of the war between the North African prince Jugurtha and the Roman state under the command of a series of generals, culminating in the great plebeian consul Gaius Marius.[1] Its preface opens with the antithesis between stability and instability embodied in excellence and chance: 'Mistakenly [*falso*] the human race complains that its nature, being feeble [*inbecilla*] and short-lived, is ruled by chance [*forte*] rather than by excellence [*virtute*]' (1. 1). Despite the traditional view that *virtus* and *fortuna* ('luck', 'chance') could cooperate to ensure success,[2] Sallust builds a contrast between the 'road of *virtus*' and *Fortuna*, the latter presiding over the bent progress of one trapped by desires (*captus pravis cupidinibus... perniciosa lubidine*, 1. 4), whose life is unstable in all its aspects (*vires tempus ingenium diffluxere*) and dangerous (*periculosa <ac perniciosa>*, 1. 5). Arrayed against *virtus*, then, is a complex force with the unpredictability of *fors/fortuna*, the lack of linearity implied in *pravitas*, and the boundary— and convention—disrespecting attributes of *cupido/lubido*, a force akin to that which ancient thought regularly identifies as the antithesis of

---

[1] A preliminary sketch of this argument appeared in Kraus and Woodman 1997: 22, 27–30. The National Endowment for the Humanities funded an early stage of this project, for which I am grateful; I thank Tony Woodman, Katherine Clarke, David Levene, Sitta von Reden, an anonymous referee for *JRS*, and (belatedly) Cynthia Damon for helpful comments. Reynolds' *Oxford Classical Text* of Sallust has been used throughout; references without book title are to the *Bellum Jugurthinum* (= *B.J.*).

[2] So Sallust presents Marius, e.g., as favoured alternately by *virtus* and *fortuna* but rarely by both together (Earl 1961: 78). On *fortuna/virtus*, see Ogilvie 1970 on Livy 5. 34. 2; Woodman 1977–1977 on Vell. Pat. 2. 97. 4; Wiseman 1971: 109–11. On *nova virtus*, which often defined itself in opposition to *fortuna*, see Hellegouarc'h 1972: 476–83, esp. 478.

Jugurthine Disorder 245

philosophical, moral, or political stability and truth.[3] It can be characterized, in shorthand, as disorderly conduct or *discordia*.[4] In Sallust's world this force operates subversively, inverting or replacing traditional labels and values, yet disguises its workings under the mask of those values, making it difficult even to know, much less to talk about, what is real and what false.[5] Like the later Tacitean universe, Sallust's is a wor(l)d where language, our principal access to reality, is itself implicated in the process of corruption and misreading that it seeks to clarify.[6]

As in the *B.C.*, the *B.J.*'s lengthy introduction argues passionately for the disciplined use of intellect, a discipline played off against the dark world of political and social corruption.[7] Yet, also as in the earlier work, the *B.J.*'s exaltation of mind over body is baffled by the main narrative, in which Sallust meticulously observes and obsessively catalogues disorderly conduct.[8] *Falso queritur* at the work's opening shows either that humans mistakenly complain about the degree to which they are controlled by outside forces, or perhaps that they deliberately misrepresent it (*falso* has two senses, 'misleadingly' and 'mistakenly', both potentially operative here). But by the end of the preface, and throughout the narrative, that complaint is shown to be more often true than false—even when the control belongs to the historian himself. The monograph's very form enacts this self-subverting tendency. In the *B.C.*, Sallust anatomizes Roman corruption by reflecting it off a single individual; his hero's story, with its 'neat dramatic arc',[9] is bounded by a neat historical narrative with a beginning, middle, and end. The historian's technique in the *B.J.* is significantly different. David Levene has argued that Sallust constructed this latter monograph as a 'fragment' whose military and political

---

[3] See Rudd 1966: 27 and Padel 1992: 68—a reference for which I thank E. E. Pender, as well as for showing me a copy of Pender 1999. For the 'curved' as a metaphor for 'wrong', cf. Hor. *Ep.* 2. 2. 44–5 with Brink 1982: 291; for an illuminating ancient discussion of morality, see Sen. *Ep.* 114.

[4] For a brief discussion, with bibliography, of the political associations of *concordia* and *discordia*, see Paul 1984: 46; for one view of discord in the *B.J.*, see Wiedemann 1993 (= Chapter 11 in this volume).

[5] Thucydides is the ultimate historiographical source for Sallust's representation of political and social corruption as a corruption of language; see Scanlon 1980: Index s.v. Corcyrean stasis, esp. 142–4; Syme 1964: 245–6 with n. 33; on the same theme in the *Bellum Catilinae* (hereafter *B.C.*), see Earl 1961: 91–7.

[6] For 'wor(l)ds', see Henderson 1998: 257–300.

[7] Especially 2. 4: 'since there are so many different intellectual skills [*artes animi*] with which the highest distinction [*summa claritudo*] is gained'.

[8] In *B.C.* there is the possible exception of the syncrisis of Cato and Caesar (on which, see Batstone 1988b); balanced characters in *B.J.* are fewer and farther between. Metellus comes closest, perhaps (45. 1); on Jugurtha's balance, see pp. 253, 262 below.

[9] Scanlon 1987: 63.

narratives are incomprehensible without continual reference to both previous and subsequent Roman history. To his arguments about the work's deferred and frustrating closure one can add the odd trick at the beginning. The preface ends with *nunc ad inceptum redeo* ('now I return to my starting point,' 4. 9), a digression-ending formula (as at 42. 5, 79. 10, Tac. *Ann.* 4. 33. 4). Yet at this point there exists no narrative for Sallust to have digressed from—unless we imagine ourselves to have started in the middle, that is, of a narrative of which only this fragment remains.[10] The author's explicit insistence that we look beyond the work at hand comes immediately thereafter with the announcement of his subject (5. 1–2):

> I am about to write the war [*bellum*] which the Roman people waged with Jugurtha, the king of the Numidians, first because it was great and terrible, with victories on both sides [*magnum et atrox variaque victoria*]; next, because this was the first challenge to the arrogance of the nobility. This struggle thoroughly confused all things divine and human [*divina et humana cuncta permiscuit*] and reached such a state of madness that only war and the devastation of Italy put an end to the civil strife [*ut studiis civilibus bellum atque vastitas Italiae finem faceret*].

In this blurb the Jugurthine war does not end: it is only shifting, faceted, various. We see *bellum* leading to *studia civilia*, which are ended—paradoxically—by (*civile*) *bellum*, by which we can understand not only the Marian/Sullan war but also the more recent conflict between Caesar and Pompey.[11] The limit to which Sallust refers with *finem* will come only after the monograph ends, with the devastation of the future, a projection into the distance mirrored by the important geographical move from Africa (*Numidarum*, 5. 1) to Italy (5. 2).[12] Yet, though

---

[10] On the 'displacement', see, e.g., Koestermann 1971 on 4. 9. Dietsch 1846 *ad loc.* argues that *inceptum* refers to Sallust's plan; this is likely enough, but the conventional use of *ad inceptum redire* suggests that something more is going on here. Wiedemann 1979 shows that Sallust is here imitating the preface to Cato's *De agricultura*; as he says, though, in *B.J.* 'the abrupt, archaic formula...is...quite out of place' (16). For the argument that 4. 2–9 does constitute a digression, see Earl 1979; on the significance of other such remarks in the *B.J.*, see Levene 1992: 58–9 (= Chapter 10, pp. 281–2 in this volume), and for bibliography on the structure of the *B.J.*, see Syme 1964: 141 n. 4; Scanlon 1988: 144–6.

[11] Levene 1992: 56, 69 (= Chapter 10, p. 278 and 301 in this volume); for extended discussion of Sallust's two themes, see Steidle 1958. Ancient readers often saw Marius and Sulla prefiguring Caesar and Pompey: cf., for one, Lucan 2. 67-233, with Fantham 1992: 91, and for the inexorable repetition encoded in civil war, see Jal 1963: 44–5 and Henderson 1998: 165–211 on Lucan's *plus quam civilia bella*. Jugurtha's fratricide will also have had contemporary resonance with the conflict between Caesar and Pompey: Bannon 1997: 142–5.

[12] It is no accident that a narrative set primarily in Africa should exhibit disorderly conduct: 'l'irrédentisme, la tendence à l'autonomie, c'est-à-dire à la dispersion, découlaient

Jugurtha's story is only part of a larger one, Sallust does centre his narrative on the life of his 'hero', starting with his birth (5. 7) and ending with his (implied) death in Marius' triumph (114. 3); he plays Jugurtha off against others (Metellus, Marius, Sulla) just as he sets Catiline against Cicero, Cato, and Caesar. This essay argues that the prince is the embodiment, cause, and effect of disorder at all levels, political, military, and historiographical; and that Sallust uses him as the focus of this 'thematics of disorder', a turmoil which ultimately threatens even the historian's project. Though credited with *virtus* by such reliable sources as Micipsa and Scipio Aemilianus, he is plagued by anger and fear; though a victim of desire, he also successfully exploits it;[13] though able to beat Roman generals in a fixed battle, he prefers to engage them with treachery and evasion. His manipulation of and affinity with money, deceit, motion, and delay enable him for years to defer any final settlement, either diplomatic or military, of the war with Rome.[14] Further, military success in Africa requires the election of the new man Marius to the consulship, a political upheaval with far-reaching, even paradigmatic consequences. The influence of Jugurthine disorder thus extends to, and indeed in Sallust's narrative causes, the historian's political theme; it thereby aggravates the collapse of ordered procedure and social boundaries in Rome itself. As each becomes less typically *nobilis*, the Roman commanders are progressively better able to deal with Jugurtha: so Metellus, who enjoys the first real success against him, has almost none of the standard aristocratic faults (43. 1, 45. 1, 64. 1). Paralleling this

nécessairement de la nature des choses [i.e., from the terrain]' (Benabou 1976: 58). Focusing on the ethnographical digressions and the relation of Numidian geography to character are Wiedemann 1993 (= Chapter 11 in this volume) and Green 1993 (= Chapter 11 in this volume); for literary discussion of the 'textual geography', see Scanlon 1988 and for Carthage in *B.J.*, see Kraus and Woodman 1997: 27–30. Relevant to the *B.J.*'s theme of boundary collapse, esp. in Sallust's digression on shifting desert sands and the Syrtes (78. 3–79. 6), is Edwards 1993: 147: diatribes against luxury often enough attack those who collapse the land/sea boundary, an 'archetypally natural distinction'.

[13] Not discussed in any detail here, but cf. 38. 10, 44. 5, 54. 5, 108. 3, where *lubido* works to Jugurtha's advantage. It clusters in the accounts of the *quaestio Mamilia* and the *mos partium*, where it fosters the atmosphere in which Jugurtha thrives (see n. 55 below); it also works with or is subordinate to Marius (63. 2, 84. 3, 85. 39, 86. 2). For the specific association of *lubido/cupido* with crookedness and passionate motion, cf. 25. 6–8 **conmotus** metu atque lubidine divorsus agitabatur... animus cupidine caecus... rapiebat. vicit tamen... pravom consilium; on Sallust's preoccupation with passion's disrupting force, see Syme 1964: 268–9 and Scanlon 1988: 170–1 n. 5 and n. 8.

[14] Finishing one's *inceptum* is a good general's attribute (e.g. Caes. *BG* 8. 3. 4, 5. 4, 19. 6 and Vell. Pat. 2. 79. 1, with Woodman 1983 *ad loc.* on *labor*, etc.). Sallust punctuates his narrative with reports of *incepta* thwarted or completed (7. 6, 11. 9, 25. 6, 7, 55. 8, 61. 1, 93. 1); the first threat to any project is (to) his own, at 4. 9 (see p. 246 above and Section V below).

movement in the field are the changes in Rome, where increasing political instability progresses from tribunician agitation undercut by bribery (30–4), through direct opposition to the aristocracy in the *quaestio Mamilia* (40), to the election of Marius (73. 7). Yet the disorder does not stop there: the *novus homo* almost immediately faces his own replacement, the patrician Sulla.[15]

Three areas of this thematics of disorder stand out: unregulated or illicit exchange, especially involving bribery; delay and its converse, rapid motion; and substitution. Though I begin by treating them separately, it will become clear that they overlap to a considerable extent, one theme flowing into another as the narrative itself exhibits the flexibility and disorder that it rehearses.

II. MONEY TALKS

As befits one who speaks very little of himself (6. 1), Sallust's Jugurtha uses direct speech only once. On the several occasions in which his words are reported, they are muted, deflected, or alien: wordless responses (only the manner, not the content, is given) at 11. 1 and 72. 1; in indirect speech at 22. 2–4 and 81. 1; in indirect speech and, as Sallust notes, in Latin, as part of a deception, at 101. 6. Once, on the point of speaking, he is silenced by a corrupt tribune, at a moment at which words would irrevocably commit him to engagement in the Roman legal process (34. 1). This repeated refusal and muting of one of the primary markers of presence displays Jugurtha as a figure for absence and deferral.[16] Even his single direct utterance, spoken while leaving Rome with a backward

---

[15] Sulla, who actually captures Jugurtha, represents a throwback to aristocratic command; but in *B.J.* he operates only as Marius' subordinate and substitute. He partakes, therefore, of non-aristocratic slipperiness. Cf. Pelling 1993: 81: 'the decline of the Jugurthine War into trickery elicits, in Sulla, the diplomatic trickster who can outsmart the African equivalents'.

[16] I am persuaded by Sternberg 1991 that indirect speech shares the 'universals of quotation' with direct speech, and that (78) 'there is no way to maintain the bond between direct quotation and literal representation'. Still, given the conventions of ancient narrative, Latin indirect speech is less flexible in form than in languages which do not use the accusative + infinitive construction. Bearing in mind, then, that 'no configuration of indirect discourse can silence the repartee's voice altogether' (Sternberg 1991: 90), I think it fair to maintain, at least formally, a distinction between the mimetic form of direct speech and the diegetic, or narrated, form of indirect (Genette 1980: 172). Given the large blocks of direct speech in *B.J.*, moreover, it is remarkable that in that medium Jugurtha speaks a total of eight words. He is relatively quiet even in indirect speech. The contrast with Catiline is instructive (two prominent direct speeches and a directly quoted letter).

glance echoing Catiline, is laden with obliquity: *sed postquam Roma egressus est, fertur saepe eo tacitus respiciens postremo dixisse: 'urbem venalem et mature perituram si emptorem invenerit.'*[17] Jugurtha barely emerges from reported speech,[18] uttering his bon mot while looking silently backwards. And though Sallust minimizes the self-contradiction of *tacitus respiciens... dixisse* by carefully indicating sequence (*postquam... saepe... postremo*), the present tense *respiciens*, usually of concomitant action,[19] hints at the paradox 'spoke silently while looking'. Finally, Jugurtha speaks only in a future condition—nothing so direct as a declarative sentence—and a condition, at that, involving a (hypothetical) financial transaction.

Accusations of bribery figure prominently both in the political propaganda of the late Republic and in Sallust's narrative of this war, especially its early stages. The historian has gone further even than the propaganda, demonstrably exaggerating both the scope and effect of bribery during those years.[20] In part, this magnifies the greed of the Roman nobles, recalling in many ways the corrupt Roman society pictured in the *B.C.* Yet the bribery motif is not randomly distributed. All of the financial transactions in the early stages of the war are initiated by or worked through Jugurtha, who has a particular affinity with tokens of exchange.[21] Like money, he goes everywhere and facilitates (potentially)

---

[17] 'But after he left Rome, he is reported finally to have said, while often looking back at it, silent: "a city for sale and ripe for perishing—if it finds a buyer!"' (35. 10). The echo of Catiline is from Cic. *Cat.* 2. 2, *retorquet oculos profecto saepe ad hanc urbem*.

[18] Appropriately enough, as this is a famous tag (*fertur*); see Paul 1984: 108. The accusative is generally taken as one of exclamation, the future perfect *invenerit* signaling the direct speech: on the future participle (not short for *perituram esse*), see Koestermann 1971: 151, Kühner 1976: I. 760–1; for *dicere* introducing direct speech, see *OLD*, s.v. 2d. Jugurtha's utterance has been printed as indirect speech, e.g. by Kritz 1828–53 and Capes 1889.

[19] The grammars explain *respiciens* as instrumental/modal, comparing 113. 1, *diu volvens... tandem promisit* ('thinking it over for a long time, he at last promised'). For *tacitus... dixisse*, cf. Hor. *Sat.* 1. 9. 11–13, where the satirist is talking (inaudibly) to himself.

[20] Steidle 1958: 51–4; Paul 1984: 261–3; see further Allen 1938 and von Fritz 1943, esp. 159–65. On the theme of greed in the first section of the *B.J.*, see Koestermann 1971 on 8. 1, 20. 1, and Leeman 1957, esp. 207–8. Braund 1984: 59 emphasizes that the 'exchange of gifts and favours was at the very heart of friendly relationships in antiquity' (cf. also 81).

[21] Just for instance: as the war heats up, Jugurtha begins to act with more free-spending abandon, *inpensius* (47. 3), a word with monetary connotations that Sallust uses only here and at 75. 1 (with *diffidens*); for its financial overtones, cf. Catullus 72. 5–6, 'though I burn more lavishly [*inpensius*], still you are much cheaper [*vilior*] in my eyes'. Despite his association with bribery, however, it does not affect him. He thus has something in common with the hero of the literary attack on luxury, in which a figure who resists corruption takes the reader on a tour of it—though Jugurtha provides precisely the reverse of that moral guidance.

treacherous dealings and changes of position; and, like it also, he can erase the distinctions that keep societies stable. For money not only corrupts; it confuses as well.[22] In its ability to erase meaning, or to replace one meaning with another, it is a fitting tool for someone who is himself polyvalent, shimmering, impossible to pin down.

This polyvalence is seen perhaps most economically at the moment when Metellus enters his new province (46. 5–6):

> The general himself, with his army on the alert and hostile, marched into Numidia, where contrary to an appearance of war [*contra belli faciem*] there were huts full of men, flocks and labourers in the fields. The king's officials came out from towns and hamlets to meet them, prepared to provide grain, to carry supplies, and do everything that they demanded. Metellus was not, for this reason, any less careful; but, just as if the enemy were present, he proceeded with an armed column, scouted all round, and believed these signs of surrender to be a sham [*ostentui*] and that a chance for ambush was being tested.

Landscape and inhabitants alike give the appearance of a peace which may or may not be real (Sallust does not tell us).[23] The narrator explains that Metellus' distrust is motivated by Jugurtha's most dangerous characteristic: *nam in Iugurtha tantus dolus tantaque peritia locorum et militiae erat ut absens an praesens, pacem an bellum gerens perniciosior esset in incerto*[24] *haberetur* ('For Jugurtha had so much craft and so much experience of the country and of warfare that it was considered uncertain whether he was more dangerous absent or present, when waging peace or

---

[22] As at *B.C.* 12. 2, where the syntax piles up evils: 'as a result of wealth, luxury and greed together with pride invaded the young: they stole, squandered, set small value on their own property while coveting others', for honour and modesty, all things human and divine mixed together [*divina atque humana promiscua*], they had no value and no respect'. See further Sekora 1977: 24, 51, 145, 242; Berry 1994: 153; and cf. Edwards 1993: 186: the flow of money 'always threatened to subvert [the] illusion of stability'. See also Barthes 1975: 215 on the 'collapse of economies' when boundaries are removed or subverted, and von Reden 1998: 255: 'the confrontation of reciprocity and commodity exchange...was a metaphorical confrontation of order and disorder, civic community and its corrosion. Menander's... representation of civic symbols as objects which have a price and are transacted arbitrarily... suggests that commodity exchange was regarded as the moral opposite of civic exchange and thus in certain circumstances detrimental to the polis.'

[23] In Livy's adaptation of this passage (6. 25. 6–11) the peace is genuine, and Livy says as much—though Camillus, like Metellus, does not trust it.

[24] *Incertus*, like *inprovisus* ('unexpected'), is a Jugurthine word, though not always in Jugurtha's control: fifteen times in *B.J.*, five in *B.C.*, nine in *Hist.*; *inprovisus*: eleven times in *B.J.*, once in *B.C.*, twice in *Hist*. Tacitus adapts 46. 5–8 to describe the impossible-to-interpret Nero (*Ann*. 15. 36. 4).

war,' 46. 8). Deceit and skill are often viewed as opposing characteristics in traditional Roman military ethics;[25] possessing both, Jugurtha cannot be evaluated, even in such antithetical situations as peace and war, presence or absence. Categories which should be stable, natural opposites are in his case confused and, Sallust may imply, liable to switch places without warning.[26] His ability to elide difference is reflected by (or causes?) Sallust's jolting zeugma, *pacem...gerens.*[27] Our evaluation of Jugurtha cannot rely even on the appearance of Sallust's words.

This Jugurtha has emerged only gradually, obliquely, from Sallust's portrait of him.[28] In the early scenes in Africa and in Numantia, the authorial voice describes a talented soldier admired by all, one who sounds very much like a virtuous young Roman (6-7):

> When Jugurtha first grew up, as he had strength and good looks, but above all being strong in intellect, he did not allow himself to be corrupted by luxury or idleness but took part in the national pursuits of riding and javelin-throwing, and competed with other young men in running; and though he outshone them all, he was dear to everyone. He also devoted much time to hunting.... He performed many feats but spoke very little of himself [*plurumum facere, minumum ipse de se loqui*]. (2) Though Micipsa was at first pleased with this, considering that Jugurtha's excellence [*virtutem*] would bring glory to his reign, once he realized that Jugurtha was in the prime of life and constantly increasing his prestige, while he himself was old and his children still small, he was violently moved by the situation and considered many things in his mind [*vehementer eo negotio permotus multa cum animo suo volvebat*]. (3) Human nature, eager for rule and rushing headlong to fill the mind's desire [*praeceps ad explendam animi cupidinem*], terrified him, together with the easy chance offered by his own age and that of his children, an opportunity which drives even average men sideways in

---

[25] Cf. Auct. *B Afr.* 73. 2, 'those who were accustomed to fight with war skill [*virtutem*] not trickery' and see Wheeler 1988, esp. 93-110.

[26] For proverbial *praesens/absens*, see Otto 1962: 286. This is a (pejorative) version of the 'unresolved alternative' in panegyric (cf. also 95. 4, Livy *Per.* 80 on Marius), for which, see Vell. Pat. 2. 122. 2, with Woodman 1977. For *varietas* confusing natural opposites, cf. Livy 5. 28. 5, 'they fought in Aequan territory with such varying success [*varie*] that it was unclear whether they had conquered or been conquered'. It is also a defining characteristic of *luxuria* (Edwards 1993: 145 n. 21). So stylistic *variatio* problematizes historical narratives and the worlds they describe: on Livy, see Kraus and Woodman 1997: 62-70; on Tacitus, 109-12.

[27] It is choice (*TLL* VI. 2. 10. 1943. 32-6 lists no earlier, and no other prose, examples) and in a different context can be totalizing, as at Verg. *Aen.* 9. 279 (see Hardie 1994 *ad loc.*). Here it dissolves totality, refusing assessment. How can one wage peace?

[28] The gradual emergence of Jugurtha's character is noted by Riposati 1978: 146-7; on the indirect technique, see Paul 1984: 29. I quote the portrait at length here, as I will return to it throughout the essay.

the hope of profit [*quae etiam mediocris viros spe praedae transvorsos agit*]; in addition there was the devotion towards Jugurtha that had been kindled in the Numidians [*studia adcensa*], which, he worried... might result in sedition or war.

(7. 1) Trapped by these difficulties, he saw that such a popular man could not be eliminated either by force or through treacherous attack. Since Jugurtha was energetic and eager for military glory, he decided to expose him to danger and thereby to test his luck. (2) And so, since during the Numantine war Micipsa was aiding the Roman people... he put him in charge of the Numidians whom he was sending to Spain, hoping that he would be killed easily, either by showing off his excellence [*ostentando virtutem*] or by the enemy's savagery. (3) But the matter came out far differently from the way he had expected [*sed ea res longe aliter ac ratus erat evenit*]. (4) For with his active and keen mind, once Jugurtha understood the nature of the Roman commander, Publius Scipio, and the character of the enemy, through much hard work and much care, by modest obedience and by often exposing himself to danger, he soon became so famous [*claritudinem*] that he was exceptionally dear [*vehementer carus*] to our men, and most terrifying to the Numantines. (5) In fact, he was both a tough fighter and a good counsellor—something which is extremely difficult, since the one usually produces fear as a product of caution, the other rashness from bold courage. (6) And so the commander conducted almost all difficult tasks through Jugurtha, considered him among his friends, and embraced him more and more each day as one whose judgements and undertakings were never in vain [*neque consilium neque inceptum ullum frustra erat*]. (7) To this was added his generosity of spirit and shrewdness of intellect, by which he joined many of the Romans to himself in close friendship.

To some degree this is a conventional picture[29] of a young warrior with brains and brawn, a doer rather than a talker, whose excellence does not attract envy—the last a particularly positive trait, given the normal Roman attitude towards competitive *virtus*. Yet King Micipsa worries that this illegitimate son of his brother Mastanabal will usurp the legitimate heirs' place. Jugurtha's origins make him both a son and a non-son, and may in the king's mind make him therefore more likely to take what is not his, a fear graphically imaged at 6. 3 by the striking metaphorical use of *transvorsum agere*.[30] Micipsa's reading of his nephew leads him to believe that Jugurtha will be tempted to 'show

---

[29] For parallels, see Paul 1984: 29–30. Green 1993, following Vretska, traces the portrait's origin to Xenophon's Cyrus, thereby mapping the Jugurthine war onto a greater precursor.

[30] *Transversus* in this figurative, moral sense is rare in Republican literature (Enn. *Scaen.* 229 J, Cato Orat. 163 ORF = fr. 95a P [Sallust's model], *B.J.* 6. 3, 14. 20; cf. Cic. *Brut.* 331 and the expression *de transverso* 'out of the blue', as at *Rhet. Her.* 4. 10. 14).

Jugurthine Disorder 253

off' (*ostentando*, 7. 2), an ambiguous word that suggests a possible disjunction between appearance and reality.[31]

At this point, however, nothing suggests that Micipsa is right. And indeed, Jugurtha's behaviour under Scipio's command allays any fear that he will disregard proper boundaries. Any doubleness in him manifests itself as a preternaturally stable mix of intellect and strength.[32] The prominent, balanced verbal decoration in 7. 5 underscores the fixity of Jugurtha's character, in which neither aspect drifts over to its less desirable version.[33] That his talents enable him to stand in for Scipio himself (7. 6) shows Jugurtha able to participate in a legitimate, controlled substitution that seems to gainsay Micipsa's fears for his own sons: if Jugurtha can take over for Scipio without taking over from him, then he might be safely entrusted with other sorts of power. By the end of Chapter 7, then, we have seen two Jugurthas, each an interpretative construction (since he hardly speaks of himself): a frightening one of Micipsa's imagination, and a competent, reassuring one as created by the narrator and perceived by Scipio and the Romans (*nostri*, 7. 4). His real character is, therefore, in some doubt—though, as Levene argues, we are surely encouraged to think that Micipsa was wrong.[34]

Or was he? With only the transitional information that Jugurtha made many Roman friends (7. 7), Sallust introduces a new way of looking at him, through the filter of Roman corruption and suspicion (8. 1–9. 1):

> At that time there were many new and noble men [*conplures novi atque nobiles*] serving in our army to whom riches were more important than what is good and honourable, men who were seditious at home and powerful among the allies, notorious [*clari*] rather than honourable. By their promises they tried to kindle Jugurtha's unaverage spirit [*non mediocrem animum pollicitando adcendebant*]: if Micipsa were dead, he would have sole power over Numidia; he had exceptional excellence; at Rome everything was for sale [*in ipso maxumam virtutem, Romae omnia venalia esse*]. (2) But when...Scipio...had rewarded Jugurtha with gifts and praised him lavishly in front of the assembly, leading him into his

---

[31] For *ostentare* of boasting or feigning—the latter found esp. in Livy and Tacitus—see *TLL* IX. 2. 8. 1147. 34–1148. 37.

[32] Precisely what the historian advocates in the prefaces to both monographs; cf. 7. 4 (*inpigro et acri ingenio*) and 7. 7 (Jugurtha's *ingeni sollertia*), the same stabilizing intellectual power—however precarious—that Sallust extols (e.g. 1. 3, 2. 2, 4).

[33] Chiasmus with correlated *ets* and homoioteleuton is followed by two precisely parallel cola in anaphora: *et proelio strenuos erat et bonus consilio, quorum alterum ex providentia timorem, alterum ex audacia temeritatem adferre plerumque solet* (see the translation on p. 252 above).

[34] Levene 1992: 60 (= Chapter 10, pp. 284–5 in this volume).

headquarters, he then in seclusion [*secreto*] advised him to cultivate the friendship of the Roman people publicly rather than privately, and not to make a habit of offering them bribes. It was dangerous (he said) to purchase from the few that which belonged to the many. If he were willing to stay firm [*permanere*] in his talents, glory and a kingdom would come to him of their own accord; but if he kept on going too fast, his own money would make him fall headlong [*suamet ipsum pecunia praecipitem casurum*]. (9. 1) After saying this, he sent him home with a letter which he was to take to Micipsa.

Narratively, this response to the *claritudo* of Chapter 7 is a disquieting replay of 6. 2–3, in which Micipsa responded to Jugurtha's *virtus* by fearing human greed. Chapter 8 shows Jugurtha as the silent recipient of two communications, first from the bad Romans, *novi atque nobiles* (8. 1)—an unholy alliance, or an even unholier hendiadys, destabilizing conventional meaning and prefiguring Marius himself.[35] These are men who wrongly assess value and who themselves embody an undesirable comparison.[36] Their disorder extends to their syntax: *in ipso maxumam virtutem, Romae omnia venalia esse*. Logically adversative, the tempters' asyndeton in fact causally (and nonsensically) connects *virtus* and bribery. The fire they (try to) kindle in the prince picks up the *studia... adcensa* of the Numidian people (6. 3). This, along with other echoes of 6. 3 (*seditiosi ~ seditio, non mediocrem animum ~ etiam mediocris viros, praecipitem ~ praeceps*) is our first confirmation of Micipsa's fears.[37]

Balancing, and (covertly) responding to, this encounter is one with Scipio (8. 2). The general's approach is double(d)—first *pro contione*, then *in praetorium... secreto*—and ironic: in private he warns against private dealings. A mirror, then—or a double?—of the (internal) doubleness of the *novi atque nobiles*. But Scipio's language is revelatory. On the

---

[35] Following Latte, Koestermann 1971: 50 takes *novi* to mean 'young' (= νέοι), so *novi atque nobiles* = *iuvenes nobiles*. Paul (1984) rightly insists instead on the political sense of *novi* here; but the possibility of taking it as a hendiadys (= *novi nobiles*) should not be eliminated. For the oxymoron, see Woodman 1977 on Vell. Pat. 2. 96. 1, *novitatem suam... nobilitaverat*.

[36] *Clari magis quam honesti* significantly contrasts appearance with inner worth; see Hellegouarc'h 1972: 237–8 on *clarus* and 462–3 on *honestus*. The latter may refer only to political honour, and hence to externals; but given *bono honestoque* just above (= καλὸν κἀγαθόν, Hellegouarc'h 1972: 462) it should here refer to inner worth. On antithesis expressed with *magis quam* as an attempt to 'uncover true human motives and overturn the apparent ones', see Scanlon 1980: 142; Kraus 1994: 146.

[37] If the ambiguous *adcendebant* is conative, as I believe, Sallust gives no explicit indication of Jugurtha's response either to the tempters or to Scipio. The textual echoes, however, may suggest to the acute reader that Micipsa was right all along.

one hand, he says, Jugurtha can have stability (*permanere*)[38]—and its rewards, glory and a kingdom that come without requiring an exchange (*ultra*). On the other, haste will bring a fall. This is, of course, a well-worn topos. But the impelling force is almost always *fortuna* or *vires*, not, as in Jugurtha's case, money.[39] This topos, then, has an unconventional (disorderly) twist. As if responding to the tempters who offer Rome for sale, Scipio couches his warning in financial terms. This first appearance of the important theme of bribery coincides with what will appear, in retrospect, as the occasion of Jugurtha's corruption.[40]

But only in retrospect. The letter Scipio sends back to the king could cause alarm: is Scipio sending Jugurtha back with his own death warrant, as Micipsa sent him to Spain to die?[41] On the contrary. The letter affirms Jugurtha's *virtus*, his dearness to the Romans (*nobis... carus*), even his legitimacy: 'you have a man worthy of yourself and of his grandfather Masinissa' (9. 2). Understanding the rumours of his nephew's performance to be true (9. 3), Micipsa adopts Jugurtha, setting a seal on the nobility that, Marius-like, he has proved through his actions (cf. 85. 15–17, 29–30). No gap, then, between reputation and reality; and no suggestion of any hidden problems. Nothing, in fact, either in story or in discourse, for years (9. 4 *paucos post annos*—in fact, fourteen).[42] Yet the collapse of narrative/narrated time may signal the magnitude of Jugurtha's disturbance. Certainly, in the next scene, as Micipsa lies dying, the deceptive gap between appearance and reality and the theme of illicit exchange come together again. His wish that Jugurtha will grow closer to his stepbrothers suggests that the adoption has not eased any dynastic tensions: *tuaque virtute nobis Romanos ex amicis amicissumos fecisti* (10. 2)...*hos qui tibi genere propinqui, beneficio meo fratres sunt,*

---

[38] Scipio is trying to induce Jugurtha to live up to his heritage. Grandfather Masinissa's 'distinguished deeds' (*praeclara facinora*) led to the gift of territory from Rome: 'therefore Masinissa's friendship with us remained good and honourable' (*bona atque honesta permansit*, 5. 5), the only other use of *permanere* in *B.J.* and a clear allusion to its part in the 'official or semi-official phrase' *in amicitia populi Romani permanere*: Powell 1988: 187. On Jugurtha's imitation of his forebears, see also Braund 1984: 138–9.

[39] Sallust uses it later of Marius, whose fall lies beyond the scope of the story, but is predicted within it: 'for afterwards his ambition sent him headlong [*praeceps*]' (63.6). For the financial element, cf. Livy 7. 25. 9, *adeo laboramus in quae sola crevimus, divitias luxuriamque* with Oakley 1997–2005: II. 235; for rich discussion of the topos, possibly originating in Latin with Sallust, see Woodman 1988b: 131–2 with n. 64.

[40] Levene 1992: 60 (= Chapter 10, p. 285 in this volume); but cf. n. 37 above.

[41] For the original of this motif, Bellerophon and his fatal letter (Homer, *Il.* 6. 168–70), see Powell 1991: 199; for folk-tale elements in the *B.J.*, see Cipriani 1988; Oniga 1990.

[42] Jugurtha returned in 132 BCE; Micipsa died in 118. *statim* at 9. 3 may itself mask a gap of a dozen years: see Paul 1984: 40–2 for a discussion.

caros habeas neu malis alienos adiungere quam sanguine coniunctos retinere (10. 3)...*quis autem amicior quam frater fratri?* (10. 5).[43] The polyptotic repetition of *amic-* and *frat-* reflects the stabilizing power of Jugurtha's *virtus*, which has the potential to bring elements together to create a unity, just as he avoided dangerous character shifts in Numantia; so too does Micipsa's exhortation to avoid unstable antithesis (*neu... malis... quam*: see n. 36 above). But by the end of the speech Jugurtha's *virtus* again poses a threat: 'But you, Adherbal and Hiempsal, tend this man and observe him, imitate his excellence [*virtutem*], and take care that I not seem to have adopted better children than [*meliores... quam*] I fathered' (10. 8).[44] Micipsa has moved from an image of Jugurtha's *virtus* as glue to one of Jugurtha's *virtus* as something that can make the worse seem the better. The centre of the speech, which enables that move, meditates on the mutability of human fortune and the tendency of power to corrupt:

> it is neither armies nor treasuries that protect a kingdom, but friends, whom you can provide for yourself neither with weapons nor with gold; they answer to kindness and loyalty.... I leave to you a kingdom that will be stable [*firmum*] if you are good, but, if you are bad, feeble [*inbecillum*].[45] For in concord small things grow, but in discord the greatest fall to pieces.
> (10. 4, 6)

Money, instability, and collapse are intimately related. The connection between money (*thesauri auro*) and the power to make illegitimate exchanges (replacing blood relatives with outsiders, friends with enemies, real sons with adopted) lies at the heart of both subversive behaviour in general and Jugurtha's character in particular.

Scipio's warning and Micipsa's fears are suddenly validated as the narrative reveals Jugurtha's duplicity: 'for the moment [*pro tempore*] he

---

[43] 'By your excellence you have made the Romans, who were already friends, exceptional friends.... [I ask you to] hold dear those who are your relatives by birth, your brothers by my favour, and do not prefer to bind strangers to you [as friends] rather than to hold onto those who are bound by blood.... What greater friend is there than a brother to a brother?'

[44] The declamatory paradoxes of Micipsa's speech illustrate language at once unruly and under tight control; one might compare Ovid's alleged license in what could be described as his most carefully controlled lines (so, e.g., Sen. *Contr.* 2. 2. 12; see Bonner 1949: 143–4).

[45] *Inbecillus*, which in 10. 6 describes the potential result of disorderly conduct, occurs in the monograph only here and at 1. 1 (see p. 244 above). The echo links the introductory themes with the current political situation in Africa, alerting the reader not only to a potential conflict between Jugurtha's *virtus* and his (still hypothetical) inner corruption, but also to a characteristic that he shares with troubled human society as a whole (this link was, of course, contradicted at 6. 1, *non se luxu neque inertiae conrumpendum dedit*; see Paul 1984: 29; Levene 1992: 59 (= Chapter 10, pp. 283–4 in this volume).

responded kindly' (11. 1). His kinship with Micipsa's treasuries and the gold they contain is demonstrated not simply through his effective bribery. All significant action in the pre-Metellan narrative reflects this connection, starting with Jugurtha's murder of his stepbrother Hiempsal, a critical step structurally linked to divisiveness and wealth. As he begins the account of the murder, Sallust backtracks slightly (12. 1–2):

> *primo conventu, quem ab regulis factum supra memoravi, propter dissensionem placuerat dividi* thesauros *finisque imperi singulis constitui. itaque tempus ad utramque rem decernitur, sed maturius ad* pecuniam *distribuendam. reguli interea in loca propinqua* thesauris *alius alio concessere.*
>
> At the first conference, which I recalled above was held by the princes, on account of their disagreement they had agreed to divide their treasuries and to establish borders of a kingdom for each of them. And so a time was decided for each matter, but an earlier one for distributing the money. In the meantime the princes went off into territory adjoining the treasuries, one to one place and one to another.

Though masquerading as incidental background, this passage in fact reports the only important decision made at the conference described in the preceding chapter: that earlier narrative concentrated instead on the kings' jockeying for position (11. 2–6). Its chronological displacement, a slight distortion weighted by the obtrusive *quem... supra memoravi*, brings it into play at a point of heightened relevance,[46] further underscored by the repeated *thesauros, pecuniam, thesauris*. That heap of money is itself confusingly mixed up with discord, which stymies limit (*dissensionem*), and regulated division, which establishes it (*dividi, decernitur, distribuendam*). The passage moves from joining (*conventu*) to separation (*concessere*: see *OLD*, s.v. 1), opposite meanings identically prefixed. The whole is bound together by *regulis... reguli*, separated polyptoton echoed by the juxtaposed but distributive *alius alio*. These elaborately introduced *thesauri* form a significant backdrop to Hiempsal's murder, which is accomplished immediately thereafter (12. 3–6) through the bribery and deceit that Micipsa deplored.

Jugurtha's act produces instant and terrifying division, both in Numidia (13. 1) and outside, as his other stepbrother, Adherbal, attempts to renew the alliance with Rome. But Jugurtha quickly passes from fear to hope via the symbiotic operators of Roman greed and his

---

[46] The use of a resumptive phrase after only a small amount of text has intervened is a feature of Caesar's writing and may be studiedly inelegant; cf. its appearance in Claud. Quad. fr. 10. 4 P (*bis*), where it is generally described as a mark of 'annalistic' style (e.g., by Eden 1962: 80 and n. 1; see also Starr 1981).

own money: 'thinking over his crime in his mind [*cum animo*] he feared the Roman people, nor... did he have hope anywhere except in the nobles' avarice and his own money' (13. 5). In his subsequent dealings with the Romans his bribery successfully establishes division (e.g., 15. 2-3, 16. 1), maintaining distance between himself and reprisals for his increasingly aggressive behaviour towards Adherbal. When he finally must face Roman armies, he finds the consul Bestia and his companions to be themselves divided, duplicitous, and liable to make disorderly appraisals (15. 4, 28. 5, 29. 2)—ready prey, in short, to Jugurtha's fiscal disorder. Negotiations for a specious surrender[47] are held in a double session reminiscent of Scipio's two communications to Jugurtha (*praesenti consilio... secreta*, 29. 5). Here the narrative juxtaposes two actions that can be understood as one, corresponding to the deceit wherein one agreement (the formal surrender, *deditio*) hides another (the secret understanding). This doubled structure is repeated a few chapters later when Cassius arrives with orders to bring Jugurtha to Rome. He finds that the specific legal and economic categories set up in the terms of the surrender have been replaced by unrestrained exchange (29. 6 ~ 32. 3-4). Rather than trying to correct this behaviour, as Metellus will do later, Cassius simply removes its primary cause. Like the negotiations for the surrender, his discussions with Jugurtha take place first (presumably) in the open, then in private (*privatim praeterea*, 32. 5). In each case, however, Cassius makes an offer of *fides*, the ultimate stabilizing force, to one who has none (*diffidenti*, 32. 5). The only difference between the two offers is that he presents public *fides* in public (32. 1, 5), his own (*suam*) in private. In contrast to Scipio's two communications, then, or to Bestia's negotiations, the content of each message is the same, the slight variation (public ~ private) precisely corresponding to the place in which it is delivered.[48]

The success of this *fides* is strictly limited. After a short but disastrous episode in Rome Jugurtha is back in Africa, where, as the war narrative moves into a new phase, the prominence of bribery gradually decreases. In its place arise two concepts whose operation resembles that of money. Delay (the gap between an action and its consequence) and motion (the quick passage of one thing into another) are two sides of the same coin;

---

[47] Whatever Bestia's intentions, the *deditio* was not genuine without the presence (= surrender) of Jugurtha's person (Paul 1984: 96-7, 102, 104-5); the prince tries an identical (absent) deal with Metellus, with no success (Paul 1984: 140 on 46. 1). For Jugurtha and presence/absence, see n. 26 above.

[48] On the rhetorical and thematic stability of sameness, see Section IV below; for the financial connotations of *fides*, see *OLD*, s.v. 5 and cf. 75. 1 cited at n. 21 above.

they have roots in the early portrait of Jugurtha, and are introduced into the military narrative as early as the surrender of 111 BCE, which begins as an attempt to purchase *mora belli* ('delay of the war,' 29. 3). The scenes between that surrender and the defeat of Aulus Albinus (38. 10) show Jugurtha still manipulating money where he can; delay and motion, however, come increasingly into their own.

III. *CUNCTA AGITARE* ('ALL SHOOK UP')

Micipsa has a remarkable, and shocking, reaction to his nephew's early talents: *vehementer eo negotio permotus multa cum suo animo volvebat* (6. 2, translated on p. 251 above). *Permovere* is at home in descriptions of sudden panic and fright, especially the panic caused by an approaching army.[49] But in Jugurtha's story it describes only the effect he has on his relatives (at 6. 3, 9. 3, 20. 4). The alarming near-metaphorical diction images a relationship more appropriate between enemies than in a family, while Micipsa's agitation is enhanced by the juxtaposition of *negotio* with *permotus*, suggesting the traditional etymology *nec otium* ('not time off').[50] *Vehementer*, too, also used of Jugurtha's (positive) effects on the Roman soldiers at Numantia (7. 4), hyperbolically qualifies emotions that verge on agitation. Even Micipsa's friendly response to his nephew, after Scipio's letter, is infected by militaristic language: 'he advanced on [*adgressus est*] Jugurtha to conquer him [*vincere*] with kindness' (9. 3), while Sallust here deploys *permovere*, once again, of the king's reaction to Jugurtha's talent and influence (*quom virtute tum gratia viri permotus*). The change of mind that Micipsa then undergoes, though presented as positive, cannot in fact be anything but sinister in the light of the surrounding vocabulary of motion and attack.

Before Metellus, no one manages to control Jugurthine mobility and delay.[51] They are at their most powerful after Adherbal's death at Cirta. Facing the new consul, Jugurtha continually defers engagement (36. 2):

---

[49] e.g., at *B.C.* 29. 1, 31. 1: 'the state was profoundly moved [*permota*] by these events and its appearance was changed'; Caes. *BCiv.* 2. 14. 3, 'our men were profoundly moved by the sudden turn of events [*repentina fortuna permoti*]'; 26. 3, 'Curio was profoundly moved by the new situation [*novitate rei...permotus*]'; Nepos, *Milt.* 4. 3, 'the Athenians were profoundly moved [*permoti*] by this emergency'.

[50] Maltby 1991: 407–8; a favourite play in the *B.J.*: elsewhere at 4. 4 (programmatic: see Section V below), 51. 1, 76. 1.

[51] Jugurtha's mobility is mirrored here, as elsewhere, by the narrative: Kraus and Woodman 1997: 45 n. 76.

at contra Iugurtha trahere omnia et alias, deinde alias morae causas facere, polliceri deditionem ac deinde metum simulare, cedere instanti et paulo post, ne sui diffiderent, instare: ita belli modo, modo pacis mora consulem ludificare.

But on the other hand Jugurtha dragged everything out and produced first some, then other reasons for delay; promised surrender and then simulated fear; yielded as they came on and a little later, lest his men lose heart, attacked; thus, now with delay of war, now of peace he mocked the consul.

War and peace, as at 46. 8 (see Section II above), become interchangeable tokens in this game. Sallust's rhetorical ornamentation highlights the stasis (in both senses, of standstill and revolution) that Jugurtha's multifarious stratagem paradoxically produces, with chiasmus in three of the four clauses, iteration (*alias, deinde alias*; *modo, modo*), word play (*instanti... instare*), and careful marking of stages (*deinde, deinde, paulo post, modo, modo*). Each of these may be read dynamically, generating comparison, slippage, even agitated motion; or statically, marking fixed relationships, balance, and stagnation.[52]

As a fitting reflection of the disorder in the field, the Roman state is racked by sedition whose uncontrolled motion (*agitabantur*, 37. 1) brings the elections to a standstill (*ea mora*, 37. 3). Against this oxymoronic background[53] the consul's brother Aulus Albinus decides to capture Jugurtha's treasury (37. 3). He could hardly have chosen a worse objective. As before, the *thesauri* can be read metaphorically for the chaotic Jugurtha. The prince simulates retreat; the Romans, following blindly, are ambushed, confused, betrayed by their own centurions and allies. Jugurthine adjectives reappear—rapid motion produces paralysis—opposites collapse into each other (38. 4–5):

He suddenly [*de inproviso*] surrounded Aulus' camp.... The Roman soldiers were struck [*perculsi*] by this unaccustomed [*insolito*] emergency; some seized weapons, some hid themselves, some reassured the frightened—there was fear everywhere. The enemy was in great strength, the sky obscured by night and clouds; whatever they did was dangerous [*periculum anceps*]; finally, they were unsure whether it was safer to flee or to remain [*postremo facere an manere tutius foret, in incerto erat*].

---

[52] So at 74. 1–2 Sallust uses telegraphic historic infinitives, short clauses, and balance of opposites to express similar ideas. For the expressive power of a list (*evidentia*, or 'vivid narration' achieved *per partes*), cf. Quint. 8. 2. 40, quoting an asyndetic passage from Cic. *Ver.* 5. 161, and see Roberts 1989: 40–2.

[53] It is, of course, standard political language, but I wish to bring out the contradiction inherent at its heart, which Sallust explores—and exploits—in the person of Jugurtha.

Jugurthine Disorder

At the last, however, Jugurtha lets the Romans go—for a price. The defeated soldiers pass under the yoke: 'though these conditions were serious and full of humiliation, nevertheless, since they were being given in exchange [*mutabantur*] for the fear of death, peace was agreed according to the king's desire [*sicuti regi lubuerat*]' (38. 10). The treasury Aulus sought to control escapes him, while it is the Romans who must give up treasure in order to live. Jugurtha's only undisputed victory is won through simulation and finalized by a trade.

Sallust underscores the particularly Jugurthine quality of this surrender by the playful semantic slippage of *foedus* from the meaning 'foul' (*foeda fuga*, 38. 7) to 'treaty' (38. 9, 39. 2–3).[54] That slippage is followed by two attempts to re-establish order in the midst of frustrating *mora/motus*: the plebeian-driven Mamilian inquiry (40) and Sallust's digression on the 'nature of political parties and factions' (41–2). In these sections characters and narrator alike attempt to stabilize the growing political disorder—described appropriately with the images of avalanche and earthquake (41. 9–10)[55]—which Sallust has set in counterpoint to the Jugurthine madness in the field. Only the digression, however, which applies the intellectual weapons of categorization and rational analysis to that political chaos, vaguely succeeds in reducing it to some sort of (retrospective) order, while both the account of the inquiry and the digression are shot through with images of internal corruption, contradiction, and identity between logical opposites. The success of these ordering devices may be judged from the state of the narrative as the war resumes: the two meanings of *foedus* now sit side by side in a temporary, but threatening truce which both establishes their separate meanings and parades their (illegitimate) synonymy: *post Auli foedus exercitusque nostri foedam fugam* ('after Aulus' agreement and the shameful flight of our army', 43. 1).

Meanwhile, the army left in Africa shows all the signs of having been in contact with Jugurthine disorder. Its unregulated commerce and motion produces a linguistic free-for-all in which active and passive states can coexist (44. 1, 5):

> Indolent, unwarlike, enduring neither danger nor hard work, readier to talk than to fight, plundering their allies and themselves plunder to the enemy [*lingua quam manu promptior, praedator ex sociis et ipsa praeda*

---

[54] See Maltby 1991: 237–8 for the ancient etymological connection.
[55] On the language, itself again conventional, see Jal 1963: 281–4 (cosmic overtones) and 462–73 (perversion and inversion of values, conflict and conflation of good and evil, etc.). Note esp. 41. 9, *semet ipsa praecipitavit* ('it caused itself to fall headlong'), of avarice, and cf. p. 255 above.

hostium]...whenever they desired [*lubebat*] the soldiers left their post; camp followers, thoroughly mixed [*permixti*] with soldiers, wandered about day and night.... They competed in leading off cattle and slaves as booty and trading them [*mutare*] with merchants for imported wine and other such things; besides, they sold the grain that was provided by the state, and bought bread each day; finally, whatever vice characteristic of cowardice and luxury can be named or imagined, every one was found in that army.

It is not only Spurius' absence and his brother's incompetence that, as Wiedemann argues, has caused this reversion to nomadism, the distinguishing characteristic of the African ethnography (17–19); the situation in the field and the political disturbances at home reflect and interpenetrate each other. Among other things, Sallust highlights the force—and contagion—of desire.[56]

Metellus combats this disorder with his own form of quintessentially Roman military discipline. Like the young Jugurtha's, his own character is balanced (*temperantia...moderatum*, 45. 1), balance which Sallust uses as an explanation (*namque*, 45. 2) of how he reforms the army. Metellus goes to the heart of Jugurthine disorder: he outlaws commerce, banning the sale of bread, the presence of camp followers, and the possession of slaves; putting the army through forced marches and disciplined activities, he keeps them in their ranks (*ordines*).[57] Above all, rather than falling victim to it, he can play Jugurtha's game against him, separating words from reality (48. 1). Still, he is eventually stymied by the prince's guerrilla tactics. Infectious disorderly conduct concentrates at the river Muthul, in a battle where the Romans are nearly undone no fewer than three times by visual confusion, mirages produced by the synergism between the terrain and Jugurtha's trickery (46. 5, 53. 1–2, 53. 7–8). In the central scene, Jugurthine confusion reigns (50. 4–51. 2):

---

[56] So at 38. 10 *lubido* is associated with Jugurtha; also 40. 3, *in partibus*; 40. 5, the *plebs*; 41. 5, the *populus*, 42. 4, the *nobilitas*; 44. 5 the army. See also n. 12 above.

[57] 45. 2, 'he moved camp daily by means of cross-country marches [*transvorsis itineribus*]', is particularly interesting, not only because Metellus is substituting controlled regular movement for the previous roaming at will. *Transvorsus* recurs thrice in the next five sections (49. 1, the battle site; 49. 6, Roman manoeuvres; 50. 1, Numidian manoeuvres). Its only other occurrences in the *B.J.* are at 6. 3 and 14. 20, both describing Jugurtha's potential for corruption, with a rare metaphor (see n. 30 above). Its reappearance here at the beginning of a battle of wits and arms adumbrates Metellus' appropriation of Jugurtha's twisting tactics. For Metellus' disciplinary moves, see Paul 1984: 139. The other famous example of this method of restoring discipline is Scipio Aemilianus, at Numantia (Livy *Per.* 57, Val. Max. 2. 7. 1–2, Frontin. *Str.* 4. 1. 1–2): does Sallust mean us to see Jugurtha challenging (or challenged by) his old mentor's stratagem? On Numantia, see further p. 270 below.

Some Numidians slaughtered the soldiers at the rear; some harassed them on left and right; enemies appeared and attacked, and everywhere they threw the Roman ranks into confusion [*ordines conturbare*]. And even those who attacked the enemy with relative courage were mocked by the uncertain mode of fighting [*ludificati incerto proelio*]....The cavalry... scattered as widely as possible [*alius alio quam maxume divorsi*]....The appearance of the whole business was changeable, indecisive [*facies totius negoti varia, incerta*], foul and pitiable; separated from their comrades, some gave ground, some attacked; they kept neither standards nor ranks [*dispersi a suis pars cedere, alii insequi; neque signa neque ordines observare*]...arms, weapons, horses, men, enemies, and citizens were thoroughly mixed together [*permixti*]; nothing was done with plan or command; chance ruled all [*fors omnia regere*]. And so, when much of the day had passed, the outcome was still uncertain [*in incerto*].

Later, Jugurtha's quickness and ability to keep opposites simultaneously in play, as he 'neither gave battle nor allowed rest', again frustrate the Roman *inceptum* (55. 8). Here too quickness is intimately connected with—and produces—delay. And even when, in the later stages, it infects Jugurtha himself, driving him like a gadfly (72. 2, 76. 1), *motus* still frustrates the Romans. Speed, a pre-eminent *virtus imperatoria* that let great generals like Caesar finish their *incepta* time and time again,[58] turns in Jugurtha's hands into a further manifestation of disorder.

IV. PLAYING THE OTHER?

This section considers a final aspect of this *discordia*, the thematics of substitution, especially in its relation to Sallust's second subject: the opposition to the aristocracy that produced *vastitas Italiae*, in which *bellum* becomes *civile bellum* (5. 2). This thematic, too, is first found in Sallust's description of the young prince (quoted pp. 251–2 above). The moment he arrives in Spain, events run far contrary to expectations (*longe aliter ac ratus erat evenit*, 7. 3). Almost the same words recur in Micipsa's deathbed scene, as the king encourages his nephew to do what is right: *te...ne aliter quid eveniat providere decet* ('you should see to it that nothing different happens', 10. 7). This is, however, the very thing that Micipsa has already learned can happen when Jugurtha is involved. His reaction—incidentally, the first time we see Jugurtha respond to any communication—also contains the narrator's first unambiguous

---

[58] See Vell. Pat. 2. 41. 2 and 2. 129. 3 with Woodman 1977 *ad loc.*

indication that the prince is not as straightforward as he seems: 'though he understood that the king had spoken lies [*ficta locutum intellegebat*], and he thought far differently in his mind [*longe aliter animo agitabat*], for the moment [Jugurtha] responded kindly [*benigne respondit*]' (11. 1). *Aliter* is at last explicitly linked to deception. But what does *ficta* mean? Micipsa's final speech contains no falsehood, comprising, as it does, only flattering exhortations and wishes. *Ficta locutum* must mean 'had spoken insincerely'—almost 'was playing a part'.[59] Commentators tend to assume, therefore, that Micipsa never really changed his mind, that Jugurtha here perceives that hypocrisy, and that at 11. 1 Sallust illustrates the prince's cleverness as well as beginning his descent into villainy.[60] But there has been nothing to indicate that *flexit animum suom* ('he changed his mind', 9. 3) was anything but sincere.[61] *Ficta locutum* goes deeper than simple questions of regal insincerity. Jugurtha understands that the verbal edifice of proverbial wisdom and good advice that the dying king has constructed is precisely that: a construct.[62] His wordlessly pleasant response, devoid of any content but *benigne*, magnifies the emptiness of Micipsa's long direct speech and emphasizes the contrast between word and fact that is implicit throughout this scene.[63]

When shortly thereafter Hiempsal suggests that the adoption be revoked, the threat to his position reveals Jugurtha's unsuspected—and dangerous—depths: 'but this utterance [*verbum*] sank deeper than anyone had thought into Jugurtha's heart. And so, from that time, anxious with anger and fear, he plotted, prepared, and considered with his mind [*cum animo habere*] how Hiempsal might be caught by stealth' (11. 7-8). The remarkable personifications of the *verbum* and of Jugurtha's *animus*, which here seems to operate separately from the rest of him,[64] intensify

---

[59] For such a connotation, see the examples of *vultus fictus* ('feigned expression') at *TLL* VI. 1. 774. 60-70 and cf. 14. 20 (where *simulare* and *fingere* are synonyms: Koestermann 1971 *ad loc.*) and Verg. *A.* 2. 107 *ficto pectore* (of the lying Sinon). An ancient glossary gives *fucatum vel coloratum* ('dyed or coloured') as equivalents for *fictum* (*TLL* VI. I. 779. 20-1), highlighting the notion of rhetorical embellishment. On Micipsa's speech, see further pp. 255-6 above.

[60] e.g., Scanlon 1980: 141, Jugurtha recognizes 'the falseness of the flattering words'; Paul 1984: 45 on 10. 2; extended discussion in Suerbaum 1964: esp. 100-6.

[61] Despite the surrounding military vocabulary, the sincerity is not in doubt; see Koestermann 1971 *ad loc.*

[62] For the proverbial elements, see Otto 1962: 13-14 (*alienus*), 20-1 (*amicus*), 89 (*concordia*), 146 (*fraternus*), 176 (*invidia*). Katherine Clarke perceptively compares *B.C.* 3. 2 *veluti ficta* [= the historian's narrative] *pro falsis ducit.*

[63] Paul 1984: 38, 45. Jugurtha gives a similar response, in a similar situation, at 72. 1.

[64] To do something *cum animo* implies a separation between the parts of a person and is not very common: there are fewer than a dozen examples before the turn of the millennium in the Packard Humanities Institute (PHI) CD texts, three in the comic playwrights

the sense that he has internalized difference. But Jugurtha also recognizes the rhetorical power of 'sameness', which he twice uses successfully to put off Roman interference while he outmanoeuvres, besieges, and eventually murders Adherbal.[65] Being 'the same' implies that he is honest, transparent, no different inside from outside; it also suggests that he is not subject to any sort of (ex)change, neither substituted nor substituting for anyone. In Sallust's world, accepting such a claim involves accepting Jugurtha's language, too, as a transparent mirror of reality (*qualis oratio talis homo*).

But the claim is dishonest. The continuing and frustrating Roman failure to trap Jugurtha stems from his talent for producing seemingly endless difference and deferral between what the Romans perceive and reality, as when Metellus enters Numidia, or in the battle at the Muthul. Throughout the central section of the narrative (43–83) Jugurtha combines delay, simulation, and rapid motion to throw the Roman offensive into disarray. With the appointment of the *novus homo* Marius, however, Jugurtha quite literally meets his match.

The kinship between Jugurtha and Marius has been much discussed.[66] It produces a curious narrative effect. Sallust chose to introduce Marius at a point when Jugurtha has again stymied the Roman enterprise in Africa (63), thereby suggesting a kinship between Metellus' two opponents. From Marius' assumption of the consulship on, however, the most remarkable feature of the monograph's final section (84–114) is Jugurtha's relative absence from it. Marius has, in effect, replaced him. At several points Sallust briefly records the prince's actions—harassing Roman allies (88. 3), sending for King Bocchus (97. l), camping near Sulla's troops (106. 2)—but, though Numidians and their allies have four major encounters (and several minor ones) with Marius' legions, their leader actively participates only in the last (101).[67] It is a typically disorderly performance, deploying stratagems of division and deceit (101. 1–2):

> So finally on the fourth day... [Roman] scouts quickly showed themselves from all quarters at once [*undique simul speculatores citi sese ostendunt*],

(Plaut. *Trin.* 305, *Aul.* 715; Ter. *Adel.* 500) and six in Sallust, all in the *B.J.*, all of cases of extreme anxiety (6. 2, 11. 8, 13. 5, 70. 5, 93. 1, 108. 3); it next clusters in the second century CE. Significantly, the oxymoronic new noble Marius is the only Roman to be so described. Tacitus borrows this Jugurthine scene for the cloaked Tiberius: *id Tiberii animum altius penetravit* (*Ann.* 1. 69. 3).

[65] At 15. 2, for instance, his legates ask the Romans not to believe that he is any different (*alium*) from his Numantine self; the same logic recurs at 22. 2 (note also Jugurtha's refusal there of invidious comparison: *sibi neque maius quicquam neque carius auctoritate senatus*).

[66] e.g., Earl 1961: 75 and n. 1; Scanlon 1987: 49; Kraus and Woodman 1997: 27.

[67] Sallust does not even mention the Numidians after the Muluccha: Paul 1984: 234.

whence it was understood that the enemy was at hand. But because they were returning, scattered, one from one direction and one from another, and yet all indicated the same thing [*divorsi redeuntes alius ab alia parte atque omnes idem significabant*], the consul, being unsure [*incertus*] how to draw up the battle line, changed no disposition, but waited in the same place prepared for everything [*nullo ordine conmutato advorsum omnia paratus ibidem opperitur*].

Jugurtha's initial tactic, which successfully collapses difference and sameness, is frustrated by the Roman's response, in which change is rejected in favour of sameness (*ibidem*) and totality (*omnia*). Jugurtha accordingly changes plan and engages. Once the battle begins, he as quickly changes again: 'he secretly turned [*clam...convortit*]...towards the infantry. There, in Latin—which he had learned to speak at Numantia—he exclaimed that our men were fighting in vain, since Marius had been killed a little while before by his own hand—at the same time displaying [*ostentans*] a sword smeared with blood which he, fighting bravely enough, had bloodied by killing our infantry' (101. 6). Complete with realistic prop, the masquerade concerning Marius is particularly relevant to the theme of substitution, and not simply as an example of Jugurtha playing a role. It forms part of a sequence of deceptions relying on the assumption of a false national identity, the others being Metellus' masking of Roman troops with Numidian cavalry at Vaga (68. 4–69. 1) and the carrying of Numidian arms by Marius' advance team at the Muluccha (94. 1).[68] Each of these is a purely military tactic; Jugurtha's Latin 'identity', on the other hand, has more substance than at first appears. It looks back to Numantia, where—as Sallust tells us parenthetically—he learned to speak the language.[69] It thereby alludes also to that first, legitimate substitution, where Jugurtha stood in for Scipio (7. 6, quoted on p. 252 above), and the ring thus formed signals one kind of narrative close.[70] For this battle is Jugurtha's final action against the Romans, from whose weapons he escapes entirely alone: *at Iugurtha...solus inter tela hostium vitabundus erumpit.*[71]

Instead, the last section of the monograph belongs, at least initially, to Marius, who manifests as much craft and knowledge of the terrain as

---

[68] On this episode, see Brescia 1997.

[69] For Numantia, see p. 270 below; cf. Braund 1984: 20 n. 66 for other examples of foreigners learning Latin while serving in the Roman army.

[70] Cirta, where this battle takes place, was also the site of Adherbal's death; on the structure, see Scanlon 1987: 59; 1989: 144.

[71] His ineffectiveness later on, when Volux and Sulla ride through his camp (107. 5), recalls a motif 'frequently associated in ancient literature with supernatural aid' (Paul 1984: 253); it may suggest both Sulla's legendary *felicitas* and Jugurtha's virtual non-corporeality at that point.

Jugurthine Disorder

Jugurtha did before him. His use of masks and surprise is best illustrated by the Sardis-type battle for a *castellum* on the Muluccha, whose capture is in fact brought about by *fors*, but is attributed to Marius' *virtus*. The build-up starts with Marius' success in the preceding campaign[72] and continues through the capture of the *castellum*, through which 'chance' sounds like a leitmotif.[73] With its last, especially telling occurrence, Marius' slipperiness reveals its fundamental weakness: *sic forte conrecta Mari temeritas gloriam ex culpa invenit* ('so Marius' rashness, having been put straight by chance, found a source of glory out of a source of blame', 94. 7). This is paradoxical, civil-war language *par excellence*. A disorderly character who like Jugurtha causes things to be different around him, Marius opens the possibility that he will himself become *alius*: that is, that he will be replaced by someone else. As if on cue, when *culpa* and *virtus* seem interchangeable, a narrative door opens, and Marius' alter ego Sulla strides in.[74]

Thus, after chapter 101—where Jugurtha claims to have killed him— Marius functions primarily to pass people and messages on.[75] And not surprisingly, perhaps, neither enemy leader is present to bring the war to a close. They work instead through substitutes. The absent Jugurtha's part is taken by his Gaetulian ally Bocchus, while Marius yields to Sulla's eloquence (102. 4). His patrician speech is less slippery, or perhaps better with kings, than Marius' own effective—and showcased (85)—demagoguery.[76] Bocchus exhibits some of the same tendency to sudden motion as Jugurtha, but in his case it can be easily explained: Sallust reduces Jugurthine disorder to a comforting commonplace, predictable regal unpredictability (*sed plerumque regiae voluntates ut vehementes*

---

[72] 'Once Marius had completed such a great deed...his already great and famous reputation became greater and more famous. Every ill-considered action was attributed to his excellence [*in virtutem trahebantur*]: the soldiers, treated with moderate discipline and enriched at the same time, praised him to the skies; the Numidians feared him as something more than mortal' (92. 1-3).

[73] 92. 6, 'this deed was accomplished by chance [*forte*] rather than by design'; 93. 1, 'worried...Marius considered with his mind [*cum animo suo*] whether to give up what he started [*inceptum*], since it was fruitless, or to wait for good luck [*fortunam*]'; 93. 2, 'by chance [*forte*] a certain Ligurian'; 93. 4, 'by chance [*forte*] in that place'. See Brescia 1997: 16-17.

[74] In a disruption so severe that it triggers a narrative digression: 'while this was happening, the quaestor Lucius Sulla arrived in camp....But since the matter has reminded me of this great man, it seems appropriate to say a few words about his nature and behaviour' (95. 1-2); see Kraus and Woodman 1997: 26. On Marius' disappearance, see Paul 1984 on 101. 4, 8, ascribing his remarkable absence from the final battle narrative to Sulla's memoirs, which Sallust may well have used as a source (see n. 93 below).

[75] He acts, therefore, like other things which facilitate chance and exchange: see n. 22 above.

[76] Kraus and Woodman 1997: 25.

sic mobiles, 113. 1).[77] Sulla's negotiations with him at first seem endless and familiar, with the same diplomacy frustrated by bribes (102), the same series of parallel meetings, first open, then secret (109; cf. 8. 2, 29. 5, 32. 5); but Bocchus is only a pale imitation, and eventually betrays Jugurtha to Sulla, who hands him over to Marius. Sulla would later have the scene engraved on a seal ring with himself as victor, (allegedly) fixing its meaning and—incidentally(?)—enraging Marius.[78] In Sallust's narrative, however, their shifting back and forth in the capture of Jugurtha must prefigure their subsequent (civil) disorder in their struggle for the possession of Rome.

V. HISTORY AS TEXT

Together with Hannibal and Cleopatra, Rome's other two great African enemies, Jugurtha focuses the themes of deceit, illegitimacy, rapid motion, frustrated action, and instability that characterize discord, especially civil strife.[79] The clusters of images and metaphors of exchange, delay, movement, and substitution 'constitute significant patterns'[80] in our reading, as in Sallust's telling, of this text, reinforcing the ways in which the content means. But it goes further than that. There are significant ways in which Jugurtha's disorder has affected Sallust's writing of history.

In the preface to the *B.J.*, as in the *B.C.*, Sallust puts contemporary politics (from which he has withdrawn) in counterpoise to his own writing of history (4. 3-4):

> I believe that because I have decided to live my life far from politics, some will give the name 'laziness' to my great and useful labour [*tanto tamque utili labori meo nomen inertiae imponant*]; certainly [those will] for whom the height of energy seems to be greeting the plebs and seeking influence through dinner parties. But if they consider both what great men were unable to hold public office at the time when I held my magistracies and what sort of men have since got into the Senate, they will certainly consider

---

[77] 'But often the desires of kings are as powerful as they are changeable.' Paul 1984: 256 notes the similar language used of the Numidians at 46. 3. Sallust's formulation at 113. 1 tames the Jugurthine adjectives *vehemens* (e.g., 4. 7, 6. 2, 7. 4) and *mobilis* (Section III).

[78] Paul 1984: 253, 256-7 for references.

[79] For Cleopatra, see Quint 1993: 28 ('the embodiment of... disorder and violence' on Aeneas' shield), 111-13 (Cleopatra, Hannibal, and Carthage).

[80] Konstan 1986: 198; see also Kurke 1991, esp. 11 on imagery as cultural symbols, transmitting the poet's message; she sees 'images as a set of systems constitutive of the poetry's social effect'.

that I exchanged my judgement [*iudicium animi mei mutavisse*] worthily rather than from sloth, and that my leisure will do the state a greater service than other men's business [*maiusque commodum ex otio meo quam ex aliorum negotiis rei publicae venturum*].

But while in the *B.C.* he is concerned lest his detractors mistake his motivation, taking criticism as a product of envy and praise as fiction (*B.C.* 3. 2), in the *B.J.* the potential confusion goes deeper. Here, he worries that the product will be ignored in favour of the process of history writing itself, which—in typical disorderly fashion—will be misread/mislabelled as *inertia* rather than *utilis labor*. Sallust counters this with a linguistic trick of his own (flagged by *mutavisse*[81]): his *otium* will bring greater benefit than others' *negotium*. Yet he frames this defence of his activity and its product with two curiously shadowed passages. Beginning with history's exceptional usefulness (*in primis magno usui est*, 4. 1), he immediately establishes distance: all such claims to utility should be passed over (*praetereundum*), as many have made them, and as people may think that the individual historian (*memet... meum*) is simply glorifying his own project. The *praeteritio*, whose explicit naming foregrounds its rhetorical function,[82] sets the stage for the equally ostentatious verbal dexterity with which Sallust defends his chosen activity (4. 3–4, above). He then repeats and specifies the claim for history's *utilitas*: it inspires imitation of ancient glory (4. 6), a claim illustrated (4. 5) with the famous comparison of history (*memoria rerum gestarum*) to ancestral portrait masks (*imagines maiorum*). As in the *B.C.*, a compound of *aequare* marks the moment of exemplary utility: as the production of history 'equals' deeds with words, proving its use to the state,[83] so the use of history, 'equalling' ancestral *fama atque gloria*, brings benefit to the republic. All of this, however, is immediately shattered by an emphatic and conclusive contradiction (*at contra*, 4. 7), as Sallust shows how the attention paid to history has vastly diminished in the face of contemporary moral and ethical debasement. He does not return to the special status of the historian, but ends the preface by turning away from the bad mores of his own time, in which traditional values are worthless, back to his subject: 'But I have gone too freely and too far out to sea, our national character being loathsome and disgusting to me. Now I return to my starting point' (4. 9).[84]

---

[81] Ahl 1985: 51; for the themes of *otium* and *negotium* in Sallust's programmatic passages, see Marincola 1997: 138–40.

[82] Earl 1979: 43.

[83] *B.C.* 3. 1; on the expression, see Kraus 1994: 214; Oakley 1997–2005: I. 560–1.

[84] See p. 246 above. For the metaphor in *altius* and the causal sense of *dum*, see Dietsch 1846 *ad loc.*, Goodyear (1972) *ad Ann.* 1. 23. 5.

It is not that Sallust believes that history has no power, either ameliorative or commemorative. He must do, as he continues to write it. But the persona of the alienated historian is more intensely drawn in the *B.J.* than it was in the *B.C.* Where Catiline was exciting as well as dangerous (*B.C.* 4. 5), Sallust's Jugurthine topic threatens the historian who has chosen it.[85] The *discordia* which he embodies challenges the utility of history, even as it does other stabilizing elements such as *virtus*,[86] the intellectual arts, and political concord. The primary task of a historian is to narrate, to finish his *inceptum* by telling the story. His Jugurthine topic compels Sallust's attention, and indeed begins as an *inceptum* which can focus Sallust's energy away from contemporary decline.[87] But as the cause of that decline, and so as a part of it, Jugurtha's story also resists and problematizes narration. So Sallust must silence Carthage, which will not fit in his narrative economy (19. 2),[88] and is disgusted by Sulla.[89] The very length and complexity of the narrative are as much a function of Jugurtha's character as they are a reflection of any action on the ground.[90] The force that Sallust invokes in the preface and that Jugurtha incarnates is most visible at the end, which famously teases us with its lack of closure.[91] In his first work Sallust bounded corruption by the limits of one man's madness. In the *B.J.* the process of corruption goes deeper, the historiographical project compromised from the very first word: *falso*.[92] The historian's subject infects his task: disorder and corruption rule at Rome, compromising Sallust's very control over his material, while the military narrative is threatened by political influence

---

[85] Perhaps by virtue of being the direct 'cause' of the first pair of dynasts, whose actions were so clearly repeated by the second pair. Catiline, though modelled in various ways on a stereotypical *regnum*-seeker, is more unique and hence more containable. On the persona of the alienated historian, see O'Gorman 1998.

[86] For the association of *virtus* with stability and related concepts, cf. 1. 1–5, 7. 5 (balance and strength); 4. 7, Livy 8. 34. 10 (direct action); 15. 2, 85. 31–2 (*virtus* superior to *dicta*); 7. 6, 76. 1, 92. 1–2 (steadfastness); Caes. *BCiv.* 3. 72. 4 (*virtus* excludes the possibility of change); Livy 6. 30. 6, *stabilis virtus*. For extended discussion of *virtus* in Sallust, see Earl 1961: 28–40; Tiffou 1973: 119–54; Batstone 1988b.

[87] Very similar is Livy's turning to ancient history, 'away from the sight of the evils which our age has seen through so many years' (Pref. 5).

[88] On Carthage and its paradoxes, see Kraus and Woodman 1997: 27–30.

[89] 95. 4, 'for I am not sure [*incertum*] whether I am more ashamed or disgusted [*pudeat an pigeat*] to narrate what he did afterwards'. On characters resisting narration, cf. the parallel case of Lucan, with the discussion of Masters 1992; for the paradox that any epic story must 'consist in delay, obstruction, deferral', see Henderson 1998: 243–4 with n. 69.

[90] On the unimportance of the war, see Paul 1984: 19–20, 264–8.

[91] Levene 1992: 54–5 (= Chapter 10, p. 275 in this volume); Kraus and Woodman 1997: 26–7.

[92] I thank Katherine Clarke for pointing this out to me.

and conflicting versions of the story, many of them going back, like Jugurtha himself, to that core experience at Numantia.[93] Sallust would go on to write more extended *annales* in a continuing search for a way to make sense of the civil disorder at the end of the Republic.[94] Like Tacitus, however, he may have found that its causes remained elusive.

ADDENDUM

I first started writing this article in the late 1980s. It threatened to become a monograph, as I tried to bring the whole Sallustian work into the mix; trimming it to a manageable length brought out the emphasis on luxury and exchange, in which I flirted with ideas of social economy and cultural capital (as formulated by Pierre Bourdieu), but never developed them; to take that further, one can learn a lot from Leslie Kurke's work (for antiquity), but Bourdieu and related thinkers have become a pervasive influence on writing since the early 1990s about Roman literature in its cultural context. On the open-endedness of ancient works, Fowler 1989 and 1997 on closure, together with the pieces in Roberts, Dunn, and Fowler 1997, are essential; the idea of building character through combination and opposition (e.g. Jugurtha and Marius) is part of the Roman ability to see one person in terms of another, on which, see above all Griffin 1982 and the voluminous subsequent work on characters in Vergil (e.g. Clausen 1987 on Dido). On the metaphor of 'the road', see Krebs 2008. I would have brought the African ethnography into the piece if it were not already too long, as it shows many of the same characteristics that I analyse in the main narrative. Good starting points on it include Green 1993, Oniga 1995, and Woolf 2011.

---

[93] Among the historians present in Scipio's entourage were Polybius (possibly), Rutilius Rufus, and Sempronius Asellio; for them as sources for the *B.J.*, see Syme 1964: 152–5, Paul 1984: 31–2, 34–5. Also present was Lucilius, who wrote about Numantia—through what filter, we cannot tell—in Book XI of his *Satires*; for a full list of those with Scipio, see Brizzi 1990: 865 n. 49. Finally, Aemilius Scaurus, a character in the *B.J.*, did cavalry service in Spain (Paul 1984: 65); he was a contemporary of Rutilius Rufus, and Paul 1984: 35 suggests that 'if suspicions of intrigue at Numantia were current, Scaurus may have touched on them in his auto-biography, if only to attempt to rebut them'. Another almost certainly recalcitrant source with a mind and voice of its own was Sulla's memoir (see n. 74 above).

[94] The *B.J.* already verges on annalistic history (Kraus and Woodman 1997: 21); on the term '*annales*' (with the relevant passages), see Verbrugghe 1989.

10

Sallust's *Jugurtha*

An 'Historical Fragment'

D. S. Levene

The ancient historian is used to dealing with texts that are fragments through the accident of transmission. This paper is concerned with a deliberate fragment: a work that is notionally complete, in that it is written and presented as something finished and whole, but which at the same time draws the reader's attention in a more or less systematic fashion to the fact that it is incomplete; it shows itself to be only part of the whole. The mode was especially popular in the Romantic period; the best-known example for English readers is Coleridge's *Kubla Khan*, but it also revealed itself in such diverse forms as the aphoristic writings of thinkers like Friedrich Schlegel,[1] or the widespread admiration of the ruins of ancient buildings.[2] I intend to argue that Sallust's *Jugurtha* is a work of this sort.

It has always, of course, been obvious that the *Jugurtha* shows an interest, not only in the Jugurthine war itself, but also in the part that it played in the development, or rather, as Sallust saw it, the decline, in

---

Versions of this paper were delivered to meetings in Oxford and to the Classical Association in Warwick, and I should thank those present for their contributions. I should also like to thank Helen DeWitt, Sally Horovitz, Andrew Laird, Raymond Lucas, and Bernard Richards for their help on specific points; and above all Doreen Innes, Chris Pelling, Leighton Reynolds, and the Editorial Committee of *JRS*, for reading and commenting on earlier drafts. I am grateful to Dr Innes also for allowing me to read her lecture notes on the *Jugurtha*.

[1] On the relationship between Schlegel's aphoristic form and his theory of the narrative fragment, see Gockel 1979; Eichner 1970: 47–8.

[2] See McFarland 1981: 25. Compare Schlegel's aphorism: 'Many works of the ancients have become fragments. Many modern works are already so when they are created' (*Athenäums-Fragmente* 25).

Roman political life. It is obvious mainly because Sallust, at several key points in the work, refers back to the events of the past or forward to those of the future, and seeks to relate them to the events of the war. Most of these passages are very well known: the most famous is the long digression at 41–2 on party strife, which sets out the decline from early harmony to the loss of *metus hostilis* after the Punic Wars, which in turn leads to the nobility using arbitrary power, and the struggles with the Gracchi. Likewise, Memmius' speech at 31 continually harks back to the same events, while Marius' speech at 85 does the same more obliquely, by his consistent adverse comparisons between the degeneracy of the contemporary nobility and the virtue of their ancestors. There are also briefer references to the past, for example at 16. 2 and 81. 1.

So too, there are several passages that refer to the still greater degeneration that will occur in the future: this theme lies at the centre of the second half of the preface, and when Marius and Sulla are each introduced, Sallust concludes their character sketches with a sinister reference to their future actions (63. 6 and 95. 4). There is also at 103. 6 a brief hint at the moral decline that is to come. I want to suggest, however, that Sallust's attempt to relate the *Jugurtha* to the wider field of Roman history goes beyond this: that he in various direct and indirect ways plays down the importance of the events of the period, and in the very structure of the work shows it as incomplete. The reader is invited to focus his attention away from the written 'fragment', and instead towards the putative unwritten whole.

I

In the creation of a 'fragment' the end of a work is likely to play a central role. This is because it is above all the end which is able to leave readers with a sense of completeness and satisfaction, so that they go away from the work feeling that it has been properly rounded off. Alternatively, if this sense is lacking, readers may feel that something more needs to be told, and that the work feels in some way incomplete. The study of how works end, the theory of 'closure', has burgeoned in recent years, with much discussion of what elements contribute to 'closure', an impression of completeness, or 'anti-closure', the sense of incompleteness.[3] With

---

[3] The essential modern discussion of closure is Smith 1968; for ancient texts, see above all Fowler 1989, which also has a substantial bibliography.

regard to Sallust, I shall consider most of the relevant factors at the appropriate points, but a couple of preliminary issues should be emphasized. First, it must be stressed that closure is a relative matter: no text can be totally closed, and it is a question of how weak or strong the closural elements are.[4] Second, it is clear that a large number of narrative and dramatic works end with references to the future. This in itself does not substantially diminish the sense of closure. However, when the future referred to is not simply the aftermath of the story, but involves the direct introduction of a substantial and important new topic, this is an anticlosural device—far from finishing, the story seems to be recommencing.[5]

What then of Sallust? The first point to observe is that the *Jugurtha* has no clear climax. The final battle at Cirta (101) is told in fairly vivid terms, and immediately after it Marius is described as 'now indubitably victorious' (102. 1), but it is hardly recounted in the dramatic manner that would emphasize that it forms the conclusion of the whole war. Moreover, after the battle about a tenth of the work is still to come; and this is entirely taken up with a detailed account of the delicate negotiations between Sulla and Bocchus to achieve the capture of Jugurtha. This whole section, too, is curiously muted, and the final betrayal and handing over of the king are described in an extremely low-key and perfunctory manner (113. 4–7). One perhaps feels it appropriate that the work ends with the taking of Jugurtha, given that it is with Jugurtha himself that the narrative began, and given the earlier stress on the importance of capturing him (e.g. 46. 4, 47. 3–4, 61–62). But this thematic closure is at least partly negated by the lack of stylistic closure—Sallust seems to be placing absolutely no emphasis on it.

Moreover, despite superficial appearances, the story of Jugurtha is not entirely completed: unlike, for example, Livy (*Per.* 67) and Plutarch (*Mar.* 12. 4–5), Sallust mentions nothing of his imprisonment and death. Of course, the *Jugurtha* is a monograph about a Roman war, not a biography. However, the Romans saw the death of Jugurtha as something that mattered to the war: at Lucan 9. 600 it is 'breaking the neck of Iugurtha' that is an example of the glorious deeds of the past. Nor are we even told that Jugurtha was led in Marius' triumph, though other writers treat this too as a key part of the victory.[6] To have given such information at the end would not have made the work a biography, but it would have provided a sense of closure comparable to that found in biography.[7]

---

[4] Smith 1968: 211; Fowler 1989: 80.
[5] Torgovnick 1981: 13 calls this a 'tangential ending'. Cf. also Smith 1968: 120.
[6] Prop. 4. 6. 66, Livy *Per.* 67, Val. Max. 6. 9. 14, Plut. *Mar.* 12. 3–4; cf. *CIL* I². 1 p. 195.
[7] See Section V below.

The overall result is that the precise point at which the work ends seems arbitrary—the narrative simply stops rather than being properly rounded off.[8] In short, it appears incomplete. The Jugurthine war's continuity with the events that followed it is brought out, and hence the fact that it forms only part of a much larger sequence.

Let us now turn to the famous last paragraph (114):

> per idem tempus advorsum Gallos ab ducibus nostris Q. Caepione et Cn. Manlio male pugnatum. quo metu Italia omnis contremuerat. illique et inde usque ad nostram memoriam Romani sic habuere, alia omnia virtuti suae prona esse, cum Gallis pro salute, non pro gloria certare. sed postquam bellum in Numidia confectum et Iugurtham Romam vinctum adduci nuntiatum est, Marius consul absens factus est et ei decreta provincia Gallia, isque Kalendis Ianuariis magna gloria consul triumphavit. et ea tempestate spes atque opes civitatis in illo sitae.

> Around the same time our generals Caepio and Manlius fought badly against the Gauls. All Italy was terrified by this; and since then up to recent times the Romans have reckoned that, while everything else was open for their courage, with Gauls one fought for life, not for glory. But after news came that the war in Numidia was over and that Jugurtha was being brought to Rome a prisoner, Marius was made consul in his absence, and was put in charge of Gaul, and he triumphed as consul with great glory on 1 January. And at that time the hopes and resources of the state were placed in him.

Clearly there are elements of closure here. For example, it matters that Sallust ends with the key figure Marius, and with a reminder of the important theme of the relationship between the Roman plebs and its leaders. We can add the penultimate sentence's accumulation of perfects, and the words *bellum* and *Iugurtham* beginning successive cola, perhaps echoing the initial statement of the theme at 5. 1. All of these contribute to the sense that the work is reaching its conclusion.

But against this are other elements that work considerably more powerfully to defeat the impression of closure. No one, I think, can be in much doubt that the last sentence is looking to the future. Sallust ends his work with an ironic contrast between the present, when Marius represents the hope of the state, and the future, when he will bring it close to destruction. It is a reminder that we are, in a sense, still only near the start of the story, and that most of the disasters are still to come. So, too, Sallust only brings his account of the African war to a close with, as it were, a preface to an even more damaging sequence of wars that

---

[8] Cf. Smith 1968: 1–2; Kuzniar 1987: 3.

is to follow. The two references to *gloria* in the passage reinforce this position:[9] the Jugurthine war, in which Marius is triumphing *magna gloria*, is, by implication, one of the lesser wars contrasted with the apparently life-and-death struggles that still lie ahead.[10] The future referred to is not only a new topic, but a significant one: what happens after the end of the work is not just 'another story', without relevance for the themes of the work, but is central to our understanding of them.[11]

It is worth adding that not only does Sallust directly introduce anti-closural devices, but he also avoids some of the most typical elements of closure. For example, there is no reference to any 'standard' closural themes, such as death[12]—indeed, as we have seen, Sallust even fails to mention the death of Jugurtha himself. Nor is the final sentence 'epigrammatic', as Smith defines the term.[13] Fowler is also suggestive: 'There is a tendency for final words to be *important* words, and nouns seem to occur more frequently at points of closure than one would expect from the rules of word-order in ancient languages.'[14] Sallust's last word, *sitae*, is a verbal adjective of no particular importance for the meaning of the sentence: it could be replaced by *erant* without significant loss. The overall effect of the ending is not to round the work off as something completed and whole, but instead to place the emphasis away from what we have seen within the work, and onto what is to come outside it.

II

Hence the end of the *Jugurtha* is set up so as to create the impression that the work is incomplete, and that its most important themes are not resolved within it. But not only the ending, but also other parts of the work contribute to this effect. We can see this from the start, where Sallust sets out his programme (5. 1–2):

> bellum scripturus sum quod populus Romanus cum Iugurtha rege Numidarum gessit, primum quia magnum et atrox variaque victoria fuit, dehinc

---

[9] Scanlon 1987: 61.
[10] It is perhaps also relevant that Sallust refers to Gauls here, when Marius was in fact due to fight the Cimbri, who were Germans. The terminology could be used loosely (Paul 1984: 257); at the same time, the inexactitude serves a purpose, as there was a longer history of Romans fighting Gauls, up to and including Caesar's recent conquest. The end thus refers all the more clearly to the wider pattern of Roman history. The *gloria* contrast also needs Gauls, since only they, and not the Germans, could be plausibly presented as the 'real enemy'.
[11] Cf. Smith 1968: 120.   [12] Cf. ibid. 101–2, 172–82.
[13] Ibid. 196–210.   [14] Ibid. 122 n. 166.

quia tunc primum superbiae nobilitatis obviam itum est; quae contentio divina et humana cuncta permiscuit eoque vecordiae processit ut studiis civilibus bellum atque vastitas Italiae finem faceret.

I am about to write of the war which the Roman people fought with the Numidian king Jugurtha, first because it was a great and terrible war with successes on both sides, secondly because then for the first time the arrogance of the nobility was opposed; this struggle threw in confusion all things, human and divine, and went to such a point of lunacy that it took war and the destruction of Italy to put an end to the civil strife.

Sallust here provides two reasons for his selection of the Jugurthine war as a topic, the first the significance of the war in itself, the second its importance for future events. The striking thing here is the relative emphasis given to the different reasons. The first, by the standards of such programmatic statements, is somewhat muted, making no reference at all to the uniqueness or unprecedented greatness of the subject.[15] The comparable statement in the *Catiline* is more typical;[16] we can see the theme originally in Thucydides, who spends a lot of time proving the point, and who is often cited as Sallust's chief model.[17] Other similar statements appear, for example, in Polybius 1. 1-2, or later in Livy *Praef.* 11, 21. 1. 1-2,[18] 31. 1. 7, and Tacitus *Hist.* 1. 2-3. True, Tacitus eschews the theme in the *Annals*, doubtless because he wished to show Rome as having declined from its glorious past, and hence not at all providing grand and magnificent subject matter; but it may also be worth noting that the preface to the *Annals* shows clear Sallustian influence.[19] All of this serves to emphasize how little Sallust is making of the Jugurthine war—indeed, even Florus' brief summary of Roman history makes more of it.[20]

Not only is Sallust's first reason played down in itself, but it is also overshadowed by the prominence given to the second reason. True, it is given second, but it is allotted rather more space, and, moreover,

---

[15] On the theme in general, cf. Herkommer 1968: 164-71.

[16] *Cat.* 4. 4: 'That crime I consider among the most memorable because the evil and the danger were unprecedented.' Cf. *Cat.* 36. 4: 'At that time the Roman empire seemed to me far and away at its most wretched.'

[17] Thuc. e.g. 1. 1. 1-2, 1. 21. 2, 1. 23. 1. On Thucydides as a model for Sallust in general, see Perrochat 1949: ch. 1; Scanlon 1980.

[18] Note in particular Livy 21. 1. 1: 'I can begin a part of my work by saying what most historians have proclaimed at the start of the whole: that I am about to describe the war that is the most memorable of all that have ever been fought.' Livy clearly regards this way of introducing one's story as standard to the point of cliché.

[19] Woodman 1988b: 167-8.

[20] Flor. 1. 36. 2: 'And in Jugurtha the Romans had the one thing that was to be feared after Hannibal.'

describes the future in such extravagant terms as to accentuate still further the contrast with the actual subject of his monograph—it is all, Sallust implies, relatively unimportant compared with what it led to. Once again, we are pointed beyond the boundaries of the work itself.

The same conclusion may be drawn if we examine the passage in its context. It comes at the end of the philosophical preface, which falls into two distinct parts.[21] The first part (1-2) examines the question of what counts as virtue; the second (3-4) is a defence of the writing of history as the activity that gives the most scope to the moral man. The only reason that Sallust gives for this—and he gives it at some length—is that his Roman contemporaries are so degenerate that political activity does more harm than good. In fact, he rather paradoxically suggests (4. 7), they are so degenerate that even the study of history does them no good, unlike their ancestors, who were inspired to virtue by the glorious deeds of their own ancestors. The paradox is especially striking: after all, usually the moral point of history was thought to be precisely its capacity for improving its readers.[22] All of this serves to set up the following sequence of thought: we see a moral theme in the abstract, and then are led to apply that theme initially to historiography as an occupation, but more centrally to the specific case of Rome, which is shown to be in a state of terminal decline—the preface to the *Jugurtha*, unlike that to the *Catiline*, does confine itself entirely to specifically Roman examples. At the end of this we find the programmatic statement discussed above; we see it now against the background of a large-scale Roman decline, and we are prepared for the idea that the important thing about the Jugurthine war is the way in which it relates to that past and future decline.

Next, where does Sallust place his major discussion of earlier events? Not at the start, but in the centre, at 41-2. This highlights its importance: it now serves as a climax to the whole of the first part of the work. Equally, it is now taken to refer to something beyond the boundaries of the monograph. Had it stood at the start, the natural way of reading it would have been as part of the war itself: in effect, the reader would have felt that the work began with the beginning of Rome, but dealt with the period up to the Jugurthine war very rapidly—compare the opening of

---

[21] I assume here what is still occasionally denied: that the preface is not intended to be unrelated to the narrative, but is there to govern the way in which we are to read the work. For various defences of this position, see Egermann 1932: 16-23; Rambaud 1946; La Penna 1968: 16-18. Earl 1961: chs. 1 and 3-5 shows more generally the continuity of ideas between the preface and the body of the work.

[22] Leeman 1955: 46-7; Lefèvre 1979: 257-8.

Tacitus' *Annals*.[23] By holding it up so long, Sallust ensures that the boundaries of the work are established essentially as those of the war, and hence that this passage is seen as looking beyond those boundaries. It also means that the many references to these same events in Memmius' speech (31) are themselves seen as looking outside the work—at that point Sallust has not had his account of the past at all. Once again, it is made clear that the monograph is not self-sufficient.

It may be objected that most of the events being referred to in the digression and by Memmius are technically contemporary with the early life of Jugurtha. Sallust, however, obscures this fact. The only point where Jugurtha's early career touches Rome is with the Numantine war and Scipio Aemilianus, and neither is mentioned in the historical digression or indeed anywhere else (apart from a few brief references back to Jugurtha's service). Moreover, and more significantly, Sallust telescopes his chronology at the start, and makes it appear that only a short time elapses between Jugurtha's return from Numantia and Micipsa's death (in fact it was at least fourteen years). After his return, Micipsa 'immediately...adopted him' (9. 3); then Micipsa dies 'a few years later' (9. 4), referring on his deathbed to Jugurtha 'recently returning from Numantia' (10. 2). Then Hiempsal says that Jugurtha 'within the last three years was adopted into the ruling household' (11. 6).[24] So too Sallust in 20. 1 fails to mention the four- or five-year gap between the division of Numidia at the beginning of the sentence and the attack on Adherbal at the end.[25] The overall result is that Jugurtha's link with Rome is presented as having come relatively shortly before the beginning of the Jugurthine war, and, correspondingly, the historical digressions appear to refer to events outside the temporal boundaries of the work.

Not only the position of the central digression, but also its ending is significant (42. 5):

> sed de studiis partium et omnis civitatis moribus si singillatim aut pro magnitudine parem disserere, tempus quam res maturius me deseret; quam ob rem ad inceptum redeo.
>
> But if I were to discuss episodes of party strife and the behaviour of the whole state individually or in proportion to their importance, I should run out of time before running out of material. So I return to my task.

---

[23] There is, of course, a little historical background at the start (*Jug.* 5. 4–7), but it is very brief, and moreover focuses closely on providing the information necessary for us to understand the personal background of Jugurtha, with whom the narrative begins.

[24] See Fritz 1943: 140–2; also Paul 1984: 40–2, though his attempt to save Sallust's historicity is implausible.

[25] Koestermann 1971: 97.

The first thing to observe is that, as before, Sallust is here emphasizing the importance of what lies outside the work, by suggesting that it is that very importance that makes it impossible to treat; the work itself, which is manifestly tractable, is implicitly diminished. But, more generally, this is an example of another technique that Sallust uses at several points in the *Jugurtha*: the direct indication that there is more to be said, about which he is however silent. It is, of course, a standard topos, related to the so-called *praeteritio*;[26] but Sallust employs it to a surprising degree and at key moments of his narrative. We see this in his digression on Africa (17–19): when he reaches the subject of Carthage, all he says is *nam de Carthagine silere melius puto quam parum dicere, quoniam alio properare tempus monet* ('for concerning Carthage I feel it is better to be silent than to say too little, since time warns me to hurry elsewhere'). Carthage is significant for Sallust, as it is the defeat of Carthage which led to the loss of the *metus hostilis* and Roman decline (41. 2–3), and moreover the Punic Wars and the Carthaginians provide a lot of his examples of heroic figures of the past (4. 5, 5. 4, 14. 5, 14. 8–10, 42. 1, 79), with whom the degenerates of the present are to be contrasted. Yet here he declines to discuss it directly, again pointing to an important and relevant matter that his work does not cover.[27] A similar thought, though less directly stated, may be seen with Memmius' speech, where both before it and after it Sallust stresses that it was only one example of many such speeches:

> sed quoniam ea tempestate Romae Memmi facundia clara pollensque fuit, decere existumavi unam ex tam multis orationem eius perscribere, et potissumum ea dicam quae in contione post reditum Bestiae huiusce modi verbis disseruit. (30. 4)

> But since at that time at Rome the eloquence of Memmius was famous and influential, I have thought it appropriate to write out one speech out of so many, and I should say that the most suitable are the things which he discussed at a meeting after the return of Bestia, speaking in the following manner.

> haec atque alia huiusce modi saepe dicundo Memmius populo persuadet.
> (32. 1)

> By often saying these and other things of this sort Memmius persuaded the people.

---

[26] We may compare the topos of 'more later', which similarly draws attention to the fact that there are topics not covered by the current work. Cf. Macleod 1974: 294; Woodman 1977: 108; also Woodman 1975: 287, who refers to this as a 'conventional method of relegating or omitting material that is unwanted for one reason or another.'

[27] Cf. Scanlon 1988: 141–3.

Jugurtha: *An 'Historical Fragment'*

There is little significance in the phrase *huiusce modi* alone—Sallust regularly introduces his speeches like this.[28] Here, however, and only here, it is combined with a substantial indication that it is not only that Sallust is paraphrasing, but also that he is selecting only one of many possibilities, and that, once again, the rest remains unsaid. Admittedly, unlike the other cases that we have been discussing, the material that is said to be missing here does not lie outside the boundaries of the *Jugurtha* in time, but this difference is only a superficial one, for, as I said earlier, the theme of this speech, and hence by implication of the other speeches to which Sallust refers, is the Roman degeneration that lies at the heart of Sallust's presentation of his overall historical theme. In each of these cases Sallust indicates the restrictions of his own work, and points out that he is failing to cover various topics fully—and not just any topics, but the very ones that are central to his work. The reader might have thought that a two-page digression on party strife was enough, but no, Sallust tells us: he has only scratched the theme's surface.

But most important of all is the final passage where Sallust directly indicates that his work is incomplete: his account of the character of Sulla (95. 2–4):

> sed quoniam nos tanti viri res admonuit, idoneum visum est de natura cultuque eius paucis dicere; neque enim alio loco de Sullae rebus dicturi sumus et L. Sisenna, optume et diligentissume omnium qui eas res dixere persecutus, parum mihi libero ore locutus videtur. igitur Sulla gentis patriciae nobilis fuit, familia prope iam extincta maiorum ignavia, litteris Graecis atque Latinis iuxta eruditus, animo ingenti, cupidus voluptatum sed gloriae cupidior; otio luxurioso esse, tamen ab negotiis numquam voluptas remorata; ... nisi quod de uxore potuit honestius consuli; facundus, callidus et amicitia facilis, ad simulanda ac dissimulanda negotia altitudo ingeni incredibilis, multarum rerum ac maxume pecuniae largitor. atque illi felicissumo omnium ante civilem victoriam numquam super industriam fortuna fuit, multique dubitavere fortior an felicior esset; nam postea quae fecerit, incertum habeo pudeat an pigeat magis disserere.

> But since the subject brings us to such a great man, it seems appropriate to speak briefly about his qualities and trappings. For I am not going to speak about Sulla's career elsewhere, and Sisenna, the best and most careful of all those who have covered this, seems to me to write too circumspectly. So Sulla was a noble of a patrician clan, but his family had been almost wiped out by his ancestors' sloth; he was equally learned in Greek and Latin literature, was eager for pleasure, still more so for glory; he spent his leisure in luxury, but

---

[28] So too Thucydides usually introduces speeches with τοιάδε: cf. Hornblower 1987: 53–4.

pleasure never kept him from business... except that he could have behaved more honourably concerning his wife; he was eloquent, clever, and ready in friendship; for invention and deception his mind was unbelievably deep; he was generous with lots of things, especially money. And his supreme luck was matched by his energy until his victory in civil war, and many have been unsure whether he was luckier or braver. I am not sure whether I would be more ashamed or sickened to discuss what he did afterwards.

In this passage Sallust explicitly says that he is not going to discuss Sulla elsewhere: this worries some people,[29] who point out that in fact Sallust did spend a substantial amount of time discussing Sulla in his *Histories*,[30] and they are led to deduce that at the time when he wrote this he had not yet planned the later work. But it seems more fruitful to suggest that this says nothing one way or the other about the author's career plan as a historian, and that the point is rather to indicate yet again the incomplete nature of the current work, and so to make it clear that this whole passage refers to something that lies outside it. Its very brevity reinforces this: the rather oblique reference, for example, to Sulla's wife, a reference which, even taking the possible lacuna into account,[31] is somewhat obscure, since Sulla was married five times, and there were suggestions in antiquity that in different ways he behaved badly to at least the last three of his wives.[32] Once again, the limitations of the monograph are stressed.

Similar is the final sentence, where Sallust hints darkly at Sulla's evil deeds after he achieved sole power. Manifestly, he had in fact no moral objections to recounting them more fully: he had already given such an account at *Catiline* 11. 4–8, and it looks as if he went on to give a still longer one in the *Histories*.[33] Rather, we can see the reasons for this statement as twofold: first, by treating the nadir as something too awful for description, it shows us the depths to which in the future the Romans will sink; at the same time, it shows that future as something that the work will not cover.

---

[29] e.g. Syme 1964: 177; Koestermann 1971: 33–4, 339.

[30] *Hist.* 1. 24–53, 58–61 M.

[31] There are probably no more than a couple of words missing: Shackleton-Bailey 1981: 355–6 suggests *erga suos humanus*.

[32] Plut. *Sull.* 6 and 35–6; cf. Sall. *Hist.* 1. 60–1 M. Paul 1984: 236 claims that *uxore* is a 'generic' singular, and hence means 'wives'. This looks like wishful thinking; such a generic singular in such a context would be unparalleled in classical Latin. It is especially improbable in an author who only very rarely uses generic singulars in any context (*LHS*: 13).

[33] No fewer than twenty of the surviving fragments of the *Histories* (1. 32–51) cover the last stages of the Civil War and Sulla's dictatorship. Cf. the attack on Sulla's dictatorship in Lepidus' speech (1. 55 M), and also Augustine *De civ. D.* 2. 18, 'Sallust then says more about the vices of Sulla,' and 2. 22, 'Who would not shudder when reading Sallust's account of the life, morals, and deeds of Sulla?'

III

I have thus shown that there are various passages in the *Jugurtha* that together create the cumulative impression that it is a 'fragment'. I now intend to argue that its overall narrative structure points to the same conclusion. In particular, I shall examine how the leading characters, Jugurtha, Metellus, Marius, and Sulla, fit into the work. Sallust's attitude to these has been much discussed: which does he support, and to which is he opposed, and how does this fit his general political views? Perhaps the analysis that I shall now establish can help resolve this vexed question: I shall argue that the chief object in Sallust's portrayal of these four characters is to show them linked to one another in a single chain of personal and general moral degeneration.

I showed above that the philosophical preface was so set up as to give us a moral theme in general, then to show the decline of Rome as a specific instance of that general theme, and finally to set the work against that background of Roman decline. Directly after this, we are introduced to Jugurtha, whose character is sketched as follows (6. 1):

> qui ubi primum adolevit, pollens viribus, decora facie, sed multo maxume ingenio validus, non se luxu neque inertiae conrumpendum dedit, sed, uti mos gentis illius est, equitare iaculari, cursu cum aequalibus certare, et quom omnis gloria anteiret, omnibus tamen carus esse... plurumum facere, minumum ipse de se loqui.

> When he first grew up, he was strong, handsome, but above all powerful of mind; he did not give himself to be corrupted by luxury or sloth, but, in the manner of his people, to the horse and the javelin; he competed at running with his contemporaries, and although he surpassed them all in glory, they all loved him... He did much, and spoke little of himself.

This is, clearly, an entirely favourable assessment: in particular, luxury and sloth are precisely the areas that in the preface Sallust has identified most closely with vicious behaviour and decline.[34] It is true that this passage is followed by an account of Micipsa's fears that Jugurtha will usurp his throne (6. 2–3), but, in context, these fears must appear unjustified:[35] there is nothing in what we have been told about Jugurtha's

---

[34] Paul 1984: 29.
[35] This is denied by Vretska 1955: 29–30, who regards Micipsa's fears as Sallust's indirect characterization of Jugurtha. However, Vretska relies on the false assumption that the ancients could not conceive of a genuinely changing character, and hence that Sallust must be presenting Jugurtha as vicious from the start; against this, see Gill 1983. Moreover, to attribute Micipsa's views uncritically to the author is to overlook the implicit irony: not

character to make one think of him in such terms. Micipsa then sends Jugurtha to fight alongside the Romans in Spain, in the hope that he will be killed in battle (7. 2), but instead Jugurtha covers himself with glory, and we are once again given an entirely favourable account of his character (7. 3–7):

> nam Iugurtha, ut erat inpigro atque acri ingenio, ubi naturam P. Scipionis, qui tum Romanis imperator erat, et morem hostium cognovit, multo labore multaque cura, praeterea modestissume parendo et saepe obviam eundo periculis in tantam claritudinem brevi pervenerat ut nostris vehementer carus, Numantinis maxumo terrori esset. ac sane, quod difficillumum in primis est, in proelio strenuus erat et bonus consilio...huc adcedebat munificentia animi et ingeni sollertia, quis rebus sibi multos ex Romanis familiari amicitia coniunxerat.
>
> Jugurtha's mind was tireless and keen, and so, when he got to know the character of Scipio (who was then the Roman general) and the behaviour of the enemy, by his hard work and diligence, by his sensible obedience and willingness to go into danger, soon became so famous that he was greatly loved by the Romans and feared by the Numantians. Indeed, he was that most rare thing: a doughty fighter and shrewd counsellor...In addition, he was generous of heart and highly intelligent, and hence became close friends with many Romans.

Still, there is plainly nothing here for Micipsa to be worrying about, and this provides confirmation that we were meant to see those earlier fears of his as unreasonable. Jugurtha is quite the paragon. But now the crunch comes (8. 1):

> ea tempestate in exercitu nostro fuere complures novi atque nobiles quibus divitiae bono honestoque potiores erant, factiosi domi, potentes apud socios, clari magis quam honesti, qui Iugurthae non mediocrem animum pollicitando adcendebant: si Micipsa rex occidisset, fore uti solus imperi Numidiae potiretur: in ipso maxumam virtutem, Romae omnia venalia esse.
>
> At that time there were in the Roman army many parvenus and nobles, for whom wealth counted for more than goodness or honour, who were factious at Rome, powerful among the allies, and famous rather than honourable; they fired Jugurtha's high spirits by promising that if King Micipsa died, he would gain sole power in Numidia; that he was a man of the highest qualities, and that at Rome everything was for sale.

So Micipsa's fears were justified after all—but for the wrong reason! Indeed, we might even say that it was his own fault. This whole passage

---

only do his ideas conflict with the tenor of the context, but at the same moment as he fears treachery in another, he is displaying it in himself (6. 3–7. 2).

is set up so as to make it clear that until now Jugurtha has been free from vice; but now he has been corrupted, and, most important of all, the corruption has come from Rome. From here on, although Sallust always recognizes Jugurtha's fine qualities of mind and body, he consistently shows these as overshadowed by his vices, and above all by the bribery and treachery that were taught to him here by his Roman friends. Sallust shows us in these opening sections the corruption of Jugurtha; and he does so directly after his presentation, first of the theme of virtue versus vice in the abstract, and then of the corruption of Rome as a whole, which is the key example of this. With Jugurtha we see the same theme focused still more narrowly: we have here the paradigm of the corruption and decline of a perfect individual, to match the corruption and decline of the perfect state. The state's corruption leads to the individual's corruption, and the latter then feeds back into the state by corrupting it still further. Moreover, Sallust never tells us the names of those who corrupted Jugurtha: this adds to the impression that it is a general malaise at Rome that is at fault, rather than particular individuals.

Let us now turn to Metellus. He is introduced in the following manner:

> Metelloque Numidia evenerat, acri viro et, quamquam advorso populi partium, fama tamen aequabili et inviolata. (43. 1)
>
> Numidia fell to Metellus, a keen man and, despite being opposed to the popular factions, universally seen as of unblemished reputation.
>
> in Numidiam proficiscitur, magna spe civium quom propter artis bonas tum maxume quod advorsum divitias invictum animum gerebat et avaritia magistratuum ante id tempus in Numidia nostrae opes contusae hostiumque auctae erant. (43. 5)
>
> He set off for Numidia; the people had great hopes in him because, along with his other fine qualities, his mind was firmly unconquered by wealth—because of official greed up to that time our forces in Numidia had been weakened and those of the enemy strengthened.

Metellus comes out of this looking nearly perfect. Unlike in the portrait of Jugurtha, Sallust has provided one discordant note in the reference to his hostility to the popular cause: this comes directly after the digression on party strife, and hence surely indicates a major flaw.[36] Nevertheless, he is respected even by his opponents, and his manifest incorruptibility is the area on which Sallust places the greatest stress—after all, bribery has so far been the chief cause of the Roman failure.

---

[36] Vretska 1955: 94–5 claims, somewhat perversely, that the fact that Metellus is said to be hostile to *populi partium*, not *populi*, shows that he is free of party strife, and hence that he is being praised here; but see Steidle 1958: 67–8.

The subsequent narrative confirms this favourable assessment. Metellus restores the discipline and morale of the army (44–5), and in the course of this Sallust again praises his virtue (45. 1):

> sed in ea difficultate Metellum nec minus quam in rebus hostilibus magnum et sapientem virum fuisse conperior: tanta temperantia inter ambitionem saevitiamque moderatum.
>
> But I reckon that in that difficulty Metellus showed himself as great and wise as he was in battle: he kept his course between ambition and harshness with such good sense.

And directly after this he refers to his *innocentia* (46. 1); and then shows his relative success against Jugurtha, first in battle, and then, when it becomes clear that this alone will not finish the war, in stratagems to persuade Jugurtha to surrender.

We do, however, begin to see some small disquieting features in Sallust's presentation. He twice directly compares Metellus to Jugurtha, first at 48. 1, where Jugurtha, seeing Metellus' trickery, *se suis artibus temptari animadvortit* ('realized that he was being assailed with his own devices'), and secondly at 52. 1:

> eo modo inter se duo imperatores, summi viri, certabant, ipsi pares, ceterum opibus disparibus.
>
> Thus, two great commanders were competing, personally matched, but unequal in resources.

This second passage invites us to see Metellus and Jugurtha as matched; apparently favourably, but 48. 1 has already shown us a negative side to their similarity. And a comparable point emerges more subtly later on (61. 3):

> neque id tempus ex aliorum more quieti aut luxuriae concedit, sed, quoniam armis bellum parum procedebat, insidias regi per amicos tendere et eorum perfidia pro armis uti parat.
>
> Nor did he spend that time, as others do, in rest and luxury, but instead, since the war was going too slowly on the military front, made ready to plot against the king through his friends, and to use their treachery rather than weapons.

Metellus, as before, shows himself incorruptible, but in abandoning straight warfare for treacherous devices, he once again seems uncomfortably close to Jugurtha in behaviour.[37]

---

[37] Koestermann 1971: 189.

So far these hints of problems with Metellus have only represented very minor features of an almost entirely favourable account; but after the introduction of Marius it is quite another story. The hatred of the commons which we were told about when he was introduced now becomes the dominant trait of his character, as he does everything in his power to prevent Marius becoming consul. 64. 1 reminds us of the initial character sketch:

> quoi quamquam virtus, gloria atque alia optanda bonis superabant, tamen inerat contemptor animus et superbia, commune nobilitatis malum.
>
> Though he surpassed the upper classes in virtue, glory and other good qualities, he had a sneering mind and arrogance, the usual fault of nobles.

There is no indication in Sallust that Metellus' dislike of Marius is anything other than class hatred; we may contrast Plutarch, who says (*Mar.* 4) that Metellus had originally been Marius' patron, and had been betrayed by him. Plutarch also says (*Mar.* 8) that he hated Marius because he had arranged the death of Turpilius, who in Plutarch's version was Metellus' client. In Sallust Turpilius is executed by Metellus himself (69. 4).[38] All of this demonstrates that Sallust is here showing Metellus in a bad light, attributing his hostility to Marius entirely to his class arrogance.[39] Indeed, for the whole of this section it is this arrogance that we see to the fore; and similarly, when at 82. 2-3 Marius is elected, and is given the command, Metellus responds extremely badly (82. 2-3):

> quibus rebus supra bonum aut honestum perculsus neque lacrumas tenere neque moderari linguam, vir egregius in aliis artibus nimis molliter aegritudinem pati. quam rem alii in superbiam vortebant, alii bonum ingenium contumelia adcensum esse, multi quod iam parta victoria ex manibus eriperetur: nobis satis cognitum est illum magis honore Mari quam iniuria sua excruciatum neque tam anxie laturum fuisse si adempta provincia alii quam Mario traderetur.
>
> He was overcome by this far more than is good or honourable; he couldn't restrain his tears or control his tongue; though a fine man in other respects he bore grief too effeminately. Some reckoned this was arrogance, others that it was that his noble mind was inflamed by the insults; many said it was because he had all but won the victory, and it was being snatched from his grasp. But I am pretty sure that he was more tormented by Marius' honour than by his own wrongs—he would not have been so worried if he had lost the province and it had gone to anyone except Marius.

---

[38] Though, unlike Plutarch, Sallust does not suggest that Turpilius was really innocent, and he has earlier harshly criticized him for his escape (67. 3).

[39] Lefèvre 1979: 266-8.

Though Sallust still tells us that he was *vir egregius in aliis artibus*, it is clear from this passage that Metellus' faults now go beyond mere upper-class arrogance. The moderation that was praised earlier has now vanished; moreover, the phrase *nimis molliter* is significant, as it carries overtones of the *luxuria* that Metellus has previously resisted.[40] The final explanation that Sallust gives us for his reaction should also be noted: to resent wrongs done to oneself might be quite acceptable in Roman eyes, but to grudge honour to someone else was *invidere*.[41] It is significant that this is the explanation behind which Sallust places his own authority, and hence the one that the reader is encouraged to find most plausible. Moreover, the growth of vice in Metellus also affects his conduct of the war. In 83 he decides that it is not worth going on, and instead wastes time in a long correspondence with Bocchus; the section ends with the phrase *ex Metelli voluntate bellum intactum trahi* ('it was deliberate on Metellus' part that the war dragged on with nothing done', 83. 3). This was more or less the state in which the previous commanders had left things when Metellus took over. True, when he returns home at 88. 1, he finds his popularity restored, but there is no indication that his character has been restored with it.

So the picture of Metellus is comparable to that of Jugurtha: an originally noble figure, but one who falls into vice. The reasons are, of course, different, but the pattern is the same; the similarity is reinforced by the earlier comparisons between them, and also the fact that, in each case, it is the decline of Rome as a whole that is a major cause of the decline of the individual, for Metellus' arrogance, as we have seen, is presented as the fault of his whole class. That this is Sallust's aim in his portrait of Metellus may perhaps be seen also from a striking omission. We have seen that at various points in the monograph he looks forward to the future. Nowhere, however, does he even hint at what was far and away the most famous event in the life of Metellus, even surpassing his actions here: his later opposition to Saturninus (and, in most versions, Marius), and his consequent exile. This is invariably treated as an example of the highest virtue; Cicero alone refers to it as such numerous times (especially, unsurprisingly, in the *post reditum* speeches, because of the obvious parallels that he wished to draw with his own exile).[42] But for

---

[40] Cf. e.g. *Cat.* 11. 5: *loca amoena, voluptaria facile in otio ferocis militum animos molliverant*.

[41] Cf. Cicero *Tusc*. 4. 16: *invidentiam esse dicunt aegritudinem susceptam propter alterius res secundas, quae nihil noceant invidenti*.

[42] Cic., *Red. sen.* 25; *Red. pop.* 9; *Dom.* 82; *Sest.* 37, 130; *Pis.* 20; *Balb.* 11; *Planc.* 89. Also Vell. Pat. 2. 15. 3–4; Val. Max. 3. 8. 4; Sen., *Ep.* 24. 4; Flor. 2. 4. 3; Plut. *Mar.* 28–9; App. *B Civ.* 1. 29–32.

Sallust even to mention such a future would spoil the schematic nature of his account: he would have to admit directly that his character's greatest moment was later than the decline we have seen here.

Marius is the next major character to be introduced, and, like Jugurtha and Metellus before him, he is given a character sketch (63. 1–2):

> per idem tempus Uticae forte C. Mario per hostias dis supplicanti magna atque mirabilia portendi haruspex dixerat: proinde quae animo agitabat fretus dis ageret, fortunam quam saepissume experiretur; cuncta prospere eventura. at illum iam antea consulatus ingens cupido exagitabat, ad quem capiundum praeter vetustatem familiae alia omnia abunde erant: industria, probitas, militiae magna scientia, animus belli ingens domi modicus, lubidinis et divitiarum victor, tantummodo gloriae avidus.

> Around the same time by chance while Marius was sacrificing to the gods at Utica a soothsayer had informed him of a great and remarkable future: henceforth he should rely on the gods and do what he was thinking over; he should try his luck as often as he could—everything was going to turn out well. He had already greatly desired the consulship, and had every quality for it except an ancient lineage: diligence, honesty, great knowledge of warfare, a mind powerful in war and moderate in peace, unaffected by pleasure and wealth, eager only for glory.

And the passage later contains the following comment (63. 6):

> tamen is ad id locorum talis vir—nam postea ambitione praeceps datus est—consulatum adpetere non audebat.

> But he, though so virtuous up to then—for later he was destroyed by ambition—did not dare to seek a consulship.

This, once again, is a largely favourable portrait. A couple of points in it, however, should give us pause. It is ambition that is said to be the cause of Marius' ultimate downfall, and the seeds of his ambition are implicit right through the passage. Moreover, we will perhaps recall that Sallust centres the first part of the preface on an attack on those who rely on fortune rather than on virtue; and, of course, that is precisely the position that Marius decides to adopt here.[43]

We have already seen Metellus' response to Marius' ambitions. Now let us see how Marius reacts to that (64. 4–5):

> quae res Marium quom pro honore quem adfectabat tum contra Metellum vehementer adcenderat. ita cupidine atque ira, pessumis consultoribus, grassari; neque facto ullo neque dicto abstinere, quod modo ambitiosum foret.

---

[43] Scanlon 1987: 55–7.

This violently fired Marius both for the office he desired and against Metellus. So he raged with desire and anger, the worst possible advisers; and he left out no word or deed that fostered his ambition.

Sallust then describes how Marius gives full rein to his *ambitio*, intriguing against Metellus in the army (64. 5-65. 5). And when he reaches Rome, he throws himself fully into the class strife (84)—note especially the first part (84. 1):

> antea iam infestus nobilitati, tum vero multus atque ferox instare, singulos modo, modo universos laedere, dictitare sese consulatum ex victis illis spolia cepisse, alia praeterea magnifica pro se et illis dolentia.
>
> He was already hostile to the nobles, but now attacked them with the greatest violence; he assailed them individually and en masse; he said that he had won his consulship as spoils from them, and said other things to glorify himself and upset them.

This is far more violent even than his speech that follows in 85—I shall discuss the significance of this shortly. For the moment, we can see how Marius has been drawn into class hatred: before, he was hostile only to Metellus as an individual; now he hates all the nobility. It may be added that, just as with Jugurtha and Metellus, it is the corruption of the city as a whole which is a substantial cause of Marius' behaviour here—Sallust has consistently made it clear that what he does is closely related to the overall class struggle at Rome, as the nobles attempt to keep a *novus homo* from office.

In war, of course, Marius' virtues are still dominant, and it is true that most of his battles come later; but it is worth observing the way in which Sallust describes his capture of the Muluccha fort (92-94). He consistently refers to the victory coming *forte* or through *fortuna* ('by chance'), thus turning the disquieting point from the soothsayer's prediction into a dominant trait. Two passages in particular should be mentioned:

> at Marius multis diebus et laboribus consumptis anxius trahere cum animo suo omitteretne inceptum, quoniam frustra erat, an fortunam opperiretur, qua saepe prospere usus fuerat. (93. 1)
>
> But Marius spent much time and effort debating internally whether he should give up the attempt, since it was useless, or to wait for luck, which he had often favoured him.

> sic forte correcta Mari temeritas gloriam ex culpa invenit. (94. 7)
>
> Thus, Marius' rashness was put right by chance, and he found glory out of his wrongdoing.

Jugurtha: An 'Historical Fragment'

The first reminds us that Marius now regularly relies on fortune; the second that he did not deserve his victory, and that reliance on chance, as we were told at the start, is not compatible with reliance on virtue.

Directly after this we come to Sulla (95. 2–4, quoted on pp. 281–2 above). This is again by and large a favourable portrait; but, by comparison with those of Jugurtha, Metellus, and Marius, the disquieting elements have multiplied. Sulla is marked by both *luxuria* and *voluptas*, though he does not usually let them interfere with his business; he is attractive, intelligent, energetic, and generous, but deceitful. And, of course, there is his most famous quality of all, his *felicitas*, which Sallust here explicitly identifies with *fortuna* ('luck')—the very quality which he criticized in his preface, and on which we have just seen Marius placing an excessive reliance.[44] And what then? Does Sulla decline, like his predecessors? Certainly he does—we are told so in this very passage. But nothing of this decline is seen within the work.

Let us put all of this together. We are shown across the work four major figures. In each case, there are general elements of syncrisis between each character and his predecessor that invite us to examine the one character in the light of the other.[45] When we make the comparison, we find that each of the four is relatively good at the start, but each at the same time is from the start less good than his predecessor. Each is in his own way in decline, and in each of the last three cases an initial element of the decline is picked up from his predecessor: thus Metellus employs the treachery and double-dealing of Jugurtha, Marius the factionalizing of Metellus, and Sulla the reliance on fortune of Marius. There is through the whole work a chain of individual corruption which is linked to and which matches the corruption of Rome as a whole which I discussed at the start. But whereas with Jugurtha and Metellus the pattern is completed, and we see each of them reach bottom, with Marius and Sulla we are told from the start that the pattern will remain incomplete, and their decline will continue beyond the end of the work; and indeed Sulla's decline never begins in the monograph at all. So here too the 'fragment' lies at the heart of Sallust's structure: he prepares the way, and sets up our expectations, but makes us aware that he is never going to fulfil them.

---

[44] The juxtaposition of Marius' *fortuna* with Sulla is observed by Avery 1967; however, he does not examine it in the light of Sallust's earlier discussion of *fortuna*, and so misses its significance.

[45] In addition to what I have discussed above, on the Metellus/Marius comparison, see Scanlon 1987: 53–5, 58, and 1988: 144–51, 153–61; on Marius/Sulla, see Scanlon 1987: 57–8 and 1988: 151–3.

IV

I now want to look at a different area. There is one rather unusual feature of the *Jugurtha* that commentators have made very little out of: its lack of dialectic. No one argues in the *Jugurtha*. There are no paired speeches, except for the brief negotiations and exchange of compliments between Sulla and Bocchus at the end. Nor are there even any speeches that are implicitly paired, for instance by presenting different views on comparable situations. There are three major speeches: one by Adherbal at 14, one by Memmius at 31, one by Marius at 85. Each analyses the state of Rome in terms of virtue and vice and corruption and decline in almost exactly the way that Sallust does when he is speaking with his own voice, for example in the preface or the digression on party strife. Not that we take any of the speakers entirely at face value.[46] Adherbal is weak and self-pitying, Memmius and Marius violent in class hatred, and Marius is boastful and overconfident to boot; and in each case these qualities come across in the speech. But in none of the cases does this affect the substance of their central analysis.[47] The same thing applies to the shorter speeches: not a single one offers a different view of the basic situation. On the rare occasion that an alternative view is put forward, as, for example, with the reply of Jugurtha's envoys to Adherbal at 15. 1, it is kept extremely brief and placed in indirect speech: Sallust reports in summary that this is what the characters say, but we can hardly see it as challenging the substantial and lengthy arguments of the author and his spokesmen. We have even seen this happening with Marius: his most violent expressions of class hatred are reserved for a brief account in indirect speech, and are excluded from his speech proper.

Jugurtha himself provides a particularly interesting example of this. He has a couple of short statements in indirect speech, but never any opportunity to put across his case in his own words. At 33. 4 Memmius invites him to reply to the charges against him, but when at 34. 1 he is about to do so, he is kept from speaking by the corrupt tribune Baebius. Only once in the whole work are we given Jugurtha's words in direct speech (35. 10):

> sed postquam Roma egressus est, fertur saepe eo tacitus respiciens postremo dixisse: 'urbem venalem et mature perituram, si emptorem invenerit.'

---

[46] Büchner 1982: 202–4.
[47] Paul 1984: 99 observes that the language of Memmius' speech is rather more violent than the actual positions set out in it would seem to warrant.

But after he had left Rome, he is said to have often looked back at it in silence and finally to have said: 'A city for sale and soon about to perish, if it finds a buyer.'

This is quoted by others, and is clearly a famous phrase, though it must be possible that it was Sallust who made it so, since the other sources for it[48] are all later. More to the point is that it too supports Sallust's analysis of Rome: everything in his account has led us to believe that the city is indeed corrupt and rushing to its destruction.[49] Thus, on the one occasion on which Jugurtha speaks, he too shows himself as a spokesman for the Sallustian viewpoint.

This absence of dialectic may seem at first sight to work against the establishment of a 'fragment'. Avoiding closure at the end of a work, while perhaps not essential to create a 'fragment', is, as I said above, in practice likely to form a major part of it. Theorists of closure, moreover, argue that there is a connection between (1) 'closure' in the sense discussed above—how far a work has a satisfying ending—and (2) what can be called 'closure of interpretation'—the degree to which a work allows new readings. These two are, of course, conceptually distinct, but in practice it is often held that they are related, and that a work which has an open ending in the first sense will be open in the second sense, rejecting clear meanings and simple solutions.[50] Dialectic's natural affinities are with this latter type of openness. It is true that there are degrees of dialectic—a work can possess other voices, while apparently clearly rejecting their point of view. But even such a work will be more open than a comparable work in which the other voices find no place, not least because it will require the active contribution of the reader, who will have to recognize which side of the argument comes out on top. There will always, to a greater or lesser degree, be the possibility that the reader will resist taking that step, and that he will find one of the 'opposing' voices at least partially persuasive.

Hence, by offering alternative viewpoints, dialectic would appear to encourage multiple interpretations. It is, therefore, surprising to find a work like the *Jugurtha*, with an open ending, but which seems to be obsessively excluding all competing voices. And the comparison with the Romantics increases one's disquiet. For them, dialectic and fragments

---

[48] Livy *Per.* 64, Flor. 1. 36. 18, App. *Numidian War* 1, Aug. *Ep.* 138. 16, Oros. 5. 15. 5.

[49] Flor. 1. 36. 18 gives us an idea of how Sallust could have shown Jugurtha up as misguided here, had he wanted to—after quoting Jugurtha, he comments, 'Now, had it been for sale, it had a buyer; but when it had escaped him, it was certain that it was not about to perish.'

[50] Fowler 1989: 78.

were generally, though not invariably, closely linked: both were held to represent the breaking of an idealized perfection.[51] Why should Sallust be so different?

The answer may be seen if we consider precisely what kind of 'fragment' Sallust is producing. 'How can a fragment be identified as a fragment unless there is also the conception of a whole from which it is broken off?' asks one critic.[52] Were Sallust, for example, to have ended his work in the middle of a battle, there would be no difficulty: this 'whole' would be a putative work in which the battle was completed. But he could hardly adopt such a solution, involving as it does an unreasonably drastic break with his historical predecessors. In the absence of such extreme methods, he can set the work up as a 'fragment' only by showing that there is a larger scheme of history, of which the *Jugurtha* forms a part.

And this is indeed what he does. He presents a clear and prominent pattern to Roman history: of decline in the past heading on to greater decline in the future. It is the fact that we accept this analysis that enables us to see much of the incompleteness in the work. It is that which allows Sallust to emphasize at the start the relatively minor role of the war itself; it is that which provides most of his opportunities to look back to the past and forward into the future; it is at least partly that which enables us to read the ending as open. And it is that which creates the possibility of having the chain of characters linked in their decline for which I was arguing earlier, and of seeing that chain as still unfinished at the end of the work.

Thus, Sallust is using the historical concepts and the historical analysis that he develops within the *Jugurtha* itself in order to establish the idea of a 'whole', and hence to show the work as a fragment broken off from that whole. Paradoxically, in such a work, dialectic could only undermine the sense that one is dealing with a 'fragment', because it would invite the reader to challenge the very historical analysis upon which its 'fragmentariness' depends. If the reader were always questioning whether he is really meant to be accepting Sallust's 'pattern' at face value, he would tend to discount this pattern's apparent lack of completeness. Indeed, the reader might even take this apparent incompleteness simply as a further indication of complexity—perhaps it is not that the pattern is incomplete, but that he has misidentified or misinterpreted the pattern, which

---

[51] Abrams 1971: 141–95; McFarland 1981: 337–9.

[52] McFarland 1981: 50. More generally, McFarland 1981: 50–4 discusses the connection (and the consequent tension) between fragments and a desire for wholeness. Cf. also Kuzniar 1987: 48–9.

Jugurtha: *An 'Historical Fragment'*

is really more complex than it superficially appears to be. The single-mindedness intensity of the monograph—the very thing which makes it so powerful to read—is thus a vital part of its fragmentary nature.

Hence we have a strong reason to suppose that not only the *Jugurtha*, but any work within the broad generic norms of ancient historiography, will have difficulty in setting itself up as a 'fragment' unless it avoids dialectic. This is a major difference between it and the Romantics, since for them, as I discussed above, 'fragments' and dialectic usually went hand in hand. On a more general level one may see certain analogies among the Romantics for this feature in Sallust too: they often set up teleologies, and desire completed stories and themes, but then employ the fragmentary form to subvert them.[53] But in Sallust the overall pattern is of far greater importance than it is for them: it must remain unchallenged, or else the 'fragment' itself would break down.

None of the arguments of this section, however, should be taken as denying that there is complexity in the *Jugurtha*. For example, we may observe that Sallust uses the digression at 41-2 to refocus the analysis, and make it less partisan than what had gone before. This, however, is far removed from dialectic: any complexity is achieved by shifts of nuance and emphasis rather than direct competition of ideas. It is still easy to discern a single unchallenged (though slightly developing) line of thought through the work.

V

The argument so far has demonstrated that the work is a 'fragment'. But this fact in itself might seem to have relatively little importance. To put it bluntly, all that I seem to have proved is that Sallust's *Jugurtha* more or less conforms to a theory of art that was employed a couple of thousand years later—and perhaps for completely different reasons.[54] Doubtless this is an interesting phenomenon in itself, and can even perhaps help us interpret the work, but has it any real significance? Since monographs by definition cover only limited topics, is it not likely that authors will employ such methods in them?

---

[53] See Kuzniar 1987: 4, 48-67.
[54] For example, Abrams 1971: e.g. 100-1, 123, 141-195, 209-14, argues that the Romantics' interest in fragments had a theological origin, and was connected with the idea of the fragmentation of an Edenic unity. No such dimension is apparent in Sallust.

There is, of course, the problem that we lack ancient historical monographs with which to compare the *Jugurtha*. Yet we do have the *Catiline*; and the *Catiline*, like the *Jugurtha*, is filled with references to the past and the future, and seems, at least at times, to be attempting to illustrate the general problems of Rome through a single symptomatic episode. In other respects, however, it does not seem to be aiming at the sort of effects that we have seen here. The philosophical preface is not nearly so obviously inviting us to see a pattern in Roman history in particular: it draws its examples from Greece and Asia. I have already indicated the more conventional way in which the subject of the work is introduced. There are no direct references to all the things that Sallust is not saying, and the subjects he is not treating. The main historical digression comes not in the centre, but right at the start, directly after the introduction of Catiline.[55] There is a moral digression in the centre, which is often compared to the one in the *Jugurtha* (*Cat.* 36. 4–39. 5), but its account of the state of Rome is much more obviously contemporary, and it looks back to the past only relatively intermittently. The end of the work has sometimes been thought abrupt,[56] but it is considerably closer to closure than is the *Jugurtha*, ending as it does with the final battle and the death of Catiline.

And when it comes to dialectic, it may be pointed out that the last part of the work is dominated by the opposing speeches of Caesar and Cato, and that Catiline himself puts his case in two major speeches and a letter. It is true that, as dialectical works go, the *Catiline* is relatively straightforward, and it is possible for the reader to extract a central political analysis not far removed from that in the *Jugurtha*. However, there are still many respects in which the dialectic complicates the historical pattern, and would hence hinder any attempt to create a 'fragment'. To select just one limited example, both Caesar[57] and Cato[58] appeal to ancient precedents, and indeed each spends part of his speech in discussing the development of the Roman state.[59] Cato's views are close to those expressed by Sallust in the narrative, but it is far from obvious that we are to reject the rather different analysis of Caesar—indeed, the syncrisis at *Cat.* 53–4 encourages us to treat them as equals. If Cato is right to suggest that the conspirators should be executed, as Sallust seems to indicate, then what of Caesar's demonstration that such a punishment

---

[55] The *Histories*, too, seem to have had their main historical digression near the start (1. 11–12).
[56] e.g. McGushin 1977: 289; but cf. Wheeldon 1989: 54–5.
[57] *Cat.* 51. 5–6; cf. also 51. 32–4.   [58] *Cat.* 52. 30–1.
[59] *Cat.* 51. 37–42; 52. 19–23.

would be contrary to ancestral precedent? These complications undercut the clear pattern of decline, and would make it harder for Sallust to show the work as an incomplete section of such a pattern.

For all of these reasons, it can hardly be said that the *Catiline* is a 'fragment', nor, consequently, can it be argued that the 'fragment' is an inevitable consequence of the monograph form.

If not inevitable, might it not at least be a fairly standard way of going about things? Here we run up against the paucity of our evidence; but we are offered a clue by Polybius:

> For how much easier it is to get hold of and read through forty books just as if woven from a single thread... than to read or get hold of the narrative of those who write piecemeal. For apart from the fact that they are many times longer than my history, it is impossible for readers to grasp anything from them with certainty, firstly because most of them do not write the same things about the same events; secondly because they leave out parallels to events, which we can look at and judge side by side, allowing each thing to be accounted for better than if we formed our opinions in isolation; and thirdly they are not able even to touch what is far and away the most important thing. For I say that above all the most vital part of history is the study of immediate and remote consequences of events and especially the study of causes.... All these things one can recognize and learn from those who write general history, but one cannot do so from those who write of the wars themselves, such as the war with Perseus or that with Philip.
> (Polyb. 3. 32. 2–8; cf. 1. 4, 8. 2)

One cannot, of course, prove the point, and we must recognize that Polybius is writing polemically, in order to advocate his particular brand of universal history, but it is perhaps unlikely that he would have said these things had writers of monographs made a habit of systematically seeking to show their work as part of a wider historical pattern. We may add that Polybius at 7. 7. 6 and 29. 12. 2–4 claims of monographs that, far from playing down the significance of their own topics, as we have seen Sallust does in the *Jugurtha*, they tend to exaggerate, and make a great deal of rather minor events. Moreover, there is some negative evidence for the same conclusions. When Cicero discusses monographs in his letter to Lucceius (*Fam.* 5. 12. 2–7), he assumes that the chief point of writing them is that they offer great opportunities for pathos and decoration. The idea that in them one might indirectly link the particular subject with wider history is never mentioned, although it is precisely to a man engaged in such a wider work that Cicero is seeking to advocate the form.

Our evidence is better for history writers in general than it is for writers of monographs, and it is perhaps here that we should look for parallels to Sallust. Little case can be made for the view that Herodotus is a 'fragment'; the fact that he has no clear movement through time, but instead continually loops and digresses through different areas of the past, means that one is not left with any sense that there are particular episodes that he has failed to cover. Indeed, it is striking that Dionysius of Halicarnassus specifically praised him for his complete coverage of his theme, and his uniting of disparate subjects into a satisfying whole.[60] Moreover, for his ending, he goes back in time to relate an episode which can be seen as providing the moral for his history as a whole, and hence rounding it off with a satisfactory conclusion.[61]

Thucydides, as I said above, is often considered the major Greek influence on Sallust, and we can see in him one or two of the features that we have been examining in the *Jugurtha*: in particular, Thucydides, like Sallust, has an extensive historical digression relatively late on in his first book. But the book had begun with a digression which surveyed an even greater period of time; in any case, the first book as a whole has a prefatory character, and in the subsequent books it is extremely rare for Thucydides to look back in time in any substantial way. Moreover, his history is unfinished, and he almost never looks beyond its conclusion. I need hardly add that he is the dialectical writer par excellence.

Nor is the field of Roman history any more promising. Many of Sallust's predecessors wrote multi-book annals, and this in itself would suggest that they were not writing 'fragmentary' works: such authors seem to have aimed at a comprehensive treatment within a strictly chronological framework. We can see something of this in their surviving successors. With Livy, even individual groups of books appear more 'complete' than the *Jugurtha*—for example, the first five seem pretty well self-sufficient, and they have a strongly closed ending. So too Tacitus' *Annals* and *Histories* seem to aim at covering events comprehensively in a way that Sallust implicitly rejects.

At least it might be expected that Sallust's open ending would find analogies in other historians. Fowler suggests that such endings may be typical of history: 'More than any other genre, history may need to suggest the simultaneous presence of a "proper" ending and the continuance of the historical process.'[62] This also finds partial support from Hayden White,[63] who argues that one type of historical writing, which he calls 'chronicles', and which narrate events comprehensively, but organize them chronologically, is marked by such endings, suggesting an

---

[60] *Pomp.* 3. 14; cf. 3. 4, 3. 8.   [61] Cf. Lateiner 1989: 44–50.
[62] Fowler 1989: 117.   [63] White 1987: 1–25.

infinitely extensible process of time; he distinguishes these from 'histories' proper, which impose on a sequence of events completed and coherent stories with strong endings. He further argues that the distinguishing feature of the latter is its moralism, without which one cannot create a real ending.

Indeed, we do find works with endings that seem open. Xenophon's *Anabasis*, like the *Jugurtha*, ends one war with a reminder of the next, while his *Hellenica* ends at an apparently arbitrary moment with an invitation for someone else to take over, just as it began at the point where Thucydides happened to break off. But in neither case are the anti-closural elements as strong as they are in Sallust; nor do they link with other aspects of the work to form a principle which dominates it. So, too, other historians picked up their work where predecessors had finished; but this does not mean that they were treating that work as a piece broken off from the whole. Thus, Polybius explicitly states that he begins his account of Greek history where Aratus had ended, but he also says that his main reason for beginning then is that 'Fortune had then as it were built the world anew' (4. 2. 1–4)—in effect, he is beginning a new subject.[64]

Moreover, the works surveyed do not seem to bear out White's general analysis. It is true that none of these histories is quite 'chronicles' as he would understand the term; however, a number of them, such as the *Hellenica* and Livy, exhibit many of the qualities that he wishes to ascribe to 'chronicles'. However, even though these works are considerably closer to 'chronicles' than is the *Jugurtha*, which bears most of the marks of an organized 'history', it is the *Jugurtha* where the opening of the ending and the suggestion of continuity seem to matter most. Moreover, the *Jugurtha* is the work that is most clearly organized around a moral conception of history; hence we cannot see the straightforward correlation between moralism and closure that White claims.

We have so far failed to find a historical work that is at all closely analogous to Sallust. However, biography at first sight looks more hopeful: we do at least there have a substantial body of material to work with, and the works tend to be much the same sort of length as the *Jugurtha*. Tacitus' *Agricola* was influenced by Sallust, and there we can see some of the elements that we saw in the *Jugurtha*, such as the references to earlier and later events, and the former, at any rate, coming out of sequence, as Tacitus narrates the earlier history of Britain. The work, however, is in no sense a 'fragment', not least because of its emphatic, panegyrical closure. Indeed, the problem with biography in general is that authors tend to keep

[64] Woodman 1988a: 152–4.

pretty closely to the limits circumscribed by the lives of their subjects.[65] It is normal to discuss their family history at the start, and one may sometimes end with an account of their descendants (as with Plutarch, *Cato Major*), or with some anecdote which summarizes their achievements (as with Plutarch, *Cicero*), or some other topic relevant to their death, such as the fates of their killers (as with Plutarch, *Caesar* and *Pompey*).[66] But only relatively rarely do writers go beyond those limits. The example closest to Sallust is perhaps Plutarch's *Cimon*, the ending of which includes a very brief summary of subsequent Greek failures against the Persians. But it is very different from the *Jugurtha*. The point in Plutarch is not to set the *Life* against the background of Greek history, but to emphasize and magnify Cimon's own achievements—it is part of a general tendency in Plutarch to end with a rehabilitation of his characters.[67] Moreover, the final paragraph returns to Cimon, and the work concludes with an account of his burial and posthumous honours (*Cim.* 19. 5). Even when the strict biographical limits are transgressed, it is usually in order to provide essential background information, or to give a final perspective on the subject. Authors do not shift the focus of the work away from the subject himself, or try to negate the sense of completeness implicit in the description of someone's whole life.

VI

So we seem to have reached the rather uncomfortable conclusion that, so far as our evidence allows us to judge, Sallust's *Jugurtha* is unique: it is the only work of historical narrative in the whole of pagan antiquity that even comes close to fitting our definition of a 'fragment'. So this leads to the obvious question: why should Sallust choose to write in such an exceptional manner?

One obvious answer might be to look back at Polybius (see Section V above). He criticizes writers of monographs for their failure to relate the subjects of their works to other events, and indeed claims that this failure is due to the defects of the form itself. Perhaps Sallust is taking up the

---

[65] Fowler 1989: 116 seems to deny this. However, his one counterexample, Plutarch's *Antony*, where the subject dies well before the end, is not a good one: uniquely, Plutarch turns the *Life* in effect into a double biography of Antony and Cleopatra together, and their joint lives now provide the limits. On differences and similarities between biography and history, cf. Moles 1988: 32–4.
[66] Cf. Pelling 1988: 323–5.   [67] Pelling 1988: 323–5, quoting J. L. Moles.

challenge, and is showing that it is possible to write a monograph that is not circumscribed so narrowly. Possibly, but this is not a complete answer. The *Catiline*, too, as I said earlier, attempts to relate its events to the wider themes of Roman history, and thus essentially fulfils Polybius' requirements; but Sallust does not, as he does in the *Jugurtha*, manipulate its structure so as to set it up as a 'fragment'.

Of course, we do not have to assume a single cause: there may be many factors working in tandem. Another factor might be the period of the *Jugurtha*'s composition: it is almost certainly being written in the early years of the Second Triumvirate, and it might be argued that a writer at a time of such profound and overwhelming social and political dislocation may feel impelled to respond to this in his work. For example, perhaps it is precisely because of the chaos around him that Sallust wrote as he did: on the one hand, he strives to impose a clear and exact pattern on Roman history,[68] to make sense of a world that is breaking down; but at the same time he shows that pattern as something whose completion is deferred—the chaos still continues, and ultimately he is disillusioned about any such overall clarity and completeness. This, then, would explain the lack of dialectic, and his treating the Jugurthine war as part—but only a relatively minor part—of a grand overall design, which, however, he never directly shows brought to fruition.

Something along these lines would be attractive, and is supported by the comparison with the Romantics. It is sometimes argued that the comparable features of their works are related to the effect of the French Revolution, which created both a great desire for and a great distrust of the view of history as something complete and total.[69] Similarly, White observes that historical writings that eschew fullness and completion are especially likely to be produced at times of political and social instability.[70] It is true that he explains this with reference to his claim that such writings are not as strongly informed by moralism, which we have seen is not the case with Sallust; but the accuracy of the specific observation is not affected by the flaws of the overall analysis.

However, the huge gaps in our knowledge of the literature of the period should lead us to hesitate before too readily accepting this account. We cannot with any confidence postulate such a Zeitgeist as an explanation when our evidence consists of just one out of a couple of

---

[68] Indeed, other literature of the period, while not 'fragmentary' by our definition, shows an interest in patterns of Roman decline: for example, Hor. *Epod.* 7, 16. 1–14, Verg. *G.* 1. 501–14.
[69] See Kuzniar 1987: 16–21.   [70] White 1987: 3; cf. 13–14.

works. The *Catiline* is written under comparable circumstances, but does not come out the same way; and if, as has been argued,[71] Livy's first pentad was originally composed in the late 30s, we have there another work which does not conform to this type.

But there is one other possibility. One can find many 'fragments' of this sort in the ancient world: in verse. There are many writers of short poems who simply select a scene or two from a longer mythological story, and not necessarily the most important scene at that: the reader is expected and desired to recognize the incompleteness of the story as it appears in the poem. And when one comes to slightly longer poems, the so-called epyllia, there are several examples that are even closer to Sallust, in so far as they are written on more of a comparable scale. Catullus 64, for example, looking forward to the future life of Achilles and the Hesiodic ages,[72] or Moschus' *Europa*, setting up the obvious aetiology and then failing to give it,[73] or Lycophron's *Alexandra*, where the bulk of the poem is a lengthy and obscure prophecy of mythological events that will only be fulfilled outside it. And, to step briefly into controversial waters, we could even add to our parallels the *Aeneid*, with its prefiguring of the whole of Roman history, and its astonishingly abrupt ending. Sallust, of course, handles it differently: a poem can directly fragment a story in the way that a history cannot, and hence does not require the abandoning of dialectic, or the employment of regular narrative patterns. But, I should like to suggest, Sallust has transformed an essentially poetic structure so as to create a historical 'fragment'.[74] And by doing so he is not playing games: he subliminally relates the rather sordid events of late Republican history to the grand tragedies of poetic myth.

---

[71] Luce 1965; Woodman 1988b: 128–35.   [72] See Townend 1983.

[73] Von Wilamowitz-Moellendorff 1906: 100–1 in fact claims that the *Europa* is genuinely incomplete, and that the aetiology would have appeared in the missing conclusion, but see Bühler 1960: 201–3; Hopkinson 1988: 214–15.

[74] History and poetry frequently fertilized one another: apart, obviously, from historical poems, such as those of Ennius, Naevius, and Lucan, there were the 'tragic historians' criticized by Polybius (e.g. 2. 56). For a discussion of this controversial issue, and more generally of the use of 'poetic' emotions and sensationalism in history (on which such borrowings from verse are usually held to centre), see, e.g., Fornara 1983: 120–34. It is claimed by Reitzenstein 1906: 84–90 (see also Ullmann 1942: 42–53) that monographs were less bound by requirements of accuracy, and hence were especially likely to show poetic influence; but against this, see La Penna 1968: 312–20. On Sallust's use of these 'poetic' techniques, see, e.g., Vretska 1955: 146–58.

ADDENDUM

This was the first scholarly article that I ever published. To me rereading it now, twenty-five years later, it seems in some ways to reveal the youth and inexperience of its author. A minor part of that is an excessive concern for perceived disciplinary proprieties (of which more below); but a more significant part is the apparent determination, not atypical of young scholars, to subsume as much of the text as possible under a single interpretation, and to ignore complexities and nuances which might compel one to qualify that interpretation. I still stand by all of the article's main conclusions, but I like to think that, were I writing it today, I would write it entirely differently. I would present the case less simplistically, and would offer more places where the discussion might be opened out in productive directions, rather than trying, as I did then, to shut out other interpretations than my own.

An example of oversimplification in the paper is the handling of the digressions within the work. I did offer some discussion of them, but the discussions did not look in much detail at their actual content, although they are an obvious place in which to consider questions of 'fragmentariness', since by definition they include material which lies outside the scope of the main narrative. For example, I placed some weight in my argument (see p. 280 above) on Sallust's *praeteritio* concerning the history of Carthage (19. 2), but did not consider the complications raised by the fact that later in the monograph he does in fact include a lengthy anecdote from Carthaginian history, namely the story of the Philaeni (79). As it happens, the digressions in Sallust, especially those concerning Africa, have been the subject of much recent scholarship, and several of those writers have attached a great deal of importance to the Philaeni within the work: important examples include Green 1993; Wiedemann 1993; Oniga 1995: esp. 37–93; Devillers 2000; Morstein-Marx 2001; and Heubner 2004. I do not think that the fundamentals of my argument are undermined by my omission, but they do indicate that Sallust's handling of his 'fragment' is richer and more multilayered than I gave him credit for.

A further weakness in the article is that I did too little to give to the idea of the 'historical fragment', which is central to my entire analysis, a proper grounding in ancient aesthetics. In the final paragraph of the article I alluded to a number of poetic parallels, which I still believe to be the key to appreciating the distinctive features of Sallust's technique in the *Jugurtha*. But if that argument is to carry conviction, it is not sufficient to refer briefly to possible parallels: there needs to be a broader and deeper analysis of the concept of 'wholes' and 'parts' in ancient poetic theory and practice. The most obvious (and most embarrassing) omission is of any reference to a book which in fact came out a couple of years before I wrote the article, but which I had at that time not yet read, namely Heath 1989: a fundamental and challenging study arguing that 'unity' was conceptualized entirely differently in antiquity from today. Heath's claims do not have a direct bearing either for or against mine, but his careful and detailed analysis of how 'unity' worked in antiquity would have provided me with a much more secure basis for developing my own argument. I should also have spent some time exploring the precise nature of the closely related Hellenistic practice of displacing the traditional centre of a story to—or outside—the margins of a poem: for various accounts of this phenomenon see, e.g., Zanker 1987: 180-2; Bing 2008: 46-8; Bing 2012: 190-7; and Schmitz 2012.

I have focused up to now on the weaknesses in the article; there are naturally strengths as well, and, as I have already noted, I still maintain that my basic thesis—that there are interlocking elements of the monograph which collectively add up to establishing it as a 'fragment'—is correct. Among later scholars who have drawn on and built on aspects of my analysis, often opening out additional complexities and subtleties in the process, I should mention in particular the essay by Christina Kraus on 'Jugurthine Disorder' reprinted as Chapter 9 of this volume, which partly draws on my ideas about the incompleteness of the monograph while demonstrating far more complex lines of moral chaos within it than the simple picture of decline by individuals and the state, with Jugurtha from the start (even when he is ostensibly virtuous) acting as the agent of social corruption. Her article should be read as both a complement to and a partial corrective of mine. Also important is Marincola 2005, who sets the open ending of the monograph in the wider context of historiographical practice, and Connolly 2015: 65-113, who uses my account of the fragmentary narrative of the *Jugurtha* (and some related aspects of the *Catiline*) as a jumping-off point for a complex meditation on what she calls 'the structural violence of political life' (113), both in Rome and today.

Others who have considered themes that I explored in the article include Benferhat 2008 on the monograph's ending and Egelhaaf-Gaiser 2010 on the speech of Marius (especially in relation to the themes of the prologue). Miller 2015, using, as I did, Catullus 64 as a major comparator, argues that the idealizing of the pre-146 past by the narrative voice and the apparent endorsement of Sallust's analysis by the speakers in the work are not to be taken at face value. Montgomery 2013-14 examines the brief account of Scipio Aemilianus in the opening pages of the monograph, arguing that, although positive, it prefigures the aristocratic arrogance that leads to the moral fall of Metellus. Dix 2006 is a systematic study of characterization in the monograph, focusing, as I did, on the four interlinked figures of Jugurtha, Metellus, Marius, and Sulla; Borzsák 2002 considers Sallust's portrayal of Marius, and Carrara 2004 (esp. 280-6), that of Sulla.

One other omission in the article—an omission of an entirely different sort—should be confessed here. My original impetus to write it did not come from my work on Roman historiography. It grew out of a term-long graduate seminar on early Romantic music that I took in 1988 with the great musicologist and pianist Charles Rosen, in which he argued for the centrality of the 'romantic fragment' in understanding music of that period. It was Rosen who introduced me to the concept; but I also, and far more significantly, learned from him the possible breadth of its application and its potency as a framework for aesthetic and ideological analysis (cf. Rosen 1995: 41-115). Nowadays, when 'interdisciplinarity' is all the rage, it may seem odd that anyone would conceal this. But in 1992 I was concerned that colleagues—and potential employers—would think it frivolous and dangerously unscholarly if I referred to a discipline so remote from my own as the origin of my work. So I suppressed in the article all references to music, and failed to give Rosen the acknowledgement that I should have done.

Charles Rosen died in December 2012. I never had any further contact with him after taking his seminar; but I can at least use the opportunity of the reprinting of this article to give him posthumously the acknowledgement and thanks that by rights I should have done in his lifetime.

11

Sallust's *Jugurtha*

Concord, Discord, and the Digressions

Thomas Wiedemann

The current fashion for emphasizing ambiguities and discontinuities in literary texts should have found Sallust's writings congenial. The *Catiline* explores competing and contradictory claims to *virtus*, exemplified by Caesar, Cato, and Catiline himself, a paragon of ambiguity in contrast to the unproblematic Cicero. The *Jugurthine War* is twice the length, with a more complicated structure and a wider range of material, including three formal digressions. A concern with the relationship between virtue and success, and with conflict between alternative virtues, is central to this monograph too; it concludes with a victory achieved not by years of military exertion but as the result of Jugurtha's treacherous betrayal to Sulla by Bocchus in contravention of all recognized moral principles ('kinship, marriage, and a formal treaty': *cognationem, affinitatem, praeterea foedus intervenisse*; cf. 'deceit', *composito dolo*, 111. 2 and 4).

Although the three digressions are a highly visible feature of the *Jugurtha*, surprisingly little attention has been directed to their functions within the narrative. Two of these digressions—the first and third—where they are discussed at all in recent commentaries, continue to be thought to have little material relevance to Sallust's theme. Where explanation of these two digressions has been attempted, as in Büchner's commentary [Büchner 1982] or Scanlon's *The Influence of Thucydides on Sallust* [Scanlon 1980], it has tended to be in stylistic terms. Histories from Herodotus onwards included digressions for a range of literary reasons: as structural devices to divide the text into distinct sections; to denote the passing of a period of time; as a way of adding variety and colour to what was ostensibly a matter-of-fact military narrative; and as a practical means to feed the reader additional material supporting the author's argument, which in a recited text (or unravelled volume) could not be done in the form of the notes or appendices that are available to writers today.[1] Such explanations in primarily literary terms are attractive in view of the digressions used by Sallust's exemplar, Thucydides. Thus, Thucydides begins his account of the Sicilian Expedition with a description of the island's geography and ethnography (6. 1-5); he describes the origins of party strife, *stasis*, at Corcyra (3. 82-4); and he uses the semi-legendary story of Harmodius and Aristogeiton to explain Athenian attitudes to tyranny (6. 53-4). These three passages clearly gave Sallust some inspiration for his own three digressions in the *Jugurtha* (for convenience, we may refer to them as A, B, and C): A. The ethnography of North Africa; B. Civil discord at Rome; C. The legend of the Philaeni. Each is carefully marked off from the preceding and following text. A: *Res postulare videtur... ad necessitudinem rei satis dictum* ('The subject seems to demand... enough has been said for what the subject requires,' 17. 1-19. 8); B: *ceterum mos partium et factionum... quam ob rem ad inceptum redeo* ('As for the tendency of division and faction... so I return to the narrative I have begun,' 41. 1-42. 5); and C: *Sed quoniam in eas regiones per Leptitanorum negotia venimus, non indignum videtur egregium atque mirabile facinus duorum Carthaginensium memorare... nunc ad rem redeo* ('Since the business of Leptis has taken me to that part of the world, it does not seem unworthy to relate the outstanding and astonishing deed of two Carthaginian brothers... now I return to the subject,' 79. 1-10).[2]

How, if at all, does their subject matter relate to Sallust's theme? The answer will depend on what we take Sallust's theme to be:

> I am going to write up the war which the Roman people waged with Jugurtha king of the Numidians, (a) firstly because it was great and bloody and with victories on both sides, (b) next because that was the first occasion when the arrogance of the nobility was challenged. That struggle brought disorder to everything divine and human, and reached such a degree of madness that war and the devastation of Italy were the only limit to civil strife. (5. 1)[3]

---

[1] Scanlon 1980: 175; 126-37; Büchner 1953: 15 emphasizes the structural role ('die gliedernde Funktion') of the first digression. Paul 1984 has little specific to say on the literary functions of the digressions: p. 72 (A), p. 198 (C). L. Watkiss's student edition (Watkiss 1971: 19) leaves the third digression out of his analysis completely.

[2] The four introductory chapters also display elements typical of a digression, ending with the standard digressory formula *nunc ad rem redeo*: see Wiedemann 1979: 13-16 and 1980: 147-9. They introduce a discrete section (chs. 5-16) containing material about the background to the war analogous to that given by Thucydides in his first book.

[3] *Bellum scripturus sum quod populus Romanus cum Iugurtha rege Numidarum gessit, primum quia magnum et atrox variaque victoria fuit, dehinc quia tunc primum superbiae*

The three commonplaces of advertising the historian's material as exciting to read because it is great, bloody, and containing many changes of fortune follow precedent.[4] Sallust's second explicit reason sounds more interesting and has been variously interpreted, depending upon whether scholars preferred to emphasize Sallust as a moralist opposing the vice of arrogance or (following Mommsen) as a political pamphleteer opposed to the *nobilitas* ('nobility', 'aristocracy', 'senatorial elite'). The view that his purpose in writing history was primarily political presupposes a picture of Roman politics as structured around two political groupings—'parties' as understood in the nineteenth century, rather than modern democratic mass parties—with Sallust supporting the 'popular' leader, Julius Caesar. This is not a view of Roman politics which many find acceptable today. There are also problems about the assumption that Sallust was Caesar's protégé; why, in that case, was he expelled from the Senate by Appius Claudius, one of the censors of 50 BCE, without protest from the other censor, Lucius Piso, who was Caesar's father-in-law and represented his interests? (There is nothing surprising about Sallust's joining Caesar in 49 BCE; like others who had been excluded from political advancement, he saw that a Caesarian victory was a precondition for any further role in public life.)[5]

Whatever our view of the historical Sallust's political affiliation, the passage explicitly advises the reader that the monograph he is about to read discusses the beginning of the sequence of events that led to the devastation of Italy: the civil wars between Sulla and the 'Marians' in the 80s, but for Sallust's contemporaries perhaps more immediately those of the 40s BCE. The external and internal conflicts are tightly connected, and Sallust links the two around the polarity of concord or cooperation versus discord and envy (there are, of course, other moral issues whose consideration binds his text together). That conceptual polarity is vividly brought to the fore by the deathbed advice given by Micipsa to his sons:

nobilitatis obviam itum est. Quae contentio divina et humana cuncta permiscuit eoque vecordiae processit, ut studiis civilibus bellum atque vastitas Italiae finem faceret.

[4] On the epic greatness of the war about to be narrated, cf., e.g., Herodotus 1. 1, Thucydides 1. 23. 1, Polybius 1. 13. 11, Livy 21. 1. 12, etc., and for verse writers, e.g., Vergil *Aeneid* 7. 44–5: *maius opus moveo*. We may also note that Sallust's account of the military operations of the final phase of the war, under Marius' command, is introduced by the phrase 'it seemed [to Marius] that it was time to undertake greater and more difficult things' (89. 3).

[5] Piso 'belonged to Caesar' and intervened to prevent the removal from the Senate of Caesar's supporter Curio: Cassius Dio 40. 63. 3. For Caesar's reinstatement of those demoted by the censors, cf. Suetonius, *Divus Julius* 41. 1. On the historical Sallust, see Malitz 1975.

'small things grow as a result of concord, but the greatest things will waste away as a result of discord'.[6]

The three digressions separate off and introduce phases of the war under various Roman commanders who represent different ethical states. A: the catastrophic Roman failures under the command of the nobles Bestia and Albinus, who notwithstanding their hereditary claim to *virtus* suffer from the vices of *avaritia* ('greed', 'avarice') and *imperitia* ('inexperience', 'ignorance'). B: the second phase, in which the aristocratic general Metellus is indeed competent, but fails to make the best use of his subordinate Marius because of his arrogance. Finally C, the last phase of the war, in which Marius is successful, but not on his own. The final surrender of Jugurtha to the Romans by the Mauretanian king Bocchus is brought about by Marius' quaestor Sulla, to whom Sallust devotes a detailed and ambiguously positive character sketch (95). The reader cannot ignore the moral: the best noble commander cannot succeed if he ignores the talent of a *novus homo* ('a new man', i.e. one whose ancestors had never served in the Senate); but a talented *novus homo* can only succeed in cooperation with a talented aristocrat. Marius and Sulla together brought success for Roman arms against the external threat; contrast the *bellum atque vastitas Italiae* later brought about by their discord, which 'I am not sure whether I would be more ashamed or more disgusted to narrate' (*incertum habeo pudeat an pigeat magis disserere*, 95. 4).

Sallust's other themes are secondary to this emphasis on cooperation. He has subordinated his selection of narrative material to this moral theme to the extent that geographical or chronological precision, as commentators constantly remind us, are of little interest to him. Thus, he fails to make explicit reference to the winters that separated the campaigning seasons of 108, 107, and 106 BCE (Syme 1964: 145; Paul 1984: 198; Watkiss 1971: 27). The break in Sallust's narrative represented by digression C probably corresponds to the first of these winters, but that only shows that Sallust's objective was not to record a sequence of campaigns, but to structure his text in terms of an account of political virtues and vices. The same applies to digression A: one of its functions may well be to cover a period of perhaps four years between Rome's division of Numidia and Jugurtha's seizure of Adherbal's portion, but that is not something Sallust chooses to tell us: rather, he wants to signal that he is about to begin his account of the events leading to direct

---

[6] *Concordia parvae res crescunt, discordia maxumae dilabuntur* (10. 6). The importance of concord as a political slogan in the Ciceronian period was discussed by Hermann Strasburger in his 1931 doctoral thesis, Strasburger 1982: 1–82.

military intervention. The three digressions separate phases of the war which illustrate different moralities, associated with a series of Roman commanders, who are not only contrasted with one another, but also with the enemies they are fighting against.

Of the three digressions, B (on *partes*, political divisions) is the one whose thematic relevance to the narrative is the easiest to identify: it gives the reader the background to popular hostility to the 'nobles' and to the Mamilian rogation. The Gracchi are treated as a separate and discrete theme, justifying Sallust's at first sight curious assertion in 5. 1 that Rome's political divisions began only at the time of the Jugurthan war. These chapters were composed at a time when the experience of civil war and of the triumviral proscriptions was still fresh; it is not illegitimate to assume that Sallust wished his readers to understand them with reference to the actions and claims of contemporary political leaders. The emphasis on civil discord is reinforced by the stylistic parallels with the analysis of *stasis* given by Thucydides on the occasion of one of the first major outbreaks of civil strife recorded in that narrative, at Corcyra in 3. 79–81.[7] Sallust's account associates other vices with civil dissension (41. 10). It is preceded by a sentence describing the court of inquiry set up by the Mamilian rogation, 'conducted harshly and violently, on the basis of uncorroborated rumours and in accordance with the caprice of the people: at that time, with things going their way, the people exercised total lack of restraint, just as the nobility had so often done' (*exercita aspere violenterque ex rumore et lubidine plebis: ut saepe nobilitatem, sic ea tempestate plebem ex secundis rebus insolentia ceperat*). *Lubido*, capriciousness, is picked up again in the digression, first applied to the people (41. 5), and then to the *nobilitas* (42. 4). To read this digression as a political attack on the 'nobility' would be naive: on the contrary, Sallust explicitly describes the Gracchi as themselves 'noble' ('the first nobles to prefer true glory to the unjust exercise of power,' *primi ex nobilitate...qui veram gloriam iniustae potentiae anteponerent*, 41. 10). If the account of civil conflict has a programme, it is to analyse rival claims to political *virtus*.

Political cooperation and discord are also the theme of the first digression, whose timbre is at first sight very different. Sallust wants it to look like the ethnographical digressions in which Hellenistic historians displayed their erudition, in competition with their predecessors.[8] He makes no claim to have learnt anything about Numidia through autopsy (there is no reference to his having governed the territory, although the description of the Numidian huts at 18. 8 looks like autopsy:

---

[7] Scanlon 1980: 127–31. [8] Syme 1964: 152, 'Greek erudition and fancies'.

see Koestermann 1971: *ad loc.*); instead, he claims to have read King Hiempsal's description, written in Punic, in a specially prepared translation. Notwithstanding such a recondite (and, to his Italian readers, inaccessible) literary source, Sallust disclaims all responsibility for the truth value of its contents (as Herodotus sometimes does). Hiempsal's myth explaining the origins of the peoples of North Africa in terms of the Median, Persian, and Armenian components of the army that accompanied Hercules on his expedition to the far west tells the reader nothing about the political structure of second-century BCE Numidia, or of the background to its relationship with Rome, outlined in a few sentences (19. 7). Its relevance to Sallust's narrative lies elsewhere: it is a statement about the difference between a well-ordered state and the anarchy of division. Hercules is to be understood as the symbol of civil society; it was as a founder of cities that he was known in the western Mediterranean.[9] Hercules' death results in the division and dispersal of his army. For the Persian contingent, civil life is abandoned, and civilized norms are transgressed: ships are turned upside down to make huts, commerce (with Spain) becomes impossible because there is no common language, and they end up as nomads like the autochthonous Gaetulians (18. 3–8). City life developed sooner among the Medians and Armenians because their proximity to Spain facilitated commerce (an argument reminiscent of Thucydides in his *Archaeology*), but it was not that particular ethnic element that established control over North Africa: it was the more warlike and nomadic ex-Persians, now calling themselves Numidians. Sallust has chosen to report Hiempsal's myth because of the moral point it makes. It explains the discord endemic in North Africa. It also glosses the division of Numidia in the immediately preceding chapter (16. 5), with Adherbal's portion 'having more harbours and fine buildings' corresponding to that originally inhabited by Libyans, and Jugurtha's 'richer in fields and population' to the Gaetulian part. The phrase *in divisione* with which that sentence begins is picked up by the first words of Sallust's account of the controversy amongst geographers as to whether Africa is a separate entity or not: *In divisione orbis terrae*... ('In dividing up the globe...', 17. 3). 'Africa' entails disagreement.

Throughout the monograph, Sallust's account of the actions of Rome's African enemies emphasizes division and disorder. This is particularly true of the final phase of the war: 'When the kings learnt about Marius' arrival, they went their separate ways to inaccessible places.' Sallust

---

[9] Galinsky 1972. At Athens, it was Theseus who became the founding hero of the 'city' and of political life: hence Theseus is associated with Herakles in some of his adventures, and takes over some of his attributes.

comments that Jugurtha hoped that he could similarly divide the Roman forces (87. 4). Even when Jugurtha's and Bocchus' armies combine to attack the Romans, there is no organization—'not in line or in any normal battle formation, but in gangs just as chance grouped them together' (97. 4). The emphasis on the role of chance, confusion, and indiscipline in explaining the outcome of particular incidents in warfare is, of course, Thucydidean in origin. But for Sallust indiscipline and division are moral weaknesses, instances of man's failure to rise above the level of the beasts, either at the individual or at the social level. In classical literature, one typical marker of the point where men are almost animals is the nomad.[10] Having destroyed his own supporters, and beginning to realize that he cannot win the war, Jugurtha declines to the level of a nomad: he is 'doubtful and uncertain', *varius incertusque*; 'He changed his itineraries and his commanders from day to day; sometimes he moved against the enemy, sometimes into the desert' (74. 1); 'After that he never stayed in one place for more than one day or one night' (76. 1), repeating 'contrary to royal dignity, he often rested in a different place each night, and sometimes he would wake from his sleep, grab his weapons and make a disturbance' (72. 2). As in other character sketches—most strikingly that of Catiline—internal and external instability go hand in hand. They are inimical to civil society, but characteristic of despots, such as Bocchus: 'Royal wishes are generally as fickle as they are emphatic, and often contradict themselves' (*plerumque regiae voluntates ut vehementes sic mobiles, saepe ipsae sibi advorsae*, 113. 1). Bocchus' *mobilitas ingeni* ('inconstancy of mind'), constant changes of plan, and treachery (explicitly called *Punica fides* (lit., 'Punic faith', implying faithlessness): 108. 3; cf. 88. 6, 102. 15) are repeatedly emphasized. To the very last moment, Bocchus is divided within himself as to whether to betray Jugurtha to Sulla or vice versa:

> During the night which preceded the day set for the conference, the Moor first summoned his friends, then changed his mind and sent everyone else away, and is said to have had a great struggle with himself, changing the expression of his face and eyes as he kept changing his mind; although he said nothing, they betrayed what was hidden in his heart. (113. 3)

But it is not just among Africans that civilized behaviour is liable to break down, to revert to unstable nomadism. The autochthonous Gaetulians and Libyans had lived like beasts; 'they were ruled by no customs or law or anyone's authority' (18. 2). Rome too is threatened by that absence of law, so Memmius claims at the beginning of his speech attacking the

---

[10] Wiedemann 1986.

Jugurtha: *Concord, Discord, and Digressions* 313

domination of the aristocracy (no justice, 31. 1; not law but caprice, 31. 7). Particularly striking is the account of indiscipline in the Roman army in Africa. Just as the pre-Herculean Gaetulians are described in epic terms as restless and roaming about (*vagi palantes*, 18. 2: cf. Koestermann 1971: *ad loc.*), so the Romans had abandoned discipline: 'they roamed about restlessly, wasting the fields' (*vagabantur et palantes agros vastare*, 44. 5). Sallust's description of the state in which Metellus found his army consciously uses phrases reminding the reader of chapter 18, but there are interesting differences: the nomads move from place to place to find fresh land, *agros temptantes*, but the Roman army moves camp only when forced to by stench or lack of fodder; while the Persians and Medes respectively find it difficult to buy or barter things with the people of Spain (*ab Hispanis emundi aut mutandi copia*) and barter amongst themselves (*mutare res inter se instituerant*, 18. 5 and 9), the Roman soldiers barter their illicit war booty with traders for imported wine (*mutare cum mercatoribus vino advecticio*). Spurius Albinus' absence and his brother's incompetence had allowed the Roman army in Africa to sink to the level reminiscent of Hercules' army after it had lost its leader.

The *virtus* of the brothers Albinus lay solely in their birth, and Spurius' support for his brother by entrusting him with command of the army in his absence brought disaster on the Romans; indeed, they cannot really be described as cooperating, since Aulus acts in Spurius' absence (and seeks to win the glory of ending the war in competition with him), and Spurius refuses to recognize his brother's treaty (37–9). Their failure as brothers is highlighted by the very peculiar theme of Sallust's third digression. It is carefully prepared by a statement about an appeal of Lepcis to Metellus (selected for no other reason than to give Sallust an excuse for introducing the story). 'Since the affairs of the people of Lepcis have brought us to this region, it seems fitting to relate the noble and memorable act of two Carthaginians' (79. 1). *Egregium atque mirabile facinus*, as the historian's material is typically supposed to be; though the reader is taken aback to find a Roman historian selecting Carthaginians as exemplars of a noble deed. In fact neither Lepcis nor its would-be tyrant Hamilcar is of significance to the progress of the war, and Sallust does not bother to mention either of them again. It is the ethical import of the story of the Philaeni that interests Sallust. Büchner suggested that Sallust intended it to reinforce the reader's appreciation of the *virtus* of Metellus (and perhaps also of Marius), as though *virtus* were unproblematic. But the qualities shown by the Philaeni are more complex than athletic energy and a willingness to be buried alive for their country. The fact that the protagonists are brothers is an essential element of the story.

To run a race, only one competitor is needed to represent each city. The fact that they are pairs of brothers places the story in a line of similar tales illustrating anxieties about the potential for rivalry between brothers. Fraternal cooperation came to represent the highest moral virtue. An example—perhaps one which triggered Sallust's story—was Solon's account of Cleobis and Biton (Herodotus 1. 31).[11]

'Who can be more of a friend than one brother to another?' asks Micipsa in his deathbed speech, and immediately continues with the warning 'And what outsider would you be able to trust if you became an enemy of your own people?' (10. 5). Brothers represent conflict more frequently than mutual support. That conflict may lead to fratricide, as in the story of Eteocles and Polynices. Twins, as the closest type of fraternal relationship, may symbolize the danger most sharply: Acrisius and Proetius quarrelled while still in the womb, and resolved their quarrel by fighting when they grew up (thus becoming the inventors of the shield: Frazer 1921: 145 n. 4). For Romans, the story of the quarrel between Romulus and Remus was a central part of the myth of their city's foundation, providing an explanation for civil discord until eventually the Christian patrons Peter and Paul replaced Romulus and Remus. Such anxieties are not limited to Greece and Rome, as the story of Jacob and Esau shows (Genesis 25. 21–8), nor to societies whose rules of inheritance gave brothers (and at Rome sisters) equal and rival claims to inherit their father's property. Shakespeare's *Lear* shows that even when, from the tenth century on, north-western Europeans developed the system of primogeniture as a means to regulate precedence and inheritance between siblings, the theme lost little, if any, of its mythical power.

What then are the parallels Sallust wishes to draw between the tale of the Philaeni and the third phase of the war? Metellus, learning of Marius' appointment, feels insulted, fails to pursue his military advantage, and final success eludes him. Even before that, Metellus' and Marius' cooperation is only at surface level: when they campaign together, they act in different places—*divorsi agebant*, 55. 6. In contrast, the Philaeni, when slandered as not having set off on the prescribed day, accept the challenge and sacrifice their lives for their country. Their cooperation with their country is symbolized by their mutual solidarity; the Romans, too, will achieve their aims, but only if the two *partes*—represented by Marius and Sulla—cooperate.

---

[11] Similar tales of races run to establish boundaries between cities may involve several runners, but not brothers. In the race between Clazomenae and Cyme, the plurality of runners is explained by the requirement to offer a sacrifice at the boundary: Diodorus 15. 1.

It is not only the two Roman pairs Metellus/Marius and Marius/Sulla who exemplify the problems of cooperation. There is also the relationship between Jugurtha and his courtier Bomilcar, and between Jugurtha and his fellow king Bocchus. In 61-2, Sallust describes how Metellus planned to entrap Jugurtha by suborning Bomilcar to persuade him to surrender unconditionally. Jugurtha initially agrees, but then changes his mind, and the war continues. Immediately after this comes Sallust's account of Marius' request for leave to bid for the consulship: just as Bomilcar treacherously and unsuccessfully tries to persuade Jugurtha to surrender, so Metellus disloyally and unsuccessfully tries to persuade Marius to put off his bid for the consulship. Sallust is scathing in his account of the behaviour of both Romans: 'he had a contemptuous and proud spirit, that common vice of the nobility' (64. 1); 'he behaved with ambition and with anger, the worst of advisers...he talked both accusingly and boastfully about the progress of the war' (64. 4–5). The episode of Bomilcar's treachery against Jugurtha is concluded a few pages later, and he is executed; in the following chapter, the episode of Metellus' lack of support for Marius is concluded when Metellus sends him home (*domum dimittit*), to stand for the consulship (72-3).

We may conclude that the material of the three digressions is far from irrelevant to the theme of Sallust's history. As Sir Ronald Syme put it, 'The digressions are often a clue to the writer's closest preoccupations.' In a text which questions different 'virtues' and explores the conflicts between them, the consistently positive emphasis on *concordia* may surprise; but both aspects are entirely consistent with the historical experience of Italians in the 40s BCE.

12

Non sunt conposita verba mea

Reflected Narratology in Sallust's Speech of Marius

Ulrike Egelhaaf-Gaiser

1. MARIUS IN SALLUSTIAN SCHOLARSHIP

Non sunt conposita verba mea: parvi id facio. ipsa se virtus satis ostendit; illis artificio opus est, ut turpia facta oratione tegant. neque litteras Graecas didici: parum placebat eas discere, quippe quae ad virtutem doctoribus nihil profuerant.

(B.J. 85. 31–2)

My words aren't finely assembled: I set little value on that. Merit displays itself well enough on its own; it is my opponents who need artistry to cloak their shameful actions with words. I haven't learned Greek either: I had no wish to learn skills which have contributed nothing to the bravery of those who teach them.

With this fictive personal statement on the occasion of his accession to the consulship in 107 BCE, Sallust's Marius not only attacks the party of the *nobiles*, which he views as equally corrupt and decadent and no longer worthy of its claim to political leadership, but also simultaneously aligns himself with two *homines novi* who defined their identity through the criterion of education.[1] Cato the Elder serves as the principal model, who, though himself a proven connoisseur of Greek literature and culture, nevertheless vehemently opposed the consequences of Hellenization

---

[1] Thanks are due to Alexander Germann for his constant readiness for discussion, diligent correction and constructive criticism of the manuscript, as well as to Meike Rühl for attentive reading and helpful improvements to the lecture version.

and the pre-eminence of the *nobiles* who depended on the reputation of their ancestors.[2] The Sallustian Marius shares with Cato a demonstratively staged construction of his own achievement,[3] which is tied to a programmatic hostility towards Greek oratory and learning. Following Cato's example,[4] the equestrian Marius obtained the consulship through his military successes alone, despite his initial handicap in comparison to aristocrats who could appeal both to their rhetorical education and to their 'commendation by ancestry' when running for office.[5] Cicero, his fellow townsman from Arpinum, paid tribute to Marius as a *rusticanus vir, sed plane vir* ('an unsophisticated man, but clearly a man', *Tusc.* 2. 53),[6] though he for his part had consistently appropriated Greek learning as a political instrument, and in doing so referred explicitly to Cato's interest in education.[7] The orator, like Marius, thus sought to appropriate the elder Cato for his own side in the late republican debate on education.[8]

So much is agreed among classical scholars. Regarding the passage's trustworthiness as a source, sub-disciplines have taken up divergent positions. In recent historical research, which has dealt in detail with the practices and media of memorial culture, the Marius speech has received wide treatment. Harriet Flower, Wolfgang Blösel, Egon Flaig, Uwe Walter, Karl-Joachim Hölkeskamp, and Lauren Kaplow have elaborated how the Sallustian Marius in his accession speech seeks to divest the *nobiles* of their symbolic capital.[9] The function of his discussion of education has been sensitively evaluated: as a member of the equestrian order, the historical Marius certainly did have access to educational institutions. It is therefore not so much the *popularis* orator's 'real' educational circumstances as his habitus in which recent research in ancient history—allowing for the acknowledged literary reworking of the original speech—has found a core of authenticity.[10]

---

[2] On Cato's position in the competition among elites and in the discourse on education in the second century, see Gehrke 1994 and 2000.

[3] Plut. *Cat. Mai.* 1.

[4] For Cato and Marius, as well as for Cato as a model for Sallust, see Skard 1956: 92–107. For the comparable rhetorical tactics of both *homines novi*, see Flaig 2004: 60–1 and 75–6.

[5] For the career of the historical Marius, see Carney 1970; Evans 1994; Thommen 2000 paints a compelling portrait of Marius.

[6] For Cicero's image of Marius, see Werner 1995: 97–214.   [7] Cic. *Sen. passim*.

[8] For the educational discourse in the late Republic, see Christes 1996.

[9] Flower 1996: 16–23; Blösel 2003: 70–1; Flaig 2004: 60–1 and 75–6; Walter 2004: 101–3 and 115; Hölkeskamp 2004: 93–105; and Kaplow 2008 (on the 'symbolic capital' of the *imagines* and ancestor tablets as a 'credit advance' for candidates for office among the leading *gentes*).

[10] For the supposed authenticity of the Marius speech in comparison with Plut. *Mar.* 8–9, see Carney 1959: 66 n. 1; Werner 1995: 54–69; Flower 1996: 17–18.

In this reading, Sallust's Marius, in close relation to the historical Marius, employs practical war experience as an argumentative weapon against the Greek learning by means of which the late republican upper class distinguished itself and sought to exclude ambitious plebeians from contested high offices. Rhetorical education is thereby an integral component of a sociopolitical discourse in which Sallust brings the *homo novus* Marius onto the stage as representative of a new ambitious nobility of achievement and simultaneously as a tradition-conscious champion of old Roman values. Marius' attack on the political ruling class is directed at its exclusive claim to mastery of skills which the *popularis* orator, on the one hand, ascribes to himself and, on the other hand, consistently depreciates: though members of the great *gentes* may have education and rhetorical technique at their disposal, without success on the battlefield, as Marius can boast of, these abilities have no value for the commonwealth.[11]

In philological scholarship, the principal interest for decades has been the literary depiction of Marius.[12] It has been convincingly shown how, first, his characterization and speech mutually reflect and complement each other and, second, how the protagonist's self-representative statements and actions contradict each other and call each other into question. While scholars in the nineteenth and early twentieth centuries saw in Marius the glorious hero of the pro-Caesarian Sallust, more recent research emphasizes the ambiguous and negative aspects of his characterization.[13]

Here, too, the speaker's conspicuous hostility to learning has received particular attention, all the more so since echoes of Plato, Lysias, and Demosthenes alongside reminiscences of a Cynic attitude and the works of Cato the Elder have been detected in the speech,[14] as well as ironizing references to the epitaphs of the Scipios.[15] Consideration of these references has raised the question whether the assimilation of the literary figure to these predecessors should be traced back to the historical

---

[11] For the image of Marius from a historical perspective, see Syme 1964: 159–76; Werner 1995: 54–69; Flower 1996: 17–18.

[12] So Vretska 1955: 101–29; Earl 1961: 70–80; Klinz 1968; La Penna 1968: 209–21; Marino 2006: 36–41; Dix 2006: 184–249. Büchner 1982: 196–9 and 202–4 treats the Marius speech in the context of other speeches as an instrument of historical representation.

[13] For summaries of older scholarship's view of Marius as a 'figure of brilliance' and exponent of *virtus*, see Vretska 1955: 101–2 and Werner 1995: 15–17, as well as Dix 2006: 295–6.

[14] Skard 1941; Skard 1956: 92–100; Picone 1976.

[15] Carney 1956; Earl 1961: 18–21 takes the epitaphs of the Scipios as a general backdrop for Sallust's concept of *virtus*.

Marius or ascribed to the narrator, and what effect such a tension between a professed lack of education and transparent literary allusions is meant to have on the reader. Is this simply the speech of a historical figure, transposed and fitted into Sallust's narrative style according to the conventions of Roman historiography? Or is the narrator trying to subvert the fictive Marius' self-portrait (itself his own creation) and present it as unreliable? Not least because of the divergent 'voices' of the text-immanent speaker and extradiegetic narrator, it has been supposed that the historian Sallust allows a radical anti-education wing of the *populares* to speak through the mouthpiece of the character Marius, since this foil enables him to cast his own retreat from politics thematized in the proem (*B.J.* 4) and the moral utility of his historiographical activity in the proper light.[16]

2. REFLECTED NARRATOLOGY IN THE *BELLUM IUGURTHINUM*

The correspondence in content between the programmatic reflection on history in its introductory proem and the plot of the monograph has been recognized by scholars.[17] This, however, is usually observed on a general level with regard to Sallust's presentation of historiography and the idea of history. Conclusions have accordingly been drawn from the proem about the late republican author's opinion of the *homo novus* Marius as exponent of the *populares*,[18] or about the aims and method of the historian as writer.[19]

Narratological inquiries in a narrower sense, however, have rarely been directed at Sallust.[20] In particular, the balance of power between speaker and narrator represented in the text has so far not been investigated. This omission is particularly remarkable in the case of the Marius speech: the propagandistic orator Marius is presented as a typical military man who follows a course of confrontation with the established *gentes* and thereby develops a new, authentically *popularis* image of

---

[16] Picone 1976: 54–8; for the composition of this passage on the model of Plato's Seventh Letter and the proem of Cato's *Origines*, see La Penna 1959: 33–4 (= 1968: 24–5) On contemporary political criticism and *otium*, see Tiffou 1973: 223–84.
[17] For a discussion of this unity, see La Penna 1959 (= 1968: 15–34); Büchner 1982: 119f; Schmal 2001: 110–27.
[18] So Werner 1995: 46–69.   [19] Büchner 1982: 244–95; Schmal 2001: 68–76.
[20] One of the few exceptions is Évrard 1990, which systematically collects the places in the text where the narrator's voice announces itself with 'I' or 'we'.

history. In doing so he breaks no new ground, but rather directly attaches himself to *popularis* predecessors such as Cato the Elder, the Gracchi, or the orator Memmius.[21] It is against the background of Memmius, who likewise appears as a *popularis* orator in the *Bellum Iugurthinum*,[22] that the distinctive features of Marius' speech become especially visible: this is by far the longest of the speeches, placed moreover at the moment of the general Metellus' replacement by Marius, a marked caesura in the plot.[23] A third characteristic that significantly differentiates Marius' speech from all others in the *Bellum Iugurthinum* is its self-referentiality: Marius not only reflects on his own rhetorical shortcomings, but actually puts them on display, as is clearly shown in the passage I chose as epigraph for this article.

In this context, my inquiry is concerned neither with the 'authenticity' of the Sallustian Marius nor with the political programme of Sallust the author. I am, rather, interested in bringing out commonalities and divergences between speaker and historian, for these indicate, in my estimation, a pointedly staged rivalry in the narrative text between two forms of memory focused on individuals, namely, between orally influenced family tradition and the historical monograph. Here it must be borne in mind that the historian's construction of this competition is essentially artificial, since he juxtaposes two forms of commemoration belonging to utterly different contexts.[24] The *memoria* of the *gentes* fulfilled a concrete political function and was deployed in particular societal situations (e.g. elections, Senate meetings, funerals, the *salutatio* in the urban house[25]) to win personal or familial prestige. It made use primarily of visual media that make an especially striking impression (*imagines*, stemmata and triumph objects in the entryway of the house, honorific and funerary monuments, coins).[26] Sallust's historical monograph, on the other hand, notwithstanding the political utility proclaimed in the proem,[27] aims at a historical analysis conceived as written from a distanced, nonpartisan perspective, addressed to an open readership. Only with the introduction into the monograph of the memorial praxis

---

[21] For the genesis of a *popularis* image of history, see Hölkeskamp 1996: 327–8.
[22] See Vretska 1955: 85–94; Büchner 1982: 190–6.
[23] For the structure of the work, see Wille 1970, here particularly 323–8.
[24] On the different purposes of historical knowledge preserved in historiography and collective memory, see Blösel 2003: 68–72.
[25] On the *imagines* in the house, see Flower 1996: 40–6; Flaig 2004: 43–4.
[26] On the various media and practices, see Plin. *HN* 35. 6–7; Flower 1996; Hölkeskamp 1996; Blösel 2003; Flaig 2004: 49–98; Walter 2004.
[27] On this, see Büchner 1982: 109–11.

of the *gentes* does the reader find an invitation to compare and counterbalance both forms of memory.

The *imagines* form an 'emblematic link' between the proem and the Marius speech:[28] they serve as a point of reference for the efficacy of historical memory in the introductory reflection on history and are invoked by the Sallustian Marius in support of his politics—not coincidentally, on the occasion of his taking up the office of consul. For it was precisely during elections that the nobility regularly exploited the symbolic capital of commendation through the *maiores*.[29] The accession speech subsequently provided a further opportunity to confirm the populace in its decision and to derive one's own policies from an appeal to the *imagines*. The importance of the praise of ancestors in this connection can be demonstrated statistically in the Marius speech: according to Harriet Flower's reckoning, the *maiores* are here mentioned eleven times, the *imagines* five times.[30] The ancestral *imagines* are thus a privilege of the ruling *gentes*, which Marius treats with positive hostility.

In light of the manifest significance of aristocratic memorial practices for the historian's self-presentation in the proem and his character portrayal in the speech, I would like to formulate three theses in advance:

1. With his appeal to the exemplary function of the *imagines*, the extradiegetic narrator in the proem does not just make general reference to the hortatory, morally instructive purpose of *historia*. Rather, he uses aristocratic memorial practice as a yardstick to help display the particular qualities and compositional freedom of his own chosen form of monographic historiography.

2. The renewed reference to the *imagines*' memorializing power in the Marius speech further develops the motif introduced in the proem within the narrative. Both levels are interwoven in such a way that narrator and speaker reciprocally cite, re-evaluate, and comment on each other.

3. The final chapter of the *Bellum Iugurthinum* programmatically refers once again back to the proem and to the Marius speech, and simultaneously constructs a virtual genealogy that leads directly from Marius, victor over the Cimbri, to Caesar, subjugator of the Gauls.

In what follows, I will elucidate these theses through noteworthy passages in the monograph which at the same time offer insight into the

---

[28] So already Marino 2006: 37–8.
[29] Flower 1996: 19, 22, 60–90; Hölkeskamp 2004: 94; Walter 2004: 99.
[30] Flower 1996: 19–20.

potential of historiographical narration. In keeping with the structure of the work, I will begin with the traces of staged orality and with the discourse on memory in the proem, and will then turn to the introductory prehistory in which the narrator, taking the Scipios as a case study, exhibits his freedom of design in contrast to the memorial practice of the *gentes*. The repurposing of gentilician *memoria* in the Marius speech will stand at the centre. A brief look at the final triumph of Marius the victor, who reaches the peak and turning point of his career in the final chapter, concludes my analysis of the text.

3. THE *MEMORIA* OF THE *NOBILES* AND MONOGRAPHIC HISTORIOGRAPHY IN THE PROEM

My starting point is the observation that the historian in the proem illustrates the affective power of *historia* through the example of the ancestor masks. In them the entire spectrum of aristocratic memorial-cultural practices that composed family tradition was symbolically concentrated—from family trees to the *pompa funebris* and *laudatio funebris*, as well as grave monuments and gentilician archives. The essential passage comes from the fourth chapter of the monograph (*B.J.* 4. 5–6):

> *nam saepe ego audivi Q. Maximum, P. Scipionem, praeterea civitatis nostrae praeclaros viros solitos ita dicere, cum maiorum imagines intuerentur, vehementissime sibi animum ad virtutem accendi. scilicet non ceram illam neque figuram tantam vim in sese habere, sed memoria rerum gestarum eam flammam egregiis viris in pectore crescere neque prius sedari, quam virtus eorum famam atque gloriam adaequaverit.*

> I have often heard how Quintus Maximus, Publius Scipio, and still other exceptional men of our nation repeatedly used to say that when they contemplated the masks of their ancestors, they felt themselves more powerfully than ever kindled to manly deeds. Of course, it was not the wax or the likeness that had such an effect—no, rather, that flame springs up in the hearts of excellent men from the memory of deeds, and it is not subdued until their own merit has equalled the reputation and glory of their forefathers.

It is undisputed that the literary tradition of historiography[31] and the primarily oral and visual *memoria* of the *gentes* enter into a direct relationship here. But the way in which historiography should be

---

[31] On this, see La Penna 1959: 27–9 (= 1968: 18–21).

evaluated in direct comparison with aristocratic *memoria* requires some clarification. Two scholarly voices that reach precisely opposite conclusions provide exemplary proof of this. In Andrew Feldherr's reading, Sallust here proclaims the superiority of the *historia* he himself practices over the traditional system of aristocratic *memoria*; for it is not the wax masks themselves, but rather the recollection presented by historiography that inspires the viewer or reader to prove themselves.[32] For Stefano Marino, on the other hand, the historian Sallust visualizes in the *imagines* the necessity of a canon of values for coming generations as a prerequisite for the continued existence of the Roman state.[33] According to this interpretation, the intentions of the *memoria* of the *nobiles* and the historiography of Sallust coincide with almost perfect congruence.

Both interpretations have, in my opinion, got something right, but not precisely grasped the meaning of the text. Credit is due to Feldherr as the first to have pointed out the competition between gentilician memorial practice and the historical monograph, though he clearly bends the original text to support his thesis.[34] Marino, on the other hand, emphasizes the overlap between the two forms of recollection, correctly in essence, but too one-sidedly: family tradition emblematized in the wax masks and monographic *historia* are different facets of a single person-centred, specifically Roman memory culture. Potential competition underlines this common affiliation, since an increased need for differentiation is motivated by the very similarity of the forms of memory.

From this perspective let us now examine what advantages and disadvantages are ascribed respectively to the *nobiles*' memory and to *historia*. With the terms *maiorum imagines*, *cera illa*, and *figura*, the ancestral masks are named three times as a medium of remembrance which must have made a particularly powerful impression on the viewer through its unmediated visibility and venerable *auctoritas*. Nevertheless, as a result of their diminished capacity for individualization,[35] the *imagines* require oral exegesis in the form of the *laudatio funebris*, which summons up the successes of the *gens* and the exemplary function of the deceased and his forebears.[36] If the entire Sallustian passage is

---

[32] Feldherr 1998: 28.   [33] Marino 2006: 38.
[34] The text speaks only of *memoria*, not of *historia*.
[35] Walter 2004: 97 n. 60 calls attention to the *imagines*' limited capacity for precise reproduction of facial expressions, as well as to their old age.
[36] Flower 1996: 129–33. Flaig 2004: 58–9 in this connection sees the *imagines* as opposed to the commentating funeral oration as an element of the highest importance, since *laudationes* were also given for common citizens, while the *imagines* remained reserved for the *nobiles*. For a reconstruction of the structure of a funeral oration, and for its development, see Kierdorf 1980.

characterized by a kind of secondary orality, this suggests in no small way the effect of the funeral oration: thus the story in the preceding chapter is transmitted exclusively through verbs of speaking and hearing (*audivi— solitos ita dicere*). The dominance of orality is further reinforced through the whole proem's approximation to the traditional style of epideictic oratory, which was already noticed by Quintilian (*Inst.* 3. 8. 8–9.).[37]

If we follow these traces of a staged orality further, the question arises on just which repeated occasions exemplary *nobiles* like Q. Maximus and P. Scipio might have made their statements about aspiring to the fame of their ancestors; alongside the *laudatio funebris*, we should think above all of speeches in the Senate and during electoral campaigns. This means, however, that the statements (constructed in the text) on the potency of familial *memoria* are motivated by an argumentative personal interest, and indeed in the most extreme case stand under suspicion of deliberately manipulating the facts. The *laudatio funebris* itself offers the best example: one need only mention the accusation levelled in the circles of *homines novi* that the funeral orations preserved in family archives claimed false triumphs and too many consulships for their members in the interest of increasing their reputation.[38]

The historian Sallust does not explicitly subscribe to this accusation of falsifying history in the proem, but he nevertheless implicitly distances himself from the commemoration of the *nobiles*. He does not present the praise of the *imagines*' impact in his own voice, but instead deliberately brings on Quintus Maximus and Publius Scipio as speakers who refer to their own respective family histories. Here the objection could be made that the narrator, by introducing such famous exempla, simply wants to lend his own voice greater authority. But it speaks against this that from a narratological perspective the statements of the introduced characters are personally focalized and—especially in comparison to the voice of the analytical narrator—inevitably coloured and partisan. In this competitive rivalry, then, the *memoria* of the *gentes* trails behind Sallust's monographic writing of history, at least in terms of its claim to objectivity.

Yet another factor shows the deficiency of gentilician memoria in the eyes of the analytical historian: because the funeral oration does not organize history as a narrative, but rather reduces the achievements of the ancestors to a scaffolding of offices and triumphs,[39] it strips the

---

[37] La Penna 1959: 24 (= 1968: 16).
[38] Cic. *Brut.* 62; Liv. 4. 16. 4, 8. 40. 4–5. On the subject, see Ridley 1983; Blösel 2003: 62–6; Walter 2004: 105–7.
[39] Walter 2004: 89–90.

persons being commemorated of all their individual contours. Egon Flaig has plausibly shown that under such conditions there was no need for a deliberate intention to deceive; rather, confusion of identities and mistaken attributions of offices were preprogrammed into the system, particularly as Roman naming conventions further exacerbated the difficulty of distinguishing individual generations.[40] From the point of view of the descendants of leading families, such confusion was no disadvantage, since they acted with a view to augmenting the prestige of the family, and the cumulative commemoration embraced all successful ancestors.[41] Only for the historian who seeks to pin down historical causes and significant dates does the need arise for an unambiguous specification of the responsible actors.

Tellingly, Sallust's text also bears witness to this problem: on closer inspection, it is not at all clear which Q. Maximus and which P. Scipio are meant. If we consider the celebrity of the names, there seems good reason to assume that we are dealing with the two great opponents of Hannibal.[42] But if we read the text from the perspective of the later generation, who imitate their forebears with burning zeal, it is perhaps rather their grandsons who are meant, i.e. the two sons of Aemilius Paulus given up for adoption.[43] The latter assumption is supported by the fact that the elder Scipio Africanus is only briefly mentioned in the prehistory to the *Bellum Iugurthinum*, whereas the younger Scipio Africanus is a crucial participant in the career of the young Jugurtha and so plays an important role in the first chapters of the monograph.[44]

Let us take stock. For the *memoria* of the *gentes* distinguishing specific generations was of secondary importance since all descendants sought to increase and lay claim to the renown of their ancestors through imitation. For the historian, however, who penetrates through to the analysis of first causes and the logical connection between events, great individuals are essential as initiators and bearers of the action. The historical monograph is doubtless far more suitable for individual characterization

---

[40] Flaig 2004: 89–90. On the problems of confused identities and on the verifiability of family histories, with the Porcii Catones as example, see Gell. *NA* 13. 20.

[41] The elegy for Gnaeus Cornelius Scipio Hispanus is representative (*CIL* 1², 15): *virtutes generis mieis moribus accumulavi / progeniem genui, facta patris petiei / maiorum optenui laudem, ut sibei me esse creatum / laetentur: stirpem nobilitavit honor* ('By my conduct I added to the virtues of my family. I produced children. I emulated the deeds of my father. I won the praise of my elders so that they rejoiced I was their progeny. My prestige ennobled the clan'). On this, see Flaig 2004: 85–6.

[42] Paul 1984: 16 identifies Q. Maximus as the famous Cunctator but leaves open the option to take P. Scipio either as the younger or the older Africanus. Beck 2000, Schwarte 2000, and Zahrndt 2000 sketch brief portraits of the figures.

[43] So Koestermann 1971: 39.   [44] See Section 4 below.

mediated through narrative and for the character portrait than the *imagines* and the *laudatio funebris*, which, however polished they may have been, were nevertheless essentially limited to a commemorative piling up of titles and triumphs.

4. NARRATED FAMILY TREES AND SUPPRESSED *COGNOMINA*: A PREHISTORY WITH UNDERTONES

The intentional staging of a competition between oral and written forms of memory is confirmed by a glance at the exposition of the work's subject in the following chapter of the monograph, which describes a transition from orality to writing (*B.J.* 5. 1):

> *bellum scripturus sum, quod populus Romanus cum Iugurtha rege Numidarum gessit, primum quia magnum et atrox variaque victoria fuit, dein quia tunc primum superbiae nobilitatis obviam itum est.*
>
> I am about to write of the war that the Roman people waged with Jugurtha, king of the Numidians, above all because it was weighty and bloody and because the fortunes of battle often changed sides, and, moreover, because the arrogance of the nobility was then opposed for the first time.

The place of speaking and hearing (*B.J.* 4) is now taken by the gesture of writing: *scripturus sum*. This new form of transmission also demands a new perspective on history. It is no longer presented as a continuous chain of successes, but rather as a decisive event in which two historical turning points coincide: the war with Jugurtha, remarkable for its scope and alternating victories, and the first resistance of the *populares* against the corrupt nobility. Marius appears as the common crystallization point of both narrative threads,[45] and of the three great Roman commanders in the *Bellum Iugurthinum* (Metellus, Marius, and Sulla) he receives special attention from the narrator.[46]

---

[45] So already Werner 1995: 18. Although, as mentioned above, the 'first resistance' of the *populares* against the political ruling class should strictly be ascribed to Tiberius Gracchus and—if we consider only the timespan of the *Bellum Iugurthinum*—Memmius, nevertheless the opposition formulated in the Marius speech stands out markedly in the narration, indeed simply through its length.

[46] Particularly in older scholarship, the textual analysis concerning the main characters is overshadowed by the question of their moral worth and *virtus*; this leads inevitably to distorted assessments that mainly declare Metellus the 'real' hero. So Vretska 1955: 95f.; Earl 1961: 119; Klinz 1968: 84–6. Even Dix 2006, already in the title of her monograph, programmatically places the moralizing aspect of characterization in the foreground.

As a result of the individualizing characterization that distinguishes the historical monograph, the exemplum of 'Scipio' introduced in the proem, whose *virtus* served as the trademark of the entire family, is concretized in the opening chapters into two clearly identifiable individuals, namely the elder and the younger Scipio Africanus. These acquire definition through the parallel constructed between the family tree of the Scipios and that of the Numidian royal family, whose lineage is precisely traced in the fifth chapter. Here the narrator takes the reader clearly from Massinissa, king of the Numidians, to his three sons Micipsa, Mastanabal, and Galussa (the last two of whom die of illness), concluding with Micipsa's biological sons, Adherbal and Hiempsal, and nephew Jugurtha, the son of Mastanabal and a concubine.

This relatively complex genealogy is now attached to that of the Scipios at key chronological points. During the Second Punic War, the elder Scipio had compacted a friendship with Massinissa (*B.J.* 5. 4). Two generations later, the latter's grandson Jugurtha earned his first laurels under the younger Scipio in the Numantine war (*B.J.* 7. 2–9. 3). Both Scipios are introduced, significantly, with the identical family name Publius Scipio (*B.J.* 5. 4 and 7. 4); grandfather and grandson only become distinguishable through the narrator's addition of the date, *bello Punico secundo* ('during the Second Punic War', *B.J.* 5. 4), which unambiguously identifies the first-named Scipio Africanus as the Elder. The younger Scipio is differentiated from him with the help of the narrative. For instead of bringing the prehistory introduced by the family trees of the Scipios and the Numidian royal family concisely to its conclusion, the narrator interposes Jugurtha's childhood and youth (*B.J.* 5. 6–7. 1). By unfolding these in comparatively extensive detail, he thus distends the narrative time—parallel to the narrated time—between the first and the second mentions of a Scipio. When he then once again comes to speak of the Scipios, he indicates with the specifying time marker *qui tum Romanis imperator erat* (*B.J.* 7. 4) the interval of two generations and attaches the military successes of the younger Scipio Africanus to the current theatre of war in Spain.

In these introductory chapters, which take in both the family background of the Scipios as *the* dominant *gens* of the second century and the Numidian royal family, the narrator demonstrates not only his historical competence and knowledge of the material, but also his independence from the family memory of the ruling republican *gentes*; the latter aim, as shown above, exclusively at the augmentation of familial glory through the agglomeration of *all* titles and victories. In contrast to this, only the elder Scipio is distinguished in the monograph with his honorific title Africanus, which the historical narrator sees as fully justified as a result of his manifest *virtus*.[47] In the case of the younger Scipio, however, the historian not only suppresses the cognomen, but also the attribute of *virtus*; only Scipio's current authority is defined through the title *imperator* (*B.J.* 7. 4 and 7. 6). This omission strikingly coincides with the implicit characterization of the younger Scipio, particularly in comparison with Jugurtha: while the latter brilliantly proves himself through his *virtus* in battle during the Numantine war, Scipio confines himself to the role of diplomatically calculating adviser who prefers to operate in the background. The narrator further elaborates the ambivalent figure of the younger Scipio[48] by supplementing Jugurtha's public commendation after the fall of Numantia with a much more extensively described private conference. There Scipio not only warns Jugurtha of the competing private interests of Roman political factions, but also seeks to indebt him to himself with a letter of recommendation to the Numidian king Micipsa.

To sum up: the *Bellum Iugurthinum* introduces in the proem and opening chapters of the narrative two competing forms of memory. In comparison to the *memoria* of the *nobiles*—which is invoked through two exemplary representatives of the ruling *gentes*, through the commemorative media of the *imagines*, and through a staged orality—the historian advertises the superiority of the historical monograph: this proves its qualification through the claim to objectivity of a distanced observer who imports gentilician *memoria* into an analytical, historical model transcending parties and, through the comparison of family trees, adapts an aristocratic commemorative medium into a narrative and appropriates it. The historical monograph further distinguishes itself through its focus on epoch-making events and through a multifaceted character depiction that allows ample space to the individuality of historical actors; this is precisely what a comprehensive and complexly composed narrative makes possible.

5. COMPETING MEMORIALIZATIONS IN THE SPEECH OF MARIUS

Let us now turn to the speech of Marius. As shown in Section 1, scholarship has addressed this speech in many ways; this allows me to focus my investigation on the memorial competition staged in the text

---

[47] *B.J.* 5. 4: *a Publio Scipione, quoi postea Africano cognomen ex virtute fuit.*
[48] Zahrndt 2000 draws an equally brief and instructive portrait of the 'machinating grandson'.

Reflected Narratology in Marius' Speech

and on the various voices of the past. I will show, first, how the *popularis* speaker appropriates the nobles' traditional 'sphere' of memory. Second, I will ask how the renewed reference to the *imagines* at this point develops and modifies the statements of the proem within the work's narrative. In this connection I will explain how the extradiegetic narrator, contrary to strict narrative logic, raises the literary character up to a higher diegetic level and allows him to present an alternative vision of history in competition with the historian's perspective. Third, it will be shown how the narrator, through the functionalization of the discourse on memory, for his part claims superior authority over the literary figure of Marius, and indeed quite disavows him.

5. 1. The antagonistic appropriation of the aristocratic memorial space

I return to the quotation that stands at the beginning of this essay: *non sunt conposita verba mea*. This fictive personal statement points in two directions: first, Marius sets himself apart from the rhetorically educated *nobiles* and, second, he casts himself with his professed renunciation of cultivated oratorical technique as the direct successor of those speakers of the early Republic who did not yet have access to the refinements of Greek rhetoric. Thus, while the contemporary representatives of the ruling elite have long since lapsed from the *mos maiorum*, the people's leader Marius alone keeps the memory of the ancestors alive through his words.

Because Marius himself verbalizes his lack of education, he leaves no doubt that his proclaimed renunciation of rhetorical technique is based not on linguistic inability, but rather on an archaizing self-comparison to exemplary representatives of republican norms and values. By presenting himself through various echoes as a new Cato, the speaker seeks to enlist Cato's *auctoritas* and the *auctoritas* of the old Romans in general for his cause.

The linguistic appropriation of the *maiores* goes together with a reshaping of the *nobiles*' memorial practice. This is most visible in Marius' construction of virtual family trees that legitimate him as a bearer of old Roman *virtus*. Here he operates with various and indeed thoroughly contradictory modes of thought, such that strategies of both pointed distancing and personal ennoblement are deployed, as well as, conversely, the communalization of gentilician memorial practice. On the one hand, the speaker self-consciously maintains that the deceased fathers of the former consuls Bestia and Albinus would only too gladly accept such a successful soldier as Marius in place of their own sons (*B.J.* 85. 16).[49] But as soon as the *popularis* has thus ennobled himself, he the next moment devalues the ruling class with his claim to surpass their honorific titles heaped up over generations with his own weapons and self-earned scars (*B.J.* 85. 29).[50]

Finally, the *homo novus* Marius—as it were to compensate for his lack of available *imagines*—lends the highest authority to his own father by uniting his admonitory voice with a chorus of other honourable men (*nam ex parente meo et ex aliis sanctis viris ita accepi*..., 'For from my own father and other revered men I have learned...' *B.J.* 85. 40). Since this illustrious circle makes up a sort of prestigious collective Roman gallery of exemplary possessors of *virtus*,[51] it can easily measure itself against any family pedigree. With an appeal to the common accessibility of the *maiores*, transcending party and class divisions, Marius divests the *nobiles* of their interpretative sovereignty over the past and transfers it to the Roman people (*B.J.* 85. 36):[52]

> *Haec atque alia talia maiores* **vestri** *faciendo seque remque publicam celebravere.*
>
> Through this and similar behaviour, your ancestors made themselves and their country celebrated.

5. 2. The stentorian voice of the orator in the power dynamics of the narrative

Up to this point, the literary transformation of authentic speeches of Marius in the Sallustian text may be plausibly supposed, in keeping with the historical scholarship. But the narrative potential of the speech of

---

[49] Carney 1959: 65–8 has called attention to a particular point: Albinus and Bestia both belong to *gentes* closely connected with the Scipios. On this basis, Carney interprets Marius' attacks as a parody of the epitaphs of the Scipios; this would be especially piquant in so far as Scipio Aemilianus, according to Plutarch (*Mar.* 3. 2–4. 1), had promoted Marius' career before Numantia, with the result that the rhetorical attack could be seen as a breach of *fides*. However, such a specific reference to the epigraphical epitaphs of the Scipios is hardly demonstrable. It therefore seems to me more appropriate merely to posit a general attack on the memorial praxis of the *nobiles*.

[50] On the semiotics of the display of scars, see Flaig 2004: 123–6.

[51] The rhetorical tactic of exploiting the collective of *maiores* as one's own virtual family tree is reminiscent of the statuary programme of *summi viri* in the Forum of Augustus conceived between 42 and 2 BCE—not least because of the temporal proximity (the *Bellum Iugurthinum* may be dated to the end of the 40s).

[52] Blösel 2003: 71; on the fundamental requirement of extra-gentilician approval on the part of the Senate and people, which actively influenced the formation of collective memory and the *mos maiorum* through selection and recognition of achievements, see Flaig 2004: 85–7.

Marius is by no means exhausted as a consequence. As I would like to show in what follows, a powerful voice of opposition to the narrator's authority is established in the speech. The historian signals through verbal reminiscences of the proem that he allows the speaker Marius to reach the level of the extradiegetic narrator. This is not only a question of a recurring motif within the work; rather, this transgression of diegetic levels in contradiction to all narrative logic gives the reader the impression that the speaker attempts to drown out the narrator with his own stentorian voice.

Marius programmatically appropriates the purpose of the historian formulated in chapter five of the *Jugurtha*. A comparison of passages reveals a significant shifting of emphasis between the historical narrator's announcement of his subject and the self-conscious statement of the newly elected consul and future general:

> *bellum scripturus sum, quod **populus Romanus** cum Iugurtha rege Numidarum gessit.* (B.J. 5. 1)
>
> I am about to write of the war that the Roman people waged with Jugurtha, king of the Numidians.
>
> *bellum **me gerere** cum Iugurtha iussistis.* (B.J. 85. 10)
>
> You have commanded me to wage war against Jugurtha.

The reader may at first recognize in the altered quotation an encouraging sign that the hitherto unsuccessful desert war will finally take a happy turn thanks to Marius. The newly elected consul casts himself as an ambitious representative of the interests of the people, who have not entrusted him with the *imperium* against Jugurtha in vain. Only with a second look does it become apparent that the renown of the *populus Romanus* is drastically curtailed by its own champion: while in the statement of the narrator it was the people who waged the war against Jugurtha, Marius styles himself as the authorized principal actor who assumes sole responsibility for the success of the war. From a historical perspective, it was, of course, never the *populus* who waged war in the proper sense, but rather always a general; this makes it all the more remarkable that the narrator, in his declaration of theme, on the one hand reduces the entire Numidian population to their king Jugurtha, but then opposes to him—rather than the executive generals Metellus and Marius—the entire *populus Romanus*, which thus becomes a symbolic principal actor in the story.[53]

---

[53] So already Wille 1970: 304.

The speaker sharpens his opposition to the nobility in a second alteration of the historian's text. First, a verbatim comparison:

> atque ego credo fore qui, quia decrevi procul a re publica aetatem agere, tanto tamque utili labori meo nomen inertiae imponant, certe quibus maxima industria videtur salutare plebem et *conviviis gratiam quaerere*. (B.J. 4. 3)

> And yet I believe, because I have decided to spend my days far removed from political activity, some will call such important and useful labour idleness; certainly those who consider it their highest mission to make themselves beloved of the masses and ingratiate themselves with banquets.

> quin ergo, quod iuvat, quod carum aestimant, id semper faciant: ament, potent; **ubi adulescentiam habuere, ibi senectutem agant, in conviviis**, dediti ventri et turpissimae parti corporis; sudorem, pulverem et alia talia relinquant nobis, quibus illa epulis iucundiora sunt. (B.J. 85. 41)

> Go on, then, let them for ever do what they enjoy and what they hold dear: let them make love and drink and spend their old age where they spent their youth, at banquets, devoted to their bellies and the basest part of their bodies; and let them leave the sweat and the dust and other such things to us, who find that pleasanter than feasting.

The representatives of the upper class, as the narrator accuses them in his proem, with their deliberately wasteful dinner parties through which they try to ensnare voters, are hardly in a moral position to rebuke the historian for his retreat into *otium*. The luxurious *convivia* are here doubly situated: first, they are pointedly introduced as an argument to support the superior utility of history writing over political activity and to defend the narrator's own *otium studiosum*. Second, the hosting of opulent *convivia* is made to serve the ends of electoral campaigning. The speaker Marius generalizes a practice linked in the proem specifically to bribing voters, making it into a byword for a decadent lifestyle that a priori disqualifies the members of the upper class for positions of honour.

With the help of these textual examples, we can now draw some conclusions about the habits of expression of the narrator and the orator: The narrator analyses events in a nuanced way and introduces characters who combine black and white. Thus, he casts a critical eye not only on the ruling class of *nobiles*, but also on *homines novi*, and in both social groups constructs a sharp antithesis between the present and periods of crisis in the past when the *virtus* of Roman generals proved itself brilliantly (B.J. 4. 7–8):

> at contra quis est omnium his moribus, quin divitiis et sumptibus, non probitate neque industria cum maioribus suis contendat? *etiam* **homines novi**, qui antea per virtutem soliti erant nobilitatem antevenire, furtim et per latrocinia potius quam bonis artibus ad imperia et honores nituntur; proinde

quasi praetura et consulatus atque alia omnia huiusce modi per se ipsa clara et magnifica sint ac non perinde habeantur, ut eorum qui ea sustinent virtus est.

Yet with the customs of today, what single person exists but that he tries to rival his ancestors in riches and expense, rather than in righteousness and industry? Even those without pedigree (*homines novi*), who once habitually used to outdo the nobility through their bravery, now grasp at military commands and honourary offices more through stealth and theft than by respectable means, as if the praetor- and consulship and everything else of the kind were brilliant and wonderful things in themselves, and not to be judged instead according to the worth of those who bear them.

The mention of social climbers confronts the reader with the unavoidable question of whether Marius, the most renowned *homo novus* of the Jugurthine war, should be assigned to the generation of highly praised bearers of *virtus* or to the furtive intriguers. The ambiguous character of the future victor of the desert war is thus already introduced in the proem. Because the narrator does not take a clear stance, he imposes this duty on the reader, whose task it is to decide whether the words and deeds of the actors—especially those of Marius—agree.

Whereas an elected consul ought to represent Roman interests that transcend class and party divisions, the Sallustian Marius sharpens partisan enmity for his own advantage: as Volker Werner has already noticed, the *res publica* plays a quite subordinate role in this speech, where it is mentioned only five times.[54] The newly elected consul Marius thereby reveals himself as an inflammatory partisan of the *populares*. Even worse, he not only attacks the nobility but also strips the Roman people of its famous achievements and makes himself supreme. Marius ultimately recognizes his obligation to no one but himself.

It is not only on the narrated level that a Marius can brook no competition. As has been shown, his character is so constructed that it even attempts to appropriate the narrator's authority by means of modified quotations. Through this behaviour, this one character in the work ascribes extraordinary privileges to himself. All other speakers in the *Bellum Iugurthinum* make reference only to other figures within the confines of the story. None apart from Marius attempts to ascend to an external diegetic level, which indeed lies in the distant future in relation to him. Through this process of metalepsis not only do the personae of the narrator and of Marius enter into competition, but their preferred forms of historical representation do so as well. The historian could hardly have set the power of oral speech more effectively on the stage.

[54] Werner 1995: 64.

5.3. Masks and masquerades: In the light and shadow of the ancestors

If the voice of the narrator finally does gain the upper hand over the speaker, this too happens through a renewed allusion to the ancestral images. We turn now to this most striking echo of the proem, which has not yet been discussed. First, the relevant passage of the speech (*B.J.* 85. 21–5):

> atque etiam, cum apud vos aut in senatu verba faciunt, pleraque oratione maiores suos extollunt: eorum fortia facta memorando clariores sese putant. quod contra est. nam quanto vita illorum praeclarior, tanto horum socordia flagitiosior, et profecto ita se res habet: **maiorum gloria posteris quasi lumen est, neque bona neque mala eorum in occulto patitur.** huiusce rei ego inopiam fateor, Quirites, verum, id quod multo praeclarius est, meamet facta mihi dicere licet. nunc videte, quam iniqui sint. quod ex aliena virtute sibi arrogant, id mihi ex mea non concedunt, scilicet quia imagines non habeo et quia mihi nova nobilitas est, quam certe peperisse melius est quam acceptam corrupisse.

> And when they speak before you or in the Senate, they also celebrate their ancestors in many fine words; and by praising their heroic deeds they reckon they make themselves more famous. But the opposite is true. For the more brilliant the life of the ancestors, the more scandalous their own lack of care. This is the way it is: the glory of the ancestors is like a bright light for their descendants; it leaves neither their virtues nor their faults in the dark. I confess my own lack of this ancestral glory, citizens; but—and this is much more outstanding—I can speak of my own actions. Now consider how unjust these people are: what they claim for themselves on the basis of others' virtue they do not allow me on the basis of my own; naturally, since I have no ancestral portraits and my nobility is still fresh. And yet it is certainly better to have engendered nobility than to have corrupted the nobility you inherited.

In the passage from the proem quoted previously, Q. Maximus and P. Scipio, two exemplary representatives of the ruling class, as may have been expected from their ancestry, had praised the affective power of the *imagines*, the sight of which sets every excellent man aflame for *virtus*. Against this Marius draws a contrasting image of history: where there is light, there must also be shadow.[55] The flame of *memoria* thus becomes a touchstone by illuminating not only the *virtutes* but also the *vitia* of future generations. The *homo novus* in this way drives a wedge into nobles' constructed historical continuity, relegating the descendants of renowned *gentes* to the shadow of their brilliant *maiores* and

---

[55] On normative power and the range of interpretations in the employment of good and bad exempla, see Walter 2004: 57–70.

letting his own deeds shine rather than theirs.[56] At the same time, he seeks to fashion capital out of his own major deficiency: since he has no *imagines*, he does not have to compete with their example. In contrast to the successful *gentes*, whose members were under enormous pressure to perform, Marius enters into the competition for titles and offices unburdened: he can count each rank he achieves as a gain.

If Marius, in the style of Cato the Elder, demands unconditional recognition for his self-won achievements,[57] he also sets a standard for his own person and deeds. The reader is thereby encouraged to compare the speaker's vaunting self-evaluation closely with the narrator's introductory judgement of history and the course of the plot so far. A review of the plot events occurring before the Marius speech is, however, quite revealing, as scholarship has shown in many ways.[58] For the image of Marius that emerges from the narration starkly contradicts the speaker's own self-representation: Marius has not yet shown much of that *virtus* that he invokes as a compensation for his lack of *imagines* and as the principle of his military career. On the contrary, the chapters immediately preceding the speech make clear that Marius has obtained the consulship primarily through inflammatory demagoguery and systematic defamation of the general Metellus. The accusation formulated by the historian in the proem that the latest generation of *homines novi* satisfy their ambitions through deceit and subterfuge rather than upright behaviour finds exemplary confirmation in Marius. Thus, while Marius attacks the *nobiles* for their ancestor masks on account of their hollow boastfulness, he himself is discredited by the narrator for his rhetorical masquerade. A glance back at the vision of history laid out in the proem reveals that such an unmasking lies precisely in the interest of the historical narrator, who wants to trace with his monograph the deterioration in values of both political parties, *nobiles* as well as *populares*.[59]

6. MARIUS THE *TRIUMPHATOR* AS JULIAN ANCESTRAL IMAGE

By way of conclusion, we may rightly ask whether this dark picture of Marius the populist demagogue is perhaps brightened by his successful war leadership in the second half of the work. Here scholarship has come

---

[56] Flaig 2004: 75–6.   [57] Cf. Plut. *Cat. Mai.* 1.
[58] For example, Klinz 1968: 82–4; Syme 1964: 162–3; Marino 2006: 38–440; Dix 2006: 225.
[59] So already Dix 2006: 298–9.

to decidedly different conclusions, depending on how much weight one ascribes respectively to the overambitious speaker and the successful officer within the work, and how one evaluates Marius' personal share in the victory over Jugurtha.[60] For all its incremental variations, the complexity of Marius' character portrait (ranging from ambiguous to dark) can, nevertheless, be called the *communis opinio*.

Therefore, only the programmatic final chapter of the work will be considered here, with respect to two aspects central to my inquiry: far-reaching thematic echoes and potentially competing forms and media of commemoration.

Retrospective allusions to the proem and to the speech of Marius reveal that the narrative macrostructure also plays an important role in the final chapter. Let us first bring the text before us (*B.J.* 114):

> *per idem tempus advorsum Gallos ab ducibus nostris Q. Caepione et Cn. Manlio male pugnatum. quo metu Italia omnis contremuerat. illique et inde usque ad nostram memoriam Romani sic habuere, alia omnia virtuti suae prona esse, cum Gallis pro salute, non pro gloria certare. sed postquam bellum in Numidia confectum et Iugurtham Romam vinctum adduci nuntiatum est, Marius consul absens factus est, et ei decreta provincia Gallia, isque Kalendis Ianuariis magna gloria consul triumphavit. et ea tempestate spes atque opes civitatis in illo sitae.*

> At the same time a defeat at the hands of the Gauls was suffered under our generals Quintus Caepio and Gnaeus Manlius, and all of Italy trembled with fear. Then and even down to our own day Romans believed that everything else would bow to their courage, but when it came to the Gauls the contest was for survival, not for glory. But after the war in Numidia was ended and the report came that Jugurtha was being brought to Rome in chains, Marius was named consul *in absentia* and Gaul was allotted to him as his province, and on the first of January as consul he held a magnificent triumph. At that time the hope and power of the state were placed in this one man.

As already in the proem, the final chapter too opens a 'historical vista' that explicitly connects the narrated past of the Jugurthine war with the lifetime of the historian (*illique et inde usque ad nostram memoriam*, 'then and even down to our own day', *B.J.* 114. 2). The Gallic Wars, in which the recent successes of Marius' nephew Caesar seem indirectly foreshadowed, following immediately after the war with Jugurtha, function as a conceptual linking device. Thus, in the final chapter a sort of

---

[60] Klinz 1968: 84–6 and Dix 2006: 226–47 represent a negative or critical assessment; Werner 1995: 69–87, by contrast, sketches a subtle picture of the general Marius, variegated according to defensive or aggressive situations.

family tree emerges which outlines not primarily the familial relationship, but rather the kinship of spirit between Marius and Caesar: both combine in their ambiguous character military *virtus* and unchecked *ambitio*, and both transform themselves fatally from successful conqueror to leader of a bloody civil war.

Through this implicit connection, the *homo novus* Marius, who himself possesses no *imagines*, unexpectedly becomes himself the ancestral image of Julius Caesar. The final chapter of the monograph, published perhaps around 40 BCE, hints not only at Marius' popularity at the time, but also at his timeless potential to be summoned into the present, of which Julius Caesar had already availed himself some thirty years before in equally provocative and propagandistic fashion: as Plutarch reports in his *Life of Caesar*, the young Caesar ordered the image of Marius to be carried in the Julian *pompa funebris* of his aunt in 69 BCE. He thereby not only established a conspicuous continuity between the Julian *gens* and Marius, but also violated the *damnatio memoriae* imposed by Sulla.[61] This contravention of the erasure of collective memory was greeted by the people with rejoicing and applause.[62]

Marius' popularity, which received a massive boost through the victory over Jugurtha, is directly addressed by the narrator in the final chapter: while Marius acquired his first consulship through a perfidious campaign against the incumbent general Metellus and ruthless electioneering, he is now as a result of his military successes elected consul even *in absentia* and entrusted with the command of the Gallic Wars. The general Marius seems at first glance to have thoroughly justified the claim to military *virtus* in his accession speech.

However, another retrospective comparison between the intention of the historian formulated at the opening, the character's speech on his accession to the consulship, and the narrator's commentary at the end of the work makes clear how the Sallustian Marius over the course of the narrative increasingly appropriates the Roman people's share in the victory for himself. The historian 'will write of the war that the Roman people waged with Jugurtha'—in *B.J.* 5. 1 the name of the victor Marius is not even mentioned. In a grand gesture, the newly elected consul Marius presents himself in his accession speech as the people's commissioned general, who offers his *virtus* to the service of Rome; accordingly, in *B.J.* 85. 10 the interests of people and consul stand in a tensed interdependency. In the final triumph of the re-elected consul, the glory of the

---

[61] On the political message and propagandistic efficacy of this gesture, see Flaig 2004: 92–4.
[62] Plut. *Caes.* 5, Suet. *Iul.* 6. 1.

war is finally attributed to Marius alone. It may, of course, be objected, from a historical viewpoint, that in a triumph the victorious general was indeed always distinguished from the multitude, and that, therefore, from a Roman perspective the focusing of the final chapter on the conqueror Marius would not have shocked a contemporary reader. But on the level of narrative technique it remains true that with the progression of the story the emphasis shifts more and more onto the protagonist Marius, until finally the *populus Romanus* completely vanishes from view.

In the analytical view of the historical narrator, the *popularis* Marius thus emerges from the Jugurthine war as the unopposed repository of hope with unlimited access to power. The temporal marker *ea tempestate spes atque opes in illo sitae*, however, makes clear that this is a snapshot of a single moment.[63] In the end, it is left open to the late republican reader whether to read the final sentence with reference only to the time window of the *Bellum Iugurthinum*, and therefore to credit Marius with an unqualified victory; or, with retrospective knowledge of the historical consequences, to detect in it an intimated warning.[64] At the very least, the reader can recognize the invitation to bridge the gap from the Jugurthine war to the later Civil War with Sulla. Against this background it is difficult not to draw a contemporary parallel with the victor over the Gauls and subsequent initiator of a civil war—Caesar.

SUMMARY

The visual emblem of the *imagines* not only points to the shared function of *memoria* and *historia*, but also proclaims the particular qualities of the historical monograph against the foil of gentilician commemorative practice; the latter's visual and textual media (from *imagines* to family trees to the *laudatio funebris*), which aim to construct, from an exclusively aristocratic perspective, stories of the uninterrupted success of politically influential families, and which consciously and deliberately suppress temporary lapses in achievement, are tendentious or at least subject to error. Precisely for this reason, they can serve as an easy target for a *popularis* partisan such as Marius, who, for his part, without regard for

---

[63] The perfect tense of the final word, indicating a completed action, also underlines the temporal limitation.

[64] A negative, indeed ironical interpretation is adopted by, among others, Büchner 1953: 62; Vretska 1955: 129; Syme 1964: 176–7; Scanlon 1987: 60–1; Dix 2006: 248–9, particularly with reference to the explicitly foreshadowing characterization of Marius (*B.J.* 63. 6: *nam postea ambitione praeceps datus est*); Werner 1995: 90–1 sees the conclusion in an overall positive light.

distortion of truth and with all the tools of rhetorical artistry, drafts a biased picture of history in his own interest.

Against these focalized and also politically functionalized forms of pictoriality and orality, the historian Sallust constructs his own interpretative authority: the superiority of his chosen form of representation is grounded in the claim to objectivity of a distanced reporter, in causal analysis and individualized characterization and, not least, in the complex structure of his narrative. Sallust's representational art is not limited to the glorifying enumeration of titles and names, nor to populist attacks on the values, norms, and behaviour of the ruling elite. Rather, he is capable of coordinating various levels and plot threads, taking a nuanced position with regard to historical persons and events, and integrating fiery speeches into his narrative as compositional highlights.

The revisionary allusion in Marius' speech to the commemorative power of the *imagines* reinscribes a discourse introduced in the proem onto the level of the narration, via the focalized speech of a character. In the final chapter the extradiegetic narrator once again takes up a programmatic position. Both voices—the extradiegetic narrator's and the character's—are interwoven through motivic references in such a way that narrator and speaker reciprocally cite, re-evaluate, and comment on each other. As characters and voices overlap, along with forms of written and oral discourse as well as the two temporal levels of the *Bellum Iugurthinum* (the time of the action, belonging to the ambivalent 'hero' Marius, and the moment of the work's composition), the programmatic passages on historiography in the proem and conclusion together with the speech of Marius come to make up a kind of narratological puzzle picture.

13

On the Introduction to Sallust's *Histories*

Friedrich Klingner

It is thanks to Augustine that we can not only hear a few disjointed phrases from the introduction to Sallust's *Histories* but see the main dimensions of the overview of Rome's historical development he constructed at the work's opening. After the pagans had used the optimistic picture of Roman development, which had dominated the imperial period since the time of Augustus, to blame the Christians for having caused the collapse of the empire, Augustine used their opponents' own weapons to defend the Christians by countering with Sallust's pessimistic view of history. For the formation of this historical picture he specifically selected the proem of the *Histories* as most suitable for his purposes because it exhibits the darkest colours. The introduction to the *Catiline* (*B.C.* 6–13) was also available to him, and he made strategic use of comparing them. In the *Catiline* (*B.C.* 5–9), Sallust had presented the old Romans as noble people and fine citizens; in the *Histories*, he filled the entire early period except for two brief stretches with signs of decay, and thereby showed how matters really stood in the good old times praised in the *Catiline*, when justice allegedly prevailed through man's natural inclination and did not yet need to be enforced through law (*De civ. D.* 2. 18). Augustine accordingly played the *Histories* against the *Catiline*[1]—and rightly, since the survey at the beginning of the *Histories* is indeed a more fully developed version of that at the beginning of the *Catiline*, but also stands in contradiction to it. He does not acknowledge the intermediary link in the *Jugurtha* (*B.J.* 41–2), and of this work he can be shown to be familiar only with the proem and the excursus on Africa (*B.J.* 17. 3; *De civ. D* 16. 17, see testimonia in Ahlberg 1915). Otherwise,

---

[1] The same procedure is used at *De civ. D.* 5. 12, 15ff., and 30ff.: here too Augustine opposes the proem of the *Histories* to the idealized treatment of the past in the *Catiline*.

he would have been able to discover a linear development in these three views of history. Only in the *Catiline* does an essentially good human race stand at the beginning. Freedom must only unleash its force, and an exemplary nation stands fully formed. Here, to reverse the course of this development, a *deus ex machina* must intervene from without: after the destruction of Carthage *saevire Fortuna und miscere omnia coepit* ('Fortune began to rage and throw all things into confusion', *B.C.* 10. 1)—a device that Sallust uses only in this one place in the earliest of the three historical works. In the *Jugurtha* (*B.J.* 41–2), the fall of Carthage is once again the turning point; but since at first only an external cause, the threat of an enemy, keeps the Romans in a healthy state, it is apparent that with the coming of peace and prosperity the decline sets in on its own. Perhaps at some earlier time good conditions had prevailed without external pressure. Or perhaps they had been maintained by continuous threats from the beginnings up until the fall of Carthage. We cannot say, since Sallust never treats the early period in this work, but nevertheless at the most important point the picture becomes much darker. As another mark of the increase in Sallust's pessimism, the *Catiline* speaks of the corruption of only one party,[2] whereas in *Jugurtha* 41. 5 both sides were equally to blame at the outset, except that the nobility gained the upper hand through its organization and in this way became both the engine of development and the bearer of guilt. Finally, in the *Histories*, Sallust paints black on black and explicitly says that the signs of decay, which spread so virulently after the fall of Carthage, had been present since the beginning; only two periods of the most terrible external compulsion had succeeded in subduing them. As far as the parties are concerned, base self-interest was the motive for all, the professed intention a mere pretext (*H.* 1.12, 1.13 M). According to *Catiline* 38. 3, this first began after the year 70 as a consequence of the total disintegration set in motion by Sulla.

This development in Sallust's conception of Roman history is related, first, to Sallust's internal transformation in the last eight years of his life and, second, to the earlier tradition of this Roman historical schema. Regarding the first, this is not the place to evaluate the thesis of Schwartz 1897—adopted and exaggerated by Lauckner 1911, Alheit 1919, Rosenberg 1921, and Baehrens 1926—and to show how, in the period after Caesar's death, Sallust's pessimism allegedly extended to everything that was at that time connected to Roman politics, including the so-called Caesarians.[3]

---

[2] Sallust does not mention the oligarchy by name, but it is evident from the context that he means it and it alone.

[3] Only the following will be briefly mentioned. According to Schwartz, Sallust's *oeuvre* is an injured man's revenge against the *optimates* who threw him off the path to power;

Here, on the other hand, the earlier tradition of this philosophy of history will be brought to light and the literary presuppositions of the proem to the *Histories* pointed out—and thereby the structure and intention of the work itself. First, however, some clarity is needed regarding the course of the proem.

> *[We here omit Klingner's comprehensive reconstruction of the first sixteen fragments of the* Histories *in Maurenbrecher's edition. A major point of this discussion is the emphasis Sallust places on the year 146 BCE as a crucial moment of moral transformation.]*

The inquiry into the models and foundations for this total picture of Roman history can now be taken up again. Where else does one encounter the view that the year 146 BCE marked the point when Roman fortunes took a turn for the worse? Among grave-minded Romans in the time of the Gracchi and earlier, it was perhaps a rather widespread sentiment that affairs had been going downhill for some time. Cato had continually presented the old times to his fellow citizens—without, however, drawing a definite boundary, as far as we can tell. His more modest successor Piso had placed the turning point in the year 154 BCE; he thought of the present pessimistically, and his history presents itself as an attempt to restore the old virtues.

Polybius 6. 57, written under the influence of the first shocks to the structure of the Roman state, is closer; though the chapter does not explicitly speak of the destruction of Carthage, this among other things is meant. When a state has survived many difficult struggles and obtains an outstanding position and undisputed dominance (ϵἰς ὑπεροχὴν καὶ δυναστείαν ἀδήριτον), then, together with prosperity, extravagant living and reckless conflict over power set in, and the second of these occurs earlier. Swindling the weak, on the one hand, and courting the favour of voters, on the other, destabilize the masses' moral equilibrium until they

---

according to Rosenberg, propagandistic service to his party, i.e. the Caesarians. These interpretations do not explain why Sallust did not return to politics in the thirties. It would have been a small matter for Octavian or Antony to retain against the opposition a man nearly, but ultimately not convicted of extortion. Second, the interpretation from the struggle over external power moves beyond Sallust's own words at *B.J.* 3, which for their part, taken together with his state of retirement at the time when Octavian was in power, yield a picture of a man inwardly withdrawing to the sidelines. Third, this interpretation reduces his writing to a mere means to a material end. An *oeuvre* that continually radiates such powerful intellectual force can never be made comprehensible in this way. In the end, the assumption that in his historical interpretation of the Sullan state Sallust carried on an intellectual battle over the picture of this state without practical purposes and intentions adequately explains the positive findings of Schwartz and his followers.

On the Introduction to Sallust's Histories

no longer submit to being governed. Thus, arise, allegedly, freedom and democracy; in reality, mob rule.

Did Sallust develop his schema out of Polybius? Or is there some intermediary source which, alongside the principal terms occurring here, also speaks of *optimi mores et concordia* ('excellent customs and concord'), *metus Punicus* ('fear of the Carthaginians'), *discordia, seditiones, ad postremum bella civilia* ('conflicts, insurrections, ultimately, civil war'), and in which all of this is explicitly grouped around the fall of Carthage? These requirements are precisely fulfilled by Diodorus 34. 33.

Scipio Nasica, the opponent of Cato, adduced the following reason for his opinion that Carthage should not be destroyed:

> As long as Carthage survived, the **fear** it generated compelled the Romans to **concord**, and to rule their subjects moderately and respectably... but once their rival was destroyed, it was obvious that **civil war** would arise among the citizens, and hatred among the allies for Rome's rule... and all of this befell Rome after the destruction of Carthage; for dangerous **demagoguery**, land confiscations, large-scale rebellions of the allies, **civil wars** that were long-lasting and terrible, and everything else Scipio predicted came to pass.[4]

As far as *luxus atque avaritia* ('luxury and greed') are concerned, this passage is complemented by Diodorus 38. 2,[5] where the primary cause of the Italian War is said to be the Romans' shift from the simple, hard lifestyle that first won them such pre-eminence to luxury; this luxury led to the rebellion of the people against the Senate, and the Senate called the Italians to its aid with the promise of citizenship.

The relation of these passages to Sallust is clear. The passage from book 34, however, is taken from the account of 111 BCE, the year in which the consul Scipio Nasica died. Diodorus takes the opportunity to acknowledge Nasica and above all his two most recent ancestors, of whom he believes the grandfather to be both the famous opponent of Cato and the man deemed by the Senate the best in Rome, and therefore worthy to receive the statue of the Great Mother goddess, the

---

[4] σωζομένης μὲν τῆς Καρχηδόνος ὁ ἀπὸ ταύτης **φόβος ἠνάγκαζεν ὁμονοεῖν** τοὺς Ῥωμαίους καὶ τῶν ὑποτεταγμένων ἐπιεικῶς καὶ ἐνδόξως ἄρχειν·…ἀπολομένης δὲ τῆς ἀντιπάλου πόλεως πρόδηλος ἦν ἐν μὲν τοῖς πολίταις **ἐμφύλιος πόλεμος** ἐσόμενος, ἐκ δὲ τῶν συμμάχων ἁπάντων μῖσος εἰς τὴν ἡγεμονίαν…. ἅπερ ἅπαντα συνέβη τῇ Ῥώμῃ μετὰ τὴν τῆς Καρχηδόνος κατασκαφήν· καὶ γὰρ ἐπικίνδυνοι **δημαγωγίαι** καὶ χώρας ἀναδασμοὶ καὶ συμμάχων ἀποστάσεις μεγάλαι καὶ **ἐμφύλιοι πόλεμοι** πολυετεῖς καὶ φοβεροὶ καὶ τἆλλα τὰ προαγορευθέντα ὑπὸ τοῦ Σκιπίωνος ἠκολούθησεν.

[5] Theißen 1912: 21 already makes Sallust *B.C.* 6ff. and *B.J.* 41–2 dependent on Posidonius through a comparison with Diodorus 37. 3 and 38. 2.

magna mater.⁶ The greatest space in the treatment of this grandfather of the consul of 111 is occupied by his prophetic attitude during the debates on the Carthaginian question.

That Diodorus inserted this entire passage himself is out of the question. His source at this point, at least in the narration of Roman affairs,⁷ is Posidonius.⁸ The passage itself seems to fit Posidonius' style—the aristocratic attitude that nevertheless disapproves of the faults of the oligarchy, the moralizing posture, the remark at the end of the chapter that the consul of 111 had studied philosophy and actually practised it in his life, rather than paying it mere lip service. It was thus Posidonius who used the death of this Nasica to erect a monument to the family that embodied his conception of aristocracy. It so happened that the prophetic attitude of that enemy of the elder Cato already contained Posidonius' own interpretation of the historical period he was representing; the phrasing of the thought clearly expresses the view that developments after the fall of Carthage *and up to the Civil Wars* of the eighties form a unity.

The passage in question—supplemented by that from book 38, which itself closely resembles attested fragments of Posidonius—gives us the main perspective from which Posidonius saw the subject of his history. The preserved passage is certainly not the only one to have contained this overall picture; one may imagine that the introduction or some expressly inserted chapters served this end, as in Sallust. It is, however, a fortunate coincidence that precisely this passage is preserved, which allows a glance at the preconditions in terms of history of ideas behind Posidonius' conception of history. Posidonius' schema has already been connected to Polybius above; but Polybius' own conception stands close to an idea which had been important in the political discussion of the first half-century, and which was adopted at the critical moment by Nasica as leader of the Scipionic party. It was already believed of the elder Africanus that he had deliberately not pursued his victory over Carthage as far as its annihilation because he wanted the Romans always to have an object of fear nearby to keep them in a sound state (App. *Pun.* 65). In 167 BCE Cato appropriated this idea and brought it to the defence of Rhodes, explicitly naming Africanus as a source, probably at the end of the speech,

---

⁶ [In fact, the Scipio who accompanied the statue to Rome was the father of Cato's opponent. (eds.)]

⁷ Baehrens 1926: 67ff. doubts whether this is true of the Jugurthine war; whether he is right need not be discussed here.

⁸ Busolt 1890: 321; Schwartz, 'Diodorus', *RE* 5. 1, p. 690; Rosenberg 1921: 117, 200. For Posidonius' picture of development, see ibid., 198.

according to Gellius *NA* 6. 3. 47, where he spoke of the repercussions the Senate's decision would have on Rome's internal circumstances and therefore on the future of the empire.[9]

Not long thereafter, when the subject was Carthage, Cato became the bitter opponent of the argument he had defended so eloquently; the Scipionic party under the leadership of Nasica, however, still clung to it. One imagines that later, when the fears had become reality, Nasica was often recalled. Posidonius, then, alluded to his opinion and saw in it the crucial insight about Roman history since the Third Punic War. The decision against Nasica in 149 BCE was fateful; its consequence was the ever-increasing rebelliousness of the masses against their leaders, which ultimately led to the Civil War. Sulla finally brought this turmoil to a halt and rebuilt the state as it had stood before that erroneous decision; for it is evident from his optimistic attitude that Posidonius in general approved of Sulla's restored state. Thus, the history of Rome, as far as it was embraced in his work, must have appeared to Posidonius as a unified tragic process, which was bounded on either side by normal circumstances and so ultimately remained an episode. Concerning the early period, it is well known that Posidonius, like the elder Cato, imagined it as exemplary, except that he regarded it with the eyes of a philosopher.

It is, therefore, this historical picture of Posidonius' which appears reflected and reshaped three times in Sallust, and which in this reshaping defines the total picture within which Sallust locates his monographs and his representation of the Sullan state. The reshaping of the idea is predictably the slightest in the *Catiline*; here the old Romans are still the exemplary people of ancient times who did not yet need statutes to compel them to be good and just, since they did it as a matter of course and purely by nature—an idea which can hardly be explained in Roman terms, but so fits all the better into Posidonius' cultural history; one need only read in Seneca how the people of antiquity, following pure nature, had no inclination to wickedness according to Posidonius, and how the need for laws arose only later as corruption crept in (*primi mortalium quique ex his geniti naturam incorrupti sequebantur, ... nec erat cuiquam aut animus in iniuriam aut causa.... sed postquam subrepentibus vitiis in tyrannidem regna conversa sunt, opus esse legibus coepit, Ep.* 90. 4–6).[10] All this and whatever else was too reminiscent of Greek theory—for example,

---

[9] Peter (P, p. 86) erroneously ascribes this thought to Cato's speech at *Orig.* fr. 88 *FRHist* (= 95b P). It is also a mistake to think that Sallust at *B.J.* 41 and *H.* 1. 11 M has Cato in mind as a model: Polybius and Posidonius stand between them.

[10] Cf. Theißen 1912: 20.

the word δικαιοσύνη ('justice') and the problems surrounding it—Sallust later expunged.[11]

The recognition of this interrelationship leads directly to the centre of Sallust's thinking. The schema that laid the foundation for Posidonius' grand historical interpretation of the Sullan state was adopted—reworked, naturally—by Sallust in all three historical works, and was deliberately presented at a prominent place: in the *Catiline* and *Histories*, at the beginning.

This historical picture, then, must have exerted a decisive influence on him. His reflection on Roman history and its large-scale progress, as visible to us in the three historical works, was developed along the lines of the Posidonian view. Moral concepts were crucial to it; here certainly is one of the two principal influences on Sallust's moralizing historiography, the other being the censorious attitude of Cato.

For Sallust, reflection on this interpretation of history must have entailed an inner struggle with Posidonius from the beginning; the result could not have been, as in Posidonius, to approve the state of the *optimates*, but rather intellectually to demolish it. Naturally he took care that the connection of his historical view with Nasica and the political ideology of the Scipios should not be recognizable; it took the vision of Augustine, which was not at all historical-philological but directed only at essentials, to restore the connection, with the result that Scipio Nasica now stands in the middle of the account of the proem to the *Histories* (*De civ. D.* 2. 18).[12] But even the overarching sense of this historical picture was inverted in Sallust. It is true that the turning point in the course of history was still the fall of Carthage; again, moral equilibrium was lost thereafter, and indeed on all sides, even among the so-called defenders of the masses, as Sallust admits with increasing frankness; again, the consequences of the general corruption were disunity and confusion that must ultimately lead to civil war. But the corruption did not, as in Posidonius, come from the side of the masses after a single erroneous and hubris-driven decision of the Senate disrupted the internal balance of the entire population, and did not consist in their wrongful rebellion against the proper government of the Senate; rather, once the cessation of pressure from without had unleashed the repressed powers of chaos into a merciless partisan struggle, the oligarchy became responsible for the ill. Indeed, the oligarchy was not from the beginning the wickeder side, but economic and social power

---

[11] *B.C.* 9. 4 *aequitate*, 10. 1 *iustitia*; cf. Klingner 1928: 173.

[12] [An appendix to Klingner's article detailing the relation between Augustine and Sallust has been omitted here. It contained further discussion of this point. (eds.)]

ruthlessly exploited put it in the wrong and catalysed the Gracchan movement, and then other insurgencies, as measures of pure self-defence. And the work of Sulla was not the admittedly grim but effectively righteous reconstruction of the old, normal status quo, but rather quite the opposite: a decisive break with the good, an agglomeration of guilt, a stabilization of wickedness. The Sullan state was the victorious evil. So the Posidonian historical picture appears after the redistribution of light and shadow worked on it by Sallust. The tragedy that begins with the destruction of Carthage does not end with Sulla, but only then really begins to darken; decline meets with no more restraint. Sulla is no longer the grim, frightful harbinger of something ultimately good, but the embodiment of evil and decay.[13]

Sallust begins his *Histories* with this figure and his achievement, the institution of the aristocratic state, the point where Posidonius left off. On two occasions he had already come close to the Posidonian historical interpretation of Sulla and the Sullan state, but only brushed up against its edges: once when he described the utmost effects of those forces in the Catilinarian crisis, and again when he depicted the nobility at the time of the Jugurthine war, whom Sulla, appearing there for the first time, had helped to victory. Now in the third work he took direct aim at the hated figure, inasmuch as he represented the Sullan state, its crimes, its hollowness, its corrosion, and its extinction in full detail. He began where Posidonius had ended: if that man had shown how the restored state was achieved, Sallust showed what became of it. He interpreted the work of Sulla from the opposite direction. Nor did he leave it to Posidonius to show how this state arose and on what preconditions it rested: in a brief survey at the work's beginning he laid out the essential processes that formed the subject of Posidonius' *Histories*, from a perspective that was indeed similar to his predecessor's in outline, but in the distribution of light and dark diametrically opposed to it. Posidonius' conception of history was reassessed. Against the background of this general view of Roman development, at the beginning of his narrative he drafted a picture of Sulla that prompted Augustine to say (*De civ. D.* 2. 22), 'Who would not shudder at this?' He then began his account of the state that arose in this way, and of this man's legacy.

If Posidonius in his history had presented a kind of hubris and its consequences, but at the end, after the chaos, had displayed something orderly and stable, and if Sallust adopted Posidonius' picture of history in its broad outline, though re-evaluating the phenomena he found in it,

[13] Cf. Alheit 1919: 31.

one might expect that he, too, at some later point eventually allowed the chaotic commotion to resolve itself into order. Now, what end did Sallust assign to the development he adopted? One must assume from his remarks in the second letter to Caesar (*Ad Caes. Sen* 2. 10. 2-3) and above all in the *Catiline* (*B.C.* 4. 2) that he began early to reflect on historical matters. If this is right, then it is probable that during his political activity he envisaged the reordering of the state at the hands of Caesar as the end of the development, and that he internally contrasted Caesar with Sulla. Compared to the re-evaluation and fundamentally divergent ethical attitudes described so far, this would amount to a merely quantitative alteration of Posidonius' schema. Whether Sallust really did mentally construct it in this way cannot be known. At any rate after Caesar's death, when he wrote his historical works, he made no such construction. At no point does he hint at anything that brought the collapse to a halt or was capable of doing so. On the contrary, he rejects alike the nobility and those who recently slipped into the Senate in the time of Caesar's successors, the conservative and now crumbled *optimates*-state and the revolutionary despotism, even if it is practicable and brings reforms. Chagrin and disgust come over him when he thinks of the moral state of the present. It is thus not the case that the turn for the worse, which set in after the fall of Carthage, in his understanding aims towards a goal and an end, however far in the future, where it will dissipate into a normal status; rather, one cannot predict where it will go. Sallust has removed the outcome of the decline in Posidonius' schema without replacing it with a new one, and thus not only quantitatively, but also qualitatively altered it: he has removed its teleology. Neither at the beginning, in the time between the foundation of Rome and the Hannibalic wars (really up to the Third Punic War), nor at the end is there anything that Sallust and his reader can approve of. In Posidonius, the tragedy was supported by the belief in an order and harmony that had existed at the beginning and was restored at the end. In Sallust there is no such supporting belief that the chaotic is ultimately encompassed by a cosmos; and thus the world as he depicts it takes on an oppressiveness and darkness beyond all measure. He does indeed employ the schema of his Greek model as a means to arrange and shape the mass of historical material—and he is perhaps the first Roman historian who thus fitted the details of his narrative into a universal vision of Roman destiny—but for him, the Roman, this ordering has a different function. It does not, as for Posidonius, fulfil the purpose of restoring chaos to meaning and harmony, but rather serves only to make a portion of the sum of ultimately meaningless, dark and chaotic events representable and relatively comprehensible.

We have now reached the point where our analysis can more deeply penetrate Sallust's character. The insight into the internal construction of his vision of history enables an assessment of the intellectual side of the polemical strain in his works, a strain which Schwartz and his followers have perhaps too closely attached to the conflicts over material power in those years. Up to the time of Caesar's victory, Sallust had fought to help destroy the Sullan state. After Caesar's death, he carried the fight forward in his writings; his target was now the intellectual representation of this state. This polemic was not merely a means to an end for him, conceived to help one group to political success or to topple a hostile one through literary propaganda. In the time after Philippi there was no longer any restored state to topple. To humiliate the still living and still hopeful republicans through a literary annihilation of the Sullan state may, of course, have been an ancillary objective of Sallust's; but that this was the case is an insupportable assumption about something that cannot be known. As far as literary propaganda for some or other power group is concerned, some external end that Sallust wished to reach must somewhere, directly or indirectly, be visible. But the historical treatment of his vision of history has shown that total pessimism reigns there, and that Sallust precisely omitted the teleology from the historical picture from which his reflection on the fate of the Roman people had developed. It would be difficult to reconcile these circumstances with the assumption that his works were oriented towards a purpose within the politics of power. One would then have to assume that Sallust intended to disseminate a kind of artificial atmosphere of decline, in order that some dynast or party would then find the population internally demoralized and so have an easier time of it. The belief in such a bizarre subterfuge is hardly justified. Thus, nothing else remains but to take Sallust's pessimism seriously. Indeed, it is understandable in a man of the period between Philippi and Actium, in a person whose belief system evidently rested above all on the inexhaustible spirit and abilities of Caesar, and, with his death, fell to pieces without finding a stable hold in any superhuman order. If Sallust's pessimism is earnest and not a mask, then his intellectual struggle against the Sullan state and its portraitist Posidonius is not merely a means to an end, but an end in itself.

14

The *Histories*

The Crisis of the *Res Publica*

Antonio La Penna

[This is a long and intricately argued chapter drawn from a long and intricately argued book. The original contains thirteen sections of which numbers two to eight each concentrate on a major figure or episode from the surviving fragments of the Histories, working closely through both the evidence of the fragments and its handling in scholarship up to the time of the book's publication in 1968 (the chapter in fact originally appeared as an article in Athenaeum in 1963). For reasons both of space and also of accessibility, we have included only one of those sections, on Pompey, a dominating presence in the work.[1] The concluding five sections, containing La

[1] For those interested in La Penna's views on these other elements of the *Histories*, we offer the following summary of the omitted sections: **Section 1** gives an overview of previous efforts to use the fragmentary *Histories* to understand Sallust's political and historiographic aims and how those efforts were shaped by twentieth-century political contexts. In **Section 2**, La Penna turns to the synopsis of the Social War and the Sullan regime with which Sallust led up to his starting point in 78 BCE; he concludes with the striking paradox that the men who in the narrative to follow would dismantle the Sullan order had learned their disruptive methods in the service of the dictator himself. **Section 3** treats the first major event of the post-Sullan period, the rebellion of Lepidus; La Penna demonstrates how this episode anticipates the political crises to follow, including the Catilinarian conspiracy, especially in the evacuation of political language that results from aristocrats' taking up the banner of *libertas*. **Section 4** turns to Sertorius, a figure whose heroization in later periods had put him at the centre of competing approaches to Roman history and to Sallust's historiography; La Penna presents him as a political agent looking for ways to stabilize the social order through a renovation of aristocratic temperance and a restraint on factional partisanship and demagoguery. The political battles between tribunes and nobles form the subject of **Section 6**; analyses of the orations of the tribune Licinius Macer in book 3 and the consul C. Aurelius Cotta in book 2 present both as exceptions to the polemical characterization of the rival factions, creating a tension between the political views that emerge from the narrative itself and the perspectives

Penna's overview of Sallust's work, have also been included complete, though with occasional light abridgment of the notes throughout. From the beginning of both the book and the chapter, La Penna differentiates his approach to Sallust from the two positions that dominated scholarship in the first half of the last century. He views the historian's works neither as written to advance specific partisan political aims nor as detached, philosophical history on the model of the Greek Posidonius. La Penna's Sallust is above all a political thinker, rather than a partisan, but one whose perspective is shaped by his own historical experiences as a member of the Italian upper class. In this respect, his argument also mediates between two then dominant models for understanding Roman History, a 'Western' emphasis on personal connections and factional politics and a 'Soviet' emphasis on economic and class structures (La Penna 1968: 10).]

5. The intensity of political polemic in the age of Caesar is even more apparent in the case of Pompey than Sertorius. Sallust's vilification of Pompey was obvious to contemporaries (*H*. 2. 16 M), and modern scholars who struggle to raise Sallust above partisan politics here run up against one of their greatest obstacles. One scholar already, though generally influenced by this tendency, has correctly contextualized Sallust's interpretation of Pompey within this contemporary debate. He interprets it as specifically opposing Pompey's idealization as the defender of the state and the martyr of the Republic, which naturally had a strong foundation in public opinion and was represented in historiography above all by Pompey's close friend Theophanes of Mytilene.[2] Varro's three-book *De Pompeio* must have also been an extensive panegyric, and there is no need to spend more words illustrating this tendency.

Pompey was produced from the Sullan fold. He was a warlord who owed his success to Sulla, and Sallust probably did not fail to emphasize that. In the work's introductory account of the Civil War of the 80s BCE, he narrated the campaign against Gnaeus Papirius Carbo (*H*. 1. 52 M),

---

directly presented in the speeches. Lucullus and his Pontic opponent Mithridates provide, in **Section 7**, an opportunity to evaluate Sallust's views on Roman imperialism; while rejecting the idea that Sallust endorsed the attack on Roman expansion expressed in Mithridates' letter, La Penna nevertheless suggests that he criticized the avarice which fed Rome's misadministration of its provinces and admired Lucullus' more enlightened approach. **Section 8**, on the slave rebellion of Spartacus, demonstrates how, for all that Sallust could not have sympathized with such a figure, his emphasis on its leader's moderation reveals a striking ability to recognize the humanity of slaves that looks forward to Seneca.

[2] Schur 1934: 259ff. I consider the chapter about Pompey the best of the book.

and the one in Africa against Gnaeus Domitius Ahenobarbus and the Numidian chief Hiarbas (*H.* 1. 53 M). We cannot say whether Sallust highlighted Pompey's ingratitude towards Carbo, who had protected him some years before, and his harshness to Domitius;[3] nor can we say if Sallust took account of the importance of the example of his father Pompeius Strabo in Pompey's development as a Sullan strongman. But perhaps only modern historians can grasp the full significance of this figure, as a study in Roman sociology, if not a consequential politician. At the head of what was virtually a private army, but with no political agenda, Strabo was prepared to pass from one side to the other according to the scope they provided for his ambition.[4] Like other personalities of the Roman Revolution, he falls somewhere between being a politician and a military adventurer. An illuminating glimpse of Pompey in the Sullan period comes from the fragment of an indirectly reported speech attributed to him in the debate over the *lex Gabinia* (*H.* 5. 20 M) where he recalls with pride the proofs of the esteem Sulla felt for him while he was still a very young man. Would Pompey in 67 really emphasize his Sullan past in this way, even in a speech obviously designed to celebrate his accomplishments? Or is it Sallust who remodels Pompey's oration to underline this past?

A character portrait of this figure appeared in the text when he was about to undertake his first action of great importance (that is, most probably, before his departure for Spain rather than his intervention in quashing Lepidus' revolt). A fragment, probably deriving from that portrait, calls Pompey 'restrained in all other things saving only domination' (*modestus ad alia omnia, nisi ad dominationem, H.* 2. 17 M). This gives the impression that the presentation of Pompey here was not completely negative, a polemic not obvious but more subtle because masked by historical objectivity. His virtues are not denied; a shame, however, that his ambition was out of control! 'Domination' is the aim of his entire life, an accusation even more bitter than Caesar's statement that 'he was unwilling that anyone be made equal to him in honour' (*neminem dignitate secum exaequari volebat,* Caes. *B Civ.* 1. 4. 5).[5] Sallust would contrast with that tone of apparent objectivity a direct and insulting accusation of hypocrisy: 'he had a seemly face but a shameless

---

[3] For further details, see van Ooteghem 1954: 59ff.

[4] So Velleius Paterculus describes him, 2. 21. 2, though he is generally favourable to the younger Pompey.

[5] Caesar and Sallust appear to be echoed and run together by Velleius Paterculus, 2. 29. 3: 'a most temperate citizen in domestic politics, except when he feared having an equal' (*civis in toga, nisi ubi vereretur ne quem haberet parem, modestissimus*).

mind' (*oris probi, animo inverecundo, H.* 2. 16 M).⁶ (However, since the fragment is quoted without book number, it is not completely certain that it comes from this opening character sketch.) The physical training of a good soldier received emphasis: 'he would compete with the agile in jumping, with the speedy in racing, and with the strong in fencing' (*cum alacribus saltu, cum velocibus cursu, cum validis vecte certabat, H.* 2. 19 M). Some praise of his moral and uncorrupted youth was very likely added, for the fragment recalls the portrait of young Iugurtha (*B.J.* 6. 1). We do not know what was said about his readiness for military command.⁷ His political and military career was retraced.⁸ To judge from *H.* 2. 21 M, which reports Sulla's cunning attempt to prevent his triumph, the historian emphasized the young general's ambition, and his lack of constitutional scruples. The triumph was illegal, as was most of the political career of this would-be defender of the Republic! In fact, Pompey's career was in itself one of the most serious signs of the crisis of the state.

Pompey's operations in the Sertorian war require no further elaboration. From Sertorius' biography in Plutarch, we get the clear impression Pompey's handling of the war was not viewed favourably. The young general comes to Spain full of glory and pride (*Sert.* 18. 3), but, during the campaign around Lauron, Sertorius famously mocks him as 'Sulla's schoolboy' (*Sert.* 18. 8). We cannot be sure that such jokes reflect Sallust's own judgement, but the negativity of that judgement emerges from the narrative itself. It is sufficient to mention the defeat at the river Sucro (*Sert.* 19. 3), for which Pompey receives all the blame since his pride and ambition did not allow him to wait for Metellus' arrival lest he have to share credit for the victory. (This verdict is confirmed in the biography of Pompey himself, *Pomp.* 19. 1.) Metellus' behaviour appears more cautious and clever, suggesting a contrast similar to the one Sertorius makes between 'the old woman' and 'the young man' (*Sert.* 19. 6). And this is the precise opposite of the praise we read in Velleius Paterculus: 'he perfected his talent with his exceptional foresight in military matters so that Metellus was more praised by Sertorius, but Pompey more feared' (*ingenium singulari rerum militarium prudentia excoluerat, ut a Sertorio Metellus laudaretur magis, Pompeius timeretur validius,* 2. 29. 5).⁹ Nor

---

⁶ Syme 1964: 206 found in the fragment a sarcastic attack on Varro, who included a tribute to Pompey's 'modest face' (*os probum*), preserved in Pliny *HN* 7. 53; 37. 14.

⁷ *H.* 2. 18 M (*belli sane sciens*—*sane* is conjecture) cannot be assigned to the character portrait with certainty, even though the book number is cited.

⁸ It is not at all clear that *H.* 2. 20 M, which describes an event completely obscure to us, is to be placed in this context.

⁹ After reporting Sertorius' squib about the old woman and the boy, Plutarch (*Pomp.* 18. 1ff.) also adds that 'in fact [Sertorius], being wary of Pompey and fearing him, used more

are objective bases lacking for an unfavourable verdict. This negative judgement of Pompey's generalship does not want for objective support: the Sertorian war, at least before 74 BCE, was the least brilliantly led of Pompey's campaigns. Overall, Pompey, while doubtless an excellent organizer of armies and operations, was no strategic genius. Metellus was perhaps more skilled and certainly more experienced in Spanish warfare. Some caution is necessary about applying this estimation to operations from 74 to 72 BCE since we have not even the vaguest idea of Sallust's treatment of the Spanish War during those years, neither from the fragments nor from Plutarch. But we seem to catch a hint of irony in the fragment where Sallust describes the notion Pompey cherished even from his early youth of being a new Alexander in deeds and decisions, a belief nourished by his own vanity and by the whisperings of flatterers: 'believing from the conversation of flatterers that he would be like King Alexander' (*sermone fautorum similem fore se credens Alexandro regi*, H. 3. 88 M). To understand the force of the irony, we have to remember the importance that the Alexander myth had had for Pompey, even, as it seems, for his hairstyle.[10] Since this fragment is assigned to book 3, it cannot belong to the character sketch and has been rightly placed almost at the end of the Sertorian war. Sallust perhaps mentioned Pompey's emulation of Alexander in connection with the trophy he erected in the Pyrenees, which recalled the one set up by Alexander in India. At the end of the Sertorian war, the vanity of the victorious general was, it seems, deflated.

But with Pompey, too, Sallust was most interested in his political behaviour. The striking aspects of the brief letter he sent to the Senate towards the end of 75 BCE (*H.* 2. 98 M) are his vanity (note that the list of glorious deeds came after two years of almost total failure) and the threat to bring war to Italy. This threat, tacked on almost as an afterthought, casts a sinister shadow on the letter and was surely more effective for Pompey than the preceding entreaties. This letter, too, then, in a sense exposes Pompey's hypocrisy. We have no reason to believe that the threat was invented by Sallust: intimidating the Senate and making it aware that his support was indispensable to its power are constant elements of Pompey's political strategy. And, specifically, Pompey's annoyance with the Senate during the Sertorian war makes the anti-senatorial attitude he adopted after his return more comprehensible.

cautious tactics'. Plutarch seems to combine Sallust's opinion with another more positive towards Pompey. The conclusion that the favourable view too comes from Sallust does not persuade me.

[10] See van Ooteghem 1954: 65ff., 69, 133ff., and *passim*.

Faithful only to his ambition, Pompey after coming back from Spain threatens the very Senate that had sent him there at the insistence of Marcius Philippus, and is set to curry favour with the common people. Sallust may have emphasized how, while Metellus had discharged his army as soon as he crossed the Alps (*H.* 4. 49 M), Pompey led his troops up to the very walls of Rome. What stands out more clearly in the few remaining fragments is Pompey's demagoguery, put in service of his desire for *dominatio*. Either during the march towards Rome or during a speech to the people by the walls of the capital, he proclaims himself as effectively the one who will decide the struggle between Senate and common people (*H.* 4. 45 M).[11] The way is paved by a tribune of the plebs, probably one of his Picene clients ('a Picene of low standing, more chatty than eloquent,' *humili loco Picens loquax magis quam facundus*, *H.* 4. 43 M). He is all subservience to the crowd in order to transform them into a tool for his ambition (*H.* 4. 47 M). As a colleague in the consulship, Pompey expects someone inferior to him in reputation to serve as admirer and stooge (*H.* 4. 48 M). Demagoguery, vanity, and hypocrisy also characterize Pompey some years later during the stormy debate over the *lex Gabinia* (*H.* 5. 20–2, 24 M).[12] Once again he makes a disreputable tribune of the plebs his instrument. And it is not without significance that Sallust reported the speech of this tribune, Gabinius. The narrative probably showed the connection between Pompey's unscrupulous ambition and the disease of tribunician demagoguery, already condemned in the central excursus in the *B.C.* (38. 1).[13] Did a connection also emerge between this plague and lower forces dangerous to the social order? This cannot be proven from the fragments we possess, but it will not be useless to recall Sallust's fleeting reflection on Catiline's revolt (*B.C.* 39. 4): even if Catiline had won, he would not have enjoyed his victory for long. Pompey (unnamed but clearly alluded to as 'the one who had more power,' *qui plus posset*) would have put the revolt down and assumed leadership of the state.[14] Subversion of the social order, because it demanded some reaction, could prepare the ground for *dominatio*.

---

[11] Whether *H.* 4. 42 M (*multisque suspicionibus volentia plebi facturus habebatur*, 'from many suspicions he was thought to be about to carry out the wishes of the common people') refers to Pompey is uncertain, since it was quoted without book number. It might also refer to Lepidus or some tribune of the plebs.
[12] *H.* 5. 19 M (*cupientissimus legis*, 'most eager for the law') can also not be securely referred to Pompey, although it would be fitting.
[13] There might have been an excursus about the politics of the years 71 and 70 BCE: *H.* 4. 46 M (*qui quidem mos ut tabes in urbem coniectus*, 'a custom indeed cast upon the city like rot'), cited with book number, leads one to suspect this.
[14] See La Penna 1968: 114.

The portrait of Pompey we can trace from the fragments of the *Histories* is unfair. While the threats and pressures he applied to the Senate are genuine, as is his recourse to tribunician demagoguery, nevertheless, Pompey neither stirred up subversive forces from the lower classes nor did he try to destroy the Senate or turn it into a mere figurehead. He wanted only to place it under his protection. And he succeeded. Yet in order to do so he had to allow the creation of a powerful anti-senatorial movement. This movement certainly would have arisen even without his permission, and he might have overcome it as well, but in the end it ruined him. Forward-looking he was not, but he saw further than the nobility. For he recognized that to remain in power the nobility had to gather around itself a broader political and social alliance, one that extended to the *boni*, the Roman and Italian economic elite. So much Cicero had understood as well. But Pompey was more perceptive than Cicero since he recognized the need for the support of the military proletariat. Cicero had a political programme more enlightened than that of the *nobilitas* and more capable of achieving a balance between the forces produced by the evolution of Roman society; but he had no idea of the means necessary to accomplish this programme. And this should warn us against any overestimation of Cicero as a politician. If Pompey's plan failed, this is due more to the obtuseness of the *nobilitas*, which accepted his protectorate too late, than to Pompey's political ineptitude or his blinding ambition. The terms on which he wanted to preserve the power of the *nobilitas* were those that made that preservation less of an illusion.

But if the picture drawn by Sallust was unfair, incomplete, or superficial, it was not in the strict sense tendentious; that is, it was not dictated by polemic in bad faith. Such tendentiousness, nevertheless, is not to be left out of account. Crassus receives no better treatment than Pompey: his opposition to Pompey derives from a base desire to denigrate him, not from a rigorous concern for the public good (*H.* 5. 51 M),[15] but the portrait of Caesar in the *B.C.*, even if it presents some shadows (which is uncertain), implies another kind of analysis. Was Caesar less ambitious than Pompey and Crassus? Did he rely less on the demagoguery of the tribunes? Was he not more tainted by plebeian filth? He could appear—and he was—more consistent in his opposition to the Senate. But for him, too, popular agitation was purely instrumental. In fact, Pompey's unscrupulous ambition becomes part of a systemic characterization of

---

[15] Clausen 1947: 297ff. tries to defend *gravis exactor*, understanding it as 'rigorously superintending'.

Roman politics, where men and factions are not bound to policies but rely from time to time on interests and social forces that may be different and even opposed in different situations. Prosopographical historiography looks especially to individuals and groups but takes little account of the forces on which they depend; but the history that gets to the heart of such forces is true history. Up to a point, Sallust understands this systemic flaw of Roman politics. And yet he makes Pompey stand out especially for this vice. This continues and amplifies a charge made by Caesar. In the *Bellum Civile*, Pompey seems ambitious for pre-eminence, vain to the point of ridiculousness, and superficial in weighing the forces that oppose him. These vices, however, appear more tolerable than those of the political group around him, and sometimes Caesar ascribes the first and most serious responsibility for the war to his personal political enemies, who stir up Pompey: 'Pompey provoked by Caesar's enemies' (*Pompeius ab inimicis Caesaris incitatus*, B Civ. 1. 4. 4); 'by which enemies Pompey was diminished and led astray' (*a quibus* [sc. *inimicis*] *deductum ac depravatum Pompeium*, B Civ. 1. 7. 1). Caesar's attack on Pompey still preserves an element of respect which seems to have fallen away in Sallust's, where Pompey stands apart from all others in his vices.

9. Let us try now to bring together the general lines of the political orientation we have detected from the analysis of the *Histories* and ask whether our picture reveals any perceptible evolution by comparison with the monographs. I would answer that it does not. The essential themes in the monographs were a polemic against the *nobilitas*, as a closed political elite that appropriated the fruits of Rome's conquests and as bearing prime responsibility for the decline of morals, and also a concern about the overturning of the social order. The danger of such unrest was perceived to derive from: (1) the destruction of values; (2) the rise of factionalism nourished both by aristocratic infighting and the demagoguery of the *populares*; and (3) the reduction, as a result of conquests, of the middle classes in both the city and the countryside to the proletariat that provided the most incendiary fuel for partisan conflict. The professionalization of the army sometimes emerges as an additional danger. The fear of social revolution was more apparent in the *B.C.*, and the polemic against the aristocracy in the *B.J.*, but neither of the monographs can be understood without taking account of all these elements together. We have found the same tendency and the same ideas in the *Histories* without perceptible changes. There is no evolution of Sallust's political thought in his written work (except for those who consider the *Epistulae* as authentic). In the *Histories*, the condemnation of the *nobilitas* is the same as in the monographs, and it has its exceptions, as it did in the *B.C.*: there Cato; here Marcius Philippus, and maybe

Lucullus too. The explanation of Catiline's plot returns, more or less, for the revolt of Lepidus. The condemnation of the demagoguery of tribunes, as we have seen, was already evident in the monographs; the condemnation of the factionalism that has reduced political ideas to simple camouflage for personal ambition recurs equally and is often expressed in similar language, and the link between factionalism and the danger of popular rebellion remains always clear.

Thus, we have two essential tendencies: the anti-aristocratic polemic that is part of an aspiration to expand the political elite, and the fear of social unrest that coincides with a need for order. These two tendencies are held in balance without either having the power to eliminate the other. The fear of social danger could have been strong enough to silence the hatred against aristocracy and to lead to absolute unity among the upper classes; the need to expand the political elite could have been strong enough to induce aristocrats to rely on free subordinate classes, if not on slaves. Neither of these two possibilities happens. Balance does not mean the mixture of the two tendencies in a coherent, organic whole. From this fact arise the most serious, the most justified, uncertainties in the interpretation of Sallust.

From an equilibrium of this sort obviously no clear and consistent political programme could emerge. It is likely that Sallust longed for order, an authoritarian order, but still a republican one, that is, one which would have left great prestige to the Senate. This new regime, in the tradition of the republican constitution and grounded on the restoration of old moral values, would eliminate at once the predominance of the aristocratic elite, the demagoguery of tribunes, the habit of factionalism, and any danger coming from the lower classes. But it is completely unlikely that Sallust had a clear idea of what constitutional, economic, or social measures to enact, or the forces to be brought together in order to achieve these ends.[16]

I have already tried to explain to what extent he may have thought that these two essential tendencies were realized in Caesar's regime.[17] What appears clear from the *Histories* is that Sallust's work takes its inspiration from those crucial political developments of the Caesarian period which Caesar himself would be called upon to address, from the complex struggle of the years and decades that came before Caesar's ultimate victory. I restate my conclusions:[18] if we are not able to trace direct connections between Sallust's historical works and the political groups of the years during which he wrote, the connections to the movements,

---

[16] La Penna 1968: 117ff. [17] La Penna 1968: 120ff.
[18] La Penna 1968: 62 n. 117.

passions, and ideas of the period of the republican crisis are clear. And the *Histories* provide further evidence. I do not see how we can understand the negative presentation of Pompey apart from the Caesarian political struggle or how we can understand the idealization of Sertorius without taking account of differences in outlook and strategy that arose among the forces opposed to the aristocracy. Undoubtedly, Sallust's work is much more than a panegyric for Caesar; and we can also believe that, when he wrote in the proem of the *Histories* 'nor does having taken an opposite side in the Civil Wars move me from the truth' (*neque me diversa pars in civilibus armis movit a vero*, H. 1. 6 M), he was in general expressing his good intentions. But I cannot bring myself to believe that he had now become an Olympian analyst and narrator, beyond or above the struggles and passions of the age of Caesar: not only was he walking 'over fires banked with treacherous ash' (Hor. *C.* 2. 1. 7–8), but he had been deeply burnt by that fire.

The interpretation of Sertorius, as we have seen, also gives us a striking hint that Sallust's point of view is more Sabine than Roman in the strictest sense. It is an Italian identity that does not arise from opposition to Rome but rather aims to participate in Roman political life and to expand the political elite of the capital, to have its weight felt in the running of the empire. This is also, however, the limit of Sallust's political mentality; the scope of the political problems he addresses involves Rome and Italy, not the empire. For him, I repeat, the problem of the empire would only have been a matter of good administration of the provinces. It is not legitimate to deduce anything beyond that either from his presentation of Sertorius or from Mithridates' letter. Sallust is almost completely absorbed in the internal moral and political crisis. Perhaps he thought that not even Caesar had satisfactorily solved this problem. In any case, after Caesar's death, Sallust saw the crisis renewed with frequent shocks and bloody violence. When Sallust died, nobody was able to foresee when and how it would be concluded. It is not surprising that his education and his intellect were dominated by it.

10. If there is no perceptible change in Sallust's political opinions in the *Histories*, or in his interpretation of the recent past, there is nevertheless a transformation of some importance in his general view of Roman history. I am referring to the expansion of the well-known theme of the *metus hostilis*: since it is so well-known and I have already spoken of it, I will be brief.[19] The *metus hostilis* as a condition, even

---

[19] La Penna 1968: 232ff. There is a treatment to be read with profit in Earl 1961: 41ff. (= Chapter 3 of this volume).

cause, of internal harmony was not present in the *B.C.* but assumed considerable importance in the central excursus of the *B.J.* It now comes to be found (*H.* 1. 11 M) in the history of Rome prior to the Punic Wars, namely at the beginning of the republican age, when internal harmony was guaranteed by the fear of Tarquin and the Etruscans. After this fear diminished, long struggles between the patricians and the common people began and continued until concord was restored through the fear of Carthage. There was thus a *metus Etruscus* before the *metus Punicus*. Scholars have used this as evidence that the historian's pessimism has deepened in his last work.[20] I would add that here the deepening of pessimism goes together with the intensification of a rationalism that lessens the idealization, partly influenced by the Athenian model, of archaic Roman history apparent in the introductory chapters of the *B.C.*[21] This would be true even if the *metus Etruscus* was not Sallust's invention but taken over from an earlier annalist who had analysed the causes and phases of internal struggles in archaic Rome (for example, Licinius Macer). Pessimism induced by the political crisis and rationalism could tend to weaken faith in the destiny of Rome, to deconsecrate the history of this exceptional city. Livy will sense the serious danger embedded in Sallust's new vision and covertly fight against it in his preface: 'no republic was ever greater or more sacred or richer in good examples' (*nulla umquam res publica nec maior nec sanctior nec bonis exemplis ditior fuit, praef.* 11).[22] The desire for glory (*cupido gloriae*) and the contest for it (*certamen gloriae*) remain in the *Histories'* vision of the republican age prior to the Punic Wars. But what in the *B.C.* (7. 3ff.) was a noble and beneficial passion becomes here a 'flaw in the character of man' (*vitium humani ingenii, H.* 1. 7 M). However, as I tried to show above,[23] we must be on our guard against seeing in the fragment a radical condemnation of human nature. Granted that the 'contest for mastery' (*dominationis*) has only a negative meaning, how could we say the same of the 'contest for glory' (*gloriae*), or even of the 'contest for freedom' (*libertatis*)? I would propose, rather, that the historian reaches an obscure awareness of the common roots of good and evil, almost a dialectic in which good itself flows into its opposite. The same restless and unconquerable energy which gives rise to the struggles for freedom and glory is also the source of civil discord. After all, he was already close to this concept when he described *ambitio* as a vice 'closer to virtue' since its goals are still glory and *imperium* (*B.C.* 11. 1). Had the ideal of

---

[20] Klingner 1928: 189 (= Chapter 13, p. 349 in this volume).   [21] La Penna 1968: 55ff.
[22] On Livy's reaction against the introduction of the *Histories*, see pp. 369–70 below.
[23] La Penna 1968: 54ff.

concord not been so deeply rooted in Sallust, he could have found in the Civil Wars a training ground for valour, a source of greatness for the Roman people, as Machiavelli would. And if he had applied such an idea to *avaritia* as well, he would have seen that greed itself had been an important spur for the expansion of empire. These suppositions are playful, but not entirely so: moralism must not be thought of as an indifferentiable mass. After all, the (originally Greek) notion of *metus hostilis* is in contradiction with moralism and offers a glimmer of a Machiavellian conception of actual political reality.

The different vision of archaic Roman history also had an effect on the pattern according to which later history was structured, before and after the destruction of Carthage. In the introduction to the *B.C.* (11), there was a distinction between a pre-Sullan phase—in which *ambitio* prevailed over *avaritia*—and a Sullan phase, when *avaritia* was raging. Already in the *B.J.*, implicitly, this schema was put aside, since according to Sallust in the Numidian war greed played a much greater role than ambition. In the *Histories* (H. 1. 16 M), the sharp moral decline may have begun quite soon after the fall of Carthage: this seems to be suggested by the echo of the passage in Velleius Paterculus (2. 1. 1).[24] And if after the destruction of Carthage the moral decline went 'like a river in flood' (*torrentis modo*), a gradual decay (*paulatim*) is demonstrated even before. Was there also a shadow on the golden age between the First and the Second Punic War? Was there any awareness of the symptoms of crisis which were noticed before the Third Punic War?[25] It is not possible to give a definite answer, but the question arises. After all, it is well known that the annalists dated the beginnings of ethical and political decline to different moments prior to the destruction of Carthage, starting from 187 BCE, when the army of Manlius Vulso came back from Asia.[26]

11. The vitality of this rationalistic streak can also be felt in the historian's attitude towards the intervention of supernatural forces, such as omens, prophecies, dreams, etc. Already in the monographs it was clear that no importance would be given to these important ingredients in so much of the Roman annalistic tradition. A typical instance is the brief mention Sallust makes of the response given to Marius by the

---

[24] This is not quite certain since Velleius might have created confusion by summarizing the ideas. Velleius gives even scanter support for the notion that *H.* 1. 18 M refers to the Gracchan period.
[25] La Penna 1968: 235ff. Earl 1961: 41 (= Chapter 3, pp. 85–6 in this volume) provides an exhaustive account of the ancient evidence.
[26] See Earl 1961: 42ff. (= Chapter 3, pp. 86–8 in this volume).

haruspex at Utica: Marius sees that the prophecy tends in the same direction 'where his mind's desire was urging him' (*quo cupido animi hortabatur, B.J.* 64. 11). Irony is not lacking: the phenomenon belongs to the normal sphere of human passions. In the *Histories*, the problem arose more frequently, even though we can glean little from the fragments. One, however, is particularly significant in this respect: *H.* 2. 28 M mentions an earthquake which struck Cordoba during one of the winters Metellus passed there.[27] This terrible event is not ascribed to divine wrath, but to 'some chance, or, as philosophers would have it, to the rush of wind through the hollows of the earth' (*alione casu an, sapientibus ut placet, venti per cava terrae citatu*). A scientific, naturalistic explanation, then. The life of Lucullus was especially rich in miraculous events and prophetic dreams (another result of his Sullan training). It was inevitable that Sallust mention this in the account of the Asian campaign. Plutarch, who enjoys such themes, surrounds the crossing of the Euphrates at the beginning of the Armenian undertaking with an aura of miracle (*Luc.* 24. 2ff.). The river suddenly dies down, and one of the cows grazing nearby offers herself spontaneously to be sacrificed. Sallust too mentions the sudden abatement of the stream: 'that such a great and sudden change seemed not to happen without some divinity' (*ut tanta repente mutatio non sine deo videretur, H.* 4. 60 M). Perhaps there is no irony (which would be in conflict with the generally favourable treatment of Lucullus); nonetheless, *videretur* does not contribute to an atmosphere of miracle.

One would expect this rationalism to be vividly present in the ethnographic digressions as well. We must acknowledge, however, that that is not the case, but neither can we speak of mere curiosity or love of the marvellous. The description of Sardinia and Corsica (*H.* 2. 1–12 M) must have contained much information about mythical traditions regarding real or supposed migrations to these two islands (those of Norax, Aristaeus, Daedalus, Trojan refugees, Iolaus, and the Ligurian bull named Corsa). The stories about other migrations to Corsica, even though less mythical, were erudite curiosities.[28] There were even some natural marvels, such as the grass which induced a sinister laughter. Similar mythical information enlivened the account of Crete (*H.* 3. 10–15 M), along with details about its position and, perhaps, its agricultural production. The excursus on

---

[27] The placement of the fragment in the winter 77–6 BCE is far from certain (La Penna 1963a: 33ff.). V. Tandoi suggests to me that with the Cordoba earthquake should probably be identified the baleful cataclysm mentioned in *Anth. Lat.* 409. 9ff.

[28] See the fragment of the Oxyrhynchus papyrus published by Roberts 1938: 60ff.

Pontus (*H.* 3. 61–80 M) was probably the most extensive and the most interesting, since it said something about the way of life of several local peoples (cf. fr. 3. 74 M, on the misery and banditry of the Tauri, and fr. 3. 76 M, on the Scythians who live on wagons, a very well-known fact). Here, too, however, we find an abundance of mythical details, both familiar and quite obscure, on the origins of these nations. The fragments of the excursus on Southern Italy and the Sicilian strait (*H.* 4. 23–9 M) give us a similar impression with their mention of Scylla, Charybdis, and Hannibal's helmsman. Nevertheless, what is said about the origin of the strait, about the coastline facing Messina (which is bowed and flat, because 'the height and harshness of Sicily smash the tide against it,' *asperitas et altitudo Siciliae aestum relidit*), and about the whirlpool and the undersea motion of Charybdis has a more scientific tone. The description of the Islands of the Blessed, of which Sertorius heard the pirates speaking (*H.* 1. 100–103 M), is a fascinating literary exercise. The mild weather, however, receives a scientific explanation based on the position of the islands and the influence of the winds (Plut. *Sert.* 2. 4, which would appear to be 'Sallustian' because of its close connection with fr. 1. 101 M). The details about the tomb of Antaeus, which aroused Sertorius' curiosity, should be attributed to a love of the marvellous. (Plut. *Sert.* 9. 6ff.; what follows about the Herakleides of Tingitana derives from Juba, according to Plutarch) And the information about Corycus of Cilicia (*H.* 2. 81M), though not unusual, bears witness to the same taste.

An obvious qualification here is that the frequency of erudite or paradoxical curiosities in the fragments of excursus might be due simply to the selection made by the learned authors who cite them. But that these elements were already present in Sallust appears likely because of the excursus on Numidia in *B.J.* 17–19: the description of weather and customs is splendid, but it takes up little space in comparison to the strange accounts of the origins of African populations which Sallust fished out of the Punic books attributed to the king Hiempsal. The interest in strange accidents is confirmed by another of the three digressions in the *B.J.* (79), devoted to the origin of the 'Altars of the Philaeni', and Sallust's introduction of the episode makes his motive explicit: 'it seems not unworthy to recall an outstanding and wonderful deed' (*non indignum videtur egregium atque mirabile facinus... memorare*).

The character of Sallust's ethnographic excursus will not appear strange if we bear in mind both the tradition of Greek ethnography (in the manner of the very influential Timaeus) and the numerous and bizarre foundation legends of Italian cities and populations, whose diffusion in literary form had been encouraged by Cato's *Origines*. However, Sallust's interest in ethnography will seem impoverished by comparison to the precedent of Posidonius. Whether Sallust used Posidonius as a source of information remains uncertain;[29] yet there is no trace of Posidonius' thought, of his unified ethnographic understanding in which climate, environment, body type and character, customs, and social organization are all related. I would add that the absence of serious ethnography in Sallust is all the more striking if we recall that Caesar's ethnographic treatments of Gauls and Germans had been known for nearly twenty years. There, again, customs, social organization, religion, and a people's habits of thought and perception were central. Caesar's account was based on direct personal experience and answered a real need for public opinion to have clearer ideas about the new peoples whom recent events had allowed them to know better and with whom they were coming into contact for the first time. There was no such context for Sallust's ethnographic digressions (at most a lively curiosity may have lingered about certain peoples of the Black Sea), and they derive entirely from books. And from the seriousness of his interests Caesar knew how to take what was best in the ancient ethnographic tradition: Sallust's excursus, however, appear thin even in what they suggest about his own learning: there is some Thucydidean spirit in the ethico-political digressions, but it has been extinguished in the ethnographic ones. All this confirms that in the final account it is experience that brings learning to life.

12. If we had more of the *Histories*, we would perhaps be able to trace some expansion in Sallust's literary horizons, in particular of his background in rhetoric and historiography (it may be, for example, that his deepened sense of the significance of the victory over Carthage as a turning point in Roman history and also the appearance of the idea of the the *metus Etruscus* were due to new readings in historiography). The fragments, however, lead us to conclude that his education and his literary preferences did not change. Here too we have to remember that Sallust's work was written in a few years, indeed scarcely more than five, and we have the impression that, for his major work, he used

---

[29] Lepore 1950: 289 ff. has tried to prove a Posidonian origin for the digression on Sardinia and Corsica. The only evidence, however, is that Posidonius may have included an excursus on the Sardi in his historical work in connection with the Sardinian revolt put down by Tiberius Gracchus. All that is certain is the close resemblance between Sallust's account of Sardinia and Corsica and Pausanias 10. 17. Since it is unlikely that Pausanias draws on Sallust, both of them probably depend on a common source, and a quite detailed one. With regard to the excursus on Pontus, we can say with certainty (or great likelihood) only that Sallust has been extensively used by Pomponius Mela. I do not know how much to make of a pair of errors shared by Strabo and Sallust's Numidian excursus. In general, scholars think that Strabo relies on Posidonius (see Syme 1964: 153).

a collection of passages already prepared at the time of the monographs. What matters, however, are the general tendencies of ideas and sentiments that are informed or reinforced in his readings and according to which the passages came to be chosen, within the limits set by the rhetorical and educational tradition. Is it possible, then, to perceive any changes in these general tendencies? A positive answer would be risky. We can glimpse, nevertheless, how the selection of passages mirrors a more brutal, more pessimistic and rational view of history and politics. In *H.* 1. 12 M, the denunciation of political slogans as empty words used to mask ambition recalls Thucydides' account of the fierce political struggles in Greek cities (3. 82. 8). Either the idea or the allusion, however, was already present in *B.C.* 38. 3. More significant for our question is the influence of the same passage of Thucydides on the notorious fragment 1. 7 M, where scholars have seen the more developed expression of a pessimistic condemnation of human nature (*vitio humani ingenii*), even if we cannot perhaps call it a categorical condemnation.[30] Thus, the increasing rationalism we have described was influenced by Thucydides' concept of *physis*. Another echo of Thucydides appears in a sarcastic barb, cutting as an epigram, directed against the youth of the age of headlong moral corruption: 'one would rightly say that a generation was born that were unable to possess their property themselves or to allow others to possess it' (*ut merito dicatur genitos esse, qui neque ipsi habere possent res familiaris neque alios pati, H.* 1. 16 M; compare the speech of the Corinthians in Thucydides 1. 70. 9).[31] This echo well documents the influence of Thucydides' sarcasm on the tone of the introduction. In the orations too, certain Thucydidean allusions are not mere ornaments, but sharp observations that bear witness to a Machiavellian analysis of human desires and powers. In *H.* 1. 55. 7 M, Lepidus begs the people not to hope that Sulla 'will with greater danger let go of what he has gained through crime' (*per scelus occupata periculosius dimissurum*); this observation with its steely realism translates, with some loss of epigrammatic force, a passage where Pericles pleads with the Athenians: 'the empire you have is like a tyranny: conquering it could be considered unjust; losing it is dangerous' (2. 63. 2). Sallust also draws on Pericles' speech (2. 61. 1) for his characterization of the political situation under Sulla, though this time he rather adds to its verbal effectiveness: 'one must either be a slave or rule; either live in fear or create fear' (*serviendum aut imperitandum, habendus metus est aut faciendus, H.* 1. 55. 10 M). The beginning of

---

[30] La Penna 1968: 54ff. For a thorough comparison of the two passages, see Avenarius 1957: 52ff. (he too denies the radical pessimism).
[31] See Perrochat 1949: 17.

Lepidus' speech itself, which has not yet deployed sarcasm but tries to combat the gullibility of the people, who, since they are merciful and honest, believe they will find the same qualities in their leaders, reproduces the orations of the Corinthians in Sparta against the Athenians.[32] The considerations of realpolitik through which Mithridates begins the letter sent to the Parthian king—to show him the need for an alliance—resemble the beginning of the speech of the Corcyraeans to the Athenians.[33]

It is no coincidence that the same sarcastic tone and brutal realism also appear in Sallust's echoes of Demosthenes. When Lepidus castigates the Romans' lack of initiative for waiting for someone else to take the lead while allowing themselves to be crushed under Sulla's heel (*H.* 1. 55. 20 M), perhaps even more than in the *B.C.*,[34] he takes his tone and almost his very imagery from Demosthenes' effort to rouse the Athenians against Philip (*Phil.* 3. 35). Sulla's vices, hidden by success now but soon to be exposed by changing fortune (*H.* 1. 55. 24 M), are denounced with an argument taken from Demosthenes (*Olynth.* 2. 20).[35] Perhaps, even the earlier condemnation of the crimes of Sulla's henchmen (*satellites*, *H.* 1. 55. 21–8 M) takes inspiration from the sketch of Philip's henchmen in the same oration (17–20),[36] as Catiline's retinue resembles Theopompus' description of Philip's.[37] From Demosthenes come some of Marcius Philippus' darts of sarcasm: the senators, among whom everyone hopes that the thunderbolt will strike his neighbour and leave him untouched (*H.* 1. 77. 12 M), behave like the Athenians in the face of threats from the Macedonian king (*Phil.* 3. 33). The truce with Philip (*Phil.* 3. 9) plays into his hands, just like the ones certain senators want to make at all costs with Lepidus (*H.* 1. 77. 18 M), another exhortation to sweep away illusions and look dangerous reality in the face. The *Philippics* and *Olynthiacs* enrich the sarcasm and bitterness of Licinius Macer's speech. The Romans beat their chests about liberty in the assemblies when they listen to orators; then they remain cowardly and slothful (*H.* 3. 48. 14 M). They resemble the Athenians, energetic during assemblies, but neglectful of danger once they are broken up (*Phil.* 4. 1).[38] The comparison of the meagre ration of food given to the citizens by the *lex frumentaria* to the rations of prisoners (*H.* 3. 48. 19 M.) was a

---

[32] The possible echo of Thucydides 1. 70. 9 (from the same speech of the Corinthians) at 1. 55. 20 would have a similar meaning (Jacobs, Wirz, and Kurfess 1922: *ad loc.*; Avenarius 1957: 49).

[33] Jacobs, Wirz, and Kurfess 1922: *ad loc.*; Avenarius 1957: 49.

[34] On the use of Demosthenes in *B.C.* (especially in Cato's speech), see La Penna 1968: 153ff.

[35] Jacobs, Wirz, and Kurfess 1922: *ad loc.*; Avenarius 1957: 75.

[36] See Guilbert 1957: 296ff.   [37] La Penna 1968: 155.   [38] Perrochat 1949: 78.

devastating and drastic argument Demosthenes used with the Athenians (*Olynth.* 3. 33).[39] The jibe directed at the plebs enslaved through those alms (*H.* 3. 48. 31 M) comes from the same passage.[40]

It was easy to find sarcasm and invective in the *Philippics* and *Olynthiacs*. Similar tones, however, are taken from the speech *On the Crown* as well. Marcius Philippus repeats a rhetorical manoeuvre from that oration when he claims not to know whether to call the senators' behaviour fear, sloth, or madness (*H.* 1. 77. 12 M).[41] Equally, his condemnation of Lepidus' thugs (*H.* 1. 77. 7 M), who were already slaves to the previous demagogues, follows a passage of *On the Crown*.[42] Sallust may even draw on Isocrates (*Paneg.* 111), whose rhetoric is rarely impassioned, for a violent depiction of Sulla's followers as enslaved to their protector in order to play the godfather to others (*H* 1. 55. 2 M).[43] We conclude that readings from Greek authors have furnished the *Histories* especially with a bitter flavour, rough, violent, and often contemptuous of reality laid bare.

13. Even if we possessed the *Histories* complete, it would not be easy to solve an important question in their evaluation: what innovation did the work bring in its way of understanding the past and constructing its narrative in comparison with previous Roman historiography? Of course, the difficulty in answering this question results from the loss of all Latin historiography before Sallust. The powerful originality of the historian is undeniable (and I will not concern myself with demonstrating that here), although it is grounded in the Catonian and annalistic tradition, but it is an originality whose premises and elements, whose choices and tendencies would be better understood if we possessed a clearer idea of certain annalistic works in their entirety; in other respects, the novelty must have been less. As far as their structure and narrative are concerned, the *Histories* clearly marked something of a return to tradition after the monographs. Their stylistic elaboration was as powerful as the monographs', whether in the general run of the narrative or in its highlights, speeches, and digressions. How much the monographs influenced the compositional structure of the larger work is hard to say: certainly they did so to a smaller degree than has been claimed and in a way that left the annalistic patterning quite visible. Sallust only departed from this scheme, at least in the division of books, for reasons having to

---

[39] Perrochat 1949: 79.   [40] Ibid.   [41] Avenarius 1957: 74.
[42] Ibid. Irony can be found in *De cor.* 212 as well, a passage echoed in *H.* 2. 15 M (Avenarius 1957: 74). The echo of *De cor.* 67 in *H.* 1. 88 M is only for the effectiveness of the conceit (Kritz 1856: v. 3, *ad loc.*; Perrochat 1949: 79ff.)
[43] Perrochat 1949: 71.

do with the inner logic of the narrative, in order not to break up the unitary development of events.[44] In any case annalistic history as mere chronicle has been plainly superseded; but even here Sallust was strongly influenced by earlier historiography; the most advanced development was perhaps achieved by Sempronius Asellio with the pragmatic, Polybian plan of his work.

Nor was it anything new to move beyond using the annalistic format to chronicle the whole of Roman history. A clear trend in writing annals had led them to reflect the strong concentration of interest in contemporary history, to devote most of their extent to recent events, and to make clear their connection with ongoing political conflicts. Already Coelius Antipater, whose responsibility also for increasing the literary value of *annales* is well known, began his work with the Second Punic War. But Sallust found in Sisenna a much more advanced experiment in this direction. Sisenna had devoted a relatively extensive work to the period from the Marsic War to Sulla's death (or to the end of 79), and he had dealt with earlier events in a brief introduction (the Marsic War was already described in book I). The relationship between the introduction (itself a narrative) and the body of the work must have been similar to what we find in Sallust. And the suspicion arises that Sallust chose to begin his introductory narrative precisely with the Marsic War to point the contrast with Sisenna's work.[45] A polemical contrast, but crucial for understanding the work's structural aims, and it may be that this reaction against Sisenna has a fundamental importance in the formation of Sallust's style as well.

Apart from stylistic experimentation, the most important contribution of the monographs to the larger work, and what gives that work its original character, was probably the acute way of framing the problem of Roman history around the analysis of the crisis of society and state. Annalistic history devoted to the propaganda of particular noble families, still prevalent in recent works like Valerius Antias', was now surpassed. The terms of the political struggle, and therefore of Sallust's historical understanding, remained those of the age of Caesar: even the goal of moving beyond factionalism in a healthier, stronger, and more authoritative Republic did not, as we have seen, exceed the parameters of that political and ideological conflict. However, it is undeniable that this aim heightened his efforts not to link his interpretation of history absolutely with the opposition to the aristocracy either and to regard its political

---

[44] On this question, see La Penna 1968: 338.
[45] For other political reasons which might have played a role, see La Penna 1968: 253.

The Histories: The Crisis of the Res Publica

activity with a certain impartiality. In any case, its anti-aristocratic thrust does not mean that Sallust's historiographic work was bound to the cause of Caesar himself. Sallust's support for Caesar's policies was anything but unconditional; and that support is based on definite political convictions, not the other way around (nor is this the case even for a Velleius Paterculus). Thus, beyond his reservations about annalistic history in the service of the great noble families, Sallust's reservations about annalistic history in the service of factionalism, which so much of the genre had been since the time of the Gracchi, were sincere and not without significance. It is clear how strongly polemical Sallust's preface was: along with praise for the truthfulness of Fannius, whom he perhaps saw as a Gracchan moderate because of the break from Gaius in 122 BCE, criticism of other historians predominates. The sketch Sallust gave of Roman historiography could not have been positive overall. The importance of the moral and political crisis was certainly nothing new in historiography; rather, it was consolidated as the crisis itself became acute. It was already clear, in addition to Polybius before, in the senatorial historiography of the time of the Gracchi (certainly not only in Piso Frugi; after all, the moralizing approach to historiography was dominated by Cato's influence). What were innovative were probably the central role Sallust attributed to the problem and his radicalization of the pessimistic interpretation of Roman history. This above all in Sallust's work made the strongest impact on Livy some ten years that made the strongest impact on Livy some ten years later. Livy's preface, as we know,[46] is an argument against the proem and the first part of the introduction of Sallust's *Histories*. In place of a fierce attack against earlier historiography, Livy rather exalts its greatness, in the face of which he takes comfort for remaining obscure himself: 'if in such a great crowd of writers my fame should remain in darkness, I would console myself with the nobility and greatness of those who block out my name' (*si in tanta scriptorum turba mea fama in obscuro sit, nobilitate ac magnitudine eorum me qui nomini officient meo consoler, praef.* 3). From the success of Sallust and Asinius Pollio, Livy knows that his audience is especially eager for the history of the Civil Wars. He, instead, wants to give its due place to archaic history in order to avoid the sight of contemporary evils and find some comfort in a story which inspires confidence (*praef.* 4ff.). In his account of civil wars he would remain unbiased, but his mind would be *sollicitus*, embittered and anxious. His quick sketch of the crisis of Roman history and its stages (*praef.* 9) is dominated by Sallust, and no phrase of Livy is more Sallustian (and Tacitean) than its epigrammatic and monumental conclusion:

---

[46] Good demonstration by Amundsen 1947: 31ff.

'we have arrived at these times in which we can endure neither our vices nor their remedies' (*ad haec tempora, quibus nec vitia nostra nec remedia pati possumus, perventum est*). But Livy wants to make clear that Roman history is not to be judged only by the epoch of crisis. Seen in its entire development, the Roman *res publica* is the greatest, the most sacred, and the richest in good examples. Corruption reached it relatively late, even if that corruption has now become very grave.

To have put the crisis at the centre of his account is the major achievement of Sallust as an interpreter of Roman history, even if its originality is only relative. It is necessary to consider how much rhetoric and imperialistic bombast he has at least partially dispelled to reach this vision. With more clarity of mind and more bravery than all of the Roman historians, he provided Latin culture with the capacity to look without sentimentality or illusion at the development of its own society. This capacity will not disappear, notwithstanding Augustus' attempts to restore full faith in the empire. Rather, it will be conspicuous in the culture of the Augustan age itself and will become a decisive element in establishing the greatness of Latin literature.

15

The Faces of Discord in Sallust's *Histories*

Andrew Feldherr

Sallust's most ambitious work, continuous *Histories* beginning in 78 BCE, survives in over 500 fragments.[1] Six speeches and letters were excerpted complete as part of a collection of rhetorical models, and there are scraps of narrative from dismantled codices and papyri. But the vast majority of these fragments are preserved indirectly, mostly in citations by grammarians or commentators on other texts. This total makes the *Histories* the best-attested lost work of Roman historiography and gives us the material to say more about it than perhaps any other Latin prose text that does not possess its own manuscript tradition. On the other hand, fragments can be made to fit into such a variety of meaningful patterns that practically no schema can be proved or disproved, and none surely captures anything like the sorts of complex readings the whole could make possible. But beyond these obvious difficulties, the very methods we necessarily use for organizing and interpreting fragments can more insidiously shape our conceptions of the text. The most convincing arguments for making sense out of what we have often involve supplementing or contextualizing fragments by adducing parallels in form or content, and this process of matching like with like inevitably makes fragmentary texts seem at once more homogeneous and familiar. Sallust, however, was an author whose extant works have themselves been claimed to approximate precisely the hermeneutic

---

[1] An early version of this paper was presented during a workshop on 'Augustus and the Destruction of History' held at the University of Cambridge in September 2013. Later drafts were read by Jennifer Gerrish and Will Batstone. I am grateful to both these colleagues and to the workshop audience for their suggestions, but all errors and infelicities remain emphatically my own responsibility.

openness of a fragment and to make productive use of incongruities and contradictions.[2] Thus, the search for coherence that forms an inevitable part even of the task of assembling fragments for publication, however well attuned to the author's predilection for inconcinnity, can in its emphasis go against the grain of the kind of interpretation applied to his surviving texts. Indeed, the greater risk in the case of Sallust will be the one described by Kraus and Woodman (1997: 30), that attention to the interpretation of individual fragments on their own will 'tend towards the atomizing'; and this tendency fits alarmingly well with a dominant view of the author.

The essay that follows embraces the latter risk perhaps all too willingly. It aims at a reading of the work that is admittedly partial.[3] But while this corrective emphasis on the text's attention to discontinuity remains equally vulnerable to the charge of circularity, there are specific justifications for the attempt beyond the general considerations that reading fragmentary texts always demands some kind of supplementation of the evidence and that not to read what we have would be more of a lost opportunity than to maintain standards of proof that might be possible for more fully accessible works. First, the very challenge of building coherence forms a particular burden of large-scale narrative history, and the reader familiar with Sallust's earlier monographs approaching the *Histories* for the first time would be especially inclined to question how and how far such coherence was achievable. The *Catiline* introduces a historian who will treat Roman history 'selectively' (*carptim*, B.C. 4. 2), concentrating on an episode whose 'newness' (*novitas*, B.C. 4. 4) marks a break from the past. The subject of the *Jugurtha* was not only variable in itself (*variaque victoria*, B.J. 5. 1), but similarly becomes a 'first', the turning point when the supremacy of the nobility was challenged (*tunc primum superbiae nobilitatis obviam itum est*, B.C. 5. 1). Will these works' emphases on transformation and discontinuity bear translation into a narrative form structured by patterns of regularity and repetition that locate any episode within the larger expanse of Roman history? Such a question takes on special importance because the very starting point Sallust chooses for his narrative, the aftermath of Sulla's

---

[2] See especially Levene 1992 (= Chapter 10 in this volume). See also the comments of Rosenblitt 2013: 467–8: 'A text which incorporates comparatively uncontrolled voices is fractured even when complete, and this suggestion that the *Historiae* may be an inherently fractured text can give us confidence in approaching its fragments.'

[3] Most obviously because of its concentration on the most truly fragmentary elements of the *Histories*, at the expense of the speeches and letters. For more comprehensive, indeed magisterial, syntheses of the work, see Syme 1964: 178–213 and La Penna 1968: 247–311 (partially reprinted as Chapter 14 of this volume).

dictatorship, could be construed either as a disruption or restoration of the former Republic, and the events of those years introduce such a host of new characters and challenges that scholars debate about where the work would have ended and what themes would have given unity to Sallust's narrative.[4]

The second justification for stressing disunity as a hermeneutic principle for the *Histories* will be its own thematization of discord as a defining characteristic of its subject matter. Of course, it is possible to produce coherent accounts of political discord, but Sallust's earlier works had demonstrated how their own narratives were themselves the product of the very disagreements they chronicled, in part by giving particular space to reproducing debate directly (as in the conclusion of the *Catiline*) and to constructing voices that in different ways compete with the historian's own in building authoritative narratives of the past.[5] While the *Histories*' fifth book may well have ended with a rhetorical contest about the passage of Gabinian Law that gave Pompey his extraordinary command against the pirates (*H.* 5. 17–27 M), the absence of any other directly paired speeches, indeed the relatively small proportion of any direct speech in the work, especially in comparison to the monographs, may in itself be an innovation as striking as the adoption of the annalistic form.[6] I will suggest that Sallust achieves an antiphonal reading of his longest work by the somewhat different means of enforcing processes of comparison and contrast through patterns of imagery and structural balance. These patterns not only formally reproduce the disharmonies of its subject matter. They themselves draw attention to aspects of likeness and difference which raise questions about unities between past and present and Roman and foreign that ultimately challenge the viability of annalistic history itself.[7]

My presentation of the *Histories* will have three parts, each focusing on a different aspect of the work that particularly emphasizes problems of historical continuity and the adequacy of representation. First, I will

---

[4] Syme 1964: 190–2 provides the best discussion.

[5] See, e.g., Egelhaaf-Gaiser 2010 (= Chapter 12 of this volume) for an argument that Marius in the *Jugurtha* constructs such a challenge, and on the particular tensions between historiographic and rhetorical voices in the *Catiline*, Feldherr 2012 and 2013. On the deconstructive aspects of the debate in that work, see esp. Sklenář 1998.

[6] See the suggestions of Levene 2007: 282–3; especially his discussion of the role of direct speech in the work.

[7] This emphasis on Sallust's response to annalistically structured history is meant as a complement to Klingner's reading of Sallust's view of Roman history as directed against the pro-optimate Posidonius (Klingner 1928: 182–8, = Chapter 13, pp. 344–49 of this volume).

analyse the vision of Roman history set out in the preface and the problems it poses for the structures and ideology of *annales*. Second, I will look at Sallust's use of physiognomy to see how history appears written on the faces of its actors. Finally, I will show how Sallust's accounts of geography and ethnography question the spatial borders of Romanness as his chronology confuses its temporal patterning. My overall aims will be to illustrate how fragmentation is made a significant theme of the work by patterns of imagery throughout and to explore the consequences of this thematic emphasis for understanding the events Sallust describes and their relationship to any larger view of Roman history. The imagery that reflects political fragmentation will often also allude to discrepancies or distortions in the narrative record, and the readers as a result must complete such partial narratives by processes not unlike those accidentally imposed by the fragmentary state of the text, using points of likeness and difference among the events that make up his subject matter and the material traces left by *imperium* on natural phenomena to construct, and deconstruct, stories of the Roman past.

I

I begin with a reading of the work's opening as a programmatic map for the oppositions it contains. *Res populi Romani M. Lepido Q. Catulo consulibus ac deinde militiae et domi gestas composui* ('The deeds of the Roman people, in the consulate of M. Lepidus and Q. Catulus and thence forward, accomplished in warfare and domestically, I have composed,' *H*. 1. 1 M). This deceptively straightforward sentence exemplifies a number of the stylistic idiosyncrasies that were probably already familiar marks of Sallust's personal style, most strikingly imbalance and exaggerated brevity.[8] It contains two rhetorical cola; the first, artificially lengthened by the delayed placement of *gestas*, comes to incorporate the entire subject of the work; the second consists of the single word *composui*. Such an abrupt ending gives this final word particular emphasis. On the one hand it has a strongly Thucydidean flavour; the prefix *com-* recalls the Greek historian's programmatic ξυνέγραψε (Thuc. 1. 1).[9] But the 'togetherness' invested in the act of 'composition' highlights the

[8] See Latte 1935: esp. 402–9 (= Chapter 2, p. 25–33 of this volume).
[9] Pasoli 1975: 375–6, in addition to demonstrating the contrast between the 'narrative ordered according to the criterion of *annales*' and the selectivity of the monographs, notes that this is the first surviving example of '*componere* used as a word that can designate

striking number of dichotomies contained by its object. Sallust has put together consuls and people, two magistrates who despite the idea of cooperation further implied by the *con-* in 'consul', did anything but work together, as well as domestic and military events.[10]

By drawing attention to his own role in yoking together opposites, therefore, Sallust allows for a deconstruction of the political balances built into the traditional annalistic representation of the past, presenting a strong contrast between the singleness of *composui*, which seems merely to be a product of the form, and the host of dualities in the earlier clause representing history's actual subject matter.[11] He uses, indeed, the conventional expectation that *annales* affirm the primacy and unity of the *populus Romanus* as well as the difference between at home and abroad as an ironic foil to the actual events he will describe. Beyond the rivalry between expected allies typical of civil war—here the demagogic Lepidus vs the reactionary Catulus—there is a larger question of whose story we are telling. The accomplishments recorded ought to be collective ones, the *res gestae* of the Roman people, with the consuls serving only to mark the work's starting point, but throughout the *Histories* the deeds of powerful individuals, including Lepidus, Pompey, Sertorius, and Mithridates will dominate the structure of the narrative, making it hard to find a unified history of the Roman people.[12] And as this list of protagonists suggests, the firm boundary between internal and external politics will be simultaneously at risk. On the one hand, where we expect unity—between *consules* and between magistrates and people, we will find division. And where we expect clear differences, between war abroad and peace at home, or simply between Pompey and Mithridates, we will find disconcerting similarities.

Another phrase in this sentence that deserves attention is *ac deinde*. For Kraus and Woodman (1997: 31) this phrase epitomizes the teleological optimism of the annalistic form: Roman history can go on and on without end. But the very uncertainty of the narrative's ending may also invite the reader to weigh the options for closure, to ask when the story that began in 78 should logically end. Correspondingly, *ac deinde*

---

historiographic activity, with a clearly pregnant force, if not actually bivalent ("to put together" and "to set out in order")'.

[10] By reversing the expected order *domi militiaeque*, 'Sallust wanted to react against the formulaic, epico-historiographic flavour of the expression' (Pasoli 1966: 37).

[11] The verb reappears in *H.* 1. 5 M to describe a historian who '[by writing] many false things about good men composed things for the worse' (*in deterius composuit*).

[12] Bauhofer 1935 argues for a largely episodic structure to the work, focusing on major personalities whose stories in turn illustrate the theme of civil war.

substitutes for a defined period a single dividing point in time, one that draws the present more closely into the narrated past than would be the case if an ending were specified. And the overcoming of this difference between past and present also has implications for understanding the very shape of Roman time. The obvious connections between the struggles after the death of Sulla and the struggles after the death of Caesar replace the promise of annual rebirth implied by new consuls with a more ominous circularity as the death of one tyrant unleashes new rivalries.[13] As we shall see, Sallust will later suggest that this happened as well at the very origins of the Roman Republic: once people were no longer afraid of the kings, they were free to struggle against one another for supremacy. The periodization we will find in Livy's second book, according to which the end of the monarchy brings 'the power of laws greater than that of individual men' (*imperia legum potentiora quam hominum*, Liv. 2. 1), seems provocatively backwards here. The state was (oxymoronically?) driven by 'an equal and measured justice' (*aequo et modesto iure agitatum*, H. 1. 1 M) only for a short period of anxiety after the expulsion of the kings, while the new republic unleashes not the transcendent potency of laws, but the 'injustices of the more powerful men' (*iniuriae validiorum*, H. 1. 1 M). Such a cycle, therefore, does not just befall the Roman people after 78 BCE, when, we might perhaps assume, Roman history reached a point of decline that severed it from its past, nor even suggest the recurrence of civil war in the triumviral period. This always was Roman history, and the annalistic structure masks its fundamental and unchanging truth. Sallust is at once rewriting the past and unwriting the historiographic model through which that past had been falsely represented.

The only substantially surviving section of the preface (H. 1. 11 M) retells precisely such a revisionist history of the Roman people. The link back to the work's own beginning is marked by the repetition of the phrase *res Romana*.[14] But the archaeology that follows so challenges fundamental assumptions about Roman history that we may well wonder whether there is such a thing as *res Romana* at all. Again, the passage proceeds not just by introducing dualities where we expect unities but by thematizing the principle of division, *discordia: discordia et avaritia*

---

[13] The importance of the triumviral context for the work has been demonstrated afresh and in detail by Gerrish 2012.

[14] For the demonstration, contra Maurenbrecher, that this was the beginning of the historical excursus, see Klingner 1928: 169–72. La Penna and Funari 2015: 131 note the occurrence of the phrase in Ennius (*Ann.* 156 and 495 Sk.), interesting in light of the Ennian resonance of the force that destroys it (see n. 18 below).

atque ambitio et cetera secundis rebus oriri sueta mala ('discord and avarice plus ambition and the other evils accustomed to arise during prosperity') increased especially after the fall of Carthage. *Avaritia* and *ambitio* will be all too familiar to readers of Sallust's earlier works as causes of Roman corruption, and the pattern of conjunctions in this clause closely connects this pair of familiar forces, but it also throws emphasis on their new partner *discordia*—the two have become a one that is itself now divided from something else.

This word *discordia* actually plays rather less of a role in Sallust's monographs than we might have expected. The modern Catiline may enjoy discord (*B.C.* 5. 2), but this marks his difference from the early Romans, who use discord against the enemy but concord at home (*B.C.* 9. 2); indeed, concord is the secret weapon of early Roman history that first unites the Trojans and Aborigines (*B.C.* 6. 2).[15] If discord is modern but not ancient in the *Catiline*, it is foreign in the *Jugurtha*. The dying Micipsa ironically reminds Jugurtha that things fall apart by discord (*B.J.* 10. 6), 'ironically' because, as Sallust will later record, the Numidian mob just are seditious and discordant by nature (*B.J.* 66. 2).[16] As discord comes to overshadow the familiar forces of immorality in the *Histories*, Sallust also reverses its associations in both his earlier works by making it both Roman and ancestral. Thus, after seeming to remind his readers of the sea change in public life that happened after the fall of Carthage—the great turning point in the *Catiline* (*B.C.* 10. 1)—he revises this view by insisting that dissensions and injustices were domestic, *domi*, even from the beginning (*iam a principio*). The addition of a perhaps superfluous *domi* at the emphatic beginning of its rhetorical colon not only contradicts assumptions from the monographs either that discord was fundamentally foreign, as in the *Jugurtha*, or an instrument in foreign affairs, as in the *Catiline*; it recalls the traditional dichotomies of the annalistic form and so again creates a tension between subject matter and the implicit ideology of the genre.

---

[15] Indeed *concordia* itself is a surprisingly rare word in the monographs. In the *Catiline*, other than in this passage, it occurs as a common noun only at 9. 1, and then twice to name the temple where the Senate meet to investigate the charges against the conspirators (46. 6 and 49. 4). There are two uses in the *Jugurtha*, once in Micipsa's speech to balance the negative reference to discord (10. 6; see below), and once, again in direct speech at 31. 23. In book one of the *Histories* alone, however, it appears six times after the preface; once in Lepidus' speech and five times in Philippus'. On the thematic significance of concord and discord in the *Jugurtha*, see especially Wiedemann 1993 (= Chapter 11 of this volume). Miller 2015: 249–50 also notes the rarity of *concordia* in the *Jugurtha* and regards its two uses in direct speech as ironic recollections of contemporary rhetorical slogans.

[16] There is another reference to the Carthaginian discord that prompts the foundation of Leptis (*B.J.* 78. 1), but these are the only occurrences of the word in the monograph.

It is common to attribute the change in Sallust's presentation of the Roman past to the author's increasing pessimism at the persistence of civic violence over the course of the second triumvirate.[17] But rather than seek such a biographical explanation, I prefer to link these reinterpretations of Rome's moral trajectory with the larger themes of the work within which it occurs. The emphasis on discord, as opposed simply to *avaritia* and *ambitio*, highlights the motifs of fragmentation and division throughout the text, while a rereading of the past in terms of the recurrence of discord suggests a quite different understanding of the relationship between past and present. Rather than imply a process of decline from ancient standards, and thus the possibility of their restoration, the present now defines the potentialities for the future, and the past is revised not as different but as identical to the present. Discord is all there ever was.[18] Indeed the very word *discordia* in this passage becomes a sort of verbal revenant[19] forcing a continual revision of

---

[17] e.g. Klingner 1928: 189 (= Chapter 13, p. 349 of this volume).

[18] Cf. especially *H.* 1. 7 M, where dissension seems not to result from specific causes but rather from a transhistorical flaw in human nature that contradicts the very language of first beginnings: *nobis primae dissensiones vitio humani ingenii evenere, quod inquies at indomitum semper in certamine libertatis aut gloriae aut dominationis agit* ('the first dissensions came about for us out of a flaw in human nature, which restless and untameable ever presses on in the struggle for liberty or glory or freedom'). See in particular the analysis of Pasoli 1966: 379–80; McGushin 1992: vol. 1, 75–6 and Funari and La Penna 2015: 129 give a more ambivalent reading of the fragment, suggesting that the propensity for dissension is less a kind of original sin than the necessary correlate of positive attributes that make us human. See especially the discussion of La Penna 1968: 301 and 306 (= Chapter 14, p. 360 and 365 in this volume).

[19] Sallust's interest in *discordia* in this passage may also evoke another important historiographic model, Ennius' *Annales*. At the start of the poet's second hexad, describing the beginning of the Second Punic War, he refers to the closing and subsequent reopening of the gates of war (*Enn. Ann.* 220–6 Sk., see the reconstruction of Skutsch 1985: 392–4). These are famously broken by *taetra Discordia*. The sudden emergence of this figure seemingly to undo the order that had just been established, as Bignone 1929 has shown, introduces the Empedoclean perspective into Roman history, for Strife was a force as old as the cosmos itself, though destined to particular periods of ascendancy. The way that *discordia* seems to undermine any attempts at periodization in Sallust's preface, even reversing the chronological flow of the passage itself, may perhaps resemble this view. One argument for this might be the way that discord's presence and absence here shadow her appearance in Ennius: Ennius introduces her to herald the beginning of the Second Punic War (although the date referred to seems to be 241 BCE), while for Sallust that same war (misleadingly) marked 'the end of discords and competition'. Of course, Sallust is talking about internal discord, and Ennius about a kind of cosmic discord causing and manifesting a new outbreak of war. Thus, it is possible to read an Ennian allusion here as affirming a general theory of domestic harmony secured by foreign threats—once foreign discord begins, domestic discords (and note the plural) end. On the other hand, if we note simply the verbal likeness of the two figures, and assimilate them into a larger image of Discord, then the conflicting chronology juxtaposing her beginning and ending seems to

every attempt at historical periodization. It returns at the beginning of a sentence that seems to describe its own ending: *discordiarum et certaminis finis fuit secundum bellum Punicum* ('the end of discords and competition was the Second Punic War'). The point is one that Sallust has already made, and the repetition seems to form a ring bounding (*finis*) the period of the conflict of the orders. Yet we already know that this impression is false—discord has no end and will return after the Third Punic War. And if we read the emphasis on discord not simply as an authorial change of heart but intertextually, as specifically evoking his earlier account of Roman history in the *Catiline*, that itself highlights the process of revision by which present experience rewrites an understanding of the past.

Before leaving Sallust's account of discord, it is important to note how fundamentally the prominence he gives its role in Roman history calls into question the very existence of Roman history as both a definable subject and a literary form. The state Sallust describes has a natural tendency to pull apart into opposite poles—the nobles aspire to act like kings, and the rest are treated as slaves.[20] The 'middle' excluded from this process is precisely the *populus Romanus* whose history Sallust was claiming to write, or perhaps put together or even compose in response to the destructive rhetoric that rips it apart. For whatever polarization may have happened in reality is matched, or maybe obscured, by an equal exaggeration in rhetoric. Kings and slaves are polemical words in Roman politics, and at this point it is hard to tell whether Sallust is actually viewing the Roman past from the perspective of those who claim oppression or highlighting rather the amplification of political language

---

amplify the Ennian effect of showing Discord almost immediately undoing the establishment of peace.

The Empedoclean underpinning of this notion tempts one to join the ranks of what Syme (1964: 10) called the 'curious and uncritical' who proposed the historian as the author of the poetic *Empedoclea*, mentioned by Cicero (*Q. fr.* 2. 9. 3). The interpenetrations of desire (*avaritia, ambitio*) and strife in shaping history would be interestingly compared and contrasted with Empedoclean notions.

[20] Note too how this polarization of the Roman people into slaves and masters will be reinforced by the itself discordant rhetoric of Lepidus (*H.* 1. 55. 2 and esp. 10 M: *hac tempestate serviendum aut imperitandum*, 'at this time one must either be a slave or a command'). On the language of this passage, see especially Venturini 1973: 646-8, who argues that in the *Histories* Sallust moves from a partisan use of this polemical language founded on post-Sullan political divisions to a more universal view of such oppositions as fundamental to Roman history from its beginnings. Another *popularis* orator in the work, Licinius Macer, strikes the same note at the beginning of his speech, *H.* 3. 48. 1 M (and again at *H.* 3. 48. 9 and 13 M).

that distorts the past. When Sallust says that discord was only held in check until the kings were driven out, he refers to the essential transformational moment that created the Roman Republic; the expulsion of the kings marks the beginning of Roman time. Yet he immediately reuses the concept of kingship to describe the new aristocracy's practice of 'having a regal disregard for lives and persons' (*de vita atque tergo regio more consulere*). The brilliant phrase *regio more consulere* thus fundamentally confounds the temporal divisions that structure Roman history as unregal.[21] At the same time, the language of kingship and slavery also recalls and recasts the polarities established at the beginning of the *Catiline*. There the ruling function of the mind was distinguished from the natural servility of the body (*B.C.* 1). The figure of the slave was used to differentiate the few who realize their human potential from the many who devote themselves to pleasures. It underlined a moral and a normative distinction. But that notion of natural hierarchies too receives a significant check when the allegorical terms of rule and servitude are returned to political reality. The better does not rule the worse, but the unchecked pursuit of property and power—the quest for actual kingship—leads to savage violence. Sallust simultaneously rewrites Rome's beginnings and his own textual origins.

As we move beyond the preface to consider the structure of Sallust's narrative (which, given the debate about the arrangement of material, must remain a very speculative project even on such a large scale),[22] we can see how both the twin problems of excessive polarization and the blurring of distinctions between Roman and foreigner adumbrated in the opening sentence and formulated in the 'archaeology' emerge from the very patterning of events.

Rome's major military campaigns in the period covered by the *Histories*, the *militiae* of the opening sentences, form a rather unusual pattern. The strictly foreign wars of the first book (some skirmishes in Macedonia, as well as a campaign against the pirates in southern Asia Minor) are overshadowed by the war against Sertorius in Spain and the rebellion begun by Lepidus in Italy. Thus, the reversal of the predicted order of the phrase *domi militiaeque* may anticipate an actual instability in the categories of domestic and foreign in the events highlighted in this book. The war with Sertorius takes place at the edge of the earth,

---

[21] See Pasoli 1966: 33.

[22] The most widely accepted schema for the content and distribution of material in the *Histories* is now McGushin's, summarized at 1992: vol. 1, 10–13, but the sketch that follows is compatible with other plausible arrangements as well.

in Hispania Ulterior, and indeed Sertorius looks outside the *oecumene* to the fabled Islands of the Blessed. But it is a war fought between Roman citizens.

Not only does Sertorius occupy a polar position at the edge of the earth which will confute annalistic expectations that the war out there will be a foreign war, but he also further blurs the temporal boundaries of the work. Lepidus' rebellion begins within the narrative period covered by the *Histories*, but the account of Sertorius at the end of the book must have contained a fairly substantial account of his campaigns during the preceding years. Thus, the parallel to Lepidus, and in a sense the reversal of chronology required by this extensive 'prequel' (*H.* 1. 84–103 M), may have recast the Sertorian war not as part of a new beginning, perhaps echoed and expanded thematically by Sertorius, but rather as itself a repetition of a pattern that began before the work itself, and before the end of the Civil Wars of the 80s.

After Lepidus' death in book two, Sertorius gains a new antithesis, Mithridates, who operates at the other extreme of the Roman world, the kingdom of Pontus.[23] Yet the pairing with the archetypal foreign king may further remind Sallust's audience that Sertorius is not such a figure. (Even his assassination at a banquet gives him a monarch's death—the death of Mithridates' own father, poisoned at a banquet in 120 BCE.) Paradoxically a far more regal presence in Spain is to be found not in the rebellious Sertorius, but in the commander of the Roman forces, Pompey, who, as we shall see, likes to imitate Alexander the Great. And like Sertorius, Mithridates transcends the temporal boundaries of the work, since his prior Roman opponent was Sulla. As Mithridates was already an enemy when the narrative begins, so too his death in 63 may well have meant that he survived the work's ending. Nor is it only through the symbolic structure of the work that Mithridates challenges Roman attempts to plot their history and impose internal boundaries. His letter in book four (4. 69 M), explicitly presents Roman actions as unified by a transhistorical motive that is the same at all times and all places: 'The Romans have only one reason for waging wars with kings, peoples, or tribes, and that an old one, their fundamental desire for power and riches.'[24]

---

[23] The exact position of Mithridates entrance in the work is somewhat debated. There was clearly some background material to the beginning of the war, including an account of the king and his antecedents (*H.* 2. 71–9 M), which probably appeared in the course of book two. For the evidence and arguments, see McGushin 1992: vol. 1, 247–55.

[24] *namque Romanis cum nationibus, populis, regibus cunctis una et ea vetus causa bellandi est, cupido profunda imperi et divitiarum*, 4. 69. 5 M.

The central third book (although Sallust may well have planned more than five) combines the rising action of the Mithridatic war in the east with the 'setting' of Sertorius in the west, but it also focuses on a figure in the centre of this geographical space, in Italy itself, who forms in his own way another opposite to Mithridates. This is Spartacus, and his presence replaces a pattern of geographical antitheses with a social one. One of Rome's new opponents is a king, and the other is a slave. The process of discord that in the prologue replaces the Roman *populus* with kings and slaves here finds an echo as a king and a slave alternately wage war on the Republic. Even within the account of the slave war, the same kind of extreme polarity seems to have been operative. Spartacus' slave troops are appropriately cast as slaves to their passions and immediate desires as well. Far from sympathetic rebels or freedom fighters, one of the manuscript fragments depicts scenes of brutal violence (*H.* 3. 98B–C M.).[25] The struggles of a single leader to regulate this unruly and easily fragmented community certainly have allegorical potential to suggest both the struggles of the mind over the body familiar from the *Catiline* and the divided Roman polity of the preface.[26] As this function of Spartacus within the narrative would suggest, the very externality of these kings and slaves becomes highly uncertain, since Sallust has taught us to see in these two ideally un-Roman figures the true reflection of the only alternatives left to Romans at home.

The structure of the work read thus gives a narrative dimension to the political analysis of the preface. The essential character of Roman historical discourse, the *populus Romanus*, fragments into a dramatis personae of diverse rulers and subjects, whose conventional significance as like or different becomes complicated through repetition. And if an annalistic account of the triumphant *res publica* forms a distinctively Roman story, the phenomena linked to its dissolution are both endlessly recurrent and ethnologically universal.

II

The aim of these next sections will be to trace the manifestations of *discordia* not only on the macrocosmic structure of the *Histories* but also

---

[25] See La Penna 1968: 296–8.

[26] For a reading of Sallust's Spartacus as 'a reflection of contemporary anxieties about the stability (or lack thereof) of the ruling triumvirate', see Gerrish 2012: 140–51 (quotation, p. 150).

within two recurring types of imagery involving the representation of the human countenance and of geography. While the relative prominence of these motifs may well be distorted by the accidents of survival, and their placement more or less conjectural, their very comparability enables a pattern of responsion which articulates the larger antitheses that emerge from the disposition of the *Histories*' subject matter. Conversely, the compositional principles of comparison and contrast revealed by the distribution of kings, slaves, and consuls in Sallust's narrative themselves encourage reading these portraits and excursus closely in relation to one another. As we shall see, both physiognomic and topographic descriptions group themselves into antitheses, fair faces versus deformed ones, and monstrous landscapes against paradisiacal ones. Yet points of similarity confuse and undermine the affirmative value of distinguishing same and other.

If this mode of analysis seems dangerously applicable to any elements in any narrative, let me point out that both bodies and space play a significant role in the preface itself precisely as problematic indices of change over the course of Roman history. The geographical extent of Rome's empire, 'at its strongest in the consulate of Ser. Sulpicius and M. Marcellus [51 BCE], with all of Gaul as far as the Rhine, from the Mediterranean to the Atlantic—except where swamps made it impassible—thoroughly conquered' (*H.* 1. 11 M), suggests a historical trajectory similar to the spatial one, of growth and expansion that will be undermined by the subsequent emphases on discord and vice. Bodies marked by violence distinguish the slave from the citizen, while physical violence against citizens (as well as the self-aggrandizing redrawing of boundaries on the smaller scale suggested by *de agro pellere*, 'to drive from their fields') was an index of un-Roman '*regnum*'.

The use Sallust makes of bodies and boundaries in the archaeology also reminds us that more generally in Roman culture both bodies and landscapes possess a historiographic dimension as well as a historical one.[27] They commemorate and depict events rather than just being affected by them. A Roman's battle-scarred body recorded his *res gestae*; *imagines* preserve the presence of great figures in contexts where they can continue to inspire or regulate behaviour in the now. Thus, the *Jugurtha* (*B.J.* 5) uses *imagines* to epitomize an effect of historical memory in recording how great figures of the past claimed to be kindled to virtue

---

[27] For a particularly interesting reading of the importance of bodies in Sallustian historiography, see Connolly 2015: 81–2. On the role of scars in Roman politics, see Leigh 1995.

by the sight of their ancestral images.[28] What is more, the commemorative value of the tough body often opposed that of *imagines* in the rhetoric of civil wars. A *novus homo* like Marius has scars, while his rivals only have *imagines* (*B.J.* 85. 29–30; cf. too *H.* 3. 48. 18 M). The conquest of territory not only affirms Roman virtue and contrasts it with the foreign practices of the defeated foe; it also places the Romans in a historical sequence of peoples and empires who have passed through each territory and so inspires comparison and contrast through time.[29] So too in examining individual countenances and landscapes depicted in the work, we will find that their portrayal often bears significance not just for the meaning of Roman history, but for the ways in which it is represented and interpreted.

Among the fragments of the *Histories*, three significant faces catch the reader's attention. Though each passage comes down to us in isolation from the others, they can be meaningfully read together as constituting a sort of portrait gallery allowing us to compare contrasting figures across the architecture of the text. The first of these faces belongs to Marius Gratidianus, and it formed one of the most memorable passages from Sallust's portrayal of the Civil Wars that brought Sulla to power: *ut in M. Mario, quoi fracta prius crura bracchiaque et oculi effossi, scilicet ut per singulos artus expiraret* ('as in the case of M. Marius, whose legs and arms were first broken and his eyes gouged out, doubtless so that he might perish limb by limb', *H.* 1. 44 M). Sallust's account of Marius' death becomes practically a topos among writers like Lucan and Seneca for the cruelty of tyranny and the excesses of civil war (cf. Luc. 2. 177–185, Sen. *dial.* 5. 18; further citations in La Penna and Funari 2015: 160–1). Marius' body provides not just an outrageous example of civic violence but almost a figure for it. The fragmentation of his members, even their individual enumeration, contrasts with the ideal unity of the *res publica*. The suggestion that Marius' killer wanted him 'to perish in each limb', further refracts one man's death into the death of a multitude, as well as offering an ironic version of the sacrificial principle of one for many. We get a sense of the historiographic significance of Marius' tortured body in the pictorial specificity of the account of the wounds, and the ironic *scilicet* which highlights the hubristic folly of his murderer who thought he could violate the fundamental rules of nature by making his victim die more than once. Whatever the identity of that murderer in Sallust's account, the word *scilicet* itself demands attention.

---

[28] Cf. the discussion by Egelhaaf-Gaiser 2010 (= Chapter 12 of this volume).

[29] A classic example of such a spatial palimpsest will be Livy's treatment of Thermopylae (36. 15–19): see Clark 2014: 93–7, and Chaplin 2010.

Marius' death was already a leitmotif of Roman polemics as early as Cicero's *In toga candida* in 64 BCE, in which Cicero accused Catiline himself of the murder (Asc. 83. 26–84. 11 C); and there was a corresponding story, recorded in Valerius Maximus (9. 2. 1), that he was killed at the tomb of the Catuli, which Lucan amplifies into an expiatory sacrifice.[30] If the historian himself describes the event in his own voice, the use of *scilicet* indicates that his narrative too took on a strong rhetorical colour. Perhaps there was some self-referential aspect to this language. The extremity of Marius' bodily torment reflects and produces an equivalent amplification in the rhetorical tradition which leaves its own trace on the historical record, and this record as a result comes to perpetuate discord in the very act of recording it.

But the thematic importance of Marius' mutilation will be further sharpened when we compare his face to another that appeared near the end of that same first book, that of the former Marian and rebel Sertorius (*H.* 1. 88 M):

> Magna gloria tribunus militum in Hispania T. Didio imperante, magno usui bello Marsico paratu militum et armorum fuit, multaque tum ductu eius <manu>que patrata primo per ignobilitatem, deinde per invidiam scriptorum incelebrata sunt: quae vivos facie sua ostentabat aliquot advorsis cicatricibus et effosso oculo. Quin ille dehonestamento corporis maxime laetabatur neque illis anxius, quia relicua gloriosius retinebat.

> As a tribune in Spain, under the command of T. Didius, he was of great glory, and of great use in the Marsic war in providing troops and weapons, and many of the accomplishments under his leadership and of his own doing were uncelebrated at first because of his own low status, then on account of the envy of writers; but he showed forth these deeds while alive in his own countenance with several front-facing scars and an eye knocked out. But he rejoiced especially in the disfigurement of his body, nor was he concerned about these things, because he had kept what was left even more gloriously.[31]

Sertorius too has lost an eye—and Sallust uses precisely the same expression here as well, *effossus oculus*. But this mutilation, together with a matching set of front-facing scars attests to his brave deeds in battle. If the depiction of Marius resembles the display of tortured bodies that in Livy indicts the cruelty of the Tarquins (1. 59, and cf. 2. 23 for the account of the body of a former soldier exposed to servile punishments as a result of debt), Sertorius belongs to the contrasting group of citizens

---

[30] For a full account of the evidence, see Marshall 1985.
[31] I use Reynolds' text of this much emended fragment.

who display their Roman *libertas* by exposing their bodies to punishment. This is, of course, the explicit claim of the equally asymmetrical Mucius Scaevola as he teaches the lesson of republican freedom by burning off his own hand to forestall being tortured by a king (Liv. 2. 12). Thus, where Marius' body measures the destruction of citizens by the tyranny of conquerors in a civil war; Sertorius' wounds are the proof of the sorts of deeds that traditionally win glory.[32] In a Sallustian moral context he also demonstrates his subordination of the body to achieve the deeds by which one wins everlasting *gloria*.[33] And the historiographic importance of his wounds as proof receives explicit emphasis. His scarred body gives the lie to attempts to slight and obscure his accomplishments, first because he was not a *nobilis*, and then out of *invidia*. Sertorius' body too thus testifies in its own way to Rome's political fragmentation in the attempts made to conceal or subvert its significance out of contempt or rivalry. And to recall the programmatic function of *invidia* in the *Catiline* preface, as part of what makes history writing itself a difficult task akin to actions (*B.C.* 3. 2), may suggest a claim here on Sallust's part that his text continues to do what the face did when it was alive, *vivos*, refute the falsities of *invidia*.

By contrast to the mutilated countenances that frame the narrative of book one, and specifically the mangled face of his opponent Sertorius, early on in book two we see the blameless face, *os probum* of the young Pompey (*H.* 2. 16 M).[34] Not only does the contrast reinforce the

---

[32] Indeed Sertorius perhaps employs a witty irony in updating this exemplum: his glory emerges not from the sacrifice of the body manifested by its losses, but in his success in retaining the rest. If scars had become a commonplace for *novi* and *imagines* for the *nobiles*, Sertorius effectively measures himself against both by a kind of triangulation, not rejoicing in the scars per se like a Cato, as signs of defeat not victory, but ironically adopting a perspective that would view scars simply as aesthetically repellent disfigurements.

Gerrish 2012: 84–5 offers a very different interpretation of the sentence: On the basis of a parallel in Plutarch (*Sert.* 4. 2), she suggests that *relicua* refers not to the remaining parts of his body, but to the scars themselves (presumably) as remnants of his deeds. Her overall interpretation of Sallust's Sertorius is markedly ambivalent, as someone whose own self-glorification was already symptomatic of the conditions of representing events in the Civil War era.

[33] Gerrish 2012: 81–3 points out that the context for the quotation of this fragment (Gell. *NA* 2. 27) was a comparison undertaken by the rhetorician T. Castricius, between Sallust's words and Demosthenes' description of Philip of Macedon (*De cor.* 67). There Castricius finds Sertorius' active rejoicing in his disfigurement 'beyond the boundaries of human nature' in contrast to Philip's mere willingness to sacrifice any part of his body for glory. However, the target of this contrast is not so much the emotions of the protagonists as the rhetorical verisimilitude of their portraits.

[34] *Oris probi, animo inverecundo*, 'of an honest face but shameless mind'. The phrase seems to have been much imitated, as will be discussed below. Though there is no indication of book number, Maurenbrecher makes it part of a background sketch of Pompey, which he

difference between winners and losers of civil wars; it also seems to symbolize a retreat from the persecutions that caused Marius' death. The adjective *probus* could convey a notion of self-restraint (cf. Festus 229, who derives it from the verb *prohibere*) strongly contrasting with the excesses of civil war, and Sallust seems to activate that aspect of its meaning by opposing it to the term *inverecundo*. If Marius' face gave evidence of the unstoppable rage of his opponents, Pompey's countenance was honourable because it revealed his modesty and respect. This was a well-known feature of Pompey, and it has been suggested that Sallust has taken the phrase itself from Varro's laudatory portrait of him.[35] But he then goes on to create a new kind of division, between inside and outside. Not only does Sallust's rebuttal of Varro—especially if it was recognized as an allusion—draw even this face under the divisive gaze of discord (and we remember that Pompey's *libertus* Lenaeus responded to his attacks on Pompey by 'lacerating' Sallust in turn, *laceravit*, Suet. *Gram.* 15), but the very deceptiveness of Pompey's appearance possesses its own historiographic significance. In the *Catiline* Sallust describes how ambition, which Sallust here calls the dominant force in Pompey's character (*modestus ad alia omnia, nisi ad dominationem*, 'moderate in all other respects, except for domination', *H.* 2. 17 M, assumed to be part of the same description) looks most like *virtus* and also compels the construction of a dishonest appearance: 'to have one thing hidden in the heart another ready on the tongue' (*B.C.* 10. 5).[36] This face too then becomes a sign of the times, and like all the other faces we have seen so far, a sign of how the forces of history conspire to falsify or rewrite the record of the past.

But as we track the historical dimension of Pompey's own visage, we meet a set of changes that further complicate its potential semantic role and recall other uses of the face as a measure of Romanness. Later in the narrative, this fair face appears not as a sign of respect for the *populus Romanus*, but a point of likeness to an un-Roman king (*H.* 3. 88 M):

> Sed Pompeius a prima adulescentia sermone fautorum similem fore se credens Alexandro regi, facta consultaque eius quidem aemulus erat.

---

locates at the beginning of his expedition against Sertorius, just after the account of Lepidus' defeat in Sardinia, at the start of book two. See, however, the discussion by La Penna 1968: 276 (= Chapter 14, p. 353 of this volume).

[35] Syme 1964: 206, citing Münzer 1897: 283–4; see the discussion below. Cf. also the contrasting phrase *ab ore improbo*, used by Cicero in his 56 BCE attack on Vatinius (*Vat.* 39) adduced and discussed by Gerrish 2012: 220–1.

[36] A point also made and more thoroughly discussed by Gerrish 2012: 220–1.

Pompey believing from his first youth on account of the speech of flatterers that he would be like King Alexander, emulated him in his deeds and acts.[37]

Plutarch (*Pomp.* 2. 1) stresses that the likeness had a physical component, and Pompey's well-known affectation of the brushed-back Alexandrian hairstyle in his portraiture again suggests that this was part of a carefully cultivated public image. Moreover, Sallust's language of emulation, and the almost programmatic doublet *facta consultaque* (cf. *B.C.* 1. 6–7) sets Pompey's adoption of Alexander as a model in a strongly historiographic context, against the traditional aristocratic use of *imagines* as patterns for future achievements. And the reference to the language of flatterers suggests opposing the false beautification of Pompey to the equally false defacement or concealment of Sertorius' scars through *invidia*.

But if the Alexandrification of Pompey shows how republican ambition metamorphoses into foreign tyranny, we should consider the possibility for Sallust's audience to supplement the text by superimposing a still later version of this visage, as a head severed by a Roman soldier at the command of a foreign king. Such 'before and after' transpositions of Pompey's image have a long afterlife in Latin literature. Thus, when Pliny describes Pompey's triumph over Mithridates, he notes that the general displayed an *imago* of himself made out of pearls.[38] Not only does this

---

[37] Full discussion of the arguments for locating the fragment in book three in Gerrish 2012: 184–5.

[38]
>erat et imago Cn. Pompei e margaritis, illa relicino honore grata, illius probi oris venerandique per cunctas gentes, illa, inquam, ex margaritis, illa, severitate victa et veriore luxuriae triumpho! numquam profecto inter illos viros durasset cognomen Magni, si prima victoria sic triumphasset! e margaritis, Magne, tam prodiga re et feminis reperta, quas gerere te fas non sit, fieri tuos voltus? sic te pretiosum videri? non ergo illa tua similior est imago quam Pyrenaei iugis inposuisti? grave profecto, foedum probrum erat, ni verius saevum irae deorum ostentum id credi oporteret clareque intellegi posset iam tum illud caput orientis opibus sine reliquo corpore ostentatum.
>
>(Plin. *HN* 37. 14–16)
>
>There was even a likeness of Pompey out of pearls, that likeness made pleasing by the distinction of the brushed-back hairstyle, a likeness of that face 'blameless' and venerable throughout all nations, that image, I repeat out of pearls!, in a triumph that was more truly of luxury itself over the defeat of austerity. Never would that name 'Magnus' have endured among the real men of that time if he had held such a triumph after his first victory. Should your face be made of pearls, Pompey? A substance so wasteful and discovered for women, which it is lawful for them—not you—to wear! Did you seem valuable so? Was not that trophy you set on the crest of the Pyrenees a truer image? That likeness would have been a weighty and foul dishonour, were it not necessary to deem it more truly an awful omen of divine anger, and were it not able to be clearly understood even then, that head shown forth in Eastern finery—without a body!

aptly convey the decadent transformation of Roman aristocratic tradition (note the word *imago*) into a sign of regal Eastern luxury, but Pliny goes on to read the head deprived of its body as a harbinger of Pompey's ultimate fate. The precise description Pliny gives of Pompey's face—*oris probi et venerandi per cunctas gentes*—not only begins just like Sallust's famous description, with an allusion to the possibly Varronian *os probi*, but his second adjective *venerandus* seems to reverse, or be reversed by, Sallust's calling Pompey's *animus inverecundus*. In place of inspiring respect in others, his mind feels no respect itself.[39] Whatever the specific intertextual lineage of the phrase, it is clear that these different verbal elements, and with them the relationship between beauty and reverence inspired by or reflected in Pompey's appearance, could be reiterated and revised as the face itself was transformed through time from an image of commanding Roman probity to one of regal extravagance, until he finally received retribution on the shores of Egypt.[40] There is a textual tradition, therefore, that evolves in parallel to the changes in the face itself. The final aspect of Pompey's face brings his story full circle by showing the boy conqueror emulating Alexander killed at the behest of another Alexandrian boy king, and imposes a similar circularity on the pattern of faces I have described in Sallust's work by linking the young champion of the restored Republic with Marius Gratidianus as a conspicuously mutilated victim of civil war.

---

[39] Either Varro may have had *venerandus*, or something equivalent, which Sallust is already answering, or maybe it is Sallust's phrase that Pliny is adapting in turn.

[40] Lucan will later activate just such a reading by recalling both Pompey's beautiful face and the Sallustian inversion of it at the moment of his murder: early in the account he asserts the unchangeability of Pompey's face in the face of death (*permansisse decus sacrae venerabile formae / iratamque deis faciem*, 'the venerable beauty of his sacred appearance endured, and the face scornful of the gods', 8. 664–5). This emphasis on the persistence of Pompey's beauty makes his countenance again a mirror of the soul, as it was not in Sallust, and in doing so rebuts the kind of reading we find in Pliny, where an apparent consistency of Pompey's image gave the measure of the enormous reversals in his fortune. On the other hand, however, Lucan may be alluding precisely to the intertextual tradition that rang so many changes on the descriptions of that face. For if *venerandus* was part of a pre-Sallustian verbal portrait, then Lucan moves closer to the Sallustian riposte of *inverecundo animo* at the moment when, with the head now severed from his body, the *generosa frons* now seems overshadowed by hair that inevitably looks more Caesarian than Alexandrian (*illa verenda / regibus hirta coma et generosa fronte decora / caesaries conprensa manu est*, 'that shaggy hair terrible to kings and the lock that beautified his well-born brow was gathered in the hand', 8. 679–81). The face may indeed be unchanging; yet the language that describes it has suffered the vicissitudes of defeat, and perhaps a trace of those vicissitudes comes in the move from '*veneranda*' to '*verenda*', which is a step closer to the Sallustian tag, *inverecundo*.

III

If these faces show individual human features deformed and misrepresented as indices of Roman historical—and historiographic—processes, another much-observed aspect of the *Histories* accomplishes something similar with features of nature on a much larger scale. Ethnographic and geographical descriptions appear quite frequently among the surviving fragments of the work.[41] While this may in part be the result of the particular interest of such information for later writers who cite or refer to Sallust, the density of attested ethnographic passages is, nevertheless, impressively high.[42] Book two began with a depiction of Sardinia (*H.* 2. 1–12 M), and also contained a much less well-attested account of the Taurus region of Asia Minor (*H.* 2. 82–6 M); book three featured the famous account of the Black Sea (*H.* 3. 61–80 M) as well as a treatment of Crete (*H.* 3. 10–15 M), while the last phase of Spartacus' rebellion in the next book highlighted the Strait of Messina (*H.* 4. 23–9 M.). To this list I would add a place that played a significant role early in the story and certainly received important mention, even if we cannot tell on what scale, the Islands of the Blessed, where Sertorius planned to sail (*H.* 1. 100–103 M).

The first point to be made about these excursus is how they too invite arrangement in patterns based on comparison and contrast, reinforcing some of the oppositions we have already encountered. Thus, two of the places featured prominently in the work lie at opposite ends of the earth, the Islands of the Blessed in the far south-west and the Black Sea in the far north-east. Crossings to islands provide another unifying category; as Sertorius hopes to sail west at the end of book one, Lepidus traces the same journey in miniature in his flight to Sardinia in book two.[43] Similar figures and themes also unite several of these passages. King Minos links Crete (*H.* 3. 15 M) to Sardinia (*H.* 2. 7 M), where he later pursues Daedalus. The Islands of the Blessed bear food unstintingly (*H.* 1. 100 M), and so, probably, does Sardinia (*H.* 2. 83 M);[44] perhaps the cultivated fertility of Crete (*H.* 3. 12 M) too provides comparison and contrast to

---

[41] On these digressions generally, see Oniga 1995: 95–115, and for a comprehensive investigation of their sources and general intellectual background, Keyser 1991. Cf. also La Penna 1968: 303–305 (= Chapter 14, pp. 362–4 in this volume).

[42] Indeed, as Oniga 1995: 95 notes, the inclusion of such descriptions was one of the distinguishing features of Sallust's writing that led Granius Licinianus, the second-century epitomator, to describe him as 'to be read not as an historian but an orator' (36. 31).

[43] Kathryn Welch (viva voce) suggests here a reflection of the escape route for opponents of Octavian across the Strait of Messina to Sextus Pompey in Sicily, and this is an important theme of Welch 2012. See esp. pp. 216–17 and 232–3.

[44] La Penna 1971 argues for reassigning this fragment to the Sardinian excursus.

this Golden Age paradise,[45] and so may the well-known abundance of fish in the Black Sea (*H.* 3. 66 M). Crete (*H.* 3. 10 M) and the Isles of the Blessed (*H.* 1. 100 M) are both far from the mainland and washed by various seas; the nearly landlocked Black Sea (*H.* 3. 62 M) is defined by the lands that surround it (*H.* 3. 70 M), and Sicily, separated by a narrow strait from the mainland (*H.* 4. 26 M), provides a geographical antithesis to both.[46] While I doubt that all of these possible points of likeness and opposition were equally developed, and some may simply be the products of ethnographic formulae and topoi, they are sufficient to establish that the geographical elements of the work can be read together as part of a larger structure of meaning and to invite investigation of how the geography itself becomes symbolic.

Nor is the functional parallel I have suggested between human features and geographical units wholly arbitrary. Places seem to take human form. The description of Sardinia notes its resemblance to a human foot (*H.* 2. 2 M), while the Black Sea looks like the drawn bow of those Scythians who in fact dwell there (*H.* 3. 63 M). And giants and monsters have become part of the landscape at least in Crete (*H.* 2. 13 M) and Sicily (*H.* 4. 27–8 M). This animation of space in itself adds traces of the uncanny and mythical that collectively put its description beyond the generic bounds of history. As both La Penna (1968: 303, = Chapter 14, p. 362 in this volume) and Tiffou (1973: 532) have suggested, the digressions manifest an abundance of supernatural and mythical events quite at odds with the general tendencies of Sallust's historical narrative. The Islands of the Blessed, of course, were described by Homer, and even though Sicily had been a Roman province for almost two hundred years before Spartacus, it is again the Homeric Sicily that dominates the description, at least what we have of it. And one interesting detail here accentuates that point. It would be easy to imagine rationalizing accounts of Scylla,[47] where the crashing waves misidentified as dogs gave rise to

---

[45] Though this passage's reference to Crete must be considered highly speculative. See McGushin 1992–4: vol. 2, 123, who cites Solinus 11. 4 for a highly idealized account of Crete.

[46] The role of Cilician pirates in preventing the crossings of both Sertorius to the Isles of the Blessed and Spartacus to Sicily may have been another linking feature. The pirates' balking at Sertorius' plans appears at Plut. *Sert.* 9. 1, though there is no evidence that Sallust mentioned them or presented a similar narrative of the attempt. Indeed, La Penna and Funari 2015: 322 tentatively suggest a possible discrepancy between an image of Odyssean heroism in Sallust's account and the desire for rest and escape stressed by Plutarch. Plut. *Crass.* 10. 6–7 describes the pirates' betrayal of Spartacus.

[47] On the ideological function of Scylla in the passage, see now Gerrish 2016, who stresses the contemporary resonances of the figure in the triumviral period as a symbol both of civil war generally and of the triumvirs' rival, Sextus Pompey.

the legend. But what Sallust seems to say is in fact almost the opposite[48] (*H.* 4. 27 M):

> Scyllam accolae saxum mari imminens appellant simile celebratae formae procul visentibus. Et monstruosam speciem fabulae illi dederunt, quasi formam hominis caninis succinctam capitibus, quia collisi ibi fluctus latratus videntur exprimere.
>
> The inhabitants named the rock jutting out over the sea Scylla, like the famous form to those who see it from far off. And they attribute the monstrous appearance of (the) fable to it, as it were the shape of a human surrounded by dog's heads, because the waves crashing there seem to make the sound of barking

What Sallust is explaining is not the origin of the myth, but why the myth was located there by the inhabitants. The Homeric myth seems to take precedence over the landscape feature, rather than vice versa. The effect is, therefore, not a demythologizing explanation of where Scylla comes from, but rather the importation of the legend into the real landscape of Sicily.[49] I make this point because one familiar way of interpreting landscape description in Roman historiography is as a trope of conquest. Knowing and mapping follow from mastery over the space itself.[50] Here, by contrast, the landscapes remain fundamentally alien; they resist incorporation into history, which is to say Roman history, like the swamps qualifying Sallust's claim that Roman arms have conquered all of Gaul (*H.* 1. 11 M). In generic terms as well they become poetic loci for mythical exploits and monstrous creatures of disorder. Some places, like the Islands of the Blessed and the far reaches of the Black Sea, remain outside the bounds of the empire, while others, like Sicily and Sardinia, show some of her earliest conquests as radically strange and perhaps dangerous. And, of course, as the site of rebellions led by Lepidus and Spartacus, they had become so again. The period of Roman domination seems bounded by the ring that links the giants to the rebels, just as it is relativized by the reminder of many previous expeditions that had passed through these crossroads of the Mediterranean.

---

[48] It is important to note, however, that we cannot be sure the source of the fragment (Isidore, *Etym.* 13. 18. 4) gives us Sallust's exact words. The basis for the attribution is the close parallel in Serv. *Aen.* 3. 420, which does explicitly cite Sallust and resembles the first sentence of Isidore quite closely. However the second sentence in Servius rather suggests that the natural features of the region explain the myth. For a full discussion of the evidence, see Keyser 1991: 415–19.

[49] Though La Penna 1968: 304 (= Chapter 14, p. 363 in this volume) goes on to note that the description of Charybdis by contrast 'gives the appearance of science'.

[50] See especially the ground-breaking articles of O'Gorman 1993 and Clark 2001.

As a final example of the self-reflexive function of these digressions, I want to turn to the account of the Strait of Messina, a passage that at once figures the overarching theme of discord,[51] continues the pattern of varied repetition, and, like the Islands of the Blessed, identifies a mythical landscape with a place of refuge just across a border which will never be passed. The band of fugitive slaves commanded by Spartacus presents in microcosm Sallust's nightmare vision of Roman politics. The truly slavish troops' desires for gratification and revenge continually frustrate any coherent strategy on the part of the rulers.[52] As a result they wander from one end of Italy to the other, destroying the landscape and disrupting patterns of civilized life instead of breaking outside to the larger spaces of the world beyond. They are at once a foil to the Roman armies we have seen crossing mountains into Spain and straits into Pontus, and an ideal metaphor for civil discord itself. Spartacus' ineffective command more directly contrasts with Crassus' use of the historic practice of decimation to punish Rome's defeated troops (*H.* 4. 22 M). But again what seems like the resuscitation of an ancient and distinctively Roman practice to restore the famous Roman discipline, against the background of the slave revolt might also look like a further brutalization of citizen bodies, treated just as one treats slaves.

If bodies are used to mark the difference between Romans and others but cannot also fail to suggest similarities as well,[53] the landscape from which Spartacus' troops make their effort to escape provides an ideal geographical expression of the same motifs. Sallust's account strongly emphasizes divisions:[54] 'All of Italy, forced into the narrows is split into two promontories.'[55] This account of the shape of Southern Italy seems to give a temporal or historical dimension to the extension of space—Italy has been forced into 'straits', *angustias*. As we turn our attention to Bruttium, we meet another division, now directly wrought by time: 'It is pretty certain (*constat*) that Sicily was joined to Italy, but the region in

---

[51] Compare Wiedemann's discussion of how the digressions in the *Jugurtha* both punctuate significant phases in the narrative and reinforce that work's own thematic preoccupation with discord (Wiedemann 1993 = Chapter 11 of this volume).

[52] Esp. *H.* 3. 96D and 3. 98B M. For the general interpretation of the disagreements among Spartacus' band as a mirror of Roman discord, see the analysis of Gerrish 2012: 140–51.

[53] And we might remember that, according to other sources, the end of the revolt saw six thousand slaves publicly tortured in the most slavish way, by crucifixion along the Via Appia from Rome to Capua (App. *B Civ.* 1. 120). Plutarch however omits this conclusion; thus, it was not an inevitable part of the narrative and may not have been in Sallust.

[54] So too Keyser 1991: 413: 'The strait as schism or rent functions not just as a topographical feature but as an ideological one.' See also Gerrish 2016: 202–3.

[55] *Omnis Italia coacta in angustias finditur in duo promunturia, Bruttium et Sallentinum*, *H.* 4. 23 M.

between was either covered over by reason of its low position or cut through by reason of its narrowness (*angustiam*).[56] As Sallust turns geography into a historical problem, speculating on the causes of what has been established by consensus, so the explanations offered for this geographical division mirror contrasting explanations of Roman discord that are themselves the rhetorical causes and instigations of division, where one side might emphasize the oppression of the lowly (cf. *humilitatem*) and the other the recourse to civic violence. Even the divider is divided, so that the strait itself features two contrasting terrors, Scylla and Charybdis, one up high, like the promontories (or *nobiles*?), the other down lower than the sea. But, for all their differences, they both mean the same thing, destruction and absorption.

So too an additional feature of this divided landscape at once reminds readers that apparent distinctions can be illusory and hints at another narrative of the past that will turn out to have a strong link to the present. Despite the narrative company it keeps, as part of a geographical 'triumvirate' with Scylla and Charybdis, Mount Pelorus recalls not a mythical monster but a historical one, Hannibal. We know, again from Servius, that Sallust gave Hannibal's steersman as the source of the toponym, and Servius and Mela supply the story of his death.[57] As Hannibal was fleeing

---

[56] *Italiae Siciliam coniunctam constat fuisse, sed medium spatium aut per humilitatem obrutum est aut per angustiam scissum. Ut autem curvom sit, facit natura mollioris Italiae, in quam asperitas et altitudo Siciliae aestum relidit*, H. 4. 27 M.

[57]
> PELORI promunctorium Siciliae est secundum Sallustium, dictum a gubernatore Hannibalis illic sepulto, qui fuerat occisus per regis ignorantiam, cum se eius dolo propter angustias freti crederet esse deceptum, veniens de Petilia: quamquam legerimus, etiam ante Pelorum dictum. Serv. Aen. 3.411~ H. 4. 29 M.

> The promontory of Pelorus was, according to Sallust, named after the steersman of Hannibal who is buried there. He had been killed on account of the ignorance of the king, who, on account of the narrowness of the sea, thought he was deceived, since he was coming from Petilia (although we have read that it was called Pelorus even before).

The circumstances of Pelorus' killing are more fully explained by Mela (2. 116):

> causa nominis Pelorus gubernator ab Hannibale ibi conditus, quem idem vir profugus ex Africa, et per ea loca Syriam petens, quia procul intuenti videbantur continua esse litora et non pervium pelagus, proditum se arbitratus occiderat.

> The source of the name is Pelorus, the steersman buried there by Hannibal, whom he himself killed. When, after his exile from Africa, he was traversing these regions on his way to Syria, because, when seen from far off, the shores seem to connect and there to be no sea route between them, Hannibal thought he had been betrayed.

More or less the same story is told by Valerius Maximus (9. 8, ext. 1), who, however, agrees with Servius that Hannibal was travelling to, not from, Africa. While only the first clause of Servius is considered a Sallustian 'fragment', and is probably a paraphrase, it is at least possible that the historian gave the etymology as well. See Keyser 1991: 423–4.

into exile from Carthage to Asia, his ship passed along the north coast of Sicily. However, when approached from that direction, Italy and Sicily seem to meet, and the strait itself is blocked from view. Hannibal therefore became convinced that his steersman was tricking him and actually meant to bring him to land in Italy and hand him over to the Romans. While we cannot be certain to what extent, if at all, the story was told by Sallust, it would make a suggestive conclusion to the excursus. First of all, as in the account of the 'inhabitants' who recognized Scylla in the rocks of the Italian coast, the hermeneutic challenges of the landscape are revealed through the perceptions of an internal spectator who misreads it. This itself draws attention to the need to interpret topographic features, and Hannibal's tragic failure to do so (tragic for Pelorus at any rate) also diametrically reverses the exaggerated emphasis on division attested in the earlier fragments. This could, on the one hand, further stress the importance of that theme by presenting Hannibal's own failure to recognize the separation as a misreading. But it also shows an important contrast within the landscape itself: from one perspective it may seem all too easy to read the setting as a 'map' figuring civil discord, but the complementary perspective of Hannibal reveals the opposite shores as contiguous so that it is hard to make any distinction at all between the divided pair. To read the space in this way also means adopting the perspective of Rome's arch-enemy, the Punic Hannibal, who was not only himself a deceiver but someone who frequently deceived precisely through the manipulation of landscape. And the focalization of this new one-eyed man also approximates that of a particular character within the time frame that is the subject of Sallust's narrative, Spartacus himself, who also seeks a refuge (whether we imagine Hannibal escaping to Africa, as in Servius, or from it, as in Mela). Is his own misreading itself a ploy, encouraging Sallust's Roman readers to forget which side they are on, the difference between *domi militiaeque* imaged as the physical separation between Italy and Rome's first province? Or does Hannibal's confusion suggest a kind of symbolic retribution for his own ability to mislead a series of consular opponents? Thus, the same topography that may have encouraged the Romans to see their own internal struggles inscribed in a foreign land simultaneously interrogates the distinction between Roman and foreign.

Whether or not the deceptive invitation to share the gaze of Hannibal was made explicit in Sallust's text, it provides an excellent parable for illustrating the larger challenges representations of landscapes offered Sallust's readers. On the one hand, they become an intimate commentary on Rome's internal history that belies both the ideology and the semiotics of conquest: the places Rome conquers signify rather than mask her internal struggles and so refute an equation between the historiographic appropriation of space and its subjection to Rome's *imperium*.[58] But, at the same time, we should not forget that such passages themselves were perceived as offering their own kind of narrative of escape and release for the reader. The instinct to differentiate distant foreign spaces from the narrative precisely as realms of myth and wonder offering amusement, if not a sense of positive superiority, often provides one of the great enticements towards reading history. And one may speculate that the confusion between the foreign and the all too identifiable, by which the potential pleasures of history draw its audience more fully into its most terrible recognitions, created a central dynamic in reading the *Histories*, one that itself makes the experience of the audience mirror the dilemmas of the characters in the text, not only incidental exiles like Hannibal. Consider, for example, the composition of book one. In contrast to the three subsequent books, the role of geographical excursus seems much reduced. However, the narrative began with a different sort of excursus, a historical precis familiar to readers of the monographs, including the social wars and culminating in a description of the horrific proscriptions during which Marius Gratidianus was dismembered. In its content as well as its structure, this excursus may perhaps have foreshadowed some of the themes of the coming descriptions of foreign places,[59] and even become a kind of ethnographic digression, presenting the bizarre and bloodthirsty customs of a foreign society that was, nevertheless, not distant or mythical but readily attested in the memory of many in Sallust's audience, and indeed in their immediate experience of the proscriptions of the 40s.[60]

Near the very end of that book, Sertorius, one of the survivors of this Civil War, someone in fact who is still fighting it and whose actions make clear that it has never ended, looks outside the bounds of the world, and conceived a longing, as Plutarch presents it, 'to dwell in the islands and to live in quiet, free from tyranny and wars that would never end'.[61] If that desire for escape itself arose as the result of a narrative he hears, as was

---

[58] Kraus and Woodman 1997: 40: 'by telling the story of conquest, an epic or historical narrative reinforces the extension and legitimization of temporal power'.

[59] In contrast to the fertility of Sardinia, the Isles of the Blessed, and Crete, Italy itself was 'laid waste by plunder, exile, and slaughter' (*vasta... rapina, fuga, caedibus*, H. 1. 23 M.). And the motif of escape that provides the context for the first two of these descriptions, in addition to the account of the Strait of Messina, also appears in the account of Marius' desperate efforts to flee the Italian coast (*H.* 1. 24–5 M; *H.* 1. 144 M).

[60] Such a strategy, of course, has an important parallel in Tacitus' presentation of Nero's Rome as a landscape of paradox, as Woodman 1992 explains it.

[61] Ταῦθ' ὁ Σερτώριος ἀκούσας ἔρωτα θαυμαστὸν ἔσχεν οἰκῆσαι τὰς νήσους καὶ ζῆν ἐν ἡσυχίᾳ, τυραννίδος ἀπαλλαγεὶς καὶ πολέμων ἀπαύστων (Plut., *Sert.* 9. 1). Gerrish 2018 argues for another form of escape provided by this incident, specifically that the prospect of

the case in Plutarch (*Sert.* 8. 2), this may have created a further parallel between Sallust's own audience and Sertorius. Yet Sertorius, and Lepidus, and Spartacus will all discover, as Daedalus had in the past, that there was no escape from the labyrinth of civil war. So too for the reader, those mythical lands that lie just beyond the generic borders of Roman historiography ('made famous in the songs of Homer', *inclitas... Homeri carminibus*, H. 1. 101 M) will offer no refuge. And, conversely, attempts to see the world from a distance, through the universalizing and perhaps recognizably foreign discourses of myth and natural description, the 'Hannibalic' perspective by which Italy and Sicily seem conjoined, continually expose the realities of the Roman present in the symbolic and linguistic links between the excursus and their larger contexts.

* * *

This effect of the *Histories* on their readers, a disorienting oscillation between the discovery of difference and disjuncture where one expects unity and of identity where one expects difference, itself recalls the hermeneutic alternatives I set out in the introduction for the interpretation of fragments. This may simply prove Kraus and Woodman's point that the fragmentary state of the text in itself can encourage us to view the original as somehow already broken. Or it may be that my emphasis on discontinuities and inconcinnities itself results from a homogenizing comparison, since these are precisely the features of the monographs that come to the fore in much recent work. And many of the suggestions made here can be only too well supported by analogies with Sallust's other surviving works. Thus, the *Catiline* challenges readers to preserve distinctions between seeming opposites like *virtus* and *ambitio*,[62] while the *Jugurtha*, as David Levene (1992 = Chapter 10 of this volume) especially has shown, uses partial similarities between paired characters, Metellus and Marius, then Marius and Sulla, to create a set of graded connections between present and past.

But Sallust's project in the *Histories* has a rather different aspect. These shorter works may stress how different the Rome of the present has become. They may also raise questions about whether any account of the past can ever be an authoritative guide to political action given how easily, indeed inescapably, its representation can only be filtered through

---

Sertorius' voyage to the Islands of the Blessed opens the door to a counterfactual history of the fall of the Republic.

[62] See esp. Batstone 1988b, 1990 (= Chapter 6 in this volume), and 2010, and Gunderson 2000 (= Chapter 7 in this volume).

the ambitions of the present. But the *Histories* much more fully and comprehensively explore the content of Roman historiography's most traditional and ideologically charged form, the *annales*. Beyond revealing how key features of *annales*, the construction of the *populus Romanus* as a subject, the subordination of individual actors to the larger story, the rigorous differentiation of home and abroad, all conflict with the historical realities of the period described, the *Histories* challenge their normative power to depict even the idealized past. Sallust's work substitutes a claustrophobic cyclicality of tyranny and disorder that seems almost ahistorical in its inevitable recurrence despite the particularities of past events. And the *Histories* raise corresponding questions about how the historical processes that lead to Roman *imperium*, and the narratives that describe it, are to be mapped against accounts of the natural world, and the paradigms of myth.

These differences from the monographs in turn suggest another comparand, Tacitus. The imperial historian's obvious evocation of Sallustian language and diction have given Tacitean parallels particular weight in arguments for the ordering and interpretation of the fragments, particularly for establishing the sequence of thought in the preface. Those later *Histories*—the coincidence of titles is accidental— too begin with a gesture toward the annalistic form that stresses the tensions between this traditional way of mapping Roman time and the work's imperial content.[63] And Tacitus too opens his narrative just after a moment of rupture that seemingly promises a new beginning, the death of Nero. Yet, just as his audience can only see that new beginning through the playing out of another cycle of tyranny, that of Domitian, so Sallust's audience inevitably perceives the restoration after Sulla left the scene as the beginning of a new cycle of civil war.

These similarities may indeed have empirical value, if we imagine Tacitus consciously imitating or alluding to Sallust. Or it may be that the perception of them has itself shaped my expectations of Sallust. Again, any attempt at a comprehensive reading of fragments will inevitably reflect the reader's models even more strongly than would be the case with extant texts, which offer a denser matrix for interpretations. And Tacitus' own rewritings of the Roman past provide a special incentive to view earlier historiography from the deconstructive perspective of its ending in empire. Consider especially the sweeping claim at the opening of the *Annales*: 'from the beginning, kings possessed the city

---

[63] On the relationship between Tacitus' preface and Sallust's, see, e.g., Scanlon 1998: 199–222.

of Rome'. The model of the *res publica* mirrored by the annalistic form now seems no longer the telos and norm in Roman history, but a mere interlude between recurrences of monarchy.

But in concluding I would like to suggest another possible explanation for these Tacitean resemblances. The spatial boundaries that I have argued constrain a reading of the *Histories* by making the alien Rome of the Civil Wars so inescapable also have a temporal element. Jennifer Gerrish (2012) has demonstrated persuasively how many features of Sallust's narrative of the 70s BCE recall events, figures, and problems of the triumviral period. This inescapability of the present, or of the past, builds from the openness of the first sentence's *ac deinde*, which challenges the reader to imagine a point of closure between the death of Sulla and the present. And the de-historicizing emphasis on likenesses between the past and the present is in accord with the model of the Roman past set forth in the preface, which replaces a never-ending trajectory of external success with one of recurrent episodes of internal violence that challenge any attempt at periodization. But these images of circularity have force beyond Sallust's contemporary audience. If Sallust, like Tacitus, rewrites the Roman past, and all earlier narratives of that past, he also predicts its future. Thus, it may not be the case simply that Sallust was a powerful model for Tacitus, teaching him how to make the forms of Roman historiography ironically expressive of new realities, nor that Tacitus effectively presents the times he recounts as a transformative new ending point for all Roman history. Rather, Sallust's view of the generative power of discord provides such a compelling way of interpreting events, in part because it explains the origins of all other dissenting historical voices, that he has already written all future histories of Rome.[64]

---

[64] On Sallust's approach to language as a 'prequel' to Lucan's verbal deconstruction of the Republic, see Batstone 2010b.

16

Princeps Historiae Romanae

Sallust in Renaissance Political Thought

Patricia J. Osmond

In the dedicatory letter of 1599 presenting his annotated edition of Sallust's *Opera* to the Senate of Nuremberg, the German philologist Christoph Coler boldly challenged the hierarchy of Roman historians recently, and authoritatively, established by the Flemish scholar Justus Lipsius.[1] It was not that Coler disliked Tacitus, whom Lipsius had been zealously editing and popularizing since the 1570s and whom he had ranked above all other ancient authors in his *Politicorum sive Civilis doctrinae libri sex* of 1589.[2] Whereas Lipsius had placed Tacitus first and Sallust second, however, Coler reversed the order. The reason, he declared, was Sallust's greater relevance to all forms of states and constitutions. 'It appears to me', he wrote, 'that Sallust teaches everyone, Tacitus only a few and learned persons; that Tacitus is useful especially to a principate, but Sallust to all forms of a commonwealth.'[3]

---

[1] Colerus 1599a: 'Ad Nobilissimum et Amplissimum Senatum Noribergensem Christophori Coleri Praefatio'. On Sallust's historical and political views in the context of his own times, see in particular the works of Earl 1961, La Penna 1969, and Syme 1964, as well as Musti 1989 and L. Canfora 1990. [See now also 'Bibliography', pts II–III, in Osmond and Ulery 2003: 217–18 and Osmond and Ulery 2014: 376, as well as the contributions and Bibliography in this volume.]

[2] For a bibliography of recent studies on Tacitus in the Renaissance, see n. 6 below.

[3] *Vereor dicere apud vos, Viri Prudentissimi, quantos Politicorum et ad quamcumque etiam rem publicam necessariorum praeceptorum thesauros in hoc auctore aperuerim, protulerim, explanaverim, ne scilicet meipsum laudem.... Ac licet neque aetate magna neque doctrina sim, conabor tamen brevi reapse planum facere, non esse solum inter veteres Tacitum, a quo Galli* πολιτεύεσθαι *hodie et Itali discant. Est certe magnus et serius scriptor Cornelius Tacitus.... De quo etiam scio quid Lipsius iudicet, nec repugno. Ego etiam aliquando utrumque diligenter inspexi et audebam alterum cum altero contendere. Videtur mihi Sallustius omnes docere, Tacitus paucos et doctos. Hic ad Principatum maxime, ille ad omnes Reipublicae formas utilis esse. Ille monere, hic cavere. Ille sapere ut docearis, hic docere*

Coler himself was an accommodating teacher, ready to apply the principle *cuius regio eius religio* to his own search for a university post in Germany; for this reason, he may have been particularly attuned to the different implications or emphases in an author's writing. Provoking a debate with the renowned Lipsius could also win instant attention. Whatever the motives, however, that prompted his interest in Sallust— and no other scholar was more enthusiastic in studying and propagating his *opera*—Coler seems to have touched upon the very aspect of Sallust's work that explains, I believe, his vast and continuing popularity throughout the early modern period: its adaptability to a changing climate of opinion.[4] In the early phases of the Renaissance, Sallust's two monographs, the *Bellum Catilinae* and *Bellum Iugurthinum*, along with the larger fragments of his *Historiae*, helped strengthen the cause of political liberty and civic humanism in the Italian city states and promote a participatory ideal of government in northern European countries. By the later sixteenth century, these works and the two *Epistulae ad Caesarem* (attributed to Sallust) were being reinterpreted in a different light—as support for authoritarian, princely government and public prudence.

Sallust's contribution to both traditions—the republican and absolutist, the civic humanist and the prudential—has been generally underestimated as attention has focused in recent scholarship on other ancient historians, notably Livy and Tacitus.[5] Both of these authors certainly influenced the development of political thought and historiography: Livy, primarily in the early, humanist stages of Renaissance intellectual life, Tacitus particularly in its later phases. As Peter Burke observed, the 'shift from virtue to prudence, from eloquence to truth' was illustrated by the decline of Livy and the rise of Tacitus.[6] For J. H. Whitfield, the change

---

ut sapias. Quid multa? Dignus Sallustio magistro Tacitus; dignior Tacito discipulo Sallustius. Ita enim ubique imitatur Sallustium ille ut eum discipulum Sallustianum merito apellem (Colerus 1599a: 'Praefatio', emphasis added). Cf. the remarks of Schindler 1939: 26–7.

[4] In 1599 Coler also published his 'Notae Politicae' on the *Epistulae ad Caesarem* (Colerus 1599b). Two of his treatises, including discussions of Sallust, are his *Sallustius sive de historia veteri oratio* (Colerus 1598) and *De studio politico ordinando epistola* (Colerus 1602). A brief biography and bibliography for Coler may be found in Ulery 1986: 136. During most of the Renaissance the *Epistulae ad Caesarem de re publica*, as well as the *Oratio* or *Invectiva in M. T. Ciceronem*, were accepted as the work of Sallust, and it was not until the latter part of the sixteenth century that scholars began seriously debating their authorship.

[5] For earlier studies on Sallust's *fortuna*, see the bibliographies in Osmond 1993 and 1994. Aside from the general surveys of Bolaffi 1949 and Schindler 1939, the most important contributions (for the period of the Renaissance) are La Penna 1969: 409–31 and McCuaig 1982: 75–98.

[6] Burke 1966: 151. Other useful studies of classical models with attention to Tacitus include Burke 1969; Whitfield 1976; La Penna 1976; Salmon 1980; and Schellhase 1976. See also Ulery 1986 for the commentaries on Tacitus; Mellor 1993; and the papers in Luce and Woodman 1993. Polybius' Renaissance *fortuna* is charted in Momigliano 1974.

in classical models of sixteenth-century Italy was succinctly represented in the title of his article 'Livy > Tacitus'. In his analysis of rhetorical and philosophical trends in sixteenth-century France, J. H. M. Salmon associated Livy and Cicero with the participatory ethic of the early decades, while linking Tacitus and Seneca to the development of political pragmatism during the Wars of Religion.

Whereas the popularity of Livy and especially of Tacitus tended to rise or fall, however, in line with these trends, that of Sallust remained comparatively steady: an indication that his work continued to exert an important influence not only in the humanist curriculum—where it provided a model of Latin prose, a source of historical and antiquarian information, and a treasure of general philosophical wisdom—but also in the field of political thought.[7] How widely he was read is evident from library inventories and publication statistics. In the fifteenth century more manuscripts of Sallust were copied and annotated than of any other classical historian.[8] From the advent of printing to the early seventeenth century, he headed the bestseller list of Roman historians. Moreover, while the Latin editions and commentaries were destined primarily for humanist teachers, students, and scholars, the translation of his *opera* into the major European vernaculars reveals his appeal to a more heterogeneous audience.

1. THE CIVIC HUMANIST TRADITION IN ITALY

The Late Medieval Background

Sallust's role in the formation of civic humanist ideology can be traced back to the later thirteenth and early fourteenth centuries.[9] The prologues and

---

[7] On Sallust in the medieval curriculum, see Smalley 1971 and Stein 1977. [On Sallust among the *auctores maiores* in the late medieval and Renaissance school curriculum in Italy, see now also the recent studies by Robert Black, including Black 2007. For further bibliography and discussion of Sallust's *fortuna* in these periods see Osmond and Ulery 2003 and 2014.]

[8] See Reynolds 1983: xxvii, citing 330 new manuscripts of Sallust in the fifteenth century alone. [See now also Osmond and Ulery 2003. For an analysis of the printed editions (texts, commentaries, translations) for the period c.1470–1650, see the Appendix to the original article (Osmond 1995) and Addendum II below.]

[9] The following sections develop themes in Osmond 1993: 410–20 and Skinner 1990. See also Skinner 1978, vol. 1, chs. 1–3, and (for traces of Sallustian influence in the art of the period) Skinner 1986. [Revised versions of many of his essays are collected now in Skinner 2002; see esp. vol. 2, *Renaissance Virtues*.] Other discussions of classical political thought in

digressions of his two monographs, as well as passages in his other works, celebrated the communal spirit and patriotism of the ancient Romans (while deploring the later decline of civic harmony). The introductory chapters of the *Bellum Catilinae* summarizing the early history of Rome supplied, in particular, a concept of republican liberty that influenced writers of both the 'rhetorical' and 'scholastic' traditions.[10] The most significant passage came from chapter 7, in which Sallust described the remarkable growth of the Roman city state after the last Tarquin had been banished and kings were replaced by two annually elected consuls:

> Sed ea tempestate coepere se quisque magis extollere magisque ingenium in promptu habere. Nam regibus boni quam mali suspectiores sunt semperque iis aliena virtus formidulosa est. Sed civitas incredibile memoratu est adepta libertate quantum brevi creverit: tanta cupido gloriae incesserat.
>
> (*B.C.* 7. 1–3)
>
> Now at that time every man began to lift his head higher and to have his talents more in readiness. For kings hold the good in greater suspicion than the wicked, and to them the merit of others is always fraught with danger; but the free state, once liberty was won, waxed incredibly strong and great in a remarkably short time, such was the thirst for glory that had filled men's minds.[11]

As early as the thirteenth century, authors of treatises on rhetoric and civic government drew upon this passage and other introductory chapters of the *Catilina* to explain the growth of their communes and describe the connection between elective government, pursuit of justice and the common good, and recent political achievements.[12] Sallust's ideas could also be combined with Aristotelian moral and political philosophy and with the growing cult of Cicero as the model citizen orator. Brunetto

---

this period include the articles of Charles T. Davis reprinted in Davis 1984; the work of Hans Baron, including 1938, 1968, and 1966; and Viroli 1992.

[10] On classical and Renaissance concepts of the city republic, see the articles cited in n. 9 above. [Although Sallust uses the term *res publica* to refer to the state or public affairs in general, even under the kings, it is the *civitas libera* governed by two annually elected magistrates that safeguards the rule of law and promotes the exceptional growth of the state (*B.C.* 6. 7–7. 7). On the emergence of the term *respublica* in the fifteenth century to refer to popular or oligarchic governments, in opposition to monarchy, see Hankins 2010.]

[11] Quotations from Sallust are taken from Reynolds's 1991 edition for the Oxford Classical Texts. Here, as in other Latin passages, the consonants 'u' and 'v' have been standardized and punctuation modernized. English versions are taken (with occasional small changes) from Rolfe's 1921 translation for the Loeb Classical Library.

[12] Cf. Skinner 1990: 123 on the use of Sallust's *Catilina* (and, to a lesser extent, the *Jugurtha*) as authorities for the newly developing civic ideology, and particularly the views on *grandezza*, civic concord and justice, and free government, as opposed to monarchy.

Brunetto Latini illustrated the four cardinal virtues of the *Nichomachean Ethics* with Sallustian *sententiae* in his *Livres dou tresor*, written during his exile in France in the early 1260s. In the French tradition of the *Faits des Romains*—also widely known in the Italian *Fatti di Cesare* (see Figure 16.1)—he used material from the *Catilina*, including the speeches of Caesar and Cato from chapters 51 and 52, to extol the consul's defence of the *res publica* in 63 BCE, the year of Catiline's conspiracy.[13] Thomas Aquinas introduced Sallustian ideas in his discussion of good and bad governments in *De regno ad regem Cypri* (1267). Repeating the words of

Figure 16.1. Catiline (left) and Q. Curius (right) (cf. *B.C.* 22. 1-2; 23. 1-2). Miniature from an early fourteenth-century Bolognese copy of *I fatti di Cesare* illustrated by the Maestro di Gherarduccio.

Florence, Biblioteca Riccardiana, MS 1538, fol. 3r (by permission of the Ministero dei Beni e delle Attività Culturali e del Turismo).

[13] Latini 1948; for the speeches of Caesar and Cato (*B.C.* 51-2), see 3: 34-8 (pp. 344-52). Italian versions (perhaps made by Latini himself) of these and other speeches and letters excerpted from Sallust's monographs appear in many later compendia. On Latini's political thought, see Davis 1967. An early fourteenth-century Bolognese manuscript of the *Fatti di Cesare* (Florence, Biblioteca Riccardiana, MS 1538), bound with Bartolomeo's translation of the *Jugurtha* and illustrated by the Maestro di Gherarduccio, depicts episodes in the conspiracy. The figure of Catiline and the story of his conspiracy were also well known (in various and often fanciful versions) in the foundation legends of Tuscan cities. [See now Addendum I: Catiline and Catilinarianism.]

Catilina 7. 2, though substituting *tyrannis* ('tyrants') for *regibus* ('kings'), he observed: *tyrannis enim magis boni quam mali suspecti sunt, semperque his aliena virtus formidolosa est*. In the following chapter, quoting *Catilina* 7. 3, he named the author himself: *et, sicut refert Salustius, 'incredibile est memoratu quantum adepta libertate in brevi Romana civitas creverit'*.[14] Although personally in favour of kingship, Aquinas appreciated the importance of liberty as a source of spiritual progress and the relevance of Sallust's words not only to conventional distinctions between kingship and tyranny but above all to a positive reappraisal of human society and political institutions.

In the early years of the fourteenth century, Sallust's monographs seem to have been especially popular among the Dominicans of S. Maria Novella, whose library housed not only works on scholastic philosophy but also a number of Latin classics.[15] Tolomeo da Lucca, in his continuation of Aquinas' work on kingship, appealed to the communal values of the ancient city state, paraphrasing Cato's words in *Catilina* 52. 19–21. The qualities that had made Rome great, he declared, were 'efficiency at home, a just rule abroad, and in counsel an independent spirit, free from guilt or passion'.[16] Bartolomeo da San Concordio, a Dominican friar and Aristotelian scholar who resided at the convent and taught at the school (1294–1304), produced the first complete Italian version of the two monographs.[17] The translation had been commissioned by Nero Cambi, a merchant banker and the leader of the Black faction, at a time of intense struggle with the rival Whites, and perhaps with a view to enlisting Sallust's authority in the service of his party. Certain Sallustian themes—the pursuit of *virtù* and *gloria*, the importance of the *bene comune*, and the denunciations of aristocratic arrogance—would undoubtedly bolster the cause of the Blacks and, after 1301, celebrate their victory. Whatever the circumstances surrounding its composition, it enjoyed an enormous success. For some two centuries, until the publication in 1518 of the first printed translation of the monographs

---

[14] Aquinas 1979: 1. 4–5, 'De regno ad regem Cypri'. For a translation of these passages, see p. 403 above.

[15] On the priors and scholars of S. Maria Novella, esp. Remigio de' Girolami, who quoted from the Sallustian-Ciceronian invectives in his *De bono comuni* (1301-2), see Panella 1979, 1985, and 1989.

[16] [*Unde*] *respublica ex parva effecta est magna, quia in illis domi fuit industria, foris iustum imperium, animus in consulendo liber, neque delicto, neque libidini obnoxius* (Tolomeo da Lucca [Bartolomeo Fiadoni]), *De regimine principum* 2. 8, Aquinas 1924: 33). On the author, see Davis 1974, as well as Panella 1979, 1985, and 1989. [See now also Blythe 2009: esp. 174–5.]

[17] Bartolomeo da San Concordio 1827. In addition to Cesare Segre's article in *Dizionario biografico degli italiani* 6: 770, see Segre 1963 and Cesareo 1924.

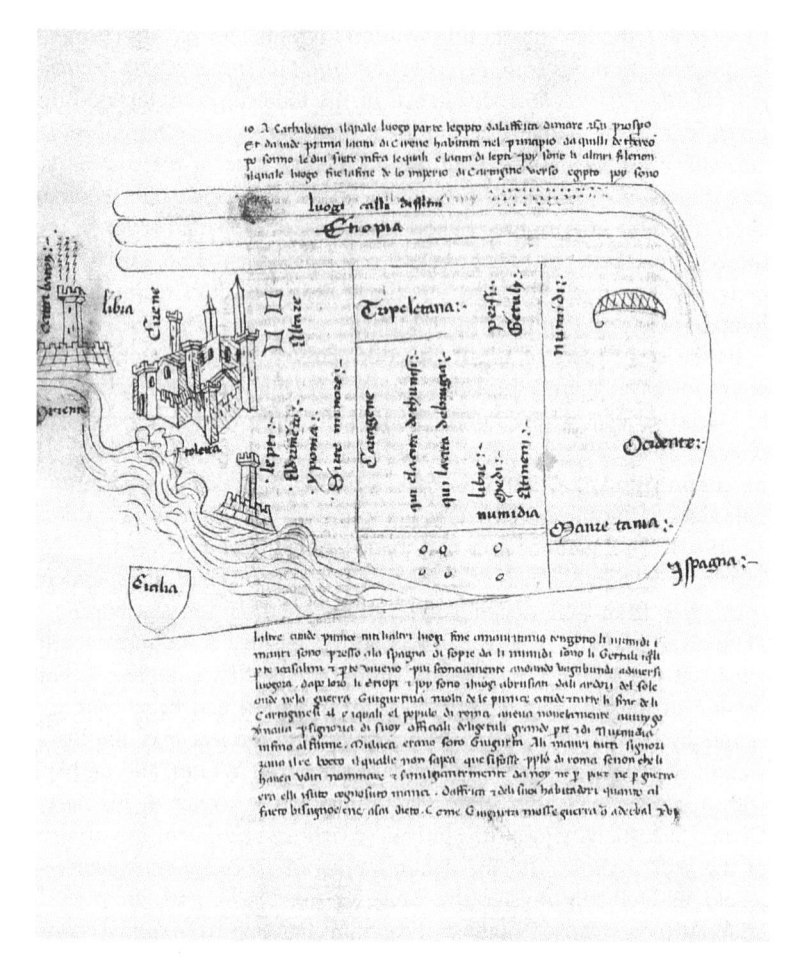

Figure 16.2. Map illustrating Sallust's *excursus* in *B.J.* 17-19 on the regions, cities, and peoples of North Africa, in a 1433 copy of San Concordio's translation of the *Bellum Iugurthinum*.

Rome, Biblioteca Corsiniana, MS 1860, fol. 27v (by permission of the Biblioteca dell'Accademia Nazionale dei Lincei e Corsiniana).

(the work of Agostino Ortica della Porta), it remained the most widely copied of the *volgarizzamenti*, and one of the most handsomely illustrated of all Sallust manuscripts (see Figure 16.2).[18]

---

[18] Figure 16.2 (Rome, Biblioteca Corsiniana, MS 1860, fol. 27v) shows an unusual map illustrating Sallust's excursus in *Jugurtha* 17-19 on North Africa in a copy of Bartolomeo's translation written by Johannes Antonius of Florence in 1433. On the so-called 'Sallust

Factional rivalries in Florence and Padua heightened the awareness of Sallust's political lessons and induced the proponents of republican government to consider the moral and social causes of its breakdown as well as its success. In two works by the Paduan jurist and poet laureate Albertino Mussato, the *De gestis Italicorum*, begun about 1315, and the *De traditione Patavii ad Canem Grandem anno 1328*, written during his exile, attention centred on the decline of *labor atque iustitia* ('hard work and justice'), the concomitant growth of *pecuniae cupido* ('desire for money'), and the dangers of encroaching despotism. In his *De lite inter Naturam et Fortunam*, Mussato also developed a theory of constitutional change inspired partly by Aristotelian schemes of rise and decline, partly by arguments in *Catilina* 6–10.[19] His younger contemporary Marsilio da Padova repeated Micipsa's words from *Jugurtha* 10. 6 to remind readers at the very outset of his *Defensor pacis* (1324) that *concordia parvae res crescunt, discordia maximae dilabuntur* ('harmony makes small states grow great, while discord undermines the mightiest empires').[20] In Florence, meanwhile, Giovanni Villani turned to Sallust, whom he reverently addressed as *grande dottore* and *maestro d'istorie*, as a trusted source of historical information, moral guidance, and political instruction for his *Nuova cronica* (begun after 1300).[21] The *Catilina*, he believed, inspired *memoria e esemplo* of ancient valour and devotion to the commonwealth, while exposing the evils of partisan quarrels and divisions.

Not all humanists who read Sallust in the fourteenth century were personally committed, of course, to the ideals of an active civic life, let alone to republican models of government. Petrarch, for instance, was attracted to Sallust's writing (as he was to that of other Roman historians and biographers) primarily for its stylistic qualities and lessons of moral excellence.[22] Yet he too was moved by the patriotic ethos of early Rome

---

maps', see 'Sallustius' in Destombes 1964: 37–8; 65–73; and Woodward 1987: ch. 18, esp. 343–4 [See now also Gautier Dalché 2003.]

[19] *De gestis Italicorum* (Mussato 1727); *De lite inter Naturam et Fortunam* (MSS Biblioteca Civica Padua B.P. 2531, ff. 1–46, and Bibl. Colombina Seville 5. 1. 5); *De traditione Patavii ad Canem Grandem anno 1328* (included as book 12 of Mussato 1727). See Rubinstein 1957: 165–83.

[20] Marsilio da Padova, *Defensor pacis*, 1. 1. The quotation is from *B.J.* 10. 7, not, as Marsilio says, the *Catilina*. Skinner 1990: 128–9 cites several writers of the earlier *Ars dictaminis* tradition who also quoted this passage.

[21] Villani 1990–1: 1. 30–2. Many orations and passages of Sallust's monographs (esp. the speeches of Memmius and Marius in the *Jugurtha*) would have resonated with the contemporary debate over 'true nobility'.

[22] On Petrarch's humanism, see in particular Billanovich 1974 and Ullman 1923. Sallust is cited in his *Epistolae familiares*, *Epistolae seniles*, and *Rerum memorandarum*

and by the stories of personal courage and devotion to the state. Quoting Sallust's words from his prologue to the *Jugurtha* (4. 5-6), he compared history to the *imagines* of the ancient Romans. It was a means of enflaming the hearts of young men with the desire for glory, of inciting them to emulate the great deeds of their ancestors.[23]

Florentine Civic Humanism

From the latter part of the Trecento into the first decades of the Quattrocento, the impact of external events, together with a growing appreciation of classical rhetoric, helped produce a still more coherent and sophisticated defence of republican government. The recurrent conflicts between Florence, Rome, and Milan, and particularly the Milanese threat to Tuscan territory, obliged Florentine statesmen and political thinkers to formulate more articulately and argue more persuasively the civic ideals they had inherited from previous generations (and their classical sources). The need for allies also impelled them to justify their foreign policy, as well as their own communal institutions, in the name of liberty. Here, as earlier, various classical authors, notably Cicero and Aristotle, contributed the weight of their authority. Yet it was again the *Catilina*, more than any other work of Roman *history*, that helped shape the city's political consciousness and public image.

Coluccio Salutati, chancellor of Florence between 1375 and 1406 and author of a work of audacious wartime propaganda, knew both monographs directly, as well as through the works of Augustine, Aquinas, and (one may assume) many of the late medieval treatises on rhetoric and politics. His personal letters were punctuated with Sallustian *sententiae*, and it is not surprising that he incorporated the arguments of *Catilina* 7-9 into a number of his public missives.[24] For Salutati, republican institutions were emphatically contrasted with any form of monarchy; moreover, liberty could be enjoyed only, or at least most fully, under a popular government. Now, too, a more explicit link was made between liberty and imperial greatness. In his missive of 1377 to the Roman

---

libri, and praised not only as a source of eloquence and moral edification but also for his truthfulness.

[23] *Profecto autem, si statue illustrium possunt nobiles animos ad imitandi studium accendere, quod Q. Fabium Maximum et P. Cornelium Scipionem dicere solitos Crispus refert, quanto magis ipsa virtus hoc efficit, claro dum proponitur non marmore sed exemplo?* (*Epistolae Familiares* 6. 4. 11, Petrarch 1934: 80).

[24] Salutati 1892-1911 and Witt 1976.

people, aimed at reinforcing opposition to the Pope, he presented the idea of civic greatness not just as an expression of civic vitality, prosperity, and prestige but in unabashed terms of territorial aggrandizement and political dominion—concluding his epistle with words clearly inspired by Sallust's text. The appeal to liberty, in other words, justified a break with Florence's traditional Guelph policy (and support of the papacy); it also set the stage for an alliance of free communes (headed naturally by Florence) against the hostile, 'tyrannical' princes of Italy.

> Do not think, o most excellent lords, that your and our ancestors—for we boast of common parents—founded such a great and memorable empire while subservient at home nor that they did it by oppressing Italy with servitude either imposed from the outside or from within. Indeed, by assisting allies and fighting for their liberty, that mighty empire of yours first set you over Italy, conquered Spain, overcame Africa and at length was brought to such heights of power that the Roman name prevailed over all nations. With liberty destroyed under the Caesars—let those who wish extol Caesar and praise Augustus with divine honors, celebrate Vespasian with admiring praise, laud Trajan's justice and military glory to the skies, and finally celebrate, however they wish, Constantine, Antonius [sic] Pius, Justinian, and the others—in their hands, without question, Italy was devastated and that pinnacle of empire was swept away. Thus, the desire of liberty alone created for the Romans empire, glory, and all their honor and influence.[25]

Salutati had another occasion to return to Sallust in the course of researching the ancient origins of Florence. In the last decade of the fourteenth century, as the city entered a crucial phase of its struggle with Giangaleazzo Visconti, it was important to bolster republican sentiments and arguments with historical documentation.[26] Thanks again, in fact, to his reading of Sallust, and of Cicero, the chancellor was able to demonstrate that Florence had been founded not at the time of Julius Caesar, the first in the line of Roman emperors,[27] but in the time of Sulla, when

---

[25] *Non putetis, excellentissimi domini, quod maiores vestri et nostri, communibus quidem parentibus gloriamur, serviendo domi, tantum tamque memorabile Imperii decus fundaverunt nec dimicetendo suam Ytaliam sub externa vel domestica servitute.... Solum itaque libertatis studium et imperium et gloriam (et) omnem Romanis peperit dignitatem.* Ed. and transl. by Witt 1976: 54, with a few changes. Other passages in Salutati's missives to Bologna of 1 and 28 July 1376 may also be compared with ideas expressed in *B.C.* 7. 2–7 (Witt 1976: 55). I thank Ronald Witt for bringing my attention to this evidence of Sallust's influence. [On the relation between liberty and empire and 'republican imperialists' in Florentine political thought, see Hörnqvist 2000: esp. 108–10.]

[26] On Salutati, see Witt 1976: Introduction, as well as Witt 1969 and 1983.

[27] According to Villani, Julius Caesar 'primo si fece chiamare imperadore' (*Cronica* 1. 19), and medieval and Renaissance histories of Imperial Rome often began with Caesar.

self-governing structures were still (formally) intact. This 'proof' of Florence's 'republican' foundation enhanced the city's status as daughter of Rome and heir to her political legacy.

By the time Salutati's pupil, and later successor in the Florentine chancery, Leonardo Bruni, set to work on his *Historiae Florentini populi* in 1415, Sallust's work was thus widely known to Florentine readers.[28] Bruni cited him admiringly early in book 1, side by side with Cicero, singling them out among the ancients as *duo praestantissimi latinae linguae auctores* ('two most outstanding Latin authors'). Indeed, for Bruni, Sallust furnished the starting point and key to his own interpretation of the historical process, in which the theme of *libertas* and *virtus* provided a meaningful and compelling conceptual framework. It explained the links between elective government, moral excellence, and a healthy, expanding commonwealth—or, on the contrary, between tyranny, moral corruption, and the decline of a state.[29] Bruni, more clearly than any of his predecessors, also understood, and elaborated upon, the particularly Sallustian notion of *virtus* as a *competitive* pursuit of honour and glory in the service of the *res publica*.

A comparison of *Catilina* 7. 1–3 with passages in book 1 of Bruni's *Historiae* describing the collapse of Etruscan and of Roman rule, then the revival of Italian city states in the Middle Ages, reveals the extent to which Bruni assimilated Sallustian concepts. As he analysed the crisis of the Etruscan cities, weakened and overcome not by arms but by loss of liberty, and as he explained the growth and later crisis of Rome's own dominion, he was expanding upon the idea of *virtus* introduced in this chapter of the *Catilina*—collating, as it were, Sallust's explanation of the rise of Rome while a *civitas libera* with Tacitus' observations in *Historiae* 1. 1 on the consequences of Octavian's victory at Actium, that is, the concentration of political powers and magistracies in the hands of one man and, with it, the disappearance of great talents:

---

[28] Bruni 1914–26: 3–288. For Bruni's life and work, as well as translations of selected texts, see Griffiths, Hankins, and Thompson 1987. [See now Bruni 2001–7].

[29] Cf. La Penna 1969: 412 on Sallust's influence in shaping Bruni's concept of the historical process:

> Più che le concordanze di lessico e di stile importa la concordanza nel concetto fondamentale: il regime tirannico e quello nobiliare deprimono i talenti, hanno paura del loro esplicarsi, il regime repubblicano o popolare pone le condizioni per una gara di virtù, offre l'incentivo alla loro piena manifestazione: il regime di libertà è innanzi tutto il regime dove le capacità dei cittadini possono competere: ecco perché negli stati non monarchici e non aristocratici la civiltà fiorisce meglio.

For liberty gave way before the imperial name, and as liberty disappeared, so did *virtus*. Before the time of the Caesars, character was the route to public honors, and... high public offices were open to men of *magnitudo animi, virtus*, and *industria*. But as soon as the republic was entrusted to one man, strength of character and magnanimity became suspect in the eyes of the rulers. Only those were acceptable to the emperors who lacked the mental vigor to care about liberty. The imperial court thus opened its gates to the lazy rather than to the strong, to flatterers rather than to hard workers, and as government fell to the worse men, little by little the empire was brought to ruin.[30]

Under the domination of Rome, Bruni argued, the Italian *municipia* had languished and declined; Rome itself, once it had succumbed to the rule of tyrants, gradually fell prey to foreign invaders. After the long interval of barbarian occupation, nevertheless, the fortunes of towns had begun to revive, and with the death of Emperor Frederick II in 1250 and the subsequent defeat of the last Hohenstaufen army, the cities were free once more to grow and expand. At the beginning of book 2, describing Florence's resurgence in the latter part of the thirteenth century, Bruni again captured the spirit of Sallust's words.[31] Both authors felt the burst of enthusiasm in the people, the exhilarating effects of liberty.

Considering the links between political liberty and *virtus*, it was also natural for Bruni, like Sallust, to identify nobility with merit, not birth.

---

[30] The translation is taken, with minor changes, from Watkins 1978: 46. In Bruni's words:

> Declinationem autem Romani imperii ab eo fere tempore ponendam reor quo, amissa libertate, imperatoribus servire Roma incepit... Cessit enim libertas imperatorio nomini, et post libertatem virtus abivit. Prius namque per virtutem ad honores via fuit, iisque ad consulatus dictaturasque et caeteros amplissimos dignitatis gradus facillime patebat iter, qui magnitudine animi, virtute et industria caeteros anteibant. Mox vero ut respublica in potestatem unius devenit, virtus et magnitudo animi suspecta dominantibus esse coepit. Hique solum imperatoribus placebant, quibus non ea vis ingenii esset, quam libertatis cura stimulare posset. Ita pro fortibus ignavos, pro industriis adulatores imperatoria suscepit aula, et rerum gubernacula ad peiores delata ruinam paulatim dedere. (Bruni 1914-26: 13-14)

Cf. La Penna 1969: 412-13.

[31]

> Ab his initiis profectum, mirabile dictu est quantum adoleverit populi robur. Homines enim, qui dudum aut principibus aut eorum fautoribus, ut vere dixerim, inservierant, gustata libertatis dulcedine, cum populus iam ipse dominus auctorque honoris esset, totis se viribus attollebant, quo dignitatem inter suos mererentur. Igitur domi consilium et industria, foris autem arma fortitudoque valebant.
> (Bruni 1914-26: 27)

Cf. La Penna 1969: 412.

In the speech composed for Giano della Bella, leader of the anti-magnate party, which in 1293 had instituted the Ordinances of Justice, he championed the rights of the people against the pretensions of the nobility, echoing Memmius' oration in *Jugurtha* 31. In the speech delivered by Giovanni de' Ricci in the year 1387, which alludes to Cato's words in *Catilina* 52. 19-21, he called upon the people to remember the *industria* of their ancestors and the virtues that had made their city great.[32] At the same time, however, Bruni did not conceal his distrust of the 'ignorant and fickle' masses and the ambitious demagogues who incited them; again, like Sallust, he tempered his criticism of the oligarchs with an appeal for restraint and respect for law.[33]

In 1427-8 Bruni had occasion to compose a public oration in honour of a distinguished military captain of Florentine extraction, Nanni degli Strozzi. By this date he had finished, or nearly finished, the first six books of the *Historiae*, and the *Oratio funebris* brought to a climax its central theme of liberty versus tyranny.[34] It was in this period too, as Bruni was entering upon his second appointment as chancellor of Florence, that Filippo Maria Visconti, Giangaleazzo's successor, had resumed Milan's expansionist policy in northern and central Italy, threatening once again the cities of Tuscany. Quoting several passages from the panegyric, Hans Baron described them as some of 'the most beautiful expressions of the civic ideal in the period when Florence was locked in struggle with the Visconti'. Yet, as Antonio La Penna has pointed out, Baron failed to recognize the influence of Sallust and to identify him with the *historicus* Bruni was citing—even when Bruni was repeating verbatim the words of *Catilina* 7. 1-3.[35] Sallustian influence is unmistakable, in fact, both in the definition of liberty and, above all, in the ideology of *virtus* and *gloria* (which recalled Marius' speech in chapter 85 of the *Jugurtha*, as well as chapter 7 of the *Catilina*). What Bruni emphasized once again was the moral vigour generated by a climate of freedom. It was the opportunity for free citizens to test their abilities and win rewards for *virtus*—rewards of public honours and offices—that set popular government above both monarchy and oligarchy:

> This is true liberty, this is fairness in a city: not to fear violence or injury from any man, and for the citizens to enjoy equality of the law and a government that is equally accessible to all. But these conditions cannot be

---

[32] Bruni 1914-26: 242-3. Cf. La Penna 1969: 425-6.
[33] On Bruni's political philosophy, see Hankins 1995. [See also Hankins 2010: 463-66 on Bruni's uses of the term *respublica* in various works.]
[34] Bruni 1764: 4: 2-7.   [35] Baron 1966: 419. Cf. La Penna 1969: 414-15.

maintained under the rule of one man or of a few.... This is why praise of monarchy has something fictitious and artificial about it, and lacks precision and solidity. *Kings, the historian says, are more suspicious of good men than of evil, and are always fearful of another's virtue.* ... Thus the only legitimate constitution left is the popular one, in which liberty is real,... in which pursuit of the virtues may flourish without suspicion. And when a free people are offered this possibility of attaining offices, it is wonderful how effectively it stimulates the talents of the citizens. When shown a hope of gaining office, men rouse themselves and seek to rise; when it is precluded they sink into idleness.[36]   (italics added)

Thanks especially to the importance of Bruni's work, Sallustian themes continued to inform the historical and political thought of Italian humanists through the mid-1400s. Bruni's protégé Buonaccorso da Montemagno adopted ideas from Marius' speech (*B.J.* 85) to defend the cause of individual merit in his *Disputatio de nobilitate*. 'Nobility', he claimed, was not a matter of illustrious ancestry; rather, it 'issued from the greatness and excellence of the soul'.[37] Matteo Palmieri, Bruni's

---

[36] Oration for the Funeral of Nanni Strozzi', transl. by G. Griffiths, in Griffiths, Hankins, and Thompson 1987: 121–27, at 125:

Haec est vera libertas, haec aequitas civitatis, nullius vim, nullius iniuriam vereri, paritatem esse iuris inter se civibus, paritatem reipublicae adeundae. Haec autem nec in unius dominatu nec in paucorum possunt subsistere.... Ex quo fit ut monarchiae laus veluti ficta quaedam et umbratilis sit, non autem expressa et solida. Regibus, inquit historicus, boni quam mali suspiciores sunt, semperque his aliena virtus formidulosa est... Ita popularis una relinquitur legitima rei publicae gubernandae forma, in qua libertas vera sit... in qua virtutum studia vigere absque suspicione possint. Atque haec honorum adipiscendorum facultas potestasque libero populo, haec assequendi proposita mirabile quantum valet ad ingenia civium excitanda. Ostensa enim honoris spe, erigunt sese homines atque attollunt, praeclusa vero inertes desidunt, ut in civitate nostra cum sit ea spes facultasque proposita, minime sit admirandum et ingenia et industriam plurimum eminere.

('Oratio funebris', 3–4, emphasis added)

Cf. La Penna 1969: 414–15. As James Hankins cautions, we should take into account Bruni's tendency to rhetorical exaggeration in what was composed after all as an epideictic oration. [See Hankins 2010: 472 and n. 69.] What is significant in this context, however, is Bruni's reliance upon Sallust for the expression of these ideas.

[37] *Nihil enim aliud est nobilitas, nisi excellentia quaedam qua digniora indignioribus praestant. Sicut igitur homo animi praestantia dignior est reliquis animantibus, ita quidem claritudine animi homo hominem antecellit... Constat igitur ex sola animi virtute veram nobilitatem defluere* (da Montemagno 1952: 142). As Gaius Flaminius declared to his imaginary panel of judges: *Etenim cum intelligerem praeclariora tantum fore mortalium ingenia cum ad rempublicam accommodantur, totum me meae patriae concessi. Neque unquam postea illius salutem et amplitudinem cogitare desii, nihil laboris pertimescens, nihil periculi, quod illi gloriam et incolumitatem parare posset* (ibid. 156).

disciple and 'theoretician' of civic humanism, and Poggio Bracciolini, Bruni's successor as chancellor of Florence, borrowed motifs from Sallust's prologues to underscore the didactic and patriotic uses of history. Palmieri inserted Sallustian-style character portraits and orations into his *De captivitate Pisarum liber* of c.1448 in order to dramatize the heroic exploits of Florence's citizen army and immortalize a victory that Bruni had not hesitated to compare with Rome's defeat of Carthage.[38] Poggio Bracciolini, introducing his account of the *Historia Florentina*, linked the early growth and vitality of the city to its free institutions.[39] A few years earlier, in 1435, he had energetically defended the cause of liberty in a controversy with Guarino Veronese over the respective merits of Julius Caesar and Scipio Africanus.[40] In the last of his letters against Guarino, who had introduced the Greek historian Dio Cassius in support of monarchy, Poggio summed up his defence of popular government, and clinched his arguments, with an appeal to Sallust:

> I was outraged when I read the words of that famous historian [Dio Cassius], who in this respect is deranged. He says, as Guarinus translates, that more, greater, and better things have issued from kings than from peoples, as the history of the Romans testifies. Here he gives pride of place to the achievements of the Roman kings over those things that were done afterwards, when the country had been freed from royal servitude. One sentence of Sallust, who said that kings are more suspicious of good men than of bad, confounds the whole of Dio.[41]

By the middle of the century, nevertheless, writers like Matteo Palmieri and Poggio Bracciolini were beginning to approach their work not only with feelings of pride, but with a certain nostalgia and, too, a certain

---

[38] Palmieri 1904. On Sallustian influences in Palmieri, see the introduction by Scaramella and (for an opposing point of view) Wilcox 1971.

[39] Bracciolini 1715. The work was begun in 1453.

[40] The letters include: Poggio on *De praestantia Scipionis et Caesaris*, addressed to Scipione Mainenti (April 1435); Guarino's reply, addressed to Francesco Barbaro (June 1435); and Poggio's *Defensio*, also addressed to Barbaro (Nov. 1435). [For the texts and commentary, see now D. Canfora 2001].

[41]
> Stomachatus sum cum legi verba illius historici [i.e. Dio Cassius] in hac parte delyrantis. Ait, ut traducit Guarinus, plura maiora et meliora obvenisse ex regibus quam ex populis, ut Romanorum gesta testantur. Hic praeponit gesta regum Romanorum his quae postmodum liberata patria a servitute regia acta sunt. Unum Salustii dictum, qui regibus bonos quam malos dixit esse suspectiores, universum Dionem confundit.
> (Bracciolini 1538: 388–9, 'Defensiuncula contra Guarinum Veronensem')

[See now the edition of D. Canfora 2001.]

caution. As Florence gradually slipped under the rule of the Medici, historians focused their attention increasingly on the 'glorious past', glossing over contemporary events; or they portrayed the recent course of history as a decline from earlier heights. From this perspective, of course, Sallust could be used to denounce the corrupting effects of power, the spread of avarice, and the dangers of factionalism.[42] Yet, by the 1470s, as Cosimo's grandson, Lorenzo, consolidated his power, little incentive or opportunity remained even for this. If writers did deplore such conditions, it was primarily to contrast the weaknesses of popular republics with the solid benefits of Medici rule.

In this changing climate of opinion, Sallust's work tended to have more impact as a literary model than as a source of political ideas. To the extent that borrowing and imitation did contain any political message, this was clearly and unequivocally the praise of civic concord and the condemnation of conspiracy. Medici supporters repeatedly quoted the lines in *Jugurtha* 10. 6 (as had Marsilio da Padova and many others): *nam concordia parvae res crescunt, discordia maxumae dilabuntur*.[43] In his apology for the Medici, composed soon after the Pazzi conspiracy of 1478, Angelo Poliziano portrayed the rebels as Catilinarian criminals, consumed by greed and envy.[44] Deliberately omitting any reference to contemporary constitutional issues and sociopolitical antagonisms, which in Sallust's own work had provided important historical background for the conspiracy of 63 BCE, he concentrated on the private vices of the Pazzi and their ingratitude towards the Medici. In the meantime, Leon Battista Alberti had already composed a commentary on another conspiracy, the attempted uprising of Stefano Porcari against Nicholas V in 1453,[45] which also underscored the blessings of *pax et princeps*.

---

[42] Brown 1992 cites a Florentine citizen who quoted Sallust on 'the need for sacrifice and unity' in the policy discussions in the 1450s. Cf. Field 1988. Apropos of avarice, see Poggio Bracciolini's *De avaritia*, in Bracciolini 1538: 1: 1–31, at 21: *Temperantia enim medii est; avaricia extremorum. Nam fortitudinem in eo esse quis dixerit cum animum virilem corpusque effeminet avaricia? Testis et autor gravis sit Sallustius.*
[43] Field 1988: 47–8 writes: 'Classical erudition in meetings of the *pratiche* is rare, but one quotation from Sallust became the political maxim of the late 1450s and the 1460s: "With harmony small states (or things) increase, with disharmony the greatest fall apart"'; cf. 214–15 and 223–4.
[44] Poliziano 1958.
[45] Alberti 1890: 257–66. [See now Addendum I: Catiline and Catilinarianism.] On Machiavelli and the conspiracy of Girolamo Olgiati, see p. XXX and n. 66 below.

2. THE TRANSITION TO NEW POLITICAL ATTITUDES

The Breakdown of Civic Humanism: 'Le calamità d'Italia'

The political upheavals in Italy in the latter part of the fifteenth and in the first decades of the sixteenth century undermined not only any surviving or (in the case of Florence) renascent ideals of municipal liberty but the humanist commitment to a life of public service, whatever the specific constitution of a city state. In the kingdom of Naples, the experience of civil war, followed by the invasion of Charles VIII, induced a more sceptical—and bitter—attitude and a more analytical approach to the writing of history. When authors like Giovanni Albino and Giovanni Pontano attempted to diagnose the cause of recent troubles, what they singled out in Sallust's monographs was above all his denunciation of human egoism and hypocrisy and his sense of the instability of human affairs.[46] Sallust, as the 'historian of calamities', offered insights into the darker recesses of the human psyche, exposed the opportunism of political leaders, and the ruthless pursuit of wealth and power.[47] At the same time, he provided a model of Latin prose noted for brevity, variation of word and syntax, and the inconcinnity that helped express the conflicts and treacheries of partisan politics, the growing disjunction between traditional ideals and contemporary realities, and a mood of deepening disillusionment. In the excursus of *Catilina* 36. 4–39. 4, Sallust had depicted the rapid deterioration of political life, especially from the time of Pompey and Crassus:

> Namque, uti paucis verum absolvam, post illa tempora quicumque rem publicam agitavere honestis nominibus, alii sicuti populi iura defenderent, pars quo senatus auctoritas maxuma foret, bonum publicum simulantes pro sua quisque potentia certabant. (*B.C.* 38. 3)
>
> For, to tell the truth in a few words, all who after that time assailed the government used specious pretexts, some maintaining that they were defending the rights of the commons, others that they were upholding the

---

[46] Giovanni Albino, 'De bello Hetrusco'; 'De bello Hydruntino'; 'De bello intestino'; 'De bello gallico' in Gravier 1769. A critical edition of the *De bello Hydruntino* by I. Nuovo is included in Gualdo Rosa, Nuovo, and Defilippis 1982.

[47] Cochrane 1981: 166 refers to Sallust as 'the most obvious ancient model for historians of calamities'. Cf. Syme 964: 56 on Sallust as 'the historian of the decline and fall'. On Neapolitan historiography in the fifteenth century, see Bentley 1987.

prestige of the Senate; but under pretence of the public welfare each in reality was working for his own advancement.

Pontano, adopting Sallustian words and rhetorical figures, described a similar struggle for power, and similar cases of deception and hypocrisy, in the war between the Neapolitan barons and King Ferrante. If the Prince of Taranto, for example, appeared to be seeking peace, in reality he was making ready for war and marking time by pretending to urge reconciliation until everything being discussed by the conspirators was ready: *ille verbis quidem pacem velle, re autem bellum parare, tempusque agitandae per speciem concordiae terere, dum quae agitabantur a coniuratis, parata essent omnia.*[48] A few years later, Pontano's Florentine friend Bernardo Rucellai wrote an account of the French invasion of 1494 modelled even more closely on Sallust. In words that again recall *Catilina* 38. 3, he cynically contrasted the base motives of popular demagogues with their lofty professions of public concern:

> pars, plebe sollicitata, bonum publicum simulantes, direptionem moliri; plerique irae atque iniuriae, pauci principatus libidini, nemo fere saluti patriae obtemperare.[49]

> Some, after the plebs had been stirred up, feigning concern for the public good, plotted its ruin; many acted out of anger and injury, a few from lust for absolute power, almost no one for the country's welfare.

Machiavelli: A New Context for Political Debate

If anyone in this period and in the decades following the collapse of the second Florentine Republic retained any confidence in human ability and any genuine hope in using that ability to control, rather than be controlled by, the course of events, it was the great Florentine political thinker Niccolò Machiavelli.[50] Like Pontano and Rucellai, he shared Sallust's cynical view of party politics and human nature. Yet he also appreciated the force of human intellect (*vis animi*), the powers of

---

[48] Giovanni Pontano, 'Historia belli quod Ferdinandus Rex Neapolitanus senior contra Ioannem Andegaviensem ducem gessit' in Gravier 1769: 1: 15. [On how 'discord is explored and revealed in the linguistic instability of Sallust's text', see Batstone 2010b: 54, and bibliography cited in his article.]

[49] Rucellai 1733: 42. On Rucellai's use of Sallust, see McCuaig 1982: 78–79, who compares this passage with the excursus of *B.C.* 38.

[50] Cf. Osmond 1993: 420–30 for a fuller discussion. Out of the vast bibliography on Machiavelli, I have relied in particular on Gaeta 1977; Gilbert 1965; Sasso 1980 and 1987; Skinner 1978, vol. 1, and 1981; Walker 1950, vol. 2, Table XIII; Whitfield 1947; and the contributions to Bock, Skinner, and Viroli, 1990.

individual talent (*ingeni opes*), which he could find in Sallust's idea of *virtus* and which characterized his own Renaissance brand of *virtù*. Both writers were recording the decline of their republics; both probably sensed the irreversibile course of that decline. But neither was prepared to rule out the potential for human effort and intervention—especially at favourable conjunctures of events—when *virtù* could not only resist but even overcome the onrushing 'river' of Fortune.[51]

Good government, Machiavelli believed, was not simply a matter of promoting *il vivere civile*; its chief function or immediate purpose was to guarantee internal order and security, and—for those states that had the potential to grow in wealth and population, and above all to expand their political dominion—to achieve *grandezza*. In constructing his new politics, he thus adapted the precepts and experience of his ancient authorities to criteria of practical success. What was needed in the contemporary crisis, he insisted, was a body of political laws aimed at discovering the means to establish, maintain, or increase the power of republics or monarchies, and based on 'quelli iudizii o... quelli remedii che dagli antichi sono stati iudicati o ordinati'.[52] Sallust was only one among many ancient authors (including Livy, Tacitus, and Polybius) whom Machiavelli drew upon in his *De principatibus*, *Discorsi*, and *Istorie fiorentine*; yet his influence was both broad and incisive.[53] In fact, his two monographs, as well as parts of the *Epistulae*, supplied many of the basic explanatory principles that could clarify the causes and dynamics of change, especially at crucial moments in the evolution of a state: in the cycle of growth and decay, in the transition from popular government to autocratic rule, or in the conditions permitting reform or provoking revolution.

Sallust's understanding of the link between liberty, *virtus*, and the growth of a republic helped explain, first of all, the salutary effects of dissension in political life.[54] For Machiavelli, as for Bruni and their late

---

[51] Even in times of political and social turmoil, perhaps especially at such times, man could still be the 'architect' of his own destiny: *sed res docuit id verum esse quod in carminibus Appius ait, fabrum esse suae quemque fortunae, atque in te maxume, qui tantum alios praegressus es, ut prius defessi sint homines laudando facta tua quam tu laude digna faciundo* (*Rep.* 1. 1. 2). [On ambiguities in the notion of *virtus*, see n. 63 below.]

[52] Machiavelli 1993: 20 (*Discorsi* 1, Proemio). Quotations are from the editions by Anselmi and Varotti, 1992 and 1993. English versions are based upon Ricci's translation of the *Prince* and Detmold's translation of the *Discourses* (Machiavelli 1950).

[53] Although much has been written about the influence of Livy and Tacitus on Machiavelli, comparatively few historians have noted the role of Sallust, and among these only a few like Whitfield and, more recently, Skinner, have recognized his *formative* influence. [See now also Fontana 2003]

[54] Skinner 1990: 135–41. According to Skinner, Machiavelli's 'defence of the "tumults"' was a novel claim, a criticism of the traditional views of Cicero on *concordia ordinum* and of

medieval predecessors, a republic founded on free competition for public office stimulated the display of individual talent. Recalling the strenuous efforts that Rome had made to subdue the peoples of Italy, he paraphrased Sallust's words in *Catilina* 7. 1–3 in *Discorsi* 2. 2:

> And it is easy to understand whence that affection for liberty arose in the people, for one sees that cities never increased in dominion or wealth unless they were free. And certainly it is wonderful to think of the greatness which Athens attained within the space of a hundred years after having freed herself from the tyranny of Pisistratus; *and still more wonderful is it to reflect upon the greatness which Rome achieved after she was rid of her kings.* The cause of this is manifest, for it is not individual prosperity, but the general good, that makes cities great; and certainly the general good is regarded nowhere but in republics.[55] (italics added)

Machiavelli perceived more clearly than Bruni, however, the natural consequences, both positive and negative, of this civic rivalry (*certamen inter civis*), or was more willing to acknowledge, as Sallust himself had, that it was not always possible to direct a man's energy and talents to the common good. On the one hand, he realized, the quarrels between the nobility and the people were in large measure responsible for the creation of good laws and a mixed form of government. Dissension was inevitable too, he insisted, in all republics that aimed at greatness, for without a large population and a well-armed citizenry the state could not hope to expand.[56] At the same time, he perceived the potentially destructive

---

Sallust 'that internal discord is invariably fatal to civic greatness'. I see Sallust's influence here, however, in Machiavelli's recognition of the *competitive* character of republican states: the element that helps him explain both the potential for expansion and the inevitable dangers of civic discord.

[55] Machiavelli 1993: 282 (*Discorsi* 2. 2):

> E facil cosa è conoscere, donde nasca ne' popoli questa affezione del vivere libero; perché si vede per esperienza le cittadi non avere mai ampliato né di dominio né di ricchezza se non mentre sono state in libertà. E veramente maravigliosa cosa è a considerare, a quanta grandezza venne Atene per spazio di cento anni, poiché la si liberò dalla tirannide di Pisistrato. Ma sopra tutto *maravigliosissima è a considerare a quanta grandezza venne Roma poiché la si liberò da' suoi Re*. La ragione è facile a intendere; perché non il bene particulare ma il bene comune è quello che fa grandi le città. E sanza dubbio questo bene comune non è osservato se non nelle republiche.
>
> (*Discorsi* 2. 2, p. 233, italics added)

[56] In Salutati and Bruni the notion of 'greatness' implies not only the prosperity and prestige of the city but also its role as one of the major territorial states of Italy. In Machiavelli, the expanding, aggressive, character of a state's growth is even more evident in what he says about the relationship between civic dissension, military power, and *grandezza* in *Discorsi* 1. 6 (Machiavelli 1993: 47–8). For Sallust, too, growth results naturally, through (just) war, in Roman *imperium* and *potentia: sed ubi labore atque iustitia res publica crevit, reges magni bello domiti, nationes ferae et populi ingentes, vi subacti* (*B.C.* 10. 1).

nature of dissension and, like Sallust, distinguished between healthy rivalry, inspired by love of the *bene comune*, and divisive factions, fostered by the *bene particulare*. Good examples and sound laws could restrain men's personal ambitions but not permanently suppress them, especially in a republic aiming to increase its political power. In *Discorsi* 1. 37 he dated the beginning of the Roman Republic's decline to the tribunates of Tiberius and Gaius Gracchus and the controversy sparked by their agrarian bills: a turning point that Sallust himself had noted in *Jugurtha* 41. 10–42. 4. In the *Istorie fiorentine* he made the *naturali inimicizie* (i.e., the causes and consequences of public discord) the central theme of his work.

Like Sallust, Machiavelli also identified two main divisions or opposing 'parties' within the citizen body: the nobility, possessed by *cura dominationis*, the people, preoccupied with *cura libertatis*.[57] Sallust had first formulated this contrast in the speech of Gaius Memmius in *Jugurtha* 31. 23: 'They [the oligarchs] wish to be tyrants, you [the commons] to be free; they desire to inflict injury, you to prevent it.'[58] Machiavelli now took up the same arguments, also tending like Sallust to radicalize the terms of the conflict (and oversimplify its causes) and ultimately laying the blame for the escalation of violence primarily on the nobles and their lust for money and power. In the *De principatibus* he set out the main lines of this antithesis;[59] in the *Discorsi*, debating whether the 'guardianship of liberty' should be entrusted to the nobles or to the people, he carried the idea a step further:

> [And] doubtless, if we consider the aims of the nobles and of the people, we will see that the first have a great desire to dominate, whilst the latter have only the wish not to be dominated, and consequently a greater desire to live in the enjoyment of liberty...; so that when the people are appointed the guardians of any liberty, and are unable to encroach upon it, it is reasonable to suppose that they will take better care of it.[60]

---

[57] Cf. Whitfield 1947: 139–42.

[58] Describing the decline of the *res publica* in *B.J.* 41. 1–5, Sallust divided the whole state into rival 'parties', denouncing the selfish aims of both *optimates* and *populares*.

[59] Machiavelli 1992: 68 (*Il Principe* 9).

[60] Machiavelli 1993: 121–2 (*Discorsi* 1. 5):

E sanza dubbio, se si considerrà il fine de' nobili e degli ignobili, si vedrà in quelli desiderio grande di dominare, ed in questi solo desiderio di non essere dominati, e per conseguente maggiore volontà di vivere liberi, potendo meno sperare di usurparla che non possono i grandi: talché essendo i popolari preposti a guardia d'una libertà, è ragionevole ne abbiano più cura; e non la potendo occupare loro, non permettino che altri la occupi.

(*Discorsi* 1. 5, p. 42; emphasis added)

Cf. 1. 4 (p. 38) on 'due umori' and the preface to book 3 of his *Istorie fiorentine*. On the greater responsibility of the nobles, see *Discorsi* 1. 5, 1. 37, and 2. 16.

Whether in ancient Rome or Renaissance Florence, as Sallust and Machiavelli agreed, the spread of ambition and avarice was accompanied by the decline of *virtus*.[61] In chapters 10–13 of the *Catilina*, Sallust had recounted the stages through which civic patriotism and harmony had given way to the pursuit of personal power and fratricidal wars. Later, in chapter 53, he concluded that only two men of eminent merit or *virtus* were left in the state: Gaius Caesar and Marcus Cato. Machiavelli, confronting the ultimate consequences of moral degeneracy and lawlessness, turned for a solution, even more unhesitatingly than Sallust, to the individual leader. If corruption had not penetrated the social fabric too deeply, he believed, it might still be possible to follow the ancient examples of Horatius Cocles, Scaevola, and Regulus and restore the state to its original principles. In times of extreme moral decay, however, only a *principe* could rescue society from impending chaos.

Machiavelli's overriding concern with successful action also made him far more willing than Sallust to depart from conventional morality.[62] Yet he may have perceived in Sallust's writing not only a similar blend of idealism and pessimism or similar notions of *virtus* and *fortuna*, but also a certain element of historical and political relativism inherent in these attitudes: a sceptical spirit that had led the Roman historian to challenge traditional judgements and lay bare the contrasts between words and actions; an ambiguity in the concept of *virtus*—on the one hand, linked to *ingenium bonum* ('good character'), on the other, an intellectual force or creative energy acting independently of ethical principles; and the realization that the moral character of the people both influenced and reflected the nature of the state's constitution and the functioning of laws.[63] It was in fact by elaborating upon such notions—and, of course, taking them well beyond such suggestions as could be found in Sallust— that Machiavelli formulated his ideas on constitutions adapted to the character of the people and the exigencies of the times.[64]

---

[61] On Machiavelli and Sallust, see Whitfield 1947: 22–107, and La Penna 1969: 53.

[62] At the same time, nevertheless, Machiavelli never lost sight of the distinction, which Sallust himself had stressed, between exercising power for the *bene comune* and the desire for mere personal aggrandizement. Caesar (whom he judged in the light of the republican tradition of tyrants) was never his ideal prince. Like Agathocles (*Il Principe* 8), he had risen to power by crime and cruelty, obtaining fame but not true glory.

[63] See La Penna 1969: 51–3 on the contradictions inherent in the concept of *virtus*: 'nei proemi soprattutto l'energia indomabile dell'uomo che agisce sulla realtà e la piega ai suoi fini' and '[la] purezza dell'animus dal corpo e dal vizio' (at 51). [See also Balmaceda 2017: esp. ch. 2, and bibliography, including Batstone 1990.]

[64] See *Discorsi* 1. 9–10 and 3. 1. Cf. Whitfield 1947: 157. When the moral character of the people had deteriorated beyond repair, it was necessary to turn to autocratic government: 'perché altri ordini e modi di vivere si debbe ordinare in uno suggetto cattivo che in uno

While Machiavelli thus developed more fully than his predecessors the civic humanist reading of Sallust—by emphasizing the expansionist drive of the Roman (and Roman-model) Republic, by asserting the dynamic nature of competition-dissension in the evolution of the state, and by exalting the importance of talent, intelligence, and ability (whether in the people collectively or in an individual leader)—he also set these ideas in a new context of political realism. If Sallust helped shape essential features of Machiavelli's political philosophy, the latter also suggested new pragmatic interpretations of his work that in the later decades of the sixteenth century became increasingly prevalent.

The detached and rational manner in which Machiavelli treated the matter of conspiracies, for example, illustrates an approach to the text that could give readers new perspectives on Sallust's work. In *Discorsi* 3. 6, where he discussed the Catilinarian conspiracy, he was, on one level, giving advice to statesmen on how to prevent or suppress such plots.[65] In fact, in the later sixteenth century, proponents of absolute monarchy quoted these and other passages to demonstrate the danger and futility of revolt. At the same time, however, by analysing in detail the causes of each conspiracy's success and failure, he could, and did, involve both himself and Sallust's *Catilina* in charges of subversiveness. In the eyes of many conservatives, such authors, by revealing the secret, behind-the-scenes preparations, might be encouraging, and actually instructing, would-be conspirators.

In the *Istorie fiorentine*, composed in the early 1520s, Machiavelli betrayed a similarly 'relativistic' approach to the question of conspiracy and, in this instance, to the use of Sallustian arguments themselves. In recounting the plot of Girolamo Olgiati against Galeazzo Sforza in 1476, he did not draw any explicit comparisons between Catiline and the Milanese humanist Cola Montano, whose 'revolutionary' teachings had supposedly inspired the conspirators. Rather, he described Montano's appeals to his students in words recalling Sallust's praises of the republic in *Catilina* 7. 2–3:

> that a people alone could be called happy and glorious whom nature and fortune had caused to be born under a republic, and not under a prince, because a republic nourishes virtuous men whilst princes destroy them; the one gains everything by the virtue of its citizens whilst the other dreads it.[66]

---

buono, né può essere la forma simile in una materia al tutto contraria' (Machiavelli 1993: 97, *Discorsi* 1. 18). Cf. 3. 8.

[65] See Osmond 1993: 428–9.

[66] Machiavelli 1976: 309 (*Florentine History* 7). Cf. La Penna 1969: 415. Corio 1855: 304–13 and 332–9 describes Olgiato's deposition in words recalling the conspirators'

Years earlier Machiavelli had evoked these same Sallustian ideals of *libertas* and *virtus* to stress the vitality of republican government and its superiority to monarchy. Now, as he reported Montano's lessons, he may have wished to convey his own—underlying or persistent—republican sympathies or even point to the demagogic perversion of Sallustian ideas. Whatever his personal feelings about the Milanese tyranny, however, what mattered in the long run was not so much the justice of this—or any—cause but rather its outcome. The plot, he commented brusquely, had 'produced no effect, because those upon whom [the conspirators] had relied for defence and support neither defended nor supported them'. Looking at the actions *ex eventu*, he concluded:

> Therefore let princes live and carry themselves in such a way that they are loved and honored, then no one can hope in killing them to escape himself, and let conspirators remember that all thoughts of relying upon the multitude are utterly vain, because although the people may be discontented they will never join or support you in danger.[67]

3. THE PRAGMATIC TRADITION: NORTHERN EUROPE IN THE SIXTEENTH AND EARLY SEVENTEENTH CENTURIES

The Humanist Background

While in early sixteenth-century Italy Sallust's work was being read in a new context of rational, pragmatic statecraft, it was just beginning to help mould a humanist political ethic in transalpine Europe. The same spirit of reform and renewal that had animated Italian humanists also encouraged their northern heirs to propagate the philosophy of an active life and public engagement. In France and England, however, and to some extent in the Habsburg Empire itself, the movement towards dynastic and centralized government naturally gave a different impetus to political and historical thought. The humanism that evolved had a national, not civic, focus, and what may be called participatory, rather than

---

feverish preparations in *B.C.* 27. Allegretti, under the year 1476 in his annals of Siena, writes: 'E questo fine ebbe la lor ferocità, con studiare el Catelinario per esser tanto più fieri e costanti a la detta impresa' (Allegretti 1733: col. 778). On Catilinarianism in the Renaissance, see n. 45 above.

[67] Machiavelli 1976: 313 (*Florentine History* 7).

communal, ideals. The patriotism of many northern humanists also revealed a militant, nationalistic character that could, in later decades, serve absolutist theories of government.

The publication of Sallust's *opera* in the late fifteenth and early sixteenth centuries, in both Latin and the vernacular, certainly helped promote this national consciousness.[68] In France in the 1470s, the first Sorbonne edition of the *Catilina* and *Jugurtha*, produced under the supervision of the visiting Italian scholar Filippo Beroaldo (and the first work of any classical historian printed at the University of Paris) enlisted Sallust's two monographs on behalf of Louis XI and his ambitious policy of territorial expansion and unification. Following the *Bellum Iugurthinum* were distichs, probably composed by the aspiring historian Robert Gaguin, rallying the French nation against the rebel Duke of Burgundy, Charles the Bold:

> Nunc parat arma virosque simul rex maximus orbis,
>   Hostibus antiquis exitium minitans.
> Nunc igitur bello studeas, gens Pariseorum,
>   Cui Martis quondam gloria magna fuit.
> Exempla tibi sint nunc fortia facta virorum
>   Quae digne memorat Crispus in hoc opere
> Armigerisque tuis Alemannos adnumeres, qui
>   Hos pressere libros, arma futura tibi.[69]
>
> Now the world's high king readies both arms and men,
>   threatening with destruction the ancient foes.
> Now may you be eager for war, people of Paris,
>   once endowed with Mars' great glory.
> May the brave deeds of men be examples for you now,
>   deeds that Crispus worthily recalls in this work,
> And may you number the Germans among your men-at-arms
>   who have printed these books, your weapons to be.

Translations of the monographs combined literary aims—and especially the French desire to enrich their native language and literature—with the humanist ideal of public service. In the introduction to his translation of the *Catilina*, published in 1528, the poet-explorer Jean Parmentier

---

[68] On the role of Sallust in early French humanism, see Osmond 1994, with bibliography including studies by J.-C. Margolin, Jacques Chocheyras, Paul Archambault, Donal Byrne, and Jean Porcher.

[69] Paris [1477–8], seen at the Bibliothèque Nationale. Cf. the verses subjoined to the *Bellum Iugurthinum* in a 1479 Lyons edition printed by Caesaris and Stol. In a letter to Robert Gaguin, appended to his *De origine et gestis Francorum compendium*, Erasmus praised his efforts to emulate the achievements of Livy and Sallust (and surpass those of the Italian humanists) (Erasmus 1906: 148–52, at 151, Ep. 45 [1495]).

reminded his patron, Jean Ango of Dieppe, how ancient history and Sallust's monograph in particular could produce 'fruict de grande utilité et d'exemple bon et salutaire à la chose publique'.[70] Guillaume Michel (Guillaume de Tours), author of the first French version of the *Jugurtha*, printed in 1532, modified the order of Sallust's last chapter in order to set in relief the famed martial qualities of the ancient (and modern) Gauls: the only enemy, Sallust acknowledged, whom the Romans had fought *pro salute non pro gloria* ('for their lives not for glory', *B.J.* 114. 2)![71]

In Germany, in the first decades of the sixteenth century, most teachers and scholars were preoccupied with adapting Sallust's work to Christian humanist and Protestant reform programmes, and correspondingly stressed the moral lessons of his writing. The Nuremberg statesman and captain Willibald Pirckheimer, however, borrowed motifs from the *Bellum Iugurthinum* to reinforce the message of his *Bellum Suitense sive Helveticum*, a monograph on the recent Swabian-Swiss war.[72] The time had come, he believed, to rescue German history from oblivion, and to record, as Sallust had done for the Romans, the memorable events and glorious exploits of the German people. Pirckheimer's history was dedicated to the Emperor Maximilian, who may well have recognized the literary allusions. Indeed it was the Habsburg ruler who, appreciating perhaps the patriotic and propagandistic value of Sallust's writing, had already commissioned Dietrich von Plieningen to compose a translation of the monographs.[73] As the latter announced in his dedicatory epistle to Maximilian, and in the accompanying letter to Ludwig, Duke of Bavaria, Sallust's *Bella* were especially relevant to his own times, providing examples of good (vs bad) government and the importance of pursuing the common interest ('der gemeine Nutz') as opposed to particularist and selfish ends. Even German philologists like Johann Rivius, who was chiefly concerned with emending the text and who produced the best critical edition to date of Sallust's *opera*, confidently recommended his work to future leaders of State and Church. The reading of ancient historians, Rivius wrote to the Bishop of Meissen, was essential training for all branches of a public career.[74]

---

[70] Parmentier 1528.   [71] Tours 1532.

[72] Pirckheimer 1737, composed in the early years of the sixteenth century. On the author, see Markwart 1886 and esp. Holzberg 1981.

[73] Plieningen 1515.

[74] *E ludis enim literariis fere proficiscuntur qui publica munera obeant, qui magistratum gerant, legesque ac iudicia administrent, qui principibus in consiliis adsint, qui rebus gerendis praeficiantur, qui gubernandis ecclesiis praesint, qui sacras ad populum conciones habeant, quique aliis hoc genus officiis muneribusque perfungantur* (Rivius 1547; the first edition appeared in Leipzig in 1539). Sallust was often cited in Catholic and Protestant sermons on

English humanists likewise turned to Sallust, not just to express their sentiments of national pride but also to train their civil servants.[75] In his popular treatise of 1532, *The Governour*, Thomas Elyot praised Sallust along with Caesar for his knowledge of political and military affairs.[76] Alexander Barclay, author of the first English translation of the *Jugurtha* (c.1520-2), was impressed by its stirring examples of patriotic spirit and martial courage (see Figure 16.3).[77] His patron, the Duke of Norfolk, had recently defeated the Scots at Flodden Field and, at the end of his preface, Barclay compared him to the 'mighty Marius'. Like the Roman consul who had triumphed over Jugurtha, 'tyran [and] usurper of the kyngdome of Numidy', Norfolk had 'vanguysshed the invasour and vyolent ennemy of the commenwayle of England'. Thomas More had taken a different approach in his *History of Richard III* (written between 1514 and 1518), using Jugurtha as a model for England's own 'tyrant' and 'usurper'.[78] Anticipating in many ways the more critical attitudes and psychological analysis of later 'politic history', he painted a dark, sinister picture of corruption, hypocrisy, and violence—the result of the *regnandi cupiditas* ('desire to rule') that Sallust had repeatedly condemned. More's *Utopia* of 1516 likewise drew on Sallust's monographs, as well as the *Epistulae*, to denounce the vices of his times, especially the evils of greed and luxury. In the tradition of civic humanism, however, he also found evidence in Sallust for the public virtues of a healthy and united society: honesty and justice, hard work, courage in warfare (when war was justified), and devotion to the *patria*—qualities that were sorely needed, More believed, to build and defend his own 'sceptred isle'.

---

the evils of avarice and luxury or the importance of peace and concord. See, for example, O'Malley 1979: 231-2. Luther also quoted from the monographs in his lectures on Genesis and Ecclesiastes.

[75] On English humanism and historiography, see in particular Weiss 1941; Levine 1970; and Levy 1967. On translations of the classics, see Lathrop 1933. [See now also the relevant contributions and bibliography in Kewes 2006.]

[76] Elyot 1907.

[77] Barclay, *The Famous Cronycle of the Warre which the Romayns had agaynst Iugurth, Usurper of the Kyngdome of Numidy*. Figure 16.3 shows the author presenting his work to the Duke of Norfolk in a woodcut from the preface to this edition (Williamstown, MA, Chapin Library, Williams College). [See now the critical edition of Barclay's translation by Waite 2014.]

[78] More 1963 (*Richard III*) and 1965 (*Utopia*). On More's use of Sallust (as well as other historians) in both the *Utopia* and *Richard III*, see the notes to these editions and Chomarat 1985.

¶ The preface of Alexander Barclay preest/ vnto the
right hye and mighty prince: Thomas
Duke of Northfolke.

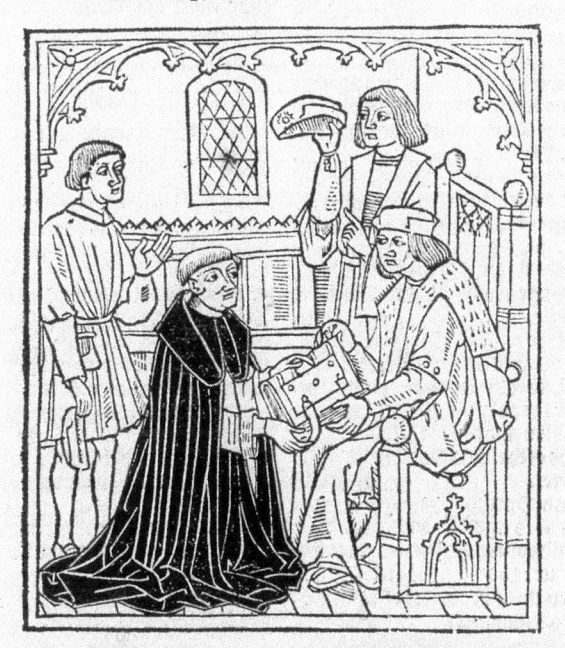

Reuerēdiſſimo in Chriſto patri ac
dño: dño Ioanni Veyſy exonienſi e-
piſcopo Alexander Barclay preſby
ter debita cum obſeruantia. S.

MEMINI me ſuperiori-
bus annis cū adhuc facel-
li regij preſul eſſes: paſtor
vigilantiſſime: tuis ſuaſi-
onibus incitatū: vt Criſpi
Saluſtij hyſtoriā (quā Iu-
gurthynū bellū dictitant) e romana lin
gua:

Right mighty/
hye/ and magnifi-
cent prince: myne
huble ſerupce/ due
vnto your grace.
And the behement
affection which I
haue vnto your honour and ppetuall
fame/ impelleth me often tymes to be-
upſe/ and to reuolue in mynde: what
ſerupce/ or pleaſure my ſympleneſſe
might

Figure 16.3. Alexander Barclay presenting his translation of Sallust's *Bellum Iugurthinum* to Thomas, duke of Norfolk. Woodcut, from the first edition (London, [1522]), sig. a 4v.

Williamstown, MA, Chapin Library, Williams College (by permission of the Williams College Special Collections).

The Radicalization of Political Thought

By the second half of the sixteenth century many of the northern European countries were experiencing—as Italy already had in the first decades of the Cinquecento—their own calamities: religious turmoil, social conflict, and political strife. Here, too, the spirit of consensus, of shared values and aspirations, that had united humanists in the service of city state or nation state, was rapidly dissolving. While most historians and political thinkers of late Renaissance Italy, however, endeavoured to reconcile *ragion di stato* with the Tridentine programme of moral and religious orthodoxy, there was a greater propensity in northern Europe to confront political issues in objective, secular terms and to develop political theory along more radical lines. Indeed, if it was Machiavelli who had set the reading of Sallust within a new pragmatic context, it was in countries north of the Alps, rather than in his native land, that the implications of this approach were actually realized. Here, in the courts, universities, and intellectual circles of France and the Netherlands, and later in England and Germany as well, political theorists not only stressed the conservative nature of Sallust's views (in advocating social stability), but also recognized the possibility of enlisting his work in support of utilitarian ethics and monarchical absolutism.

France during the Religious Wars

The new pragmatic approach to Sallust was foreshadowed in treatises like Jean Bodin's *Methodus ad facilem historiarum cognitionem* of 1566, in which Sallust was linked with such 'serious and sober' authors as Polybius and Tacitus and recommended for his political experience and careful reporting of events.[79] By the mid-1570s, at the height of the religious wars, the reading of Sallust, in the company of such political historians as Tacitus, Machiavelli, and Guicciardini, undoubtedly helped bolster the call for a strong royal authority. His work was well known and appreciated at the court of Henry III, and a letter of 1575 from Jacopo Corbinelli, *lecteur du roi* (as well as apologist for the St Bartholomew's Day Massacre) requests a copy of Sallust for the king, perhaps to be read at one of the gatherings of the court or in one of the private *réunions* in

---

[79] Bodin 1945. Cf. Baudouin 1579.

the king's apartments.[80] In the annotations to his own copy of the *Bella* (a 1576 edition by Pier Vettori) Corbinelli devoted most of his attention to textual questions and literary analysis, comparing and contrasting the styles of Sallust and Tacitus. But he did not overlook the practical value that the monographs could have for his own *patria* (Florence) as well as for the monarchy of Henry III, and he borrowed *sententiae* and *exempla* from Sallust, as well as from Tacitus and other Roman historians and philosophers, to illustrate his 1576 edition of Guicciardini's *Ricordi* and his copy of Machiavelli's *Discorsi*. Meanwhile, Jérôme de Chomedey, another member of the French court and translator of Guicciardini's *Storia d'Italia*, completed new French versions of the *Catilina* and *Jugurtha*. In the dedicatory letter of his *Histoire de la conjuration de Catilina*, he praised the superior efficiency of monarchy in suppressing revolts and called for unconditional obedience to the French throne:

> Sire,... God always grants to the Prince who lives in such a way [in piety and justice] the means to punish rebels and bring them to reason. And when such troubles arise, Princes can bring things to order more easily than Republics, as witnessed in the Roman Republic which was saved from such a disaster more by its good fortune than by its great virtue. Now if Princes who possess absolute power never speak more worthily than when they call themselves ministers of God and acknowledge themselves bound to the law, what, I pray, will be the duty of subjects?[81]

Considering the number of recent conspiracies in France (despite the supposed superiority of monarchy) and the conspiratorial atmosphere at court, Chomedey's translation of the *Catilina* could not have been more germane. To make sure readers understood the message, nevertheless, he had the following epigram inscribed on the title page: 'Ceux qui usurperont le glaive, periront par le glaive.' He also added to his work a translation of *Discorsi* 3. 6: the 'discours de Machiavel touchant les

---

[80] On Corbinelli and his annotated copy of Sallust's monographs (Paris, BnF, J. 13,457), see Osmond 1994.

[81] Dieu baille tousiours au Prince qui vit de telle façon, le moyen de chastier les mutins et les faire venir à la raison. Et quand tels inconveniens surviennent, les Princes plus aisement que les Republiques y peuvent donner ordre, temoing la Rep. romaine qui fut sauvé d'un tel desastre, plustost par sa bonne fortune, que par sa grande vertu. Or si les Princes qui ont puissance absolue, ne parlent jamais plus dignement que quand ils se disent ministres de Dieu, et qu'eux mesmes se confessent estre obligez à la loy, quel sera je vous prie le devoir des sujets?

conjurations'.[82] While Sallust had demonstrated the fate of revolutionaries like Catilina, who had taken up arms against lawful government, so Machiavelli, quoting Tacitus (*Hist.* 4. 8. 2), had exhorted the subjects of a prince to bear with *all* rulers, good or bad, lest, as he warned, rebellion involve them and their country in ruin.

This tendency to couple Sallust with Tacitus was indicative of the new attitude towards his work. In the early Renaissance, Sallust had regularly been linked with Livy and Caesar in a triumvirate of Roman historians: models of historical writing and sources of patriotic inspiration. Each had excelled in a different genre of history: the annals of a city state, the commentary, and the monograph; moreover, each had his distinctive style, ranging from Livy's 'milky richness' to Sallust's brevity and abruptness. Yet all three authors concentrated on the political and military affairs of the Roman Republic and endorsed (albeit for various reasons) the aristocratic ethos of *virtus* and *gloria*. Historical writing itself was understood as a means of serving the *res publica*: preserving the memory of ancient valour and heroic feats of arms, inculcating civic virtues, inspiring pride in an expanding empire.

If, in the later Renaissance, Sallust was paired more frequently with Tacitus, it not only reveals a greater sensitivity to affinities in style and mood, but also a re-evaluation of his work in light of new political and moral priorities. Both authors, to quote Sir Ronald Syme, 'belonged to that company of searching and subversive writers, preoccupied with power and the play of chance..., finding their delectation in disillusionment'.[83] While Tacitus excelled in exposing the *arcana imperii*, Sallust unmasked the self-seeking aims of party leaders. If Tacitus recognized the advantages, or necessity, of a new regime (where the old rule by the Senate and people had failed) and was even prepared to suffer tyrants (rather than encourage futile opposition), Sallust too sympathized with the need for public order and a strong government to enforce that order. Certainly, he was no proponent of monarchy, let alone autocracy, but his repeated denunciations of factional strife, his aversion to *res novae* ('revolutionary change'), and his appeals for vigorous, decisive action could lend support to apologies for authoritarian regimes—as could many *sententiae* taken (in or out of context) from

---

[82] Chomedey mentions in his preface to the king that he has added to his translation of the *Catilina* 'un discours de Machiavel touchant les conjurations, pourceque là dedans y a une fort bonne instruction, tant pour les Princes que pour les sujets, accompagnée d'une infinité de beaulx exemples, entre lesquels celuy de Catilin n'est oublié'.

[83] Syme 1964: 256.

the speeches in his various works. Passages in the *Catilina*, especially in Cato's oration in chapter 52, appeared to condone the use of extralegal methods in times of emergency. The second *Epistula ad Caesarem* called for *lasting peace* and proffered advice to a leader whose position, at least from the standpoint of the Renaissance, was clearly monarchical. A French translation of this letter was published by Chomedey in 1582, and the increasing popularity of both *Epistulae* in the later Renaissance testifies to the appeal of these writings (still generally ascribed to Sallust) in a period of bitter civil wars.

In the academic year 1578-9, the French scholar Marc-Antoine Muret lectured on Sallust at the University of Rome as a prelude, it seems, to the course he hoped to teach (and, two years later, did teach) on Tacitus' *Annales*.[84] Prominent members of the Farnese Circle, the Spanish philologist Pedro Chacòn and the librarian to 'il Gran Cardinale', Fulvio Orsini—whose collection of antiquities included a Roman contorniate with Sallust's portrait (see Figure 16.4)—both pointed out Tacitus' borrowings from Sallust in their annotations on his texts.[85] Montaigne, who had been a pupil of Muret at the Collège de Guyennes, and who may have heard his lectures on Tacitus in Rome in 1580-1, recognized the similar stylistic features of the two historians. In fact, the growing preference for the *genus humile* reflected not only a change in literary and rhetorical taste, from the elaborate Asianism of forensic oratory to the simpler, more sober style of neo-Attic prose, but also a different intellectual atmosphere. The qualities of brevity and conciseness, the figures of wit and thought, suited the reflective mood of philosophical essays, the confidential correspondence of royal counsellors, the conversation at court, and the subtle, rational analysis of political interest.[86]

---

[84] Muretus 1789: 'Oratio' and 'In Sallustium Notae'.

[85] Chacòn 1594 (published posthumously); Orsini 1595. See Figure 16.4 for the drawing of the contorniate, accompanied by the drawing of a funeral inscription from the Horti Sallustiani, and Orsini's notes explaining what he believes to be the origin of this nummus (Orsini 1570: fig. 90). On the reverse are three female figures, probably musicians, with the legend *MONE GEAS*. I thank Katherine Geffcken for relating Orsini's exemplar to the series of contorniates bearing portraits of Sallust (Alföldi and Alföldi 1976: 1: 28-32, #106; 2: 101; and 6, pt. 1, Tafel 34-37, 11). She suggests that the legend is probably a misreading of the phrase *PETRONI PLACEAS* found on all other exemplars of this group.

[86] Montaigne 1931. See especially 1. 21 and 2. 17, where he compares Sallust with other historians and praises his style. Voisin de La Popelinière 1599: 321-2. On changes in rhetorical tastes and ancient models, see esp. Morris W. Croll's essays in Patrick and Evans 1966 and Fumaroli 1980 and 1981.

> M·POBLICIVS· M· L· MODES
> TVS·EROTI·C·SALLVSTI·CRISPI
> SERVO·METELLIANO·FRATRI·SVO

M·AVRELIVS· PACORVS
M·COCCEIVS·STRATOCLES
AEDITVI·VENERIS·HORTORVM
SALLVSTIANORVM·BASEM·CVM
PALMENTO MARMORATO
DEANAE
·D·   ·D·

C· Sallustius Crispus, ex nobili Sallustiorum familia, Amiterni, in agro Sabino natus esse dicitur: ibiquoq̃ annum agens lxij aliquot post occisum Cæsarem annis, obijsse traditur. itaq̃ facile adducor ut credam. Amiterninos ciuis sui, & historici clarissimi imaginem, nobilitandæ urbis causa nomismate signasse! quod certe à multis alijs Ciuitatibus factum esse animaduertimus illud tamen ex ipsa literarῠ & nomismatis forma satis constat, aliquot post Sallustium seculis numum hunc ex ere signatum fuisse. qui Sallustij ne historici, an eius qui consul multis post annis fuit imaginem referat, cum pro certo affirmare non possim: sequor tamen eorum opinionem, qui ad historicum pertinere existimant. de Sallustianis autem hortis, quorum in antiqua inscriptione fit mentio, ita Cornelius Tacitus scribit, uentitabat Nero ad pontem Miluium quo solutius urbem extra lasciuiret; igitur regredienti per uiam Flaminiam, compositas insidias, ...euitatas, quoniam di uerso itinere Sallustianos in hortos remeauerit &c. horum autem hortorum meminit etiam Plinius li vij cap. ib hodieq̃ uestigia apparent in colle: non longe à porta Collina, ubi inscriptio e marmore patrum nostrorum temporibus fuit eruta, & in hortis tunc Angeli Colotij uiri optimi, et de omni antiquitate bene meriti collocatα.

Figure 16.4. Portrait of Sallust on a Roman contorniate in the collection of Fulvio Orsini, with other drawings and notes.

Imagines et elogia virorum illustrium (Rome, 1570), p. 90 (by permission of the Ministero dei Beni e delle Attività Culturali e del Turismo).

Justus Lipsius and 'Prudentia Mixta'

The scholar who was most influential, nevertheless, in reshaping Sallust's reputation as an exponent of political prudence was the Flemish-born editor and annotator of Tacitus, Justus Lipsius.[87] In the 1570s, as Spanish troops overran the Netherlands, Lipsius began his long peregrinations through European courts and universities, anxious to avoid polemics and ready to change his religion as the occasion demanded. Seneca and Tacitus, to whom he devoted most of his studies in the following years, helped sustain his faith in the inner freedom and dignity of man, while guiding him in a policy of outward conformity.

In Lipsius' hierarchy of ancient historians, Sallust occupied a distinguished second place, just below Tacitus and above both Livy and Caesar. In the Preface to his *Notae*, appended to his 1574 edition of Tacitus' *Opera*, he credited Sallust alone, among all historians of this age, with combining in his work *delectatio, fides*, and *vita* ('pleasure', 'trustworthiness', and 'what is important for life', namely, moral and political instruction).[88] Sallust, he concluded, deserved the title *princeps Senatus historici* ('leader of the Senate of historians'); Tacitus was in turn introduced as his successor and imitator. In his major political work, the *Politicorum sive Civilis doctrinae libri sex* of 1589, Lipsius drew frequently on Sallust to demonstrate the benefits of monarchy and the necessity of public order.[89] Passages from the *Bella* and *Historiae* illustrated the antiquity of kingship, the superiority of *iusti domini* to popular government, and the Stoic virtues of *clementia, modestia*, and *constantia* in the ideal ruler. The chapters on *civilis prudentia* quoted Lepidus on the importance of *severitas* and Cato on the necessity of strong, preventive punishments. If the use of fraud and deception in governing a state created a moral dilemma, Lipsius attempted to reach a compromise. He could not bring himself to agree with Lepidus' remark that any and all means of securing power were honourable.[90] But the practice of *diffidentia* and *corruptio*, as Sallust had described elsewhere,

---

[87] Lipsius 1675. On Lipsius' Neostoicism and political thought, see esp. Oestreich 1982 and Morford 1991.

[88] For the Preface see Ulery 1986: 6: 113–14. Cf. Morford 1991: 50 and n. 54, who also states, however, that Lipsius emphasized Tacitus' superiority in *prudentia* (political wisdom), *iudicium* (choice of material, historical truth, moral-psychological insight), and *utilitas*, especially in his later work (ibid. 149–50 and 156).

[89] Lipsius 1675, vol. 4. On *civilis prudentia* see book 4, esp. chs. 5–6 and 9–10; on *prudentia mixta*, chs. 13–14.

[90] 'Oratio Lepidi', *Historiarum fragmenta selecta*, 1. 55. 8.

could reasonably be mixed with *prudentia*—providing they were used in moderation and the end (the common good) justified the means.

In summarizing his views on history and historians in the notes to book 1 of the *Politica*, Lipsius again ranked Sallust next to Tacitus in importance. He was even inclined, it seems, to place Sallust on the same level as Tacitus, or higher—were it not so difficult to judge his work from the few samples that survived. If the author of the *Annales* and *Historiae* was 'the true leader of both wisdom and prudence'(*dux Sapientiae simul et Prudentiae*), he concluded, then 'let the other be C. Sallustius; indeed the first, if only we had [all] his books' (*alter esto C. Sallustius; omnino primus, si libros modo eius haberemus*). Comparing him to Thucydides, he praised his work for its truthfulness, explanation of causes, and careful judgement, as well as its brevity and gravity of style—all indispensable qualities of pragmatic history.[91]

Lipsius' Influence in France and England

In Northern Europe, especially in France and England, Lipsius' view of Sallust as an exponent of prudential ethics found numerous and articulate spokesmen. The French author Pierre Charron borrowed Sallustian *sententiae* to illustrate Neostoic doctrines and *politique* principles in his treatise *De la sagesse* of 1601.[92] Rulers, he urged, must not only curb the mutinous temper of the crowd but also learn to exercise diffidence, even deception, in conducting affairs of state. The king's ministers and counsellors should learn the art of dissimulation, especially when kingship had degenerated into tyranny. As Sallust (and Tacitus) had advised, it was better to practise discretion and moderation than attempt a perilous opposition. Gabriel Chappuys, author of *La citadelle de la royauté* of 1604, improved upon Jean Bodin's concept of *la souveraine puissance* by repeating a famous phrase from Memmius' speech in *Jugurtha* 31. 26: *impune quaelibet facere, id est Regem esse* ('to do with impunity whatever one likes, that is to be king').[93] In order to underscore the absolute nature of royal power and the subjects' duty of unconditional obedience, he also drew freely upon the history of Persian and Roman rulers and the theory of divine right monarchy. Other examples from Sallust, as well as from Tacitus, helped Gabriel Naudé illustrate his theory of *raison d'état*.[94]

---

[91] Lipsius 1675: 216 (Notes to 1. 9). Cf. 214.
[92] Charron 1836: esp. 1. 52 and 2. 2–5.
[93] Quoted in Thuau 1966: 392. Cf. Sallust, *B.J.* 31. 26: *nam inpune quae lubet facere, id est regem esse*.
[94] Naudé 1633; 1639; 1646.

Taking Lipsius' and Charron's ideas of prudence one step further, he postulated a *prudence extraordinaire* designed for political emergencies. When the survival of the state was at risk, he argued, all means of deception and force were legitimate. Paraphrasing the advice to Caesar in *Epistula* 1. 6. 1 he commented: *sic multorum saluti potius quam libidini consulendum* ('so one must look after the safety rather than the pleasure of the multitude').

The only conspicuous departure from this trend was the young Abbé de Gondi's *La conjuration du comte Jean-Louis de Fiesque* of 1638–9, an audacious apology for revolution aimed against Cardinal de Richelieu, the perceived enemy of the French nobility.[95] While purportedly translating Agostino Mascardi's *La congiura di Gio. Luigi de' Fieschi* of 1629, he turned the figure of Fieschi from a perverse and treacherous criminal into an impassioned, heroic rebel, bent on overthrowing the oppressive Doria faction. Like Sallust's Catiline, he possessed immense daring and energy; like Caesar (in Sallust's ch. 54), he sought for opportunities to display his prowess and dreamed of *actions éclatatantes*. Even the future Cardinal de Retz, however, shared the practical concerns of his age. As a manual for conspirators, his *Conjuration* did not simply exalt the pursuit of *gloire* as an end in itself; it aimed at teaching the *successful* conquest of power.

In early seventeenth-century England, the popularity of Lipsius' *Politica*, along with the spread of 'politic history' and Neostoic philosophy, also encouraged a pragmatic reading of Sallust's *opera*.[96] In an atmosphere of political intrigue and escalating religious tensions, contemporary conspirators were branded as dangerous and sinister Catilines; the figure of Cato was represented as a model of Stoic wisdom and constancy; *sententiae* and *exempla* drawn from the *Historiae* and *Epistulae ad Caesarem*, as well as from the monographs, demonstrated lessons of public and private prudence. Here, too, Sallust was cited in tandem with Tacitus, often along with Machiavelli and Guicciardini. Whereas Tacitus, however, served chiefly as a 'vehicle of discontent' for embittered members of the Jacobean court,[97] Sallust was called upon to strengthen royal authority in the face of growing opposition.

---

[95] Gondi (Cardinal de Retz) 1880.
[96] On trends in English historical and political thought in this period, with attention to classical sources and models, see Levy 1972 and 1987: 1–34; Salmon 1989; and contributions to Burns 1991. [See also the additional references in n. 75 above and Osmond and Ulery 2017: Introduction.]
[97] Salmon 1989: 224.

Robert Dallington, author of the *Aphorismes Civill and Militarie*, published in 1613, drew upon Sallust as one of his principal ancient authorities.[98] Guicciardini's *Storia d'Italia* had recently been translated into English from the earlier French rendering by Jérôme Chomedey (the same Frenchman who had translated Sallust's monographs) and Dallington now set out to elucidate his history with examples from contemporary events and political axioms. Sallust could counsel rulers and statesmen on a wide variety of civil and military affairs, but Dallington relied upon him particularly in his chapters on diplomacy and public relations. Sallustian aphorisms warned the prince to take heed of his rivals' personal interests in seeking alliance, to avoid the advice of persons he had previously injured, and, in the event of popular insurrections, to curry the favour of the masses by singling out only the leaders of the revolt for (exemplary) punishment.[99] Other maxims, which Dallington may have borrowed indirectly from Charron and Lipsius, recommended swift, severe, and preventive punishments at even the slightest suspicion of treason. In times of emergency, even force and deception could be allowed. The importance of suppressing immediately any threat of sedition was a recurrent theme in the *Aphorismes*, and Dallington reinforced Machiavellian precepts and Lipsius' doctrine of *prudentia mixta* with Cato's warnings to his fellow senators, paraphrasing B.C. 52. 11–12: *nec ista mansuetudo et misericordia... in miseriam vertat* ('let not that kindness and mercy... turn into [our] suffering') and *dum paucis sceleratis parcis, bonos omnes is perditum* ('be not prodigal of our blood, and in sparing a few scoundrels, bring ruin upon all good men').[100]

In general, Dallington, like Lipsius, tried to steer a middle course between conventional ethics and political realism, and drew upon Sallust in the same spirit. When it came to summing up his views on morality and the state towards the end of his work, however, he used Tacitus to illustrate a moderate position and Sallust the extreme:

> All (1) Morallists hold nothing profitable that is not honest. (2) Some Politicks have inverted this order.... Howsoever those former may seeme

---

[98] Dallington 1613.
[99] Ibid. 3 (1. ii). Dallington commented on international alliances, saying: 'Hence is it that Leagues are made betweene States for the mutuall supplement and support one of another. But the colleagues have commonly their particular ends, besides the generall good pretended.' He then illustrated this with two statements from Sallust: (1) *Bocchum legati monuerunt ne florentes res suas cum Iugurthae perditis misceret* (B.J. 83. 1) and (2) *Amicitias inimicitiasque non ex re sed ex commodo aestimare magisque vultum quam ingenium bonum habere* (B.C. 10. 5).
[100] Ibid. 245 (4. xviii); 321 (5. xxiv).

too streight laced, these surely are too loose. (3) For there is a middle way betweene both, which a right Statesman must take.
(1) Nullum utile est, quod non sit honestum (Cic. *off.* l. 2) [Nothing is profitable which is not (also) good.] ...
(2) Cui omnia cum pretio honesta videntur. (Salust. *Iug.*) [To whom all things seem honest for a price.] ...
(3) Velimus Principem alto animo, sed tamen eruditum utilia honestis miscere. (Tacit. *Agric.*) [We would like a prince of noble mind, but nevertheless brought up to mix the useful with the good.] ...
Intuta quae indecora. (Tacit. *hist.*) [What is dishonorable is unsafe.][101]

In this particular instance, it seems, Sallust outdid Tacitus himself as a 'politic historian'.

Recent events in England, from the Essex rebellion in 1601 to the Gunpowder Plot of 1605, had meanwhile awakened popular interest in Sallust's *opera*, especially the *Catilina*. King James not only labelled the Plotters 'worse than Catilines', but also paraphrased Sallust's words in *Catilina* 52. 3 (cf. 59. 5): *qui patriae parentibus, aris atque focis suis bellum paravere*[102] ('who have plotted warfare upon their country, parents, altars, and hearths'). Thomas Heywood, poet, playwright, and actor as well as translator, published the first English version of the *Bella* in 1609, based upon the earlier French rendering by Louis Meigret.[103] There was, moreover, a special feature of Heywood's edition that emphasized Sallust's role as a 'politic historian': the inclusion of an English translation of Bodin's chapter 4 of the *Methodus*, devoted to the aims and methods of historical writing and the criteria for evaluating ancient historians. The passage on Sallust described him as 'a most sincere Author and deepe Statist'.[104] Coming as it did from the spokesman of 'la puissance souveraine', it was a fitting introduction and an authoritative endorsement.

Some two years later, in 1611, the story of Catiline's conspiracy was enacted on the London stage. As a theatrical representation, Ben Jonson's drama proved a dismal failure (although Jonson himself continued to consider it one of his best works).[105] As a political statement, however, it made its point. Catiline, the villain of the play, was transformed into a Senecan-like monster of cruelty and impiety. Cicero and Cato appeared as the saviours of the commonwealth, steadfast defenders of public order,

---

[101] Ibid. 314–15 (5. xix).   [102] Quoted in De Luna 1967: 74 and 91.
[103] Heywood 1609.
[104] Ibid. 'On the Choice of History, by Way of Preface' (unnumbered p. 8).
[105] Jonson 1973: Introduction and Appendix B, 'Jonson's Classical Sources'. [See now also Addendum I: The *Catilina* and *Jugurtha* in Renaissance and Early Modern drama.]

who also, however, lent support to policies of public prudence. Cicero, for instance, shrewdly exploited favourable situations in order to ensnare the conspirators. Cato frankly urged the consul to adapt his course to the needs of the moment. The captain of state, he declared, 'must know his tides, his currents, how to shift his sails' according to the winds and seas. Sallust's *Catilina*—buttressed with Costanzo Felici's *De coniuratione L. Catilinae liber unus*[106] and Cicero's orations—offered Jonson an opportunity to write the kind of academic drama he preferred while professing his loyalty to the Stuart monarchy.

The Oxford professor Degory Wheare quoted both Lipsius and the German scholar Christoph Coler in his lectures on history, first published in 1623 as the *De ratione et methodo legendi historias dissertatio*.[107] Sallust, he agreed, surely deserved Lipsius' title of 'President of the Senate of Historians'. As Coler had written to Stanislas Zelenius in 1601, he was the 'perfect historian', endowed with a profound knowledge of public affairs. Tacitus, on the other hand, still aroused a certain distrust. Quoting Casaubon this time, Wheare reminded his king that the *Annales* might spread pernicious examples and precepts of tyranny.

4. SURVIVING TRADITIONS AND MINOR CURRENTS

Not every historian or political thinker naturally interpreted Sallust in this new pragmatic mode. Throughout most of Italy, for instance, writers, especially of *ars historica* treatises, focused primarily on the stylistic or moralizing aspects of Sallust's *opera*—character portraits and battle scenes, speeches and aphorisms—while scholars assembled the scattered fragments of the *Historiae* and debated textual problems.[108] There was also a current, or undercurrent, of anti-Sallustian criticism

---

[106] Costanzo Felici's *De coniuratione L. Catilinae liber unus*, with *De exilio M. Tullii Ciceronis liber unus, De reditu M. Tullii Ciceronis liber unus*, and *Epistola M. T. Ciceronis ad Lu. Luceium*, dedicated to Pope Leo X, was published in Rome in 1518. It was intended as a revised version of Sallust's monograph, which, according to its young author, had not given Cicero the credit he deserved in suppressing the conspiracy of 63 BCE. See Osmond and Ulery 1995. In the dedicatory letter of his English translation of 1541 (reprinted in 1557) to Henry VIII, Paynell underscored the fate of recent rebels against the English throne and the necessity of extralegal measures in punishing crimes against the kingdom.

[107] Wheare 1685: 104–8.

[108] On aspects of Italian historiography and political thought in the later sixteenth and early seventeenth centuries, see: Bertelli 1973; Cochrane 1973 and 1970, as well as 1981; Cotroneo 1971; Spini 1948; Toffanin 1972; plus the studies on rhetoric by Croll in Patrick and Evans 1966, and Fumaroli 1980 and 1981.

that denounced Sallust for his supposed neglect of Cicero and his bias in favour of Caesar. Its origins can be traced to an early sixteenth-century humanist, Costanzo Felici of Castel Durante, who was anxious to win the favour of Leo X and to prove himself as a Ciceronian stylist. Although his name and identity were often ignored or forgotten in the following decades, his arguments—which foreshadowed the criticisms of Mommsen and Schwartz in the late 1800s—survived in the writings of a number of authors, particularly Francesco Robortello, Gianantonio Viperano, Melchior Cano, Famiano Strada, and Agostino Mascardi (as well as in the English translation of 1541 by Thomas Paynell, which preceded the English version of Sallust's own *Catilina* by more than half a century). In the early seventeenth century these criticisms culminated in the work of Paolo Beni of Gubbio.[109]

To the extent that Sallust's work was cited in a political context, the message simply contrasted the benefits of peace with the dangers and evils of rebellion. Earlier interpretations of the same nature had already appeared in fifteenth-century Rome and Florence, where writers like Alberti and Poliziano had celebrated the 'Ciceronian' victory of stable government over the forces of violence and disorder. Now, in post-Tridentine Italy, historians who recounted the 1547 uprising of Gianluigi Fieschi in Genoa or the earlier barons' war in the kingdom of Naples mingled Sallustian maxims with lessons of Divine Providence. The failure of Catilinarian conspirators, ancient or modern, was proof of God's judgement: an example of divine retribution and warning to would-be rebels.[110] Moreover, many authors who did perceive a pragmatic element in Sallust's *opera* reacted with dismay. The Genoese historian Iacopo Bonfadio, writing an account of Fieschi's conspiracy in his *Annales Genuenses* (c.1448–1550), placed the *Catilina* in the same class of dangerously subversive books as 'the life of Nero' and the *Prince*. Agostino Mascardi, author of *La congiura di Gio. Luigi de' Fieschi* of

---

[109] See Osmond and Ulery 1995 and n. 105 above. As Schindler pointed out, these criticisms foreshadowed the 'Mommsen-Schwartz thesis' of the late nineteenth century.

[110] Historians hastened to condemn the attempted coup of Gianluigi Fieschi in Genoa in 1548, contrasting the *concordia civium* formerly enjoyed under the 'just and benevolent' guidance of Andrea Doria with the factional discord that had fostered the criminal ambitions of the young Fieschi. See, for example, Foglietta 1571. Cf. La Penna's 1969: 'Appendice seconda'. The Neapolitan historian Camillo Porzio introduced Sallustian character sketches and speeches into his own account of the uprising, while paraphrasing Machiavelli's warnings against potential conspirators (Porzio 1839). In his *Congiura de' baroni* of 1565 (Porzio 1958) he adapted Sallust's analysis of moral and social corruption to his account of the Neapolitan kingdom in the late 1400s, and particularly the 'pravi passioni' of the barons.

1629, warned that, by teaching those wicked *materie di Stato*, the *Catilina* (like the works of Tacitus and Machiavelli) might actually inspire revolutionary schemes.[111]

On the other hand, where civic institutions retained some degree of vitality—as they did (for a time) in Venice and in a few cities of the German Empire—or where popular governments supplanted foreign rulers—as in the Dutch confederation—Sallust's work could offer fresh support to republican and participatory ideals. In the Netherlands, the classical scholar and jurist Theodorus (Dirk) Graswinckel published a new commentary on the *Catilina* with an eye to defending the Dutch constitution.[112] At a time of escalating conflict between the republican forces of Holland and the monarchist movement of the Orangists, Sallust's work, as Graswinckel suggested in his preface, might strengthen the resolve of his fellow citizens and help preserve their hard-won liberties.

5. PRINCEPS HISTORIAE ROMANAE

If Sallust remained the most popular of ancient historians from the fifteenth to the early seventeenth centuries, it was largely due to the versatility and adaptability of his thought and writing. More effectively than any other classical historian, he helped stimulate and shape, sustain and legitimize the new directions in Renaissance political life—while still giving voice to conventional attitudes and traditional values. Cristoph Coler seems to have understood these qualities of Sallust's work when he recommended the *Opera* to his patrons in the Senate of Nuremberg. He himself had studied and propagated Sallust's political thought in the broadest possible ways. His 1599 edition of the *Epistulae* with its *Notae politicae* dedicated to two young noblemen, called upon Sallust, counsellor of princes, in advocating stern measures of repression to eliminate opposition and restore peace in a politically troubled country. In the same year, he proposed Sallust's work to the Senate of Nuremberg, recommending his history as 'none other than a mirror' of the city's

---

[111] Bonfadio 1586; Mascardi 1629. Such judgements were often accompanied by criticisms of Sallust's 'unfair' treatment of Cicero (as, for example, in Mascardi's *Dell'arte istorica* of 1636)—criticisms that originated in Felici's *De coniuratione L. Catilinae liber*. To the extent that there was any prudential reading of Sallust, it might be found in the identification of Sallust the historian with his great-nephew, C. Sallustius Crispus II of Tacitean fame. See, for instance, Botero 1948 and esp. Boccalini 1910–48.

[112] Graswinckelius 1642. Hugo Grotius, meanwhile, recommended Sallust's *Epistulae ad Caesarem* to royal counsellors and envoys in his 'Epistola de studio politico'. See Naudé 1633.

own *res publica aristocratica*, the model of a free imperial city and the example of how a healthy, harmonious polis should be constituted and governed.[113]

Throughout the Renaissance, editors and commentators quoted the verses by the Roman poet Martial praising Sallust as 'first' or 'foremost' in Roman history:

> Hic erit, ut perhibent doctorum corda virorum,
> Primus Romana Crispus in historia. (14. 191)

This Crispus, as the hearts of learned men declare, will be the first in Roman history.

Justus Lipsius had recently hailed Sallust as *princeps Senatus historici*.[114] Coler now entitled his new edition of Sallust's works: *C. Sallustii Crispi Historiae Romanae Principis Opera* and, in his dedicatory letter to the Nuremberg Senate, improvised on the same theme. *Principi civitati Germaniae*, he wrote, *principem historicum Romanum commendo* ('To the leading city of Germany I commend the leading Roman historian.').

* * *

The story of Sallust's *fortuna* in the Renaissance elucidates the changing mental climate of a complex and protean age. The Renaissance has often been described as an age of crisis and transition, and the varying uses of Sallust throughout these centuries clarify important developments in the intellectual and moral currents of the period: a shift from the ideals, or ideologies, of civic humanism and republican liberty to the philosophies of absolutism and *raison d'état*. At the same time, the study of Sallust's reception in this era illustrates the rich potential for meaning inherent in his work, and his capacity as a historian and literary artist to elicit new interpretations in a continuing dialogue between the reader and the text.[115]

The writers who cited, borrowed, imitated, and appropriated Sallust's ideas were not seeking, for the most part, to understand his point of view and to interpret his thought and writing in its original (Roman) context.[116] On the contrary, they sought to make his work relevant to

---

[113] Colerus 1599a.
[114] Preface to his *Notae* to the 1574 edition of Tacitus, transcribed in Ulery 1986: 6: 113.
[115] Cf. the theory of *Rezeptionsgeschichte* developed by the Constance School and particularly by Hans Robert Jauss in a number of studies including 1972, 1982a, and 1982b.
[116] Renaissance modes of reading classical texts and, in particular, the question of allegorical or imitative approaches, as opposed to historical and critical reading, are examined by Anthony Grafton in a number of his books and articles, including 1977, 1983, 1985, and 1991. See also Hankins 1990, vol. 1: Introduction.

their own experience and, in the process, did not scruple to pick and choose those *sententiae* and *exempla*, ideas and themes, character studies and philosophical digressions that best suited their own interests and purposes.[117] Yet, influenced or biased though they were by personal and professional concerns or by political loyalties, they discovered in his *opera* a variety and range of meanings that other generations have often overlooked: interpretations that reveal the complexity, and ambiguities too, of the author's mind and personality.[118] Sallust's own life and political career fell within one of the most critical periods in the history of the ancient world, a period that witnessed the early stages in the transformation of senatorial Republic into Principate and the evolution from civic and collectivist values to apologies for monarchy and philosophies of individualism. As the defender of liberty, critic of Rome's corruption, or champion of established order, Sallust, as the historian of transition, could speak to the entire Renaissance.

APPENDIX I

Notes on Recent Scholarship

Since this article was first published in 1995 important new work has appeared on different aspects of Roman and Renaissance political thought, as well as new editions, translations, and studies of Sallust and of major Renaissance authors,

---

[117] In similar fashion, much of the Renaissance scholarship on Sallust seen in the textual and antiquarian commentaries from the mid-sixteenth century on aimed at recovering the original text 'for its own sake', or of reconstructing the past 'as it really was', but at making the author's work more *accessible* and, in turn, *relevant* to contemporary conditions and issues. The Swiss antiquarian Henricus Glareanus, for example, pointed out Sallust's errors in his description of Africa (*B.J.* 17–19) but praised his accuracy when a passage on the ancient Gauls (*B.J.* 114) corroborated his own patriotic image of his Swiss ancestors. The German philologist Johannes Rivius questioned Sallust's fairness to Cicero more for the sake of pleasing a Ciceronian friend, it seems, than from any independent analysis of the evidence.

One could argue of course that just as a 'present-minded' approach to an author's work could offer fresh perspectives and reveal new dimensions of meaning, so the practical and polemical aims of philologists could lead, indirectly, to the establishment of a better text and more rigorous source criticism. Despite signs of a more sceptical attitude towards Sallust's reputation for truthfulness, however, most defenders of Sallust's accuracy and impartiality continued throughout this period to appeal to tradition and authority (namely the classical *testimonia* and, above all, Augustine), while his critics repeated the objections raised by Costanzo Felici and the early sixteenth-century Ciceronians. The discussion of Sallust's *fides* as a historian, moreover, had little impact on the *political* interpretations and uses of his work, although there is an occasional connection between the charges of anti-Ciceronian bias and the tendency to view his work as politically subversive.

[118] For an analysis of the contradictory and ambiguous elements in Sallust's thought, see the references in n. 63 above.

new explorations into the history of the book, and new theories of cultural change. Much of this scholarship can provide fresh insights into the historical and historiographical contexts in which Sallust was read and suggest new ways of looking at questions of reception and transformation. Due to limits of space, however, I add only a few titles relevant to topics in this article. For fuller bibliographies see the *Catalogus translationum et commentariorum*, vols. 8 (Brown, Hankins, and Kaster 2003) and 10 (Dinkova-Bruun, Hankins, and Kaster 2014), s.v. 'Survival and Influence' in the articles on Sallust.

Surveys of Sallust's *fortuna*: Ulery 1999; Osmond 2010b; and Osmond and Ulery 2003 and 2014.

Studies on aspects of Sallust's thought and writing, with further bibliographies: Balmaceda 2017 and Batstone 2010b.

Renaissance editions and translations of the monographs: Waite 2014 and Minisci 2017.

Renaissance commentaries on the monographs (in addition to *CTC*, vols. 8 and 10, cited above): Farenga 2003; Osmond 2003, 2005, 2010a; Ulery 2003 and 2005.

Sallust in Renaissance historiography, political thought, and drama: Dati 2000; Hörnqvist 2000; Fontana 2003; Ferente 2013; and Osmond 2015b.

Catiline and Catilinarianism: Boehrer 1997; Osmond 2000 and 2015a; and Lovascio 2011.

Sallustian influences in medieval and Renaissance art: Funari 2002 and Guerrini 2008.

APPENDIX II

Latin Editions of Sallust's Works, 1470–1650

The popularity of Sallust's monographs in the Middle Ages, attested by hundreds of codices, continued uninterrupted into (and beyond) the Renaissance; indeed, with the invention of printing and a growing reading public, it quickly gained new momentum. The Appendix to my article in *Memoirs of the American Academy* (Osmond 1995) documented his popularity in print by comparing the number of editions for a core group of historians from *c.*1470 to 1650.[119] As the tables demonstrated, he was the most published Latin historian for nearly the entire period; only in the first half of the seventeenth century did he begin to slip into second place, behind the new favourite, Tacitus, and then by only a small margin. Whereas Sallust's popularity remained remarkably constant, however, throughout this era, that of other authors fluctuated, at times dramatically. The number of editions and corresponding rank of Livy, Florus, and Caesar, for instance, began to drop or level off, especially after the later sixteenth century,

---

[119] On the selection of Latin historians, the works and types of editions included in the survey, and the bibliographic sources used, see the Appendix in *MAAR* 40 (1995), 132–9. The Appendix also contains sections on the geographical diffusion of Sallust's work in Italy and northern Europe, its popularity in Latin commentaries, and the translations into vernacular languages.

444   *Patricia J. Osmond*

while Tacitus experienced an even more striking change in the opposite direction, soaring from last place on the list in the late 1400s and early 1500s to first place by 1650. In so far as changes in popularity tend to reflect mutations in historiographical tastes and political interests, the fact that Sallust found himself in the company of different authors in the course of this long period also supports what has been argued in this article, namely that, while his work was being continuously read, studied, cited, and imitated, it was appreciated for different reasons in different periods.

In the course of the last twenty-five years, dozens of other editions of the Roman historians have been identified thanks to the new national and international online databases. It would thus seem that the time had come to update the 1995 survey, which was based on the limited standard printed catalogues then available. However, while the British Library's Incunabula Short Title Catalogue (ISTC) provides an authoritative source for fifteenth-century books, the current state of many databases for sixteenth- and seventeenth-century editions makes it extremely difficult to compare numbers for these periods with any degree of accuracy. As vast amounts of library records are being imported into these systems from contributing institutions, we have to navigate various obstacles: misidentification of authors and works; confusion of Latin and vernacular titles; and inconsistencies in recording composite editions or different volumes of the same work. Even more challenging is the lack of common criteria for recording the title and printer's/publisher's imprint of a given edition, which often makes it impossible to distinguish between separate editions of a work and copies of the same.

It thus seems advisable to postpone a new review of the comparative popularity of ancient historians until we have data that can be more reliably evaluated. A quick sampling of major catalogues[120] (keeping in mind the caveats mentioned above) confirms, nevertheless, the general trends previously described, that is, both the *continuously* leading position of Sallust from the fifteenth well into the early seventeenth century and the *changing* rank of other historians, above all Tacitus—an indication of the varying interests of the reading public and the shifting attitudes towards Sallust's work in the course of these centuries.[121]

---

[120] I have consulted the online catalogues of the BnF, British Library, Gateway Bayern, and OPAC-SBN, as well as ISTC and CERL's Heritage of the Printed Book Database (HPB).

[121] This article was originally published in 1995. It is republished here with corrections and small changes, slightly abridged notes, and two addenda. Occasional references to more recent bibliography are inserted in the notes in square brackets. I thank Robert W. Ulery, Jr and the editors of this volume for their helpful comments and contributions.

This article presents a summary of work to date [1995] on the political interpretations of Sallust in the Renaissance. Portions of the text summarize material or expand upon themes in two of my recent articles: Osmond 1993 and 1994. I would like to express my appreciation to the readers who have suggested improvements in the original manuscript, to the directors and staff of the library of the American Academy in Rome, and to John H. M. Salmon [†], Russell T. Scott, and Ann Reynolds Scott for valuable advice and assistance during earlier stages of my work on Sallust at Bryn Mawr College. Grants from the National Endowment for the Humanities and the American Philosophical Society have made it possible to continue my research in libraries in Paris and northern Italy.

Bibliography

Abrams, M. H. (1971). *Natural Supernaturalism: Tradition and Revolution in Romantic Culture*. New York: Norton.
Adler, E. (2006). 'Who's Anti-Roman? Sallust and Pompeius Trogus on Mithridates'. *CJ* 101: 383–407.
Ahl, F. (1985). *Metaformations: Soundplay and Wordplay in Ovid and Other Classical Poets*. Ithaca, NY: Cornell University Press.
Ahlberg, A. W. (ed.) (1915). *C. Sallusti Crispi Bellum Iugurthinum*. Gothenburg: Eranos, and Leipzig: Harrassowitz.
Ahlberg, A. W. (ed.) (1919). *C. Sallusti Crispi Catilina, Iugurtha, Orationes et Epistulae Excerptae de Historiis*. Leipzig: Teubner.
Ahlheid, F. (1988). 'Oratorical Strategy in Sallust's Letter of Mithridates Reconsidered'. *Mnemosyne* 41: 67–92.
Alberti, L. B. (1890). 'De Porcaria coniuratione epistola'. In G. Mancini (ed.), *Opera inedita et pauca separatim impressa*. Florence: Sansoni, 257–66.
Alföldi, A. (1956). 'The Main Aspects of Political Propaganda on the Coinage of the Roman Republic'. In R. A. G. Carson and C. H. V. Sutherland (eds.), *Essays in Roman Coinage Presented to Harold Mattingly*. Oxford: Oxford University Press, 63–95.
Alföldi, A. and Alföldi, E. (1976). *Die Kontorniat-Medaillons*. Berlin: De Gruyter.
Alheit, L. (1919). Charakterdarstellung bei Sallust. *NJb* 43: 17–54.
Allegretti, A. (1733). *Diari scritti da Allegretto Allegretti delle cose sanesi del suo tempo*. Ed. by L. A. Muratori. *RIS* 23: cols. 767–860.
Allen, W., Jr (1938). 'The Source of Jugurtha's Influence in the Roman Senate'. *CPh* 33: 90–2.
Amundsen, L. (1947). 'Notes to the Preface of Livy'. *SO* 25: 31–35.
Aquinas, T. (1924). *De regimine principum ad regem Cypri et De regimine judaeorum ad ducissam Brabantiae*. Ed. by J. Mathis. Turin: Marietti.
Aquinas, T. (1979). *Sancti Thomae de Aquino opera omnia*. Ed. by R. A. Gauthier et al. Rome: Commissio Leonina.
Astin, A. E. (1978). *Cato the Censor*. Oxford: Oxford University Press.
Austin, J. L. (1975). *How to Do Things with Words*. Cambridge, MA: Harvard University Press.
Avenarius, W. (1957). 'Die griechischen Vorbilder des Sallust'. *SO* 33: 48–86.
Avery, H. C. (1967). 'Marius Felix (Sallust, *Jug*. 92–94)'. *Hermes* 95: 324–30.
Aymard, A. (1948). 'Deux anecdotes sur Scipion Émilien'. *Mélanges de la société toulousaine d'études classiques* 2: 106–109.
Badian, E. (1962). 'Waiting for Sulla'. *JRS* 52: 47–61.
Badian, E. (1971). Review of A. La Penna, *Sallustio e la 'rivoluzione' romana*. *AJPh* 92: 103–7.

Baehrens, W. A. (1926). *Sallust als Historiker, Politiker und Tendenzschriftsteller. Neue Wege zur Antike* 4. Leipzig: Teubner.
Balmaceda, C. (2017). *Virtus Romana: Politics and Morality in the Roman Historians*. Chapel Hill, NC: University of North Carolina Press.
Bannon, C. (1997). *The Brothers of Romulus*. Princeton, NJ: Princeton University Press.
Baron, H. (1938). 'Cicero and the Roman Civic Spirit in the Middle Ages and Early Renaissance'. *Bulletin of the John Rylands Library, Manchester* 22: 72–97.
Baron, H. (1966). *The Crisis of the Early Italian Renaissance*, 2nd edn. Princeton, NJ: Princeton University Press.
Baron, H. (1968). *From Petrarch to Bruni: Studies in Humanistic and Political Literature*. Chicago: University of Chicago Press.
Barthes, R. (1975). *S/Z*. Transl. by R. Miller. London: Hill and Wang.
Batstone, W. W. (1986). '*Incerta pro Certis*: An Interpretation of Sallust's *Bellum Catilinae* 48.4–49.4'. *Ramus* 15: 105–21.
Batstone, W. W. (1988a). '*Quantum ingenio possum*: On Sallust's use of *ingenium* in *Bellum Catilinae* 53.6'. *CJ* 83: 301–6.
Batstone, W. W. (1988b). 'The Antithesis of Virtue: Sallust's *Synkrisis* and the Crisis of the Late Republic'. *ClAnt* 7: 1–29.
Batstone, W. W. (1990). 'Intellectual Conflict and Mimesis in Sallust's *Bellum Catilinae*'. In J. W. Allison (ed.), *Conflict, Antithesis, and the Ancient Historian*. Columbus, OH: Ohio State University Press, 112–32.
Batstone, W. W. (2009). 'Postmodernism and Roman Historiography'. In Feldherr (ed.), 24–40.
Batstone, W. W. (2010a). 'Catiline's Speeches in Sallust's *Bellum Catilinae*'. In D. H. Berry and A. Erskine, (eds.), *Form and Function in Roman Oratory*. Cambridge: Cambridge University Press, 227–46.
Batstone, W. W. (2010b). 'Word at War: The Prequel'. In B. Breed, C. Damon, and A. Rossi (eds.), *Citizens of Discord: Rome and its Civil Wars*. Oxford: Oxford University Press, 45–67.
Baudouin, F. (1579). 'De institutione historiae universae et eius cum iurisprudentia coniunctione prolegomenon libri II'. In *Artis historicae penus*. Ed. by J. Wolfius. Basle: Petrus Perna.
Bauhofer, K. (1935). 'Die Komposition der *Historien* Sallusts'. Diss. Munich.
Baumbach, M. and Bär, S. (eds.) (2012). *Brill's Companion to Greek and Latin Epyllion and its Reception*. Leiden: Brill.
Beck, H. (2000). 'Quintus Fabius Maximus—Musterkarriere ohne Zögern'. In Hölkeskamp and Stein-Hölkeskamp (eds.), 79–91.
Becker, C. (1973). 'Sallust'. *ANRW* 1.3: 720–54.
Bellen, H. (1985). *Metus Gallicus—Metus Punicus; zum Furchtmotiv in der römischen Republik*. Mainz: Akademie der Wissenschaften und der Literatur.
Benabou, M. (1976). *La Résistance africaine et la romanisation*. Paris: Maspero.
Benferhat, Y. (2008). 'Ubi est? La Fin chez Salluste'. In B. Bureau and C. Nicolas (eds.), *Commencer et finir: débuts et fins dans les littératures grecque, latine et*

Bibliography 447

néolatine. Actes du colloque organisé les 29 et 30 septembre 2006 par l'Université Jean Moulin Lyon 3 et l'ENS-LSH. Lyons: Université Jean Moulin 3, 621–35.

Beni, P. (1622). *In Sallustii Catilinariam commentarii.* Venice: Guerilium.

Bentley, J. H. (1987). *Politics and Culture in Renaissance Naples.* Princeton, NJ: Princeton University Press.

Berry, C. (1994). *The Idea of Luxury.* Cambridge: Cambridge University Press.

Berry, D. H. (1996). *Cicero: Pro Sulla.* Cambridge: Cambridge University Press.

Bertelli, S. (1973). *Ribelli, libertini e ortodossi nella storiografia barocca.* Florence: La Nuova Italia.

Besser, J. (1880). 'De Coniuratione Catilinaria'. Diss. Leipzig.

Bignone, E. (1929). 'Ennio ed Empedocle'. *RFIC* 7: 10–30.

Bignone, E. (1950). *Storia della letteratura latina III.* Florence: Sansoni.

Bikerman, E. (1946). 'La Lettre de Mithridate dans les *Histoires* de Salluste'. *REL* 23: 131–151.

Billanovich, G. (1974). 'Il Petrarca e gli storici latini'. In G. Bernardoni Trezzini, O. Besomi, et al. (eds.), *Tra latino e volgare: per Carlo Dionisotti. Medioevo e Umanesimo* 17. Padua: Antenore, 67–45.

Bing, P. (2008). *The Well-Read Muse: Present and Past in Callimachus and the Hellenistic Poets*, 2nd edn. Ann Arbor, MI: Michigan Classical Press.

Bing, P. (2012). 'A Proto-Epyllion? The Pseudo-Hesiodic Shield and the Poetics of Deferral'. In Baumbach and Bär (eds.), 177–97.

Black, R. (2007). *Education and Society in Florentine Tuscany.* Leiden: Brill.

Bloch, H. (1961). 'The Structure of Sallust's *Historiae*. The Evidence of the Fleury Manuscript'. in S. Prete (ed.), *Didascaliae: Studies in Honor of A. M. Albareda.* New York: Rosenthal, 59–76.

Blösel, W. (2003). 'Die *memoria* der *gentes* als Rückgrat der kollektiven Erinnerung im republikanischen Rom'. In U. Eigler, U. Gotter, N. Luraghi, and U. Walter (eds.), *Formen römischer Geschichtsschreibung von den Anfängen bis Livius.* Darmstadt: Wissenschaftliche Buchgesellschaft, 43–72.

Bluck, R. S. (1949). *Plato's Life and Thought.* London: Routledge.

Blyth, J. M. (2009). *The Life and Works of Tolomeo Fiadoni (Ptolemy of Lucca).* Turnhout: Brepols.

Boccalini, T. (1910-48). *Ragguagli di Parnaso*, 3 vols. Ed. by G. Rua (vols. 1–2) and L. Firpo (vol. 3). Bari: Laterza.

Bock, G., Skinner, Q., and Viroli, M. (eds.) (1990). *Machiavelli and Republicanism.* Cambridge: Cambridge University Press.

Bodin, J. (1945). *Method for the Easy Comprehension of History [1566].* Transl. by B. Reynolds. New York: Norton.

Boehrer, B. (1997). 'Jonson's *Catiline* and Anti-Sallustian Trends in Early Modern Historiography'. *SPh* 94: 85–102.

Bolaffi, E. (1949). *Sallustio e la sua fortuna nei secoli.* Rome: Perrella.

Bolgar, R. R. (ed.) (1971). *Classical Influences on European Culture, A.D. 500–1500.* Cambridge: Cambridge University Press.

Bolgar, R. R. (ed.) (1976). *Classical Influences on European Culture, A.D. 1500–1700.* Cambridge: Cambridge University Press.

Boll, F. (1920). *Vita Contemplativa. SHAW* 8. Heidelberg: Winter.
Bolton, W. F. and Gardner, J. F. (1973). Introduction and Appendix B: 'Jonson's Classical Sources'. In W. F. Bolton and J. F. Gardner (eds.), *Catiline His Conspiracy*, by B. Jonson. Lincoln, NE: University of Nebraska Press.
Bonamente, G. (1975). 'Il "metus Punicus" e la decadenza di Roma in Sallustio, Agostino ed Orosio'. *GIF* 27: 137–69.
Bonfadio, I. (1586). *Annales Genuenses*. Genoa: Bartolus.
Bonner, S. F. (1949). *Roman Declamation*. Liverpool: University Press of Liverpool.
Borzsák, S. (2002). 'Marius Ἀλεξανδρώδης. Zum Marius-Porträt des Sallustius'. In P. Defosse (ed.), *Hommages à Carl Deroux II: Prose et linguistique, Médecine*. Brussels: Latomus, 57–63.
Bosselaar, D. E. (1915). 'Quomodo Sallustius historiam belli Iugurthini conscripserit'. Diss. Utrecht.
Botero, G. (1948). *Della ragion di stato*. Ed. by L. Firpo. Turin: UTET.
Bourdieu, P. (1977). *Outline of a Theory of Practice*. Transl. by R. Nice. Cambridge: Cambridge University Press.
Boyd, B. W. (1987). '*Virtus effeminata* and Sallust's Sempronia'. *TAPhA* 117: 183–201.
Bracciolini, P. (1538). 'Defensiuncula contra Guarinum Veronensem'. In *Poggii Florentini Oratoris et Philosophi Opera*. Basle: Petri, 388–89.
Bracciolini, P. (1715). *Historia florentina*. Ed. by J. Baptista Recanatus. Venice: Hertz.
Braund, D. (1984). *Rome and the Friendly King*. London: Routledge.
Brescia, G. (1997). *La 'Scalata' del Ligure*. Bari: Edipuglia.
Brink, C. O. (1982). *Horace on Poetry*, vol. 3, *Epistles, Book II: The Letters to Augustus and Florus*. Cambridge: Cambridge University Press.
Brink, C. O. and Walbank, F. W. (1954). 'The Construction of the Sixth Book of Polybius'. *CQ* 4: 97–122.
Briscoe, J. (1981). *A Commentary on Livy Books XXXIV–XXXVII*. Oxford: Oxford University Press.
Brizzi, G. (1990). 'Giugurta, Calama e i Romani sub iugum'. In A. Mastino (ed.), *L'Africa romana*. Sassari: Università degli Studi, 855–70.
Broilo, F. (ed.) (1985). *Scritti in onore di Piero Treves*. Rome: L'Erma.
Brosses, C. de (1777). *Histoire de la république romaine dans le cours du VIIe siècle, par Salluste*. Dijon: Frantin.
Broughton, T. R. S. (1936). 'Was Sallust Fair to Cicero?'. *TAPhA* 67: 34–46.
Broughton, T. R. S. (1948). 'More Notes on Roman Magistrates'. *TAPhA* 79: 63–78.
Brown, A. (1992). *The Medici in Florence: The Exercise and Language of Power*. Florence: Olschki.
Brown, V., Hankins, J., and Kaster, R. A. (eds.) (2003). *Catalogus Translationum et Commentariorum: Mediaeval and Renaissance Latin Translations and Commentaries*, vol. 8. Washington DC: Catholic University of America Press.
Bruennert, G. (1873). 'De Sallustio imitatore Catonis Sisennae aliorumque veterum historicorum Romanorum'. Diss. Jena.

Bruggisser, P. (2002). 'Audacia in Sallusts Verschwörung des Catilina'. Hermes 130: 265-87.

Bruni, L. (1764). 'Oratio in funere Nannis Strozae Equitis Florentini'. In G. D. Mansi (ed.), Stephani Baluzii Tutelensis Miscellanea novo ordine digesta et non paucis ineditis monumentis opportunisque animadversionibus aucta. Lucca: Riccomini, 4: 2-7.

Bruni, L. (1914-26). Historiarum florentini populi libri XII. Ed. by E. Santini. RIS n.s. 19. 3. Città di Castello: Lapi.

Bruni, L. (2001-7). History of the Florentine People, 3 vols. Ed. and transl. by J. Hankins. Cambridge, MA: Harvard University Press.

Bruns, I. (1896). Das literarische Porträt der Griechen im fünften und vierten Jahrhundert vor Christi Geburt. Berlin: Hertz.

Brunt, P. A. (1980). 'On Historical Fragments and Epitomes'. CQ 30: 477-94.

Brunt, P. A. (1988). The Fall of the Roman Republic and Related Essays. Oxford: Oxford University Press.

Büchner, K. (1953). Der Aufbau von Sallusts Bellum Iugurthinum. Hermes Einzelschriften 9. Wiesbaden: Steiner.

Büchner, K. (1960). Sallust. Heidelberg: Winter.

Büchner, K. (1967). Sallustinterpretationen. In Auseinandersetzung mit dem Sallustbuch von Ronald Syme. Altsprächliche Unterricht 10 Beiheft 2. Stuttgart: Klett.

Büchner, K. (1982). Sallust, 2nd edn. Heidelberg: Winter.

Buecheler, F. (1915). Kleine Schriften. Leipzig: Teubner.

Bühler, W. (1960). 'Die Europa des Moschos'. Hermes Einzelschriften 13. Wiesbaden: Steiner.

Burke, P. (1966). 'A Survey of the Popularity of Ancient Historians, 1450-1700'. H&T 5: 135-52.

Burke, P. (1969). 'Tacitism'. In T. A. Dorey (ed.), Tacitus. London: Routledge, 149-71.

Burns, J. H. (ed.) (1991). Cambridge History of Modern Political Thought, 1450-1700. Cambridge: Cambridge University Press.

Busolt, G. (1890). 'Quellenkritische Beiträge zur Geschichte der römischen Revolutionszzeit'. Jahrbuch für klassische Philologie 141: 321-349.

Cadoux, T. (1980). 'Sallust and Sempronia'. In B. Marshall (ed.), Vindex Humanitatis: Essays in Honour of John Huntly Bishop. Armidale: University of New England, 93-122.

Canfora, D. (ed.) (2001). La controversia di Poggio Bracciolini e Guarino Veronese su Cesare e Scipione. Florence: Olschki.

Canfora, L. (1972a). 'Il programma di Sallustio'. Belfagor 27: 137-148.

Canfora, L. (1972b). Totalità e selezione nella storiografia classica. Bari: Laterza.

Canfora, L. (1985). 'Sallustio e i triumviri'. In Broilo (ed.), 19-23.

Canfora, L. (1990). 'L'autobiografia intellettuale'. In Cavallo, Fedeli, and Giardina (eds.), vol. 3., 11-51.

Canfora, L. (1991). 'Vera vocabula rerum amisimus'. In Pani (ed.), 103-108.

Capes, W. W. (ed.) (1889). C. Sallusti Crispi De Coniuratione Catilinae liber; De Bello Jugurthino liber, 2nd edn. Oxford: Oxford University Press.

Carney, T. F. (1959). 'Once again Marius' Speech after Election in 108 B.C.'. *SO* 35: 63-70.
Carney, T. F. (1970). *A Biography of C. Marius*, 2nd edn. Chicago: Argonaut.
Carrara, L. (2004). 'Silla e la nascita del ritratto "paradossale"'. *SCO* 50: 267-94.
Carrera de la Red, A. (2007). 'Cultura clásica y educación para la humanidad en una edición renacentista de Salustio'. *EClás* 132: 87-106.
Caspari, M. O. B. (1913). 'On some Problems of Roman Agrarian History'. *Klio* 13: 184-98.
Castorina, E. (1975). 'Sul proemio delle *Historiae* di Sallustio (frr. I, 1-18 M.). La sentenziosità e il pessimismo'. *StudUrb* (Ser. B) 49: 355-366.
Cavallo, G., Fedeli, P., and Giardina, A. (eds.) (1989-91). *Lo spazio letterario di Roma antica*, 5 vols. Rome: Salerno Editrice.
Cesareo, E. (1924). *Le traduzioni italiane delle monografie di Sallustio*. Palermo: Scuola Tip.
Chacòn, P. C. (ed.) (1594). *Sallustii Crispi Opera omnia quae exstant cum Petri Ciacconii Toletani novis ad eadem notis*. London: Lownes.
Charron, P. (1836). *De la sagesse, trois livres*. Paris: Lefèvre.
Chassignet, M. (ed.) (1986). *Cato: Les Origines*. Paris: Les Belles Lettres.
Chomarat, J. (1985). 'More, Erasme, et les historiens latins'. *Moreana* 86: 71-107.
Chouet, M. (1950). *Les Lettres de Salluste à César*. Paris: Les Belles Lettres.
Christes, J. (1996). 'Der Gebildete im republikanischen Rom im Spannungsfeld von *negotium* und *otium*'. In R. W. Keck, E. Wiersing, and K. Wittstadt (eds.), *Literaten, Kleriker, Gelehrte: zur Geschichte der Gebildeten im vormodernen Europa*. Cologne: Böhlau.
Cipriani, G. (1988). *Sallustio e l'immaginario: per una biografia eroica di Giugurtha*. Bari: Adriatica.
Clark, V. (2014). 'Landscapes of Conquest: Space, Place, and Environment in Livy's *Ab Urbe Condita Libri*'. Diss. Princeton University.
Clarke, K. (2001). 'An Island Nation: Re-Reading Tacitus' *Agricola*. *JRS* 91: 94-112.
Clausen, W. (1947). 'Notes on Sallust's *Historiae*'. *AJPh* 68: 293-301.
Clausen, W. (1987). *Virgil's* Aeneid *and the Tradition of Hellenistic Poetry*. Berkeley, CA: University of California Press.
Clift, E. H. (1945). *Latin Pseudepigrapha: A Study in Literary Attributions*. Baltimore, MD: Furst.
Cochrane, E. (1970). *The Late Italian Renaissance: 1525-1630*. London: Macmillan.
Cochrane, E. (1973). *Florence in the Forgotten Centuries: 1527-1800*. Chicago: University of Chicago Press.
Cochrane, E. (1981). *Historians and Historiography in the Italian Renaissance*. Chicago: University of Chicago Press.
Colerus, C. (1598). *Sallustius sive de historia veteri oratio*. Nuremberg: Kauffman.
Colerus, C. (1599a). *C. Sallustii Crispi Historiae Romanae Principis Opera, cum fragmentis*. Nuremberg: Kauffman.

Colerus, C. (1599b). *C. Sallustii Crispi Epistulae ad Caesarem senem de republica*. Hamburg: Forster.

Colerus, C. (1602). *De studio politico ordinando epistola*. Hanover: Wechel.

Collingswood, R. G. (1961). *The Idea of History*. Oxford: Oxford University Press.

Collins, J. H. (1959). 'On the Date and Interpretation of the *Bellum Civile*'. *AJPh* 80: 113–32.

Compagno, B. (1991). 'Gloria nelle *Epistulae ad Caesarem* e nelle monografie di Sallustio'. In *Studi di filologia classica in onore di G. Monaco*, vol. 2. Palermo: Università di Palermo, 869–877.

Connolly, J. (2014). *The Life of Roman Republicanism*. Princeton, NJ: Princeton University Press.

Corio, B. (1855). *Storia di Milano*, vol. 1. Ed. by E. de Magri. Milan: Colombo.

Cotroneo, G. (1971). *I trattatisti dell' 'Ars Historica'*. Naples: Giannini.

Coulter, J. A. (1964). 'The Relation of the *Apology of Socrates* to Gorgias' *Defense of Palamedes* and Plato's Critique of Gorgianic Rhetoric'. *HSPh* 68: 269–303.

Dahlmann, H. (1934). '*Clementia Caesaris*'. *NJb* 10: 17–26.

Dallington, R. (1613). *Aphorismes Civill and Militarie*. London: Field.

Damon, C. (2010). 'Déjà Vu or Déjà Lu? History as Intertext', *Papers of the Langford Latin Seminar* 14: 375–88.

da Montemagno, B. (1952). 'De nobilitate'. In E. Garin (ed. and transl.), *Prosatori latini del Quattrocento*. Milan: Ricciardi, 141–65.

da San Concordio, B. (1827). *Il Catilinario ed il Giugurtino*. Ed. by B. Puoti. Naples: Stamperia Francese.

Dati, L. (2000). *Hyempsal*. Ed. by A. Onorato. *Quaderni di filologia medievale e umanistica* 3. Messina: Centro interdipartimentale di studi umanistici.

Davis, C. T. (1967). 'Brunetto Latini and Dante'. *Studi medievali* 8: 421–50. (= C. T. Davis 1984: 166–97).

Davis, C. T. (1974). 'Ptolemy of Lucca and the Roman Republic'. *PAPhS* 118: 30–50. (= C. T. Davis 1984: 254–89).

Davis, C. T. (1984). *Dante's Italy and Other Essays*. Philadelphia, PA: University of Pennsylvania Press.

Della Corte, F. (1985). 'La furia nella saeua Pelopis domus'. In Broilo (ed.), 77–81.

Deltour, F. (1859). 'De Sallustio Catonis imitatore'. Diss. Paris.

De Luna, B. N. (1967). *Jonson's Romish Plot: A Study of 'Catiline' in its Historical Context*. Oxford: Oxford University Press.

Delz, J. (1985). 'Verachtete Sallust die Beschäftigung mit der Landwirtschaft?'. *MH* 42: 168–73.

Deroux, C. (ed.) (1998). *Studies in Latin Literature and Roman History IX*. Brussels: Latomus.

Derrida, J. (1988). *Limited Inc*. Evanston, IL: Northwestern University Press.

De Sanctis, G. (1923). *Storia dei romani*, vol. 4, *La fondazione dell'impero*. Parte 1: *Dalla battaglia di Naraggara alla battaglia di Pidna*. Turin: Bocca.

Destombes, M. (ed.) (1964). *Mappemondes, A.D. 1200–1500*. Amsterdam: Israel.

Devillers, O. (2000). 'Regards romains sur les autels des frères Philènes'. In M. Khanoussi, P. Ruggeri, C. Vismara (eds.), *L'Africa romana: Atti del XIII convegno di studio Djerba, 10–13 dicembre 1998*. Rome: Carocci, 118–44.

Dietsch, R. (1846). C. *Salusti* [sic] *Crispi Catilina et Iugurtha*, vol. 2, *Iugurtha*. Leipzig: Teubner.

Dillery, J. (2007). Review of C. S. Kraus, *The Limits of Historiography: Genre and Narrative in Ancient Historical Texts*. BMCR 01.02.07.

Dinkova-Bruun, G., Hankins, J., and Kaster, R. A. (eds.) (2014). *Catalogus Translationum et Commentariorum: Mediaeval and Renaissance Latin Translations and Commentaries*, vol. 10. Washington DC: Catholic University of America Press.

Dix, C. V. (2006). *Virtutes und vitia: Interpretationen der Charakterzeichnungen in Sallusts Bellum Iugurthinum*. Bochumer altertumswissenschaftliches Colloquium 70. Trier: Wissenschaftlicher Verlag Trier.

Döpp, S. (2011). 'Fasziniert von Thukydides: zu zwei Rezeptionstypen bei Sallust'. In A. Heil, M. Korn, and J. Sauer (eds.), *Noctes Sinenses: Festschrift für Fritz-Heiner Mutschler zum 65. Geburtstag*. Heidelberg: Winter, 189–95.

Drummond, A. (1995). *Law, Politics and Power: Sallust and the Execution of the Catilinarian Conspirators*. Stuttgart: Steiner.

Dué, C. (2000). 'Tragic History and Barbarian Speech in Sallust's *Iugurtha*'. *HSPh* 100: 311–35.

Due, O. (1983). 'La Position politique de Salluste'. *C&M* 34: 113–39.

Earl, D. C. (1961). *The Political Thought of Sallust*. Cambridge: Cambridge University Press.

Earl, D. C. (1965). Review of Syme, *Sallust*. *JRS* 55: 232–40.

Earl, D. C. (1966). 'The Early Career of Sallust'. *Historia* 15: 302–11.

Earl, D. C. (1972). 'Prologue-Form in Ancient Historiography'. *ANRW* 1.2: 842–56.

Earl, (1979). '*Nunc ad inceptum redeo*, Sallust, *BJ* 4. 9: An Unreal Problem?'. *LCM* 4: 43.

Eden, P. T. (1962). 'Caesar's Style: Inheritance versus Intelligence'. *Glotta* 40: 74–117.

Edwards, C. (1993). *The Politics of Immorality in Ancient Rome*. Cambridge: Cambridge University Press.

Egelhaaf-Gaiser, U. (2010). '*Non sunt conposita verba mea*: Gespiegelte Erzählkunst in der Mariusrede des Sallust'. In D. Pausch (ed.), *Stimmen der Geschichte: Funktionen von Reden in der Antiken Historiographie*. Berlin: De Gruyter, 157–82.

Egermann, F. (1932). *Die Proömien zu den Werken des Sallust*. SAWW 214.3. Vienna: Hölder-Pichler-Tempsky.

Eichner, H. (1970). *Friedrich Schlegel*. New York: Twayne.

Elyot, T. (1907). *The Boke Named The Governour*. London: Dent.

Erasmus, D. (1906). *Opus Epistolarum Des. Erasmi Roterodami*, vol. 1. Ed. by P. S. Allen. Oxford: Oxford University Press.

Ernout, A. (1941). *Salluste: Catilina; Jugurtha; Fragments des histoires*. Paris: Les Belles Lettres.
Ernout, A. (1946). *Salluste: Catilina; Jugurtha; Fragments des histoires*, 2nd edn. Paris: Les Belles Lettres.
Ernout, A. (1949). 'Salluste et Caton'. *Information Littéraire* 1: 61–5.
Ernout, A. (ed.) (1962). *Pseudo-Salluste. Lettres à César, Invectives*. Paris: Budé.
Evans, R. J. (1994). *Gaius Marius: A Political Biography*. Pretoria: University of South Africa Press.
Évrard, É. (1990). 'L'Émergence du narrateur principal dans le *Bellum Iugurthinum* de Salluste'. *Lexis* 5–6: 127–46.
Fantham, E. (1987). 'Lucan, his Scholia, and the Victims of Marius'. *AHB* 1: 89–96.
Fantham, E. (ed.) (1992). *Lucan, De Bello Ciuili* Book II. Cambridge: Cambridge University Press.
Farenga, P. (2003). 'In the Margins of Sallust. Part I. Di un incunabulo non del tutto sconosciuto e del commento di Pomponio agli Opera di Sallustio'. In M. Miglio (ed.), *Antiquaria a Roma. Intorno a Pomponio Leto e Paolo II*. Rome: Roma nel Rinascimento, 1–11.
Feeney, D. C. (1994). 'Beginning Sallust's *Catiline*'. *Prudentia* 26: 139–46.
Feldherr, A. (1998). *Spectacle and Society in Livy's History*. Berkeley, CA: University of California Press.
Feldherr, A. (ed.) (2009) *The Cambridge Companion to the Roman Historians*. Cambridge: Cambridge University Press.
Feldherr, A. (2010). 'Hannibalic Laughter: Sallust's Archaeology and the End of Livy's Third Decade'. In W. Polleichtner (ed.), *Livy and Intertextuality*. Trier: Wissenschaftlicher Verlag Trier, 203–32.
Feldherr, A. (2012). '*Magna mihi copia est memorandi*: Modes of Historiography in the Speeches of Caesar and Cato (Sallust, *Bellum Catilinae* 51–4)'. In J. Grethlein and C. Krebs (eds.), *Time and Narrative in Ancient Historiography*. Cambridge: Cambridge University Press, 95–112.
Feldherr, A. (2013). 'Free Spirits: Sallust and the Citation of Catiline'. *AJPh* 134: 49–66.
Ferente, S. (2013). 'The Liberty of Italian City-States'. In Q. Skinner and M. van Gelderen (eds.), *Freedom and the Construction of Europe*, vol. 1, *Religious and Constitutional Liberties*. Cambridge: Cambridge University Press, 157–75.
Field, A. (1988). *The Origins of the Platonic Academy of Florence*. Princeton, NJ: Princeton University Press.
Flaig, E. (2004). *Ritualisierte Politik: Zeichen, Gesten und Herrschaft im Alten Rom. Historische Semantik* 1. Göttingen: Vandenhoeck und Ruprecht.
Flower, H. (1996). *Ancestor Masks and Aristocratic Power in Roman Culture*. Oxford: Oxford University Press.
Flower, H. (2010). *Roman Republics*. Princeton, NJ: Princeton University Press.
Foglietta, U. (1571). *Ex universa historia rerum Europae suorum temporum*. Naples: Cacchi.
Fontana, B. (2003). 'Sallust and the Politics of Machiavelli'. *HPTh* 24: 86–108.

Fornara, C. W. (1983). *The Nature of History in Ancient Greece and Rome*. Berkeley, CA: University of California Press.

Foucault, M. (1977a). 'Nietzsche, Genealogy, History'. In *Language, Countermemory, Practice: Selected Essays and Interviews*. Ithaca, NY: Cornell University Press, 139–64.

Foucault, M. (1977b). 'What is an Author?'. In *Language, Countermemory, Practice: Selected Essays and Interviews*. Ithaca, NY: Cornell University Press, 113–38.

Fowler, D. P. (1989). 'First Thoughts on Closure: Problems and Prospects'. *MD* 22: 75–122.

Fowler, D. P. (1997). 'Second Thoughts on Closure'. In Roberts, Dunn, and Fowler (eds.), 3–22.

Fraenkel, E. (1922). *Plautinisches im Plautus*. Berlin: Weidmann.

Fraenkel, E. (1951). Review of M. Chouet, *Les Lettres de Salluste à César*, *JRS* 41: 192–4.

Fränkel, H. (1933). 'Über philologische Interpretation am Beispiel von Caesars gallischen Krieg'. *NJb* 9: 26–41.

Frassinetti, P. (1975). 'I fatti di Spagna nel libro II delle *Historiae* di Sallustio'. *StudUrb* (Ser. B) 49: 381–98.

Frazer, J. G. (ed. and transl.) (1921). *Apollodorus: The Library*, vol. 1, *Books 1–3.9*. Loeb Classical Library. Cambridge, MA: Harvard University Press.

Freud, S. (1963a). 'Further Recommendations in the Technique of Psychoanalysis: Recollection, Repetition, and Working Through'. In *Therapy and Technique*. Ed. by P. Rieff. New York: Collier, 157–66.

Freud, S. (1963b). 'Mourning and Melancholia'. In *General Psychological Theory*. Ed. by P. Rieff. New York: Collier, 164–179.

Friedländer, P. (1945). 'Socrates Enters Rome'. *AJPh* 66: 337–51. (=Friedländer 1968, 323–32.)

Friedländer, P. (1968). *Plato*. Transl. by H. Meyeroff. Bollingen Series 59, vol. 12. Princeton, NJ: Princeton University Press.

Fritz, K. von (1943). 'Sallust and the Attitude of the Roman Nobility at the Time of the Wars against Jugurtha (112–105 B.C.)'. *TAPhA* 74: 134–68.

Fumaroli, M. (1980). *L'Âge de l'éloquence: rhétorique et 'res literaria' de la Renaissance au seuil de l'époque classique*. Geneva: Droz.

Fumaroli, M. (1981). 'Aulae arcana. Rhétorique et politique à la cour de France sous Henri III et Henri IV'. *JS* 2: 137–89.

Funari, R. (ed.) (1996). *C. Sallusti Crispi Historiarum fragmenta*. Amsterdam: Hakkert.

Funari, R. (2002). *Un ciclo di tradizione repubblicana nel Palazzo Pubblico di Siena: le iscrizioni degli affreschi di Taddeo di Bartolo, 1413–1414*. Siena: Accademia senese degli Intronati.

Funari, R. (ed.) (2008). *Corpus dei papiri storici greci e latini. B. Storici latini. 1. Autori noti. 2. Caius Sallustius Crispus*. Pisa: Serra.

Gaeta, F. (1977). 'Sull'idea di Roma nell'Umanesimo e nel Rinascimento'. *StudRom* 25: 169–186.

Galinsky, G. K. (1972). *The Herakles Theme*. Oxford: Blackwell.

Gärtner, T. (2011a). 'Cotta bei Sallust und Perikles bei Thukydides—eine übersehene Parallele'. *Historia* 60: 122-5.

Gärtner, T. (2011b). 'Das griechische Vorbild der Strafdebatte in der sallustischen *Coniuratio Catilinae*'. *Klio* 93: 149-57.

Gärtner, T. (2011c). 'Die Thukydidesremineszenz im Prooemium zu Sallusts *Bellum Catilinae*'. *Prometheus* 37: 163-8.

Gautier Dalché, P. (2003). 'Les Diagrammes topographiques dans les manuscrits des classiques latins (Lucain, Solin, Salluste)'. In P. Lardet (ed.), *La Tradition vive: Mélanges d'histoire des textes en l'honneur de Louis Holtz*. Turnhout: Brepols, 291-306.

Gehrke, H.-J. (1994). 'Römischer *mos* und griechische Ethik. Überlegungen zum Zusammenhang von Akkulturation und politischer Ordnung im Hellenismus'. *HZ* 258: 593-622.

Gehrke, H.-J. (2000). 'Marcus Porcius Cato Censorius—ein Bild von einem Römer'. In Hölkeskamp and Stein-Hölkeskamp (eds.), 147-58.

Gelzer, M. (1931). 'Nasicas Widerspruch gegen die Zerstörung Karthagos'. *Philologus* 86: 261-302. (= (1963). In H. Strasburger and C. Meier (eds.), *Kleine Schriften* II. Wiesbaden: Steiner, 39-72.)

Genette, G. (1980). *Narrative Discourse*. Transl. by J. Lewin. Ithaca, NY: Cornell University Press.

Gerrish, J. (2012). 'Sallust's *Histories* and Triumviral Historiography'. Diss. University of Pennsylvania.

Gerrish, J. (2016). '*Monstruosa species*: Scylla, Spartacus, Sextus Pompeius, and Civil War in Sallust's *Histories*'. *CJ* 111: 193-217.

Gerrish, J. (2018). 'The Blessed Isles and Counterfactual History in Sallust'. *Histos* 12: 49-70.

Gerrish, J. (2019). *Sallust's* Histories *and Triumviral Historiography: Confronting the End of History*. New York: Routledge.

Gibbon, E. (1796). *Miscellaneous Works*. Basle: Tourneisen.

Gilbert, C. D. (1973). 'Marius and Fortuna'. *CQ* 23: 104-107.

Gilbert, F. (1965). *Machiavelli and Guicciardini*. Princeton, NJ: Princeton University Press.

Gill, C. (1983). 'The Question of Character-Development: Plutarch and Tacitus'. *CQ* 33: 469-87.

Glücklich, H.-J. (1988). 'Gute und schlechte Triebe in Sallusts *Catilinae coniuratio*'. *AU* 31.5: 23-41.

Gockel, H. (1979). 'Friedrich Schlegels Theorie des Fragments'. In E. Ribbat (ed.), *Romantik: ein literaturwissenschaftliches Studienbuch*. Königstein: Athenäum, 22-37.

Gold, B. (ed.) (1982). *Literary and Artistic Patronage in Ancient Rome*. Austin, TX: University of Texas Press.

Gondi, J.-F.-P. de [Cardinal de Retz] (1880). 'La Conjuration du comte Jean-Louis de Fiesque'. In A. Feillet, J. Gourdault, and R. Chantelauze (eds.), *Œuvres du Cardinal de Retz*, vol. 5. Paris: Hachette, 472-658.

Goodyear, F. R. D. (1972). *The Annals of Tacitus, Books 1–6*, vol. 1, *Annals 1. 1–54*. Cambridge: Cambridge University Press.
Grafton, A. (1977). 'On the Scholarship of Politian and its Context'. *JWI* 40: 152–62.
Grafton, A. (1983). *Joseph Scaliger: A Study in the History of Classical Scholarship*. Oxford: Oxford University Press.
Grafton, A. (1985). 'Renaissance Readers and Ancient Texts: Comments on Some Commentaries'. *RenQ* 38: 615–49.
Grafton, A. (1991). '*Discitur ut agatur*; How Gabriel Harvey Read his Livy'. In S. A. Barney (ed.), *Annotation and its Texts*. Oxford: Oxford University Press, 108–29.
Graswinckelius, T. (1642). *C. Crispi Sallusti Catilina. Theod. I. F. Graswinckelius commentario illustravit*. Leiden: Commelin.
Gravier, G. (ed.) (1769). *Raccolta di tutti i più rinomati scrittori dell'istoria generale del Regno di Napoli*, vol. 5. Naples: Gravier.
Green, C. M. J. (1993). '*De Africa et eius incolis*: The Function of Geography and Ethnography in Sallust's History of the Jugurthine War (*B.J.* 17–19)'. *AncW* 24: 199–212.
Grene, D. (ed. and transl.) (1959). *The Complete Greek Tragedies*, vol. 1, *Aeschylus*. Chicago: University of Chicago Press.
Grethlein, J. (2006a). '*Nam Quid Ea Memorem*: The Dialectical Relation of *Res Gestae* and *Memoria Rerum Gestarum* in Sallust's *Bellum Jugurthinum*'. *CQ* 56: 135–48.
Grethlein, J. (2006b). 'The Unthucydidean Voice of Sallust'. *TAPhA* 136: 299–327.
Grethlein, J. (2013). *Experience and Teleology in Ancient Historiography*. Cambridge: Cambridge University Press.
Griffin, J. (1982). 'The Creation of Characters in the *Aeneid*'. In Gold (ed.), 118–34.
Griffiths, G., Hankins, J., and Thompson, T. (eds. and transl.) (1987). *The Humanism of Leonardo Bruni*. Binghamton, NY: Center for Medieval and Renaissance Studies, State University of New York.
Gruen, E. (1974). *The Last Generation of the Roman Republic*. Berkeley, CA: University of California Press.
Gsell, S. (1913–28). *Histoire ancienne de l'Afrique du Nord*. Paris: Hachette.
Gualdo Rosa, L., Nuovo, I., and Defilippis, D. (eds.) (1982). *Gli umanisti e la guerra otrantina*. Bari: Dedalo.
Gudeman, A. (ed.) (1916). *P. Corneli Taciti De Germania*. Berlin: Weidmann.
Guerrini, R. (2008). 'Idem velle idem nolle. Sallustio nel Palazzo Pubblico di Siena'. In *Presenza del passato: Political ideas e modelli culturali nella storia e nell'arte senese. Convegno internazionale, Siena, 4 maggio 2007*. Siena: Cantagalli, 187–200.
Guilbert, D. (1957). 'Salluste, oratio Lepidi consulis et la IIe Olynthienne'. *LEC* 25: 296–299.
Gunderson, E. (2000). 'The History of Mind and the Philosophy of History in Sallust's *Bellum Catilinae*'. *Ramus* 29: 85–126.
Hache, F. (1907). 'Quaestiones Archaicae'. Diss. Breslau.
Hackl, U. (1980). 'Poseidonios und das Jahr 146 v. Chr. als Epochendatum in der antiken Historiographie'. *Gymnasium* 87: 151–66.

Bibliography 457

Haffter, H. (1934). *Untersuchungen zur altlateinischen Dichtersprache*. Berlin: Weidmann.

Hammer, D. (2014). *Roman Political Thought: From Cicero to Augustine*. Cambridge: Cambridge University Press.

Hand, F. (1829-45). *Tursellinus seu de particulis Latinis commentarii*, 4 vols. Leipzig: Weidmann.

Hankins, J. (1990). *Plato in the Italian Renaissance*, 2 vols. Leiden: Brill.

Hankins, J. (1995). 'The "Baron Thesis" after Forty Years and some Recent Studies of Leonardo Bruni'. *JHI* 48: 309-38.

Hankins, J. (2010). 'Exclusivist Republicanism and the Non-Monarchical Republic'. *Political Theory* 38: 252-82.

Hardie, P. (ed.) (1994). *Virgil, Aeneid Book IX*. Cambridge: Cambridge University Press.

Hardie, P. (2012). *Rumour and Renown: Representations of Fama in Western Literature*. Cambridge: Cambridge University Press.

Harding, B. (2011). *Augustine and Roman Virtue*. London: Continuum.

Hardy, R. (2007). '"A Mirror of the Times": The Catilinarian Conspiracy in Eighteenth-Century British and American Political Thought'. *IJCT* 14: 431-54.

Hatzfeld, J. (1919). *Les Trafiquants italiens dans l'Orient hellénique*. Paris: Boccard.

Heath, M. (1989). *Unity in Greek Poetics*. Oxford: Oxford University Press.

Hegel, G. (1956). *The Philosophy of History*. Transl. by J. Sibree. New York: Dover Publications.

Hegel, G. (1974). *Lectures on the History of Philosophy*, 2 vols. Transl. by E. S. Haldane and F. H. Simson. New York: Humanities Press.

Hegel, G. (1977). *Phenomenology of the Spirit*. Transl. by A. V. Miller. Oxford: Oxford University Press.

Heinze, R. (1925). *Von den Ursachen der Grösse Roms*. Leipzig: Teubner.

Heldmann, K. (1993). *Sallust über die römische Weltherrschaft: ein Geschichtsmodell im* Catilina *und seine Tradition in der hellenistischen Historiographie*. Stuttgart: Teubner.

Hellegouarc'h, J. (1963). *Le Vocabulaire latin des relations et des partis politiques sous la République*. Paris: Publications de la Faculté des Lettres et Sciences Humaines de l'Université de Lille.

Hellegouarc'h, J. (1972). *Le Vocabulaire latin des relations et des partis politiques sous la République*, 2nd edn. Paris: Les Belles Lettres.

Henderson, J. (1998). *Fighting for Rome*. Cambridge: Cambridge University Press.

Herkommer, E. (1968). 'Die Topoi in den Proömien der römischen Geschichtswerke'. Diss. Tübingen.

Heubner, F. (2004). 'Die Fremden in Sallusts Afrika-Excurs (Sall. *Iug.* 17-19)'. In J. Dummer and M. Vielberg (eds.), *Der Fremde, Freund oder Feind*. Stuttgart: Steiner, 93-111.

Heywood, T. (transl.) (1609). *The two most worthy and notable histories which remaine unmaimed to posterity*. London: Jaggard.

458 Bibliography

Hinds, S. (1998). *Allusion and Intertext: Dynamics of Appropriation in Roman Poetry*. Cambridge: Cambridge University Press.
Hock, R. (1988). 'Servile Behavior in Sallust's *Bellum Catilinae*'. *CW* 82: 13–24.
Hoffmann, W. (1960). 'Die römische Politik des 2. Jahrhunderts und das Ende Karthagos'. *History* 9: 309–44.
Hofmann, J. B. (1926). *Lateinische Umgangssprache*. Heidelberg: Winter.
Hölkeskamp, K.-J. (1996). '*Exempla* und *mos maiorum*'. In H.-J. Gehrke and A. Moller (eds.), *Vergangenheit und Lebenswelt: Soziale Kommunikation, Traditionsbildung und historisches Bewußtsein*. Tübingen: Narr, 301–38.
Hölkeskamp, K.-J. (2004). *Rekonstruktionen einer Republik: Die politische Kultur des antiken Rom und die Forschung der letzten Jahrzehnte*. HZ Beihefte 38. Munich: Oldenbourg.
Hölkeskamp, K.-J. and Stein-Hölkeskamp, E. (eds.) (2000). *Von Romulus zu Augustus: Große Gestalten der römischen Republik*. Munich: Beck.
Holzberg, N. (1981). *Willibald Pirckheimer: Griechischer Humanismus in Deutschland*. Munich: Fink.
Hopkinson, N. (ed.) (1988). *A Hellenistic Anthology*. Cambridge: Cambridge University Press.
Hornblower, S. (1987). *Thucydides*. London: Duckworth.
Hörnqvist, M. (2000). 'The Two Myths of Civic Humanism'. In J. Hankins (ed.), *Renaissance Civic Humanism*. Cambridge: Cambridge University Press, 105–42.
Jacobs, R., Wirz, H., and Kurfess, A. (eds.) (1922). *C. Sallusti Crispi De coniuratione Catilinae liber; Orationes et epistulae ex historiis excerptae*. 11th edn. Berlin: Weidmann.
Jaeger, W. (1928). 'Über Ursprung und Kreislauf des philosophischen Lebensideals'. *SPAW, phil.-hist.Kl.* 25: 390–420.
Jaeger, W. (1938). *Demosthenes: The Origin and Growth of his Policy*. Berkeley, CA: University of California Press (=Jaeger 1940, *Demosthenes: Der Staatsman und sein Werden*. Berlin: Verlag Walter de Gruyter).
Jaeger, W. (1945). *Paideia*. Transl. by G. Highet. Oxford: Oxford University Press.
Jal, P. (1963). *La Guerre civile à Rome*. Paris: Presses Universitaires de France.
Jauss, H. R. (1972). *Kleine Apologie der ästhetischen Erfahrung*. Constance: Universitätsverlag.
Jauss, H. R. (1982a). 'Literary History as a Challenge to Literary Theory'. In *Toward an Aesthetic of Reception*, vol. 2 of *Theory and History of Literature*. Transl. by T. Bahti. Minneapolis, MN: University of Minnesota Press, 3–45.
Jauss, H. R. (1982b). *Aesthetic Experience and Literary Hermeneutics*. Transl. by M. Shaw. Minneapolis, MN: University of Minnesota Press.
Jenkins, K. (1991). *Re-Thinking History*. New York and London: Routledge.
John, C. (1876a). 'Sallustius über Catilinas Candidatur im Jahr 688'. *RhM* 31: 401–31.
John, C. (1876b). 'Die Entstehungsgeschichte der catilinarischen Verschwörung: Ein Beitrag zur Kritik des Sallustius'. *Jahrbücher für classische Philologie*, Supp. 8: 703–819.

Bibliography

Jonson, B. (1973). *Catiline His Conspiracy*. Ed. by W. F. Bolton and J. F. Gardner. Lincoln, NE: University of Nebraska Press.
Jordan, H. (1860). *M. Catonis praeter librum de re rustica quae extant*. Leipzig: Teubner.
Kaplow, L. (2008). 'Redefining *Imagines*: Ancestor Masks and Political Legitimacy in the Rhetoric of New Men'. *Mouseion* 8: 409–416.
Katz, B. R. (1981a). '*Dolor, invidia* and *misericordia* in Sallust'. *AClass* 24: 71–85.
Katz, B. R. (1981b). 'Sallust and Varro'. *Maia* 33: 111–23.
Katz, B. R. (1981c). 'Sertorius, Caesar, and Sallust'. *AAntHung* 29: 285–313.
Katz, B. R. (1982). 'Sallust and Pompey'. *RSA* 12: 75–83.
Katz, B. R. (1983). 'Did Sallust have a guilty conscience?'. *Eranos* 81: 101–11.
Kewes, P. (ed.) (2006). *The Uses of History in Early Modern England*. San Marino, CA: Huntington Library.
Keyser, P. T. (1991). 'Geography and Ethnography in Sallust'. Diss. Univ. of Colorado at Boulder.
Kierdorf, W. (1980). *Laudatio funebris: Interpretationen und Untersuchungen zur Entwicklung der römischen Leichenrede*. Beiträge zur klassischen Philologie 106. Meisenheim am Glan: Hain.
Klingner, F. (1928). 'Über die Einleitung der *Historien* Sallusts'. *Hermes* 63: 165–92.
Klinz, A. (1968). 'Die große Rede des Marius (*Iug.* 85) und ihre Bedeutung für das Geschichtsbild des Sallust'. *AU* 11: 76–90.
Knoche, U. (1934). 'Der römische Ruhmesgedanke'. *Philologus* 89: 102–124.
Koestermann, E. (1971). *C. Sallustius Crispus: Bellum Iugurthinum*. Heidelberg: Winter.
Koestermann, E. (1973). 'Das Problem der römischen Dekadenz bei Sallust und Tacitus'. *ANRW* 1.3: 781–810.
Kojève, A. 1980. *Introduction to the Reading of Hegel*. Ithaca, NY: Cornell University Press.
Konrad, C. F. (1988). 'Why not Sallust on the Eighties?'. *AHB* 2: 12–15.
Konstan, D. (1986). 'Narrative and Ideology in Livy: Book I'. *ClAnt* 5: 198–215.
Kortte, G. (ed.) (1724). *Caii Crispi Sallustii quae exstant*. Leipzig: Gleditsch.
Kraus, C. (ed.) (1994). *Livy, Ab Vrbe Condita Book VI*. Cambridge: Cambridge University Press.
Kraus, C. (1999). 'Jugurthine Disorder'. In C. Kraus (ed.), *The Limits of Historiography: Genre and Narrative in Ancient Historical Texts*. Leiden: Brill, 217–47.
Kraus, C. S. and Woodman, A. J. (1997). *Latin Historians*. Greece & Rome New Surveys in the Classics 27. Oxford: Oxford University Press.
Krebs, C. B. (2008). 'The Imagery of "the Way" in the Proem to Sallust's *Bellum Catilinae* (1–4)'. *AJPh* 129: 581–94.
Kretschmer, P. (1910). 'Zur Erklärung des sogenannten Infinitivus historicus'. *Glotta* 2: 270–87.
Kritz, F. (ed.) (1828–53). *C. Sallusti Crispi Opera quae Supersunt*. Leipzig: Teubner.

Kritz, F. (ed.) (1856). *C. Sallusti Crispi Opera quae Supersunt*. 2nd edn. Leipzig: Hahn.
Kroll, W. (1927). 'Die Sprache Des Sallust'. *Glotta* 15: 280–305.
Kuhner, R. (1976). *Ausführliche Grammatik der lateinischen Sprache*, vol. 2, *Satzlehre*. Ed. by C. Stegmann. 5th edn. Hannover: Hahnsche.
Kunze, A. (1892-7). *Sallustiana*, 3 vols. Leipzig: Simmel.
Kurfess, A. (ed.) (1981). *C. Sallusti Crispi Catilina, Iugurtha, fragmenta ampliora. Post A. W. Ahlberg*. Leipzig: Teubner.
Kurke, L. (1991). *The Traffic in Praise: Pindar and the Poetics of Social Economy*. Ithaca, NY: Cornell University Press. (2nd expanded edn, 2013, Berkeley, CA: University of California Press.)
Kuzniar, A. A. (1987). *Delayed Endings: Nonclosure in Novalis and Hölderlin*. Athens, GA: University of Georgia Press.
Lacan, J. (1977). 'The Function and Field of Speech and Language in Psychoanalysis'. In *Écrits: A Selection*. Transl. by A. Sheridan. New York: Norton, 30–113.
Lacan, J. (1988). *The Seminar of Jacques Lacan, Book I: Freud's Papers on Technique, 1953-1954*. Transl. by J. Forrester. New York: Norton.
Laistner, M. L. W. (1947). *The Greater Roman Historians*. Berkeley, CA: University of California Press.
La Penna, A. (1959). 'Il significato dei proemi sallustiani'. *Maia* 11: 23–43, 89–119.
La Penna, A. (1963a). 'Le *Historiae* di Sallustio e l'interpretazione della crisi repubblicana'. *Athenaeum* 41: 201–74.
La Penna, A. (1963b). 'Per la ricostruzione delle *Historiae* di Sallustio'. *SIFC* 35: 5–68.
La Penna, A. (1968). *Sallustio e la 'rivoluzione' romana*. Milan: Feltrinelli.
La Penna, A. (1969). *Sallustio e la 'rivoluzione' romana*, 2nd edn. Milan: Feltrinelli.
La Penna, A. (1971). 'Sallustio, *Hist*. II, 83 M'. *RFIC* 99: 61–62.
La Penna, A. (1973). 'Una polemica di Sallustio contro l'oratoria contemporanea?'. *RFIC* 101: 88–91.
La Penna, A. (1976). 'Vivere sotto i tiranni: un tema taciiano da Guicciardini a Diderot'. In R. R. Bolgar (ed.), 295–304 (= La Penna 1983, 233–46.)
La Penna, A. (1983). *Aspetti del pensiero storico latino: con due scritti sulla scuola classica*, 2nd edn. Turin: Einaudi.
La Penna, A. (1985). 'Il *Bellum civile* di Petronio e il proemio delle *Historiae* di Sallustio'. *RFIC* 113: 170–3.
La Penna, A. (1987). '*Rapere, trahere*: uno slogan di Catone contra i ladri di stato?'. In S. Boldrini et al. (eds.), *Filologia e forme letterarie: studi offerti a Francesco della Corte*, vol. 2. Urbino: Università degli Studi di Urbino, 103–10.
La Penna, A. and Funari, R. (eds.) (2015). *C. Sallusti Crispi Historiae I: Fragmenta 1.1-146*. Berlin: De Gruyter.
Last, H. M. (1923). 'On the Sallustian *Suasoriae*'. *CQ* 17: 88–100, 151–62.

Last, H. M. (1948). 'Sallust and Caesar in the *Bellum Catilinae*'. In *Mélanges de philologie, de littérature et d'histoire anciennes offerts à J. Marouzeau par ses collègues et élèves étrangers*. Paris: Les Belles Lettres, 355–69.

Lateiner, D. (1989). *The Historical Method of Herodotus*. Toronto: University of Toronto Press.

Lathrop, H. B. (1933). *Translations from the Classics into English from Caxton to Chapman 1477–1620*. University of Wisconsin Studies in Language and Literature 35. Madison, WI: University of Wisconsin Press.

Latini, B. (1948). *Li livres dou tresor*. Ed. by F. J. Carmody. Berkeley, CA: University of California Press.

Latta, B. (1988). 'Der Wandel in Sallusts Geschichtsauffassung: Vom *Bellum Catilinae* zum *Bellum Iugurthinum*'. *Maia* 40: 271–88.

Latta, B. (1989). 'Die Ausgestaltung der Geschichtskonzeption Sallusts. Vom *Bellum Jugurthinum* zu den *Historien*'. *Maia* 41: 41–57.

Latte, K. (1935). *Sallust. Neue Wege zur Antike* 2.4. Stuttgart: Teubner.

Lauckner, C. (1911). 'Die kunstlerischen und politischen Ziele der Monographie Sallusts über den Jugurthinischen Krieg'. Diss. Leipzig.

Lebek, W. (1970). *Verba Prisca: Die Anfänge des Archaisierens in der lateinischen Beredsamkeit und Geschichtsschreibung*, Hypomnemata 25. Göttingen: Vandenhoeck and Ruprecht.

Leeman, A. D. (1954–5). 'Sallusts Prologe und seine Auffassung von der Historiographie'. *Mnemosyne* 7: 323–39 and 8: 38–48.

Leeman, A. D. (1955). 'Sallusts Prologe und seine Auffassung von der Historiographie. II. Das Jugurtha-Proömium'. *Mnemosyne* 8: 38–48.

Leeman, A. D. (1957). *Aufbau und Absicht von Sallusts* Bellum Jugurthinum. Amsterdam: Noord-Hollandsche Uitgevers Maatschappij.

Leeman, A. D. (1965). *A Systematical Bibliography of Sallust*, 2nd edn. Leiden: Brill.

Leeman, A. D. (1967). 'Formen sallustianischer Geschichtsschreibung'. *Gymnasium* 74: 108–15.

Lefèvre, E. (1979). 'Argumentation und Struktur der moralischen Geschichtsschreibung der Römer am Beispiel von Sallusts *Bellum Iugurthinum*'. *Gymnasium* 86: 249–77.

Leigh, M. (1995). 'Wounding and Popular Rhetoric at Rome'. *BICS* 40: 195–215.

Leisner-Jensen, M. (1997). 'P. Ventidius and Sallust'. *C&M* 48: 325–46.

Leo, F. (1896–1906). *Analecta Plautina de figuris sermonis*, 3 vols. Göttingen: Vandenhoeck and Ruprecht.

Lepore, E. (1950). 'I due frammenti Rylands delle Storie di Sallustio'. *Athenaeum* 28: 280–91.

Leumann, M., and Hoffman, J. B. (1965). *Lateinische Grammatik*, vol. 2, *Lateinische Syntax und Stilistik*. Rev. by A. Szantyr. Munich: Beck.

Levene, D. S. (1992). 'Sallust's *Jugurtha*: An "Historical Fragment"'. *JRS* 82: 53–70.

Levene, D. S. (2000). 'Sallust's *Catiline* and Cato the Censor'. *CQ* 50: 170–91.

Levene, D. S. (2007). 'Roman Historiography in the Late Republic'. In J. Marincola (ed.), *Companion to Greek and Roman Historiography*, vol. 1. Malden, MA: Blackwell, 275–89.

Levene, D. S. (2010). *Livy on the Hannibalic War*. Oxford: Oxford University Press.

Levine, J. M. (1970). *Humanism and History*. Ithaca, NY: Cornell University Press.

Levy, F. J. (1967). *Tudor Historical Thought*. San Marino, CA: Huntington Library.

Levy, F. J. (1972). 'Introduction'. In *The History of the Reign of King Henry the Seventh*, by Francis Bacon. Ed. by F. J. Levy. New York: Bobbs-Merrill.

Levy, F. J. (1987). 'Hayward, Daniel, and the Beginnings of Politic History in England'. *Huntington Library Quarterly* 50: 1–34.

Lindholm, E. (1931). *Stilistische Studien zur Erweiterung der Satzglieder im Lateinschen*. Lund: Gleerup.

Lintott, A. W. (1999). *Violence in Republican Rome*. 2nd edn. Oxford: Oxford University Press.

Lipsius, J. (1675). *Opera omnia*, 4 vols. Wesel: Hoogenhuysen.

Lloyd-Jones, H. (1971). *The Justice of Zeus*. Berkeley, CA: University of California Press.

Löfstedt, E. (1933). *Syntactica: Studien und Beiträge zur historischen Syntax des Lateins*, vol. 2, *Syntaktisch-stilistische Gesichtspunkte und Probleme*. Lund: Gleerup.

Lovascio, D. (ed. and transl.) (2011). *La congiura di Catilina*, by Ben Jonson. Genoa: ECIG.

Luce, T. J. (1965). 'The Dating of Livy's First Decade'. *TAPhA* 96: 209–40.

Luce, T. J. and Woodman, A. J. (eds.) (1993). *Tacitus and the Tacitean Tradition*. Princeton, NJ: Princeton University Press.

Lyotard, J.-F. (1984). *The Postmodern Condition: A Report on Knowledge*. Transl. by G. Bennington and B. Massumi. Minneapolis, MN: University of Minnesota Press.

McCuaig, W. (1982). 'Bernardo Rucellai and Sallust'. *Rinascimento* 32: 75–98.

Machiavelli, N. (1950). *The Prince and the Discourses*. Transl. by L. Ricci and C. E. Detmold. New York: The Modern Library.

Machiavelli, N. (1976). *Florentine History*. Transl. by W. K. Marriott. London: Dent.

Machiavelli, N. (1992). *Le grandi opere politiche*, vol. 1, *Il Principe*. Ed. by G. M. Anselmi and C. Varotti. Turin: Bollati Boringhieri.

Machiavelli, N. (1993). *Le grandi opere politiche*, vol. 2, *Discorsi sopra la prima Deca di Tito Livio*. Ed. by G. M. Anselmi and C. Varotti. Turin: Bollati Boringhieri.

McDonald, A. H. (1944). 'Rome and the Italian Confederation (200–186 B.C.)'. *JRS* 34: 11–33.

McFarland, T. (1981). *Romanticism and the Forms of Ruin*. Princeton, NJ: Princeton University Press.

Bibliography

McGing, B. C. and Mossman, J. M. (eds.) (1996). *The Limits of Ancient Biography*. Swansea: Classical Press of Wales.

McGushin, P. (1977). *C. Sallustius Crispus, Bellum Catilinae: A Commentary*. Leiden: Brill.

McGushin, P. (1992-4). *Sallust, the Histories*. 2 vols. Oxford: Oxford University Press.

MacKay, L. A. (1962). 'Sallust's *Catiline*, Date and Purpose'. *Phoenix* 16: 181-94.

McKeown, J. C. (1987). *Ovid: Amores. Text, Prolegomena, and Commentary*, vol. 1. Liverpool: Cairns.

MacLeod, C. W. (1974). Review of A. Pelletier (ed.), *Legatio ad Gaium*, by Philo of Alexandria. *CR* 24: 293-4.

Malitz, J. (1975). *Ambitio Mala: Studien zur politischen Biographie des Sallust*. Saarbrücker Beitr. z. Altertumskunde 14. Bonn: Habelt.

Maltby, R. (1991). *A Lexicon of Ancient Latin Etymologies*. Leeds: Cairns.

Marin, M. (1997). 'Crisi morale e decadenza politica della repubblica romana: la rilettura agostiniana di Sallustio'. *VetChr* 34: 15-31.

Marincola, J. (1997). *Authority and Tradition in Ancient Historiography*. Cambridge: Cambridge University Press.

Marincola, J. (2005). 'Concluding Narratives: Looking to the End in Classical Historiography'. *Papers of the Langford Latin Seminar* 12: 285-320.

Marincola, J. (2010). 'The Rhetoric of History: Allusion, Intertextualtiy, and Exemplarity'. In D. Pausch (ed.), 259-289.

Marino, S. (2006). 'Personenkritik bei Sallust und Catull. Konträre Lebensentwürfe im Rom der ausgehenden Republik'. *AU* 49.1: 35-45.

Markwart, O. (1886). *Wilibald Pirckheimer als Geschichtschreiber*. Zurich: Meyer and Zeller.

Marshall, B. (1985). 'Catilina and the Execution of M. Marius Gratidianus'. *CQ* 35: 124-33.

Marx, F. (ed.) (1905). *C. Lucilii carminum reliquiae*, 2 vols. Leipzig: Teubner.

Marx, K. (1978). *The Eighteenth Brumaire of Louis Bonaparte*. Peking: Foreign Languages Press.

Mascardi, A. (1629). *La congiura del conte Gio. Luigi de' Fieschi*. Venice: Scaglia.

Masters, J. (1992). *Poetry and Civil War in Lucan's Bellum Ciuile*. Cambridge: Cambridge University Press.

Melchior, A. (2010). 'Citizen as Enemy in Sallust's *Bellum Catilinae*'. In R. M. Rosen and I. Sluiter (eds.), *Valuing Others in Classical Antiquity*. Leiden: Brill, 391-415.

Mellor, R. (1993). *Tacitus*. New York: Routledge.

Meyer, E. A. (2010). 'Allusion and Contrast in the Letters of Nicias (Thuc. 7.11-15) and Pompey (Sall. *Hist.* 2.98M)'. In C. S. Kraus, J. Marincola, and C. Pelling (eds.), *Ancient Historiography and its Contexts: Studies in Honour of A.J. Woodman*, Oxford: Oxford University Press: 97-117.

Millar, F. (1998). *The Crowd in Rome in the Late Republic*. Ann Arbor, MI: University of Michigan Press.

Miller, J. (2015). 'Idealization and Irony in Sallust's *Jugurtha*: The Narrator's Depiction of Rome before 146 B.C.'. *CQ* 65: 242–52.

Milner, N. P. (1993). *Vegetius: Epitome of Military Science*. Liverpool: Liverpool University Press.

Minisci, A. (ed.) (2017). *Le traduzioni da Sallustio di Ludovico Carbone*. Pisa: ETS.

Moles, J. L. (1988). *Plutarch: Life of Cicero*. Warminster: Aris and Phillips.

Molho, A. and Tedeschi, J. A. (eds.) (1971). *Renaissance Studies in Honor of Hans Baron*. Florence: Sansoni.

Mollmann, E. (1878). *Quatenus Sallustius e scriptorum graecorum exemplo pendeat*. Königsberg: Dalkowski.

Momigliano, A. (1974). 'Polybius' Reappearance in Western Europe'. *Entretiens Hardt* 20: 345–72.

Mommsen, T. (1854–60). *Römische Geschichte*, 3 vols. Berlin: Weidmann.

Mommsen, T. (1905–13). *Gesammelte Schriften*, 8 vols. Berlin: Weidmann.

Montaigne, M. de (1931). *Essais*, 3 vols. Ed. by J. Plattard. Paris: Roches.

Montgomery, P. A. (2013–14). 'Sallust's Scipio: A Preview of Aristocratic *Superbia* (Sal. *Jug*. 7. 2–9. 2)'. *CJ* 109: 21–40.

More, T. (1963). *The Complete Works*, vol. 2, *Richard III*. Ed. by R. L. Sylvester. New Haven, CT: Yale University Press.

More, T. (1965). *The Complete Works*, vol. 4, *Utopia*. Ed. by E. Surtz and J. H. Hexter. New Haven, CT: Yale University Press.

Morford, M. (1991). *Stoics and Neostoics: Rubens and the Circle of Lipsius*. Princeton, NJ: Princeton University Press.

Morgan, L. (2000). 'The Autopsy of C. Asinius Pollio'. *JRS* 90: 51–69.

Morstein-Marx, R. (2001). 'The Myth of Numidian Origins in Sallust's African Excursus (*Iugurtha* 17. 7–18. 12)'. *CPh* 122: 179–200.

Morstein-Marx, R. (2004). *Mass Oratory and Political Power in the Late Roman Republic*. Cambridge: Cambridge University Press.

Mouritsen, H. (2017). *Politics in the Roman Republic*. Cambridge: Cambridge University Press.

Moxon, I. S., Smart, J. D., and Woodman, A. J. (eds.) (1986). *Past Perspectives*. Cambridge: Cambridge University Press.

Münzer, F. (1897). *Beiträge zur Quellenkritik der Naturgeschichte des Plinius*. Berlin: Weidmann.

Münzer, F. (1920). *Römische Adelsparteien und Adelsfamilien*. Stuttgart: Metzler.

Muretus, M. A. (1789). 'Oratio' and 'In Sallustium Notae'. In D. Ruhnkenius (ed.), *M. Antonii Mureti Opera omnia*. 4 vols. Leiden: Luchtmans, vol. 1: 275–83 and vol. 4: 173–87.

Mussato, A. (1727). *De gestis Italicorum post Henricum VII Caesarem*. Ed. by L. A. Muratori. *RIS* 10: cols. 573–768.

Musti, D. (1989). 'Il pensiero storico romano'. In Cavallo, Fedeli, and Giardina (eds.), vol. 1, *La produzione del testo*, 177–240.

Naudé, G. (1633). *Bibliographia politica*. Venice: Baba.

Naudé, G. (1639). *Considérations politiques sur les coups d'éstat*. Rome.
Naudé, G. (1646). *Advis pour dresser une bibliothèque*. Paris: Targa.
Németh, B. (1992). 'To the Authenticity of Sallust's *Invectiva in Ciceronem*'. *ACD* 28: 73–7.
Newbold, R. (1990). 'Patterns of Anxiety in Sallust, Suetonius, and Procopius'. *AHB* 4: 44–50.
Nippel, W. (1995). *Public Order in Ancient Rome*. Cambridge: Cambridge University Press.
Nisbet, R. G. M. (1959). 'Notes on Horace, *Epistles* 1'. *CQ* 9: 73–7. (= (1995). In S. J. Harrison (ed.), *Collected Papers on Latin Literature*. Oxford: Oxford University Press, 1–3.)
Norden E. (1898). *Die antike Kunstprosa vom VI Jahrhundert vor Chr. bis in die Zeit der Renaissance*, 2 vols. Leipzig: Teubner.
Oakley, S. P. (1997–2005). *A Commentary on Livy Books VI–X*, 4 vols. Oxford: Oxford University Press.
O'Daly, G. (1999). *Augustine's City of God: A Reader's Guide*. Oxford: Oxford University Press.
Oestreich, G. (1982). *Neostoicism and the Early Modern State*. Ed. by B. Oestreich and H. G. Koenigsberger, transl. by D. McLintock. Cambridge: Cambridge University Press.
Ogilvie, R. M. (1970). *A Commentary on Livy Books 1–5*, 2nd edn. Oxford: Oxford University Press.
O'Gorman, E. (1993). 'No Place Like Rome: Identity and Difference in the *Germania* of Tacitus'. *Ramus* 22: 135–54.
O'Gorman, E. (1998). 'Alienation and Misreading: Narrative Dissent in the *Annals* of Tacitus'. Diss. Bristol.
O'Gorman, E. (2009). 'Intertextuality and Historiography'. In Feldherr (ed.), 231–42.
O'Malley, J. W. (1979). *Praise and Blame in Renaissance Rome*. Durham, NC: Duke University Press.
Oniga, R. (1990). *Il confine conteso. Lettura antropologica di un capitolo sallustiano (*Bellum Jugurthinum *79)*. Bari: Edipuglia.
Oniga, R. (1995). *Sallustio e l'etnografia*. Pisa: Giardini.
Oppermann, H. (1933). *Caesar, der Schriftsteller und sein Werk*. Leipzig: Teubner.
Orsini, F. (1570). *Imagines et elogia virorum illustrium et eruditorum ex antiquis lapidibus et nomismatibus expressa cum annotationibus*. Rome: Lafrery-Formeis.
Orsini, F. (1595). *Fragmenta historicorum collecta ab Antonio Augustino emendata a Fulvio Ursino*. Antwerp: Plantin-Moretus.
Osmond, P. J. (1993). 'Sallust and Machiavelli'. *Journal of Medieval and Renaissance Studies* 23: 407–38.
Osmond, P. J. (1994). 'Jacopo Corbinelli and the Reading of Sallust in Late Renaissance France'. *Medievalia et Humanistica* 19: 85–109.

Osmond, P. J. (1995). '"Princeps Historiae Romanae": Sallust in Renaissance Political Thought'. *MAAR* 40: 101–43.

Osmond, P. J. (2000). 'Catiline in Fiesole and Florence: The After-Life of a Roman Conspirator'. *IJCT* 7: 3–38.

Osmond, P. J. (2003). 'In the Margins of Sallust. Part III. Pomponio Leto's Notes on "Ars Historica"'. In M. Miglio (ed.), *Antiquaria a Roma. Intorno a Pomponio Leto e Paolo II*. Rome: Roma nel Rinascimento, 35–49.

Osmond, P. J. (2005). 'The Valla Commentary on Sallust's *Bellum Catilinae*: Questions of Authenticity and Reception'. In M. Pade (ed.), 29–48.

Osmond, P. J. (2010a). 'Pomponio Leto's Unpublished Commentary on Sallust: Five Witnesses (and More)'. In B. Wagner and M. Reed (eds.), *Early Printed Books as Material Objects. Proceedings of the Conference Organized by the IFLA Rare Books and Manuscripts Section, Munich, 19–21 August 2009*. Berlin: De Gruyter, 135–49.

Osmond, P. J. (2010b). 'Sallust'. In A. Grafton, G. W. Most, and S. Settis (eds.), *The Classical Tradition*. Cambridge, MA: Harvard University Press, 856–8.

Osmond, P. J. (2011). '*Lectiones Sallustianae*. Pomponio Leto's Annotations on Sallust: A Commentary for the Academy?'. In M. Pade (ed.), *On Renaissance Academies: Proceedings of the International Conference 'From the Roman Academy to the Danish Academy in Rome = Dall'Accademia Romana all'Accademia di Danimarca a Roma': The Danish Academy in Rome, 11–13 October 2006*. ARID Supplementum 42. Rome: Edizioni Quasar, 91–108.

Osmond, P. J. (2015a). 'Catiline in Renaissance Conspiracy Histories: Hero or Villain? The Case of Stefano Porcari'. In M. Chiabò, M. Gargano, A. Modigliani, and P. Osmond (eds.), *Congiure e conflitti: L'affermazione della signoria pontificia su Roma nel Rinascimento: politica, economia e cultura*. Rome: Roma nel Rinascimento, 203–15.

Osmond, P. J. (2015b). 'Pomponio Leto's Life of Sallust: Between *vita* and *invectiva*'. In M. Pade (ed.), *Vitae Pomponianae. Lives of Classical Writers in Fifteenth-Century Humanism*. *Renæssanceforum* 9: 35–62.

Osmond, P. J. and Ulery, R. W., Jr (1995). 'Constantius Felicius Durantinus and the Renaissance Origins of Anti-Sallustian Criticism'. *IJCT* 1: 29–56.

Osmond, P. J. and Ulery, R. W., Jr (2003). 'Sallustius Crispus, Gaius'. In Brown, Hankins, and Kaster (eds.), 183–326.

Osmond, P. J. and Ulery, R. W., Jr (2014). 'Sallustius Crispus, Gaius. Addenda et Corrigenda'. In Dinkova-Bruun, Hankins, and Kaster (eds.), 375–91.

Osmond, P. J. and Ulery, R. W., Jr (eds.) (2017). *Averrunci or The Skowrers: Ponderous and New Considerations on the First Six Books of the* Annals *of Cornelius Tacitus concerning Tiberius Caesar (Genoa, Biblioteca Durazzo, MS. A IV 5) by E. Bolton*. Renaissance English Text Society 38. Tempe, AZ: Arizona Center for Medieval and Renaissance Studies.

Otto, A. (1890). *Die Sprichwörter und sprichwörtlichen Redensarten der Römer*. Hildesheim: Olms.

Paananen, U. (1975). 'Die Echtheit der 'pseudosallustischen' Schriften'. *Historiallinen Arkisto* 68: 22–68.

Pade, M. (ed.) (2005). *On Renaissance Commentaries. Noctes Neolatinae* 4. Hildesheim: Olms.
Padel, R. (1992). *In and out of the Mind*. Princeton, NJ: Princeton University Press.
Paladini, V. (1948). *Sallustio*. Milan: Principato.
Palmieri, M. (1904). *De captivitate Pisarum liber*. Ed. by G. Scaramella. *RIS*, n.s. 19. 2. Città di Castello: Lapi.
Panella, E., O.P. (1979). 'Per lo studio di Fra Remigio dei Girolami (†1319)'. *Memorie domenicane*, n.s. 10: 1–313.
Panella, E., O.P. (1985). 'Dal bene comune al bene del comune. I trattati politici di Remigio dei Girolami nella Firenze dei bianchi-neri'. *Memorie domenicane* n.s. 16 (1985): 1–198.
Panella, E., O.P. (1989). 'Livio in Tolomeo da Lucca'. *Studi Petrarcheschi* 6: 43–52.
Pani, M. (ed.) (1991). *Continuità e transformazioni fra Repubblica e Principato: istituzioni, politica, società: Atti dell'incontro di studi organizzato da Università di Bari (Dipartimento di Scienze dell'Antichità), École française de Rome*. Bari: Edipuglia.
Pantzerhielm, T. S. (1936). 'The Prologues of Sallust'. *SO* 15: 140–62.
Parmentier, J. (1528). *L'Hystoire Catilinaire de Salluste*. Paris: Simon du Goys. [Reprinted 1969, Dublin: Aquila]
Paschkowski, I. (1966). 'Die Kunst der Reden in der 4. und 5. Dekade des Livius'. Diss. Kiel.
Pasoli, E. (1966). 'Pensiero storico ed espressione artistica nelle *Historiae* di Sallustio'. *Bolletino del comitato per la preparazione dell'edizione nazionale dei classici greci e latini*, 14: 23–50.
Pasoli, E. (1970). *Problemi delle* Epistolae ad Caesarem *sallustiane*. Bologna: Pátron.
Pasoli, E. (1975). 'Osservazioni sul proemio delle *Historiae* di Sallustio'. *StudUrb* (Ser. B) 49: 367–80.
Patrick, J. M. and Evans, R. O. (eds.) (1966). *Style, Rhetoric, and Rhythm*. Princeton, NJ: Princeton University Press.
Paul, G. M. (1984). *A Historical Commentary on Sallust's* Bellum Jugurthinum. Liverpool: Cairns.
Paul, G. M. (1985). 'Sallust's Sempronia: The Portrait of a Lady'. *Papers of the Liverpool Latin Seminar* 5: 9–22.
Pausch, D. (ed.) (2010). *Stimmen der Geschichte: Funktionen von Reden in der antiken Historiographie*. Berlin: De Gruyter.
Pelling, C. B. R. (ed.) (1988). *Plutarch: Life of Antony*. Cambridge: Cambridge University Press.
Pelling, C. B. R. (1993). 'Tacitus and Germanicus'. In Luce and Woodman (eds.), 59–85.
Pelling, C. B. R. (1996). 'Breaking the Bounds: Writing about Julius Caesar'. In McGing and Mossman (eds.), 255–80.
Pelling, C. B. R. (2013). 'Intertextuality, Plausibility, and Interpretation'. *Histos* 7: 1–20.

Bibliography

Pender, E. E. (1999). 'Plato's Moving Logos'. *PCPhS* 45: 75–107.
Perl, G. (1969). 'Sallusts politische Stellung'. *WZRostock* 18: 379–90.
Perrochat, P. (1932). *L'Infinitif de narration en latin. L'utilisation d'une forme d'expression esquissée*. Paris: Les Belles Lettres.
Perrochat, P. (1949). *Les Modèles grecs de Salluste*. Paris: Les Belles Lettres.
Petrarch, F. (1934). *Le familiari*, vol. 2, *Libri V–XI*. Ed. by V. Rossi. Florence: Sansoni.
Petrone, G. (1976). 'Per una ricostruzione del proemio delle *Historiae* di Sallustio'. *Pan* 4: 59–67.
Picone, G. (1976). 'La polemica anticulturale nel discorso di Mario (*B. Iug.* 85)'. *Pan* 4: 51–8.
Pirckheimer, W. (1737). *Bellum Suitense sive Helveticum cum Maximiliano Imperatore atque dynastis et civitatibus Suevicis feliciter gestum anno MCCCXCIX*. Zurich: Orell.
Plieningen, D. von (1515). *Des hochberompten Latinischen historischreibers Salustij: zwo schon historien, nemlichen von des Catilinen und auch des Jugurthen kriegen*. Landshut: Weyssenburger.
Poignault, R. (ed.) (1997). *Présence de Salluste*. Tours: Centre de recherches A. Piganiol, Université de Tours.
Poliziano, A. (1958). *Della congiura dei Pazzi (Coniurationis commentarium)*. Ed. by A. Perosa. Padua: Antenore.
Pontano, G. (1769). 'Historia belli quod Ferdinandus Rex Neapolitanus senior contra Ioannem Andegaviensem ducem gessit'. In Gravier (ed.), 1: 15.
Porzio, C. (1839). *L'istoria d'Italia nell'anno MDXLVIII e la descrizione del Regno di Napoli*. Naples: Tramater.
Porzio, C. (1958). *La congiura de' baroni del Regno di Napoli contra il Re Ferdinando Primo e gli altri scritti*. Ed. by E. Pontieri. Naples: Edizioni scientifiche italiane.
Pöschl, V. (1940). *Grundwerte römischer Staatsgesinnung in den Geschichtswerken des Sallust*. Berlin: De Gruyter. (Reprinted 1967).
Pöschl, V. (1970). 'Die Reden Caesars und Catos in Sallusts *Catilina*'. In V. Pöschl (ed.), *Sallust*. Darmstadt: Wissenschaftliche Buchgesellschaft, 368–97.
Powell, B. (1991). *Homer and the Origin of the Greek Alphabet*. Cambridge: Cambridge University Press.
Powell, J. G. F. (ed.) (1988). *Cicero, Cato Maior de Senectute*. Cambridge: Cambridge University Press.
Quint, D. (1993). *Epic and Empire*. Princeton, NJ: Princeton University Press.
Rambaud, M. (1946). 'Les Prologues de Salluste et la démonstration morale de son œuvre'. *REL* 24: 115–130.
Ramsey, J. T. (ed. and transl.) (2007). *Sallust's* Bellum Catilinae, 2nd edn. Oxford: Oxford University Press.
Ramsey, J. T. (ed.) (2015). *Sallust: Fragments of the Histories; Letters to Caesar*. Loeb Classical Library 522. Cambridge, MA: Harvard University Press.

Bibliography 469

Reckzey, A. (1888). *Über grammatische und rhetorische Stellung des Adjektivums bei den Annalisten, Cato und Sallust*. Berlin: Gaertner.

Reden, S. von (1998). 'The Commodification of Symbols: Reciprocity and its Perversions in Menander'. In C. Gill, N. Postlethwaite, and R. Seaford (eds.), *Reciprocity in Ancient Greece*, 255–78. Oxford: Oxford University Press.

Regenbogen, O. (1932). *Lukrez: Seine Gestalt in seinem Gedicht*. Leipzig: Teubner.

Reitzenstein, R. (1906). *Hellenistische Wundererzählungen*. Leipzig: Teubner.

Renehan, R. (1962). 'Duo loci Sallustiani'. *RhM* 105: 257–60.

Renehan, R. (1976). 'A Traditional Pattern of Imitation in Sallust and his Sources'. *CPh* 71: 97–105.

Renehan, R. (2000). 'Further Thoughts on a Sallustian Literary Device'. *AncW* 31: 144–7.

Reynolds, L. D. (1983). *Texts and Transmission*. Oxford: Oxford University Press.

Reynolds, L. D. (ed.) (1991). *C. Sallusti Crispi Catilina, Iugurtha, Historiarum fragmenta selecta, Appendix Sallustiana*. Oxford Classical Texts. Oxford: Oxford University Press.

Richter, W. (1973). 'Der Manierismus des Sallust und die Sprache der römischen Historiographie'. *ANRW* 1.3: 755–80.

Ridley, R. T. (1983). 'Falsi triumphi, plures consulatus'. *Latomus* 42: 372–83.

Riposati, B. (1978). 'L'arte del ritratto in Sallustio'. In A. Pastorino (ed.), *Sallustio: letture critiche*. Milan: Mursia, 135–49.

Rivius, J. (1547). Preface to 'Castigationum libri II ... in historiam de Coniuratione Catilinae, alter vero in Jugurthinum Bellum. Item in fragmenta Historiarum Sallustii'. In *Opera*, by Sallust. Venice: In aedibus Venturini Roffinelli.

Roberts, C. H. (ed.) (1938). *Catalogue of the Greek and Latin Papyri in the John Rylands Library*, vol. 3, *Theological and Literary Texts (Nos. 457–551)*. Manchester: Manchester University Press.

Roberts, D. H., Dunn, F. M., and Fowler, D. P. (eds.) (1997). *Classical Closure: Reading the End in Greek and Latin Literature*. Princeton, NJ: Princeton University Press.

Roberts, M. (1989). *The Jeweled Style*. Ithaca, NY: Cornell University Press.

Rolfe, J. C. (ed. and transl.) (1921; rev. 1931, rep. 1985). *Sallust*. Loeb Classical Library. Cambridge, MA: Harvard University Press.

Rosen, C. (1995). *The Romantic Imagination*. Cambridge, MA: Harvard University Press.

Rosenberg A. (1921). *Einleitung und Quellenkunde zur römischen Geschichte*. Berlin: Weidmann.

Rosenblitt, J. A. (2011). 'The *"devotio"* of Sallust's Cotta'. *AJPh* 132: 397–427.

Rosenblitt, J. A. (2013). 'Sallust's *Historiae* and the Voice of Sallust's Lepidus'. *Arethusa* 46: 447–70.

Rosenblitt, J. A. (2016). 'Hostile Politics: Sallust and the Rhetoric of Popular Champions in the Late Republic'. *AJPh* 137: 655–88.

Rosenblitt, J. A. (2019). *Rome after Sulla*. London: Bloomsbury.

Rubinstein, N. (1957). 'Some Ideas on Municipal Progress and Decline in the Italy of the Communes'. In D. J. Gordon (ed.), *Fritz Saxl 1890–1948. A Volume of Memorial Essays*. London: Nelson, 165–83.

Rucellai, B. (1733). *De bello Italico commentarius*. London: Bowyer.

Rudd, N. (1966). *The Satires of Horace*. Cambridge: Cambridge University Press.

Rutledge, H. C. (1964). Review of D. C. Earl, *The Political Thought of Sallust*. *CJ* 58: 136–8.

Salmon, J. H. M. (1980). 'Cicero and Tacitus in Sixteenth-Century France'. *AHR* 85: 307–31.

Salmon, J. H. M. (1989). 'Stoicism and Roman Example: Seneca and Tacitus in Jacobean England'. *JHI* 50: 199–225.

Salutati, C. (1891–1911). *Epistolario di Coluccio Salutati*, 4 vols. Ed. by F. Novati. Rome: Forzani.

Samotta, I. (2009). *Das Vorbild der Vergangenheit: Geschichtsbild und Reformvorschläge bei Cicero und Sallust*. Historia Einzelschriften 204. Stuttgart: Steiner.

Sanders, H. A. (1932). 'The So-Called First Triumvirate'. *MAAR* 10: 55–68.

Santangelo, F. (2012). 'Authoritative Forgeries: Late Republican History Re-Told in Pseudo-Sallust'. *Histos* 6: 27–51.

Sasso, G. (1980). *Niccolò Machiavelli: Storia del suo pensiero politico*, 2nd edn. Bologna: Il Mulino.

Sasso, G. (1987). *Machiavelli e gli antichi*. Milan: Ricciardi.

Scaliger, J. S. (1561). *Poetices libri septem*. Lyon: Petrus Santandreanus.

Scanlon, T. F. (1980). *The Influence of Thucydides on Sallust*. Heidelberg: Winter.

Scanlon, T. F. (1987). *Spes Frustrata: A Reading of Sallust*. Heidelberg: Winter.

Scanlon, T. F. (1988). 'Textual Geography in Sallust's *The War with Jugurtha*'. *Ramus* 17: 138–175.

Scanlon, T. F. (1998). 'Reflexivity and Irony in the Proem of Sallust's *Historiae*'. In Deroux (ed.), 186–224.

Schellhase, K. (1976). *Tacitus in Renaissance Political Thought*. Chicago: University of Chicago Press.

Schindler, F. (1939). 'Untersuchungen zur Geschichte des Sallustbildes'. Diss. Breslau.

Schmal, S. (2001). *Sallust*. Hildesheim: Olms.

Schmid, W. (1993). *Frühschriften Sallusts im Horizont des Gesamtwerks*, Neustadt-Aisch: Schmidt.

Schmidt, P. L. (2008). 'Sallust'. In H. Cancik and H. Schneider (eds.). *Brill's Encyclopedia of the Ancient World: New Pauly*. (English edition by C. F. Salazar), vol. 12. Leiden: Brill, 890–4.

Schmitz, T. A. (2012). 'Herakles in Bits and Pieces: *Id.* 25 in the *Corpus Theocriteum*'. In Baumbach and Bär (eds.), 259–82.

Schur, W. (1934). *Sallust als Historiker*. Stuttgart: Kohlhammer.

Schuster, M. (1926). 'Zu den Theorien über die Entstehung und das Wesen des sogenannten historischen Infinitivs'. In *Festschrift für Paul Kretschmer: Beitrage zur griechischen und lateinischen Sprachforschung*. Vienna: Verlag für Jugend und Volk.

Schwarte, K.-H. (2000). 'Publius Cornelius Scipio Africanus der Ältere—Eroberer zwischen West und Ost'. In Hölkeskamp and Stein-Hölkeskamp (eds.), 106–19.
Schwartz, E. (1896a). Review of E. Meyer, *Untersuchungen zur Geschichte der Gracchen. GGA* 158: 792–811.
Schwartz, E. (1896b). *Fünf Vorträge über den griechischen Roman*. Berlin: Reimer.
Schwartz, E. (1897). 'Die Berichte über die catilinarische Verschwörung'. *Hermes* 32: 560–608.
Schwartz, E. (1905). 'Diodorus'. In A. Pauly, G. Wissowa, W. Kroll, K. Witte, K. Mittelhaus, and K. Ziegler (eds.), *Paulys Realencyclopädie der classischen Altertumswissenschaft: Neue Bearbeitung*, vol. 5.10. Stuttgart: 658–704.
Scullard, H. H. (1951). *Roman Politics, 220–150 B.C.* Oxford: Oxford University Press.
Seel, O. (1930). *Sallust von den Briefen ad Caesarem zur Coniuratio Catilinae*. Leipzig: Teubner.
Seel, O. (1966). *Sallusts Briefe und die pseudosallustische Invektive*. Nuremberg: Carl.
Segre, C. (1963). *Lingua, stile e società: Studi sulla storia della prosa italiana*. Milan: Feltrinelli.
Sekora, J. (1977). *Luxury: The Concept in Western Thought, Eden to Smollett*. Baltimore, MD: John Hopkins University Press.
Shackleton Bailey, D. R. (1981). 'Sallustiana'. *Mnemosyne* 34: 351–6.
Sherwin-White, A. N. (1939). *The Roman Citizenship*. Oxford: Oxford University Press.
Shimron, B. (1967). 'Caesar's Place in Sallust's Political Theory'. *Athenaeum* 45: 335–45.
Skard, E. (1933). *Ennius und Sallustius; eine sprachliche Untersuchung*. Oslo: Dybwad.
Skard, E. (1941). 'Marius' Speech in Sall. *Iug*. 85'. *SO* 21: 98–102.
Skard, E. (1956). *Sallust und seine Vorgänger. SO fasc. supplet.* 15. Oslo: Brøgger.
Skinner, Q. (1978). *Foundations of Modern Political Thought*, 2 vols. Cambridge: Cambridge University Press.
Skinner, Q. (1981). *Machiavelli*. New York: Hill and Wang.
Skinner, Q. (1986). 'Ambrogio Lorenzetti: The Artist as Political Philosopher'. *PBA* 72: 1–56.
Skinner, Q. (1990). 'Machiavelli's *Discorsi* and the Pre-Humanist Origins of Republican Ideas'. In G. Bock, Q. Skinner, and M. Viroli (eds.), *Machiavelli and Republicanism*. Cambridge: Cambridge University Press, 121–41.
Skinner, Q. (2002). *Visions of Politics*, 3 vols. Cambridge: Cambridge University Press.
Sklenář, R. (1998). 'La République des Signes: Caesar, Cato, and the Language of Sallustian Morality'. *TAPhA* 128: 205–220.
Skutsch, O. (1985). *The Annals of Quintus Ennius*. Oxford: Oxford University Press.

Smalley, B. (1971). 'Sallust in the Middle Ages'. In Bolgar (ed.), 165–75.
Smith, B. H. (1968). *Poetic Closure: A Study of How Poems End*. Chicago: University of Chicago Press.
Souilhé, J. (ed. and transl.) (1931). *Platon: Œuvres complètes. Tome XIII, 1re partie: Lettres*. Paris: Budé.
Spielberg, L. (2017). 'Language, *Stasis* and the Role of the Historian in Thucydides, Sallust and Tacitus'. *AJPh* 138: 331–73.
Spini, G. (1948). 'I trattatisti dell'arte storica nella Controriforma italiana'. In *Contributi alla storia del Concilio di Trento e della Controriforma. Quaderni del Belfagor*. Florence: Vallecchi, 109–136.
Starr, R. J. (1981). 'Cross-References in Roman Prose'. *AJPh* 102: 431–7.
Steed, K. S. (2017). 'The Speeches of Sallust's *Histories* and the Legacy of Sulla'. *Historia* 66: 401–41.
Steel, C. (2013). *The End of the Roman Republic, 146–44 B.C.* Edinburgh: Edinburgh University Press.
Steele, R. B. (1891). 'Chiasmus in Sallust, Caesar, Tacitus, and Iustinus'. Diss. Johns Hopkins University.
Steidle, W. (1958). *Sallusts historische Monographien: Themenwahl und Geschichtsbild. Historia* Einzelschriften 3. Wiesbaden: Steiner.
Stein, P. (1930). 'Die Senatssitzungen der ciceronischen Zeit'. Diss. Münster.
Stein, R. M. (1977). 'Sallust for his Readers, 410–1550'. Diss. Columbia.
Stern, E. von (1883). *Catilina und die Parteikämpfe in Rom der Jahre 66–63*. Tartu: Laakmann.
Sternberg, M. (1991). 'How Indirect Discourse Means: Syntax, Semantics, Poetics, Pragmatics'. In R. D. Sell (ed.), *Literary Pragmatics*. London: Routledge, 62–93.
Stone, M. (1999). 'Tribute to a Statesman: Cicero and Sallust'. *Antichthon* 33: 48–76.
Strasburger, H. (1982). *Studien zur Alten Geschichte*, vol. 1. Hildesheim: Olms.
Suerbaum, W. (1964). 'Rex ficta locutus est'. *Hermes* 92: 85–106.
Syme, R. (1939). *The Roman Revolution*. Oxford: Oxford University Press (rev. repr. 1952).
Syme, R. (1964). *Sallust*. Berkeley, CA: University of California Press (repr. with a new foreword by R. Mellor, 2002).
Taisne, A.-M. (1997). 'Salluste chez saint Augustin (Cité de Dieu, I–V)'. In Poignault (ed.), 119–28.
Theißen, W. (1912). 'De Sallustii Livii Taciti digressionibus'. Diss. Berlin.
Thommen, L. (2000). 'Gaius Marius—oder: der Anfang vom Ende der Republik'. In Hölkeskamp and Stein-Hölkeskamp (eds.), 187–98.
Thraede, K. (1977). 'Zur Häufigkeit einiger Satzschlußrhythmen bei Sallust und in den Briefen an Caesar'. *GB* 6: 133–47.
Thraede, K. (1978). 'E. Skards sprachstatistische Behandlung der *Epistulae ad Caesarem Senem*'. *Mnemosyne* 31: 179–95.
Thuau, É. (1966). *Raison d'état et pensée politique à l'époque de Richelieu*. Athens: Institut français d'Athènes.

Tiffou, E. (1973). *Essai sur la penseé morale de Salluste à la lumière de ses prologues*. Paris: Klincksieck.

Toffanin, G. (1972). *Machiavelli e il 'Tacitismo'*, 2nd edn. Naples: Guida.

Torgovnick, M. (1981). *Closure in the Novel*. Princeton, NJ: Princeton University Press.

Tours, M. de (1532). *Salluste autheur romain de la guerre que les Romains feirent a lencontre de Iugurtha, Roy de Numidie*. Paris: Galliot de Pré.

Townend, G. B. (1983). 'The Unstated Climax of Catullus 64'. *G&R* 30: 21-30.

Tränkle, H. (1971). *Cato in der vierten und fünften Dekade des Livius*. Mainz: Verlag der Akademie der Wissenschaften und der Literatur.

Ulery, R. W., Jr (1986). 'Cornelius Tacitus'. In F. E. Cranz, V. Brown, and P. O. Kristeller (eds.), *Catalogus Translationum et Commentariorum: Mediaeval and Renaissance Latin Translations and Commentaries*, vol. 6. Washington DC: Catholic University of America Press, 87-174.

Ulery, R. W., Jr (1999). 'Sallust'. In W. W. Briggs (ed.), *Dictionary of Literary Biography*, vol. 211, *Ancient Roman Writers*. Detroit, MI: Gale, 267-76.

Ulery, R. W., Jr (2003). 'In the Margins of Sallust. Part II. The Sources and Method of Commentary'. In M. Miglio (ed.), *Antiquaria a Roma. Intorno a Pomponio Leto e Paolo II*. Rome: Roma nel Rinascimento, 13-33.

Ulery, R. W., Jr (2005). 'Sallust's *Bellum Catilinae* in the Edition of Venice, 1500: The Medieval Commentary and the Renaissance Reader'. In M. Pade (ed.), 7-28.

Ullmann, B. L. (1923). 'Petrarch's Favorite Books'. *TAPhA* 54: 21-38.

Ullmann, B. L. (1942). 'History and Tragedy'. *TAPhA* 73: 25-53.

Ullmann, R. (1927). *La Technique des discours dans Salluste, Tite-Live et Tacite*. Oslo: Dybwad.

Van den Hout, M. P. J. (1999). *A Commentary on the Letters of M. Cornelius Fronto*. Leiden: Brill.

Van Ooteghem, J. (1954). *Pompée le Grand bâtisseur de l'empire*. Brussels: Palais des Académies.

Vassiliadès, G. (2015). 'Écrire l'histoire sous les Triumvirs: Salluste et sa position politique'. *Historiographies antiques*. https://storioant.hypotheses.org/55, accessed 30 Apr. 2019.

Venturini, C. (1973). '*Libertas* e *dominatio* nell'opera di Sallustio e nella pubblicistica dei *populares* (osservazioni e problemi)'. In *Studi per Ermanno Graziani*. Pisa: Pacini: 636-58.

Verbrugghe, G. (1989). 'On the Meaning of *Annales*, On the Meaning of Annalist'. *Philologus* 113: 192-230.

Villani, G. (1990-1). *Nuova cronica*, 3 vols. Ed. by G. Porta. Parma: Guanda.

Viroli, M. (1992). *From Politics to Reason of State: The Acquisition and Transformation of the Language of Politics 1250-1600*. Cambridge: Cambridge University Press.

Voisin de La Popelinière, L. (1599). *L'Histoire des histoires avec l'idée de l'histoire accomplice. Plus le dessein de l'histoire nouvelle des français*. Paris: Orry.

Voit, L. (1982). Review of G. Lehmann, *Politische Reformvorschläge in der Krise der späten römischen Republik. Cicero* De legibus III *und Sallusts Sendschreiben an Caesar*'. *Gymnasium* 89: 340–2.

Voss, G. J. (1627). *De Historicis Latinis Libri III*. Leiden: Maire.

Vretska, K. (1937). 'Der Aufbau des *Bellum Catilinae*'. *Hermes* 72: 202–22.

Vretska, K. (1955). *Studien zu Sallusts* Bellum Jugurthinum. *SAWW* 229.4. Vienna: Rohrer.

Vretska, K. (1961). *C. Sallustius Crispus: Invektive und Episteln*, 2 vols. Heidelberg: Winter.

Vretska, K. (1976). *C. Sallustius Crispus: De Catilinae Coniuratione*. Heidelberg: Winter.

Wackernagel, J. (1920–4). *Vorlesungen über Syntax mit besonderer Berücksichtigung von Griechisch, Lateinisch und Deutsch*, 2 vols. Basle: Birkhaüser.

Waite, G. (ed.) (2014). *The Famous Cronycle of the Warre which the Romayns had agaynst Iugurth, Usurper of the Kyngdome of Numidy: Alexander Barclay's Translation of Sallust's* Bellum Iugurthinum. Oxford: Oxford University Press.

Walker, L. J. (transl.) (1950). *The Discourses of Niccolò Machiavelli*, 2 vols. New Haven, CT: Yale University Press.

Walter, U. (2004). *Memoria und res publica. Zur Geschichtskultur im republikanischen Rom*. Studien zur Alten Geschichte 1. Frankfurt: Verlag Antike.

Watkins, R. N. (1978). *Humanism and Liberty: Writings on Freedom from Fifteenth-Century Florence*. Columbia, SC: University of South Carolina Press.

Watkiss, L. (ed.) (1971). *Gaii Sallusti Crispi Bellum Iugurthinum (The Jugurtha)*. London: University Tutorial Press.

Wegehaupt, H. (1932). 'Die Bedeutung und Anwendung von *dignitas* in den Schriften der republikanischen Zeit'. Diss. Breslau.

Weiss, R. (1941). *Humanism in England during the Fifteenth Century*. Oxford: Oxford University Press.

Welch, K. E. (2012). *Magnus Pius: Sextus Pompeius and the Transformation of the Roman Republic*. Swansea: Classical Press of Wales.

Werner, V. (1995). Quantum bello optimus, tantum pace pessimus. *Studien zum Mariusbild in der antiken Geschichtsschreibung*. Habelts Dissertationsdrucke, Reihe Alte Geschichte 39. Bonn: Habelt.

Wheare, D. (1685). *The Method and Order of Reading both Civil and Ecclesiastical Histories*. Transl. by E. Bohun. London: M. Flesher for Charles Brome.

Wheeldon, M. J. (1989). '"True Stories": The Reception of Historiography in Antiquity'. In A. M. Cameron (ed.), *History as Text: The Writing of Ancient History*. Chapel Hill, NC: University of North Carolina Press, 33–63.

Wheeler, E. (1988). *Stratagem and the Vocabulary of Military Trickery*. Leiden: Brill.

White, H. (1973). *Metahistory: The Historical Imagination in Nineteenth-Century Europe*. Baltimore, MD: Johns Hopkins University Press.

White, H. (1987). *The Content of the Form: Narrative Discourse and Historical Representation*. Baltimore, MD: John Hopkins University Press.
White, H. (2010). *The Fiction of Narrative: Essays on History, Literature, and Theory*. Ed. and intr. by R. Doran. Baltimore, MD: Johns Hopkins University Press.
Whitfield, J. H. (1947). *Machiavelli*. Oxford: Oxford University Press.
Whitfield, J. H. (1976). "Livy > Tacitus." In Bolgar (ed.), 281–94.
Wiedemann, T. (1979). '*Nunc ad inceptum redeo*. Sallust, *Jugurtha* 4.9 and Cato'. *LCM* 4: 13–16.
Wiedemann, T. (1980). 'Sallust, *Jugurtha* 4.9. A Misplaced Formula?'. *LCM* 5: 147–149.
Wiedemann, T. (1986). 'Between Men and Beasts'. In Moxon, Smart, and Woodman (eds.), 189–211.
Wiedemann, T. (1993). 'Sallust's *Jugurtha*: Concord, Discord, and the Digressions'. *G&R* 40: 48–57.
Wilamowitz-Moellendorff, U. von (1906). *Die Textgeschichte der griechischen Bukoliker*. Philologische Untersuchungen 18. Berlin: Weidmann.
Wilcox, D. (1971). 'Matteo Palmieri and the "De Captivitate Pisarum Liber"'. In A. Molho and J. A. Tedeschi (eds.), *Renaissance Studies in Honor of Hans Baron*. Florence: Sansoni, 265–81.
Wilkins, A. T. (1994). *Villain or Hero: Sallust's Portrayal of Catiline*. New York: Lang.
Wille, G. (1970). 'Der Mariusexkurs Kap. 63 im Aufbau von Sallusts *Bellum Iugurthinum*'. In D. Ableitinger and H. Gugel (eds), *Festschrift für Karl Vretska*. Heidelberg: Winter, 304–31.
Wirszubski, C. (1950). *Libertas as a Political Idea at Rome during the Late Republic and Early Principate*. Cambridge: Cambridge University Press.
Wirz, H. (1864). *Catilinas und Ciceros Bewerbung um den Consulat für das Jahr 63*. Zurich: Höhr.
Wiseman, T. P. (1971). *New Men in the Roman Senate*. Oxford: Oxford University Press.
Wiseman, T. P. (1979). *Clio's Cosmetics: Three Studies in Greco-Roman Literature*. Leicester: Leicester University Press.
Wiseman, T. P. (1981). 'Monuments and the Roman Annalists'. In Moxon, Smart, and Woodman (eds.), 87–100.
Wiseman, T. P. (2009). *Remembering the Roman People: Essays on Late-Republican Politics and Literature*. Oxford: Oxford University Press.
Witt, R. G. (1969). "Coluccio Salutati and the Origins of Florence." *PPol* 2: 161–72.
Witt, R. G. (1976). *Coluccio Salutati and his Public Letters*. Geneva: Librairie Droz.
Witt, R. G. (1983). *Hercules at the Crossroads: The Life, Works, and Thought of Coluccio Salutati*. Durham, NC: Duke University Press.
Wölfflin, E. (1876). 'Bemerkungen über das Vulgärlatein'. *Philologus* 34: 137–65.

Woodman, A. J. (1973). 'A Note on Sallust, *Catilina* 1.1'. *CQ* 23: 310.
Woodman, A. J. (1975). 'Questions of Date, Genre, and Style in Velleius: Some Literary Answers'. *CQ* 25: 272–306.
Woodman, A. J. (ed.) (1977). *Velleius Paterculus: The Tiberian Narrative (2.94–131)*. Cambridge: Cambridge University Press.
Woodman, A. J. (ed.) (1983). *Velleius Paterculus: The Caesarian and Augustan Narratives (2.41–93)*. Cambridge: Cambridge University Press.
Woodman, A. J. (1977–83). *Velleius Paterculus: The Caesarian, Augustan, and Tiberian Narratives*. 2 vols. Cambridge: Cambridge University Press.
Woodman, A. J. (1988a). 'Contemporary History in the Classical World'. In A. Seldon (ed.), *Contemporary History: Practice and Method*. Oxford: Oxford University Press, 149–64.
Woodman, A. J. (1988b). *Rhetoric in Classical Historiography: Four Studies*. Portland, OR: Areopagitica.
Woodman, A. J. (1992). 'Nero's Alien Capital: Tacitus as Paradoxographer (Annals 15.36-7)'. In A. J. Woodman and J. Powell (eds.), *Author and Imitation in Latin Literature*. Cambridge: Cambridge University Press, 173–88, 251–5.
Woodward, D. (1987). *The History of Cartography*, vol. 1, *Cartography in Prehistoric, Ancient, and Medieval Europe and the Mediterranean*. Ed. by J. B. Harley and D. Woodward. Chicago: University of Chicago Press.
Woolf, G. (2011). *Tales of the Barbarians: Ethnography and Empire in the Roman West*. Chichester: Wiley-Blackwell.
Woytek, E. (2004). 'Klärendes zu den pseudo-sallustischen *"epistulae"*' In H. Heftner and K. Tomaschitz (eds.), *Ad Fontes!: Festschrift für Gerhard Dobesch zum fünfundsechzigsten Geburtstag*. Vienna: Privately Published, 329–41.
Zahrndt, M. (2000). 'Publius Cornelius Scipio Aemilianus—der intrigante Enkel'. In Hölkeskamp and Stein-Hölkeskamp (eds.), 159–71.
Zanker, G. (1987). *Realism in Alexandrian Poetry: A Literature and its Audience*. London: Croom Helm.

Acknowledgements

Permission to reprint the following items is gratefully acknowledged:

K. Latte, 'Sallust: Diction and Sentence Structure, Narrative Style and Composition, Personality and Times', in *Sallust, Neue Wege zur Antike* 2.4 (Stuttgart: Teubner, 1935), 401–59.

D. C. Earl, 'The Moral Crisis in Sallust's View', in *The Political Thought of Sallust* (Cambridge: Cambridge University Press, 1961), 41–59. © Faculty of Classics, University of Cambridge, published by Cambridge University Press, reproduced with permission.

R. Renehan, 'A Traditional Pattern of Imitation in Sallust and his Sources', *Classical Philology* 71 (1976): 95–105. © 1976 by the University of Chicago Press.

E. Schwartz, 'Die Berichte über die catilinarische Verschwörung', *Hermes* 32 (1897), 560–608.

W. W. Batstone, 'Intellectual Conflict and Mimesis in Sallust's *Bellum Catilinae*', in J. W. Allison (ed.), *Conflict, Antithesis, and the Ancient Historian* (Columbus, OH: Ohio State University Press, 1990), 112–32 (text), 189–94 (notes).

E. Gunderson, 'The History of Mind and the Philosophy of History in Sallust's *Bellum Catilinae*', *Ramus* 29 (2000): 85–126.

D. S. Levene, 'Sallust's *Catiline* and Cato the Censor', *Classical Quarterly* 50 (2000): 170–91.

C. S. Kraus, 'Jugurthine Disorder', in C. Kraus (ed.), *The Limits of Historiography: Genre and Narrative in Ancient Historical Texts* (Leiden: Brill, 1999), 217–47.

D. S. Levene, 'Sallust's *Jugurtha*: An "Historical Fragment"', *Journal of Roman Studies* 82 (1992), 53–70.

T. Wiedemann, 'Sallust's *Jugurtha*: Concord, Discord, and the Digressions', *Greece & Rome* 40 (1993), 48–57. © The Classical Association, published by Cambridge University Press, reproduced with permission.

U. Egelhaaf-Gaiser, '*Non sunt conposita verba mea*: Reflected Narratology in Sallust's Speech of Marius', in D. Pausch (ed.), *Stimmen der Geschichte: Funktionen von Reden in der antiken Historiographie* (Berlin: De Gruyter, 2010), 157–82.

A. La Penna, 'The *Histories*: The Crisis of the *Res Publica*', in *Sallustio e la 'rivoluzione' romana* (Milan: Feltrinelli, 1968), 247–311.

F. Klingner, 'Über die Einleitung der *Historien* Sallusts', *Hermes* 63 (1928): 165–92.

P. J. Osmond, '*Princeps Historiae Romanae*: Sallust in Renaissance Political Thought', *Memoirs of the American Academy in Rome* 40 (1995): 101–43.

Index of Passages

Aesch. *Sept.* 592: 105, 106, 228
  597–614: 106
Anth. Lat. 409.9ff.: 362 n. 27
App. *B Civ.* 1.12–13: 101 n. 81
  1.22: 101 n. 84, 101 n. 85
  1.29–32: 288 n. 42
  1.120: 393 n. 53
  2.2: 62
  5.5: 101 n. 84
  Hisp. 49: 85 n. 5, 94 n. 47
    51–5: 85 n. 3
    59–61: 85 n. 3
    70: 93 n. 40
    79: 94 n. 43
    83: 94 n. 43
    84–5: 94 n. 41
    85–6: 94 n. 42
  Num. 1: 60, 293 n. 48
    3: 66
  Pun. 65: 91 n. 29, 236–237, 344
    69: 91 n. 27, 93 n. 34
Arist. II 255.5 Dind.: 51 n. 44
  Pol. 7.1334a–b: 91 n. 26
Asc. 23 C: 94 n. 45
  37.16–21 C: 3 n. 8
  49.6–8 C: 73
  49.24–50.1 C: 3 n. 8, 73
  51.10–11: 73
  83.20–2: 119 n. 21, 119 n. 23
  83.26–84.11 C: 385
Ath. 6.108: 85 n. 4
  6.274C: 85 n. 4
  6.274–5: 86–87 n. 7
Auct. *Bell. Afr.* 73.2: 251 n. 25
August *De civ. D.* 1.30: 91 n. 23
  2.18: 282 n. 33, 340, 346
  2.22: 282 n.33, 347
  5.12: 340 n. 1
  5.15ff.: 340 n. 1
  5.30ff.: 340 n. 1
  16.17: 340
  Ep. 138.16: 293 n. 48
BAfr. 22.2: 98 n. 67
C. Gracchus frr. 48–9 *ORF*: 97 n. 58
Caecil. 204 R: 38

Caes. *B Civ.* 1.4.4: 97 n. 63, 357
  1.4.5: 352
  1.7.1: 357
  1.7.7: 97 n. 64
  1.9.2: 97 n. 64
  1.22.5: 98
  2.14.3: 259 n. 49
  2.26.3: 259 n. 49
  3.72.4: 270 n. 86
  3.91.2: 97 n. 64
  B Gall. 2.18: 48
  4.32: 45
  4.33: 46
  4.34: 46
  4.38: 32
  5.4: 247 n. 14
  8.3.4: 247 n. 14
  19.6: 247 n. 14
CAH[1] 8.377: 93 n. 39
Cato *Agr.* 1.2: 82
  141: 34
  Carmen de Moribus frs. 2–3: 216 n. 10
  Orat. 17–18 *ORF*: 85 n. 2
  21 *ORF*: 222
  35 *ORF*: 38
  58 *ORF*: 216 n. 11
  58–65 *ORF*: 85 n. 3
  59 *ORF*: 238 n. 71
  62 *ORF*: 238 n. 71
  66 *ORF*: 85 n. 3
  69–71 *ORF*: 93 n. 35
  78 *ORF*: 216 n. 10
  94 *ORF* (=Fronto 227 VDH):
    86–87 n. 7, 93 n. 35, 220 n. 26
  110 *ORF*: 93 n. 35, 220 n. 27
  111 *ORF*: 216 n. 10
  117 *ORF*: 234
  121 *ORF*: 92 n. 30
  122 *ORF*: 89 n. 15
  128 *ORF*: 220 n. 27
  131 *ORF*: 93 n. 35
  132 *ORF*: 216 n. 10
  136 *ORF*: 220 n. 26
  139 *ORF*: 216 n. 10
  141 *ORF*: 220 n. 27
  142 *ORF*: 216 n. 10
  144 *ORF*: 216 n. 10
  145–6 *ORF*: 93 n. 35

Index of Passages

Cato *Agr.* 1.2: (*cont.*)
  146 *ORF*: 86–87 n. 7, 216 n. 10
  148 *ORF*: 220 n. 25
  154 *ORF*: 220 n. 26
  154–5 *ORF*: 85 n. 3
  163 *ORF*: 223, 224, 235, 252 n. 30
  163 M (=fr. 95a P): 252 n. 30
  163, 164 *ORF* (=*Orig.* 95a–b P): 92 n. 30
  164 *ORF*: 236
  164.4 *ORF*: 226–227 n. 45
  173 *ORF*: 216 n. 11, 217 n. 14, 220 n. 26
  173–5 *ORF*: 85 n. 4
  174 *ORF*: 220 n. 27
  174–5 *ORF*: 93 n. 35, 239
  177 *ORF*: 216 n. 11, 220 n. 26, 238 n. 71
  185 *ORF*: 220 n. 27
  186 *ORF*: 220 n. 25
  212 *ORF* (=57.1 Jordan): 36 n. 18
  213 *ORF*: 220 n. 27
  217 *ORF* (= 67.5 Jordan): 37
  224 *ORF*: 93 n. 35, 216 n. 11, 220 n. 26, 232 n. 59
  247 *ORF*: 93 n. 35
  254 *ORF*: 93 n. 35
Orig. 1 P: 217
  2 P: 219 n. 22, 232
  5 P (=Serv. *Aen.* 1.6): 220
  20 P: 221–222
  34 P: 36
  81 P (=85 *FRHist*): 37
  82 P: 222 n. 35
  83 P (=76 *FRHist*): 67, 221 n. 32
  95a P (=87 *FRHist*): 89 n. 15
  95a–b P (=87–8 *FRHist*): 92 n. 30
  95b P (=88 *FRHist*): 345 n. 9

Catull. 72.5–6: 249 n. 21

Charis. p. 146.31: 119 n. 21

Cic. *Acad. Pr.* 2.62: 138 n. 56
  Arch. 3.14: 9 n. 15
  Att. 1.14.4: 137 n. 54
    1.14.5: 138 n. 56
    1.16.15: 116 n. 2
    1.17.9: 101 n. 84
    1.19.10: 117 n. 6, 117 n. 7
    2.1.1: 117 n. 5
    2.1.2: 117 n. 3
    2.1.7: 137 n. 54
    2.2.2: 117 n. 4
    2.6.2: 119 n. 15
    2.7.4: 79
    2.12.4: 79

    2.16.3: 79
    2.24.4: 129 n. 37
    3: 118 n. 12
    3.7.2: 117 n. 8
    3.8.4: 117 n. 8
    4: 118 n. 12
    4.3.5: 117 n. 8
    4.5: 117 n. 8
    4.6.3: 117 n. 8
    4.6.4: 117 n. 9, 118 n. 10
    4.9.2: 118 n. 11
    5.13.1: 101 n. 84
    5.20.6: 78
    7.1: 119 n. 15
    7.7.6: 126 n. 32
    7.11.1: 97 n. 64
    8b: 118 n. 12
    8.1: 119 n. 15
    9.2: 117 n. 8
    11.2: 118 n. 11
    12.3: 119 n. 15
    12.5b: 94 n. 45
    12.21.1: 138 n. 55
    12.21.2: 63
    12.22.2: 44 n. 38
    12.44.4: 80
    12.52.3: 80
    13.2: 117 n. 8
    13.52.2: 79
    14.2: 119 n. 15
    14.17.6: 119 n. 16, 119 n. 17
    15.2: 117 n. 8
    15.3.3: 119 n. 17, 119 n. 19
    15.4.3: 119 n. 17
    15.13.6: 80
    16.5.5: 119 n. 20
    16.11.3: 119 n. 16, 119 n. 19
    16.11.12: 119 n. 19
    17.10: 137 n. 54
    18.3: 137 n. 54
    19.3: 117 n. 8
    20.1: 117 n. 8
  Balb. 11: 288 n. 42
  Brut. 3: 77 n. 74
    62: 324 n. 38
    212: 98–99
    255: 80
    331: 252 n. 30
  Cat. 1.1: 107, 108, 139 n. 60, 206 n. 82
    1.7: 135 n. 49
    1.7.8: 135 n. 50
    1.10: 138 n. 56
    1.11: 61
    1.16: 61, 137 n. 52

1.18: 138 n. 58
1.20: 61
1.21: 61
1.31: 138 n. 58
1.33: 61
2.2: 249 n. 17
2.7: 138 n. 58
2.8: 137 n. 52
2.12: 61
2.13: 62
2.20: 130 n. 44
3.12: 44
4.15.22: 137 n. 54
De or. 2.260: 93 n. 38
Div. 1.132: 73 n. 70
Div. Caec. 67: 93 n. 38
Dom. 24: 100 n. 80
29: 117 n. 8
82: 288 n. 42
130: 132 n. 47
Fam. 1.7.2: 117 n. 8
1.9: 116 n. 1
1.9.23: 118 n. 12
1.10ff.: 116 n. 1
2.5.2: 100 n. 75
4.2.1–4: 299
5.5.2: 138 n. 56
5.12: 117 n. 9
5.12.2–7: 297
5.12.6: 54
7.7ff.: 116 n. 1
9.2.5: 79
9.3.2: 79
9.17.1: 44 n. 38
9.22.2: 65–66 n. 58
10.31.2: 126 n. 32
10.31.5: 100 n. 75
12.16.4: 119 n. 20
Fin. 1.23: 222 n. 33
1.24: 94 n. 44
1.35: 222 n. 33
2.28.92: 109
2.54: 94 n. 43, 94 n. 45
4.77: 94 n. 45
5.62: 94 n. 45
Flacc. 19: 101 n. 84
25: 100 n. 75
28: 69 n. 64
Font. 23: 94 n. 43
Leg. 1.5ff.: 118 n. 13
3.20: 93 n. 39
Leg. agr. 2.2.4: 100 n. 75
Leg. Man. 14–15: 101 n. 84
Lig. 18: 97 n. 64
Marcell. 25: 97 n. 64

Mil. 47: 3 n.8
Mur. 32: 230
49: 130 n. 43
50: 130 n. 41
51: 61, 62
58: 93 n. 38
66: 229
76: 69 n. 64
Nat. D. 1.63: 94 n. 45
Off. 1.2: 437
1.109: 99 n. 70
2.27: 69 n. 63
2.84: 139 n. 59
3.109: 94 n. 43
Or. 32: 26 n. 4
129: 62
170: 26 n. 4
Phil. 2.11: 137 n. 51
2.16: 137 n. 54
2.30: 100 n. 75
Pis. 7: 137 n. 54
20: 288 n. 42
Planc. 66: 219 n. 22
89: 288 n. 42
Q. fr. 1.3.8: 117 n. 8
1.4.4: 117 n. 8
2.9.3: 378–379 n. 19
3.5.1: 119 n. 18
Red. pop. 9: 288 n. 42
13.21: 117 n. 8
Red. sen. 25: 288 n. 42
32: 137 n. 54
Rep. 1.26ff.: 79
1.27 (= fr. 130 *FRHist*, fr. 127 P): 76
2.1.2: 132 n. 46
Sen. 51–60: 219 n. 23, 219 n. 24
Sest. 28: 137 n. 54
37: 288 n. 42
46: 117 n. 8
101: 129 n. 37
105: 100 n. 80
130: 288 n. 42
144: 100 n. 75
Sull. 32: 222 n. 33, 233 n. 63
67: 138 n. 58
67ff.: 128 n. 35
Tusc. 1.37: 73 n. 70
3.35.100: 109
4.16: 288 n. 41
Vat. 14: 73 n. 70
39: 387 n. 35
Verr. 1.38: 101 n. 84
2.3.12: 101 n. 84
2.3.168: 101 n. 84
2.5.175: 97 n. 58

Cic. *Acad. Pr.* 2.62: (*cont.*)
   5.161: 260 n. 52
   5.5: 76
Cicero (Quintus) *Comment. pet.* 10: 137 n. 52
CIL I².1: 274 n. 6
CIL I².15: 325 n. 41
Claud. Quad. fr. 10.4 P:
   257 n. 46
De vir. ill. 58.9: 93 n. 37
Dem. *De cor.* 67: 386 n. 33
   97: 43 n. 34
   212: 367 n. 42
   Olynth. 2.17–20: 366
   2.20: 366
   3.15: 43
   3.25–6: 69
   3.33: 367
   Phil. 3.9: 366
   3.33: 366
   3.35: 366
   3.36: 43
   4.1: 366
Dio Cass. 37.31.1: 129 n. 39
   37.40.2: 66
   37.46.3: 129 n. 37
   37.55.3–56.4: 97 n. 61
   39.10: 119 n. 21, 119 n. 22
   40.5a: 61
   40.63.3: 308 n. 5
   40.63.4: 4
   42.52: 4
   43.9.2: 73
   43.9.2–3: 4, 140 n. 62
   fr. 76: 93 n. 37
Diod. Sic. 12.64.3: 222 n. 33
   15.1: 314 n. 11
   28a: 123 n. 25
   31.8.11: 85 n. 4
   31.26: 87 n. 9
   34.3.3–6: 91 n. 27
   34.33: 343
   34.33.3–6: 226 n. 44
   34.33.4–6: 92 n. 33, 93 n. 34
   34.34a: 60
   34–35: 123 n. 25
   34–35.2–3: 101 n. 83
   37.3: 343 n. 5
   37.3.9: 101 n. 85
   38.2: 343, 343 n. 5
   40.5: 65
Dion. Hal. *Ep. ad Amm.* 2.2: 26 n. 4, 41 n. 30

Donat. *Vita Pers.* 8: 44 n. 36
   Vita Verg. 22: 44 n. 36
Enn. *Ann.* 151 Sk.: 151, 151 n. 27
   156 Sk.: 376 n. 14
   220–6 Sk.: 378–9 n. 19
   495 Sk.: 376 n. 14
   Scaen. 22 J: 76
   229 J: 252 n. 30
Fest. 229: 387
   285 L: 87 n. 9
   360 L: 85 n. 3, 87–88 n. 11
Flor. 1.31.5: 91 n. 27
   1.33.1: 91 n. 23
   1.34.18: 91 n. 23
   1.36.2: 277 n. 17
   1.36.18: 293 n. 48, 293 n. 49
   1.47.2: 91 n. 23
   2.4.3: 288 n. 42
   2.13.11: 97 n. 61
   2.13.14: 97 n. 62, 97 n. 63
   3.13: 88 n. 12
Frontin. *S.* 4.1.1–2: 262 n. 57
Fronto 44 VDH (=I 14 H): 25
   56 VDH (=I 4 H): 88 n. 13, 214 n. 2
   100 VDH (=II 158 H, 107 N): 25
   123 VDH (=II 150 H)
   132 VDH (=II 48 H): 25
   148.8 VDH: 10 n. 18
   227 VDH (=II 2 H, Cato fr. 96 *ORF*): 86–87 n. 7
Gell. *NA* 1.13.10: 222 n. 33
   1.15.18: 25
   2.24.1–6: 85 n. 4
   2.27: 386 n. 33
   3.1.5: 31
   4.15.1: 25
   5.19.15 (=Scipio fr. 17 *ORF*): 93 n. 38
   6.3.7: 235 n. 65
   6.3.14: 235
   6.3.15: 236
   6.3.47: 345
   6.3.52: 235, 235 n. 67
   6.12.1 (=Scipio fr. 19 *ORF*): 93 n. 38
   6.20.1 (=Scipio fr. 13 *ORF*): 93 n. 38
   9.13.20: 222 n. 33
   10.26.1: 25 n. 3
   13.20: 325 n. 40
   17.18: 8, 81
   17.21.17: 222 n. 33
Granius Licinianus 36.31: 390 n. 42

Index of Passages

Hdt. 1.1: 308 n. 4
   1.31: 314
   1.136: 108 n. 11
Hippoc. *Aer.* 17: 108 n. 11
Hirtius *B Gall.* 8.52.4: 97 n. 64
   8.53.1: 97 n. 64
Hom. *Il.* 6.168–70: 255 n. 41
Hor. *Carm.* 2.1.7–8: 359
   2.15.13: 69 n. 64
   3.1.25: 150 n. 23
   Ep. 2.2.44–5: 245 n. 3
   Epod. 7: 301 n. 68
   16.1–14: 301 n. 68
   Sat. 1.9.11–13: 249 n. 19
Isid. *Etym.* 13.18.4: 392 n. 48
Inv. in Sall. 3.19: 4
Isoc. *Pan.* 48: 69
   76: 69
   79: 68
   80: 69
   85: 68
Jer. *Chron.* 1930: 2–3
   1981: 4
Livy *Praef.* 3: 369
   Praef. 4ff.: 369
   Praef. 5: 270 n. 87
   Praef. 9: 369–370
   Praef. 11: 277, 360
   1.59: 385
   2.1: 376
   2.12: 386
   2.23: 385
   4.16.4: 324 n. 38
   4.6.11: 97 n. 60
   4.29: 222 n. 33
   4.29.6: 222 n. 33
   5.28.5: 251 n. 26
   5.34.2: 244 n. 2
   6.18.5: 107
   6.25.6–11: 250 n. 23
   6.30.6: 270 n. 86
   7.25.9: 255 n. 39
   7.33.3: 97
   8.7: 222 n. 33
   8.34.10: 270 n. 86
   8.40.4–5: 324 n. 38
   21.1.1: 277 n. 18
   21.1.1–2: 277
   21.1.12: 308 n. 4
   21.4: 51
   21.5–8: 51
   29.29.6: 60
   31.1.7: 277
   33.3.2–7: 85 n. 2
   34.2–4: 232, 232 n. 62
   34.2.13–13.3: 232 n. 62
   34.3.9: 232 n. 62
   34.4.1–2: 232
   34.4.2: 232 n. 62
   34.4.3: 232 n. 62
   34.4.14: 232 n. 62
   34.56.9: 85 n. 2, 85 n. 5
   35.3: 85 n. 3
   35.20.6: 85 n. 3
   35.21.7ff.: 85 n. 3
   36.38: 85 n. 3
   37.46.1–2: 85 n. 3
   37.57.9ff.: 85 n. 3
   39.2–4: 220 n. 27
   39.5.14–17: 85 n. 4
   39.6.5ff.: 90 n. 20
   39.6.5–6: 85 n. 2
   39.6.7: 86–87 n. 7
   39.7: 85 n. 4
   39.8–19: 85 n. 5
   39.38.6–12: 85 n. 2
   39.40.4: 219 n. 23
   39.42.5–43.5: 85 n. 5
   39.44.9: 85 n. 5
   40.1.4: 85 n. 2
   40.16.9: 85 n. 2
   40.35.7: 85 n. 2
   40.39.4: 85 n. 2
   40.40.14: 85 n. 2
   40.41.8–11: 85 n. 2
   41.10.6–10: 85 n. 2
   42.3.1–4: 85 n. 3
   42.3.1–11: 85 n. 3
   42.7.3–9.6: 85 n. 3
   42.10.5: 85 n. 3
   42.10.9–15: 85 n. 3
   42.21.1–22.8: 85 n. 3
   42.28.12: 85 n. 3
   42.32–5: 94 n. 48
   42.32.7–35.2: 85 n. 2
   43.1.4–12: 85 n. 3, 87–88 n. 11
   43.2.1–12: 85 n. 3
   43.4.5–13: 85 n. 3
   43.5.1–10: 85 n. 3
   43.6.2–3: 85 n. 3
   43.7.5–8: 85 n. 3
   43.11.10: 85 n. 2, 94 n. 48
   43.14.7: 85 n. 2, 94 n. 48
   43.16.1–16: 85 n. 5
   45.25.3: 61 n. 51, 235 n. 65
   45.40.1: 85 n. 4

Index of Passages

Livy *Praef.* 3: (*cont.*)
  Oxy. Per. 54: 93 n. 40, 94 n. 44
    55: 93 n. 38, 93 n. 39, 93 n. 40
  Per. 43: 85 n. 3
    47: 85 n. 3, 87–88 n. 11
    48: 85 n. 5, 87–88 n. 11, 94 n. 47
    49: 61 n. 51
    54: 93 n. 40, 94 n. 43, 94 n. 44
    55: 93 n. 39
    57: 94 n. 41, 94 n. 42, 262 n. 57
    58: 101 n. 82
    62: 60
    64: 60
    67: 274, 274 n. 6
    80: 251 n. 26

Luc. 1.2: 25
  1.125: 97 n. 63
  2.67–233: 246 n. 11
  2.177–185: 384
  8.664–5: 389 n. 40
  8.679–81: 389 n. 40
  9.600: 274

Lucr. 1.42: 77

Lycurg. *Leoc.* 126: 231

Lys. 16.18: 51 n. 44

Macrob. *Sat.* 3.13.13: 85 n. 4
  3.16.4: 85 n. 4
  3.17.3–5: 85 n. 4
  3.17.6: 94 n. 46

Mart. 14.191: 441

Mela 2.116: 394 n. 57

Nep. *Cato* 2.3: 220 n. 27
  3.1: 219 n. 23
  3.4: 217 n. 17, 221 n. 30
  Milt. 4.3: 259 n. 49

Oros. 5.8.1: 103 n. 89
  5.8.2: 91 n. 23
  6.3.1: 129 n. 38
  6.15.8: 4

Paus. 10.17: 364

Piso 34 P (= Plin. *HN* 34.14, 36 *FRHist*): 86–87 n. 7
  38 P (=Plin. *HN* 17.244, 40 *FRHist*): 65–66 n. 58, 87 n. 9
  40 P (= fr. 42 *FRHist*): 65–66 n. 58

Pl. *Ep.* 7.324b: 70, 109
  7.324d: 70
  7.325a: 109
  7.325cff.: 70
  7.325e–326a: 109
  Leg. 3.698bff.: 91 n. 26

Menex. 247d: 69
Phd. 80a: 69
Resp. 473c–d: 113–114
  479b–c: 113–114
  544d–e: 158 n. 45
  9.586a: 69

Plaut. *Aul.* 715: 264–265 n. 64
  Capt. 297: 44 n. 38
  Curc. 257: 44 n. 38
  Persa 410: 224
  Trin. 288: 224
    305: 264–265 n. 64
    613: 38
    622: 38

Plin. *HN* 8.11: 221 n. 30
  10.139: 85 n. 4
  17.244 (=38 P, Piso fr. 40 *FRHist*): 87 n. 10
  33.148: 88 n. 12
  33.150: 91 n. 23
  34.14 (= Piso fr. 36 *FRHist*.): 86–87 n. 7
  35.6–7: 320 n. 26
  37.14–16: 388 n. 38

Plut. *Aem.* 32.3: 85 n. 4
  38: 85 n. 4
  Apophth. 198D: 216 n. 10
  198E: 232
  Caes. 5: 337 n. 62
  Cat. Mai. 1: 317 n. 3, 335 n. 57
  7.1: 216 n. 10
  8.1: 86–87 n. 7
  8.9: 232
  9.5: 216 n. 10
  10.4: 229 n. 50
  16–19: 85 n. 5
  18.1: 86–87 n. 7
  19.4: 89 n. 17
  25.1: 219 n. 23
  27: 91 n. 27
  32: 93 n. 34
  Cic. 15: 129 n. 39
  21.5: 63
  Cim. 19.5: 300
  Crass. 10.6–7: 391 n. 46
  13: 119 n. 22, 119 n. 23, 129 n. 39
  Luc. 24.2ff.: 362
  Mar. 3.2–4.1: 330
  4: 287
  5.1–2: 61
  8: 287
  8.8: 61
  8–9: 317 n. 10

12.3-4: 274 n. 6
12.4-5: 66, 274
28-9: 288 n. 42
Per. 28.3: 67
Pomp. 2.1: 388
  18.1ff.: 353-354 n. 9
  19.1: 353
Sert. 2.4: 363
  4.2: 386 n. 32
  8.2: 397
  9.1: 391 n. 46, 396-397 n. 61
  9.6ff.: 363
  18.3: 353
  18.8: 353
  19.3: 353
  19.6: 353
Sull. 6: 282 n. 32
  35-36: 282 n. 32
Ti. Gracch. 8: 97 n. 58
  20: 101 n. 81

Polyb. prol. 3: 158 n. 45
  1.1-2: 277
  1.4: 297
  1.13.11: 308 n. 4
  2.56: 302 n. 74
  2.56.6: 67
  2.59.1: 67
  3.32.2-8: 297
  6.10.2: 132 n. 46
  6.18: 91 n. 26
  6.57: 342
  6.57.5: 87 n. 9, 91 n. 26
  7.7.6: 297
  8.2: 297
  10.3.6: 181 n. 40
  10.36.5-7: 112 n. 19
  12.28.2-5: 113-114
  29.12.2-4: 297
  31.23.11: 76
  31.23-30: 113
  31.25.3ff.: 87 n. 9, 91 n. 26, 93 n. 36
  31.25.5: 86-87 n. 7, 220 n. 27
  32.13.6: 87-88 n. 11, 91 n. 26, 92 n. 31
  35.4: 85 n. 5, 94 n. 47
  38.5.1ff.: 93 n. 36
  38.35.4: 85 n. 4

Porphyr. *Hor. serm.* 1.1.102: 74 n. 71

Posidonius 112 *FGrH*: 91 n. 28

Prisc. 18.169 1 H: 41 n. 28

Prop. 4.6.66: 274 n. 6

Ps.-Acr. *ad Hor. Serm.* 1.2.41: 44 n. 36

Quint. *Inst.* 1.4.8: 36 n. 19
  3.8.8-9: 324

3.8.9: 5
4.2.25: 26
8.2.40: 260 n. 52
8.3.29: 88 n. 14, 214 n. 2
9.3.17: 40
10.1.101: 25
10.2.7: 26
10.3.8: 44 n. 36
12.11.23: 219 n. 23

Rhet. Her. 4.10.14: 252 n. 30

Sall. [*Ad Caes. sen.*] 1.1.2: 418 n. 51
  2.3.4: 224 n. 37
  2.10.2-3: 348
  B.C. 1: 380
  1.1: 10 n. 18, 33, 74, 150-152,
    150 n. 24, 162, 172-173, 192,
    215 n. 8, 216
  1.1-4: 154
  1.2: 69, 160-161, 216
  1.3: 27 n. 5, 33, 154, 215 n. 8
  1.4: 74, 81, 155 n. 38, 216
  1.5: 74
  1.5-2.6: 75, 154
  1.6-7: 388
  1.7: 216
  1-2: 215
  1-4: 55, 215
  2: 185, 188, 189, 194, 195 n. 58
  2.1: 155, 177, 178, 181, 216
  2.2: 152-153, 154, 155, 155 n. 38,
    177-178, 209, 216
  2.3: 156, 156 n. 40, 180, 216
  2.4-6: 112 n. 19
  2.5: 156, 157, 181, 216, 226 n. 42
  2.5-6: 241
  2.6: 157, 157 n. 44
  2.7: 182
  2.8: 74, 152 n. 31, 162 n. 53, 173-174,
    182, 216
  2.9: 74, 158
  2.9-3.2: 216
  2.20: 130 n. 43
  3: 184, 196 n. 61
  3.1: 155
  3.1-2: 7, 158, 205
  3.2: 2, 141-142 n. 2, 158, 158 n. 47,
    184 n. 44, 264 n. 62, 269, 386
  3.3: 70, 109, 159, 160, 184
  3.3-4.1: 217
  3.3-4.2: 9, 109
  3.4: 10, 110, 160
  3.4-5: 109
  4: 185
  4.1: 4, 11, 70, 82, 154, 162, 185, 218
  4.1-2: 109

Sall. [*Ad Caes. sen.*] 1.1.2: (*cont.*)
   4.2: 73, 217, 348, 372
   4.2.45: 161 n. 52
   4.3: 187
   4.4: 160, 187, 189, 209, 277 n. 16, 372
   4.5: 186, 270
   5: 187, 188, 189
   5.1: 126, 153 n. 33, 160–161, 372
   5.1–8: 55
   5.2: 377
   5.4: 25
   5.6: 127, 153, 187, 189
   5.7: 208
   5.8: 30
   5.8–14.1: 127
   5.9–13: 55
   5–9: 340
   5–22: 55, 57
   6: 182
   6ff.: 343 n. 5
   6.1: 155 n. 37, 189, 220, 221
   6.2: 89 n. 18, 377
   6.3: 158 n. 48, 221
   6.5: 42, 68, 220, 228, 228 n. 46
   6.6: 188, 190, 220
   6.7: 222
   6.7–7.7: 403 n. 10
   6–7: 72
   6–10: 407
   6–13: 68, 215, 220, 340
   7: 193, 412
   7–9: 86
   7.1: 220
   7.1–3: 403, 410, 412, 419
   7.2: 220, 405
   7.2–3: 422
   7.2–7: 409
   7.3: 405
   7.3ff.: 360
   7.4: 41, 190, 190 n. 52, 220, 228
   7.4–7: 220
   7.5: 89, 95, 220, 228
   7.6: 35, 68, 191, 220
   7.7: 29
   8: 110–111, 185 n. 47, 193, 207
   8.1: 5, 191
   8.2: 154
   8.2–4: 153 n. 33, 159, 159 n. 49
   8.4: 153, 176, 192, 220
   8.5: 192, 192 n. 54, 220
   9: 193
   9.1: 69, 86, 377 n. 15
   9.1–3: 85 n. 1
   9.2: 69, 220, 228, 377
   9.2–4: 220
   9.3: 220, 222, 230
   9.4: 222, 233–234, 346 n. 11
   9.5: 69, 220, 228, 238
   10: 181–182, 195 n. 58
   10.1: 89 n. 15, 91 n. 24, 93, 194, 220, 230, 341, 346 n. 11, 377, 419
   10.1–2: 225, 226–227 n. 45, 228
   10.3: 194
   10.3–5: 68
   10.5: 195, 195 n. 57, 228, 387
   10–13: 421
   11: 127, 196, 201, 360
   11ff.: 97 n. 58
   11.1: 110 n. 15, 151 n. 29, 196 n. 59, 360
   11.2: 34, 101–102
   11.3: 196 n. 60, 196–197, 197 n. 62
   11.3–13.2: 221
   11.4: 28, 197 n. 64, 200, 221
   11.4–8: 223, 282
   11.5: 197 n. 65, 224, 288 n. 40
   11.5–6: 90 n. 20
   11.7–8: 223
   12.1: 34, 81, 228
   12.2: 250 n. 22
   12.3: 69
   12.5: 198
   13: 198, 201, 202
   13.1: 198
   13.3: 69, 145 n. 13, 199 n. 66
   13.5: 199
   14: 55, 197 n. 65
   14.1: 145 n. 13
   14.1–4: 63
   14.2: 34, 65–66 n. 58, 145 n. 13
   14.4: 63
   14.6: 145 n. 13
   14.7: 65–66, 142 n. 3, 144 n. 11, 145 n. 14
   14.7–15.2: 144–145
   15: 55, 123, 208
   15.2–5: 208–209
   15.4: 37
   15.5: 26, 31
   16: 55, 203 n. 75
   16.2: 35
   16.4: 127
   17: 55, 126, 203 n. 75
   17.1: 39, 124 n. 26
   18: 65, 205
   18.2: 35, 41, 129
   18.4: 126
   18.5: 124 n. 27
   18.6: 124 n. 27

Index of Passages

18–19: 55
19: 205
19.4: 34
20: 57, 206
20.1: 6, 35
20.7: 33, 99 n. 71, 99 n. 72, 130 n. 42
20.7–8: 99 n. 73
20.8: 90 n. 21
20.9: 29–30, 107, 137, 206 n. 82
20.12: 206
20.14: 34
20–22: 55
21.2: 34, 188
21.4: 127
22: 66
22.1–2: 404
22.1–4: 145 n. 14
22.5: 6
23.1: 126
23.1–2: 124 n. 30, 404
23.1–3: 40
23.1–4: 56
23.3: 126
23.3–4: 65
23.4: 145 n. 14
23.5–24.1: 56
23.6: 41
23–55: 57
24: 56, 204
24.1: 35
24.2–4: 56
24.4: 45, 144
25: 51, 56, 124 n. 29, 204
25.1: 33
25.2: 51
25.2–3: 204, 204 n. 79
25.3–4: 51
25.5: 51, 205
26: 49
26.1: 49, 56
26.2: 49
26.2–4: 56
26.4: 49
26.5: 49, 56
27: 422–423 n. 66
27.1: 49
27.2: 28
27.2–28.2: 49
27–28.3: 56
28: 202 n. 70
28.2–3: 49
28.4: 49, 56, 130 n. 45
29: 49, 56
29.1: 135 n. 48, 138, 145 n. 14, 259 n. 49
30: 57

30.1: 124 n. 26, 143–144, 143 n. 10, 145 n. 14
30.2: 71, 144
30.6: 144
31: 124 n. 31
31.1: 29, 259 n. 49
31.1–3: 55, 57
31.3: 39
31.4–32.1: 57
31.5: 62
31.5–32: 61
31.6: 107 n. 8, 134
31.7: 90 n. 22
31.8: 61
31.9: 62
32.3–34.1: 144
33.1: 35
33.3: 29
34.3: 145 n. 14
35: 129
36.1: 65
36.2–3: 57
36.4: 277 n. 16
36.4–39.4: 416
36.4–39.5: 57, 296
37.2: 71
38: 210 n. 89
38.1: 355
38.3: 42 n. 33, 68, 153 n. 34, 341, 365, 416, 417
38.4: 31
39.4: 31, 355
39.5: 55, 124 n. 28
39.6–41: 57
39.6–43: 55
40.1: 36
40.5: 56
42: 57
42.2: 144
43: 57, 191
43.1: 137–138
43.2: 145 n. 14
43.4: 124 n. 30
44.1: 37
44.5: 44
44–45: 57
45.1: 245 n. 8
46.2: 82
46.3: 37
46.6–9: 57, 377 n. 15
47.1: 37, 145 n. 14
48: 124 n. 31, 148
48.1: 31
48.1–2: 57, 137 n. 53
48.3: 6, 35

Sall. [*Ad Caes. sen.*] 1.1.2: (*cont.*)
    48.4–49.4: 145–146
    48.5: 146, 146 n. 16
    48.7–8: 147
    48.9: 145 n. 14, 148, 148 n. 17
    49: 129, 148–149
    49.1: 148, 148 n. 19
    49.4: 6, 149 n. 20, 377 n. 15
    50.1: 32
    50.1–2: 57
    50.1–3: 163
    50.3–53: 57
    50.3–53.1: 63
    50.4: 63 n. 55, 240
    51: 404
    51.1: 235
    51.1–4: 230 n. 51
    51.4: 35
    51.5: 234
    51.5–6: 296 n. 57
    51.6: 237–238
    51.22: 234
    51.26–36: 238–239
    51.32–4: 296 n. 57
    51.33: 37, 239 n. 72
    51.37–42: 296
    51.38: 106–107 n. 6
    51.39–40: 234
    51–52: 404 n. 13
    51–4: 215
    52: 404, 431
    52.3: 437
    52.4: 231
    52.7: 232
    52.8: 232
    52.11: 2, 68, 153 n. 34, 157, 157 n. 42, 157 n. 43, 169–170, 230 n. 51
    52.11–12: 436
    52.12: 157 n. 43
    52.19–21: 405, 412
    52.19–23: 296 n. 59
    52.21–2: 42
    52.24: 126
    52.26: 11, 160
    52.27: 230 n. 51
    52.30: 222 n. 33
    52.30–1: 233, 296 n. 58
    52.35: 231
    52.36: 233
    53: 421
    53.1: 31, 63
    53.3: 35
    53.6: 7, 101, 105 n. 4
    53.6–54.6: 227–8
    53–54: 296
    54: 435
    54.2: 228, 230 n. 51
    54.2–6: 50
    54.3: 7, 34, 228
    54.4: 228, 230
    54.6: 105, 228
    55.5: 35, 66
    55.6: 126
    56.4: 28 n. 8
    56.5: 41, 144
    56–61: 57
    57.2–4: 57
    58.8: 34
    58.11: 34
    58.19: 34
    59.2: 48
    59.3: 49, 145 n. 14
    59.4–6: 57
    59.5: 34, 437
    60: 46
    60.4: 39, 46
    60.5: 46
    61.1: 37, 163
    61.1–6: 142 n. 4
    61.4: 163
    61.5: 37
    61.8: 32
B.J. 1.1: 10 n. 18, 244
    1.1–5: 270 n. 86
    1.2: 36
    1.3: 27 n. 5, 253 n. 32
    1.4: 244
    1.5: 244
    1–2: 278
    2.2: 253 n. 32
    2.4: 245 n. 7, 253 n. 32
    3: 341–342 n. 3
    3.1: 142 n. 4
    3–4: 278
    4: 319, 326
    4.1: 269
    4.2: 9
    4.2–9: 246 n. 10
    4.3: 75, 332
    4.3–4: 268–269
    4.4: 9, 75, 217 n. 18, 259 n. 50
    4.5: 269, 280
    4.5–6: 8, 322, 408
    4.6: 9, 269
    4.7: 8, 268 n. 77, 269, 270 n. 86, 278
    4.7–8: 332–333
    4.9: 246, 247 n. 14, 269
    5.1: 246, 275, 307, 307–308 n. 3, 310, 326, 331, 337
    5.1–2: 246, 276–277

Index of Passages

5.2: 1, 246, 263
5.4: 280, 327, 328 n. 47
5.4–7: 279 n. 23
5.6–7.1: 327
5.7: 60, 247
5–16: 58
5–26: 55
6.1: 108, 248, 256 n. 45, 283, 353
6.2: 82, 259, 264–265 n. 64, 268 n. 77
6.2–3: 254, 283
6.3: 252, 252 n. 30, 259, 262 n. 57
6.3–7.2: 283–284n. 35
6–7: 251–252
7: 254
7.1: 35
7.2: 252–253, 284
7.2–9.3: 327
7.3: 263
7.3–7: 284
7.4: 253, 253 n. 32, 259, 268 n. 77, 327, 328
7.5: 42 n. 33, 253, 270 n. 86
7.6: 247 n. 14, 253, 266, 270 n. 86, 328
7.7: 253, 253 n. 32
8: 254
8.1: 41, 254, 284
8.1–9.1: 253–254
8.2: 254, 268
9.2: 255
9.3: 255, 255 n. 42, 259, 264, 279
9.4: 255, 279
10.2: 38, 256 n. 42, 279
10.3: 255–256, 256 n. 42
10.4: 69, 256
10.5: 256 n. 42, 314, 436 n. 99
10.6: 89, 102 n. 87, 256, 256 n. 45, 309 n. 6, 377, 377 n. 15, 407, 415
10.7: 263, 407
10.8: 256
11.1: 248, 256–257, 264
11.2–6: 257
11.3–4: 49
11.5: 49
11.6: 49, 279
11.7–8: 264
11.7–9: 49
11.8: 264–265 n. 64
11.9: 247 n. 14
12: 60
12.1–2: 257
12.3–6: 257
12.5: 39, 66
13.1: 29, 257

13.5: 258, 264–265 n. 64
14: 292
14.5: 280
14.8–10: 280
14.9: 34
14.18: 38
14.20: 34, 252 n. 30, 262 n. 57, 264 n. 59
14.23: 34
15.1: 292
15.2: 265 n. 65, 270 n. 86
15.2–3: 258
15.4: 34, 258
15.5: 71
15–16: 307
16.1: 258
16.2: 273
16.5: 311
17.1: 32
17.1–19.8: 307
17.3: 42, 311, 340
17–19: 58, 262, 280, 363, 406, 406 n. 18, 442 n. 117
18: 313
18.2: 312, 313
18.3–8: 311
18.5: 313
18.8: 310–311
18.9: 313
19.2: 270, 303
19.7: 311
20.1: 35
20.4: 259
20–21: 58
20–42: 58
21.4–22: 58
22.2–4: 248, 265 n. 65
23: 58
24–25: 58
25.3: 71
25.6: 247 n. 14
25.6–8: 247 n. 13
25.7: 247 n. 14
26: 58
26.2: 108 n. 12
27.4: 35
27–28.3: 58
28.4–29: 58
28.5: 258
29.2: 258
29.3: 259
29.5: 258, 268
29.6: 258
29.7: 35
30.4: 31, 280

Sall. [*Ad Caes. sen.*] 1.1.2: (*cont.*)
  30–32: 58
  30–34: 247–248
  31: 97 n. 58, 273, 292, 412
  31.1: 313
  31.2: 31
  31.7: 313
  31.10: 32
  31.17: 42 n. 33, 86
  31.20: 90 n. 21
  31.23: 38, 377 n. 15, 420
  31.25: 29
  31.26: 434, 434 n. 93
  32.1: 258, 280
  32.2–35: 58
  32.3–4: 258
  32.5: 258, 268
  33.4: 292
  34: 292
  34.1: 40, 248
  35: 60
  35.5: 38
  35.9: 60
  35.10: 249, 249 n. 17, 292–293
  36.2: 28, 259–260
  36–38: 58
  37.1: 260
  37.3: 260
  37–39: 313
  38.4–5: 260
  38.7: 261
  38.9: 261
  38.10: 247 n. 13, 259, 261, 262 n. 56
  39.1: 27 n. 5
  39.2–3: 261
  39–40: 58
  40: 247–248, 261
  40.3: 262 n. 56
  40.5: 262 n. 56
  41: 89 n. 19, 345 n. 9
  41.1: 89 n. 15, 91 n. 24, 102 n. 88
  41.1–42.5: 307
  41.2: 85 n. 1
  41.2–3: 50, 225 n. 40, 280
  41.3: 40
  41.5: 50, 96, 99 n. 72, 224, 262 n. 56, 310, 341
  41.5–8: 50, 68
  41.6: 102 n. 88
  41.7: 90, 97 n. 56, 102 n. 88
  41.7–8: 99 n. 71
  41.8: 97 n. 57
  41.9: 50, 98 n. 69, 261 n. 55
  41.9–10: 261
  41.10: 50, 310
  41.10–42.1: 98
  41.10–42.4: 420
  41–42: 50, 58, 72, 96, 261, 273, 278, 295, 340, 341, 343 n. 5
  42.1: 50, 100 n. 79, 102 n. 88, 280
  42.2: 101
  42.2–4: 50
  42.3: 101
  42.4: 68, 102, 262 n. 56, 310
  42.5: 246, 279
  43.1: 247, 261, 285
  43.4: 32
  43.5: 285
  43–45: 58
  43–79: 58
  43–83: 265
  44.1: 261–262
  44.5: 42 n. 33, 247 n. 13, 261–262, 262 n. 56, 313
  44–45: 286
  45.1: 247, 262, 286
  45.2: 49, 262, 262 n. 57
  46.1: 286
  46.3: 108 n. 12, 268 n. 77
  46.4: 274
  46.5: 262
  46.5–6: 250
  46.5–8: 250 n. 24
  46.8: 108 n. 12, 250, 260
  46–47: 58
  47.3: 249 n. 21
  47.3–4: 274
  48.1: 108 n. 12, 262, 286
  48.3: 31–32, 48
  48–53: 58
  49.1: 262 n. 57
  49.4: 34
  49.5: 29
  49.6: 262 n. 57
  50.1: 262 n. 57
  50.4–51.2: 262–263
  51.1: 259 n. 50
  52.1: 286
  53.1–2: 262
  53.6: 108 n. 12
  53.7–8: 262
  54.1: 29, 38–39
  654.4: 37
  54.5: 247 n. 13
  54–62: 58
  55.6: 314
  55.8: 35, 247 n. 14, 263
  56.1: 29
  56.5: 108 n. 12
  57.4: 28 n. 8, 35, 42

Index of Passages

60.2: 68
60.4: 28, 68
61.1: 247 n. 14
61.3: 30, 286
61.4: 30
61.5: 108 n. 12
61–62: 274, 315
62: 58
62.5: 35 n. 15
62.9: 35
63.1: 61
63.1.1: 6
63.1–2: 289
63.2: 247 n. 13
63.6: 273, 289
63.4: 30, 35
63.4–5: 61
63.6: 90 n. 22, 255 n. 39
63–65: 59
64.1: 29, 247, 287, 315
64.4–5: 289, 315
64.5: 30
64.5–65.5: 290
64.11: 362
66.2: 27 n. 5, 71, 377
66–67: 59
66.2–67: 64
67.1: 30
67.3: 37, 287 n. 38
68–69: 59
68.4–69.1: 266
69.2: 31
69.3: 66
69.4: 64, 287
70.2: 45
70.5: 31, 264–265 n. 64
70–72: 59
71.1ff.: 65
72.1: 248, 264 n. 63
2.2: 39, 82, 263, 312
72–73: 315
73.5: 42
73.6–7: 59
73.7: 247–248
74.1: 32, 312
74.1–2: 260 n. 52
74.3: 35
74–77: 59
77.4: 32
75.1: 249 n. 21
76.1: 259 n. 50, 263, 270 n. 86, 312
78.1: 377 n. 16
78.3–79.6: 246–247 n. 12
78–79: 58
79: 280, 303, 363

79.1: 313
79.1–10: 307
79.10: 246
80.6: 60
80–81: 59
81.1: 72, 248, 273
82.3: 41
82–83: 59
83: 288
83.1: 436 n. 99
83.3: 288
84: 290
84.1: 59, 290
84.2: 35, 35 n. 15
84.3: 41, 247 n. 13
84–86.3: 59
84–114: 265
85: 97 n. 58, 267, 273, 292, 412, 413
85.10: 331
85.12: 43
85.15–17: 255
85.16: 329
85.21–5: 334
85.29: 330
85.29–30: 255, 384
85.31–2: 270 n. 86, 316
85.36: 330
85.39: 247 n. 13
85.40: 330
85.41: 332
85.49: 69
86.2: 247 n. 13
86.4–94: 59
87.4: 312
88.3: 265
88.6: 312
89.3: 308 n. 4
91.7: 108 n. 12
92.1–2: 270 n. 86
92.1–3: 267 n. 72
92.6: 267 n. 73
92–94: 290
93.1: 247 n. 14, 264–265 n. 64, 267 n. 73, 290
93.3: 71
93.4: 267 n. 73
94.1: 266
94.2ff.: 65
94.3: 37
94.7: 267, 290
95: 59, 309
95.1: 59
95.1–2: 267 n. 74
95.2–4: 281–282, 291
95.3ff.: 51

Sall. [*Ad Caes. sen.*] 1.1.2: (*cont.*)
  95.4: 251 n. 26, 270 n. 89, 273, 309
  96.1: 59
  96.2–4: 39
  96.3: 71
  96–101: 59
  97.1: 265
  97.4: 35, 312
  98.5ff.: 67
  99.2–3: 37
  100: 39–40
  100.1: 39
  100.2: 39–40 n. 26, 47
  100.2/3: 39
  100.2–4: 39
  100.4: 39, 41, 47
  100.5: 39, 47
  100.6: 47
  100.7: 47
  100.8: 47
  101: 47, 265, 267, 274
  101.1–2: 47, 265–266
  101.4: 267 n. 74
  101.6: 248, 266
  101.8: 267 n. 74
  101.11: 39
  102: 268
  102.1: 274
  102.4: 267
  102.6: 41
  102.9: 5
  102.15: 312
  102–113: 59
  103.6: 273
  106.2: 265
  106.6: 37
  107.1: 69
  107.5: 266 n. 71
  108.1: 35
  108.3: 6, 247 n. 13, 264–265 n. 64, 312
  109: 268
  110.2: 30
  110.6: 30
  111.2: 306
  111.4: 306
  113.1: 249 n. 19, 267–268, 268 n. 77, 312
  113.3: 312
  113.4–7: 274
  114: 275, 336, 442 n. 117
  114.2: 336, 425
  114.3: 247
  H. 1.1 M: 374, 376
  1.4 M: 10 n. 18, 217 n. 17
  1.5 M: 42, 375
  1.6 M: 359

1.7 M: 70, 360, 365, 378 n. 18
1.11 M: 85 n. 6, 89 n. 15, 91 n. 24, 345 n. 9, 360, 376, 383, 392
1.11–12 M: 72, 225 n. 40, 296 n. 55
1.12 M: 42 n. 33, 85 n. 6, 89 n. 15, 91 n. 24, 225 n. 40, 365
1.16 M: 42, 85 n. 6, 361, 365
1.18 M: 25, 361 n. 24
1.23 M: 396 n. 59
1.24–5 M: 396 n. 59
1.24–53 M: 282 n. 30
1.32–51: 282 n. 32
1.44 M: 384
1.52 M: 351
1.53 M: 352
1.55: 282 n. 33
1.55.2 M: 367, 379 n. 20
1.55.7 M: 365
1.55.10 M: 365, 379 n. 20
1.55.15 M: 43 n. 34
1.55.20 M: 366, 366 n. 32
1.55.21–8 M: 366
1.55.24 M: 366
1.58–61 M: 282 n. 30
1.60–1 M: 282 n. 32
1.77 M: 35, 51
1.77.2 M: 52
1.77.5 M: 52
1.77.7 M: 367
1.77.7–8 M: 52
1.77.9 M: 52
1.77.10 M: 52
1.77.10–11 M: 52
1.77.12 M: 366, 367
1.77.12–13 M: 52
1.77.13 M: 52
1.77.14–16: 52
1.77.17 M: 52, 107
1.77.17–18 M: 53
1.77.18 M: 366
1.77.19 M: 53
1.77.20 M: 53
1.77.22 M: 53
1.84–103 M: 381
1.88 M: 385
1.100 M: 390, 391
1.100–103 M: 363, 390
1.101 M: 363, 397
1.144 M: 396 n. 59
2.1–12 M: 362, 390
2.2 M: 35, 391
2.7 M: 390
2.13 M: 391
2.15 M: 367 n. 42
2.16 M: 351, 353, 386

2.17 M: 352, 387
2.18 M: 353 n. 7
2.19 M: 353
2.20 M: 353 n. 7
2.21 M: 353
2.28 M: 362
2.69 M: 42
2.70 M: 36, 67
2.71–9 M: 381 n. 23
2.81 M: 363
2.82–86 M: 390
2.83 M: 390
2.98 M: 354
2.98D M: 54
2.98.1 M: 53
2.98.2 M: 53
2.98.4 M: 53
2.98.4–6 M: 53
2.98.6 M: 53
2.98.7–8 M: 53
2.98.9 M: 53
3.10 M: 391
3.10–15 M: 362, 390
3.12 M: 390
3.14 M: 42
3.15 M: 390
3.26 M: 36
3.36 M: 29
3.48.1 M: 379 n. 20
3.48.9 M: 379 n. 20
3.48.13 M: 379 n. 20
3.48.14 M: 366
3.48.18 M: 384
3.48.19 M: 366–367
3.48.31 M: 367
3.61–80 M: 363, 390
3.62 M: 391
3.63 M: 391
3.66 M: 391
3.70 M: 391
3.74 M: 363
3.84–5 M: 66
3.88 M: 354, 387–388
3.96D–3.98B M: 393 n. 52
3.98B–C M: 382
4.22 M: 393
4.23 M: 393 n. 55
4.23–9 M: 363, 390
4.26 M: 391
4.27 M: 392, 394 n. 56
4.27–8 M: 391
4.29 M: 394 n. 57
4.42 M: 355 n. 11
4.43 M: 355
4.45 M: 355
4.46 M: 355 n. 13
4.47 M: 355
4.48 M: 355
4.49 M: 355
4.54: 10 n. 18
4.60 M: 362
4.69 M: 72, 381
4.69.5 M: 381 n. 24
5.17–27 M: 373
5.19 M: 355 n. 12
5.20 M: 352
5.20–2 M: 355
5.24 M: 355
5.51 M: 356
12 M: 341
13 M: 341
55.12M: 35 n. 15

Sen. (the Elder) *Controv.* 2.2.12: 256 n. 44
   9.1.13: 25
   9.2.19: 222 n. 33
   10.3.8: 222 n. 33

Sen. *Constant.* 18.1: 27
  Dial. 5.18: 384
  Ep. 24.4: 288 n. 42
   49.5: 77
   90.4–6: 345
   114: 245 n. 3
   114.17: 26

Serv. *Aen.* 1.6 (= Cato *Orig.* fr. 63 *FRHist.*,
   5 P): 89 n. 16
  3.411: 394 n. 57
  3.420: 392 n. 48

Sisenna 13 P (= 32 *FRHist*): 66 n. 59
  45 P (= 33 *FRHist*): 66 n. 59
  103 P (= 14 *FRHist*): 66 n. 59

Stat. *Silv.* 3.5.88: 69

Suet. *Aug.* 86: 88 n. 13, 214 n. 2
  89.2: 69 n. 64
  Iul. 6.1: 337
   9: 119 n. 14, 129 n. 36
   14.1: 63
   19: 7 n. 13
   41.1: 308 n. 5
   72: 126 n. 32
  Gramm. 10: 25, 81, 88 n. 14, 120 n. 24
   15: 214 n. 2, 387
   15.1: 25

Tac. *Agr.* 7.3: 106–107 n. 6
  Ann. 1.23.5: 269 n. 84
   1.69.3: 264–265 n. 64
   4.33.4: 246
   15.36.4: 250 n. 24
   15.63: 61 n. 51

Tac. *Agr.* 7.3: (*cont.*)
  Germ. 19.5: 69
  Hist. 1.1: 410
    1.2–3: 277
    4.8.2: 430
Ter. *Adel.* 500: 264–265 n. 64
  Haut. 141: 239 n. 72
Theopomp. 224 *FGrH*: 63
  224–5 *FGrH*: 63 n. 56
Thuc. 1.1.1–2: 277 n. 17
  1.10.2: 111
  1.17: 42
  1.110.4: 41
  1.21.1: 42
  1.21.2: 277 n. 17
  1.22.1: 41
  1.23.1: 277 n. 17, 308 n. 4
  1.70.9: 42, 365, 366 n. 32
  1.73–8: 112
  1.77.6: 112
  1.126.3: 108 n. 10
  2.40.3: 42 n. 33
  2.40.4: 42, 68
  2.61.1: 365
  2.61.6: 42 n. 33
  2.63.2: 365
  2.65.4: 40
  3.8.4: 288 n. 42
  3.48.1: 230 n. 51
  3.79–81: 310
  3.81–5: 104
  3.81.5: 42 n. 33
  3.82.2: 70
  3.82.4: 68
  3.82.8: 42 n. 33, 68, 153 n. 34, 365
  3.82–84: 307
  3.87ff.: 68
  4.43.2: 42
  5.73.1: 41
  5.84–115: 112
  5.90: 113
  6.1–5: 307
  6.37.1: 41
  6.53–54: 307
  7.28.2: 41
  7.71.3: 68
Val. Max. 2.4.2: 85 n. 5, 87–88 n. 11
  2.7.1–2: 262 n. 57
  2.7.6: 222 n. 33
  5.6: 49
  5.8: 94 n. 44
  6.4.2: 93 n. 37, 93 n. 38
  6.9.1: 222 n. 33
  6.9.10: 85 n. 3, 87–88 n. 11
  6.9.14: 274 n. 6
  7.2.3: 91 n. 29
  8.1.1: 93 n. 38
  8.5.1: 94 n. 43
  9.2.1: 385
  9.3.4: 222 n. 33
  9.6.4: 93 n. 40
  9.8.1: 394 n. 57

Valerius Probus fr. I Aistermann: 25

Veg. *Mil.* 1.13 (=Cato *De Re Militari* fr. 3): 231

Vell. Pat. 1.9.6: 85 n. 4
  1.15.3: 85 n. 5, 87–88 n. 11
  2.1.1: 91 n. 23, 361
  2.1.5: 94 n. 43
  2.3.2: 101 n. 82
  2.15.3–4: 288 n. 42
  2.21.2: 352 n. 4
  2.29.3: 352 n. 5
  2.29.5: 353
  2.33.3: 97 n. 63
  2.36.2: 25, 110, 110 n. 17
  2.41.2: 263 n. 58
  2.79.1: 247 n. 14
  2.96.1: 254 n. 35
  2.97.4: 244 n. 2
  2.122.2: 251 n. 26
  2.129.3: 263 n. 58

Verg. *Aen.* 2.107: 264 n. 59
  6.824–5: 222 n. 33
  7.44–45: 308 n. 4
  9.279: 251 n. 27
  12.552: 151, 151 n. 27
  G. 1.501–14: 301 n. 68

Xen. *Cyr.* 3.1.26: 91 n. 26
  3.3.45: 69
  8.7.13: 69
  Hell. 2.2.10: 112
  3.5.8–15: 112
  Mem. 2.1.30: 69